From the Foundations to the Legacy of Minoan Archaeology

Published in the United Kingdom in 2018 by
OXBOW BOOKS
The Old Music Hall, 106-108 Cowley Road, Oxford, OX4 1JE

and in the United States by
OXBOW BOOKS
1950 Lawrence Road, Havertown, PA 19083

Paperback: ISBN 978-1-78570-926-5 (PB)
Digital Edition: ISBN 978-1-78570-927-2 (epub)

A CIP record for this book is available from the British Library

Library of Congress Control Number: 2017963323

For a complete list of Oxbow titles, please contact:

UNITED KINGDOM
Oxbow Books
Telephone (01865) 241249
Email: oxbow@oxbowbooks.com
www.oxbowbooks.com

UNITED STATES OF AMERICA
Oxbow Books
Telephone (800) 791-9354, Fax (610) 853-9146
Email: queries@casemateacademic.com
www.casemateacademic.com/oxbow

Oxbow Books is part of the Casemate Group

Front cover: Crete, Mesara-type tomb Krasi A: alignment with midsummer dawn rising over "horns" of Khalikas mountain. Photograph © Carlos Guarita. Part of a joint long-term project with Lucy Goodison to establish a pattern of dawn alignments at significant Minoan buildings.

Contents

Preface vii
List of contributors ix

1. Keith Branigan: Introductory 1
   Peter Warren

2. Roots and routes: Technologies of life, death, community and identity 10
   Maria Relaki

3. Inspecting the foundations: The Early Minoan Project in review 36
   Peter Tomkins

4. Early Minoan Knossos: A few new thoughts 68
   Gerald Cadogan

5. Caves in Crete and their use as architectural space 83
   Philip P. Betancourt

6. Mortuary variability, social differentiation and ranking in Prepalatial Crete: The evidence from the cemetery of Phourni, Archanes 96
   Yiannis Papadatos

7. Variables and diachronic diversities in the funerary remains of the Kamilari tholos tombs 115
   Luca Girella

8. Managing with death in Prepalatial Crete: The evidence of the human remains 141
   Sevi Triantaphyllou

9. The house tomb in context: Assessing mortuary behaviour in north-east Crete 167
   Ilse Schoep

10. Visible and invisible death. Shifting patterns in the burial customs of Bronze Age Crete 190
Eleni Hatzaki

11. Recognising polities in prehistoric Crete 210
Todd Whitelaw

12. The relevance of survey data as evidence for settlement structure in Prepalatial Crete 256
Donald C. Haggis

13. Comparative issues in archaeological field survey in the Asterousia region 275
Andonis Vasilakis and Kostas Sbonias

14. Beyond the collective ... The Minoan Palace in action 291
Jan Driessen

15. The "emergence of the individual" revisited: Memory and trans-corporeality in the mortuary landscapes of Bronze Age Crete 314
Yannis Hamilakis

Preface

It is our great privilege to produce this volume in honour of Professor Keith Branigan deriving from the 14th Sheffield Round Table in Aegean Archaeology (29–31 January 2010). As founder and principal member of the Sheffield Centre for Aegean Archaeology (SCAA), Professor Branigan has been the instigator of the Sheffield Round Tables in Aegean Archaeology, organised annually since 1995, aiming to address each time a specific topic of Aegean Prehistory in a manner that showcases new research and promotes constructive debate within the discipline. Keith is also to be credited for establishing the series of Sheffield Studies in Aegean Archaeology publications deriving from the round tables that have tackled as diverse themes as Neolithic Society, Urbanism, Landscape and Land Use, Feasting and Craft Technologies to name but a few. It seemed a very fitting way to mark Keith's retirement by organising a Round Table in his honour and dedicating it to the subject of Minoan Crete to which he has contributed so vastly over the years.

Colleagues were invited to discuss topics from four distinct areas of interest that have informed Keith's work and have helped to shape the current picture of Minoan archaeology: general frameworks for understanding Minoan society; regional analysis, survey and settlement; technology and craft activity; and funerary archaeology. Keith has contributed to all these themes through major fieldwork and especially wide-influencing publications that still constitute the cornerstone of our knowledge of Bronze Age Crete. The breadth and depth of his influence is demonstrated in the articles of this volume, benefiting from his research and the intellectual legacy he established in Minoan archaeology.

We take this opportunity to warmly thank a number of people who have contributed to the production of the Round Table and this volume. John Bennet, Paul Halstead, Sue Sherratt, Peter Day, Roger Doonan, John Barrett, Michael Parker Pearson at the Department of Archaeology in Sheffield, for being gracious hosts, offering logistical support, and facilitating the conference organisation in every possible way. In addition, John Bennet, Peter Day, Gerald Cadogan, Paul Halstead, Sue Sherratt and Peter Warren chaired the conference sessions most effectively and guided a lively and stimulating discussion. Glynis Jones, Ben Chan, Christina Tsoraki and Ioanna Moutafi kindly hosted several of the Round Table participants. Debi Harlan and Valasia Isaakidou were the driving forces behind the organisation of the magnificent customary feast to open up the proceedings on Friday night, and continued the wonderful task that Nong Branigan has been performing since the Round Table's inception in hosting the Saturday night party. They were supported by an enthusiastic army of coffee makers, dish washers, room re-arrangers, and general helpers from the students of the Department of Archaeology as well as conference attendants. We also wish to acknowledge the contribution of colleagues who delivered oral presentations but were unable to submit an article for the publication: Cyprian Broodbank, Evangelia Kiriatzi, Myrto Georgakopoulou, Tim Campbell-Green, Tristan Carter, Despina Catapoti, and Roger Doonan. As always, we are grateful to the Institute of Aegean Prehistory (INSTAP) for the financial support provided for the organisation of the Round Table and for taking this opportunity to honour Professor Branigan by awarding him the Medal of the Institute for Aegean Prehistory, presented to Keith by Professor Philip Betancourt. We are indebted to the pool of reviewers who offered comments and advice on the submitted articles and we thank the authors for engaging with these suggestions to produce what we hope is a stimulating and thought-provoking volume on Minoan archaeology. Finally, we are grateful to the Editorial Team at Oxbow for their patience and support during the lengthy gestation of this volume.

Maria Relaki and Yiannis Papadatos

List of contributors

PHILIP P. BETANCOURT
Department of Art History, Temple University, 2001 North 13th Street, Philadelphia, PA 19122, USA.

GERALD CADOGAN
3 The Old Rickyard, Moreton Pinkney, Daventry NN11 3TL, UK.

JAN DRIESSEN
Université Catholique de Louvain, Faculté de philosophie, arts et lettres (FIAL), Collège Erasme, Place Blaise Pascal 1 bte L3.03.13, Louvain-la-Neuve 1348, Belgium.

LUCA GIRELLA
Università Telematica Internazionale Uninettuno, Facoltà di Lettere, Corso Vittorio Emanuele II, 39 00186 Rome, Italy.

DONALD C. HAGGIS
Department of Classics, The University of North Carolina at Chapel Hill, 212 Murphey Hall, CB 3145, Chapel Hill, NC 27599-3145, USA.

YANNIS HAMILAKIS
Joukowsky Institute for Archaeology & the Ancient World, Brown University, Box 1837/60 George Street, Providence, RI 02912, USA.

ELENI HATZAKI
Department of Classics, The University of Cincinnati, 410 Blegen Library, PO Box 210226, Cincinnati, OH 45221-0226, USA.

YIANNIS PAPADATOS
Department of History and Archaeology, National and Kapodistrian University of Athens, University Campus, 15784 Zografou, Athens, Greece.

MARIA RELAKI
Université Catholique de Louvain, Faculté de philosophie, arts et lettres (FIAL), Belgium and Faculty of Arts and Social Sciences, The Open University, UK. 29 Smeeton Road, Kibworth Beauchamp, LE8 0LG, UK.

KOSTAS SBONIAS
Department of History, Ionian University, 72 I. Theotoki str., 49100 Corfu, Greece.

ILSE SCHOEP
Department of Archaeology, Katholieke Universiteit Leuven, Blijde-Inkomststraat 21-box 3313, 3000 Leuven, Belgium.

PETER TOMKINS
SCAA Research Associate, Department of Archaeology, University of Sheffield, UK. Brusselsestraat 188, 3000 Leuven, Belgium.

SEVI TRIANTAPHYLLOU
Faculty of Philosophy, School of History and Archaeology, Aristotle University of Thessaloniki, 54124 Thessaloniki, Greece.

ANDONIS VASILAKIS
Director Emeritus, Hellenic Ministry of Culture, Ephorate of Antiquities of Heraklion, Hatzidaki and Xanthoudidi, 71202 Herakleion Crete, Greece.

PETER WARREN
Department of Archaeology and Anthropology, University of Bristol, 43 Woodland Road, Clifton, Bristol BS8 1UU, UK.

TODD WHITELAW
Institute of Archaeology, University College London, 31–34 Gordon Square, London WC1H 0PY, UK.

Chapter 1

Keith Branigan: Introductory[1]

Peter Warren

It was hot, hot with the particular strength of the sun built up through the day to the middle of the afternoon. The ancient bus lurched along the unmetalled road, its full complement of passengers and animals interchanging gossip and queasiness. The bus eventually arrives, passengers and packages emerge, among them a pale, not to say pallid foreigner. “Where on earth have you brought us to? The back of beyond?”, he asks, none too cheerfully.

Ladies and Gentlemen, Κυρίες και Κύριοι, welcome to the moment of arrival at the village of Myrtos at the beginning of August 1967 of the young (well, 27-year-old) Dr Keith Branigan.

Keith had agreed to be a trench supervisor in some excavations two and half kilometres walk away from the village, but what I would like to do in these introductory remarks at what, to judge by the Abstracts, will be an outstandingly interesting and successful International Round Table, is to try, albeit briefly and 42½ years later, to put Keith in context, αφού έτσι είναι ο ρόλος των γέρων μας σήμερα.

So, let us indulge not in Cretan Early Bronze Age history but rather Cretan Early Bronze Age historiography. For this, true to the sound heuristic principle of periodisation in evolutionary studies, here are some stages in the brief 116 year-old study of the Cretan EBA. We of course need period names; given the very recent and very exciting discoveries of apparent Lower Palaeolithic occupation in the area of Preveli-Plakias and Loutro and Gavdos we may borrow the nomenclature of deep time, though using investigators rather than sites investigated (Fig. 1.1).

I EVANSIAN–TARAMELLIAN 1894–1897

The beginning. Almost immediately after his first visit to Crete in 1894, in his first Cretan book, *Cretan Pictographs and Prae-Phoenician Script* (1895), that is long before he proposed any Minoan periods, Evans brilliantly realised that the Hagios Onouphrios Deposit published in the book could be dated as intermediate between the first

I	EVANSIAN - TARAMELLIAN	1894-7
II	SEAGERIAN-XANTHOUDIDIAN	1904 -1924
III	MARINATOSIAN-BANTIAN	1926-1930s
IV	ALEXIOUIAN	1950-1960
V	BRANIGANIAN	1968-1990s
VI	HELLENIAN	1990s →

Figure 1.1: A historiography of the Cretan Early Bronze Age.

prehistoric stratum of Troy and the early remains of Thera, and as about contemporary with the graves of Amorgos. At the very same time Antonio Taramelli investigated the little cave at Miamou with its contemporary remains. What is more, Taramelli included not only a careful plan but two drawn stratigraphical sections to indicate sequential occupation (Taramelli 1897). So, a good start, to be followed by a much longer period.

II SEAGERIAN–XANTHOUDIDIAN 1904–1924

The great age of discovery and the beginning of interpretation. Evans published his *Essai de classification des époques de la civilisation minoenne* in 1906, presented first at the Prehistoric Congress in Athens in 1904. In this little work he assigns contents to each of his periods, thus introducing the notions of development and of substantive stages, i.e. something well beyond the definition of a period as a block of time in which pottery of a certain style was characteristic or predominant. Furthermore he includes settlement evidence along with funerary. He also, by the way, anticipates and at least in part disposes of two modern, supposedly fundamental criticisms of his whole approach. First, Yannis Hamilakis (2002: 5–15) attacked evolutionists and neo-evolutionists such as Renfrew, Warren and Branigan on the grounds that such an approach, in highlighting the acme of a civilisation, fails to do justice to pre-acme periods worthy of interpretation in their own right; but Evans, while promoting the necessity of "une systématisation logique" and indeed of a Minoan palatial acme, was fully aware that the fundamental position was one of continuity and thus of the importance of each period in its own terms, since his periods were (in translation) only the artificial boundaries of a course uninterrupted in reality. Second, Cyprian Broodbank's (2004: 50–54) attempted questioning of the term Minoan (rejection of supposedly ethnic labels is currently very p.c.) is met by this anticipatory comment of Evans (in translation): "The term 'Minoan' at least has the advantage of not passing beyond the confines of ethnographic neutrality. To make use of 'Minos' like 'Caesar' or 'Pharaoh' avoids giving rise to the embroiling questions of Carians, Pelasgians, Achaeans or even Libyans" (Evans 1906: 4).

Alongside Evans's periodic classification the most important stratigraphical statement for the Cretan EBA was Seager's presentation in 1907 of the evidence of Vasilike (Seager 1907: especially 113–14). Later this became the basis for EMII A and EMII B. Meanwhile the British School's excavations at Palaikastro had produced good EM settlement evidence, including, as Keith fully recognised, parts of a monumental building, and ossuaries covering several EM periods; Gournia too was yielding settlement evidence, especially Early Minoan III from the North Trench, and Xanthoudides had starting excavating Mesara round tombs in 1904; the tombs of Mochlos, and its settlement, soon followed, Seager publishing the tombs in 1912. A few years later Xanthoudides dug and published in some detail in 1918 the Pyrgos burial cave and his fundamental *The Vaulted Tombs of Mesara* came out in 1924. We should remember that in these publications much was said and quite detailed interpretations were offered of the burial and funerary remains – they were far from just presentations of the finds.

III MARINATOSIAN[2]–BANTIAN 1926–1930s

In this period the pace of discovery, and so too of interpretation, slackened but was far from negligible. Marinatos excavated and published the tomb of Krasi, the first round tomb outside the Mesara, and those of Vorou, overlooking it. The Vorou larnakes and pithoi required specific discussion. He also brought Early Bronze Age cave and rock shelter evidence into the picture with his investigations at three sites, Amnisos-Eileithyia – later to be reinvestigated by his daughter Nanno and Phil Betancourt , at Partira and at Elenes in West central Crete, as did those of Pendlebury and BSA colleagues at Trapeza. In this period too Luisa Banti published the long excavated large tholos of Hagia Triada, adding a wealth of new evidence. The excavations at Mallia and Phaistos had penetrated into the Prepalatial levels and demonstrated substantial occupation, published by Pernier and Banti for Phaistos in 1935. So by 1939 Pendlebury could summarise. Although the 48 pages in *The Archaeology of Crete* devoted to the Early Minoan period may seem a mere trifle by today's luxuriating standards, given the wealth of evidence even then at his disposal, his account, by periods and slightly evolutionary in character (note how his "The second Early Minoan Period is the climax of the so-called early Bronze Age in the Aegean"

[Pendlebury 1939: 59] anticipates Colin Renfrew's major EBA thesis), goes beyond much excellently descriptive detail in emphasising regional variation, anthropology, technology and foreign contacts.

IV ALEXIOUIAN[3] 1950–1960s

After a hiatus caused by the Second World War (a little German EBA work at Koumarospelio on the Akrotiri and MM I at Apesokari, both published in 1951) we have the major excavations, all burial sites, by Alexiou at the EM I rock shelter of Kanli Kastelli and the five Lebena tombs at three separate sites, as well as the recovery of a large number of stone vessels by Platon in an annex at Platanos. There was also the Neolithic house and adjacent Neolithic-Late Minoan rock shelter burials at Katsamba, excavated by Alexiou in 1953–4. The two Lebena tombs at Yerokambos produced a wealth of evidence, including the deep EM I basal level in tomb II, very carefully excavated and then reported in the *Illustrated London News* in 1960 (6th August). In 1959, the same year as Yerokambos, Levi excavated the Kamilari tholos, with a long report in the *Annuario* (1961–2), and Hood the EM I Well under the palace at Knossos, to be published by him and Gerald Cadogan in 2011. But in this period (1950–1960s) there was not much synthetic or analytic study of the Cretan EBA as such. One exception to this was the remarkable contribution of the late Paul Faure. His work in a huge number of Cretan caves, many including early use, is matched only by that of Eleutherios Platakis, and was brought to fruition in his book of 1964, *Fonctions des cavernes crétoises.*

V BRANIGANIAN 1967–1990s

1967 and 1968 can now be seen as two golden years in terms of Early Minoan publication. 1967 was the year of Zois' *Έρευνα περί της μινωϊκής κεραμεικής*, that is his systematic publication of the pottery of what he termed the Koumasa Style, followed in 1968 by his *Der Kamares-Stil. Werden und Wesen*, with four of its initial chapters devoted to EM pottery. This was also the year of Pini's still fundamental, albeit rarely cited, *Beiträge zur minoischen Gräberkunde*, carefully examining not merely the burial customs and practices of the EM and later communities, but also discussing the beliefs underlying them. And 1968 was also the year of Keith's first Cretan EBA book, *Copper and Bronze Working in Early Bronze Age Crete*, the publication of his doctoral dissertation of 1966. It is a systematic and thorough presentation by typology of the wealth of evidence and it includes valuable work on metal sources and technology, with compositional analyses. Keith's book and those of Zois mark the beginning of a significant advance in Cretan EBA studies, that is the study and publication of discrete *corpora*; the *Corpus der minoischen und mykenischen Siegel* is the outstanding example, though we certainly should not forget Matz's great pioneer work of this kind, *Die frühkretische Siegel* in 1928. These works, themselves interpretative, provided a new basis for future work and they have been followed by many of the same type. Keith of course was soon to place the Cretan metalwork within a pan-Aegean frame with his magisterial compendium of 1974, *Aegean Metalwork of the Early and Middle Bronze Age.*

Keith meanwhile had published *The Foundations of Palatial Crete* in 1970. This book is not simply the first book-length study of the period (Pendlebury's 48 pages have become 232). Its organisation transforms the study of the subject, its main chapters being no longer periods but themes and topics, architecture, economy, religion and ritual, society and social organisation, art, funerary architecture and trade and communications, and he ended with a summary of the sequential development, that is the history of the period. The first chapter of the book, "Background to the enquiry", ably sets Neolithic and EBA Crete within the contemporary Anatolian, Near Eastern, central and west Mediterranean context. It and the final, historical chapter are mildly diffusionist (local emergence in EM I is tentatively given preference over migrations from the Palestinian area) and certainly evolutionist in character: "the society of palatial Crete, like its art, architecture, religion, economy, and crafts, was brought about not by revolution but by evolution. This was perhaps the finest achievement of Early Minoan Crete and its most valuable contribution to palatial civilisation". It is no criticism of the book to say that it is not at all concerned with theory or with explicit generalised propositions or models which are tested against evidence; its great merit is that its overall framework or conception is thematic; Pendlebury, by contrast, had worked from periods; the content of each, however, was also thematic, but on a much briefer base than Keith's. I perhaps labour this point because at its heart is the central issue of the validity of the "grand narrative" approach for the explanation of change, as against the explicitly theoretical approach. At its best the "grand narrative" approach, while fundamentally evolutionist *and* processualist, recognises short term factors as also having valid explanatory power. So in the second edition of *Foundations*, published eighteen years later in 1988, Keith added a chapter which rightly recognised the Renfrew versus Cherry debate on state formation and supported Renfrew's later work on Catastrophe Theory, since within the theory "the underlying causative factors" promoted change as much as relatively sudden behavioural factors did. Keith therefore concluded that long-term developments in EM II and III could explain Cherry's "quantum leap", out of which latter palatial societies emerged. Keith also liked Paul Halstead's at that time innovative work on social storage as relevant to the creation of the palatial system.

Of *The Tombs of Mesara*, the second book of 1970, and the 1993 book, *Dancing With Death*, I say very little, for the simple reason that I think these are Keith's best books, remaining standard works for the twofold reason of their inclusion of comprehensive factual data on the Mesaran and Asterousian tombs and their analyses of the relationships between cemeteries and society. I think the non-funerary role of paved and open areas beside tombs is still an open question; ritual activity in a liminal zone is surely established, in no small measure because of Keith's work; in my own view such liminal action corresponds well with a Minoan conception of liminality in their ordering of the cosmos. But a purely secular use of these spaces I think invites further discussion.

Still within our Period V, the BRANIGANIAN, we must recognise Keith's joint survey work with David Blackman in the Hagiopharango, including the most praiseworthy excavation of the looted Hagia Kyriaki tomb, and on the coast eastwards of the gorge, followed by their publication in several substantial papers from 1975–82. Keith's survey work was later extended to upland Ziros in the remote south-east corner of the island and has more recently returned to the head of the Hagiopharango, that is to Moni Odigitria and its khora, in synergasia with Andonis Vasilakis, who has himself done so much in the Asterousia and whom it is such a pleasure to see again here in Sheffield. (Since the Round Table we greatly welcome the substantial publication of Moni Odigitria [Vasilakis and Branigan 2010]). This brings us appropriately to our final period.

VI HELLENIAN 1990s to today

Keith's contributions certainly did not stop in the 1990s but the final part of our historiographical summary merits a new period and a new name. This is the HELLENIAN and is so called for three reasons. Before I come to them a contribution must be highlighted which may suitably be called adopted-Hellenian, since it has involved life largely among Cretan shepherds and farmers. This is the remarkable work of Krzysztof Nowicki primarily in the Cretan mountains and lowland hills, where he has discovered and reported on dozens of Final Neolithic-Early Minoan I hilltop sites. These radically enlarge our picture of what was happening in the island at that time.

The first of three reasons for the HELLENIAN is that over about the last twenty years there has been a huge amount of new Cretan EBA fieldwork and most of it has been directed by our Greek colleagues, solely or, in the case of some of the intensive surveys, in synergasia. Of surveys – we have mentioned Keith's Ziros and his and Andonis' Moni Odigitria – the list is almost too long to cite, though in this context those of the Western Mesara under Watrous, Hadzi-Vallianou and Blitzer, with an important methodological contribution by John Bennet, and that of Andonis Vasilakis, necessarily extensive in character, in the Asterousia and now around Trypiti in particular may be highlighted. Of excavations and site-specific surveys with Final Neolithic and EBA material, moving from east to west, we have the settlements at Hagia Eirini: Kastri and at Livari: Kastrokephalaki; the Goudouras: Livari-Skiadi round tomb, with highly interesting osteological results from Sevi Triantaphyllou; the stratified FN-EM I settlement at Petras: Kephala; the very early palatial building at Hagia Photia; the final publication of the preceding huge EM I-II cemetery at the same site; Chrysokamino, copper ore processing centre for its region in Prepalatial EM III and possibly earlier; a rich EM III pottery deposit found in 2007 in a small cave near Pacheia Ammos; Kalo Chorio (Donald Haggis can count as ancestrally Hellene); vertiginous Katalimata in the Final Neolithic; the site of Tis Aphrodites to Kephali, exceptionally interesting for its pithos storage already in EM I; the EMIII Alatzomouri rock shelter; the Haghios Charalambos reburial cave (but how much Prepalatial?); the cemetery of Gournes, resembling that of Hagia Photia; the Herakleion: Poros harbour settlement with evidence of metalworking; the rich excavation of the rock shelter burial site at Kyparissi (Kanli Kastelli), north of the one excavated by Alexiou in 1951; the Tou Adami to Kephali settlement perched on its little flat hilltop above Trypiti; the careful excavation of what was left at the Moni Odigitria tombs after the appalling looting; the new and highly interesting Final Neolithic and EM work at Phaistos; the Atsipades peak sanctuary (or was it settlement occupation at the start of the Bronze Age?), Final Neolithic or EM I Gavdos; Psathi west of Khania; EM II Nopigeia: Troulia, and certainly other sites I have omitted. Such a wealth of new sites transforms our knowledge of the period. There have been numerous other surveys, both site-specific and regional, with results primarily post-EBA.

The second reason for our HELLENIAN is the detailed final publication of the well preserved and very well excavated EM tombs of Archanes, tholoi Gamma (Papadatos 2005) and Epsilon (Panagiotopoulos 2002) and Burial Building 19, by Greek colleagues. From these tombs, already reported in some detail in earlier years by their excavator, the late Yiannis Sakellarakis, we are able to analyse osteological and artefactual evidence at levels never previously achievable and thus to provide a much strengthened basis for both funerary and social reconstruction. The Anglo-Hellenic publication of Moni Odigitria has been referred to. Another such is the publication of the five Lebena tombs (Alexiou and Warren 2004).

This brings us to the third HELLENIAN component. In the 1980s debate concentrated on state formation, that is on the Protopalatial period and the reasons for its emergence. The debate took place not only in published papers much given to theoretical considerations but also at the level of fieldwork, expressed most fully in the reasoning behind and the interpretative discussion of the data from the Western Mesara Survey. In the last ten years the debate has changed. It has become focussed on the Early Bronze Age as such and in international conference fora in which, it is a joy to note, younger scholars, especially again Greek colleagues, take the lead. Already in 1998 the Sheffield Round Table, *Cemetery and Society in the Aegean Bronze Age*, had several papers on the Cretan EBA. We have also had the 2006 Round Table of Peter Tomkins and Valasia Isaakidou on the Cretan Neolithic, *Escaping the Labyrinth. The Cretan Neolithic in Context*, published in 2008. The Athens BSA conference *Back to the Starting Line: New Theoretical & Methodological Approaches to Early Bronze Age Crete* in December 2007 and the immediately following and very similarly titled Leuven conference *Back to the Beginning. Reassessing Social, Economic and Political Complexity in the Early and Middle Bronze Age on Crete* in February 2008 are the cutting edge expression of the debate. Yannis Hamilakis's edited volume *Labyrinth Revisited. Rethinking Minoan Archaeology* (2002) has two papers devoted to the Prepalatial period: that of Donald Haggis invites critical discussion of the definition of the term "integration", while that of Peter Day and David Wilson, notwithstanding its frequent citations of Hamilakis in support of individual points, is wholly evolutionist. And now we are about to start the present meeting, which, to judge by the abstracts, will go further.

So I will finish by making one observation and posing three questions. The observation is that it has become clear, even before Philip Betancourt wrote his latest book (Betancourt 2008), that already in EM I, that is by 2800 BC at the latest and very possibly several centuries earlier, the economies of Crete were more complex, more advanced and more organised than had previously been thought. The questions. (1) Was there a ranked or stratified society in EBA Crete or was it essentially egalitarian? These are of course very broad terms, but the evidence, especially the clear differentials in the placements of grave goods, increasingly suggests there was at least some ranking, more than I for one had long ago thought, but that Keith had thought. This would, with Todd Whitelaw, indeed have been the case at places the size of Knossos, with a possible population of a thousand, above the threshold for hierarchical organisation. (2) Was EBA Crete internationalist? Again the answer, as I am sure Tristan Carter among many others would agree, is, increasingly, yes. (3) Are there already signs, if not of nucleation at least of centralisation? Again, if a touch more hesitantly, yes. We may indeed be seeing the beginnings of such nucleation, or at least focus on a communal centre, already in the Final Neolithic at Phaistos.

Whatever the answers, indeed whatever the questions, I am confident that Keith himself will be very happy with all these recent developments, not least because to no small extent they express the leadership which the Sheffield Aegean School has offered for so many years, not least under Keith's own leadership and direction.

At the end of the 1967 excavation season at Myrtos: Phournou Koryphi Keith threw his worn out sandals to the ground and declared that I owed him a new pair. With apologies for some delay I am delighted now to oblige.

Notes

1 The printed text is close to and deliberately retains the tone of that given as an Introduction at the Round Table. The primary aim of this historiographic summary, including its illustrations, was for Keith, friend for more than forty years, to enjoy it.

2 For Marinatos see now Marinatos, N. 2015.

3 If this sounds assonantly discordant I challenge you to produce an appropriate alternative with seven vowels in a ten-letter word.

Bibliography

Alexiou, S. and P. Warren

2004 *The Early Minoan Tombs of Lebena, Southern Crete* (Studies in Mediterranean Archaeology 30). Sävedalen: Paul Ästroms Förlag.

Betancourt, P. P.

2008 *The Bronze Age Begins. The Ceramics Revolution of Early Minoan I and the New Forms of Wealth that Transformed Prehistoric Society*. Philadelphia: INSTAP Academic Press.

Broodbank, C.

2004 Minoanisation. *Proceedings of the Cambridge Philological Society* 50: 46–91.

Evans, A. J.
1895 *Cretan Pictographs and Prae-Phoenician Script. With an Account of a Sepulchral Deposit at Hagios Onuphrios Near Phaestos in Its Relation to Primitive Cretan and Aegean Culture*. London: Bernard Quaritch. New York: G. P. Putnam's Sons.
1906 *Essai de Classification des Époques de la Civilisation Minoenne*. Londres: B. Quaritch.
Hamilakis, Y. (ed.)
2002a *Labyrinth Revisited. Rethinking "Minoan" Archaeology*. Oxford: Oxbow.
2002b What future for the "Minoan" past? Re-thinking Minoan archaeology. In Y. Hamilakis (ed.), *Labyrinth Revisited. Rethinking "Minoan" Archaeology*: 2–28. Oxford: Oxbow.
Marinatos, N.
2015 Sir Arthur Evans and Minoan Crete. Creating a Vision of Knossos. London: I.B. Tauris.
Panagiotopoulos, D.
2002 *Das Tholosgrab E von Phourni bei Archanes: Studien zu einem frühkretischen Grabfund und seinem kulturellen Kontext* (BAR IS 1014). Oxford: Archaeopress.
Papadatos, Y.
2005 *Tholos Tomb Gamma: A Prepalatial Tomb at Phourni, Archanes* (Prehistory Monographs 17). Philadelphia: INSTAP Academic Press.
Pendlebury, J. D. S.
1939 *The Archaeology of Crete. An Introduction*. London: Methuen & Co. Ltd.
Seager, R. B.
1907 Report of excavations at Vasiliki, Crete, in 1906. *University of Pennsylvania. Transactions of the Free Museum of Science and Art (University Museum)* 2 (2): 111–32.
Taramelli, A.
1897 Cretan Expedition VIII. The prehistoric grotto at Miamou. *American Journal of Archaeology* 1: 287–312.
Vasilakis, A. and K. Branigan (eds.)
2010 *Moni Odigitria. A Prepalatial Cemetery and Its Environs in the Asterousia, Southern Crete* (Prehistory Monographs 30). Philadelphia: INSTAP Academic Press.

Chapter 2

Roots and routes:[1] Technologies of life, death, community and identity

Maria Relaki

> "... it is impossible even to conceive of an artefact that does not incorporate social relations, or to define a social structure without the integration of non-humans into it. Every human interaction is socio-technical." (Latour 1994: 805–6)

Forty six years since the publication of Keith Branigan's seminal work *The Foundations of Palatial Crete* (1970a, henceforth *Foundations*), Minoan archaeology is still grappling with the challenges of developing a coherent general framework of interpretation that allows us both to capture a broader interpretative picture, as well as fleshing out the details that make each area and period of Cretan prehistory stand autonomously within the historical trajectory of the island (see Tomkins; Haggis this volume). While the striking diversity of the Cretan Bronze Age societies (Whitelaw 2012: 115; see also Schoep this volume) has rightly been emphasised by the continuous fieldwork and research of the last forty odd years, it has also made difficult the production of synthetic works with the kind of unified agenda that the *Foundations* had. At the same time though, this new emphasis on diversity has also accelerated the initially slow realisation that our existing analytic categories are proving too rigid for accommodating the more versatile and fluid patterns that archaeological research has been observing in the last couple of decades, planting the theoretical seed that, without re-evaluating the existing categories, we may never be able to come close to the interpretative goals set by works such as the *Foundations*.

All the contributions in this volume highlight this analytic conundrum by emphasising the various ways in which our categories stumble upon diffuse and interchangeable boundaries: in the ways territories and polities are defined (Whitelaw; Vasilakis and Sbonias this volume) with implications for the reach of political structures (Whitelaw; Haggis; Girella this volume); in understanding dwelling practices and the construction of space (Haggis; Betancount; Driessen; Hatzaki; Schoep this volume); in analysing the fabric of social units and conceptualising personhood and group identities (Hamilakis; Triantaphyllou; Haggis; Papadatos; Driessen; Hatzaki this volume); in figuring out the periodisation and temporality of social action (Tomkins; Cadogan; Hatzaki this volume); in defining value in both extra-ordinary (Papadatos; Hamilakis; Girella; Hatzaki; Schoep this volume) as well as more routine interactions (such as technological practice – see discussion below). Thus, Tomkins argues for abandoning a narrative of revolutionary change, pigeon-holing social action in distinct chronological phases, in favour of a long period of more diffuse evolution characterised by profound continuities, multiple episodes of change and diversity of regional and local development. Cadogan illustrates the methodological challenges presented by efforts to co-ordinate the basic tools of chronological resolution, ceramic development and stratigraphic phasing, using Knossos as a case study. Betancourt in turn considers the transformation of the physical space of caves into a multitude of settings for social action, be it mortuary, domestic or ritual, often undifferentiated from one another. Papadatos critically illustrates the limitations of existing analytic categories as shown in the flawed relationship between wealth and social ranking, particularly pertaining to how funerary goods are interpreted. Girella uses ceramic variability from a single cemetery to reconstruct internal social differentiations that also reflect broader social dynamics in Protopalatial Mesara, underscoring the linkage of small and medium scale processes. Triantaphyllou uses the study of the skeletal material from Prepalatial cemeteries to argue for a more nuanced understanding of secondary burial as a continuum of mortuary treatment rather than as a set of disparate actions and to illustrate the complex interplay between individual burial and collective mortuary ritual. Schoep criticises the use of funerary data to support a normative view of mortuary practice as a passive reflection of social structure, using the distribution of house tomb architecture to demonstrate the intricate processes of status negotiation at intra- and supra-community level. Hatzaki offers a much needed diachronic overview of mortuary practice by emphasising the continuum of social behaviour that links the fluctuating visibility of funerary display and other contexts favouring public social action. Moving from the mortuary sphere and the more local considerations of social pattern to the wider processes of political formation, Whitelaw evaluates the ways in which polities can be defined in Crete, questioning the naturalisation of palatial centres as the dominant scenario and concluding that political developments on the island are far more locally varied, fluid and dynamic than traditional interpretations have recognised. Haggis corroborates this view by using survey data to illustrate the remarkably long-term adherence of Bronze Age societies to local social landscapes, reflecting centripetal developments rather than resulting from economic expansion or socio-political centralisation, a pattern which he sees repeated across the island's micro-regions. Vasilakis and Sbonias also employ a variety of survey data to illuminate the interconnections between settlements and mortuary landscapes in the Asterousia, simultaneously documenting dynamic changes and emphasising the remarkable continuity of habitation in pockets of this landscape. In the final two articles of the volume, Driessen and Hamilakis, each tackle the dialectic constitution of individual and collective practices: Driessen emphasises the ways in which various aspects of the Protopalatial social landscape emanate from group power strategies, in contrast to more traditional perspectives seeing the Palaces as the triumph of individualism; Hamilakis, looking at the extremely fluid corporeal landscape of Prepalatial mortuary practices, discusses a series of practices which marked intentional strategies of forgetting individuals as social agents by remembering them as part of the collective of ancestors. In continuing the discussion on research themes reflected by Branigan's work all contributions demonstrate vividly how pertinent these issues remain within contemporary Cretan archaeology, while by making reference to dynamic practices that often defy neat categorisation, all articles emphasise the need for intermediate conceptual levels to fill the gaps appearing within our existing scales of analysis and for capturing more effectively the fluidity of social action.

Deconstructing the purity of categories is not a new venture in anthropology, philosophy and material culture studies (e.g. Strathern 1980; Haraway 1991; Latour 1993; Ingold 2000; Knappett 2005; Barrett 2014), with the most important task being to move beyond humano-centric perspectives and to embrace more symmetrical approaches (e.g. Shanks 2007; Knappett and Malafouris 2008; Hall 2011; Overton and Hamilakis 2013). No category has been immune to this rethinking and even the boundaries of concepts thought to be ontologically secure, such as the individual, are shown to be permeable (e.g. Strathern 1988; Busby 1997; Nanoglou 2012; Hamilakis this volume). The realisation that conventional analytic categories have lost much of their explanatory potential has been particularly striking in the discussion of wider historical processes of Cretan prehistory, such as palatial formation and more specifically the nature and format of the palatial institution (e.g. articles in Driessen *et al.* 2002; Hamilakis 2002). What we are now coming to terms with in Minoan archaeology is that a whole host of categories at smaller and medium-scale levels that we had considered to be well-defined and fixed are actually porous and often dissolvable, as many of the articles in the volume show. This categorical fuzziness (Knappett 2005: 16–17) tends to cause an analytical insecurity as it can make it appear difficult to find order in the richness and diversity of life in the past. Having no clear-cut categories in which the material remains of the past can fit neatly may also give the impression that we can only ever look at the minutiae of very specific and localised contexts, without the potential to draw rigorous general conclusions about broader, larger-scale processes, and this tension is reflected in many of the discussions presented in the volume.

Fuzziness, however, by embodying the realisation that things may not always be tidily and securely ordered, has many benefits: it allows us to perceive the common ground between entities, it makes it easier to detect links and connections between different fields, and thus emphasises a continuum of perception and action that reflects better the reality – and the messiness – of life in any period. Instead of perceiving fuzziness as an analytic problem, we should be making it our ontological starting point. Adopting this perspective would provide us with a more dynamic perception of the past as a constant flow of materials, energy, and information (Barrett 2014). Our new research task then would be to find, out of this constant flow, the structural nodes that link different people, things, places and temporalities together by providing a grounding point where meaning is concentrated, negotiated and re-affirmed (Relaki 2013: 110).

To achieve this we will need to work with new kinds of *assemblages*[2] that can simultaneously reflect this dynamic flow, but also allow us to identify contexts and practices that facilitate a crystallisation of meaning, even if fleetingly and temporarily. Such assemblages should not be made up of things only, as in their more traditional definitions in archaeological practice, but they should incorporate humans and non-human entities as well. Deleuze and Guattari's (1987) philosophical work has laid the foundations for conceptualising such fluid structures, by perceiving the world as constituted through a multiplicity of relations between humans, non-humans and materials that affect and are affected in a myriad of directions and levels. Such affective flows create assemblages which operate in a rhizomatic way, forging connections at every level, plane of interaction or point of entry, expanding in all directions and creating links that are not linear or hierarchical, but can be best described as taking the form of a map, which "fosters connections between fields; is open and connectable in all its dimensions" (Deleuze and Guattari 1987: 7–12). This kind of assemblages are in a constant state of becoming, continuously defined by the *relations* they facilitate and embody. The boundaries of any assemblage can become sharper and its composition homogenised through territorialisation processes, which solidify and concretise the defining elements of the assemblage. Since the components of any assemblage, however, retain their autonomy and are not fused into a seamless whole, deterritorialisation processes can detach any of the components and plug it into a different assemblage, thereby destabilising its identity, breaking down its boundaries and making the assemblage prone to change (Deleuze and Guattari 1987: 88; De Landa 2006: 253). These interchangeable and continuous territorialisations and deterritorialisations are the means by which lives, social action and history unfold (Fox and Alldred 2014: 401), in "a world that is constantly becoming" (Thrift 2004: 61).

The most crucial methodological and ontological advantages in these constructs are that they focus on processes and interactions, striving to grasp the continuous becoming of entities rather than any static or fixed state of being (Fox and Alldred 2014: 401) and that they are operating through a post-humanist perspective which allows key roles for materials and non-human entities and the affordances that these present for action. The latter is a central concern of the present discussion, which seeks to capture the dynamics of technological practice by placing equal emphasis on the transformative and crystallising qualities of human interactions with materials and techniques.

My aim in this article is to explore how human interactions with materials and techniques create *assemblages* that operate as structural nodes that can concentrate meaning and reconfigure identities. As Latour (1994) points out, social relations are impossible without engagement with non-human agents, such as things and materials. His argument is that "social interactions ... are extremely labile and transitory. They are either negotiable, but transient, or, if they are encoded, for instance, in the genetic make-up, they are extremely durable, but impossible to easily negotiate." Non-humans on the other hand "are at once pliable and durable; they can be shaped very fast, but once shaped, they last much longer than the interaction that fabricated them. [...] By bringing in non-humans, the contradiction of durability and negotiability [in social interactions] is solved" (Latour 1994: 803). This argument underscores the inherent ephemeral nature of human interactions and highlights the organic role that materials and things play in facilitating social interactions and negotiating social identities. Such an approach is echoed in calls to reassess the perception of organisms and their boundaries (and by extension, the way we understand any categorical formation and its boundaries) as semi-permeable "because the organism can only exist relative to sources of energy whilst maintaining its organisational integrity" (Barrett 2014: 70; see also Ingold 2000; Knappett 2005). In other words, in the same way that humans cannot exist outside of the affordances that their environments offer, their social interactions cannot take shape or place without the involvement of and engagement with materials and things. Such a perspective also destabilises conventional categorisations of subject (creator) and object (creation) by emphasising the reciprocity and inter-reliability of the two roles; one cannot be without the other, or, as Serres (1982: 223) explains, the two converge into a "quasi-object" which "is not an object; but it is one nevertheless, since it is not a subject, since it is in the world; it is also a quasi-subject, since it marks or designates a subject who, without it would not be a subject." This mutual constitution of subject and object is particularly useful for exploring the dialectic relationship that exists in the creative processes between human agents, materials, techniques and artefacts. What is more, such an approach allows us more fruitful insights into the role that technological practice and artefacts play in the constitution of social identities.

I will examine these ideas in some detail through a case study looking at the way that particular interactions of people with diverse materials and techniques in the Mesara and Asterousia area in south central Crete during the Prepalatial and early Protopalatial periods helped create distinctive *assemblages* of people, places and things that focused identities and meaning out of a constant flow of matter, energy and information. In the process of doing so I aim to critically examine the ways in which the concepts of local and non-local are constructed and the significance of this contrast for shaping boundaries and defining social interactions. Because these human-social-technical interactions can operate as territorialising processes that can sharpen identities and condense the consistency of the assemblages of relations and meaning they generate, they are particularly useful for exploring and evaluating what makes something local (i.e. belonging) or non-local (i.e. external to the assemblage, potentially diluting its texture). *Exotica* will thus be examined as part of deterritorialising strategies that threaten the links keeping these assemblages together and undermining their meaning.

Roots: humans, materials, techniques

Reflecting the theoretical trends explored above, in recent years archaeological investigations of ancient technologies have moved away from strict categorisations based on raw material towards emphasising interrelationships between craft practices. These attitudes emerge out of a reaction against the limitations posed by these categorical boundaries to attaining a deeper understanding of technical engagement that spans different materials, but they also draw on a self-critical recognition that such categorical ordering reflects more modern concerns which do not capture the whole gamut of ways that people interacted with materials and techniques in the past. Under the influence of concepts such as the *chaîne opératoire* (Leroi-Gourhan 1993), more emphasis is placed on gestures and technical processes that cross-cut the manipulation of different raw materials and the creation of diverse artefacts, offering a more holistic approach to the study of technological practice (e.g. Dobres 1999). In a similar vein, the usefulness of concepts such as materiality have been re-evaluated by examining in detail how they may allow a better understanding of human engagement with techniques (Ingold 2007; Knappett 2007; Tilley 2007). In re-addressing categorical boundaries, even the fixity of the properties of materials, which had traditionally operated as a defining criterion for ordering artefacts and establishing categories of analysis, has been called into question; for example, it has been emphasised how several materials may exhibit certain properties when they are being worked (e.g. clay being pliable, dissolvable, soft) which they lose once the technical process is complete and the artefact has been formed (e.g. fired clay being hard, rigid, static) (Ingold 2007: 13). Such observations underline the importance of approaching socio-technical interactions as an ongoing process, in which neither the interaction, nor the resulting artefact are ever fixed, casting the dialectic between transformation and continuity under sharper focus.

A substantial range of craft goods was produced in the Mesara and Asterousia area from the earliest Prepalatial until the palatial periods, including ceramics (Wilson and Day 1994; Todaro 2012; 2013; Mentesana *et al.* 2016), stone vases (Warren 1969; Bevan 2007; Todaro 2013), seals (Sbonias 1999; 2000), metal daggers (Branigan 1967), figurines (Branigan 1971a; Papadatos 2007; Alexiou and Warren 2004), and obsidian blades (Carter 1998; 2010). Despite the standard division of these objects into different categories on the basis of their raw material and form, a striking set of close similarities and associations can be observed from the perspective of both their *chaînes opératoires* and the spatial and temporal configuration of the productive process, while all these artefacts also played a key role in strategies of social negotiation during the Prepalatial and early Protopalatial periods.

One of the most evident affinities in technological practice concerns the knowledge of pyrotechnology and the application of heat during the technical process. Both ceramic and metal production relies equally on the detailed knowledge and skilled manipulation of fire and firing conditions for the manufacture of ceramic and metal artefacts (Doonan and Day 2007: 12). While for the earliest Mesaran ceramics these skills can be inferred by the quality of the finished product and particularly the control of the firing conditions (Wilson and Day 1994: 70–76), for later Prepalatial and Protopalatial ceramics there is evidence of kilns and kiln wasters from the area (Carinci 1997; Van De Moortel 2006; Todaro 2012; 2013), which testifies to the investment of knowledge, energy and resources associated with this craft activity. Other, less obvious, categories of materials also make use of heat in their productive routine: the manufacture of a category of sealstones known as "white pieces" entails the mixing of pulverised talc with a binding agent, the mixture then being heat treated in order to solidify (Krzyszkowska 2005: 73; Sbonias 1995: 113–18). More surprising applications of pyrotechnology are emerging from recent studies of Prepalatial cemeteries across the island, this time concerning ways of destroying rather than creating objects. For example, heat has been applied to facilitate the breakage of stone vases before deposition at the Prepalatial cemetery of Petras Kephala in east Crete (Relaki and Tsoraki 2017), unsurprisingly suggesting specialised knowledge of the raw material and its behaviour, but rather unexpectedly revealing technical expertise in the use and control of fire to achieve the desired effect for an artefact category that does not routinely use heat in the manufacture process. Such expertise is also mirrored in the extensive uses of fire in the handling of the dead bodies during various stages of deposition in several Prepalatial cemeteries (Triantaphyllou 2009; 2010: 232; 2017; this volume). Examples of twisted metal daggers are also known from tombs in the Mesara (e.g. Platanos A; Xanthoudides [1924: 107] suggests that the triangular daggers might have been "twisted by the great heat" of fire used to presumably fumigate the tomb) and eastern Crete (e.g. Hagia Photia, Hamilakis 1998: 123, fig. 8.2) for which a suggestion of intentional, ritual killing has been made (Hamilakis 1998). While the latter examples illustrate practices that do not manipulate fire and its effects to construct, as in the case of firing a ceramic vase, or smelting copper to manufacture metal tools and weapons, but rather to deconstruct, as Hoffman argued (1999: 103), "breaking is as much about technological practice ... as is making". In breaking apart what is considered a bounded whole, these practices serve to emphasise the role that technique and technical knowledge played in creating meaningful *assemblages*: in life, this technology was used to bring together elements, to mix, to amalgamate, to territorialise a set of identities and social interactions; in death, the same practice was used to break apart these connections, to deterritorialise these identities and insert them into a new assemblage, where personhood (see Hamilakis this volume) and thing-hood played different roles, subsumed to a larger, undifferentiated collectivity. In living, by mixing materials, energy and forms to create artefacts that could anchor social interactions, and in dying, by diffusing the boundaries between humans and things, these assemblages created distinct social identities mediated by technique.

A further blurring of traditional artefact categories is also noted in the selection and manipulation of raw materials to manufacture a suite of diverse craft goods. Stone vessels and seals produced in the Mesara are commonly made of chlorite, steatite and serpentine locally occurring in the ophiolitic complex in the Asterousia and the southern Ida slopes (Warren 1969: 129–30; Becker 1976; Bevan 2007: 85), which is also the source of clays and non-plastic inclusions used in a range of pottery fabrics produced in the area (Wilson and Day 1994: 54–57; Mentesana *et al.* 2016: 491). Similarly, the main ingredient of the white paste seals discussed above, appearing from the MMIA onwards across the region (Krzyskowska 2005: 73), is pulverised talc, a component of steatite, available in the same geological outcrop. Analysis of Prepalatial and Protopalatial ceramics from the wider Mesara and Asterousia area has also demonstrated that talc had been used to produce the white colour in the surface decoration of polychrome pottery, this being a very localised pattern, characteristic of Mesaran production as other areas of Crete seem to be using a calcite-based white pigment (Day *et al.* 2006: 56). The use of a common suite of raw materials suggests a close dialogue between presumably different crafts, not only highlighting the shared knowledge of the location and harvesting of these raw materials and implying common understanding of a range of techniques and gestures necessary for their processing, but also underscoring a shared appreciation of the value of these materials for facilitating social interaction. Such sharing of knowledge, technique and practice maps an *assemblage* of technical and social relations that highlight the embeddedness of such activities in social life and their central role in processes of social negotiation.

Perhaps this sharing ethos can account for another common element between these categories of objects, a common repertoire of decorative principles and motifs, as well as some interchangeable forms and types crosscutting different media, such as the various zoomorphic objects (Fig. 2.1). Such similarities may often be dismissed as superficial fashion trends, particularly if viewed through the somewhat distorting prism of chronological periods and sub-periods, however, the repetition of specific motifs across different supports, such as ceramics and seals, consumed in common contexts and embedded in similar collective practices, has been convincingly shown in other areas of Crete to reflect the articulation of close-knit, symbolically-charged collective networks (Haggis 2007). By the same token, working within broad chronological horizons presents certain advantages as it allows us to observe wider trends in technical engagement. A number of technical changes, such as the introduction of drilling for the manufacture of stone vases and seals from EMIIB onwards (Warren 1969: 161; Bevan 2007: 58; Krzyskowska 2005: 60) or the production of polychrome ceramic wares and white paste sealstones at the beginning of the MBA – both making use of pulverised talc as noted above – are strikingly contemporaneous (Day *et al.* 2006), suggesting that these technical features and choices might have been part of the same horizons of technological innovation. Such observations further illustrate the existence of an undifferentiated technical milieu in which artefact creation reflected and materialised an *assemblage*

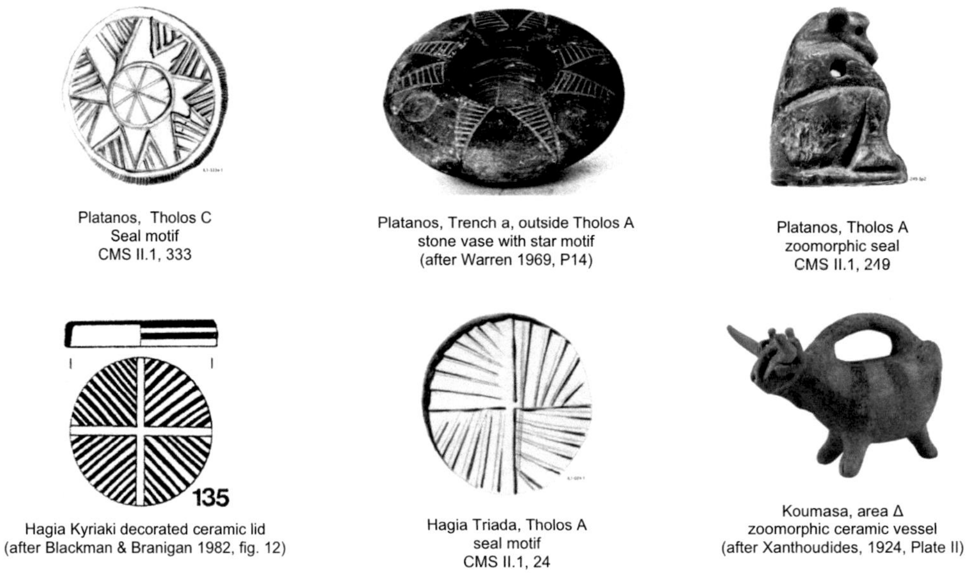

Platanos, Tholos C
Seal motif
CMS II.1, 333

Platanos, Trench a, outside Tholos A
stone vase with star motif
(after Warren 1969, P14)

Platanos, Tholos A
zoomorphic seal
CMS II.1, 249

Hagia Kyriaki decorated ceramic lid
(after Blackman & Branigan 1982, fig. 12)

Hagia Triada, Tholos A
seal motif
CMS II.1, 24

Koumasa, area Δ
zoomorphic ceramic vessel
(after Xanthoudides, 1924, Plate II)

Figure 2.1: Selection of objects sharing decorative principles and motifs.

of social relations, being expressed as much in the manufacturing processes as in the appearance and use of the objects.

In that respect, it is noteworthy that the object types showing the greatest affinities seem to also make the most pronounced reference to collective social practices. This is more obvious for ceramics which are produced in bulk and have been convincingly shown to be embedded in practices of large scale food and drink consumption (Hamilakis 1998; 2000; 2008; Day and Wilson 1998; Haggis 2007; Day *et al.* 2010; Todaro 2012; 2013: 260–66). However, similar patterns may also be observed for stone vases, particularly in terms of their deposition in Prepalatial cemeteries as shown, for example, in the more than 300 stone vases that were found outside Tholos A in Platanos (Xanthoudides 1924: 90, 98–104; Gerontakou 2003). Thus, even though stone vase manufacture may necessitate longer amounts of time than ceramic production (although see Todaro [2013: 196–201] for a discussion of layering, a particularly time-consuming and labour intensive method of ceramic production, specific to Mesaran technological traditions), such instances of bulk stone vase use may mirror ceramic practices and situate both types of objects within equivalent consumption strategies. Similarly, although it has been suggested that the use of daggers and seals reflected an increasing emphasis on individual identities, to the extent of representing a shift of emphasis from more collective to more personal strategies (see also Hamilakis this volume), increasing evidence also highlights their instrumental role in collective representation. It has been suggested that the combined presence of seals and daggers in Prepalatial cemeteries in the Mesara and Asterousia marks the burial of clan leaders (Renfrew 1972: 387–88), or heads of nuclear families (Whitelaw 1983: 343, n. 16),

Table 2.1: Distribution of seals and daggers in the Mesara tholos tombs

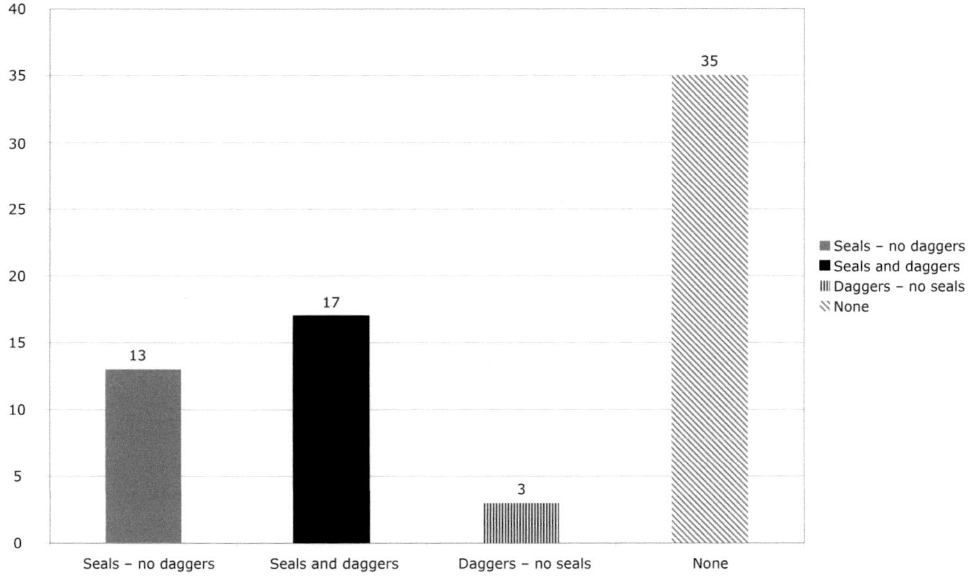

on the basis that these items would have functioned as insignia of personal status. However, these two types of objects were not always complementary in their burial deposition: there are cemeteries where seals, but not daggers have been included in the burials (e.g. Hagia Kyriaki A, Lebena Papoura 1b, Platanos C) whereas in the lower level of Platanos Tholos A only daggers were deposited and no seals (Table 2.1). Moreover, whenever they are found together seals are always more numerous, as seen in the more undisturbed contexts of the Lebena tombs (Alexiou and Warren 2004). Therefore, this lack of a clear association between seals and daggers may imply that these artefacts might have represented different kinds of personal strategies, as well as different consumption practices on a collective level, as is implied by their concentrations in certain cemeteries, particularly in the case of daggers (e.g. Hagia Triada and Platanos-Xanthoudides 1924; Branigan 1970b). Moreover, although seals are generally considered "items of identity", the kind of identities they reflected combined features geared towards personal identification (e.g. they are invariably perforated, occur in a great variety of shapes and sizes, and have a possible amuletic function therefore suggesting that they were meant to be worn by a person [Sbonias 1999: 35; Krzyskowska 2005: 76]) at the same time as displaying elements more suited to collective representation and use (e.g. motif groups are associated with specific cemeteries [Sbonias 1999: 42–43; 2000: 287]; motifs are inherited through generations and reproduced as look-alikes; and both Prepalatial and Protopalatial sealing practices in the Mesara reflect collective representation [Relaki 2009; 2012]). Therefore their morphological elements, patterns of deposition and use all point, once again, to a blurring of collective and personal strategies.

These patterns of collective association and crosscutting of the barriers between different techniques and craft activities are further expounded by more recent discoveries of shared production settings at Phaistos (Todaro 2012; 2013). Evidence for the production of stone and ceramic vases, obsidian blades, and bone tools has been unearthed on various locations of the hill throughout several phases of the Prepalatial and Protopalatial (Todaro 2013: 246, 260 and *passim*) at consistently common settings, using shared tools and resources despite any differential requirements in the productive process of each object. Furthermore, analysis of bone material from recent excavations at Phaistos has also demonstrated the consumption of large amounts of cattle and sheep/goat, butchered in the vicinity of the hill (Masala 2009), a pattern consistent with meat consumption reserved for special, largely collective events (Halstead 2007: 27). The presence of such a large amount of bone material has been linked with large-scale food and drink consumption events at Phaistos, in which ceramic implements played a vital role, while large-scale ceramic production events have also been isolated, possibly catering for such feasts (Todaro 2013: 261). Interestingly the meat consumption might have also provided raw material for a range of other craft activities. For example, cattle metatarsals and metacarpals (parts of the hind- and forefoot) have been commonly used for the production of bone seals, most notably of ring-shaped seals and the *epomia* style (Krzyszkowska 2005: 62), which is a local tradition limited to the Mesara and the Asterousia (Sbonias 2000: 281–82). The evidence from Phaistos thus presents a fascinating glimpse not only of the ways in which diverse materials were embedded in shared technical processes, but also, more importantly, of the ways in which artefacts and people participated in, and generated *assemblages* of meaning that validated and consolidated their social interactions and identities.

What is even more interesting about these events is that they consistently blur any division between production and consumption, both in the sense of situating the two activities within the same spatial and temporal framework, as well as through the performativity of both actions. While it has been relatively easy to amplify the significance of performance in consumption events, particularly in large scale feasting (e.g. Dietler and Hayden 2001; Day and Wilson 2004; Haggis 2007; Hamilakis 2008) it has been perhaps more difficult to argue the same for production, mainly by virtue of technological activity often necessitating remote locations due to pollution, noise, or lack of space within built up areas. However, recent technological investigations have demonstrated that, even when physically removed from the public eye, particular kinds of technical activity displayed a combination of withholding trade secrets while simultaneously treating craft production as a practical drama (Doonan *et al.* 2007: 115–17), while the performative role of a range of craft activities has also been emphasised within the "theatrics" of technological practice (Carter 1998; 2010: 152, 165; Catapotis 2007; Todaro 2013: 288). This blurring of productive and consumptive processes further illustrates that the categorical divisions we had imposed on these activities rather hindered our understanding of the ways social roles and identities were negotiated in these contexts. Instead, by looking at these activities as a series of human interactions with materials and techniques, we can see an *assemblage* of meaningful associations between people, places, materials and objects, mediated by technological practice, taking shape and informing the active negotiation of social identities in Prepalatial and Protopalatial Mesara and Asterousia.

Routes: exotica and the deterritorialisation of value

The picture painted above of craft production informing a set of shared practices, experiences and belonging, which territorialised a very local perception of value, should be embellished through a parallel consideration of the role that imported goods and materials played in shaping social interactions at both a local and supra-regional level. Cretan communities did not exist in isolation at any chronological period, however, an intensification of long distance exchange that increased the influx of materials and finished goods, particularly emanating from the Cyclades and the southern Aegean has been suggested from the EMII period onwards (Renfrew 1972; Broodbank 2000; Vavouranakis 2011) although more recent work has placed such intensification at an even earlier stage (Papadatos and Tomkins 2013; 2014). Similarly, interactions with Egypt and the eastern Mediterranean begin rather slowly and sporadically from the EMII and become more pronounced in the late Prepalatial although the pace and intensity of such interactions is also characterised by fluctuations (Warren 1965; 1969; Lambrou-Philipson 1990; Watrous 1998; Bevan 2004; Phillips 2005; 2008). The range of materials, artefacts and influences noted as imports on Crete have, to a large extent, been categorised as such on the basis of raw material provenance and style/external appearance of the finished goods, thus mirroring the traditional categorisations of technological objects explored above for "local" products.

The main objections to this picture have been mounted from an analytic perspective, particularly of ceramics and metals, able to go underneath the "foreign" veneer of any presumed imports to reveal a much more complex image. Thus, ceramic analysis from a number of sites along the north-east coast of the island has demonstrated that a significant amount of Cycladic-style pottery found there was actually produced in Crete, using local raw materials (Dimopoulou-Rethemiotaki *et al.* 2007: 88, 90; Papadatos and Tomkins 2013: 356–65; 2014: 331–34), while EMI cemeteries like Hagia Photia in eastern Crete consumed a combination of imports, from both the Cyclades and other areas of Crete (Day *et al.* 1998). Although imports of Cycladic pottery are rare in the Mesara (Wilson 2008: 85), arguments have been made about the broader stylistic influences noted on Cretan EMI-EMII types, such as the Dark Grey Pattern Burnished ware which appears very similar to many dark surface Cycladic ceramics (Vavouranakis 2011: 97), large quantities of which have been documented from contexts in Hagia Triada and Phaistos (Wilson 2008: 84), while Cycladicising features also extend on other Mesaran ceramic wares and types (e.g. fine burnished and painted ware pyxides with slashed handles and stamped triangular and incised decoration; Wilson 2008: 87). On the whole, divergent ceramic traditions seem to co-exist on the island, encompassing both Cycladic-style and Minoan "proper" pottery, but certainly being characterised by very localised spatial distribution; Cycladic-style ceramics seem to be limited to the north coast, despite a variety of other Cycladic goods and materials regularly reaching south-central Crete, and in spite of Mesaran imports being documented in gateway communities with good access to Cycladic materials, such as Poros-Katsambas in EMI and EMII (Dimopoulou-Rethemiotaki *et al.* 2007: 88–89) and even as far as Hagia Photia in east Crete (Day *et al.* 1998: 138, 146). This pattern of exchange thus presents itself as multi-directional and multi-dimensional, the spatial extent of this network being affected by more than just the provenance or style of the exchanged ceramics.

For metal objects, even more intriguing patterns emerge through the analysis of both raw materials as well as technological processes. Metal daggers, frequently encountered in the mortuary record of Prepalatial Crete, occur in two distinct types: the short, triangular type, the overwhelming distribution of which in the Mesara, with nearly half of these deriving from Hagia Triada (Branigan 1967: 230) branding them a quintessentially local type (Nakou 1995: 9), and the long, mid-rib daggers, which, although also well documented on Crete (Branigan 1967; 1974), their affinities with Cycladic types situate them as largely foreign imports (Renfrew 1973). However, once again, evidence from local production in the presence of moulds found at Poros-Katsambas (Doonan *et al.* 2007: 114) casts doubts to such straightforward characterisations, while the examination of the sources of the raw materials used in the production of these artefacts paints an even more complex picture. Although some evidence for copper mineralisation can be found in south Crete, at Chrysostomos on the edge of the Mesara (Branigan 1971b: 14; Stos-Gale 1993: 119; Doonan *et al.* 2007: 100), scientific analysis has shown that the copper used for the production of most of the triangular daggers was of Kythnian origin, while the tin included in the alloy more likely derived from Anatolia (Branigan 1974). Similarly, recent investigations from the FN-EMIII metallurgical facility at Chrysokamino (Betancourt 2006) have shown that minerals from two different sources had been used to produce freshly smelted copper (Catapotis and Bassiakos 2007: 72), indicating that "mixed provenance" can extend to raw materials as well as finished goods (Doonan and Day 2007: 7). Moreover, secondary production sites such as Poros-Katsambas on the north coast further complicate the suggestion of a clear geographical origin for craft objects, by utilising imported raw materials to produce "foreign"-looking items locally on Crete (Doonan *et al.* 2007).

Obsidian blades constitute another typically Cycladic import, also regularly deposited in funerary contexts in the Mesara and across the island. Their raw material derives from Melos and the necrotaphic consumption of fine obsidian blades also draws on Cycladic mortuary traditions (Carter 1998; 2010: 151). However, obsidian blades are in their majority deposited un-used and in quite fresh condition, suggesting that their manufacture took place shortly before deposition, something that is unparalleled to the ways in which the same artefacts were used in the Cyclades (Carter 1998: 69; 2010: 161). Furthermore, the way the blades were produced shows a significant departure from the technological principles characterising obsidian production in the Cyclades, and on the basis of several obsidian assemblages from the island, it has been suggested that the manufacturing process observed in Crete was part of a technological *koine*, reserved for Cretan sites and quite distinct from its contemporary Cycladic counterparts (Carter 2010: 161).

Similar fuzzy amalgamations of origin and technology are reflected in folded-arm figurines included in the funerary consumption of the Prepalatial period. A number of figurines have been recovered in Crete, only a small portion of which has direct parallels in Cycladic types and can therefore be considered as imports. Some figurines found in Archanes display peculiarities such as denoting the mouth (very common in Cretan, but rare in Cycladic examples) or displaying separate legs, an important departure from Cycladic-proper convention (Papadatos 2007: 427). Several Cretan varieties also exist, such as Koumasa, Sivas and Trapeza (Branigan 1971a), which occur in a range of lithic sources, such as steatite, schist and limestone, all available locally, while there are also examples made of animal bone, which nevertheless faithfully reproduce Cycladic types such as the Spedhos variety (Papadatos 2007: 427). While varieties such as the Koumasa type are considered local "imitations" developed and produced in Crete (Renfrew 1969: 19), examples of this local type occur on distinctly Cycladic raw material, such as marble, as the figurines from Lebena show (Alexiou and Warren 2004: 52, 53, 127–28, 187). Thus taking both raw material and style as our guiding criteria for artefact categorisation would not help us clearly distinguish the provenance and ethnic or cultural origin of such objects, something that has significant implications for the ways these might have been perceived as being "local" or "foreign". Instead we may get more critical insights if we consider the "blended" connotations of distance and belonging that such objects embody as part of a larger *assemblage* of people, things and technical practices that validate certain kinds of social relations.

Stone vases represent another category of artefact where diverse off-island influences have been noted. In contrast to stone vase manufacture in the Cyclades that stretches back to the last phases of the Neolithic period (Bevan 2007: 80–85), stone vase production on Crete begins rather suddenly in the EMIIA period (Warren 1969: 182–83). However, given the influx of Cycladic material on Crete and the noted intensity of exchanges, there are no overt Cycladic influences on Cretan stone vase production. Bevan (2007: 86) notes that although early chlorite stone vases in Cycladic and Cretan traditions share a set of decorative principles, particularly demonstrated in their incised decoration, both represent distinct and spatially separated manufacturing traditions. This rather oblique relationship with Cycladic influences is further demonstrated by the lack of verified imports of finished vases while examples of what has been considered local "imitations" do not have straightforward parallels in the Cyclades (Bevan 2007: 94).

Intermingled with this picture, Egyptian influences which were rather sporadic in the early Prepalatial seem to become more prominent from the MMIA onwards (Bevan 2004), although these include a rather mixed bag of features. Evidence for actual imported Egyptian stone vases to the Mesara in the Prepalatial period is limited to an anorthosite gneiss jar from Hagia Triada Tholos A (Karetsou and Andreadaki-Vlazaki 2000: no. 5; Bevan 2004: 113), while the same tomb also included the largest concentration of Egyptianising vessels found at a single context at that time. Discussion of Cretan exchange patterns with Egypt has focused on local "imitations" of Egyptian stone vases, presenting a set of distinct characteristics: they concentrate mainly on Mochlos and the Mesara; they seem to copy the most common of contemporary Egyptian oil container shape, in contrast to the small and more eclectic sample of actual Egyptian imports; and local imitations reproduce mainly miniature versions of shapes found in a variety of sizes in Egypt (Bevan 2004: 112; 2007: 96–97). Aside to rightfully illustrating a complex exchange pattern with Egypt, the suggestion of local imitations presents some difficulties. On the one hand, although there is no doubt that particular features of the shapes and the local materials used for the production of these vases make reference to examples known from Egypt, a particular stage of the "imitation" process is missing, as Bevan (2007: 97) also concedes, in that there are no known imports of the shapes that the local versions are supposed to be copying. While these may have been lost to the vagaries of site preservation, the extensive number of "copies" and the long curation of certain imported vases would probably warn against all such examples not surviving. Therefore pinpointing the source and method of inspiration by Egyptian prototypes remains quite unclear. On a more theoretical level, if anything has been learnt from the preceding discussion is that local engagement with materials and techniques of any provenance makes it very difficult to specify "prototypes" and "imitations" as the technical process blurs and distorts these artificial distinctions in forceful and consistent ways.

Such complex interrelations between "exotic originals" and "local versions" are also reflected in seals and scarabs from the Prepalatial and early Protopalatial period. Seals are introduced in the panoply of Minoan material culture from the EMIIA onwards, generally produced in a variety of local soft stones and bone (Krzyszkowska 2005: 59–60). From the same period and more prominently during the EMIII-MMIA, they are also produced in hippopotamus ivory imported from either Egypt or the Near East (Krzyszkowska 2005: 59; Sbonias 2000: 283). In addition to such foreign raw materials, the cylinder shape seal variety is also thought to be introduced on Crete from the Near East, although Cretan cylinder seals are not engraved on the barrel and then rolled (as the Near Eastern examples), but rather continue the local practice of stamp sealing by using the two flat faces of the cylinder to carry the engraved motifs (Krzyszkowska 2005: 64). Scarabs occur as both actual imports and local varieties, the latter exceeding the former in number. Certain aspects of the imported scarabs betray local consumption preferences irrespectively of what was popular at the time in Egyptian contexts: for example, only half of the imported scarabs have a lunate head, in contrast to the stronger popularity of this type in Egypt (Phillips 2008: 122), a preference which seems to replicate in some ways the "imitation" patterns observed for stone vases. On the other hand, the Minoan examples clearly chose not to illustrate the indigenous horned scarab species, opting instead for the Egyptian scarab form while they are also exclusively made of white paste, which, although a distinctly local innovation (see discussion above) it has been suggested that it emerged out of efforts to replicate the Egyptian scarab raw material (Phillips 2008: 132). However, taking all the idiosyncracies of the Minoan scarabs into consideration, in comparison to other areas in the eastern Mediterranean where Egyptian scarabs were imported and imitated in more straightforward manners, Philips (2005: 44; 2008: 123–125, 132) concludes that the Minoan scarabs should not be seen as imitations of the Egyptian prototypes, but rather as a new element introduced in the already developed repertoire of zoomorphic seals widely circulating on Crete at the time, the preference for scarabs probably explained by their flat shape offering a larger surface for carving a seal design, at the time when Cretan seals were transitioning from tall narrow shapes to short and wide forms. Whether imported or locally made, scarabs are almost invariably deposited in mortuary contexts, with significant concentrations in the Mesara and Asterousia tholoi. However, even though imports are distributed more widely across the island, locally made scarabs are almost exclusively found in the Mesara, concentrated particularly around Moni Odigitria and Kaloi Limenes, suggesting the existence of a production centre in this region (Phillips 2008: 123, 224), which would also comply with the suggested production location of other white paste seals (Sbonias 2010). Thus the patterns of exchange and importation for both stone vases and seals underline an emphasis on the appropriation of exotic raw materials and influences by assimilating them into local preferences and concerns, manifested both by the technical process of production as well as the patterns of consumption.

To further flesh out the multi-layered nature of such exchange patterns, another very important consideration is the direction of travel that the various imported goods followed in order to reach the Mesara. While the travel path for the Cycladic goods seems to be more self-evident, varied opinions exist suggesting either a N–S axis, originating in north coast gateway communities such as Poros Katsambas, reaching the south central communities in the Mesara and Asterousia via Archanes (Papadatos 2007; this volume), or privileging the option of cosmopolitan sites in the north-east of the island, such as Mochlos (Branigan 1991), feeding imported material via communities on the south-east coast of the island and reaching the Mesara through a maritime route (Carter 2010: 164), although it is quite possible that both routes might have been operational but channelling different goods. For the Egyptian and Near Eastern material reaching the Mesara region, opinions are even more varied, possibly reflecting temporal variability as well as differential distribution of goods. Thus, the suggestion has been made that although maritime contact with Egypt might have included direct southwards journeys from the Mesara to Egypt with return voyages going through the Levantine coast, the dominance of Egyptian imitations in the Mesara as opposed to the more frequent presence of actual imports along the north-central coast may imply rather limited access to Egyptian goods which might have been channelled to the Mesara via the north (Bevan 2007: 93). Phillips (2005; 2008) also corroborates part of this suggestion by observing a chronological pattern in Egyptian goods being imported via the north in the earlier part of the Prepalatial period, with more direct routes coming to play from the EMIII onwards. The idea of a direct route of communication between Egypt and the Mesara has been challenged by considerations of sea currents and prevalent winds across the eastern Mediterranean (Agouridis 1997), which make the suggestion of an intermediary route, including the Levant, southern Anatolian coast, Cyprus and Rhodes, more probable (Legarra-Herrero 2011: 268; also Bevan 2004: 120).

A major implication of all these suggestions, irrespectively of the route favoured, is that any items reaching the Mesara were transported there via down-the-line exchanges, which would have made the appreciation of an original provenance rather diluted and diffuse, significantly filtered through other areas of Crete and the eastern Mediterranean (Carter 1998; Bevan 2004: 120; Phillips 2005; Papadatos 2007: 438; Legarra-Herrero 2011). Accordingly, the Cretan adoption of such foreign objects has been variably interpreted as characterised primarily by local consumption concerns (Phillips 2005; Legarra-Herrero 2011), while other approaches oscillate between a rather uncritical direct replication of Near Eastern status and power strategies (Colburn 2008: 214) and a more nuanced appreciation and manipulation of foreign symbolism for elite building (e.g. Schoep 2006).

While it is a valid point that the south-central communities would have had rather indirect awareness of the Cycladic (Papadatos 2007: 438) and possibly the Egyptian world, the suggestion that a long line of exchanges would have completely removed the original meaning and the value of these objects as *exotica* (Legarra-Herrero 2011: 274) has some problematic implications. In the latter scheme, the value of the objects is seen as something fixed, inherent in the raw material and/or in the social connotations surrounding the object in its "original" context. What's more, if what makes an object valuable as *exotica* is the meaning imbued in it in its original context of provenance, and if this is removed or lost along its travels, then this leaves raw material as the only criterion of value and the main explanation for this sustained investment in the maintenance of long-distance acquisition networks. However, what the above discussion has demonstrated is that the appreciation of raw materials is not static, but drawing its value from the set of practices and experiences it can facilitate and the *assemblage* of relations within which it is embedded. Similarly, technical goods, artefacts, do not carry some finite value inscribed on them through abstract perceptions of wealth or status (see also Papadatos, this volume), but rather their value constantly emerges out of the social relations they facilitate and embody. The value of these objects is not fixed in their molecular structure, their geological origin or their exchange rate. It is rather constituted from being integral for interactions that can crystallise human identities on a local, regional and supra-regional level.

Value constantly emerges out of social interactions that are not circumscribed, but continuously looking for new ways to both negotiate and cement particular relations and identities.

More importantly, the very idea of imitation implies a one-directional traffic, from an "original" to a "derivative" copied at secondary level, with the subtle implication that the resulting imitation is of less value. However, nothing/no-one exists in isolation and everything and everybody relies and builds upon the generosity of others (Clark 2007: 57). Even the Egyptian "prototypes" would have referenced some tangible or intangible influences further afield which were incorporated and appropriated in their technical fashioning and/or use to facilitate specific social interactions. The very notion of an original type and its imitations distracts us from the more important aspect of such interactions: that they are all parts in a continuous process whereby a combination of form, substance and meaning takes on a specific crystallisation that can, at a later stage, be dismantled and re-formed into new and different *assemblages* of relations and practices.

Conclusion

Looking at the ways in which human interactions with materials and techniques were constituted through both local concerns and off-island influences allows us to appreciate the crucial significance of these interactions in negotiating and creating social identities and the ways in which local and wider scales can be brought together. The sophisticated and versatile engagement with materials and techniques gave rise to specific technologies of life, death and community, which created dynamic *assemblages* able to territorialise a specific set of social relations and identities. What we can observe by analysing the material culture of the Prepalatial and early Protopalatial periods in the Mesara and Asterousia, is that objects, techniques and practices are singled out and perpetuated by virtue of the relations they embody and facilitate and the perceptions of value they create. This value is channelled through an emphasis of collective practice, whether by its striking visibility in the mortuary sphere at the earliest periods, or by its transfer to communal settings of production and consumption later on. The fact that the materials and techniques that validate these relations remain constant is testament to the long and continuous territorialisation of identities that these socio-technical interactions have facilitated. However, even within this territorial circumscription, the flow of materials, energy and information remains perpetual and off-island influences came to destabilise these emergent social identities by broadening the scale of interaction and introducing new elements in the socio-technical milieu.

What all the exchange patterns noted above illustrate is that the Mesara and Asterousia regions were permeable from all directions, irrespectively of the original source of goods and materials. Perhaps then what was important was the act of exchange and its ability to create new *assemblages* of relations, therefore opening up the possibilities for new kinds of interactions which could fuel and forge new types of identities. However, it is critical that we tread carefully between recognising the preponderance of local concerns in influencing what gets imported and dismissing all such imports as mere expressions and adaptations of local values. These local values could only have been constructed as such through comparison and juxtaposition to non-local elements. The periodic and chronologically variable influx of non-local materials and artefacts illustrates pressures on the familiar *assemblage* of the south-central communities by spreading its notional spatial boundaries through the incorporation of broader perceptions and understandings of belonging. *Exotica* thus, as agents that blur spatial boundaries, acted as deterritorialising elements which threatened the consistency of the existing *assemblage*. Assimilating non-local elements and influences through well-known practices of technical engagement could restore (even if fleetingly) the boundaries of the *assemblage*, absorbing change into the familiar territory of established practice, while crucially injecting new life and rejuvenating the familiar routines, protecting them from stagnation, and ultimately safeguarding against the complete breakdown of the structures that give meaning to the everyday experience of the world.

While this case study focuses on a single area of the island, its analytic value can be appreciated more broadly through its potential to bridge different scales of analysis without succumbing to the hierarchical impasses posed by fixed categorical boundaries that view local patterns as circumscribed and isolated, receiving only top-down influences. By approaching the interactions of people, things and materials in the past as part of distinct *assemblages* which facilitate and validate particular kinds of relations that do not remain static, but are continuously renegotiated and re-affirmed, we come closer to a way of grasping and interpreting the dialectic of change and continuity, across the island and its many historical trajectories. We can use this perspective as a small step towards renewing the interpretative aspirations of works such as the *Foundations* and those that built upon it.

Notes

1 The title draws its inspiration from Urry (2000).

2 This volume had been wrapped up by the time Y. Hamilakis and A. Jones published a special issue on "Archaeology and Assemblage" at *Cambridge Archaeological Journal* vol. 27(1) and therefore I was not able to include their perspective in the theoretical discussion of this article. I very much look forward to reading it and engaging with it in future research.

Bibliography

Agouridis, C.

1997 Sea routes and navigation in the third millennium Aegean. *Oxford Journal of Archaeology* 16: 1–24.

Alexiou, S. and P. Warren

2004 *The Early Minoan Tombs of Lebena, Southern Crete.* Sävedalen: Paul Åströms Förlag.

Barrett, J. C.
2014 The material constitution of humanness. *Archaeological Dialogues* 21(1): 65–74.
Becker, M. J.
1976 Soft stone sources on Crete. *Journal of Field Archaeology* 3: 361–374.
Betancourt, P. P.
2006 *The Chrysokamino Metallurgy Workshop and Its Territory.* Princeton, N.J.: American School of Classical Studies at Athens.
Bevan, A.
2004 Emerging civilised values? The consumption and imitation of Egyptian stone vessels in EMII-MMI Crete and its wider eastern Mediterranean context. In J. C. Barrett, & P. Halstead (eds.), *The Emergence of Civilisation Revisited*: 107–126 (Sheffield Studies in Aegean Archaeology 6). Oxford: Oxbow.
2007 *Stone Vessels and Values in the Bronze Age Mediterranean.* Cambridge: Cambridge University Press.
Blackman, D. and K. Branigan
1982 The excavation of an Early Minoan tholos tomb at Ayia Kyriaki, Ayiofarango, southern Crete. *Annual of the British School at Athens* 77: 1–57.
Branigan, K.
1967 The Early Bronze Age daggers of Crete. *Annual of the British School at Athens* 62: 211–239.
1968 *Copper and Bronze Working in Early Bronze Age Crete.* (Studies in Mediterranean archaeology 19). Lund: Paul Åströms Förlag.
1970a *The Foundations of Palatial Crete: A Survey of Crete in the Early Bronze Age.* States and cities of ancient Greece. London: Routledge & K. Paul.
1970b *The Tombs of Mesara: A Study of Funerary Architecture and Ritual in Southern Crete, 2800–1700 B.C.* London: Duckworth.
1971a Cycladic figurines and their derivatives in Crete. *Annual of the British School at Athens* 66: 57–78.
1971b An Early Bronze Age metal source in Crete. *Studi Micenei ed Egeo-Anatolici* 1: 10–14.
1974 *Aegean Metalwork of the Early and Middle Bronze Age.* (Oxford monographs on classical archaeology). Oxford: Clarendon Press.
1991 Mochlos - an early Aegean 'gateway community'?. In R. Laffineur, & L. Basch (eds.), *"Thalassa. L'Egée préhistorique et la mer." Actes de la 3e Rencontre égéenne internationale de l'Université de Liège, Station de recherches sous-marines et océanographiques, Calvi, Corse, 23–25 avril 1990:* 97–105. (Aegaeum 7). Liège: Universite de Liège.
Broodbank, C.
2000 *An Island Archaeology of the Early Cyclades.* Cambridge: Cambridge University Press.
Busby, C.
1997 Permeable and partible persons: a comparative analysis of gender and body in South India and Mealanesia. *Journal of the Royal Anthropological Institute* 3(2): 261–278.
Carinci, F.
2000 Western Mesara and Egypt during the Protopalatial period: a minimalist view. In A. Karetsou (ed.), *Crete-Egypt: Three Millennia of Cultural Interactions:* 31–37. Athens: Kapon.
Carter, T.
1998 Reverberations of the International Spirit: Thoughts upon 'Cycladica' in the Mesara. In K. Branigan (ed.), *Cemetery and Society in the Bronze Age:* 59–77. (Sheffield Studies in Aegean Archaeology 1). Sheffield: Sheffield Academic Press.
2010 Of blades and burials, flakes and funerals: the chipped stone from Moni Odigitria. In A. Vasilakis & K. Branigan (eds.), *Moni Odigitria. A Prepalatial Cemetery and Its Environs in the Asterousia, Southern Crete (Prehistory Monographs 30):* 151–170. Philadelphia: INSTAP Academic Press.

Catapotis, M.
2007 On the spatial organisation of copper smelting activities in the southern Aegean during the Early Bronze Age. In P. M. Day & R. C. P. Doonan (eds.), *Metallurgy in the Early Bronze Age Aegean:* 207–223. (Sheffield Studies in Aegean Archaeology 7). Oxford: Oxbow.

Catapotis, M. and Y. Bassiakos
2007 Copper smelting at the Early Minoan site of Chrysokamino on Crete. In P. M. Day & R. C. P. Doonan (eds.), *Metallurgy in the Early Bronze Age Aegean:* 68–83. (Sheffield Studies in Aegean Archaeology 7). Oxford: Oxbow.

Clark, N.
2007 Animal interface: the generosity of domestication. In R. Cassidy & M. Mullin (eds.), *Where the Wild Things Are Now: Domestication Reconsidered:* 49–70. Wenner-Gren International Symposium Series. Oxford-New York: Berg.

Colburn, C. S.
2008 Exotica and the Early Minoan elite: eastern imports in Prepalatial Crete. *American Journal of Archaeology* 112: 203–224.

Day, P. M., M. Relaki and E. Faber
2006 Pottery making and social reproduction in Bronze Age Mesara. In M. H. Weiner, J. L. Warner, J. Polonsky & E. E. Hayes (eds.), *Pottery and Society. The Impact of Recent Studies in Minoan Pottery. Gold Medal Colloquium in Honor of Philip P. Betancourt, 104th Annual Meeting of the Archaeological Institute of America, New Orleans, 5 January 2003:* 22–72. Boston: Archaeological Institute of America.

Day, P. M., M. Relaki and S. Todaro
2010 Living from pots? Ceramic perspectives on the economies of Prepalatial Crete. In D. J. Pullen (ed.), *"Political Economies of the Bronze Age Aegean", Proceedings of the Langford Conference held at FSU Tallahassee Florida, 22-24 February 2007:* 205–229. Oxford: Oxbow.

Day, P. M. and D. E. Wilson
1998 Consuming power: Kamares ware in protopalatial Knossos. *Antiquity* 72: 350–358.
2004 Ceramic change and the practice of eating and drinking in Early Bronze Age Crete. In P. Halstead & J. C. Barrett (eds.), *Food, Cuisine and Society in Prehistoric Greece:* 45–62. (Sheffield Studies in Aegean Archaeology 5). Oxford: Oxbow.

Day, P. M., D. E. Wilson and E. Kiriatzi
1998 Pots, labels and people: burying ethnicity in the cemetery of Ag. Photia, Siteias. In K. Branigan (ed.), *Cemetery and Society in the Bronze Age:* 133–149. (Sheffield Studies in Aegean Archaeology 1). Sheffield: Sheffield Academic Press.

De Landa, M.
2006 Deleuzian social ontology and assemblage theory. In M. Fuglsang & B.M. Sørensen (eds.), *Deleuze and the Social:* 250–266. Edinburgh: Edinburgh University Press.

Deleuze, G. and F. Guattari
1987 *A Thousand Plateaus: Capitalism and Schizophrenia.* Minneapolis: University of Minnesota Press.

Dietler, M. and B. Hayden
2001 *Feasts: Archaeological and Ethnographic Perspectives on Food, Politics, and Power.* Washington, D.C. & London: Smithsonian Institution Press.

Dimopoulou-Rethemiotaki, N., D. E. Wilson and P. M. Day
2007 The earlier Prepalatial settlement of Poros-Katsambas: craft production and exchange at the harbour town of Knossos. In P. M. Day & R. C. P. Doonan (eds.), *Metallurgy in the Early Bronze Age Aegean:* 84–97. (Sheffield Studies in Aegean Archaeology 7). Oxford: Oxbow.

Dobres, M. A.
1999 Technology's links and chaînes: the processual unfolding of technique and technician. In M. A. Dobres & C. R. Hoffman (eds.), *The Social Dynamics of Technology. Practice, Politics and World Views:* 124–146. Washington DC & London: Smithsonian Institution Press.

Doonan, R. C. P. and P. M. Day
2007 Mixed origins and the origins of mixing: alloys and provenance in the Early Bronze Age Aegean. In Day, P. M. & R. C. P. Doonan (eds.), *Metallurgy in the Early Bronze Age Aegean:* 1–18. (Sheffield Studies in Aegean Archaeology 7). Oxford: Oxbow.
Doonan, R. C. P., P. M. Day and N. Dimopoulou-Rethemiotaki
2007 Lame excuses for emerging complexity in Early Bronze Age Crete. In P. M. Day & R. C. P. Doonan (eds.), *Metallurgy in the Early Bronze Age Aegean:* 98–122. (Sheffield Studies in Aegean Archaeology 7). Oxford: Oxbow.
Driessen, J., I. Schoep and R. Laffineur (eds.),
2002 *Monuments of Minos: Rethinking the Minoan Palaces. Proceedings of the International Workshop "Crete of the Hundred Palaces?" held at the Université Catholique de Louvain, Louvain-la-Neuve, 14–15 December 2001.* Liège: Université de Liège.
Fox, N. J. and P. Alldred
2014 New materialist social inquiry: designs, methods and the research-assemblage. *International Journal of Social Research Methodology* 18(4): 399–414.
Gerontakou, E.
2003 Δύο Μεσομινωικοί αποθέτες απο το νεκροταφείο του Πλατάνου. In A. Vlachopoulos & K. Mpirtacha (eds.), *ΑΡΓΟΝΑΥΤΗΣ. Τιμητικός τόμος για τον Καθηγητή Χρίστο Ντούμα από τους μαθητές του στο Πανεπιστήμιο Αθηνών (1980–2000):* 303–330. Athens: Kathimerini A.E.
Haggis, D. C.
2007 Stylistic diversity and diacritical feasting at Protopalatial Petras: A preliminary analysis of the Lakkos deposit. *American Journal of Archaeology* 111: 715–775.
Hall, M.
2011 *Plants as Persons. A Philosophical Botany.* Albany: State University of New York Press.
Halstead, P.
2007 Carcasses and commensality: investigating the social context of meat consumption in Neolithic and Early Bronze Age Greece. In C. Mee & J. Renard (eds.), *Cooking Up the Past. Food and Culinary Practices in the Neolithic and Bronze Age Aegean:* 25–48. Oxford: Oxbow.
Hamilakis, Y.
1996 Wine, oil and the dialectics of power in Bronze Age Crete: A review of the evidence. *Oxford Journal of Archaeology* 15: 1–32.
1998 Eating the dead: Mortuary feasting and the politics of memory in the Aegean Bronze Age Societies. In K. Branigan (ed.), *Cemetery and Society in the Aegean Bronze Age:* 115–132. (Sheffield Studies in Aegean Archaeology 1). Sheffield: Sheffield Academic Press.
2000 The anthropology of food and drink consumption and Aegean archaeology. In S., J., Vaughan & W. D. E. Coulson (eds.), *Palaeodiet in the Aegean: Papers from a colloquium held at the 1993 meeting of the Archaeological Institute of America in Washington D.C.:* 55–63. (Wiener Laboratory Monographs 1). Oxford: Oxbow.
2002 (ed.) *Labyrinth Revisited. Rethinking "Minoan" Archaeology.* Oxford: Oxbow.
2008 Time, performance and the production of a mnemonic record: from feasting to an archaeology of eating and drinking. In L. Hitchcock, R. Laffineur & J. L. Crowley (eds.), *Dais: The Aegean Feast; Proceedings of the 12th International Aegean Conference, University of Melbourne, Centre for Classics and Archaeology, 25–29 March 2008:* 3–19. (Aegaeum 29). Liège: Université de Liège.
Haraway, D. J.
1991 *Simians, Cyborgs and Women: The Reinvention of Nature.* London: Free Association Books.
Hoffman, C. R.
1999 Intentional damage as technological agency: breaking metals in Late Prehistoric Mallorca, Spain. In M.-A. Dobres & C. R. Hoffman (eds.), *The Social Dynamics of Technology: Practice, Politics and World Views:* 103–123. Washington, DC: Smithsonian Institution Press.

Ingold, T.
2000 *The Perception of the Environment: Essays on Livelihood, Dwelling and Skill.* London: Routledge.
2007 Materials against materiality. *Archaeological Dialogues* 14(1): 1–16.

Karetsou, A. and M. Andreadaki-Vlazaki (eds.),
2000 *Κρήτη-Αίγυπτος. Πολιτισμικοί δεσμοί τριών χιλιετιών. Κατάλογος: Αρχαιολογικό Μουσείο Ηρακλείου, 21 Νοεμβρίου 1999–21 Σεπτεμβρίου 2000 (με τη συνεργασία του Νίκου Παπαδάκη).* Herakleion: Ypourgeio Politismou - KG', KD', KE' Eforeies Proistorikon kai Klassikon Archaiotiton.

Karytinos, A.
1998 Sealstones in cemeteries: a display of social status? In K. Branigan (ed.) *Cemetery and Society in the Aegean Bronze Age:* 76–86. (Sheffield Studies in Aegean Archaeology 1). Sheffield: Sheffield Academic Press.

Knappett, C.
2005 *Thinking Through Material Culture : An Interdisciplinary Perspective.* Archaeology, culture, and society. Philadelphia: University of Pennsylvania Press.
2007 Materials with materiality? *Archaeological Dialogues* 14(1): 20–23.

Knappett, C. and L. Malafouris (eds.),
2008 *Material Agency: Towards A Non-anthropocentric Approach.* New York: Springer.

Krzyszkowska, O.
2005 *Aegean Seals: An Introduction.* London: Institute of Classical Studies, School of Advanced Study, University of London.

Lambrou-Phillipson, C.
1990 *Hellenorientalia: The Near Eastern Presence in the Bronze Age Aegean ca. 3000–1100 B.C.: Interconnections Based on the Material Record and the Written Evidence, plus Orientalia: A Catalogue of Egyptian, Mesopotamian, Mitannian, Syro-Palestinian, Cypriot and Asia Minor objects from The Bronze Age Aegean.* Göteborg: Åströms Editions.

Latour, B.
1993 *We Have Never Been Modern.* London: Harvester Wheatsheaf.
1994 Pragmatogonies: a mythical account of how humans and nonhumans swap properties. *American Behavioral Scientist* 37(6): 791–808.

Legarra-Herrero, B.
2011 New kid on the block: the nature of the first systemic contacts between Crete and the Eastern Mediterranean around 2000 BC. In T. C. Wilkinson, S. Sherratt & J. Bennet (eds.), *Interweaving Worlds. Systemic Interactions in Eurasia, 7th to 1st Millennia BC:* 266–281. Oxford: Oxbow.

Leroi-Gourhan, A.
1993 *Gesture and Speech.* Cambridge, Mass. & London: MIT Press.

Masala, S.
2009 I resti faunistici provenienti dal saggio sotto il vano XIX a Festos. *Creta Antica* 10(I): 97–103.

Mentesana, R., P. M. Day, V. Kilikoglou and S. Todaro
2016 United in our differences: The production and consumption of pottery at EM IB Phaistos, Crete. *Journal of Archaeological Science: Reports* 7: 489–498.

Nakou, G.
1995 The cutting edge: a new look at Early Aegean metallurgy. *Journal of Mediterranean Archaeology* 8(2): 1–32.

Nanoglou, S.
2012 From embodied regulations to hybrid ontologies: questioning archaeological bodies. In B. S. Turner (ed.), *The Routledge Handbook of Body Studies:* 157–170. Oxford & New York: Routledge.

Overton, N. J. and Y. Hamilakis
2013 A manifesto for a social zooarchaeology. Swans and other beings in the Mesolithic. *Archaeological Dialogues* 20(2): 111–136.

Papadatos, Y.
2007 Beyond cultures and ethnicity: a new look at material culture distribution and inter-regional interaction in the Early Bronze Age Southern Aegean. In S. Antoniadou & A. Pace (eds.), *Mediterranean Crossroads: Selected Papers of the International Conference, Athens, 10-13 may 2005:* 419–451. Athens: Pierides Foundation Publications.

Papadatos, Y. and P. Tomkins
2013 Trading, the longboat, and cultural interaction in the Aegean During the late fourth millennium B.C.E.: the view from Kephala Petras, east Crete. *American Journal of Archaeology* 117: 353–381.
2014 The emergence of trade and the integration of Crete into the wider Aegean in the late 4th millennium: new evidence and implications. In B. Horejs & M. Mehofer (eds.), *Western Anatolia Before Troy. Proto-urbanisation in the 4th Millennium BC. OREA* 1: 329–343.

Phillips, J.
2005 A question of reception. In J. Clarke (ed.), *Archaeological Perspectives on the Transmission and Transformation of Culture in the Eastern Mediterranean:* 39–47. Oxford: Oxbow.
2008 *Aegyptiaca on the Island of Crete in Their Chronological Context: A Critical Review.* Contributions to the Chronology of the Eastern Mediterranean 18. Wien: Verlag der Ōsterreichischen Akademie der Wissenschaften.

Platon, N.
1969 *Iraklion, Corpus der Minoische Siegel (CMS II, 1) Archäologisches Museum. Teil 1.* Die Siegel der Vorpalastzeit. Berlin.

Relaki, M.
2009 Rethinking administration and seal use in third millennium Crete. *Creta Antica* 10(II): 353–372.
2012 The social arenas of tradition. Investigating collective and individual social strategies in the Prepalatial and Protopalatial Mesara. In I. Schoep, P. Tomkins & J. Driessen (eds.), *Back to the Beginning. Reassessing Social and Political Complexity on Crete During the Early and Middle Bronze Age:* 290–324. Oxford: Oxbow.
2013 Pervasive assumptions of ownership: land, gender and reproductive narratives. In M. Relaki & D. Catapoti (eds.), *The Archaeology of Land Ownership:* 93–125. (Routledge Studies in Archaeology 9). Oxford & New York: Routledge.

Relaki, M. and C. Tsoraki
2017 Variability and differentiation: a first look at the stone vase assemblage in the Petras cemetery. In M. Tsipopoulou (ed.), *Petras-Siteia. The Pre- and Protopalatial Cemetery in Context. The 2nd International Petras Symposium, The Danish Institute at Athens, 14-15 February 2015:* 159–178 (Monographs of the Danish Institute at Athens 21). Athens: Danish Institute at Athens.

Renfrew, C.
1969 The development and chronology of the Early Cycladic figurines. *American Journal of Archaeology* 73(1): 1–32.
1972 *The Emergence of Civilisation: the Cyclades and the Aegean in the Third Millennium B.C.* Studies in prehistory, London: Methuen.
1973 *Before Civilization. The Radiocarbon Revolution and Prehistoric Europe.* London: Jonathan Cape.

Sbonias, K.
1995 *Frühkretische Siegel: Ansätze für eine Interpretation der sozial-politischen Entwicklung auf Kreta während der Frühbronzezeit.* BAR IS, 620. Oxford: Tempus Reparatum.

1999 Social development, management of production, and symbolic representation in Prepalatial Crete. In A. Chaniotis (ed.) *From Minoan Farmers to Roman Traders. Sidelights on the Economy of Ancient Crete*: 25–51. Stuttgart: Franz Steiner Verlag.

2000 Specialization in the Early Minoan seal manufacture: craftsmen, settlements and the organisation of production. In I. Pini (ed.), *Minoisch-mykenische Glyptik: Stil, Ikonographie, Funktion*: 277–293. CMS Beiheft, 6. Berlin.

2010 Seals from the cemetery. In A. Vasilakis & K. Branigan (eds.), *Moni Odigitria. A Prepalatial Cemetery and Its Environs in the Asterousia, Southern Crete* (Prehistory Monographs 30): 201–228. Philadelphia: INSTAP Academic Press.

Schoep, I.

2006 Looking beyond the First Palaces: elites and the agency of power in EMIII-MMII Crete. *American Journal of Archaeology* 110: 37–64.

Serres, M.

1982 *The Parasite*. Baltimore: Johns Hopkins University Press.

Shanks, M.

2007 Symmetrical archaeology. *World Archaeology* 39(4): 589–596.

Stos-Gale, Z. A.

1993 The origin of metal used for making weapons in Early and Middle Minoan Crete. In C. Scarre & F. Healy (eds.), *Trade and Exchange in Prehistoric Europe*: 115–130. Oxford: Oxbow.

Strathern, M.

1980 No nature, no culture: the Hagen case. In C. P. MacCormack & M. Strathern (eds.), *Nature, Culture and Gender*: 174–222. Cambridge: Cambridge University Press.

1988 *The Gender of the Gift: Problems with Women and Problems with Society in Melanesia*. Berkeley London: University of California Press.

Thrift, N.

2004 Intensities of feeling: Towards a spatial politics of affect. *Geografiska Annaler, Series B: Human Geography* 86(1): 57–78.

Tilley, C.

2007 Materiality in materials. *Archaeological Dialogues* 14(1): 16–20.

Todaro, S.

2012 Craft production and social practices at Prepalatial Phaistos: the background to the First 'Palace'. In P. Tomkins, I. Schoep & J. Driessen (eds.), *Back to the Beginning: Reassessing Social, Economic and Political Complexity in the Early and Middle Bronze Age on Crete, Proceedings of the International conference held at Leuven, 1-2 February 2008*: 195–235. Oxford: Oxbow.

2013 *The Phaistos Hills Before the Palace: A contextual Reappraisal*. Prehistorica Medterranea 5. Monza: Polimetrica.

Triantaphyllou, S.

2009 EM/MM human skeletal remains from East Crete: the Kephala Petras rock shelter, Siteia, and the Livari tholos tomb, Skiadi. *Kentro, The Newsletter of the INSTAP Study Center for East Crete* 12: 19–23.

2010 Analysis of the human bones. In A. Vasilakis & K. Branigan (eds.), *Moni Odigitria: A Prepalatial Cemetery and its Environs in the Asterousia, Southern Crete* (Prehistory Monographs 30): 229–250. Philadelphia: INSTAP Academic Press.

2017 Όσο ψηλά κι ανεβείς λέξη μην πείς μεγάλη 'πο χώμα σε έφτιαξε ο θεός κι εκειά γυρίζεις πάλι. Cretan madinada on death. In M. Tsipopoulou, (ed.) *Petras-Siteia. The Pre- and Protopalatial Cemetery in context. The 2nd International Petras Symposium, The Danish Institute at Athens, 14-15 February 2015*: 271–290. (Monographs of the Danish Institute at Athens 21). Athens: Danish Institute at Athens.

Urry, J.

2000 *Sociology Beyond Societies: Mobilities for the Twenty-First century*. London: Routledge.

Van de Moortel, A.
2006 Middle Minoan A and Protopalatial pottery. In J. W. Shaw & M. C. Shaw (eds.), *Kommos V. The Monumental Buildings at Kommos:* 264–377. Princeton & Oxford: Princeton University Press.

Vavouranakis, G.
2011 Funerary customs and maritime activity in Early Bronze Age Crete. In G. Vavourakis (ed.), *The Seascape in Aegean Prehistory:* 91–118. (Monographs of the Danish Institute at Athens 14). Athens: Danish Institute at Athens.

Warren, P.
1965 The first Minoan stone vases and EM chronology. *Κρητικά Χρονικά* 19:7–43.
1969 *Minoan Stone Vases.* Cambridge Classical Studies, Cambridge: Cambridge University Press.

Watrous, L. V.
1998 Egypt and Crete in the early Middle Bronze Age: a case of trade and cultural diffusion. In E. H. Cline & D. Harris-Cline (eds.), *The Aegean and the Orient in the Second Millennium: Proceedings of the 50th Anniversary Symposium, Cincinnati, 18–19 April April 1997:* 19–28. (Aegaeum 18). Liège: Université de Liège.

Whitelaw, T. M.
1983 The settlement at Fournou Koryfi Myrtos and aspects of Early Minoan social organisation. In O. Krzyszkowska & L. Nixon (eds.), *Minoan Society, Proceedings of the Cambridge Colloquium 1981:* 323–345. Bristol: Bristol Classical Press.
2012 The Urbanisation of prehistoric Crete: settlement perspectives on Minoan state formation. In I. Schoep, P. Tomkins & J. Driessen (eds.), *Back to the Beginning. Reassessing Social and Political Complexity on Crete During The Early and Middle Bronze Age:* 114–176. Oxford: Oxbow.

Wilson, D. E.
2008 Early Prepalatial Crete. In C. W. Shelmerdine (ed.), *The Cambridge Companion to the Aegean Bronze Age:* 77–104. Cambridge: Cambridge University Press.

Wilson, D. E. and P. M. Day
1994 Ceramic regionalism in Prepalatial central Crete: the Mesara imports at EM I to EM II A Knossos. *The Annual of the British School at Athens* 89: 1–87.

Xanthoudides, S.
1924 *The Vaulted Tombs of Mesara: An Account of Some Early Cemeteries of Southern Crete.* London: University Press, Hodder & Stoughton.

Chapter 3

Inspecting the foundations: The Early Minoan Project in review[1]

Peter Tomkins

Between the fourth and late third millennia BC Crete was transformed from a landscape of hamlets and villages – a mosaic of "small worlds" composed of egalitarian, mixed-farming communities connected by networks of gift-exchange (Tomkins 2008; 2010) – to one where cities sat among hamlets and villages, where forms of livelihood and trajectories of development differed, often dramatically, between communities and regions, where inequalities could be sharp and enduring and where cultures of acquisition and consumption were geared towards the marking of difference (Tomkins and Schoep 2010). In other words, Crete had in certain key respects come to look more like modern western societies. This resemblance demanded investigation and, ever since its birth research into later Cretan prehistory – or what was termed the Bronze Age – has been wrestling with the "emergence of civilisation" (hereafter *emergence*), seeking not just insights into a history of human progress towards modernity, but also prophecies for Europe's future (Evans 1921; Childe 1958; Renfrew 1972: 52–53; 1973: 192–213; Cherry 1983: 33–34, 38–41; Bintliff 1984; Hamilakis 2002; McEnroe 2002; Papadopoulos 2005; Hamilakis and Momigliano 2006; Gere 2009; Schoep and Tomkins 2012).

Arthur Evans claimed the role of interpreter of "Minoan civilisation" and established a particular vision of its development, shaped by prevailing trends in the study of the human past and focused by his own agenda for Aegean prehistory (McNeal 1973; McEnroe 1995; 2002; Hamilakis 2002; Papadopoulos 2005; Hamilakis and Momigliano 2006; Schoep 2010a; 2010b). In this developmental scheme (Evans 1906; 1921) the beginning of the Early Minoan phase (EM I) saw the initial emergence of Minoan civilisation, which then developed up until the next significant horizon marked by the construction of the "First Palaces" at the beginning of the Middle Minoan phase (MM I). During MM this civilisation "matured" and reached an acme early in Late Minoan (LM I and into LM II), after which it declined up to the close of the Bronze Age (LM III). Building on recent interest in the modern production of the Aegean prehistoric past (Hamilakis 2002; McEnroe 2002; Papadopoulos 2005; Hamilakis and Momigliano 2006; Gere 2009; see also McNeil 1973; Bintliff 1984; McEnroe 1995) this paper considers the recent (1960–present) history of this EM developmental phase and assesses its cogency, paying particular attention to the shape, timing and trajectory of *emergence* implied in the richer datasets for the fourth and third millennia BC that are now available. In the process the paper reflects upon the pivotal role played by the work of Keith Branigan, most notably *The Foundations of Palatial Crete* (published in 1970, but written by 1968; Branigan 1988: 233), but also his pioneering field projects.

Between rhetoric and reality. Early Minoan before *Foundations*

In Evans' developmental scheme *emergence* takes place early, that is *at the beginning of* EM I. The EM period is therefore not a formative phase prior to the emergence of civilisation in MM I, but a phase in the *development* of a civilisation that had already emerged. The complexity of Minoan civilisation is seen as developing gradually during EM (also Mackenzie 1906b: 226), largely under its own internally-driven momentum, but also stimulated by specific, transformative links with other East Mediterranean civilisations, until by MM I it had evolved "palaces" and "priest-kings". What is perhaps most remarkable about this vision of EM is that it had already been sketched well before the Knossos excavations began (e.g. Evans 1897: 371–72; see MacGillivray 2000; Papadopoulos 2005; Schoep 2010b). In papers published in the decade before 1900 Evans was keen to establish parity in timing and sophistication between the pre-hellenic, European civilisation that was emerging in the Aegean and the longer known civilisations of Egypt and Mesopotamia. He thus arrived at Knossos already with key elements of his developmental scheme in mind and inevitably this structured his interpretation of what he found. While he was a principled scientist, and saw no virtue in fabricating evidence to suit his vision, he was certainly not immune to imposing a preferential order upon poorly defined data (for Evans' justification of this approach see Momigliano 2002: 265, 303–04). Throughout Evans' lifetime EM artefacts remained loosely positioned in a relative chronology that itself was only coarsely defined, even at Knossos. This meant an EM dataset that was amenable to multiple *rhetorical* re-orderings to suit different agendas for Cretan prehistory.

Although Evans' gradualistic, externally stimulated but internally-driven model for a rapid, early emergence (EM I) and long evolution of Minoan civilisation has been profoundly influential (e.g. Branigan 1970; Warren 1987), it constitutes only one of two dominant visions. An alternative model takes issue with the notion that EM Crete qualifies to be termed a civilisation and instead views EM as no more than a *formative* phase *predating* civilisation (e.g. Renfrew 1971; 1972; 1973; Cherry 1983; 1984; 1986). In this view civilisation emerges, not in EM I, but much later, in or around MM I, in a rapid, revolutionary phase of reconfiguration marked by the sudden appearance of "palaces", rulers and a ranked or class-based society. This alternative vision, typified by the notion of a MM I horizon or revolution, is now most commonly associated with John Cherry (Cherry 1983; 1984; 1986). However, the origins of this alternative vision go back much further in time than commonly realised. We can, for instance, detect its influence upon Renfrew's *Emergence* (1972; see below) and upon Hutchinson's 1962 synthesis of prehistoric Crete, back indeed until we reach Gordon Childe, in whose work this alternative view first crystallises.

Childe, who entered Evans' milieu when studying at Oxford in 1914–17 and generally followed his interpretations closely (Sherratt 2006: 108–09), evolved this alternative view during the three decades that preceded his death in 1958. The impulse to do so was his hugely ambitious project to submit the disparate regional sequences and research traditions of Europe to a single, universal grand narrative of the emergence of European civilisation (Rowlands 1984; Sherratt 1989; 2006). From the late 1920s, Childe's leftist leanings and Marxist readings, combined with the security of a permanent academic post, encouraged him to develop a more rigorous definition of civilisation, one based not so much on loosely formulated, personalised appreciations of artistic, aesthetic and technical achievements, but on clearly defined, cross-cultural indices of complexity, such as the presence of cities, writing, central buildings and a class-based society (Childe 1934; 1954; 1958).

Childe grew to believe that the initial emergence of civilisation in the Near East and Egypt was driven by an Urban Revolution (1934; 1954). The key turning point in his narrative of the origins of European civilisation thus came when this Urban Revolution first became manifest on European soil. This, for Childe, was Central Crete during MM I when a critical concentration of wealth and power at the end of EM rapidly evolved into a civilised class society, ruled by kings who resided in purpose-built "palaces" (1958: 114–16, 150–61). This lead him to re-date the emergence of Minoan civilisation to MM I and to recast EM as a formative phase preceding civilisation which, while seeing the development of metallurgy, trade networks, craft specialists and chiefs, lacked the critical scale (e.g. absence of large urban populations, surplus accumulated resources) and qualities (e.g. writing, class society, central buildings) that he deemed integral to a definition of civilisation (1950: 3–4; 1958: 110–15). Accordingly in his cross-cultural evolutionary scheme the EM period came to be grouped with the other early metal-using societies of Europe's copper-age and termed "higher barbarism". With its emphasis on MM I as a pivotal phase of rapid structural reconfiguration, this alternative vision of *emergence* encouraged the view that the societies of EM and MM were qualitatively different and contrasting (e.g. Hutchinson 1962: 161).

However, at the same time as these confident narratives were being penned at desks far from Crete, fieldworkers of the 1950s and 1960s were experiencing a growing sense of unease at the shaky foundations upon which understandings of EM were based. The fact that it was possible for two quite different visions of the emergence of Minoan civilisation to exist side by side provides eloquent testimony to their rhetorical nature and to the very coarse and loose understanding of EM that was then the reality. Not only had the pioneering field projects of the 1950s and 1960s recovered a significant amount of new EM data, which remained to be fully synthesised (Branigan 1970: 13–17), but also there remained fundamental concerns about chronology. Not all of the pre-war objections to Evans' scheme had gone away and new challenges had in the meantime emerged (Levi 1951; 1958; Platon 1956; 1961; Palmer 1963). For many researchers working outside Knossos there were not only technical issues of intra- and inter-site phasing, but also genuine unease that the phases defined at Knossos might not have exact equivalents at other sites and/or that the timing of the transitions between phases at some sites (e.g. Knossos) may have been different from others.

In the context of such uncertainty (notably Levi's objections), and under the influence of Childe's alternative model of *emergence*, Nicolas Platon (1956; 1961) revived the less resolved chronological and developmental scheme first proposed by Åberg (1933), which was based on the timing of major phases of construction, destruction and renewal at the principal palatial centres of Knossos, Phaistos and Malia. In contrast to Åberg, however, Platon's version respected the existence and integrity of Evans' phases, but grouped them together to form longer developmental phases, such that the entirety of EM together with MM IA became a single, "Prepalatial" phase, which was followed by a "Protopalatial phase" divided into three sub-phases: Protopalatial I (MM IB), Protopalatial II (MM IIA) and Protopalatial III (MM IIB) (Platon 1956: 511–12). While simplifying the task of chronological attribution, and thus relieving those working amid poorer stratigraphical resolution of the burden of specificity (a burden that weighed particularly heavily on Platon himself in the case of his excavations at Viannos, Myrsini and Gonies Maleviziou; Branigan 1970: 14), this scheme also encouraged researchers to oversimplify chronological and cultural development within EM (Branigan 1970: 208 n. 1). More fundamentally it enshrined a specific, Childean vision of *emergence* in the conceptual architecture of Minoan archaeology. In deeming finer chronological resolution to be unnecessary or irrelevant for the EM period, but essential to the phases thereafter, Platon's Prepalatial scheme most effectively served those who, like Childe, saw Minoan civilisation as first emerging in a MM I revolution.

Founding the Early Minoan Project

Completed in 1968 and published in 1970, Keith Branigan's *The Foundations of Palatial Crete* tackled these issues in typically forthright style and with a new clarity born of a close familiarity with the data and the issues surrounding its interpretation. *Foundations* was written as the first comprehensive, book-length account of EM Crete and sought to correct a tendency hitherto to neglect the study of what happened prior to an emergence of "palaces" in MM IB (Branigan 1970: xv). Its principal aim in doing this was to make clear "the debt of palatial Crete to the Early Bronze Age civilisation". While such statements now strike us as straightforward, in the context of the late 1960s they signalled a subtly subversive agenda that sought to break with the prevailing Childean orthodoxy in three important ways.

From externalist to more fully autonomist explanations of the emergence of civilisation

First, and perhaps most obviously, *Foundations* sought to break with the externalist paradigm that had hitherto informed explanations of the timing and nature of key cultural changes in the Cretan prehistoric sequence. Thus, while Evans and thence Childe were of the view that most Cretan prehistoric development was internally driven (e.g. Evans 1921: 19, 25, 30), a view which had the twin virtue of according with their Eurocentric agenda and being a logical reading of cultural succession, they nevertheless both sought external (Egyptian/Oriental) triggers (migration, diffusion) for specific "pivotal" phases of transformation, notably EM I (Evans) and MM I (Childe). In contrast, *Foundations* sought to develop a narrative of indigenous, internally-driven development, in which the existence of external influences, even during these "pivotal" phases of transformation, is preferably explained in terms of indigenous evolution and acculturation (Branigan 1970: 196–201; 1988: 247). While the reaction against the externalist paradigm would subsequently be taken further (perhaps even to extremes; Sherratt 2006) in Renfrew's *Emergence* (1972), *Foundations* is noteworthy for being the first significant attempt to break with the prevailing orthodoxy and seek alternative, more fully autonomist explanations (Renfrew 1971; Halstead 2004).

Civilisation and the "shape" of its emergence in Crete

Foundations also broke with Childe by rejecting his Prepalatial model of a rapid, late emergence of civilisation associated with an appearance of "palaces" in MM I. Instead *Foundations'* review of the EM data led it to develop a reading of the shape of *emergence* more akin to Evans' original vision, where the emergence of civilisation and the appearance of "palaces" are treated as different phenomena, the latter evolving out of the former. *Foundations* took the line that the rise of something that we might call Minoan civilisation first emerges early and rapidly in what might be termed an EM I revolution (Branigan 1970: 202; cf. Evans 1921: 1, 13): variously marked by a "sudden flowering of the ceramic art" (in contrast to the "uninspiring" and "unimaginative" Neolithic pottery that came before; Branigan 1970: 11), the probable emergence of craft specialisation (1970: 73–74, 202), social and commercial contacts on a scale hitherto unknown (1970: 179), the "sudden flowering of village life" (1970: 37; cf. Pendlebury 1939: 277–79), population increase, the emergence of the "clan", social inequality and possibly already some sort of permanent central authority (1970: 118, 202). Briefly touching upon themes that have since become central to recent work on EM and MM social organisation (i.e. heterarchical power relations between corporate groups; Schoep 2002; Schoep and Tomkins 2012), *Foundations* notes the important role played by large groups (i.e. "clans", "tribes" and "communities") in EM social organisation and the existence of multiple entities of equal status (Branigan 1970: 116–19; see also Glotz 1925: 131–38; Pendlebury 1939: 279–80).

Following this EM I revolution, civilisation is presented as developing and increasing in complexity, without obvious interruption or external intervention, until it evolved the institutions thought to characterise MM "palatial society" (Branigan 1970: 196–97; cf. Evans 1921: 30). In conscious opposition to Childe, *Foundations* explicitly viewed a coming of the "palaces" in MM IB as "brought about not by revolution, but by evolution" (Branigan 1970: 204). The beginning of Childe's Urban Revolution is tacitly pushed back to EM II, marked by the first development of towns at Phaistos and Knossos (1970: 42, 118, 120; also Warren 1975: 2, 36), while EM II-III more generally is favoured as decisive in the breakdown of the "clan" and the formation of some of the key elements of "palatial civilisation" (1970: 203–04). It is suggested that late in the EM and into MM I central authorities changed and extended their control, the number of classes increased (and their differences deepened), villages became towns, towns became "city-states"; and centralised "palatial" control over trade accelerated an expansion in foreign contacts that had begun in EM III (Branigan 1970: 119–22, 180–82, 189–95; cf. Pendlebury 1939: 281). Viewed in such terms an emergence of "palaces" in MM IB becomes a catalyst accelerating processes (e.g. urbanism, social inequality) that were already well underway in EM.

In order to demonstrate this evolution – and thus make good on its promise of revealing "the debt of palatial Crete to the Early Bronze Age civilisation" (Branigan 1970: xv, note the term "Early Bronze Age *civilisation*") – *Foundations* searched the EM dataset for the origins and predecessors of MM complexity. This agenda for the EM period may be variously glimpsed in the emphasis given to the status of EM material culture as "art" (Branigan 1970: 126–51), in the placing of an emergence of craft specialisation in EM I (e.g. pottery; Branigan 1970: 11, 73–74; cf. Glotz 1925: 33; Pendlebury 1939: 280), in the desire to establish both conceptual precursors and an indigenous architectural tradition out of which "palaces" might be seen to develop (Branigan 1970: 48–52, 118; also Warren 1987), in the argument that a common religion, containing the main elements of palatial religion, had already emerged during EM (Branigan 1970: 103, 108–13) and in the willingness to see central authorities, classes and the earliest stages of urbanism as present already by EM II-III (Branigan 1970: 42, 118, 120).

Although not all of these claims have stood the test of time, *Foundations* nevertheless deserves greater recognition for having initiated a process whereby Childe's MM I revolution has been deconstructed. *Foundations*' key role in this has tended to be overlooked, the principal reason for this coming in the form of Renfrew's *Emergence* (1972). *Emergence* took up the main elements of *Foundations*' vision of EM development (e.g. Renfrew 1973: 205–10), but framed them within a resuscitated Childean vision of civilisation and its emergence. In contrast to *Foundations*, but like Childe, *Emergence* defined civilisation in such terms (i.e. urban centres of 5000+, monumental ceremonial centres and/or writing; Renfrew 1972: 7) as to raise the bar to attainment and thus push its appearance down to MM I (Renfrew 1972: 15, 47, 98). *Emergence* thus explicitly revived Childe's alternative vision of a late and revolutionary emergence of Minoan civilisation in MM I that had been implicitly rejected in *Foundations*. With its publication coming so soon after *Foundations*, and with its greater theoretical and methodological ambition and broader chronological and geographical range, inevitably it was *Emergence*'s Childean vision that exercised the more profound influence over those that followed. Developments prior to MM I were returned to the status of background, significant only in the sense that they exercised a "formative" influence on the emergence of "palatial civilisation" (e.g. Renfrew 1973: 205, 211) and MM I once again became *the* critical "horizon of change", "take-off point" or "revolution" that any serious narrative of *emergence* had to explain (Renfrew 1972: 27, 39, 98).

In this respect, it is worth noting that the shape of emergence depicted in *Emergence* makes it much closer to Cherry's "revolutionary model" (1983; 1984; 1986) than is generally recognised (and indeed Cherry's own critique of *Emergence*'s "gradualist" narrative seems somewhat misplaced; 1983: 36). In *Emergence* (also Renfrew 1978) Childe's notion of revolutions is re-worked in the context of systems theory to become the "multiplier effect", the operation of which:

> "produces a 'revolution' in the sense intended by Gordon Childe. This applies equally to the Neolithic, Urban and Industrial Revolutions. Each may take a long time to mature, since these are not sudden quantum shifts, but continuous processes of change. But in each case the rate of innovation and the speed of structural change in the society are much faster over a considerable period, which we regard as the duration of the revolution itself" (Renfrew 1972: 43).

Where Cherry's model differs most obviously from *Emergence* – and diametrically opposes *Foundations* – is in the extremity with which it plays down EM complexity, particularly during EM I-II, and its extremely pessimistic view of the possibility that significant continuities can be usefully traced between the societies of EM and the "palatial civilisations" of MM and LM (Cherry 1983; 1986; also Boardman 1972; Watrous 1987).

From universalist to particularist narratives of emergence

A third, significant departure from Childe is marked by the differing narrative ambitions of *Foundations*. In the case of Childe (and subsequently also *Emergence*) a core ambition – to develop an understanding of *emergence* that might have genuine cross-cultural validity (Childe 1925: xiii; 1934: 1–41; Renfrew 1972: 3) – led to the assumption of a unilineal trajectory of development and a single set of underlying processes, which in turn meant that the regional diversity inherent in the data tended to be underrepresented (Whitelaw 2004; Schoep and Tomkins 2012: 5–6). While *Foundations* did not explicitly take issue with the validity of this type of universalising grand narrative, its narrative ambitions for the EM dataset are notably different. Rather than viewing EM Crete top-down and through the prism of a grand narrative for the emergence of civilisation in Europe, *Foundations* pursued a more explicitly particularist and historical approach, in which EM Crete is viewed, more from the bottom up and in its own terms, as something distinctive and diverse. This meant that *Foundations* was better able to represent regional variation, at least as it appeared in 1968, and was much less interested in reducing that variation to conform to a single unilineal developmental model (e.g. "The historical development which I have outlined was not of course identical all over the island", Branigan 1970: 204). In its aim to develop a historical narrative of EM in its own terms *Foundations* was original and ground-breaking, and was immediately appreciated as such by prehistorians (Renfrew 1971; Shaw 1971), if not by some more traditionally-minded classical archaeologists (Boardman 1972). It is important to recognise that, in seeking to recognise and represent regional variation, *Foundations* anticipated, by some two decades or so, the eventual rejection of the doctrine of unilinearity espoused by Childe and *Emergence*, and the development of multilinear models of complexity that embrace diversity and divergent trajectories of development (Whitelaw 2004; Tomkins and Schoep 2010; Schoep and Tomkins 2012: 4–6).

In order to fulfil this ambitious narrative objective *Foundations* needed to transform EM from a sketchily defined monolith, upon which different developmental visions with equal apparent validity might be projected, to a data-led, goal-oriented research project, geared towards clarifying the precise nature and timing of EM developments in different regions of Crete. Looming large on the agenda of this Early Minoan Project was the lack of "a really solid framework" into which the "very large body of Early Bronze Age material" might be fitted and clarified (1970: 14–15). The solution followed was to restate the validity of the Evans-Mackenzie chronological system by tackling criticism, by rigorously checking and deepening the characterisation of its phases (EM I-MM IA) and by demonstrating its relevance to deposits and sequences from sites beyond Knossos (1970: xv; 17–35; also Pendlebury 1939). Through the hard spadework of chronological re-evaluation, *Foundations* sought to work at the highest possible chronological resolution and thereby clarify the actual nature and timing of material changes within EM and foreclose the rhetorical reordering and wishful thinking found in previous treatments.

The Early Minoan Project as a programme for future research

Foundations ends with a discussion of major problems requiring solution in 1968 (Branigan 1970: 206–08). First and foremost was EM chronology. While *Foundations* (and subsequently *Emergence*) improved the rigour and resolution of EM chronology, this exercise also served to highlight the many serious gaps in the understanding of different regional sequences around the island (1970: 204–06). *Foundations* looked forward to the definition of stratified sequences in all regions of the island, wisely predicted it would take "many years" and tempered its ambition to "the publication of the Early Minoan deposits from Knossos, Lebena and Fournou Korifi" (1970: 206). It also hoped that we would know more about two types of EM site: (1) settlements (especially a Mesara village); and (2) coastal trading communities (1970: 206–07). In the category of settlements *Foundations* saw as particularly problematic the scarcity of evidence for what was happening in EM at sites that subsequently saw the construction of "palaces" (i.e. Knossos, Phaistos, Malia; 1970: 16–17). It also expressed a desire to see further detailed artefactual characterisation work (1970: 207).

Looking back over the last four decades one can see that even this modest programme of remedial research has taken far longer to realise than could be envisaged in 1970. While the Phournou Koryphi excavations were rapidly published (Warren 1972; also Whitelaw 1983; Whitelaw *et al.* 1997; 2007), publication of Lebena (Alexiou and Warren 2004) and the EM deposits from Knossos (e.g. Wilson 1985; Wilson and Day 1994; 2000; Momigliano 2007b; Hood and Cadogan 2011) has taken much longer. Nevertheless, thanks to work at these and other sites, we have finally begun to close in on the chronological clarity and resolution that Keith sought, largely in ways that he foresaw (for recent overviews of EM chronology see Wilson 2007; 2008; Momigliano 2007b). The main chronological issues of the 1960s, such as confusion about the use of the Evans-Mackenzie scheme to refer to both pottery styles, which can overlap, and periods of time, which cannot (Branigan 1970: 208; Renfrew 1972: 54; Momigliano 2011), have largely been resolved by improved methodological and terminological rigour (e.g. Cadogan *et al.* 1983; Momigliano 2007a; 2011). The Evans-Mackenzie chronological framework thus remains, but its relevance to sequences outside Knossos is now broadly accepted and the characteristics of its phases, as represented in different regions of Crete, are now more clearly defined, thanks in no small part to detailed, analytically-supported, ceramic characterisation work (Wilson and Day 1994; 2000; Whitelaw *et al.* 1997; Todaro 2005; 2013). The resolution of the Evans-Mackenzie chronology has been further extended by the definition of a series of sub-phases, not just of EM (Wilson 1985; Wilson 2007; 2008; Todaro 2005; Momigliano 2007b; Papadatos and Tomkins 2013), but also of the preceding FN period (FN I-IV; Tomkins 2007b; 2008; Todaro and Di Tonto 2008). While issues and lacunae persist, the "really solid framework" sought by *Foundations* (1970: 14–15) is in view and we are now able, like never before, to map continuity and change in Crete during FN and EM.

Running parallel to this increase in temporal resolution has been a tremendous expansion in our knowledge base of EM settlement and funerary contexts. There have been excavations and studies at a host of funerary sites, including some notably more complex cemeteries (e.g. Archanes-Phourni: Panagiatopoulos 2002; Papadatos 2005; Schoep 2012; for overviews see Branigan 1993; Legarra Herrero 2012). But perhaps, the biggest gains have been made with regard to smaller settlements, specifically hamlets and villages. There are now many more dots on the distribution map thanks to the many survey projects that followed Keith's pioneering 1971–72 Agiopharango survey (Blackman and Branigan 1975). Improved resolution in our mapping of site distribution means we can now begin to characterise small-scale settlement systems for the late FN and EM (e.g. Branigan 1998; Whitelaw 2000; 2004; Haggis 2002; this volume; Tomkins 2008), although working solely at the coarse resolution and partial sample provided by survey data inevitably limits the extent to which meaningful insights into social life, livelihood and connectivity can be generated.

In some areas of Crete this shortfall has been significantly offset by the excavation and publication of assemblages from a select group of EM hamlets and villages, notably Myrtos Phournou-Koryphi (Warren 1972), Debla (Warren and Tzedakis 1974) and Trypeti (Vasilakis 1989). In addition, excavation at certain coastal sites has brought major insights into the EM trading communities that Keith originally identified as a major research priority (1970: 206–07; 1991), notably Hagia Photia (Davaras and Betancourt 2004; Tsipopoulou 2007) Mochlos (Soles 1992), Poros-Katsambas (Wilson *et al.* 2004; 2008) and, most recently Kephala Petras (Papadatos 2007; Papadatos and Tomkins 2013). However, there is undoubtedly still a great deal left to learn. While the recovery of well-stratified samples of organic and inorganic materials from all EM contexts represents an urgent, ongoing priority, there remain some very obvious, specific gaps. Chief among these is a Mesara village, which sat prominently on Keith's original wish-list for excavation (1970: 206–07) and is urgently needed to balance and contextualise our rich funerary dataset from this region.

Another yawning gap in our knowledge, and one that few, until recently, saw any significant prospect of being filled (Branigan 1970: 16–17), concerns the nature of EM (and earlier) activity in the locations occupied by the MM and LM "palaces". Ever since Evans the orthodoxy has been that levelling and terracing activity in advance of "palatial" construction in and after MM I had seriously disrupted or removed all significant traces of EM activity at Knossos. Naturally here and there, mainly beneath the "First Palace" at Malia and on the periphery of the palace hills of Knossos and Phaistos, pockets of EM material survived to be recovered and published (Levi 1951; 1957; Wilson 1985; Hue and Pelon 1992; Pelon 2005; Hood and Cadogan 2011). But on the whole the picture seemed too fragmentary and incomplete to admit meaningful insight.

What has been less widely appreciated is that this seemingly small gap in our sample – so what if we know next to nothing about an area of a hectare or so at one or two EM settlements? – translates into a major potential gap in our sample of EM complexity. As has long been appreciated (Branigan 1970: 42, 118, 120; Warren 1975: 2, 36; Whitelaw 1983; 2012) Knossos, Phaistos and Malia are among a very small number of settlements to exceed the size and organisational threshold of villages and embark upon urbanisation well before the end of the EM period. Ironically, therefore, it is at the very locations, where we might expect to encounter top-end EM complexity, that we seemingly lack the possibility for insight. Perfecting this irony is the fact that our knowledge of smaller (and thus organisationally less complex) sites is steadily increasing, feeding the illusion that our sample is complete and thus representative. Because this irony is *ex silentio*, discussions of EM complexity have been free either to recognise it, and thus factor in the possibility of unappreciated forms of greater complexity at a handful of sites (Branigan 1970), or to ignore it and thus form a more pessimistic view of the extent of EM complexity (Cherry 1983; Watrous 1987; 2001). And so, while the Early Minoan Project has, on the whole, been extremely successful in achieving the objective of *Foundations* to banish the prospect of alternative and opposing readings of the same EM data, these multiple readings still jostle with each other in the vacuum of understanding that, until recently, engulfed the Neolithic-EM periods at locations occupied by the main MM "palaces".

Two controversies for Arthur Evans, Gordon Childe and the Early Minoan Project

In this regard, therefore, recent insights into late FN and EM activity in the area of the MM "palaces" at Knossos (Wilson and Day 2000; Day and Wilson 2002; Tomkins 2008; 2010; 2012a) and Phaistos (Todaro and Di Tonto 2008; Todaro 2012) might be seen as significantly advancing the ambitions of the Early Minoan Project. Finally a more specific picture of what happened at these locations prior to MM I is crystallising and as a result the "shape" of *emergence* in these larger, more complex EM communities has, in certain respects, become clearer. At the same time, however, it is necessary to recognise that this new picture poses certain problems or controversies for the Early Minoan Project, at least as most scholars currently conceive and pursue it.

Controversy 1. The Bronze Age before the Bronze Age

The first controversy concerns the specific way we – or rather our forebears – have framed the beginning of the Bronze Age. Ever since Evans our investigations and narratives of the Cretan Bronze Age have begun, where Evans intended, at the beginning of his EM period (e.g. Branigan 1970; Betancourt 1999) and have privileged an EM I phase beginning around 3100/3000 BC as the point when something definably different, that is "Minoan", rapidly first emerged out of an insignificant Neolithic (Betancourt 1999; 2008). However, with recent clarification of FN-EM I chronology (Tomkins 2007b; Todaro 2013), and thereby the nature and timing of developments prior to EM I (Tomkins 2008; 2014), has come the realisation that the EM I *emergence* horizon is inaccurate and artificial, created out of an over-estimation of the newness of what was happening in EM I and an ignorance of what took place before (Tomkins 2010; Tomkins and Schoep 2010). It is worth recalling that Evans' decision to enshrine EM I as the beginning of the Bronze Age was based on his perception of differences in material culture, primarily pottery, between "latest" Neolithic and "EM I" deposits in the Knossos sequence. Although these material differences are substantive, they represent an overly narrow perspective from which to define the limits of the Bronze Age as a social phenomenon. Moreover it is now clear that Evans' reading was based on pottery from deposits that are neither closely related in time nor always internally coherent. Thus his "EM I" deposit from the 1904 West Court tests is actually EM IIA in date (c. 2700–2500 BC), while the latest Neolithic deposits available to him for the first two decades of his work at Knossos are no later than FN I-II (c. 4600/4500–4000/3900 BC), leaving more than a millennium unaccounted for.

If, however, we pay attention to the period from FN II (c. 4200–4000/3900 BC) until an early phase of EM I present at Phaistos (c. 3600/3500-3200 BC; see

Todaro 2005; 2013 Phaistos III phase) and elsewhere (e.g. Knossos), it becomes apparent that a series of significant changes take place during the first half of the fourth millennium BC. These changes include the emergence of new strategies for livelihood, *marginality* and *trading*, alongside the continuing exploitation of the most productive *agricultural* locations (for a discussion see Tomkins 2010; 2014; Tomkins and Schoep 2010; also Whitelaw 2004; Papadatos and Tomkins 2013). Together these and other changes testify to a transformation of later Neolithic society and the emergence of lifeways, values and trajectories of development that hitherto had been considered to characterise the "Bronze Age" and thus not thought to appear before what might now be termed "mature" (i.e. post-Phaistos III) EM I (c. 3200/3100 BC), if not much later.

Marginality may be defined as the settlement of agriculturally less extensive or productive areas of the landscape, such as small upland valleys, islands and coastal plains. Prior to FN IV such areas generally appear to have been empty of settlement, save perhaps for a ritual usage of certain cave sites (Tomkins 2008; 2009; 2010). The little that we know about these early marginal settlement systems in Crete has a great deal to do with Keith's survey projects, notably the carpet of FN IV and EM I sites scattered in the valleys around Ziros in East Crete (Branigan 1998) and through the Asterousia (Branigan and Blackman 1975). In both these cases marginal colonisation seems to be characterised by a new dispersed notion of community, where a community does not reside in a single location, but is spread across multiple locations, sometimes occupied by no more than a single co-residential group, in a landscape where agricultural productivity is more dispersed and discretely located (Whitelaw 2000; Tomkins 2008: 38–40; 2010: 39–40). In order to maintain a shared sense of community these dispersed settlement systems typically do two things: (1) they situate their dispersed residential components, wherever possible, so that they are inter-visible; and (2) they develop and maintain common ritual gathering places, usually at nodal points in networks of movement and/or prominent natural places, such as peaks or caves (Branigan 1998; Tomkins 2008; 2009; 2013). In the EM I Asterousia these ritual gathering places most obviously take the form of the tholos cemeteries (Whitelaw 2000), but cave sites, such as Miamou, may also have played a role (Tomkins 2013).

Trading as a livelihood needs rather less introduction and may be defined as the establishment of long-distance exchange relationships in order to secure privileged access to high-value raw materials, objects, and practices (technologies, consumption) and the exploitation of their distribution as a means of negotiating power and livelihood (Tomkins 2010). Trading in the late FN, however, certainly does require justification and is currently most clearly illustrated by the metal, stone and ceramic assemblages from the FN IV-EM I coastal site of Kephala Petras in East Crete (Papadatos and Tomkins 2013 for a discussion). Study of these materials indicates that, despite its position at the eastern end of Crete, opposite Kasos and Karpathos, Kephala Petras maintained an especially close and directed connection with the

organisation of ritual space from open, equal and unrestricted access to a plurality of locales, to one where ritual space is defined and confined to specific central places. Once created these central places create the possibility of developing spatial hierarchies of axis, where access and residential proximity serve as more permanent and inheritable indices of social status.

And so, drawing these various strands together, it may be suggested that the fourth millennium (late FN-earlier EM I) saw a fundamental shift in social rights and obligations within Cretan communities. This shift represented a radical rewriting of the rules governing what households and communities could (and could not) be and do that is tantamount to a breakdown in the egalitarian contract that hitherto had underwritten the stability of later Neolithic village life. In a recent paper (Tomkins 2010) I have characterised this change in terms of the emergence of a new form of household, which I have termed "modular" because households now appear to have been more free to operate in isolation as fully separate and separable socioeconomic units that might combine in new and different ways to meet new and different circumstances. Prior to this point communities had effectively managed and curtailed the competitive desire of households to capitalise on periodic productive advantage and solidify more permanent inequalities in status and resources. The erosion of these communal controls not only facilitated increased organisational flexibility, but also meant that households were now more free to accumulate and appropriate in ways that encroached upon previously sacrosanct domains of household and communal practice. These changes facilitated the emergence of new forms of identity, more permanent forms of inequality and new forms of livelihood, such as trading and marginality, which enabled communities to exploit a wider range of the resources configured across the land and seascapes of the Aegean. In this way, the process of local and regional socioeconomic diversification, held to be typical of the third millennium BC Aegean, should be understood to begin at least a millennium earlier.

Controversy 2. Palaces before Palaces

The second controversy concerns the nature and timing of the emergence of the "palaces", specifically the orthodoxy that this took place during MM I. Ever since *Foundations* first took issue with Childe's vision of *emergence*, the precise nature of what is conventionally termed the MM I horizon has been a major research question for the Early Minoan Project. Clarification has taken considerable time and effort and as recently as the mid-1980s it was still possible for the clash between Evansian evolution (Warren 1987) and Childean revolution (Cherry 1983; 1984) to be prominently replayed. Ultimately, however, research, particularly over the last two decades, has demonstrated that the defining elements of the MM I revolution, as Childe and others saw it, actually emerge before (e.g. craft specialisation, social hierarchy, urbanism), during (e.g. writing) or after (e.g. state formation) MM I, in many cases substantially so (for recent discussions see Haggis 2002; Schoep and Knappett 2004; Tomkins and Schoep 2010; Schoep and Tomkins 2012).

Hitherto the one element that has resisted this reappraisal is the MM I emergence date for the "palaces" themselves. For those taking issue with this orthodoxy the challenge has been to identify convincing EM predecessors that might lengthen the process of palatial emergence and thus lessen the apparent suddenness of what happened in MM I (Branigan 1970; Hood 1971: 36, 40, 50; 2005: 45; Schoep 2002; 2004; Schoep and Knappett 2004). Generally, such attempts have struggled to convince the majority, primarily because the pre-MM IB evidence is perceived to be absent, equivocal or else inaccessible to scrutiny (Cherry 1983; Watrous 2001: 167–72, 175; Macdonald 2005; Macdonald and Knappett 2007; Whitelaw 2012). In this way, still seemingly fixed in MM I, but now stripped of other "significant developments" palatial emergence seems more miraculous and paradoxical than ever: a seemingly sudden and significant expenditure of resources that surely implies a new revolutionary social order, but one now lacking the associated horizon of changes that such a revolution might be expected to set in train.

In this regard recent insights into the nature of EM consumption and deposition on the palace hills at Knossos and Phaistos (Wilson and Day 2000; Day and Wilson 2002; 2004; Todaro 2012; Tomkins 2012) and the mapping of major episodes of EM construction (Wilson 1994; Todaro 2012; 2013; Tomkins 2012) represent a long awaited (Branigan 1970: 41–43, 206) transformation in our knowledge of these sites in the period up to MM I. At both sites, the late FN-EM I evidence for communal ritual focused on open spaces or courts (see above) is succeeded, at a point early in EM IIA, by a large-scale episode of clearance, construction and spatial reorganisation oriented on and around these older open spaces. On the palace hill at Phaistos there is evidence for a massive terracing operation taking place early in EM IIA as part of which a large south ramp was constructed (see Todaro 2012; 2013). In EM III a major building project substantially altered the appearance of the hill, extending the west slope and constructing a paved ramp that zigzagged up from the south slope and opened out onto a Court at the westernmost edge of the hilltop. This western Court, a possible predecessor of the Middle West Court, was connected eastwards, via a cobbled passageway, to an open, unpaved area at the centre of the hilltop. Between EM III and MM IA the area between these western and central open areas was occupied by one or more buildings with floors of red ochre or stucco. While the precise nature and form of the EM II-MM IA hilltop building(s) remain unclear (discrete residences or "palatial predecessor"?), it is notable that the articulation of space, with architecture located between western and central open areas and reached by a ramped access point (relaid in MM IB and II), essentially mirrors that of the MM IB–II Northwest and Southwest Buildings of the "First Palace" (Militello 2012).

At Knossos, early in EM IIA, there is evidence in the form of stratigraphic truncation, the deposition of construction fills and the construction of new walls, to suggest a major transformation of the Kephala Hill. In the area of the Central Court this involved the demolition, clearance and levelling of Buildings H and J, and the creation of a considerably larger Court. This large Court was initially surrounded

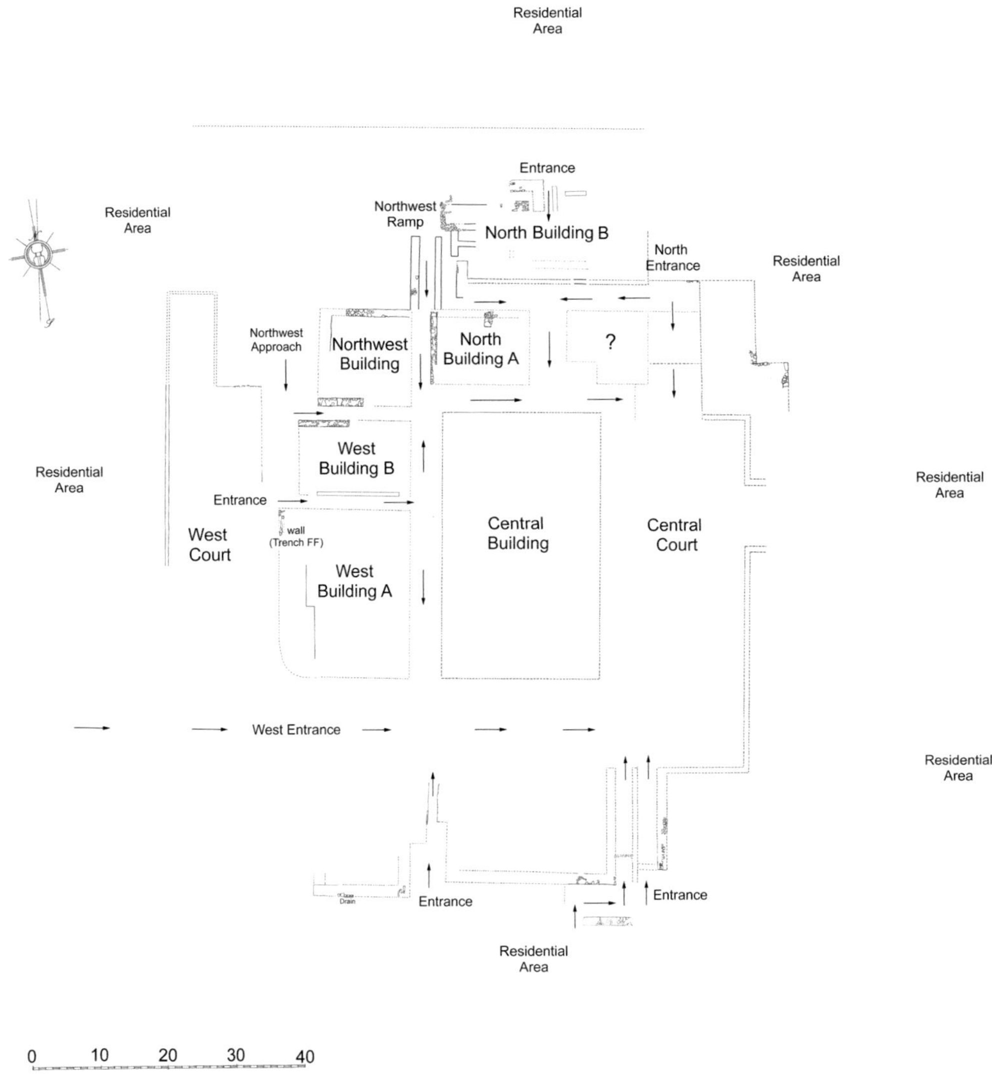

Figure 3.2: The Kephala Hill at Knossos at the end of EM IIB.

by a series of aligned buildings (or "insulae", *pace* Evans 1921: 141 *et passim*) (see Tomkins 2012), which subsequently expanded further during EM IIA late and EM IIB, through the construction of additional, similarly aligned insulae (Figure 3.2), to achieve a similar form and footprint to north and west as the later "palace". The subsequent history of this EM II Court Complex may be traced via further episodes of expansion and modification through EM III, MM IA and into MM IB at which point it becomes what convention terms the MM IB "First Palace" (Figures 3.3–3.5). It should be stressed, however, that this MM IB Court Complex is not a new building, but rather a phase of use in the history of an existing complex. MM IB certainly saw

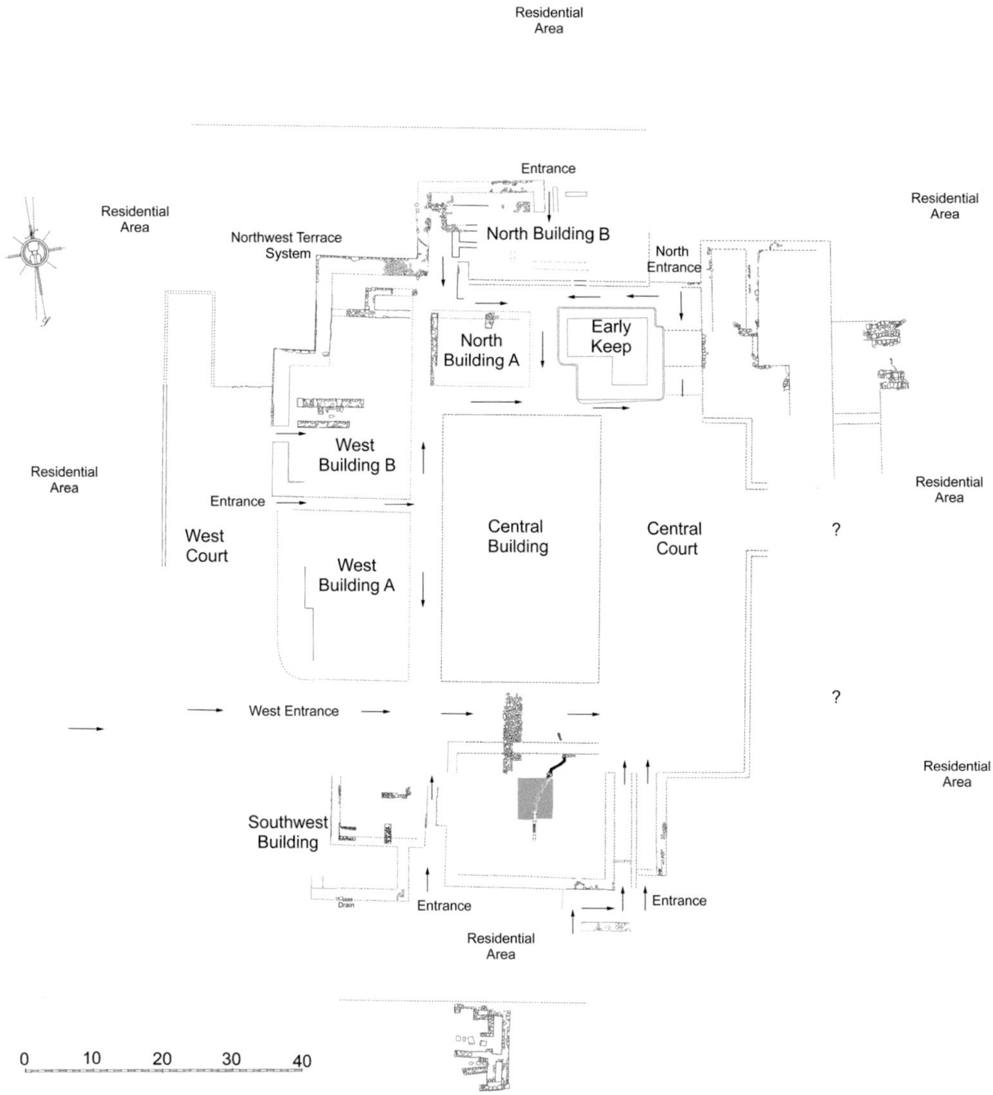

Figure 3.3: The Kephala Hill at Knossos during EM III.

significant investment in this complex, most obviously in its peripheral spaces and western and northern facades (Tomkins 2012: 59–63), but probably also within its west (Macdonald 2012) and northern wings (e.g. Early Keep; Branigan 1992: 160–61; Tomkins 2012: 62). Nevertheless, many of its EM II, EM III and MM IA components, including many of their original walls, seem to have continued to exist in some form or other.

What is the precise nature of the late FN and EM activity on the palace hills at Knossos and Phaistos and how should we conceptualise its relationship to what takes

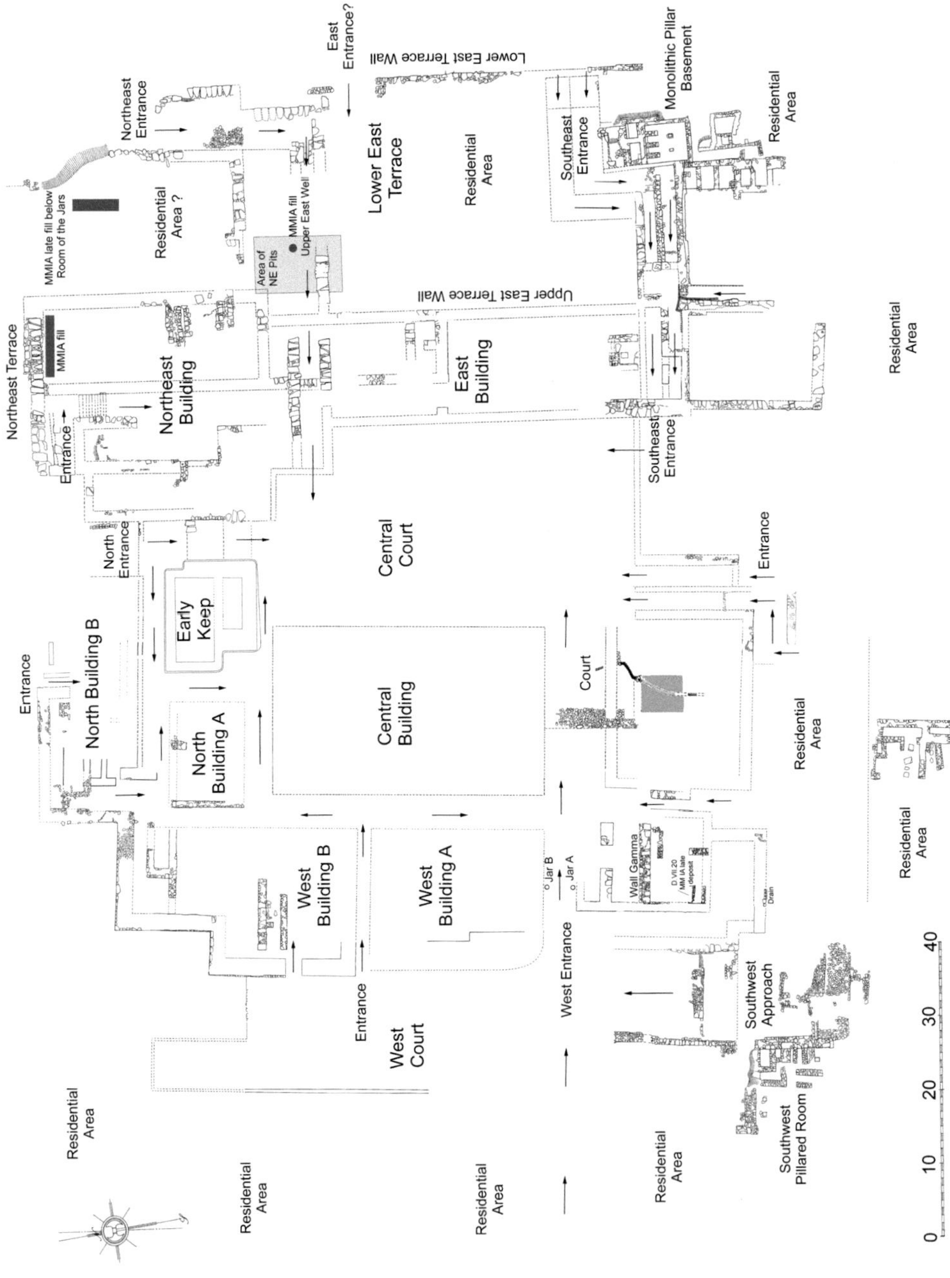

Figure 3.4: The Kephala Hill at Knossos at the end of MM IA.

Figure 35: The Kephala Hill at Knossos at the end of MM IB.

place later during MM and LM? This is not a question that currently admits of detailed answers and much remains to be clarified. What does seem clear, however, is that the emergence of the "Minoan palaces" unfolded over different timescales in different places and in very different ways to that understood by Evans, Childe and twentieth century scholarship as a whole (Schoep and Tomkins 2012: 8–11). Currently the most obviously striking elements of this new view are, first, that the ritual significance of the locations occupied by the MM I "palaces" at Knossos and Phaistos around 2000 BC, together with key details of spatial organisation and practice, can now be traced back a further 1500–2000 years to the late FN; and second, that the basic architectural form of the MM "palaces", namely a complex of aligned buildings around a large Court, now appears to emerge early in EM II, possibly as much as 700 years earlier than previously thought.

In view of these differences, and given the preliminary nature of our understanding, it is important that we avoid falling into the trap of allowing our new engagement with the late FN-EM data to be structured by our early twentieth century conceptual inheritance of ideas (e.g. Schoep 2010a; 2010b). At Knossos, at least, the terms "First Palace", "Second Palace" (etc) are particularly problematic because they suppose a genesis scenario that is no longer compatible with the EM II-MM I evidence. There is no single commissioning Minos, no single Daedalic vision, no unitary building project playing out over one or two generations, and thus no end point where one can say that this is the "First Palace" as it was originally intended by a specific architect. What we have instead is an architectural complex that is a palimpsestic sum of the diverse intentions and efforts of a multitude of people, reaching back many, many generations to a point still early in EM. This is emphatically not the scenario envisaged by Evans and Childe and thus not the scenario implied in the conceptual architecture that we have inherited from them.

Final thoughts. Early Minoan and the shape of *emergence*

Armed with four decades of data from the Early Minoan Project, we can now assess how well this picture accords with the competing visions of the shape of *emergence*, first proposed by Arthur Evans and Gordon Childe, and so influential on subsequent twentieth century Minoan scholarship. Of the two it is the vision of Childe, together with the Prepalatial-Protopalatial chronological scheme that it inspired, that is most obviously obsolete. EM makes little sense as a single developmental phase and is no longer "pre-palatial" at the main centres, "palaces" no longer emerge abruptly and paradoxically in MM I and MM I-II is no longer "proto-palatial". The death of Childe's vision of a formative EM followed by an MM I revolution has been a slow one and, despite the marshalling of an extensive body of evidence to the contrary, is still not quite complete for some. It is appropriate, and not just in the context of the present volume, that we give credit to Keith for initiating the deconstruction of Childe's vision with *Foundations* and for his pioneering role in the fieldwork and research upon which our present, more secure understanding of EM is based. It is important also that we recognise how this process of deconstruction came to be marginalised by the appearance of Renfrew's *Emergence*, which, though of profound consequence to our understanding of the Aegean, also repackaged and thus perpetuated Childe's ideas about civilisation, his universalist narrative ambitions and his reading of the Cretan data for the New Archaeology generation and others that followed. Indeed it is only in the last decade or so, as we have finally moved out of the shadow of *Emergence* and gained purchase on the modernist production of the "Minoan" past (Hamilakis 2002; Barrett and Halstead 2004; Schoep and Tomkins 2012), that the deconstruction of Childe's vision of MM I has again gained coherence, credibility and some sort of conclusion (Schoep and Knappett 2004; Tomkins and Schoep 2010; Schoep and Tomkins 2012).

Moreover, as data for the fourth and third millennia in Crete gain depth and resolution, so it becomes clearer that the very notion of a single, revolutionary origin point for the emergence of "civilisation" – or however one chooses to gloss the array of phenomena consequent upon increased social complexity and more permanent forms of inequality – whether placed in EM I or MM I – only makes sense in rhetorical terms, as a device to bring simplicity and structure to a particular sort of (grand) narrative (Gamble 2007 for a general discussion). In dispensing with the artificiality of the MM I revolution, we not only improve our understanding of how complexity evolved during FN and EM, but also clarify the MM I reality. While the emergence of the "palaces" is clearly, as Keith emphasised, an evolution, the origins of which now lie considerably earlier than MM IB, and while we now routinely trace fundamental continuities between the societies of EM and MM I Crete (Schoep 2012), the changes that take place in and around MM I remain significant. Thus the emergence of script, changes in trade and connectivity, the marked increase in the size of the communities at "palatial" centres (with all the implications for organisation that this entails; see Whitelaw 2012) and the scale and nature of the investments made in the Court Complexes (Macdonald 2012; Militello 2012; Tomkins 2012) all represent significant MM I developments for "Minoan civilisation".

And so, although Evans sought an early emergence of "civilisation" on Crete in order to satisfy a set of now dubious personal objectives for Cretan and European prehistory and on the basis of a preferential ordering of the limited data then available, it is this longer chronology, first effectively laid out in *Foundations*, that appears to be the least incorrect rendering of the shape of emergence now apparent in the data. Where Evans' conceptualisation of EM, and that of *Foundations*, most clearly falls down is in its failure to incorporate the earliest phases of *emergence* within its frame of enquiry. Faced with the data now available, Evans and Childe would hopefully recognise the significance of developments taking place in the fourth millennium BC (i.e. FN-earlier EM I) and the artificiality of the divide with EM I that is enforced by our inherited chrono-developmental terminology. Much as with MM I, the evidence now suggests we should abandon the notion of a single, revolutionary phase of change in mature EM I (e.g. Branigan 1970; Betancourt 2008) or indeed EM II (e.g. Renfrew 1972) in favour of a longer period of evolution extending back into earlier phases of EM I and FN. It is during this period, at least on current evidence, that we see the first clear signs of a transformation in the egalitarian constitution of "Neolithic" societies and the emergence of a new emphasis on acquisition, accumulation and the stabilisation of social difference that is more typical of "Bronze Age" societies (Tomkins 2010; 2014).

Once mature EM I is understood, not as a beginning in an emergence of greater complexity (*contra* Evans 1921; Branigan 1970; Betancourt 2008), but as a late phase in a longer period of reconfiguration, the changes that take place within it, such as those in pottery or the funerary realm, take on new clarity and meaning. Thus, in the case of pottery, the appearance of new forms (e.g. pithos) and distinctive surface treatments (e.g. fine dark-on-light painted ware, dark grey burnished ware) might make sense as consequences of a new late FN culture of consumption that privileged the acquisition of prestige forms, commodities and practices through which differential identity and status might be performed and stabilised (Papadatos and Tomkins 2013). Similarly the appearance of dedicated environments for intense funerary deposition, whether natural (rock-shelters) or artificial (i.e. constructed "tholoi" mimicking the physical characteristics of rock-shelters), may be understood both as a new development (specialised places of memory for specific [supra-household] groups?) and as referencing a Neolithic tradition of ritual cave usage in which the (occasional) deposition of human remains played a role (Tomkins 2013).

The ultimate lesson to learn from the Early Minoan Project would appear to be that Evans' Early Minoan period, at least as conventionally defined, has little, if any, of the developmental relevance with which it was originally imbued and little congruence with the timing of change or with the complexity and diversity now apparent in the data. It is neither the formative period preceding *emergence*, as Childe and Renfrew argued, nor does EM I mark the "emergence of Minoan civilisation" or MM I the beginning of the "palaces", as Evans intended. In short, Evans' scheme represents a noble, but ultimately doomed attempt to create a unilineal ordering of a partial dataset that exhibits multilineal lines of development. However, with EM embedded in our chronological architecture, we are in effect stuck with it. What we can do, nevertheless, is resist the temptation to ascribe any sort of historical or developmental meaning to our relative chronological terminology and simply treat it as a shorthand for sequential units of time. Recognising that phenomena, such as trading, a "prestige-goods economy" and cultures of accumulation and difference, begin in the late FN may pose problems for those who like neatness in prehistory and seek congruity in the timing of chronological and developmental schemes. Nevertheless it is essential that we acknowledge that our investigation of *emergence* is partial and has been unduly compromised by our having the "Bronze Age" begin part way through it. Rectifying this represents a new challenge for the Early Minoan

Project and requires a change in awareness among fieldworkers, which we can only hope to fill if we extend the temporal limits of investigation to include the FN and pursue field projects that treat the detailed investigation of FN assemblages, sites and landscapes as a priority, not a serendipity.

Finally, we might return to the question of *emergence* and attempt to sketch some of the key developments that punctuated its development between the fourth and early third millennia BC. Staying within a discourse that would be familiar to Evans and Childe, the data now suggest that *emergence* began earlier than hitherto thought, in the late FN, and that by EM II a new threshold of complexity had been reached that we might consider calling civilisation, even on the basis of Childe's (or Renfrew's) more stringent criteria (i.e. writing/sealing, central buildings, and urbanising communities). Not only is the timing of *emergence* different, but also the timeframe over which it unfolds. The notion that civilisation emerges rapidly in a single, revolutionary phase of reconfiguration and follows a single, unilineal trajectory of development simply does not match what we now know about the nature, timing and diversity of change in Crete during late prehistory. Rather *emergence* is a long, complex, multilineal evolution playing out between the late FN and EM I (c. 4000–2700 BC), composed of *multiple* episodes of change and reconfiguration and characterised by multiple, divergent "pathways to complexity". From the late FN one sees a critical shift in social rights and obligations that opened up the possibility for new cultures of accumulation and new forms of difference and inequality to emerge that were, in turn, instrumental in the development of new livelihoods, such as marginality, trading and new forms of craft specialisation. From an early point in EM II the largest, most complex communities had constructed the first central buildings and a definable process of urbanisation was underway.

We might (semi-seriously) term this late FN-EM II period the Urban Evolution (*pace* Childe 1950). While urban centres continued to evolve and greater complexity was reached after EM II, these represent episodes in the subsequent *development* of civilisation. After EM II the relevant question for the Bronze Age is no longer how did more permanent forms of inequality, trade and urbanism *emerge* out of Neolithic egalitarianism, but how they *developed* in scale, complexity and articulation. Although the changes that took place between the late FN and EM II might seem unimpressive, when viewed against subsequent developments, once they are considered from the less distorting perspective of what came before their full significance becomes clearer. This period of transformation is of fundamental significant for social evolution in the Aegean because it marks a shift in the constitution of Aegean societies that (so far at least!) has never been reversed and is thus, in effect, a permanent condition. Once the Aegean societies of what we call the Stone Age moved, from being constructed around communality and subjugated to the interests of the many, to being constructed around inequality and driven by the interests of the few, there was, it would seem, no going back.

Acknowledgements

I would like to thank the editors for the invitation to contribute to the original Round Table workshop and for their patience during the long gestation period of this paper. In pursuing the research upon which this paper is based I have greatly benefited from conversations with John Evans, Peter Day, David Wilson, Colin Macdonald, Carl Knappett, Simona Todaro, Todd Whitelaw and Ilse Schoep. I would like also to thank the BSA Committee and a series of Knossos Curators, both permanent and acting, for providing access to the collections in the Knossos Stratigraphical Museum. Over the last decade my research at Knossos has been funded by grants from INSTAP, the European Community Marie Curie Programme (Contract No. HPMF-CT-2001-01385), the White-Levy Foundation and the British School at Athens. Nicoletta Momigliano provided useful comments on an earlier draft of this paper.

Bibliography

Åberg, N.

1933 *Bronzezeitliche und Fruheisenzeitliche Chronologie, IV, Griechenland.* Stockholm: Historie och Antikvitets Akademien.

Alexiou, S. and P. Warren,

2004 *The Early Minoan Tombs of Lebena, Southern Crete* (Studies in Mediterranean Archaeology 30). Sävedalen: Paul Åströms Förlag.

Barrett, J. and P. Halstead (eds.)

2004 *The Emergence of Civilization Revisited* (Sheffield Studies in Aegean Archaeology 6). Oxford: Oxbow.

Betancourt, P. P.

1999 What is Minoan? FN/EM I in the gulf of Mirabello region. In P. P. Betancourt, V. Karageorghis, R. Laffineur and W.-D. Niemeier (eds.), *Meletemata. Studies in Aegean Archaeology Presented to Malcolm H. Wiener* (Aegaeum 20): 33–40. Liège: Université de Liège.

2008 *The Bronze Age Begins. The Ceramics Revolution of Early Minoan I and the New Forms of Wealth that Transformed Prehistoric Society.* Philadelphia: INSTAP Press.

Bintliff, J.

1984 Structuralism and the Minoan Myth. *Antiquity* 83: 33–38.

Blackman, D. and K. Branigan

1975 An archaeological survey on the South Coast of Crete, between the Ayiofarango and Chrisostomos. *Annual of the British School at Athens* 70: 17–36.

Boardman, J.

1972 Review of "The Foundations of Palatial Crete. A Survey of Crete in the Early Bronze Age". *English Historical Review* 87.342: 151.

Branigan, K.

1970 *The Foundations of Palatial Crete: A Survey of Crete in the Early Bronze Age.* London: Routledge.

1988 Foundations reviewed. In K. Branigan, *Pre-Palatial. The Foundations of Palatial Crete: A Survey of Crete in the Early Bronze Age*: 233–53. London: Adolf M. Hakkert.

1991 Mochlos: An Early Aegean "Gateway Community"? In R. Laffineur and L. Basch (eds.), *Thalassa. L'Egée préhistorique et la mer. Actes de la troisième rencontre égéenne internationale de l'Université de Liège, Station de recherches sous-marines et océanographiques (StaReSo), Calvi, Corse, 23-25 avril 1990* (Aegaeum 7): 97–105. Liège: Université de Liège.

1992 The early keep, Knossos: a reappraisal. *Annual of the British School at Athens* 87: 153–63.

1993 *Dancing with Death. Life and Death in Southern Crete, c. 3000–2000 B.C.* Amsterdam: A. M. Hakkert.

1998 Prehistoric and early historic settlement in the Ziros region, eastern Crete. *Annual of the British School at Athens* 93: 23–90.

Broodbank, C.

1989 The Longboat and society in the Cyclades in the Keros-Syros culture. *American Journal of Archaeology* 93: 319–37.

2000 *An Island Archaeology of the Early Cyclades.* Cambridge: Cambridge University Press.

Burrows, R. M.

1907 *The Discoveries in Crete and their Bearing on the History of Ancient Civilisation.* London: John Murray.

Cadogan, G., P. Day, C. F. MacDonald, J. A. MacGillivray, N. Momigliano, T. Whitelaw and D. Wilson

1993 Early Minoan and Middle Minoan pottery groups at Knossos. *Annual of the British School at Athens* 88: 21–28.

Cherry, J.

1983 Evolution, revolution, and the origins of complex society in Minoan Crete. In O. Krzyszkowska and L. Nixon (eds.), *Minoan Society. Proceedings of the Cambridge Colloquium 1981*: 33–45. Bristol: Bristol Classical Press.

1984 The emergence of the state in the prehistoric Aegean. *Proceedings of the Cambridge Philological Society* 30: 18–48.

1986 Polities and palaces: some problems in Minoan state formation. In C. Renfrew and J. Cherry (eds.), *Peer Polity Interaction and Socio-political Change*: 19–45. Cambridge: Cambridge University Press.

Childe, V. G.

1925 *The Dawn of European Civilization.* London: Kegan Paul.

1934 *Man Makes Himself.* London: Watts and Co.

1950 The Urban Revolution. *Town Planning Review* 21.1: 3–19.

1954 *What Happened in History.* Hardmondsworth: Penguin.

1958 *The Prehistory of European Society.* Harmondsworth: Penguin.

Davaras, C. and P. P. Betancourt

2004 *The Hagia Photia Cemetery I. The Tomb Groups and Architecture* (Prehistory Monographs 14). Philadelphia: INSTAP Press.

Day, P. and D. Wilson

2002 Landscapes of memory, craft and power in Pre-Palatial and Proto-Palatial Knossos. In Y. Hamilakis (ed.), *Labyrinth Revisited. Rethinking "Minoan" Archaeology*: 143–66. Oxford: Oxbow.

2004 Ceramic change and the practice of eating and drinking in Early Bronze Age Crete. In P. Halstead and J. Barrett (eds.), *Food, Cuisine and Society in Prehistoric Greece* (Sheffield Studies in Aegean Archaeology 5): 45–62. Oxford: Oxbow.

Dickinson, O.

1994 *The Aegean Bronze Age.* Cambridge: Cambridge University Press.

Evans, A.

1896 "The Eastern Question" in Anthropology. *Report of the 66th Meeting of the British Association for the Advancement of Science* 1896: 906–22.

1897 Primitive Pictographs and a Prae-Phoenician Script, from Crete and the Peloponnese. *Journal of Hellenic Studies* 14: 270–372.

1906 *Essai de classification des époques de la civilisation Minoenne: résumé d'un discours fait au Congrés d'archéologie à Athènes.* London: B. Quaritch.

1921 *The Palace of Minos.* Volume 1. London: Macmillan.

Gamble, C.
2007 *Origins and Revolutions: Human Identity in Earliest Prehistory*. New York: Cambridge University Press.
Gere, C.
2009 *Knossos and the Prophets of Modernism*. Chicago: University of Chicago Press.
Glotz, G.
1925 *The Aegean Civilization*. London: Kegan Paul.
Haggis, D.
2002 Integration and complexity in the late pre-Palatial period. A view from the countryside in eastern Crete. In Y. Hamilakis (ed.), *Labyrinth Revisited: Rethinking "Minoan" Archaeology*: 120–42. Oxford: Oxbow.
Hall, H. R.
1928 *The Civilization of Greece in the Bronze Age*. London: Methuen.
Halstead, P.
2004 Life after Mediterranean polyculture: the subsistence subsystem and the Emergence of Civilization revisited. In J. Barrett and P. Halstead (eds.), *The Emergence of Civilisation Revisited* (Sheffield Studies in Aegean Archaeology 6): 189–206. Oxford: Oxbow.
Hamilakis, Y.
2002 What future for the Minoan past? In Y. Hamilakis (ed.), *Labyrinth Revisited. Rethinking "Minoan" Archaeology*: 2–28. Oxford: Oxbow.
Hamilakis, Y. and N. Momigliano (eds.)
2006 *Archaeology and European Modernity: Producing and Consuming the "Minoans"* (Creta Antica 7). Padua: Bottega d'Erasmo.
Hitchcock, L.
2010 Minoan architecture. In E. Cline (ed.), *The Oxford Handbook of the Bronze Age Aegean*: 189–99. New York: Oxford University Press.
Hood, S.
1971 *The Minoans. Crete in the Bronze Age*. London: Thames and Hudson.
2005 Dating the Knossos frescoes. In L. Morgan (ed.), *Aegean Wall Painting. A Tribute to Mark Cameron* (BSA Studies 13): 45–81. London: British School at Athens.
Hood, S. and G. Cadogan
2011 *Knossos Excavations 1957-61* (BSA Supplementary Volume 46). London: British School at Athens.
Hue, M. and O. Pelon
1992 La salle à piliers du palais de Malia et ses antécédents. *Bulletin de Correspondance Hellénique* 116: 1–36.
Hutchinson, R. W.
1962 *Prehistoric Crete*. London: Penguin.
Latour, B.
2005 *Reassembling the Social: An Introduction to Actor-Network-Theory*. Oxford: Oxford University Press.
Legarra Herrero, B.
2012 The construction, deconstruction and non-construction of hierarchies in the funerary record of Prepalatial Crete. In I. Schoep, P. Tomkins and J. Driessen (eds.), *Back to the Beginning. Reassessing Social and Political Complexity on Crete during the Early and Middle Bronze Age*: 325–57. Oxford: Oxbow.
Levi, D.
1951 La ripresa dello scavo a Festòs. *Bollettino d'Arte della Pubblica Istruzione* 1951: 333–48.
1957 L'archivio di cretule a Festòs. *Annuario della Scuola archeologica di Atene e delle Missioni italiane in Oriente* 19–20: 193–361.

Macdonald, C. F.

2005 *Knossos.* London: Folio Society.

2012 Palatial Knossos: The early years. In I. Schoep, P. Tomkins and J. Driessen (eds.), *Back to the Beginning. Reassessing Social and Political Complexity on Crete during the Early and Middle Bronze Age*: 81–113. Oxford: Oxbow.

Macdonald, C. F. and C. Knappett

2007 *Knossos: Protopalatial deposits in Early Magazine A and the South-west Houses* (BSA Supplementary Volume 41). London: British School at Athens.

McEnroe, J.

1995 Sir Arthur Evans and Edwardian archaeology. *Classical Bulletin* 71: 3–18.

2002 Cretan questions: politics and archaeology 1898–1913. In Y. Hamilakis (ed.), *Labyrinth Revisited. Rethinking "Minoan" Archaeology*: 59–72. Oxford: Oxbow.

McNeal, R.

1973 The legacy of Arthur Evans. *University of California Studies in Classical Antiquity* 6: 205–20.

MacGillivray, J. A.

2000 *Minotaur. Arthur Evans and the Archaeology of the Minoan Myth*. London: Jonathan Cape.

Mackenzie, D.

1903 The pottery of Knossos. *Journal of Hellenic Studies* 23: 157–203.

1906a The Middle Minoan pottery of Knossos. *Journal of Hellenic Studies* 26: 243–67.

1906b Cretan Palaces and the Aegean Civilization. *Annual of the British School at Athens* 12: 216–58.

Manning, S.

2008 Formation of the palaces. In C. Shelmerdine (ed.), *The Cambridge Companion to the Aegean Bronze Age*: 105–20. Cambridge: Cambridge University Press.

Militello, P.

2012 Emerging authority: a functional analysis of the MM II settlement of Phaistos. In I. Schoep, P. Tomkins and J. Driessen (eds.), *Back to the Beginning. Reassessing Social and Political Complexity on Crete during the Early and Middle Bronze Age*: 236–72. Oxford: Oxbow.

Momigliano, N.

2002 Federico Halbherr and Arthur Evans: an archaeological correspondence (1894–1917). *Studi Micenei ed Egeo-Anatolici* 44: 263–318.

2007a *Knossos Pottery Handbook. Neolithic and Bronze Age (Minoan)* (BSA Studies 14): 79–103. London: British School at Athens.

2007b Late Prepalatial (EM III-MM IA). In N. Momigliano (ed.), *Knossos Pottery Handbook. Neolithic and Bronze Age (Minoan)* (BSA Studies 14): 79–103. London: British School at Athens.

2011 On the Knossos pottery sequence and the Evans-Mackenzie chronological scheme for the "Minoan Age". *Πεπραγμένα του Ι' Διεθνούς Κρητολογικού Συνεδρίου*, vol. A3: 107–25. Χανιά: Φιλολογικός Σύλλογος "Ο Χρυσόστομος"

Palmer, L.

1963 *The find places of the Knossos tablets.* Oxford: Clarendon Press.

Panagiotopoulos, D.

2002 Das Tholosgrab E von Phourni: Studien zu einem frühkretische Grabfund un seinem Kulturellen Kulturkontext (BAR IS 1014). Oxford: Archaeopress.

Papadatos, Y.

2005 *Tholos Tomb Gamma: A Prepalatial Tholos Tomb at Phourni, Archanes* (Prehistory Monographs 17). Philadelphia: INSTAP Academic Press.

2007 The beginning of metallurgy in Crete: new evidence from the FN – EM I settlement at Kephala Petras, Siteia. In P. M. Day and R. C. P. Doonan (eds.), *Metallurgy in the Early Bronze Age Aegean* (Sheffield Studies in Aegean Archaeology 7): 154–167. Oxford: Oxbow.

Papadatos, Y. and P. Tomkins
2013 Trading, the longboat and cultural interaction in the late FN-early EB I Aegean. The view from Kephala Petras, East Crete. *American Journal of Archaeology* 117: 353-81.
Papadopoulos, J.
2005 Inventing the Minoans: archaeology, modernity and the quest for European identity. *Journal of Mediterranean Archaeology* 18: 87–149.
Pelon, O.
2005 Les deux destructions du palais de Malia. In I. Bradfer-Burdet, B. Detournay and R. Laffineur (eds.), *ΚΡΗΣ ΤΕΧΝΙΤΗΣ. L'Artisan Crétois: Recueil d'articles en l'honneur de Jean-Claude Poursat, publié à l'occasion des 40 ans de la découverte du Quartier Mu* (Aegaeum 26): 185–97 Liège: Université de Liège.
Pendlebury, J.
1939 *The Archaeology of Crete*. London: Methuen.
Perlès, C.
1992 Systems of exchange and organization in Neolithic Greece. *Journal of Mediterranean Archaeology* 5: 115–64.
Platon, N.
1956 La *chronologie minoenne*. In C. Zervos (ed.), *L' Art de la Crète Neolithique et Minoenne*: 509–12. Paris: Cahiers d' Art.
1961 Chronologie de la Crète et des Cyclades à l' Âge du Bronze. In G. Bersu (ed.), *Bericht über den V. Internationalen Kongress für Vor- und Frühgeschichte, Hamburg 1958*: 671–74. Berlin: Mann.
Relaki, M.
2012 The social arenas of tradition. Investigating collective and individual social strategies in the Prepalatial and Protopalatial Mesara. In I. Schoep, P. Tomkins and J. Driessen (eds.), *Back to the Beginning. Reassessing Social and Political Complexity on Crete during the Early and Middle Bronze Age*: 290–324. Oxford: Oxbow.
Renfrew, C.
1971 Review of "The Foundations of Palatial Crete. A Survey of Crete in the Early Bronze Age". *Classical Review* 21: 434–35.
1972 *The Emergence of Civilisation*. London: Methuen.
1973 *Before Civilization. The Radiocarbon Revolution and Prehistoric Europe*. London: Pimlico.
1978 Trajectory discontinuity and morphogenesis: the implications of catastrophe theory for archaeology. *American Antiquity* 43: 203–22.
Rowlands, M.
1984 Conceptualising the European Bronze and Early Iron ages. In J. Bintliff (ed.), *European Social Evolution: Archaeological Perspectives*: 147–56. Bradford: University of Bradford.
Schoep, I.
2002 Social and political organization on Crete in the Proto-Palatial period: the case of Middle Minoan II Malia. *Journal of Mediterranean Archaeology* 15: 101–32.
2004 Assessing the role of architecture in conspicuous consumption in the Middle Minoan I-II Periods. *Oxford Journal of Archaeology* 23: 243–69.
2010a Middle Bronze Age: Crete. In E. Cline (ed.), *The Oxford Handbook of the Bronze Age Aegean*: 113–25. New York: Oxford University Press.
2010b The Minoan "Palace-Temple" reconsidered: a critical assessment of the spatial concentration of political, religious and economic power in Bronze Age Crete. *Journal of Mediterranean Archaeology* 23: 219–44.
2012 Bridging the divide between the "Prepalatial" and the "Protopalatial" Periods? In I. Schoep, P. Tomkins and J. Driessen (eds.), *Back to the Beginning. Reassessing Social and Political Complexity on Crete during the Early and Middle Bronze Age*: 403–28. Oxford: Oxbow.

Schoep, I. and C. Knappett
2004 Dual Emergence: evolving heterarchy, exploding hierarchy. In J. Barrett and P. Halstead (eds.), *The Emergence of Civilisation Revisited* (Sheffield Studies in Aegean Archaeology 6): 21–37. Oxford: Oxbow.

Schoep, I. and P. Tomkins
2012 Back to the beginning for the Early and Middle Bronze Age on Crete. In I. Schoep, P. Tomkins and J. Driessen (eds.), *Back to the Beginning. Reassessing Social and Political Complexity on Crete during the Early and Middle Bronze Age*: 1–31. Oxford: Oxbow.

Shaw, J. W.
1971 Review of "The Foundations of Palatial Crete. A Survey of Crete in the Early Bronze Age". *American Journal of Archaeology* 75: 220.

Sherratt, A.
1989 V. Gordon Childe: archaeology and intellectual history. *Past and Present* 125: 151–85.
2006 Crete, Greece and the Orient in the thought of Gordon Childe (with an Appendix on Toynbee and Spengler: The Afterlife of the Minoans in European Intellectual History). In Y. Hamilakis and N. Momigliano (eds.), *Archaeology and European Modernity: Producing and Consuming the "Minoans"* (Creta Antica 7): 107–26. Padua: Bottega d'Erasmo.

Soles, J.
1992 *The Prepalatial Cemeteries at Mochlos and Gournia and the House Tombs of Bronze Age Crete* (Hesperia Supplement 24). Princeton: American School of Classical Studies at Athens.

Televantou, C.
2008 Strofilas: a Neolithic settlement on Andros. In N. Brodie, J. Doole, G. Gavalas and C. Renfrew (eds.), *Horizon, A colloquium on the prehistory of the Cyclades*: 43–53. Cambridge: McDonald Institute for Archaeological Research.

Todaro, S.
2005 EMI-MMIA ceramic groups at Phaistos: towards the definition of a Prepalatial ceramic sequence in South Central Crete. *Creta Antica* 6: 11–46.
2012 Craft production and social practices at Prepalatial Phaistos: the background to the First "Palace". In I. Schoep, P. Tomkins and J. Driessen (eds.), *Back to the Beginning. Reassessing Social and Political Complexity on Crete during the Early and Middle Bronze Age*: 195–235. Oxford: Oxbow.
2013 *The Phaistos Hills Before the Palace. A Contextual Reappraisal* (Praehistorica Mediterranea 5). Monza: Polimetrica.

Todaro, S. and S. Di Tonto
2008 The Neolithic settlement at Phaistos revisited: evidence for ceremonial activity on the eve of the Bronze Age. In V. Isaakidou and P. Tomkins (eds.), *Escaping the Labyrinth. The Cretan Neolithic in Context* (Sheffield Studies in Aegean Archaeology 8): 177–90. Oxford: Oxbow.

Tomkins, P.
2004 Filling in the "Neolithic Background": social life and social transformation in the Aegean before the Bronze Age. In J. Barrett and P. Halstead (eds.), *The Emergence of Civilization Revisited* (Sheffield Studies in Aegean Archaeology 6): 38–63. Oxford: Oxbow.
2007a Communality and competition. The social life of food and containers at Aceramic and Early Neolithic Knossos, Crete. In C. Mee and J. Renard (eds.), *Cooking Up the Past. Food and Culinary Practices in the Neolithic and Bronze Age Aegean*: 174–99. Oxford: Oxbow.
2007b Neolithic: Strata IX-VIII, VII-VIB, VIA-V, IV, IIIB, IIIA, IIB, IIA and IC Groups. In N. Momigliano (ed.), *Knossos Pottery Handbook: Neolithic and Bronze Age (Minoan)* (BSA Studies 14): 9–48. London: British School at Athens.
2008 Time, space and the reinvention of the Cretan Neolithic. In V. Isaakidou and P. Tomkins (eds.), *Escaping the Labyrinth. The Cretan Neolithic in Context* (Sheffield Studies in Aegean Archaeology 8): 21–48. Oxford: Oxbow.

2009 Domesticity by default: ritual, ritualisation and cave use in the Neolithic Aegean. *Oxford Journal of Archaeology* 28: 125–53.
2010 Neolithic antecedents. In E. Cline (ed.), *The Oxford Handbook of the Bronze Age Aegean*: 31–49. New York: Oxford University Press.
2012 Behind the Horizon. Reconsidering the genesis and function of the "First Palace" at Knossos (Final Neolithic IV-Middle Minoan IB). In I. Schoep, P. Tomkins and J. Driessen (eds.), *Back to the Beginning. Reassessing Social and Political Complexity on Crete during the Early and Middle Bronze Age*: 32–80. Oxford: Oxbow.
2013 Landscapes of ritual, identity and memory. Reconsidering Neolithic and Early Bronze Age cave-use in Crete, Greece. In H. Moyes (ed.), *Sacred Darkness. A Global Perspective on the Ritual Use of Caves*: 59–79. Colorado: University Press of Colorado.
2014 Tracing complexity in "the missing millennium". An overview of recent research into the Final Neolithic period on Crete. In B. Horejs and M. Mehofer (eds.), *Western Anatolia before Troy. Proto-urbanisation in the 4th millennium BC*. OREA 1: 345–64.

Tomkins, P. and I. Schoep
2010 The Early Bronze Age: Crete. In E. Cline (ed.), *The Oxford Handbook of the Bronze Age Aegean*: 66–82. New York: Oxford University Press.

Vagnetti, L.
1996 The Final Neolithic: Crete enters the wider world. *Cretan Studies* 5: 29–39.

Vasilakis, A.
1989 Ο πρωτομινωικός οικισμός Τρυπητής. *Αρχαιολογία* 30: 52–56.

Warren, P.
1972 *Myrtos: An Early Bronze Age Site in Crete* (BSA Supplementary Volume 7). London: Thames and Hudson.
1975 *The Aegean Civilizations*. New York: Phaidon Press.
1987 The genesis of the Minoan palace. In R. Hägg and N. Marinatos (eds.), *The Function of the Minoan Palaces*: 47–56. Stockholm: Swedish Institute in Athens.

Warren, P. and V. Hankey
1989 *Aegean Bronze Age Chronology*. Bristol: Bristol Classical Press.

Warren, P. and Y. Tzedakis
1974 Debla, an Early Minoan settlement in Western Crete. *Annual of the British School at Athens* 69: 299–342.

Watrous, L. V.
1987 The Role of the Near East in the rise of the Cretan Palaces. In R. Hägg and N. Marinatos (eds.), *The Function of the Minoan Palaces*: 65–70. Stockholm: Swedish Institute in Athens.
2001 Crete from the Earliest Prehistory through the Protopalatial Period. In T. Cullen (ed.), *Aegean Prehistory: A Review* (AJA Supplement 1): 157–223. Boston: Archaeological Institute of America.

Whitelaw, T.
1983 The settlement at Fournou Korifi. Myrtos and aspects of Early Minoan social organization. In O. Krzyszkowska and L. Nixon (eds.), *Minoan Society. Proceedings of the Cambridge Colloquium 1981*: 323–45. Bristol: Bristol Classical Press.
2000 Settlement instability and landscape degradation in the Southern Aegean in the third Millennium. In P. Halstead and C. Frederick (eds.), *Landscape and Land Use in Postglacial Greece* (Sheffield Studies in Aegean Archaeology 3): 135–61. Sheffield: Sheffield Academic Press.
2004 Alternative pathways to complexity in the southern Aegean. In J. Barrett and P. Halstead (eds.), *The Emergence of Civilisation Revisited*. (Sheffield Studies in Aegean Archaeology 6): 232–56. Oxford: Oxbow.

2007 Houses, households and community at Early Minoan Fournou Korifi: methods and models for interpretation. In R. Westgate, N. Fisher and J. Whitley (eds.), *Building Communities. House, Settlement and Society in the Aegean and Beyond* (BSA Studies 15): 65–76. London: British School at Athens.

2012 The Urbanisation of Minoan Crete. Settlement perspectives on Minoan state formation. In I. Schoep, P. Tomkins and J. Driessen (eds.), *Back to the Beginning. Reassessing Social and Political Complexity on Crete during the Early and Middle Bronze Age*: 114–76. Oxford: Oxbow.

Whitelaw, T., P. Day, E. Kiriatzi, V. Kilikoglou and D. Wilson

1997 Ceramic traditions at EM IIB Myrtos, Fournou Korifi. In R. Laffineur and P. Betancourt (eds.), *TEXNH: Craftsmen, Craftswomen and Craftsmanship in the Aegean Bronze Age* (Aegaeum 16): 265–74. Liège: Université de Liège.

Wilson, D.

1985 The pottery and architecture of the EM IIA West Court House at Knossos. *Annual of the British School at Athens* 80: 281–364.

1994 Knossos before the palaces: an overview of the Early Bronze Age (EM I-III). In D. Evely, H. Hughes-Brock and N. Momigliano (eds.), *Knossos: A Labyrinth of History. Papers Presented in Honour of Sinclair Hood*: 23–44. Oxford: Oxbow.

2007 Early Prepalatial (EM I-EM II). In N. Momigliano (ed.) *Knossos Pottery Handbook. Neolithic and Bronze Age (Minoan)* (BSA Studies 14): 49–77. London: British School at Athens.

2008 Early Prepalatial Crete. In C. Shelmerdine (ed.), *The Cambridge Companion to the Aegean Bronze Age*: 77–104. Cambridge: Cambridge University Press.

Wilson, D. and P. Day

1994 Ceramic regionalism in Prepalatial central Crete: The Mesara imports at EM I to EM IIA Knossos. *Annual of the British School at Athens* 89: 1–87.

2000 EM I chronology and social practice: pottery from the early palace tests at Knossos. *Annual of the British School at Athens* 95: 21–63.

Wilson, D., P. Day and N. Dimopoulou-Rethemiotaki

2004 The pottery from Early Minoan I-IIB Knossos and its relations with the harbour site of Poros-Katsambas. In G. Cadogan, E. Hatzaki and A. Vasilakis (eds.), *Knossos: Palace, City, State* (BSA Studies 12): 67–74. London: British School at Athens.

2008 The gateway port of Poros-Katsambas: trade and exchange between north-central Crete and the Cyclades in EB I-II. In N. Brodie, J. Doole, G. Gavalas and C. Renfrew (eds.), *Horizon, A colloquium on the prehistory of the Cyclades*: 261–270. Cambridge: McDonald Institute for Archaeological Research.

Zois, A.

1992 Vasiliki. In J. W. Myers, E. E. Myers and G. Cadogan (eds.), *The Aerial Atlas of Ancient Crete*: 276–281. Berkeley: University of California Press.

Chapter 4

Early Minoan Knossos: A few new thoughts

Gerald Cadogan

This paper presents some thoughts about Early Minoan Knossos that have come from working with Sinclair Hood on publishing his Early Minoan excavations there of 1958 to 1961 (Hood and Cadogan 2011: this should be consulted for illustrations, details and further references). After I gave it at Sheffield, it was revised for the Minoan Seminar in Athens a year later, and has since been revised again. I offer it in memory of Yannis Sakellarakis, a founding father of the Minoan Seminar, and in honour of Keith Branigan: they have both made many pioneering contributions to our understanding of Crete in the third millennium BC. I must stress that Sinclair is not responsible for what I say – except through having introduced me to Minoan culture and Minoan pottery and Early Minoan Knossos, and also to Yannis and Efi back in 1964; for all of which I am most grateful.

Hood excavated three Early Minoan sites inside the fenced area of the Palace (Fig. 4.1): the EM I Palace Well; at Royal Road North, best known for its LM IB deposit (Hood 2011), a small trial (called Area A) produced a sequence of EM IIA–III domestic deposits; and the so-called Early Houses (Area B) just downhill from the south front of the Palace, where EM IIB–III domestic deposits include the EM III South Front House (SFH) (Momigliano and Wilson 1996).

Before we look at these, it is worth recalling the state of study of EM Knossos in the 1950s and earlier 1960s. The EM settlement and its sequence were scarcely known then, as is apparent from the first chapters of the first volume of *The Palace of Minos* where Arthur Evans (1921) fills out his account of Early Minoan with results from the Pyrgos burial cave, excavated by Stefanos Xanthoudides (1918), and Mochlos and Vasiliki, excavated by Richard Seager (1905; 1907; 1909; 1912; Boyd *et al.* 1908). *The Vaulted Tombs of Mesará* was still to be published (Xanthoudides 1924). In the 1930s, John Pendlebury excavated the Trapeza cave in Lasithi (Pendlebury *et al.* 1936) and produced an extensive and pioneering overview of Early Minoan in *The Archaeology of Crete* (Pendlebury 1939), with some attention to Knossos, thanks to his having seen its EM pottery when arranging the Stratigraphical Museum (Pendlebury 1933; Pendlebury and Pendlebury 1933; Eccles *et al.* 1933; Money-Coutts and Pendlebury 1933). In the post-war period came the important tomb excavations of Stylianos Alexiou at Kyparissi (Alexiou 1951) and Lebena, the latter published in 2004 (Alexiou and Warren 2004). At Phaistos, Doro Levi had excavated EM I and II, but came to believe in a truncated EM sequence of 100 years starting around 2000 BC (Levi 1960: 116–18, 121)! Antonis Zois made a robust rebuttal at the time (Zois 1965: 53–65); Simona Todaro has since produced a ten-phase sequence for Prepalatial Phaistos (Todaro 2013; also 2005; 2009a; 2012).

Consequently, when Nikolaos Platon, then Ephor of Crete, came upon a well that turned out to be EM I, and also EM III floors in the Early Houses, and entrusted them to the British School for further investigation, these were excellent opportunities for Hood to explore and test the early part of Evans's Minoan sequence, which was the principal aim of his 1957–61 stratigraphic excavations at Knossos; while the EM excavation in Royal Road North began as an investigation of what was under the Late Minoan I floors there. Hood was expecting Middle Minoan, as in his excavations in Royal Road South. At the first Cretological Conference in 1961 he gave his first synoptic account (Hood 1962) of the Minoan sequence he had found in the 1957–61 excavations at Knossos. Early Minoan I and II figure, but "Early Minoan III, as this was defined by Evans, does not seem to exist at Knossos" (Hood 1962: 93). He did, however, recognise a pre-polychrome phase of Middle Minoan IA, which "might therefore perhaps be called Early Minoan III".

In 1964–65, EM Knossos changed, when study of the pottery from the three excavations made it obvious that here was a major settlement – at least in ceramic terms – of the third millennium BC and identified an EM III deposit in the Early Houses (Area B), with more deposits in Royal Road North (Area A). In autumn 1965 Hood presented this new EM sequence at the Mycenaean Seminar (Hood 1966) and rehabilitated Knossos's Early Minoan III. A few months later, and independently of Hood, Zois gave an important paper at the second Cretological Conference entitled "Υπάρχει ΠΜ ΙΙΙ εποχή;" (Zois 1967). He reached the same straightforward answer as Hood: Yes, there is.

Hood then began writing the account of his Early Minoan excavations but, for many reasons, there were big delays. However, the pottery from the three sites was available for others and was referred to, and to varying extents included, in an impressive series of studies, from the 1970s until today, of the ceramics and contexts of EM Knossos, including reports on the EM IIA West Court House (WCH) and the SFH excavations (Andreou 1978; Wilson 1985; Momigliano 1990; 1991; Cadogan *et al.* 1993; Wilson 1994; Wilson and Day 1994; Momigliano and Wilson 1996; Wilson and Day 1999; 2000; Momigliano 2000; Day and Wilson 2002; 2004; Wilson *et al.* 2004; Momigliano 2007; Tomkins 2007; Wilson 2007; 2010; Tomkins 2012; Whitelaw 2012). These publications have established the present picture of Early Minoan Knossos and its Neolithic predecessor(s), and agree on the historical value of the fill in the EM I Palace Well and the stratigraphic sequences of Hood's other two sites. The focus of

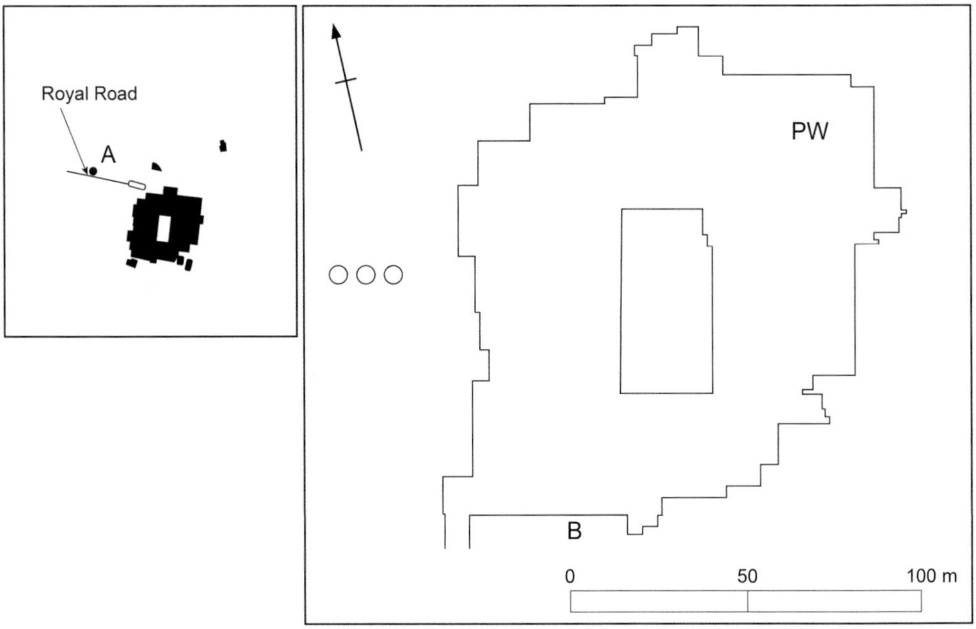

Figure 4.1: Early Minoan excavations in the Palace area at Knossos. PW: Palace Well; A: Royal Road North; B: Early Houses.

this latter-day research has been mainly (but not wholly) on ceramic development, including provenance studies that reveal inter-regional pot exchanges. The chapters by Tomkins (2007), Momigliano (2007) and Wilson (2007) in the *Knossos Pottery Handbook* make succinct, easily available accounts of present ceramic knowledge of Neolithic and EM Knossos.

We can turn now to the three excavation sites and then review their implications for the history of third millennium BC Knossos.

The EM I Well

The Palace Well (Fig. 4.1: PW), the first Bronze Age well known at Knossos, is key evidence for society and community organisation in EM I, when it was dug, used, went out of use, and finally filled with debris. In the NE part of the Palace, close to the later Animal Pens (Hood and Taylor 1981: no. 182; Shaw 1978), it was 17.2 m deep, measuring from the modern surface – the ancient one may have been much the same. If it seems surprising to find a well less than 200 m from the Kairatos, it is not alone. Nearby are both the EM III Upper East Well (at least 19.4, possibly over 22.5 m deep) and another, later well (14.5 m deep) (which Todd Whitelaw kindly told me of) upslope from the East Bastion but downslope from, and excavated before, the Upper East Well (UEW). This less known well can explain how the UEW came to be named, since it was dug first and became in effect a "Lower East Well" following the discovery of the UEW. On the W side of the Kephala hill two, perhaps three, other EM III wells emphasise the importance of water provision in late Prepalatial times, when the settlement was expanding fast. This may be the message too of the Hypogaeum on the south side (Belli 1999), probably of much the same date – if it was a large public well, a round pit with staircase winding down its side (similar to Neolithic Jericho), and not a granary (cf. Halstead 1981: 198).

The Palace Well had three separate deposits. The bottom 3 m (deposit 1) produced mainly big scored/wiped ware water jugs that were missing their handles, where the jugs had broken when drawing water. This is the primary use level of the Well and has to be earlier – but we cannot say how much earlier – than the main deposit (2), a vertically mixed fill 10–11 m deep mostly of pottery, often burnt, which was seen originally as debris from a destruction in, or of, the settlement. Above it was deposit 3, with debris from cutting the well through the layers of the Neolithic tell.

Two elaborate, high-quality shapes in deposit 2 that needed time and skill in manufacture, and are known from burial deposits such as the Pyrgos cave, are the chalice (very common) and pedestal bowl (common). They are part of a broad range of domestic pottery including a little otherwise known from tombs but here, significantly, found in a settlement context, such as suspension pots (which are often called pyxides). One of these suspension pots in light grey ware is about the earliest example at Knossos of this fabric, which is generally seen as typical of EM IIA and produced in, and imported from, the Mesara (Wilson and Day 1994). The Well also produced "baking plates", a type that then carried on throughout the Minoan Bronze Age, and plenty of pithos sherds, as well as probable bins in unbaked clay (if, that is, they are not ovens).

The sometimes burnt, and often gnawed, animal bones studied by Valasia Isaakidou (2011a) include cattle, pigs, sheep and goats – and one bone of a dog. Among other finds are two olive pips; a vine leaf impression on a pot base; and small round pebbles used as pot boilers for stew or soup, and oddly little recognised for Minoan Crete; and obsidian blades and flakes.

Area A (Royal Road North)

The principal EM excavation in Area A (Fig. 4.1: A) was a test in 1961, measuring 2.75 × 2.45 m, that produced seven domestic deposits (A7–A1) from late EM III down to EM IIA, which form the longest stratigraphic and ceramic sequence yet known at EM Knossos. Beneath them is a Neolithic scatter or soil wash (deposit A0: some of it is as early as Early or Middle Neolithic, Peter Tomkins kindly tells me; I am following his Knossos sequence). The EM IIA deposits lay then on basically virgin ground and mark the growth northwards of the Kephala settlement, which seems to have followed after an expansion westwards that we see best in the West Court

House (WCH) (Wilson 1985) and, farther out, in Peter Warren's Royal Road South excavations (Warren 1973; 1974) close to the modern road and the bus stop (see also Whitelaw 2012).

EM IIA (deposit A1) saw the introduction of tripod cooking pots to Knossos and the relatively short-lived use of horned stands in cooking pot ware: their *floruit* seems to have been EM IIA but at present they have not been recognised outside Knossos. Goblets had now shrunk to one-person size; and there was a little, very little, of the light grey and fine painted wares from the Mesara.

EM IIB is marked by a fairly substantial, if vestigial, building, which may connect with the EM structures that Evans found under the adjacent Armoury (or Arsenal). If so, we may infer a building or building complex of some size and importance on the N edge of the probably still expanding settlement. But it may not have lasted long if, as we tend to think, a destruction brought it to an end (deposit A2). Rebuilding followed, still within EM IIB (deposits A3–A4); above (deposits A5–A7) were two main floor levels of EM III, beneath Floor II of Late Minoan IA, which was under LM IB Floor I with the well known deposit of ivories (Hood 2011).

The EM II levels produced 232 pieces of obsidian, the EM III 73: all seem Melian except 1–2% of the smoky, shiny obsidian that is often called "Anatolian". The work area may have been close by.

Area B (Early Houses)

The Early Houses, as Evans and Duncan Mackenzie called them, of our Area B (Fig. 4.1: B) lie immediately south of the south front of the Palace and east of the cutting for the South House. To their east is the Hypogaeum mentioned above. Mackenzie was the first to excavate here in 1907–1908, reporting EM II and EM III houses. The number of whole vessels found suggests floor deposits of what is now EM IIB and, possibly, a destruction that could be of the same horizon as what we are suggesting in Area A: the pottery is now dispersed between Heraklion, Oxford, London and New York, but we have attempted to re-group it and, in effect, publish it for the first time.

The excavation was triggered by Platons's discovery of two pink/red plaster floors, and related EM pottery (some of which could be classified as EM III white-on-dark) during conservation in 1957, which led to his inviting Hood to investigate further. On behalf of Sinclair Hood and myself I should like to thank most warmly Lefteris Platon for sending us copies of the pages of his father's notebook and photographs, which he is letting us publish. We excavated in 1960, when Spyros Vasilakis, father of Andonis, was the guiding hand for a young supervisor with his first trench of his own. Then in 1993 Nicoletta Momigliano and David Wilson excavated parts that we had not (Momigliano and Wilson 1996): our results are broadly complementary.

The (eroded) Early Houses were founded in EM IIB on LN I open air surfaces, but there is little to say about the EM II structures. If the EM IIB deposits of Evans and Mackenzie look mainly like dumps behind terraces (Wilson and Day 1999), the floors that we identified (deposits B1 and B2) did not have sufficient whole vessels to match what they found.

EM III is different. The South Front House set on top of the EM II structures is a building of quality with distinctive floors, and likely minimum dimensions of 13 m N–S × 9 m E–W; and there could have been a link with the Hypogaeum. At the north end of the SFH we excavated an E–W passage, with two pink/red plaster floors, and a fill of sherds and stones 5–10 cm thick between them (deposit B3), which can date a remodelling of the House and became, after Hood (1966), a key deposit in the rehabilitation of Knossian EM III; Momigliano (2007) assigns it to the Upper East Well Group of EM III late. It has no polychrome pottery but there is part of an imported east Cretan EM III jar – and others are known in EM III–MM IA contexts at Knossos. It may be significant that these east Cretan EM III imports all seem to be jars (Hood and Cadogan 2011: 225, no. 1124, pls. 48 and 64).

Other artefacts include, in EM III, a stone vessel in serpentinite (an early use), and the much discussed and very well dated clay stopper, shaped like a truncated champagne cork, with impressions of an ivory seal belonging to the Parading Lions group. Judith Weingarten (2005: 764–65 and n. 34) suggests that this motif may be a "symbol of chiefdom, perhaps even of an emergent royalty", and a mark of power adapted/adopted from Egyptian originals. As for the stopper and its sealings, it may have had a simple domestic purpose; or there may have been something more public and external, perhaps connected with an emerging practice of documentation and administration at Knossos in the late third millennium. There is nothing, however, as Ilse Schoep has said (2004: 285–86, 290), to point to any "centralised authority".

We do not know what sort of vessel the stopper stoppered, or what its important contents were. It had a narrow mouth, which may suggest a tall upright neck like a bottle. But that is a shape that we do not find in the EM III pottery repertoire, until flasks appeared some centuries later. I wonder then if it could have been a gourd or a leather bottle/flask, perhaps containing a scented oil, or perhaps a rare beverage.

As in Area A, obsidian is about three times more plentiful in the EM IIB levels than in those of EM III; and again there is a little, very little of the "Anatolian" smoky variety in EM IIB, although it is as many as four out of nine pieces of obsidian in the EM III B3 deposit.

How do these three sites help fill out our picture of Early Minoan Knossos?

EM I

The Palace Well gives the most new evidence.

The Well reveals a considerable degree of communal organisation. As well as a squad of shovellers and basket-boys, it needed a master well-digger and, probably, a water diviner (who may have been the same person) to locate the aquifers deep underground. These persons, or this person, may have been itinerant specialists, since there would hardly have been enough work at Knossos to support them if wells were their full-time work. Equally, it needed a "chief" or, probably less likely, a committee of elders to commission the job and ensure, once it was working, that it was properly maintained. It would have been a welcome addition to the resources of the community, as well as giving opportunities to meet people, especially of the other sex, when drawing water. It was probably used by more than one household and could have been the main water supply for the whole EM I community, since it could hold up to 2 tonnes of water, to guesstimate the volume of deposit 1. Tomkins (2012) detects further evidence for communal organisation and civic planning in the levelings that led to a FN IV–EM I Court that would be the first of the Central Courts of Knossos, with an enlargement in EM IIA. The Well would have been a very short walk from the heart of the community.

Its going out of use during Early Minoan I must have been a big blow to the Kephala community. It then became a dump, as is often the case with dead wells. Much of the pottery that filled it was badly burnt. This may indicate a destruction with fire (which would become the first of a long series of such destructions at Knossos variously attributed to enemies or earthquakes or both) of part or all of the settlement, or may not. The bones were lying around for a time and had been gnawed by scavengers, and only a few were burnt – which argues against a general destruction – while the temperature of the fire was too high for straightforward roasting and grilling (Isaakidou 2011a) – which argues against this being part of feasting. The fire/fires could equally have been a bonfire to burn the rubbish or accidental, even a bonfire that got out of control and burnt the settlement.

The pottery was prestigious and of high quality, which tends to suggest specialist potters, as do the water jugs and pithoi: we may imagine separate workshops with different products for different requirements. None of the Cycladic-style pottery so prominent at Poros at the mouth of the river Kairatos (Wilson *et al.* 2004; see also Dimopoulou-Rethemiotaki 2004 and Dimopoulou-Rethemiotaki *et al.* 2007) was found in the Well, which would argue for two completely separate, and quite possibly hostile, communities a few kilometres apart.

The chalices and pedestalled bowls held too much for one person, and imply eating together by groups of people, perhaps different households – or commensality. While this does not preclude heavy drinking and much eating of meat at feasts – we are talking about Cretan γλέντια – these symbolically important events need not have been the only times when the chalices and big bowls were used. In any event, the animal bones' being less burnt than the pottery tends to argue against feasts involving smashing the pottery and throwing the bones all at once into the fire. It is also the case that the painted jugs do not form sets of tableware with the pattern-burnished chalices and bowls.

The Well shows (probably improved) farming at Knossos, and improved storage to hold it in the new fired pithoi, as well as the likely unfired clay bins. The pithoi are among several groups of them that appear across the island in Early Minoan I (Betancourt 2008; 2010; 2013), suggesting generally improved agriculture at the start of the Bronze Age. Note that their Neolithic predecessors do not have relief rope patterning, which may be a skeuomorphic sign of better logistics: a hint perhaps of more donkeys being available for roping the pithoi to. But it would be good to have some faunal evidence to support this.

The Well also offers the first baking plates (for some kind of flat breads) and apparent pot boilers – a rarity in Minoan culinary studies – for stews and soup involving all four main species of farmyard animals, to judge from their bones. There was also a dog in deposit 2.

The evidence for other crafts is slight: obsidian from Melos; mud plastering and perhaps the first evidence for lime plaster; and the first Bronze Age roundels (discs cut from sherds, not superior sealings) although they are known back to MN Stratum VII at Knossos. At Phaistos, Todaro (2009b: 341–43, figs. 6c, 7d; 347) has linked them to the management of EM potting.

What do the Well and its pottery tell us about continuity from the Neolithic and/or the possible arrival of newcomers? Clearly, like Phaistos and Petras-Kephala (Papadatos 2008), there was continuity in Knossos's location, with its advantages for defence and farming. But if it was unbroken continuity from FN IV to EM I is hard to say. Beneath the Central Court there was an EM I house overlying one of FN IV, as Hood (2006) and Tomkins (2007: 45) have shown, and Duncan Mackenzie (see Hood 2006) pointed out long ago. Mackenzie remarked on how the EM I architecture was much sloppier than that of the Neolithic building below. Tomkins suggests that the first levelling of the Kephala hill was in FN IV, making the cobbled south-east platform the first central gathering place; an EM I surface was later made on top of it. But we have no idea of what spurred these building works.

The considerable changes in the range and wares of the pottery, and huge progress in ceramic technology, could well suggest newcomers. So could the short-lived new feature of carinated or rounded bases, not in Neolithic and not in EM IIA. Might this habit, Hood has suggested to me, come from somewhere where people were used to setting pottery in the sand? In any event, the swathe of sites with Cycladic-style pottery and burials along the north coast from Poros to Hagia Photia shows that the notion of incomers is quite acceptable, and cannot be rejected on determinist *a priori* grounds.

So can we find any sources for possible incomers in the rest of the Aegean (other than the Cyclades) and/or further east? Pattern burnishing and scoring are not of much help, since they occur widely across the Aegean; but the numbers of other changes and improvements, especially the appearance of painted ware, suggest that it is foolish to reject incomers, even if it is hard to say where they come from! But Hood and I have been heartened that Phil Betancourt (2008) espouses newcomers in FN IV–EM I, and I like Yiannis Papadatos's observation (2008: 268) that the wider Aegean world "intrudes" (a good and helpful word) into Crete in comparing the new traditions starting in FN IV at Petras-Kephala and Nerokourou in the west.

Finally in EM I, we have the question of whether to place the Well in EM IA or EM IB. While we should prefer to have it in EM IA (as Sinclair Hood has written several times), with EM IB represented by chalices with ring-stems or grooved stems as known from the Pyrgos burial cave and elsewhere, and while we note that both Todaro (Todaro 2005: 34–38, 44; 2012; also Todaro and Di Tonto 2008: 177–79) for Phaistos and Papadatos (2008) for Petras–Kepahala identify EM IA and EM IB, we feel that for the time being it is wiser to stick with an unitary EM I in view of the reported occurrence of "EM IA" and "EM IB" features together at Poros – which is the view of David Wilson (2007) in assembling his EM I Well Group in the *Knossos Pottery Handbook*. Furthermore, we are unable to identify any specifically "EM IB" deposits from Evans's excavations at Knossos or from ours. But one must now see EM I as a flexible term, which may change for Knossos when the Poros material is fully published, and realise the inherent fluidity in the chronological and cultural divisions we impose. Two examples come to mind: the light grey ware suspension pot, normally a hallmark of EM IIA (early) in the EM I Well; and the few pieces of Vasiliki ware in the EM IIA levels of Area A which one would assign, if they were out of context, to EM IIB.

EM II

Our EM II and III sites were on the edges of the Knossos settlement, and so cannot tell us about the core of it below the Central Court and the West Court and the space between, and have little to add to debates about "proto-palace" predecessors of the so-called "Palace".

In Area A, the early occurrence of Vasiliki ware in the lowest floor deposit is matched by some pottery with white-on-dark decoration, which became regular from EM IIB (albeit found first in stage F of Lebena Yerokambos II, but not in the Knossos Well). New shapes now include tripod cooking pots, which may perhaps be dateable to EM I in the Hagia Photia cemetery although I think a case can be made for continuity there into EM IIA, in terms of a little light grey ware and a jug painted with Myrtos style fans. This all reinforces the argument for fluidity in the terminology. The cooking pots suggest further culinary progress in Minoan Crete, as may the horned stands that are a remarkable feature of Knossian EM IIA (and occur in the WCH, with its large EM IIA deposits) and were perhaps intended as stands for pottery and other vessels to keep them upright and off the floor. It might be that they were placed over hearths but, if so, the heat had gone out, since we do not see signs of burning. Three badger bones occur in EM IIB levels in Area A, and one in an EM III level: perhaps they had joined the menu (Isaakidou 2011b).

Architecturally, Area A revealed a little of a building of some quality in EM IIB. In newly occupied Area B at that time we have scrappy walls and floors, and pits, over Neolithic surface scatter, but no evidence of a more solid floor that could have had the whole vessels that Evans and Mackenzie found – which may be a destruction deposit, that may also be matched in Area A. If this was (to some extent) the case, we may consider adding a destruction in EM IIB at Knossos to add to that of EM IIA found in the WCH and the possible EM I destruction as seen in the Well.

No imports were recognised from the Cyclades or the Mesara at either site, other than some Melian obsidian; and there is also a little of the smoky "Anatolian" variety. Two phalli are a curiosity and something to include in discussions of gender and the roles of males in Cretan Bronze Age society.

EM III

In Area B the construction in EM III of the SFH was a significant statement of importance in placing such a building, with its views towards Gypsades and Iuktas, on top of the EM IIB Early Houses: the two pink/red floors show at least two building phases, while it may have continued into MM IA. In Area A the architectural evidence is sketchy.

The SFH belongs to a time of vigorous growth of Knossos beyond the Kephala hill, notably to the west and north-west, which continued into MM IA. Todd Whitelaw (2012) has recently suggested a settlement of 20 ha as a minimum and possibly twice that, as against 6.5 ha in EM II. It sits then with the first known built road at Knossos, houses and a large terrace wall below the level of the West Court, the Upper East Well and perhaps the Hypogaeum and the Keep (Branigan 1992; 1995) and, not least, the very large and well laid north-west terrace wall which, it has been suggested, may have been part of the first truly monumental building at Knossos (Hood 1994; Macdonald 2012; Tomkins 2012; Whitelaw 2012. The wall is well illustrated, and briefly discussed, by McEnroe [2010: 41–42, figs. 4.16–4.17] – or, can we say, palace or proto-palace?

I should like to see the South Front House as having been built with some protective and/or ceremonial purpose at the southern threshold of the Kephala settlement. It is close to the route that came over the Viaduct and up the Stepped Portico, which may have been there already: there is a little MM IA evidence to support this, but this route could be centuries older. Thus it commanded this approach, as the South House did later. If this interpretation is more or less correct, we might then see it as a southern counterpart to the Keep on the north side of the centre of the settlement.

The material culture also shows innovations and improvements, with slightly more smoky obsidian and some stone vessels (still rare in settlement contexts). An east Cretan Early Minoan III jar is one of several imported into Knossos in EM III and MM IA – one also reached Lerna VA (Zerner 1978), as well as a north-central Cretan eggcup goblet that could be EM III or MM IA in Knossian terms (Caskey 1956: 160 and n. 28, pl. 43c; Cadogan 1994: 64, n. 34) and the much cited sealing with the Parading Lions. These noble beasts may indicate high rank, as may the very fact that the sealing was found as a discard in a fill in the South Front House: the fill could well have come from the House or somewhere nearby. As for its use, the glyptocrats are sceptical of it just being for household use, but further than that is hard to say what it tells us about administration. In view of its findspot, there is no necessity to relate it to a central authority; but that is not impossible, especially if the South Front House had some official role (as is quite likely).

In conclusion

Hood's excavations are probably most valuable for their stratigraphic sequences in which ceramic changes and development are easily recognisable. But they also help to document the growth of the settlement on the NW and S–SW sides of the Kephala hill, and add to the valuable evidence for terracing (and planning) on the west side – in the West Court dip – in EM IIA and again in EM III–MM IA. For all of this, the papers by Tomkins, Whitelaw and Macdonald in the Leuven volume (published in 2012) are essential, and raise questions that I have not touched on.

As for the Palace Well, apart from its ceramic importance, it raises intriguing questions of shades of social interpretation that are still being debated. The trouble is that it is such a blockbuster deposit that our views may be skewed! We need a new EM I excavation, or two, inside the Palace fence to compare it with. For EM II and III we are in a better state as there have been several excavations over the last half-century offering sound comparanda.

All the same, several new excavations, and preferably more than keyhole tests, would be welcome to fill the gaps and reveal the expansion and vicissitudes of Early Minoan Knossos, once all the work now in progress has been published. And the discovery of the cemetery/ies for Early Minoan Knossos is fervently to be desired.

Acknowledgements

I thank Maria Relaki and Yiannis Papadatos for inviting me to the Round Table, and Yiannis and Colin Macdonald for inviting me to the Minoan Seminar.

Bibliography

Alexiou, S.

1951 Πρωτομινωικαί ταφαί παρά το Καvλί-Καστέλλι Ηρακλείου. *Κρητικά Χρονικά* 5: 275–94.

Alexiou, S. and P. M. Warren

2004 *The Early Minoan Tombs of Lebena, Southern Crete* (SIMA 30). Sävedalen: Paul Åströms Förlag.

Andreou, S.

1978 *Pottery Groups of the Old Palace Period in Crete*. PhD dissertation, University of Cincinnati.

Belli, P.

1999 The "Early Hypogaeum" at Knossos: some hints for future investigations. In P. P. Betancourt, V. Karageorghis, R. Laffineur and W.-D. Niemeier (eds.), *MELETEMATA. Studies in Aegean Archaeology Presented to Malcolm H. Wiener as He Enters his 65th Year* (Aegaeum 20): 25–32. Liège: Université de Liège.

Betancourt, P. P.

2008 *The Bronze Age Begins: the Ceramics Revolution of Early Minoan I and the New Forms of Wealth that Transformed Prehistoric Society*. Philadelphia: INSTAP Academic Press.

2010 The EM I pithoi from Aphrodite's Kephali. In O. Krzyszkowska (ed.), *Cretan Offerings: Studies in Honour of Peter Warren* (BSA Studies 18): 1–9. London: British School at Athens.
2013 *Aphrodite's Kephali. An Early Minoan I Defensive Site on Eastern Crete.* (Prehistory Monographs 41). Philadelphia: INSTAP Academic Press.

Boyd Hawes, H., B. Williams, R. Seager and E. Hall
1908 *Gournia, Vasiliki and Other Prehistoric Sites on the Isthmus of Hierapetra, Crete.* Philadelphia: American Exploration Society, Free Museum of Science and Art.

Branigan, K.
1992 The Early Keep, Knossos: a reappraisal. *Annual of the British School at Athens* 87: 153–63.
1995 The Early Keep at Knossos reviewed. *Πεπραγμένα του Ζ' Διεθνούς Κρητολογικού Συνεδρίου, vol.* A1: 87–96. Ρέθυμνο: Δήμος Ρεθύμνης, Ιστορική και Λαογραφική Εταιρεία Ρεθύμνης.

Cadogan, G.
1994 An Old Palace period Knossos state? In D. Evely, H. Hughes-Brock and N. Momigliano (eds.), *Knossos: A Labyrinth of History. Papers Presented in Honour of Sinclair Hood*: 57–68. London: British School at Athens.

Cadogan, G., P. M. Day, C. F. Macdonald, J. A. MacGillivray, N. Momigliano, T. M. Whitelaw and D. E. Wilson
1993 Early Minoan and Middle Minoan pottery groups at Knossos. *Annual of the British School at Athens* 88: 21–28.

Caskey, J. L. 1956. Excavations at Lerna, 1955. *Hesperia* 25: 147–73.

Day, P. M. and D. E. Wilson
2002 Landscapes of memory, craft and power in Prepalatial and Protopalatial Knossos. In Y. Hamilakis (ed.), *Labyrinth Revisited: Rethinking "Minoan" Archaeology*: 143–66. Oxford: Oxbow.
2004 Ceramic change and the practice of eating and drinking in Early Bronze Age Crete. In P. Halstead and J. C. Barrett (eds.), *Food, Cuisine and Society in Prehistoric Greece* (Sheffield Studies in Aegean Archaeology 5): 45–62. Oxford: Oxbow.

Dimopoulou-Rethemiotaki, N.
2004 Το επίνειο της Κνωσού στον Πόρο–Κατσαμπά. In G. Cadogan, E, Hatzaki and A. Vasilakis (eds.), *Knossos: Palace, City, State* (BSA Studies 12): 363–80. London: British School at Athens.

Dimopoulou-Rethemiotaki, N., D. E. Wilson and P. M. Day
2007 The earlier Prepalatial settlement of Poros–Katsambas: craft production and exchange at the harbour town of Knossos. In P. M. Day and R. C. P. Doonan (eds.), *Metallurgy in the Early Bronze Age Aegean* (Sheffield Studies in Aegean Archaeology 7): 84–97. Oxford: Oxbow.

Eccles, E., M. B. Money-Coutts and J. D. S. Pendlebury
1933 *Dating of the Pottery in the Stratigraphical Museum* 2. London: British School at Athens.

Evans, A. J.
1921 *The Palace of Minos at Knossos. Volume I.* London: Macmillan.

Halstead, P.
1981 From determinism to uncertainty: social storage and the rise of the Minoan palace. In A. Sheridan and G. Bailey (eds.), *Economic Archaeology: towards an Integration of Ecological and Social Approaches* (BAR IS 96): 187–213. Oxford: British Archaeological Reports.

Hood, S.
1962 Stratigraphic excavations at Knossos, 1957–61. *Πεπραγμένα του Α' Διεθνούς Κρητολογικού Συνεδρίου* 1: 92–98.
1966 The Early and Middle Minoan periods at Knossos. *Bulletin of the Institute of Classical Studies* 13: 110–11.
1994 Knossos: soundings in the Palace area, 1973–87. *Annual of the British School at Athens* 89: 101–02.

2006 Mackenzie and the Late Neolithic/Early Minoan I interface at Knossos. *Πεπραγμένα Θ΄ Διεθνούς Κρητολογικού Συνεδρίου, vol. A2*: 9–21. Ηράκλειο: Εταιρεία Κρητικών Ιστορικών Μελετών.

2011 Knossos, Royal Road North, LM IB deposits. In E. E. Hallager and T. Brogan (eds.), *LM IB Pottery: Examining New Evidence for Relative Chronology and Regional Differences* (Monographs of the Danish Institute at Athens 11): 153–74. Athens: Danish Institute at Athens.

Hood, S. and G. Cadogan

2011 *Knossos. Excavations 1957-1961: Early Minoan* (BSA Supplementary Volume 46). London: British School at Athens.

Hood, S. and W. Taylor

1981 *The Bronze Age Palace at Knossos: Plan and Sections* (BSA Supplementary Volume 13). London: British School at Athens.

Isaakidou, V.

2011a Faunal remains and taphonomy. In S. Hood and G. Cadogan, *Knossos. Excavations 1957-1961: Early Minoan* (BSA Supplementary Volume 46): 63–67. London: British School at Athens.

2011b Faunal remains. In S. Hood and G. Cadogan, *Knossos. Excavations 1957-1961: Early Minoan* (BSA Supplementary Volume 46): 229–33. London: British School at Athens.

Levi, D.

1960 Per una nuova classificazione della civiltà minoica. *La parola del passato* 72: 81–121.

Macdonald, C. F.

2012 Palatial Knossos: the early years. In I. Schoep, P. Tomkins and J. Driessen (eds.), *Back to the Beginning. Reassessing Social and Political Complexity on Crete during the Early and Middle Bronze Ages*: 81–113. Oxford: Oxbow.

McEnroe, J. C.

2010 *Architecture of Minoan Crete: Constructing Identity in the Aegean Bronze Age*. Austin: University of Texas Press.

Momigliano, N.

1990 The development of the footed goblet ("Egg-Cup") from EM II to MM III at Cnossos. *Πεπραγμένα του ΣΤ΄ Διεθνούς Κρητολογικού Συνεδρίου*, Vol. A1: 477-87. Χανιά: Φιλολογικός Σύλλογος "Ο Χρυσόστομος".

1991 MM IA pottery from Evans' excavations at Knossos: a reassessment. *Annual of the British School at Athens* 86: 149–271.

2000 Knossos 1902, 1905: the Prepalatial and Protopalatial deposits from the Room of the Jars in the Royal Pottery Stores. *Annual of the British School at Athens* 95: 65–105.

2007 Late Prepalatial (EM III–MM IA): South Front House Foundation Trench, Upper East Well and House C/RRS Fill Groups. In N. Momigliano (ed.), *Knossos Pottery Handbook: Neolithic and Bronze Age (Minoan)* (BSA Studies 14): 79–103. London: British School at Athens.

Momigliano, N. and D. E. Wilson

1996 Knossos 1993: excavations outside the South Front of the Palace. *Annual of the British School at Athens* 91: 1–57.

Money-Coutts, M. B. and J. D. S. Pendlebury

1933 *Dating of the Pottery in the Stratigraphical Museum* 3. *The Plans*. London: British School at Athens.

Papadatos, Y.

2008 The Neolithic–Early Bronze Age transition in Crete: new evidence from the settlement at Petras Kephala, Siteia. In V. Isaakidou and P. D. Tomkins (eds.), *Escaping the Labyrinth: the Cretan Neolithic in Context* (Sheffield Studies for Aegean Archaeology 8): 258–72. Oxford: Oxbow.

Papadatos, Y. and P. Tomkins

2013 Trading, the longboat, and cultural interaction in the Aegean during the late fourth millennium B.C.E.: the view from Kephala Petras, East Crete. *American Journal of Archaeology* 117: 353–81.

Pendlebury, H. W., J. D. S. Pendlebury and M. B. Money-Coutts

1936 Excavations in the plain of Lasithi I. The cave of Trapeza. *Annual of the British School at Athens* 36: 5–131.

Pendlebury, J. D. S.

1933 *A Guide to the Stratigraphical Museum in the Palace at Knossos.* London: British School at Athens.

1939 *The Archaeology of Crete: an Introduction.* London: Methuen.

Pendlebury, J. D. S. and H. W. Pendlebury

1933 *Dating of the Pottery in the Stratigraphical Museum* 1. London: British School at Athens.

Schoep, I.

2004 The socio-economic context of seal use and administration at Knossos. In G. Cadogan, E. Hatzaki and A. Vasilakis (eds.), *Knossos: Palace, City, State* (BSA Studies 12): 283–93. London: British School at Athens.

Seager, R. B.

1905 Excavations at Vasiliki, 1904. *University of Pennsylvania, Transactions of the Department of Archaeology, Free Museum of Science and Art* 1: 207–21.

1907 Report of excavations at Vasiliki, Crete, in 1906. *University of Pennsylvania, Transactions of the Free Museum of Science and Art (University Museum)* 2: 111–32.

1909 Excavations on the island of Mochlos. *American Journal of Archaeology* 13: 273–303.

1912 *Explorations in the Island of Mochlos.* Boston and New York: American School of Classical Studies at Athens.

Shaw, J. W.

1978 Sliding panels at Knossos. *Annual of the British School at Athens* 83: 235–48.

Todaro, S.

2005 EM I–MM IA ceramic groups at Phaistos: towards the definition of a Prepalatial ceramic sequence in South Central Crete. *Creta Antica* 6: 11–46.

2009a The latest Prepalatial period and the foundation of the first palace at Phaistos: a stratigraphic and chronological re-assessment. *Creta Antica* 10: 105–45.

2009b Pottery production in the Prepalatial Mesara: the Artisans' Quarter to the west of the Palace at Phaistos. *Creta Antica* 10: 335–52.

2012 Craft production and social practices at Prepalatial Phaistos: the background to the first "Palace". In I. Schoep, P. Tomkins and J. Driessen (eds.), *Back to the Beginning. Reassessing Social and Political Complexity on Crete during the Early and Middle Bronze Ages*: 195–235. Oxford: Oxbow.

2013 *The Phaistos Hills Before the Palace: a Contextual Reappraisal* (Praehistorica Mediterranea 5). Monza: Polimetrico.

Todaro, S. and S. Di Tonto

2008 The Neolithic settlement of Phaistos revisited: evidence for ceremonial activity on the eve of the Bronze Age. In V. Isaakidou and P. D. Tomkins (eds.), *Escaping the Labyrinth: the Cretan Neolithic in Context* (Sheffield Studies in Aegean Archaeology 8): 177–90. Oxford: Oxbow.

Tomkins, P.

2007 Neolithic: Strata IX–VIII, VII–VIB, VIA–V, IV, IIIB, IIIA, IIA and IC Groups. In N. Momigliano (ed.), *Knossos Pottery Handbook: Neolithic and Bronze Age (Minoan)* (BSA Studies 14): 9–48.

2012 Behind the horizon. Reconsidering the genesis and function of the "First Palace" at Knossos (Final Neolithic IV–Middle Minoan IB). In I. Schoep, P. Tomkins and J. Driessen (eds.), *Back to the Beginning. Reassessing Social and Political Complexity on Crete during the Early and Middle Bronze Ages*: 32–80. Oxford: Oxbow.

Warren, P. M.

1973 Knossos. Excavation in the area of the Royal Road. *Αρχαιολογικόν Δελτίον* 28 (Χρονικά): 574–76.

1974 Knossos 1973. Royal Road excavations and study season. *Αρχαιολογικόν Δελτίον* 29 (Χρονικά): 903–04.

Weingarten, J.

2005 How many seals make a heap: seals and interconnections on Prepalatial Crete. In R. Laffineur and E. Greco (eds.), *EMPORIA. Aegeans in the Central and Eastern Mediterranean* (Aegaeum 25): 759–66. Liège and Austin: Université de Liège and University of Texas at Austin.

Whitelaw, T. M.

2012 The urbanisation of prehistoric Crete: settlement perspectives on Minoan state formation. In I. Schoep, P. Tomkins and J. Driessen (eds.), *Back to the Beginning. Reassessing Social and Political Complexity on Crete during the Early and Middle Bronze Ages*: 114–76. Oxford: Oxbow.

Wilson, D. E.

1985 The pottery and architecture of the EM IIA West Court House at Knossos. *Annual of the British School at Athens* 80: 281–364.

1994 Knossos before the Palaces: an overview of the Early Bronze Age (EM I–EM III). In D. Evely, H. Hughes-Brock and N. Momigliano (eds.), *Knossos: a Labyrinth of History. Papers Presented in Honour of Sinclair Hood*: 23–44. London: British School at Athens.

2007 Early Prepalatial (EM I–EM II): EM I Well, West Court House, North-East Magazines and South Front Groups. In N. Momigliano (ed.), *Knossos Pottery Handbook: Neolithic and Bronze Age (Minoan)* (BSA Studies 14): 49–77. London: British School at Athens.

2010 Knossos 1955–1957: early Prepalatial deposits from Platon's tests in the Palace. *Annual of the British School at Athens* 105: 97–155.

Wilson, D. E. and P. M. Day

1994 Ceramic regionalism in Prepalatial central Crete: the Mesara imports at EM I to EM IIA Knossos. *Annual of the British School at Athens* 89: 1–87.

1999 EM IIB ware groups at Knossos: the 1907–1908 South Front tests. *Annual of the British School at Athens* 94: 1–62.

2000 EM I chronology and social practice: pottery from the early Palace tests at Knossos. *Annual of the British School at Athens* 95: 21–63.

Wilson, D. E., P. M. Day and N. Dimopoulou-Rethemiotaki

2004 The pottery from Early Minoan I–IIB Knossos and its relations with the harbour site of Poros–Katsambas. In G. Cadogan, E. Hatzaki and A. Vasilakis (eds.), *Knossos: Palace, City, State* (BSA Studies 12): 67–74. London: British School at Athens.

Xanthoudides, S.

1918 Μέγας πρωτομινωϊκός τάφος Πύργου. *Αρχαιολογικόν Δελτίον* 4: 136–70.

1924 *The Vaulted Tombs of Mesara: an Account of some Early Cemeteries of Southern Crete*. Liverpool: University Press of Liverpool; London: Hodder & Stoughton.

Zerner, C. W.

1978 *The beginning of the Middle Helladic period at Lerna*. PhD dissertation, University of Cincinnati.

Zois, A. A.

1965 Φαιστιακά. *Αρχαιολογική Εφημερίς*: 27–109.

1967 Υπάρχει ΠΜ ΙΙΙ εποχή; *Πεπραγμένα του Β' Διεθνούς Κρητολογικού Συνεδρίου vol.* A1: 141–56. Αθήνα: Φιλολογικός Σύλλογος "Ο Χρυσόστομος" εν Χανίοις.

Chapter 5

Caves in Crete and their use as architectural space

Philip P. Betancourt

Even though a cave is a natural rather than a man-made space, it can be used as architecture for a variety of activities, and its interior rooms can be modified to better accommodate their intended functions. Because conscious choices are involved in the original selection of a cavern for a specific purpose, the acceptance or rejection of a cave's interior spaces and their component parts, and the ways that those underground rooms are used, modified, or ignored, caverns can be regarded as a specialised aspect of a society's architectural tradition. This is especially true of a society like that of Bronze Age Crete where the residents of the island used caves on a regular basis. Cretan caverns were important for both funerary and ceremonial purposes, and they have been the focus of many general studies (Halbherr and Orsi 1888; Marinatos 1941; Faure 1960; 1964; Boardman 1961; Tyree 1974; Rutkowski 1986: 47–71; Rutkowski and Nowicki 1996).

The choice of a natural cave for use as architecture involves some slightly different concerns from those used for a structure that is entirely man-made. The final form of a constructed building is limited by the nature of the materials to be used, the available resources, the topography of the site, and other factors; the use of a natural cave presents an additional set of limitations and characteristics. Caves have particular features that involve both practical and aesthetic/emotional elements. They are composed of rooms with a high degree of safety (particularly in comparison with stone architecture in a land like Crete that is subject to severe earthquakes). The rooms are already present, and they can be spacious, but they may also have some characteristics like dampness, darkness, or difficult access that can render them unsuitable for some purposes. Some caverns only require a minimum amount of labour to adapt them to specific classes of human use. Caves can also evoke strong emotions by the contrast in environment as the visitor moves from bright sunlight and the familiar natural world into spaces that are dark, humid, and silent.

The conversion from natural cavern to human architecture may involve man-made modifications, not just a simple choice to use the underground rooms. The natural cave can be the starting point, comparable to the topographic site chosen for a new building. Just as an architect who is building above-ground may choose to incorporate aspects of the building site into the final structure, so someone who is choosing a cave may wish to combine aspects of the natural setting into the completed interior spaces. The difference is more of degree than of concept – the architectural modifications of the Minoan builders were often very modest, but the actual use of the spaces could also completely transform the rooms from their original natural state into chambers whose new ambience was completely dominated by the result of human actions.

The Minoans used caves in at least four ways: a) as a source for water; b) as shelter; c) for burial and d) for religious ceremonies.

The first two of these uses did not always involve strict selection and caves of many sizes and types could be used. Modifications were not always necessary. The last two classes involved more specialised choices in the type of cavern that was considered appropriate and in the architectural modifications that made it suitable as architecture. Architectural modifications were often employed for both of these uses to adapt the natural space to its intended purpose.

Especially in the Neolithic and in EM I, caves were used as sources of water and as shelters from sun, rain, snow, or other inclement weather. One good example of this use is a small cave at Aphrodite's Kephali, an EM I fortified site in the Isthmus of Ierapetra (Fig. 5.1). Rescue excavations at Aphrodite's Kephali were conducted by the 24th Ephorate in 1996 under the direction of Theodore Eliopoulos, supervised by Nikos Panagiotakis, as a part of the investigation in anticipation of the possibility of building a new airport north of

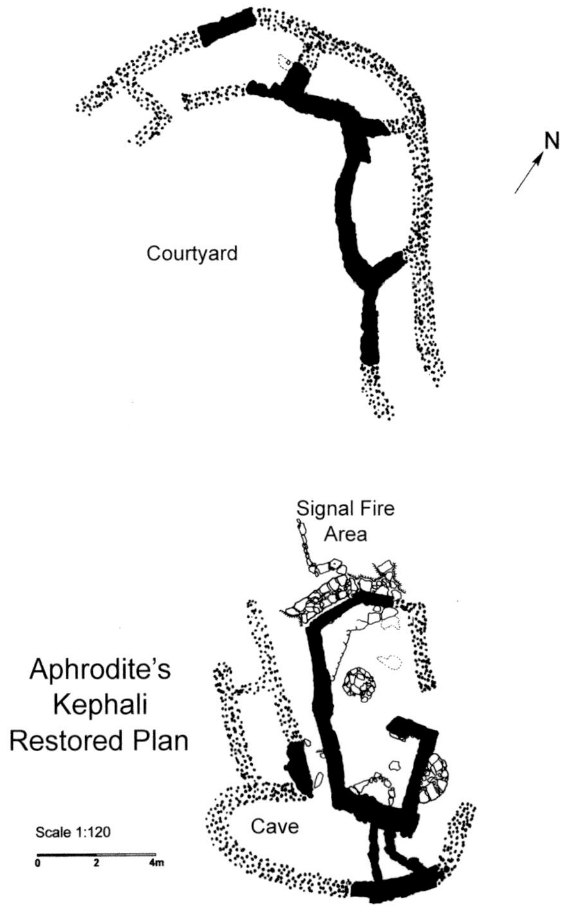

Figure 5.1: Plan of the walls around the summit of Aphrodite's Kephali showing the location of the cave at the south (dotted lines are restored).

Ierapetra (Eliopoulos 1998: 312). Work was continued in 2003 under the direction of Stavroula Apostolakou, with the work supervised by Maria Kyriakaki (Betancourt 1998: 106). The excavations took place after the property owner was stopped from levelling the entire hill with bulldozers to make an olive field larger. The hill rises above the valley near modern Episkopi, overlooking the north-south road across the Isthmus of Ierapetra. The pale coloured soil from the bulldozer work is clearly visible all around the periphery of the upper part of the hill. A cave entrance is located at the south of the hill. The cave was filled with soil and boulders when the edges of the site were removed with power equipment. The site is a fortified small hilltop with a fortification wall, a large exterior fire area whose soil is burned to a red colour, a courtyard, and one small building. It had an impressive amount of storage for this early period, with a minimum of nine pithoi (Betancourt 2008: 78–83). All the pottery is from EM I, including sherds of Hagios Onouphrios Style and burnished grey pottery. The cave was an integral part of this little complex, and it may be one of the reasons this site was chosen, as a more easily fortified location without any cave is situated nearby, at a slightly higher elevation to the west. The cave will have given the fort a source of water as well as a place for additional storage. Unfortunately, the interior of the cave is no longer accessible, but its situation and the reasons for its use are easily comprehended. The fortification wall that enclosed its entrance is sufficient to document its human use as an integral part of the fortified complex.

Many caves are known to have had a funerary use in Crete. One good example is located at Hagios Charalambos in the Plain of Lasithi (Fig. 5.2). The site is a natural cavern used as a secondary ossuary (Betancourt *et al.* 2008). Before the underground rooms in this cavern received human bones and their accompanying offerings in MM IIB, the cave required some architectural modifications. The original cave consisted of a vertical entrance shaft that led down into Room 1. From here, the visitor could enter six additional rooms. Two of the rooms, nos. 6 and 7, were considered too small for use, and Room 7 (at the lowest level of the cave) was surely very wet at some times during the year. Except for Room 5, the rooms had level floors and they did not need any modification to make them suitable for use as an ossuary. The bedrock of Room 5 had a substantial inclination, so it was modified by the addition of two terrace walls to help support the deposit of human bones and other objects that was placed there. The stone blocks for this work were brought into the cave from outside and used to build two walls across the room from north to south. After this work was completed, human leg bones were placed in a grid to create a sort of platform for the deposit over cracks in the floor, and the human bones and offerings were then placed within the room (Fig. 5.3). The deposit was completed with a pile of human skulls placed on top of the other bones (Fig. 5.4).

Although the architectural modification was modest, the final result was very dramatic. The feeling evoked by the rooms filled with bones, with skulls over the deposits (Fig. 5.4), was very different from the appearance of the clean cave before its new use. The sense of a foreign, exotic environment was created by the choice of

Figure 5.2: Plan of the Hagios Charalambos Cave.

the underground setting and by the presence of the offerings themselves, especially the human skulls that were placed on top of the new deposit.

A second example of this funerary use was the Trapeza cave, a cavern located part way up the mountain that rises above Tzermiado at the eastern side of the Lasithi Plain (Fig. 5.5). It served as a shelter during the Final Neolithic period, and it was used as an ossuary during MM II (Pendlebury *et al.* 1935–36). The cave was entered through a natural doorway that led into a series of small rooms, some of which contained stalactites and stalagmites. The ancient remains consisted of a small deposit of Final Neolithic date on bedrock, plus a much larger mixed deposit of human bones, complete vases, sherds, and various offerings that had been deposited with the dead.

Figure 5.3: Grid of long bones in situ *below part of the deposit of disarticulated human bones in the Room 4/5 Entrance in the Hagios Charalambos cave.*

Although Pendlebury and others regarded the mixed deposit of human bones and Minoan artefacts inside the cave as a mass of disturbed primary burials (Pendlebury *et al.* 1935–36; Faure 1964: 68; Rutkowski and Nowicki 1996: 69), the only evidence for this conclusion was that the finds were not stratified. The mixed nature of the deposit could not have been caused by looting, however, because of the many important finds that had not been removed (they consisted of whole vessels, figurines, seals, metal objects, ivory carvings, and other items), and the other suggestion of Pendlebury, that it had been converted into a sacred cave for offerings in MM I, is contradicted by the completely mixed nature of the deposit at the time of excavation. The cave was almost certainly an ossuary whose contents were mixed at the time they were deposited, just like the cave at Hagios Charalambos.

This class of ossuary, with the collective remains of a community's ancestors placed underground, must have been much more common than was once thought. For example, the Pyrgos cave was surely similar (Xanthoudides 1918). The cave no longer exists because it was discovered inside a quarry and quarrying operations resumed

Figure 5.4: Pile of human skulls as found on the top of the deposit of human bones next to the north wall in Room 5, Hagios Charalambos cave.

after the excavation. The remains consisted of a mass of disarticulated bones with artefacts mixed in. Most objects dated to the EM I, but larnakes were added at a later time, near the front of the cave.

The fourth type of cave use involved visiting underground chambers for the performance of ceremonies. Because of the nature of these ceremonies, sometimes additions to suit the activities were needed. Ceremonial use of caves was already present in Crete during the Neolithic (Tomkins 2009). A list of caves with interior walls was compiled by Faure in the index to his 1964 volume (Faure 1964). He listed Karteros, Ida, Melidoni, Psychro, and Kamares, and several additions can be made to his list, including Kleisidi (Younger 1976) and Pelekita (Rutkowski and Nowicki 1996: 33). An altar or table was built inside the cave of Arkalochori (Rutkowski and Nowicki 1996: 25).

The Psychro cave, the most dramatic cavern in the Lasithi region, is a good example of this class of use (Figs. 5.6, 5.7). Its large size and impressive stalactite formations are very different from the more modest aspects of the other caves near the Lasithi Plain, and these characteristics must have inspired the choice to adapt the large cavern to cult use. It has a long bibliography (Halbherr and Orsi 1888; Hogarth 1899–1900; Demargne 1902; Bosanquet 1939–40; Platakis 1973; Faure 1964: 151–59; 1996: 33–38; Tyree 1974: 14–20; Rutkowski 1972: 34–36; Rutkowski and Nowicki 1996; Watrous 1996).

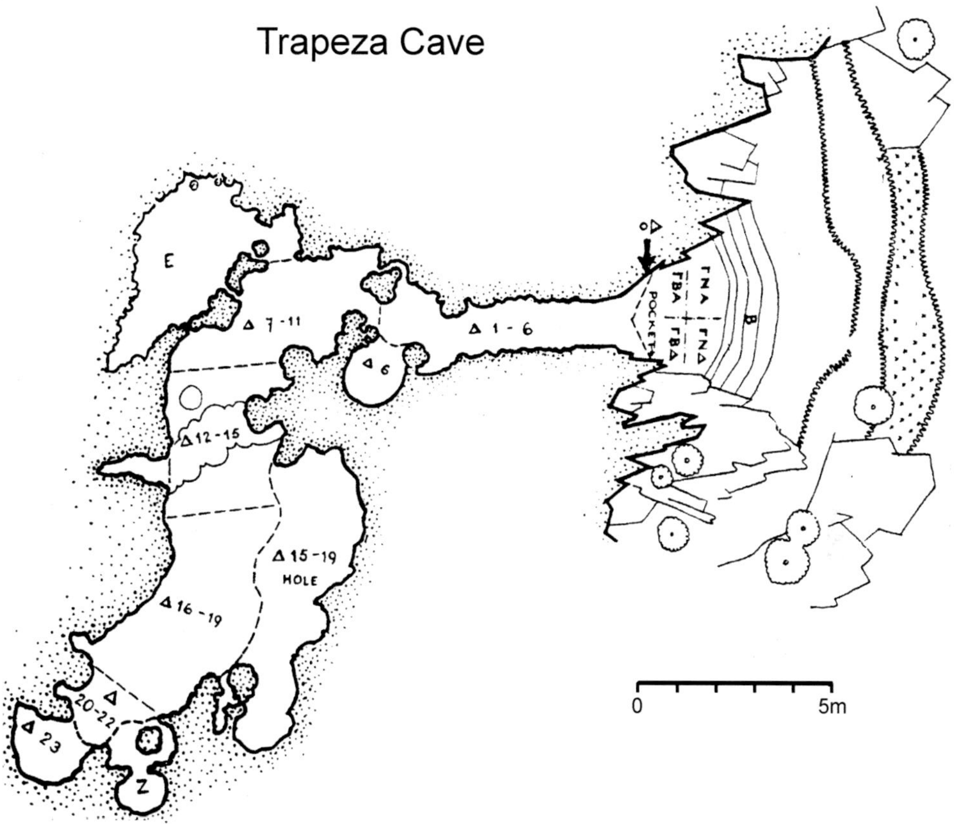

Figure 5.5: Plan of the Trapeza cave. Redrawn after Pendlebury, Pendlebury, and Money-Coutts 1935–36: 15, fig. 3.

The earliest objects found in the cave were Neolithic (Watrous 2004: 142), and it was probably used for shelter and as a source of water at this time. Water still collects every spring in a pool at the deep end of the cavern. Psychro was a centre of cult activity from the Early Minoan period until Roman times, and many bronzes and other objects have been found inside it. The many offerings in the cave suggest that it was a focus of ritual action.

Little can be seen of the cave's upper gallery today. At the time of excavation by Hogarth, it had black soil with evidence for feasting and the giving of offerings in its Middle Minoan levels, while in LM I the worshippers added an area with a stone bench-like platform regarded by the excavators as an altar (Fig. 5.6). It was surrounded by paving stones where elaborate offerings were left. These architectural constructions made the space more suitable for the ceremonies that occurred there, but the main aesthetic attraction of the site must have been the natural cave formations that were reached by descending a long downward slope (Fig. 5.7). As a visitor descended into

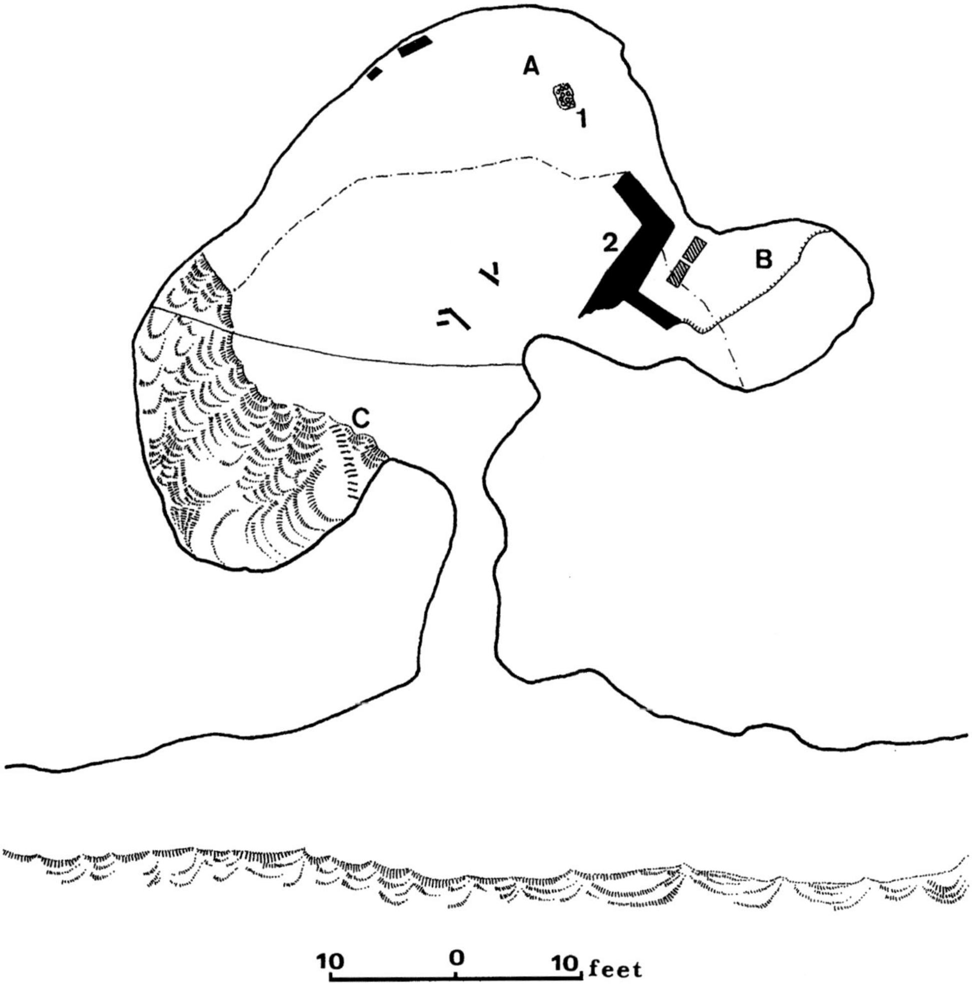

Figure 5.6: Plan of the Upper Room in the Psychro cave. Drawing courtesy of K. Nowicki.

the lower level of the underground spaces, the beautiful displays of stalactites and stalagmites would have been visible. These cave formations make this cavern more impressive than the other underground chambers in the Lasithi region. They must have been a focal point for the Minoan worshippers, because especially rich finds were discovered within and near the pool of water in the lower part of the cavern, in front of the largest natural stalactite display.

A second example of this category is a cave at Amnisos, regarded by the original excavator as the Cave of Eileithyia mentioned by Homer, an identification that is seriously doubted by this writer (Betancourt *et al.* 2000). Human bones inside the cave suggest it was either an ossuary or a place for primary burial before it was used for the ceremonies that required the construction of a small stone building inside the cave.

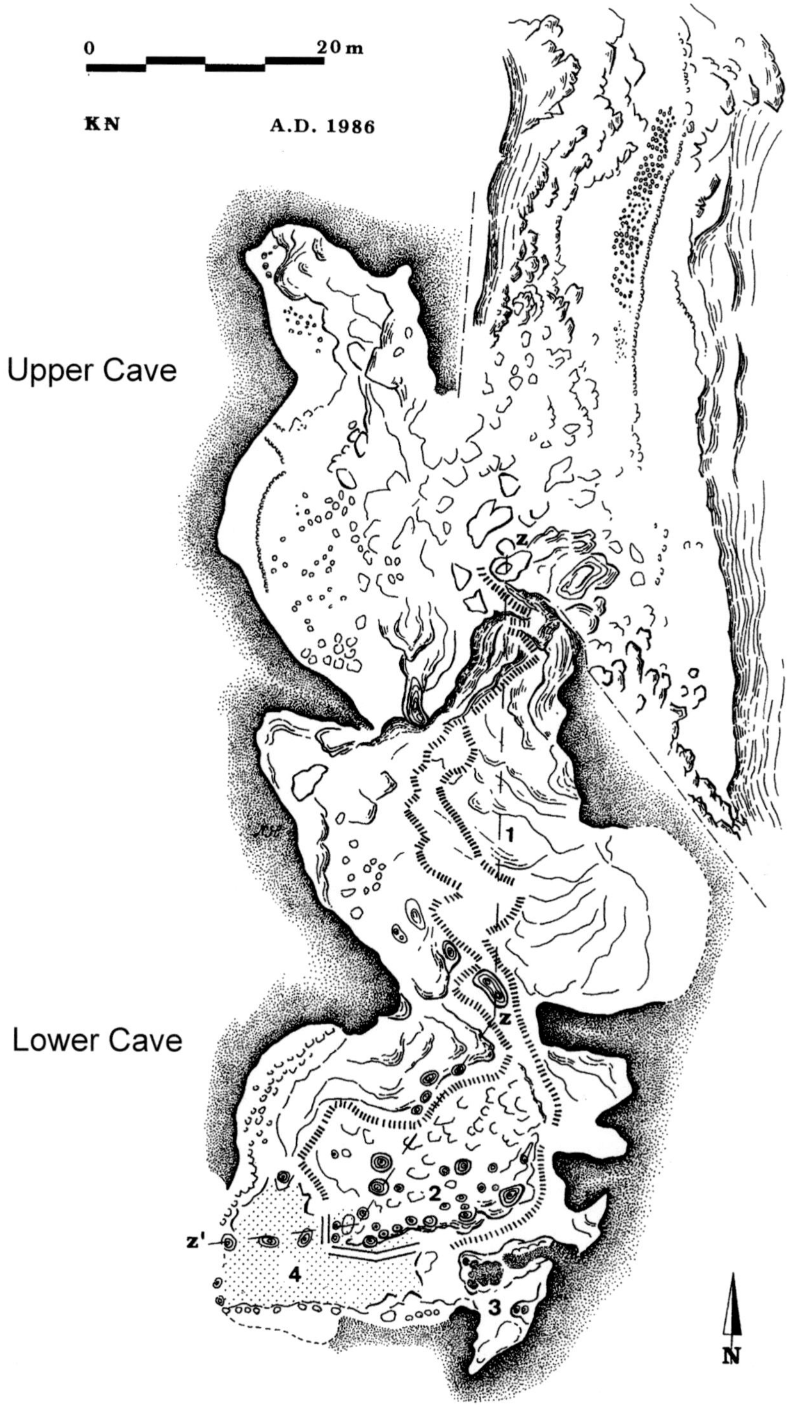

Figure 5.7: Plan of the Psychro cave. Drawing courtesy of K. Nowicki.

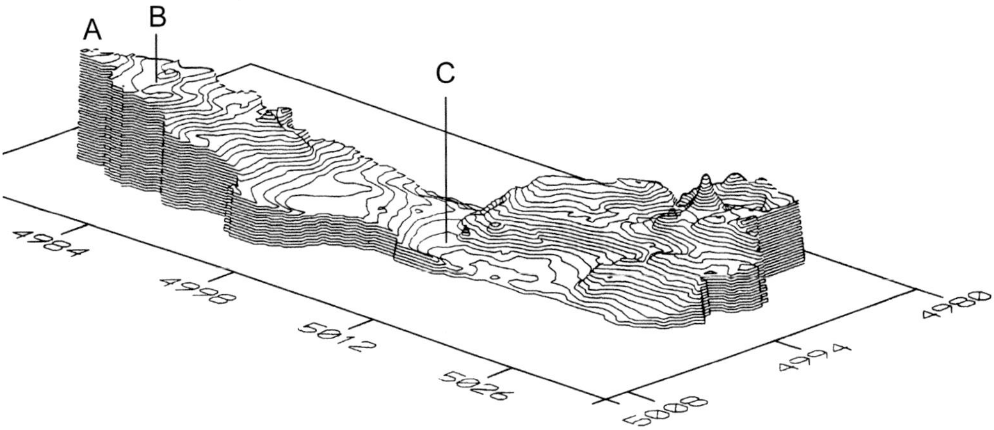

Figure 5.8: Elevation model of the Amnissos cave. Drawing by Senta German and Shannon McPherron.

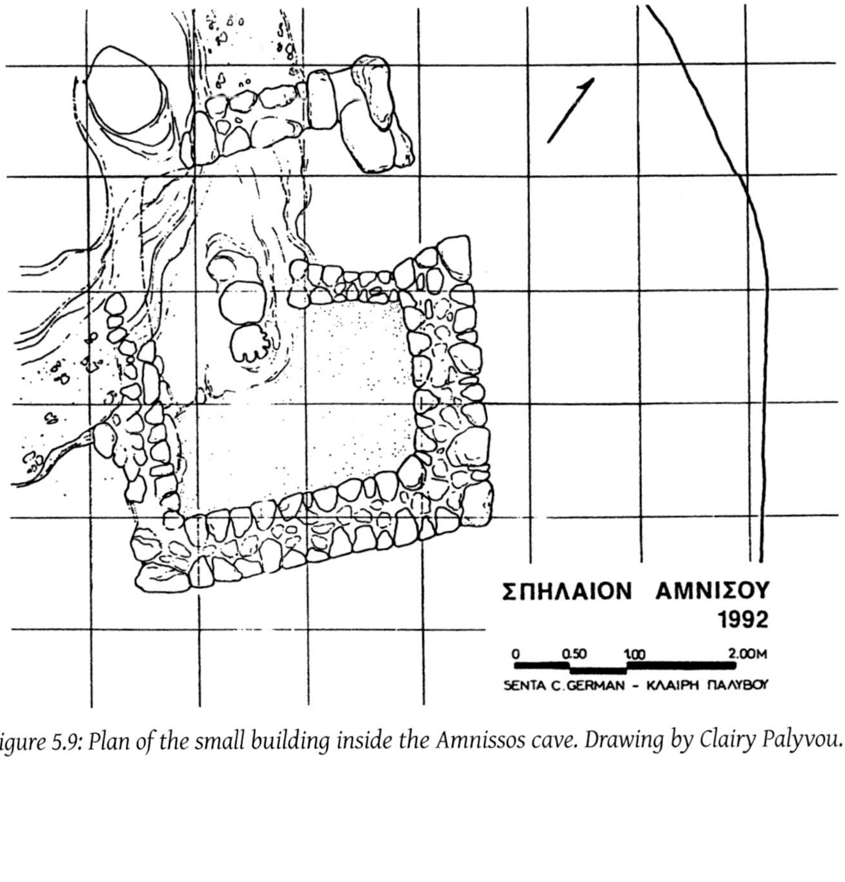

Figure 5.9: Plan of the small building inside the Amnissos cave. Drawing by Clairy Palyvou.

Work here in collaboration with Nanno Marinatos and Clairy Palyvou in the early 1990s resulted in a new plan of the cave and the architectural study of its small underground building (Figs. 5.8, 5.9). Several architectural modifications were made by the Minoans. Just inside the entrance are stone walls that create a terrace or platform where visitors could stand to observe ceremonies enacted in the largest room of the cave (Fig. 5.8, at location A). Directly in front of the terrace but at a somewhat lower level was a great display of stalactites and stalagmites next to a small building (Fig. 5.9). The small building, constructed around a stalagmite, was designed to force anyone entering it to take an indirect route to the innermost part. This type of plan, which has been called the bent axis system, forced the visitor to pass to the right and make several right-angle turns before entering the tiny space in front of the stalagmite at the focal point of the building. The plan is well known from other Minoan ceremonial contexts, such as a Middle Minoan shrine at Malia (for discussion, see Betancourt 2007: 81). The private and secret nature of the inner sanctum in this building must have been heightened by its location deep inside the earth.

Comments

These examples and many others illustrate the diverse ways that Cretan caves were adapted for various human uses. Both burials and ceremonies took place underground. Some caverns had terraces supported by constructed stone walls, while others did not. Occasionally, the caves received architectural features that look like benches, altars, walls, or small buildings. Many of these architectural adaptations have to do with ceremonial use, burial practices, and cult ceremonies, which seem to have varied from community to community, and this diversity is obviously reflected in the way the caves were modified and used.

The intended use helped determine the choice of cave as well as the modifications that were made to it. The Minoans made few modifications if the cavern was just used for casual shelter or for water or storage, but they undertook more extensive building operations if a slope needed to be made more level, a terrace was needed for a large audience for a ceremony, or the ceremony itself required a bench, an altar, or a small walled enclosure or building. As is the case with other aspects of Minoan architecture, the modifications to caves were generally similar (often, for example, consisting of walls and platforms of stone blocks), but the uses were never systematised. The building operations seem to have been designed and built differently for each cave, with the builders adapting their modifications to the new situation in an individual way. In all of these examples, however, the intent was to create a series of architectural spaces for human activities. Some of the aspects of the underground architecture were created by nature, while others were added by the Minoan builders, and additional aspects of the spaces were generated by the uses to which they were put. The results of the human activities inside these caverns, like the addition of human bones and offerings, added a final and very important dimension to the effect the rooms created for those who used them.

Bibliography

Betancourt, P. P.
2007 *Introduction to Aegean Art.* Philadelphia: INSTAP Academic Press.
2008 *The Bronze Age Begins: The Ceramics Revolution of Early Minoan I and the New Forms of Wealth that Transformed Prehistoric Society.* Philadelphia: INSTAP Academic Press.
Betancourt, P. P., C. Davaras, E. Stravopodi, P. Karkanas, L. Langford-Verstegen, H. M. C. Dierckx, S.C. Ferrence, J. Hickman, D. S. Reese, J. D. Muhly, P. J. P. McGeorge, and S. Chlouveraki
2008 Excavations in the Hagios Charalambos Cave: A Preliminary Report. *Hesperia* 77: 539–605.
Betancourt, P. P., N. Marinatos, T. Albani, K. Palyvou, N. Poulou-Papadimitriou, S. German, and S. McPherron
2000 Το Σπήλαιο της Αμνισού, η έρευνα του 1992. *Αρχαιολογική Εφημερίς* 2000: 179–236.
Boardman, J.
1961 *The Cretan Collection in Oxford: The Dictaean Cave and Iron Age Crete.* Oxford: Oxford University Press and the Clarendon Press.
Bosanquet, R. C.
1939–40 Dicte and the temples of Dictaean Zeus. *Annual of the British School at Athens* 40–41: 60–77.
Demargne, P.
1902 Antiquités de Praesos et de l'antre dictéen. *Bulletin de Correspondance Hellénique* 26: 571–83.
Eliopoulos, T.
1998 A preliminary report on the discovery of a temple complex of the Dark Ages at Kephala Vasilikis. In V. Karageorghis and N. C. Stampolidis (eds.), *Eastern Mediterranean: Cyprus—Dodecanese—Crete 16th-6th cent. B.C. Proceedings of the International Symposium Held at Rethymnon, Crete in May 1997*: 301–13. Athens: The University of Crete and The A.G. Leventis Foundation.
Faure, P.
1960 Nouvelles recherches de spéléologie et de topographie crétoises. *Bulletin de Correspondance Hellénique* 84: 189–220.
1964 *Fonctions des cavernes crétoises.* (*École française d'Athènes, Travaux et Mémoires* 14). Paris: Boccard.
Halbherr, F., and P. Orsi
1888 Scoperte nell'antro di Psychro. *Museo Italiano di antichità Classica* 2: 905–12.
Hogarth, D. G.
1899–1900 The Dictaean cave. *Annual of the British School at Athens* 6: 94–116.
Marinatos, S.
1941 The cult of the Cretan caves. *Review of Religion* 1941: 129–36.
Pendlebury, J. D. S., H. W. Pendlebury, and M. B. Money-Coutts
1935–36 Excavations in the plain of Lasithi. I: The cave of Trapeza. *Annual of the British School at Athens* 36: 1–131.
Platakis, E. K.
1973 Το Δικταίον άντρον. *Αμάλθεια* 4 (16–17): 274–80.
Rutkowski, B.
1972 *Cult Places in the Aegean World.* Warsaw: Polish Academy of Sciences.
1986 *The Cult Places of the Aegean.* New Haven and London: Yale University Press.

Rutkowski, B., and K. Nowicki
1996 *The Psychro Cave and Other Sacred Grottoes in Crete (Studies and Monographs in Mediterranean Archaeology and Civilization Ser. II vol. 1)*. Warsaw: Polish Academy of Sciences.

Tomkins, P.
2009 Domesticity by default. Ritual, ritualization and cave-use in the Neolithic Aegean. *Oxford Journal of Archaeology* 28: 125–53.

Tyree, L.
1974 *Cretan Sacred Caves: Archaeological Evidence*. PhD dissertation, University of Missouri.

Watrous, L. V.
1996 *The Cave Sanctuary of Zeus at Psychro. A Study of Extra-Urban Sanctuaries in Minoan and Early Iron Age Crete* (*Aegaeum* 15). Liège : Université de Liège.
2004 New pottery from the Psychro cave and its implications for Minoan Crete. *Annual of the British School at Athens* 99: 129–47.

Xanthoudides, S.
1918 Μέγας Πρωτομινωικός Τάφος Πύργου. *Αρχαιολογικόν Δελτίον* 4: 136–70.

Younger, J. G.
1976 The cave *To Kleisidi* near Myrtos in Southern Crete. *Αρχαιολογικά Ανάλεκτα εξ Αθηνών* 9: 166–69.

Chapter 6

Mortuary variability, social differentiation and ranking in Prepalatial Crete: The evidence from the cemetery of Phourni, Archanes

Yiannis Papadatos

Introduction

The identification of social ranking has always been a focal point of Prepalatial studies, as a principle indicator of social complexity. The initial consensus for a simple, unranked, even egalitarian society (Branigan 1970: 130) was followed in the 1980s and 1990s by strong dispute over the degree of social complexity in the Prepalatial period with the supporters of the evolutionary model arguing that social ranking appeared already in the earlier part of the period (Whitelaw 1983; Branigan 1984; Soles 1988), while the supporters of the revolutionary model suggested that it appeared only at the very end of it, just before the emergence of the palaces (Cherry 1983; Watrous 1994). The most recent debate about the character of the first palaces kept the issue in the front line. The basic idea of a complex, ranked Prepalatial society seems now to be widely accepted, but most studies focus on the later part of the period (EM III-MM IA phases), connecting it to the social dynamics, mainly social competition and emulation that led to the emergence of the palaces (Haggis 2002; Whitelaw 2004; Schoep 2006; Colburn 2008; Tomkins and Schoep 2010).

To identify social ranking, a broad array of issues attracted attention including demography and settlement size, architecture, craft specialisation, exchange, consumption and use of material culture, and sealing practices. However, mortuary practices are traditionally considered one of the principal domains to investigate social inequality and ranking. This is partly because the majority of the Prepalatial archaeological evidence comes from funerary contexts, but also because they offer the opportunity to study individuals or groups against each other when comparing burials, tombs and cemeteries. Traditionally, mortuary variability and differences identified between cemeteries or tombs within the same cemetery are regarded as evidence for social differentiation, inequality and ranking. However, there are certain reservations that should be kept in mind:

First, due to the collective character of the Prepalatial burial facilities it is more feasible to identify differences between burial groups rather than individuals. Therefore, it is important that any analytic approach (a) should identify the character and social composition of the various burial groups, (b) distinguish between position within the burial group and position within society at large, and (c) examine how the former affects the latter. Furthermore, it should be considered that mortuary variability may often correspond to horizontal differentiation, i.e. membership of a clan, kin-group or sodality, rather than vertical, i.e. ranking (Parker Pearson 1999: 74–75).

Second, despite the fact that most studies focus on differences in burial offerings, the relationship between wealth and ranking has not been adequately discussed. Wealth and economic inequality may exist but not necessarily used to generate social inequality or to create power relations (Wason 1994: 125–26). This has to be proven rather than *a priori* assumed. Consequently, the value of funerary goods as indicators of ranking is quite controversial, since any observed differences may correspond to differences in wealth. Markers of wealth are those items of material value that everyone can possess if one has the means, while status markers are items of symbolic value (although they may have material value as well), which can be possessed only by those who have the appropriate status. To distinguish between the two is not an easy task and a combination of factors needs to be taken into account, such as the quantity, quality and form of such markers, as well as their distribution between, or within cemeteries and tombs.

Third, it is important not only to recognise wealth and/or status differences within a community but also to identify whether wealth and social status are achieved through life or ascribed through heredity, since this reflects the level of socio-political complexity of a particular society (O'Shea 1984: 251–52; Pader 1982: 61–62; Parker Pearson 1999: 74). The problem becomes more complex in collective tombs, like the Prepalatial, in which it is almost impossible to identify specific individuals. In these cases it is important to understand how horizontal social position and membership of a burial group affect the vertical social position and wealth of the deceased.

Finally, burial offerings are traditionally regarded as personal possessions passively reflecting the social position and rank of the deceased (Soles 1992: 226; Branigan 1993: 75). It has been shown, however, that material culture can play a more active role in the negotiation of social values, including social position and rank, particularly in contexts of ritual behaviour, such as mortuary practices (Pader 1982: 60–61; Barrett 1988; Parker Pearson 1999: 72–94). Mortuary practices should not be approached as normative practices, passively reflecting social structure; rather they constitute powerful means for the establishment, display or even distortion of what happens in real life (Barrett 1988; Parker Pearson 1982; Shanks and Tilley 1982; 1987). In other words, equality or inequality in death does not necessarily mean equality or inequality in life.

With the above in mind we will examine the available evidence for mortuary variability in the cemetery of Phourni (Figs. 6.1–6.2) in an effort to investigate the existence of social ranking in the corresponding Archanes community during the Prepalatial period. In comparison to other Prepalatial cemeteries Phourni provides an excellent case study for a number of reasons (Sakellarakis and Sapouna-Sakellaraki 1997: 152–267): it comprises a large number of tombs, allowing meaningful

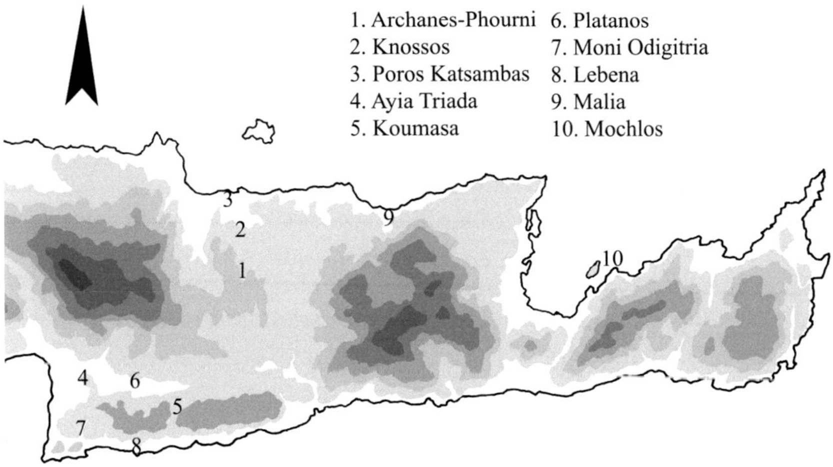

Figure 6.1: Map of the sites mentioned in the text.

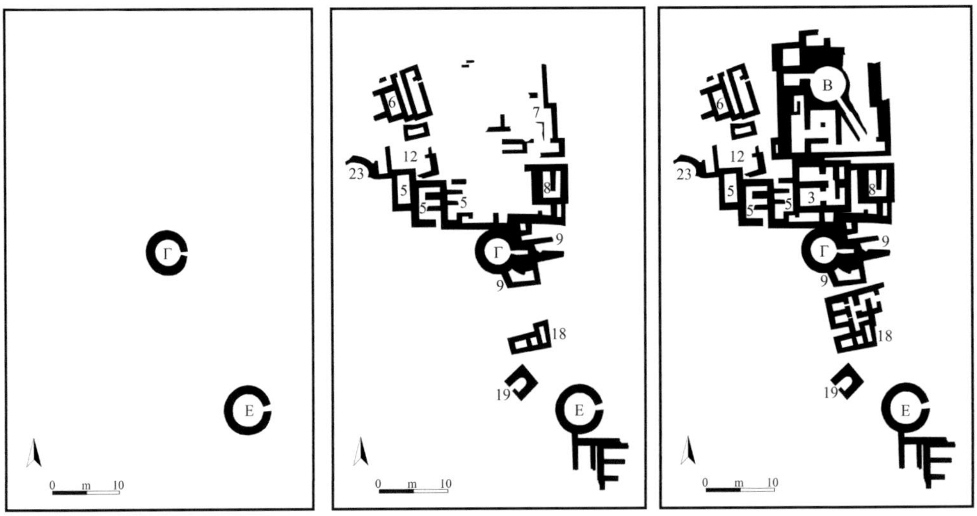

Figure 6.2: Plan of the Phourni cemetery in EM IIA, EM III–MM IA and the end of MM IA.

comparisons and identification of patterns of spatial distribution; it has a long history of use throughout most of the Prepalatial period, allowing the identification of patterns and changes in mortuary variability through time; because the cemetery has not been affected by looting, the archaeological data have not suffered later disturbance and can provide a rather accurate picture of mortuary practices and past ritual activities; finally, it was excavated relatively recently, and, although not fully published, the detailed preliminary reports (Sakellarakis 1966; 1967; 1971; 1972; 1973; 1975; Sakellarakis and Sakellaraki 1976; 1978; 1982; 1991), a thorough two-volume synthetic work (Sakellarakis and Sapouna-Sakellaraki 1997) and the study and publication of specific tombs and materials (Lahanas 1993; 1994; Maggidis 1994a; 1994b; Karytinos 1997; 1998; Panagiotopoulos 2002; Papadatos 1999; 2005) provide the necessary basis for a comprehensive discussion of the archaeological evidence. To the above we can also add the location of Archanes; the proximity of the site to the north coast (12 km) allowed the Archanes people to have easy, probably direct, contacts with the gateway communities and harbours to the north; the proximity to Knossos (8 km) allowed the local community to directly feel the impact, and follow diachronically the major socio-political changes of this important centre; finally, its position on inland routes connecting the north coast with south central Crete (the Mesara) allowed the community to play a significant role in the exchange, interaction and communication between the important centres that existed in these areas. As will be seen below, all these were strongly imprinted on the material culture deposited in the cemetery of the Archanes Prepalatial community.

Early Prepalatial period (EM IIA)

The evidence from Phourni

The cemetery was founded in EM IIA (Fig. 6.2a; Sakellarakis and Sapouna-Sakellaraki 1997: 379). A few EM I sherds may suggest earlier use of the area, though not necessarily for funerary purposes (Papadatos 2005: 63). During this period the cemetery consisted of two tholos tombs, Tholos Γ (Papadatos 2005) and Tholos E (Panagiotopoulos 2002), used contemporaneously by two different burial groups following similar mortuary practices (Papadatos 2005: 55–61). The two tombs are similar in form, plan, size, architecture and method of construction, but show sharp differences in the material contained therein (Papadatos 1999: 79–80; 2007: 435–36).

In absolute numbers, Tholos Γ outnumbers Tholos E in the total number of artefacts (196 to 80) and in objects made of imported raw materials that could be regarded as “exotic” (Table 6.1). The latter include objects made of raw materials originating from the Cyclades, namely marble figurines (Fig. 6.3a–e), silver (Fig. 6.4d) and copper objects (Fig. 6.4a–c) and obsidian blades, and from the east Mediterranean, namely gold jewellery and ivory handles (Fig. 6.4e–f). In contrast, Tholos E is wealthier only in locally available materials such as chipped stone tools made of chert and vases, beads and seals made of steatite and schist.

Table 6.1: Distribution of finds in EM IIA Phourni (evidence from: Panagiotopoulos 2002; Papadatos 2005)

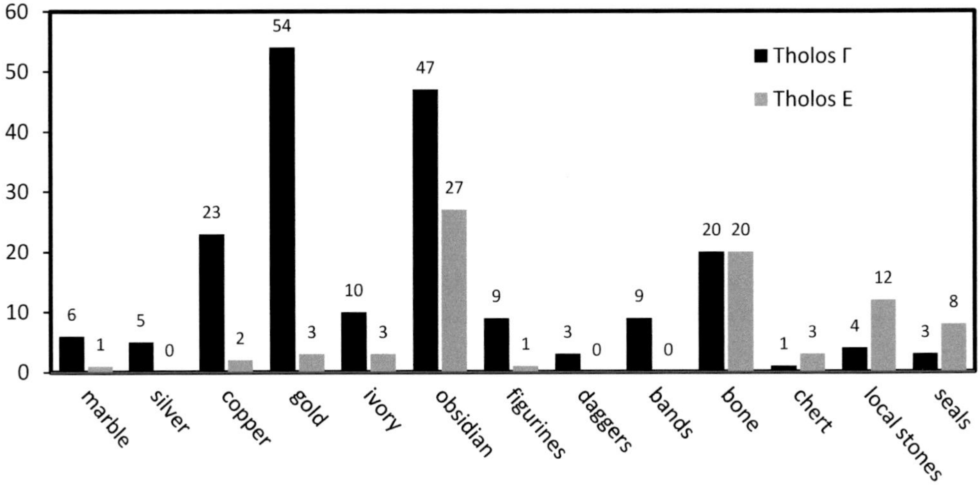

Sharp differences between the two tombs can also be seen in the quality of the material deposited in each. The marble objects of Tholos Γ, namely five figurines and one bowl, are of large size and exceptional quality; some were imported from the Cyclades (Fig. 6.3c–e), while others were probably Cretan imitations of elaborate craftsmanship (Fig. 6.3a–b) (Papadatos 2003; 2007); in contrast, the only marble object of Tholos E was a rather crudely made marble bowl, probably locally made (Fig. 6.4h; Panagiotopoulos 2002: 93). Most of the beads of Tholos Γ are made of gold, belong to a variety of shapes, some of them are rather complex and of elaborate craftsmanship, and a few have parallels from off-island areas, such as the Aegina, Poliochni and Troy treasures (Papadatos 2005: 38–39); in contrast, the Tholos E beads are simpler, and made of locally available stones, apart from a gold one (Panagiotopoulos 2002: 96). Finally, objects of high level of craftsmanship found in Tholos Γ, such as the copper mid-rib daggers (Fig. 6.4a–c), the marble Cycladic-type figurines (Fig. 3a–e) and the ivory handles (Fig. 6.4e–f) are totally absent from Tholos E. The latter contained only a crudely made imitation of a Cycladic-type figurine (Fig. 6.3g), made of widely available limestone (Panagiotopoulos 2002: 98), which again is inferior to the Cycladic-type figurine made of bone from Tholos Γ (Fig. 6.3f). The copper daggers in particular are traditionally regarded as artefacts of emblematic character signalling masculinity and special social status (Nakou 1995: 9–13; Whitelaw 1983: 343, n. 16), and the same was probably the case for the gold bands which belong to diadems; therefore, their absence from Tholos E could be related to differences in social position rather than wealth.

Before assessing the evidence presented above, it is important to consider whether these differences are the result of taphonomic or post-depositional factors. This seems a reasonable possibility considering that in the following period (EM III-

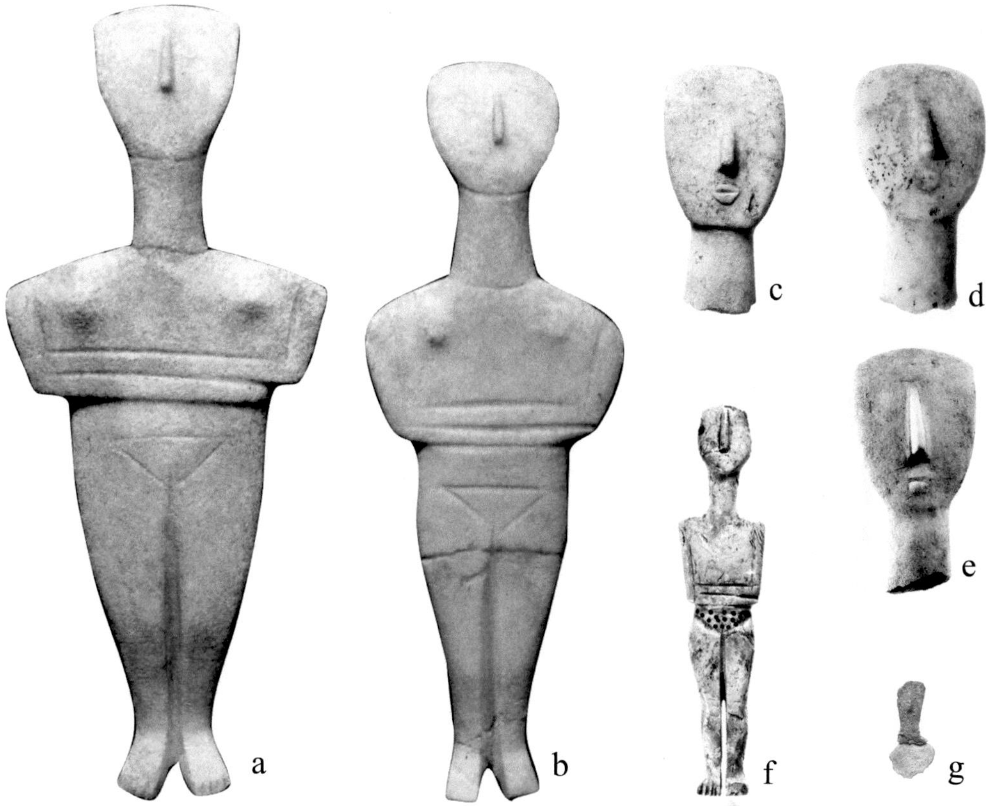

Figure 6.3: Cycladic-type figurines from Tholos Γ (a–f) and Tholos E (g).

MM I) both tombs suffered extensive clearing operations, causing the removal and re-deposition of a certain portion of the original EM IIA funerary material outside the tombs, particularly in the so-called Area of the Rocks (Papadatos 2005: 58). However, it should be noted that the observed differences are not only of quantitative but also of qualitative character, involving objects of special character. This would seem to support the idea that they constitute real differences and are not the result of random clearing operations. In addition, the character and aim of the clearing operations were similar in both tombs: to lower and level the floor before the introduction of the burial containers of the EM III-MM IA phases (Papadatos 2005: 58–61). Finally, differences between the two tombs involved both recyclable (metals) and non-recyclable raw materials (marble, ivory). For the above reasons it seems rather improbable that people cleared deliberately all the valuable objects of high quality, elaborate craftsmanship and recyclable character from Tholos E, but they ignored such artefacts during the clearance of Tholos Γ. Therefore, the increased mortuary differentiation seen in the funerary material of the two tombs represents real distinctions between the dead buried in the two tholoi.

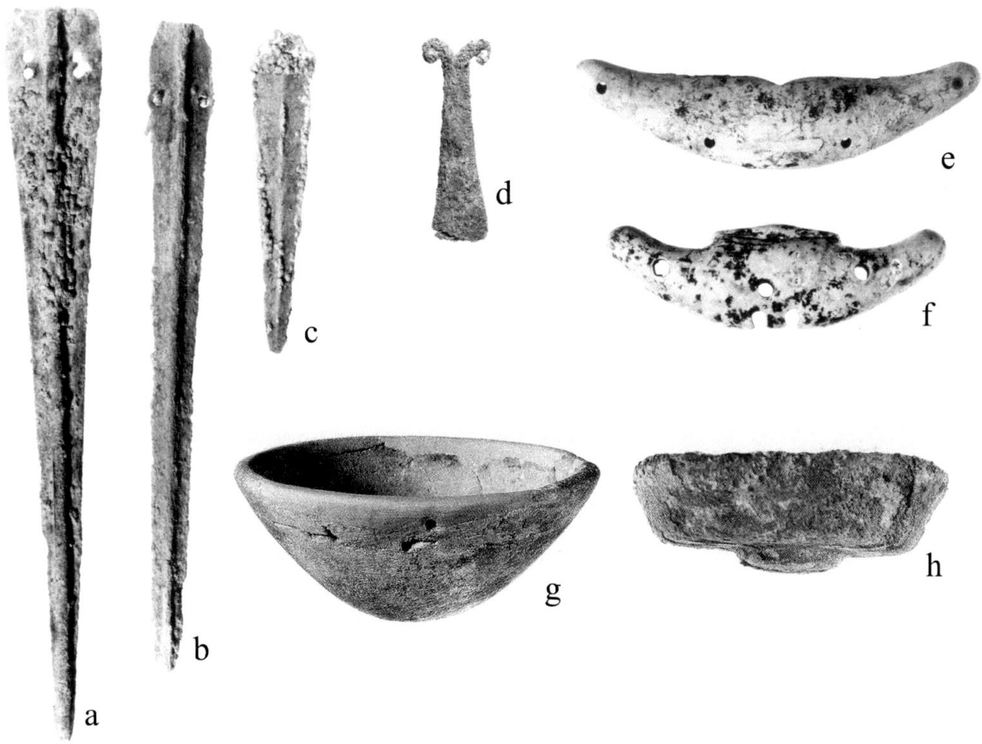

Figure 6.4: Various finds from Tholos Γ (a–g) and Tholos E (h).

Discussion: mortuary variability and social structure in EM IIA

On the basis of the above evidence, it appears that in EM IIA the cemetery of Phourni was characterised by high degree of mortuary differentiation, which was manifested through the deposition of funerary material inside the tombs. Tholos Γ was superior to Tholos E in objects that could be regarded as symbols of status and prestige, particularly objects of display, such as the copper daggers and the marble figurines, and personal adornment, such as the gold jewels. These objects were made of imported materials and were of exceptional quality of manufacture. Moreover, in many object categories the difference between the two tombs was on the basis of presence or absence, not merely relative frequency (e.g. copper daggers and ivory handles). This observation reinforces the suggestion that they were related not only to wealth, but also to special social position, otherwise we would expect to find them in both tombs, albeit in different numbers. On this basis, it seems reasonable to suggest that mortuary differentiation at Phourni corresponds to differences of status within the Archanes society and not just differences in wealth achieved on the basis of personal abilities.

The absence of such objects from Tholos E suggests that special social position was not achieved, but transmitted within the burial group. It could be suggested that only the members of the Tholos Γ burial group had the right or the ability to be buried with such objects. Restriction of access to such status symbols, and by extension, to special social positions, stresses the existence of social ranking within the Archanes society. Also, it is possible to suggest hereditary inequality, since the individuals of only one burial group possessed special social positions, which were expressed in the mortuary ritual through the use of emblematic funerary goods. It seems, therefore, that membership in a specific burial group was the basic criterion for social position and status. Unfortunately, it is not possible to make inferences about individual burials, and consequently about the number of the individuals who had these special social positions in the Archanes society. However, it is possible to identify the character of these positions and infer about their social significance.

On the basis of evidence from Archanes (Carter 1998; Papadatos 2007: 437–41) and Poros Katsambas (Wilson *et al.* 2008; Doonan *et al.* 2007) it has been suggested that communities in north central Crete played a significant role in the circulation of finished objects and raw materials of Cycladic origin to south central Crete (the Mesara and the Asterousia), where such goods were highly desirable for display and conspicuous consumption in mortuary contexts. The Archanes community was located at a strategic position on the inland communication routes connecting the gateway communities of the north coast, such as Poros Katsambas, with the agricultural settlements of the Mesara to the south, via the large and important settlement of Knossos and along the natural pathway following the bed of the Kairatos river. Thus, it was in a favourable location not only to get involved in the flow of such objects, raw materials and "exotic" knowledge, but also to control them. The procurement of imported artefacts and the skilled craft of exotic raw materials were activities with great social potential. They could be of exclusive character and be controlled by a few individuals or groups in order to establish, maintain, increase and legitimise social differentiation. Thus, the basic criterion of social distinction in the Archanes community was probably the ability of the members of one burial group to participate in the social networks and control the interaction through which objects and raw materials of Cycladic origin moved to south Crete.

The way the Archanes community expressed itself in death may support the idea that in real life its economy was structured around trading networks in the context of a prestige good economic system (Whitelaw 2004: 245). Although, the importance of the large and fertile Archanes plain for the prosperity of the community cannot be underestimated, it seems that social position was based on the participation in trading networks and was expressed through the deposition of off-island artefacts and raw materials in funerary contexts. The basic criterion for social position was membership of a specific burial group. Consequently, the right or the ability to participate in these networks was not widely accessible, but deliberately restricted and exclusive, and only a specific group of individuals, the members of the burial group that used Tholos Γ, benefited from them.

It seems rather improbable that this type of social structure was a phenomenon limited to Archanes, especially since Poros Katsambas and perhaps other trading communities were operating alongside the north Cretan coast in the EM IIA period. However, because of the lack of adequate mortuary evidence, it is not possible to identify ranking in other trading communities. The closest parallel is Mochlos, a rich gateway community further east on the north Cretan coastline (Branigan 1991; Carter 2004). The evidence from the cemetery shows sharp differences between the tombs of the West Terrace and the South Slope, suggesting social inequality and ranking in the local trading community (Soles 1988; 1992; Soles and Davaras 1992: 417, 420–28; 1996: 175–80; Whitelaw 2004: 245). However, it is important to note that the increased mortuary differentiation at Mochlos is a later phenomenon, dated to the EM IIB-III period.

Comparison of Phourni with similar tholos tomb cemeteries in south Crete (the Mesara and the Asterousia) shows that prestige objects similar to those found at Phourni, such as Cycladic figurines, copper daggers, and silver and gold jewellery, probably signalling special social status, are also found in these cemeteries. However, the picture of salient mortuary differentiation seen in Phourni is not the case in south Crete since the status markers show a relatively equal distribution between cemeteries and between tombs of the same cemetery. Long ago, Branigan (1984) has identified a series of differences between the cemeteries of the Mesara and the Asterousia in items of wealth and display, artefacts of elaborate manufacture or imported from exotic places, and in evidence for communal ritual, such as paved areas and enclosures. However, such differences should be re-evaluated under the light of recent publications of the large and rich Asterousia cemeteries at Lebena and Moni Odigitria (Alexiou and Warren 2004; Vasilakis and Branigan 2010). Furthermore, it has also be noted (Branigan 1984) that in the three larger Mesara cemeteries (Koumasa, Hagia Triada and Platanos) one tomb differed remarkably from the others in terms of wealth, size and construction, suggesting social differentiation within these Mesara communities. However, the differentiation in items of wealth and display between the tombs was based on objects mostly dated to the later Prepalatial period, such as the elaborate ivory and white paste seals, almost all of the stone vases, a large number of long mid-ribbed daggers, and the gold jewellery with filigree and granulated decoration. Furthermore, such objects are found in all the tombs, albeit in different quantities. Therefore, it seems that, unlike Phourni, in south Crete members of all social groups were buried with objects of special status. Consequently, special social positions were not of limited access. On the basis of what has been argued above, it is possible that the difference between Archanes and the communities of south Crete may be related to the way society was structured in life. Unlike Archanes, which due to privileged location could control the circulation of imported objects along routes of communication and trade, the south Cretan communities were the consumers of these goods. Thus, the deposition of such objects did not reflect exclusive access to networks of interaction at the level of the community but rather wealth and/or special position at the level of the social group that used each tomb. In the Mesara the wealth and social importance of particular individuals were probably based on agricultural production and land use, rather than control of exchange and interaction.

Before proceeding to the following period, a final point has to be made concerning tomb architecture and burial treatment at Phourni. Although social distinction and hereditary inequality in the Archanes society were manifested through sharp differences in the deposited funerary goods, they do not seem to be institutionalised through mortuary variability in tomb architecture and burial treatment. Individuals of high social status do not seem to be treated in a special way or separately from the rest of the community or their corresponding burial group. This contradiction between individualism in status markers and collectiveness in burial treatment reinforces the idea that special social status was affected by or achieved through membership of a social group rather than through personal accomplishments. Consequently, special statuses had to be expressed *only* through the deposition of elaborate funerary goods of personal display and adornment, *not* by interment in distinct individual graves, separately from the rest of the burial group.

Late Prepalatial period (EM III-MM IA)

The evidence from Phourni

A rather different picture is observed at Phourni in the later Prepalatial period. No EM IIB tomb has been identified so far, but this does not necessarily mean a break, as suggested by small quantities of EM IIB pottery found in open areas of the cemetery and in excavations within the Archanes settlement (Sakellarakis and Sapouna-Sakellaraki 1997: 382–5). In any case, the decreased quantity of EM IIB in the cemetery may suggest disruptions, something reinforced by the major changes occurring in EM III-MM IA in many aspects of mortuary practices. The burial containers (larnakes and pithoi) and the rectangular, multi-room house tombs were introduced and their use became widespread (Papadatos 2005: 57). The cemetery expands (Fig. 6.2b), comprising the two old tholos tombs (Γ and E) alongside at least nine house tombs (Tombs 5, 6, 7, 8, 9, 12, 16, 18 and 19). Tholos Γ was used in EM III and perhaps until MM IA (Papadatos 2005: 63–5), Tholos E from MM IA until MM II (Panagiotopoulos 2002: 8), while the house tombs were built at various stages from EM III to MM IA and most of them continued to be used until MM IB or MM II (Sakellarakis and Sapouna-Sakellaraki 1997).

The contemporary use of two different types of tombs, the old reused tholoi and the newly built house tombs, may be regarded as evidence for mortuary variability, at least in tomb architecture. It is tempting to suggest that the individuals buried in the old tholoi had a special social position within Archanes society, being or claiming themselves descendants of the earlier inhabitants of the settlement. However, there is no additional evidence to support this hypothesis. The house tombs were of similar construction as the two tholoi and their spatial distribution in the cemetery does not reveal any significant pattern. Moreover, there was a high degree of similarity among the house tombs themselves in terms of form, size, plan and quality of construction. Differences in size do exist, with some tombs (e.g. Tombs 5, 6 and 7) being larger and with more rooms, but there are no differences in the way of construction.

The evidence for variability in the treatment of the corpse is also rather limited. Most burials seem to have been made inside clay containers, pithoi or larnakes, which were always placed inside the collective tombs (Sakellarakis and Sapouna-Sakellaraki 1997: 246–52). The tombs and the clay containers placed in them received many successive burials, making necessary the secondary treatment of the corpse and the cleaning of the earlier burial remains (Papadatos 2005: 57–60). Burial deposits were also found in the open areas of the cemetery, particularly the so-called Area of the Rocks (Sakellarakis and Sapouna-Sakellaraki 1997: 234). However, the number of the burials is not higher than those made inside the tombs and it is difficult to regard them as commoners' burials. Furthermore, a large part, if not all, of the skeletal material and the finds from the Area of the Rocks does not belong to primary burials, but it has been cleared from nearby tombs and disposed off in this area (Sakellarakis and Sapouna-Sakellaraki 1997: 232; Papadatos 2005: 58–59). Therefore, it is doubtful that they imply differential burial treatment for individuals of lower social status (*contra* Maggidis 1998: 97–98).

The same picture of low mortuary variability can also be seen in the case of the funerary goods (Table 6.2). With the exception of Tholoi Γ and E (Papadatos 2005; Panagiotopoulos 2002) and Tomb 19 (Maggidis 1998), most of the tombs have not

Table 6.2: Distribution of finds in EM III-MM IA Phourni (evidence from: Sakellarakis 1966; 1967; 1971; 1972; 1973; 1975; Sakellarakis and Sakellaraki 1976; 1978; 1982; 1991; 1997; Maggidis 1994a; Panagiotopoulos 2002; Papadatos 2005)

Tomb	Date	Clay vases	Stone vases	Special vases	Seals	Copper	Gold	Beads	Pendants	Special objects
Tholos Γ Upper stratum	EM III-MM IA	2			6	3			3	
Tholos E Upper stratum	MM IA		3		3	1			3	
Tomb 5	EM III-MM IA	90	2	1	5	1		Few	Few	1
Tomb 6	EM III-MM IB	70	2		17	2		Few	Few	1
Tomb 7	MM IA	few			4	3	8	Few		2
Tomb 8	EM III-MM IA	2								
Tomb 9	EM III-MM II	163		4	5		Few	Few	Few	1
Tomb 12	EM III-MM I	20	2		1		4	Few	Few	
Tomb 16	MM IA	5			3	2			3	
Tomb 18 Early rooms	EM III-MM IA	4			3		Few	Few		
Tomb 19 Lower stratum	EM III-MM IA	51	1		4			9	12	

been fully studied yet, so it is not always possible to distinguish between the funerary material of EM III and MM IA, and in some cases even between the later Prepalatial (EM III-MM IA) and the Protopalatial (MM IB-II). Thus, Table 6.2 is not a complete and accurate account of all the artefacts found in the tombs of Phourni. However, it provides sufficient evidence to allow some interesting observations on the character and distribution of funerary goods in the cemetery.

First, the comparison between the earlier (EM IIA) and the later (EM III-MM IA) Prepalatial phases reveals interesting shifts in the quantity, quality and character of the burial offerings. Objects of exceptional craftsmanship seen in EM IIA, such as metal daggers, gold and silver jewels and figurines decrease considerably. It is worth noting that Tholos Γ in EM IIA contained more such artefacts than the entire cemetery in EM III-MM IA. Only two categories seem to follow an opposite trajectory. The seals increase in number and become more elaborate, a change that is usually connected to a higher degree of individualism (Karytinos 1998; Branigan 1993: 140–1), marking identity and social difference (Schoep 2004: 2006). Clay vases constitute the second category of objects indicating sharp increase. They mainly comprise drinking (cups) and pouring shapes (jugs) and special ritual forms, such as kernoi, anthromorphic and zoomorphic rhyta (Sakellarakis and Sapouna-Sakellaraki 1997: 386–405, 540–44; Lahanas 1993). The increase in the number of clay vases may be related to changes in rituals, including their character and the number of participants.

Second, the comparison between tombs shows that none can be distinguished in terms of the quantity, quality and character of the funerary goods they contained. The latter comprise mainly clay vases, necklaces made of simple stone beads and seals. There are only a few objects that could be regarded of special character, signalling social difference: two copper daggers and two Egyptian scarabs from Tombs 6 and 7 (Sakellarakis and Sapouna-Sakellaraki 1997: 357, 595–6), and a clay imitation of an Egyptian sistrum from Tomb 9 (Sakellarakis and Sapouna-Sakellaraki 1997: 351). Furthermore, these objects and the seals were not concentrated but dispersed in several tombs of the cemetery. Differences in quantity do exist, but only Tomb 6 with 17 seals can be clearly distinguished from the others. It should be noted, however, that this tomb has a long period of use extending into the Protopalatial period; consequently, some of the seals could be dated after the MM IA.

Mortuary variability and social structure in EM III-MM IA

To summarise, in EM III-MM IA Phourni no tomb can be distinguished by its position in the cemetery, the mortuary practices, or the funerary goods deposited in it. With the exception of seals, high status objects decrease from the previous period. All objects that can be regarded as signalling social position and status show a relatively equal distribution across the cemetery. However, it is difficult to accept that in the late Prepalatial period the Archanes society became poorer or less differentiated. Instead it could be related to changes in the attitudes of people towards death and the dead, or in the way material culture was used in funerary rituals to signal special social position and differences in wealth and status. The distribution of these objects in all the tombs of Phourni, and in comparable numbers, may indicate that they signified special status within the burial group (e.g. head of family, elders, etc.), or that special social positions were not restricted, as in EM IIA, but open to all the groups.

The decrease in the number of imported "exotica" at Phourni and the shift in their origin from the Cyclades to the east Mediterranean may suggest that in the late Prepalatial the Archanes community ceased to play any significant role in off-Cretan trading networks connecting the Cyclades with south Crete. Consequently, participation in these networks ceased to be important for social prominence and differentiation of status. On this basis, a change towards a more agriculturally-based economy may be inferred, with land-holding groups competing with each other (Whitelaw 2004: 245). Collectiveness in death remained important, but the increase in the number of the tombs and the use of burial containers may be seen as evidence for increased individuality (Branigan 1993: 141) or better for mortuary segregation into smaller burial units (Papadatos 1999).

Furthermore, what mostly differentiates EM III-MM IA from EM IIA is the considerable increase in the amount of clay vases, found inside tombs but also in extensive deposits of discarded pottery. The special character of the EM III-MM IA ceramic assemblages, which comprise kernoi, anthropomorphic and zoomorphic rhyta, jugs and cups with elaborate painted decoration (Sakellarakis and Sapouna-Sakellaraki 1997: 386–405, 540–44; Lahanas 1993), suggests rituals taking place in the open areas of the cemetery with the participation of large numbers of people. It could be suggested that the Phourni cemetery continued to be an arena for the communication of, or competition over social status, but this was achieved through participation in collective rituals, rather than through the deposition of markers of status with the dead inside the tombs.

The degree of mortuary differentiation at Phourni increases again at the very end of the Prepalatial period, but it also takes an entirely different character than before. At a late stage of MM IA two imposing, monumental tombs were built, after the demolition of earlier tombs: Tholos B was built on top of Tomb 7 and Tomb 3 on top of the east wing of Tomb 5 (Fig. 6.2c; Sakellarakis and Sapouna-Sakellaraki 1997: 169–79, 194–98). These are large, multi-roomed, two-storey complexes, with thick walls built with dressed stones and special architectural features, such as internal staircases. Unfortunately, very little is known about the earliest material deposited inside them, since both continued to be used for a long period of time. However, they can be clearly distinguished from all the tombs of the cemetery, earlier or contemporary, in terms of size, method of construction, and form. It is the first time that mortuary differentiation is expressed so profoundly in burial architecture. The monumentalisation of mortuary differentiation may be regarded as evidence for the institutionalisation of social inequality in the Archanes community. This is reinforced by the fact that it is contemporary with broader social dynamics and processes related to the foundation of the first monumental palatial buildings in neighbouring Knossos and further afield, at Malia and Phaistos.

Unfortunately, very little is known about the settlement of Archanes at this period, and, therefore, it is not possible to make any comparisons with the above palatial centres. However, a similar process of funerary aggrandisement and monumentalisation can be seen in the cemetery of Malia. The cemetery largely consists of an open area with many burials made inside natural crevices in the bedrock. Some sort of mortuary differentiation possibly emerged in EM IIB with the erection of the Ossuaire Renaudin and increased in EM III-MM IA with the construction of the House of the Dead, the East Ossuary (Soles 1992: 172–76, 255; Van Effenterre 1980; Van Effenterre & Van Effenterre 1963) and the earlier of the Chrysolakkos monumental buildings (Soles 1992: 163–66; Poursat 1993; Driessen 2010: 559–60; note that the funerary use of the latter is in doubt). The burials made in these built tombs can be regarded as different, but almost nothing is preserved from their contents, so it is not possible to draw conclusions about differences in wealth and status. However, the simple inhumations that continued to be made in the open areas of the cemetery were poorly furnished and they never received secondary treatment, suggesting differences in burial treatment. At some point between the end of the MM IA or the beginning of MM IB, the impressive, monumental second Chrysolakkos building was erected on top of the earlier structure (Soles 1992: 166–71; Poursat 1993). Although the funerary use of this structure is also in doubt (Treuil 2005: 214; Driessen 2010: 560), its monumentality, size and canonical plan resembles that of Phourni Tholos B and Tomb 3; furthermore, not only the Chrysolakkos and Phourni buildings were erected above earlier structures, but their construction is also roughly contemporary. As in the case of Phourni, very little is preserved from the original contents of the Chrysolakkos building, but the few finds, including a gold pendant with two wasps, clearly indicate elite burials.

On the basis of the above evidence it seems reasonable to suggest that the elite group(s) of Archanes and Malia manipulated mortuary practices and exploited the old cemeteries to legitimise social position and/or authority. Display and deposition of rich funerary offerings and symbols of status may have continued to play the same role as in previous periods, but for the first time we observe an increased investment in burial architecture. As in the case of contemporary settlements, where monumental palatial buildings and mansions begin to emerge (e.g. Quartier Mu at Malia), the mortuary arena is also characterised by a tendency for architectural elaboration, which by the end of the Prepalatial constitutes a new media for the communication and institutionalisation of social difference and ranking.

Final remarks

The above analysis, although largely based on a single cemetery, provides valuable insights on the issue of social ranking, especially when the evidence from Phourni is considered within the broader spatial and temporal context of Prepalatial Crete. What Phourni clearly illustrates is that mortuary variability and ranking do not follow a unilinear trajectory from low to high degree. They may decrease over time, as seen from the comparison between the early (EM IIA) and the late Prepalatial period (EM III-MM IA), or change character and way of expression, as seen in the monumental tombs that first appear at the end of MM IA.

On this basis, our research goal should be to identify changes in the degree and character of mortuary differentiation and understand the social, economic, political or ideological reasons behind these changes. After all, there are no static frames of ranking or absolute measures of social complexity, but rather historical trajectories of successive political acts in which the living used the dead as a powerful means to achieve social goals and express social values (Parker Pearson 1999: 94). In the case of Phourni, the observed changes in mortuary differentiation had to do more with shifts in the economic conditions and the base of power not only of the community as a whole, but also of the elite groups and/or individuals. Archanes, from an important trading community along the exchange networks connecting the north coast and the Mesara in the EM IIA, shifts towards a more agriculturally-based economy in EM III-MM IA. Competing land-holding groups may have existed in the latter period, as implied by the increased mortuary segregation into many house tombs, with small rooms and burial containers placed within them. However, differences between these groups were not expressed through the conspicuous consumption of objects of personal adornment, as before, but rather through rituals taking place in the area of the cemetery. Finally, the monumentalisation of the end of MM IA should be seen as result of the institutionalisation rather than the first appearance of social hierarchy in the local community.

The case of Phourni shows that, instead of trying to identify when social differentiation appeared for the first time, or whether ranking was present or absent in Prepalatial Crete, it is far more promising to: (a) identify the particular characteristics of mortuary variability in successive phases and in various cemeteries across Crete, (b) understand the extent to which mortuary variability corresponds, reflects or masks social organisation in real life, and (c) investigate why social organisation was expressed in these particular ways, at these particular cemeteries, in a given time-frame.

Acknowledgements

It is an honour and a pleasure to contribute in a volume celebrating the work and the personality of Keith Branigan. Keith has been a supportive supervisor, a constant source of inspiration, and a person always willing to discuss any opinion, even those that were opposing his own ideas. Because of these qualities, Sheffield became a cradle of scholarship on Prehistoric Aegean for many years.

Bibliography

Alexiou, S. and P. Warren.

2004 *The Early Minoan Tombs of Lebena, Southern Crete*. (Studies in Mediterranean Archaeology 30). Sävedalen: Paul Åströms Förlag.

Barrett, J. C.
1988 The living, the dead and the ancestors: Neolithic and Early Bronze Age mortuary practices. In J. C. Barrett and I. Kinnes (eds.), *The archaeology of context in Neolithic and Bronze Age: recent trends*: 30–41. Sheffield: Department of Archaeology and Prehistory, University of Sheffield.

Branigan, K.
1970 *The Foundations of Palatial Crete. A Survey of Crete in the Early Bronze Age*. London: Routledge and Kegan Paul.
1984 Early Minoan society: the evidence of the Mesara tholoi revisited. In C. Nicolette (ed.), *Aux origines de l'Hellénisme. La Crète et la Grèce. Hommage à Henri van Effenterre présenté par le Centre G. Glotz*. Publications de la Sorbonne, Histoire Ancienne et Mediévale 15: 29–37. Paris: Université de Paris I Panthéon-Sorbonne.
1991 Mochlos: an Early Aegean "gateway community"?. In R. Laffineur and L. Basch (eds.), *Thalassa: L'Egée préhistorique et la mer*, (Aegaeum 7): 97–105. Liège: Université de Liège.
1993 *Dancing with Death: Life and Death in Southern Crete, c. 3000–2000 BC*. Amsterdam: Adolf M. Hakkert.

Carter, T.
1998 Reverberations of the International Spirit: Thoughts upon "Cycladica" in the Mesara. In K. Branigan (ed.), *Cemetery and Society in the Aegean Bronze Age* (Sheffield Studies in Aegean Archaeology 1): 59–77. Sheffield: Sheffield Academic Press.
2004 Mochlos and Melos: A special relationship? Creating identity and status in Minoan Crete. In L. P. Day, M. S. Mook and J. D. Muhly (eds.), *Crete Beyond the Palaces*, (Prehistory Monographs 10): 291–307. Philadelphia: INSTAP Academic Press.

Cherry, J. F.
1983 Evolution, revolution, and the origins of complex society in Minoan Crete. In O. Krzyszkowska and L. Nixon (eds.), *Minoan Society, Proceedings of the Cambridge Colloquium 1981*: 33–45. Bristol: Bristol Classical Press.

Colburn, C. S.
2008 Exotica and the Early Minoan elite: eastern imports in Prepalatial Crete. *American Journal of Archaeology* 112: 203–224.

Doonan, R. C. P., P. M. Day, and N. Dimopoulou-Rethemiotaki
2007 Lame excuses for emerging complexity in Early Bronze Age Crete: The metallurgical finds from Poros-Katsambas and their context. In P. M. Day and R. C. P. Doonan (eds.), *Metallurgy in the Early Bronze Age Aegean* (Sheffield Studies in Aegean Archaeology 7): 98–122. Oxford: Oxbow.

Driessen, J.
2010 Malia. In E. H. Cline (ed.), *The Oxford Handbook of the Bronze Age Aegean (ca. 3000–1000 BC)*: 556–70. Oxford: Oxford University Press.

Haggis, D. C.
2002 Integration and complexity in the Late Pre-Palatial Period. A view from the countryside in Eastern Crete. In Y. Hamilakis (ed.), *Labyrinth Revisited. Rethinking "Minoan" Archaeology*: 120–42. Oxford: Oxbow.

Hodder, I.
1980 Social structure and cemeteries: a critical re-appraisal. In P. Ratz, T. Dickinson and L. Watts (eds.), *Anglo-Saxon cemeteries 1979* (BAR 82): 161–69. Oxford: Archaeopress.

Karytinos, A.
1997 *Minoan Prepalatial sealstones in their economic and social context. A study based on the new material from Archanes-Phourni*. Unpublished PhD thesis, University of Sheffield.
1998 Sealstones in cemeteries: a display of social status? In K. Branigan (ed.), *Cemetery and Society in the Aegean Bronze Age* (Sheffield Studies in Aegean Archaeology 1): 78–86. Sheffield: Sheffield Academic Press.

Lahanas, A.
1993 Ein Keramikdepot aus Archanes und seine Bedeutung für die Entwicklung der Mittelminoischen Keramik. Unpublished PhD thesis, Albert Ludwigs University, Freiburg.
1994 Η πρώιμη κεραμεική των Αρχανών. *Αρχαιολογία* 53: 36–41.
Maggidis, C.
1994a *Burial Building 19 at Archanes: A study of Prepalatial and Early Protopalatial Funerary Architecture and Ritual.* Unpublished PhD thesis, University of Pennsylvania.
1994b Ταφικό Κτήριο 19: Ένας μοναδικός ημιθολωτός τάφος στις Αρχάνες. *Αρχαιολογία* 53: 47–52.
1998 From Polis to Necropolis: social ranking from architectural and mortuary evidence in the Minoan cemetery at Phourni, Archanes. In K. Branigan (ed.), *Cemetery and Society in the Aegean Bronze Age* (Sheffield Studies in Aegean Archaeology 1): 87–102. Sheffield: Sheffield Academic Press.
Nakou, G.
1995 The cutting edge: a new look at early Aegean metallurgy. *Journal of Mediterranean Archaeology* 8(2): 1–32.
O'Shea, J.
1984 *Mortuary Variability. An Archaeological Investigation.* Orlando: Academic Press.
Pader, E. J.
1982 *Symbolism, Social Relations and the Interpretation of Mortuary Remains.* (BAR IS 130). Oxford: Archaeopress.
Panagiotopoulos, D.
2002 *Das Tholosgrab E von Phourni bei Archanes. Studien zu einem frühkretischen Grabfund und seinem kulturellen Kontext.* (BAR IS 1014). Oxford: Archaeopress.
Papadatos, Y.
1999 Mortuary practices and their importance for the reconstruction of society and life in Prepalatial Crete: The evidence from Tholos Tomb Γ, in Archanes-Phourni. Unpublished PhD Thesis, University of Sheffield. Sheffield.
2003 Ένα παλίμψηστο λοιπόν.... In A. Vlachopoulos and K. Birtacha (eds.), *ΑΡΓΟΝΑΥΤΗΣ. Τιμητικός τόμος για τον Καθηγητή Χρίστο Ντούμα από τους μαθητές του στο Πανεπιστήμιο Αθηνών (1980-2000)*: 277–291. Athens: Kathimerini A.E.
2005 *Tholos Tomb Gamma: A Prepalatial Tholos Tomb at Phourni, Archanes.* (Prehistory Monographs 17). Philadelphia: INSTAP Academic Press.
2007 Beyond cultures and ethnicity: a new look at material culture distribution and inter-regional interaction in the Early Bronze Age Southern Aegean. In S. Antoniadou and A. Pace (eds.), *Mediterranean Crossroads*: 419–51. Oxford: Pierides Foundation.
Parker Pearson, M.
1982 Mortuary practices, society and ideology: an ethnoarchaeological study. In I. Hodder (ed.), *Symbolic and structural archaeology*: 99–113. Cambridge: Cambridge University Press.
1999 *The Archaeology of Death and Burial.* Stroud: Sutton Publishing.
Poursat, J.-C.
1993 Notes de céramique maliote. A propos de "La céramique de Chrysolakkos". *Bulletin de Correspondance Hellénique* 117: 603–07.
Sakellarakis, Y.
1966 Αρχαιότητες και μνημεία της Ανατολικής Κρήτης. *Αρχαιολογικό Δελτίο* 21, B2: 411–419.
1967 Ανασκαφή Αρχανών. *Πρακτικά της εν Αθήναις Αρχαιολογικής Εταιρείας*: 151–161.
1971 Ανασκαφή Αρχανών. *Πρακτικά της εν Αθήναις Αρχαιολογικής Εταιρείας*: 276–283.
1972 Ανασκαφή Αρχανών. *Πρακτικά της εν Αθήναις Αρχαιολογικής Εταιρείας*: 310–353.
1973 Ανασκαφή Αρχανών. *Πρακτικά της εν Αθήναις Αρχαιολογικής Εταιρείας*: 167–187.
1975 Ανασκαφή Αρχανών. *Πρακτικά της εν Αθήναις Αρχαιολογικής Εταιρείας*: 255–321.

Sakellarakis, Y. and Sakellaraki, E.
1976 Ανασκαφή Αρχανών. *Πρακτικά της εν Αθήναις Αρχαιολογικής Εταιρείας*: 342–399.
1978 Ανασκαφή Αρχανών. *Πρακτικά της εν Αθήναις Αρχαιολογικής Εταιρείας*: 309–322.
1982 Ανασκαφή Αρχανών. *Πρακτικά της εν Αθήναις Αρχαιολογικής Εταιρείας*: 467–530.
1991 Ανασκαφή Αρχανών. *Αρχαιολογική Εφημερίς*: 205–18.
Sakellarakis, Y. and Sapouna- Sakellaraki, E.
1997 *Αρχάνες. Μια νέα ματιά στη Μινωική Κρήτη*. Αθήνα: Εκδόσεις Άμμος.
Schoep, I.
2004 The socio-economic context of seal use and administration at Knossos. In C. Gerald, E. Hatzaki and A. Vasilakis (eds.), *Knossos: Palace, City, State*: 283–293. London: The British School at Athens.
2006 Looking beyond the First Palaces: elites and the agency of power in EM III-MM II Crete. *American Journal of Archaeology* 110: 37–64.
Shanks, M. and Tilley, C.
1982 Ideology, symbolic power and ritual communication: a reinterpretation of Neolithic mortuary practices. In I. Hodder (ed.), *Symbolic and structural archaeology*: 129–54. Cambridge: Cambridge University Press.
1987 *Reconstructing archaeology: theory and practice*. Cambridge: Cambridge University Press.
Soles, J. S.
1988 Social ranking in prepalatial cemeteries. In E. B. French and K. A. Wardle (eds.), *Problems in Greek Prehistory. Papers Presented at the Centenary Conference of the British School of Archaeology at Athens*: 49–61. Bristol: Bristol Classical Press.
1992 *Prepalatial Cemeteries at Mochlos and Gournia and the House Tombs of Bronze Age Crete* (Hesperia Supplement 24). Princeton: American School of Classical Studies.
Soles, J. S. and C. Davaras
1992 Excavations at Mochlos, 1989. *Hesperia* 61: 413–45.
1996 Excavations at Mochlos 1992–3. *Hesperia* 65: 175–230.
Tomkins, P. and I. Schoep
2010 Early Bronze Age: Crete. In E. H. Cline (ed.), *The Oxford Handbook of the Bronze Age Aegean (ca. 3000–1000 BC)*: 66–82. Oxford: Oxford University Press.
Treuil, R.
2005 Entre morts et vivants à Malia. La "zone de nécropoles" et les quartiers d'habitation. In I. Bradfer-Burdet, B. Detournay and R. Laffineur (eds.), ΚΡΗΣ ΤΕΧΝΙΤΗΣ. *L'Artisan Crétois: Recueil d'articles en l'honneur de Jean-Claude Poursat, publié à l'occasion des 40 ans de la découverte du Quartier Mu*: 209–20. *Aegaeum* 26. Liège: Université de Liège.
Van Effenterre, H.
1980 *Le Palais de Mallia et la cité Minoenne: Étude de Synthèse*. Incunabula Graeca 76. Rome: Ateneo e Bizarri.
Van Effenterre, H. and Van Effenterre, M.
1963 *Fouilles exécutées à Mallia, Étude du site et exploration des nécropoles (1915–1928)* (Études Crétoises XIII). Paris: Guenther.
Vasilakis, A. and K. Branigan
2010 *Moni Odigitria: A Prepalatial Cemetery and Its Environs in the Asterousia, Southern Crete*. (Prehistory Monographs 30). Philadelphia: INSTAP Academic Press.
Wason, P. K.
1994 *The Archaeology of Rank*. Cambridge: Cambridge University Press.
Watrous, L. V.
1994 Crete from earliest prehistory through the Protopalatial Period. *Americal Journal of Archaeology* 98: 695–753.

Whitelaw, T. M.
1983 The settlement at Fournou Korifi, Myrtos and aspects of Early Minoan social organization. In O. Krzyszkowska and L. Nixon (eds.), *Minoan Society, Proceedings of the Cambridge Colloquium 1981*: 323–45. Bristol: Bristol Classical Press.
2004 Alternative pathways to complexity in the Southern Aegean. In J. C. Barrett and P. Halstead (eds.), *The Emergence of Civilisation Revisited* (Sheffield Studies in Aegean Archaeology 5): 232–256. Oxford: Oxbow.

Wilson, D. E., P. M. Day and N. Dimopoulou-Rethemiotaki
2008 The gateway port of Poros-Katsambas: trade and exchange between north-central Crete and the Cyclades in EB I-II. In N. Brodie, J. Doole, G. Gavalas and C. Renfrew (eds.), *Horizon, A colloquium on the prehistory of the Cyclades*: 261–70. Cambridge: McDonald Institute for Archaeological Research.

Chapter 7

Variables and diachronic diversities in the funerary remains of the Kamilari tholos tombs

Luca Girella

Introduction: some preliminary statements

For over thirty years Kamilari and Keith Branigan have represented a special bond as emerging in two fundamental books published in 1970 and 1993. Firstly, at the end of the 1960s, the cornerstone book *The tombs of Mesara* offered the first reasoned essay after the work of Xanthoudides (1924), in which Kamilari, thanks to its extraordinary state of preservation, presented the newest and most remarkable funerary evidence from the Mesara, which gave Branigan new grounds for considering the issue of the vaulted roof (Branigan 1970: 28–55; Girella *et al.* 2013). Secondly, in the 1990s, the admirable *Dancing with Death* took a new turn in interpretation, as the author argued for the existence and consistency of post-funerary rituals: again Kamilari, alongside the Hagia Kyriaki cemetery, provided rich evidence for the ceremonies conducted outside the tomb (Branigan 1993). A few years later, in the proceedings of the first Sheffield Round Table, Branigan used aspects of landscape archaeology to analyse the relationship between cemeteries and social landscapes (Branigan 1998).

What separates Branigan's two major books is the growing awareness of a more complex society behind the mortuary data of the Mesara plain during the EBA (Branigan 1984; 1991). While the picture of the EBA Mesara drawn in the 1970s was one characterised by egalitarian societies (Branigan 1970), Branigan later opted for a "ranked society that stands somewhere between the egalitarian community and the full chiefdom with a clearly social hierarchy" (Branigan 1984: 35; 1993). With the nineties came a more profound awareness that Kamilari, together with other tholos cemeteries, manifest a more complex regional mortuary language that reveals a "juxtaposition of cemetery and settlement" (Branigan 1998: 19; Murphy 1998). Building on this insight, new theoretical approaches (Papadatos 1999; Relaki 2004; Murphy 2011; Legarra Herrero 2014), new publications (Panagiotopoulos 2002; Gerontakou

2003; Alexiou and Warren 2004; Papadatos 2005; Campbell-Green 2006; Vasilakis and Branigan 2010), and new gazetteers of tholos tombs (Belli 1984; Panagiotopoulos 2002: 164–68, tables 5–7; Goodison and Guarita 2005) provide fresher food for thought: we now see such cemeteries not necessarily as a reflection of the social structure of the groups that used the tombs, but also as a social arena where such groups actively played a role in constructing and modifying positions and status within the communities (Pader 1982; Shanks and Tilley 1984; Barrett 1988; Parker Pearson 1993; 1999; Robb 1994; 2007; Hamilakis 2013).

Certainly the Kamilari cemetery has attracted much interest among the scholars of Crete. However, its importance, like that of other tholos cemeteries in Crete, relies largely on old data, incomplete publication, and unsustainable interpretative models, which are often exasperated by such problems as looting, communal use, and limited rescue excavations. Because of their long use, our vision of the Cretan tholos tombs has always reflected what we basically know from the final use of the graves. Consequently, not enough attention has been paid to the variability of these cemeteries through time and space. While cemeteries, in fact, spatially reflect the human groups that used them, chronologically they may represent social groups resulting from a combination of local histories (Relaki 2004; Legarra Herrero 2009). Therefore, the study of variables and diachronic diversities within a cemetery is an essential tool for reconstructing its entire history and the interaction with the social and political landscape in which it is situated.

The tholos tombs of Kamilari are the ideal case study as, not only were they used for a long period, but the largest tomb was found almost untouched and well preserved. Notwithstanding the exhaustive preliminary report provided by D. Levi after excavations in 1959 (Levi 1961–62; 1976: 703–43), the present picture of the cemetery still suffers from vague interpretations for two reasons: a) not enough attention has been paid to the changes that occurred during the history of the tombs; and b) most of the artefacts have been studied independently of their architectural setting.

A new project focusing on the complete re-publication of the Kamilari cemetery started a few years ago (Girella 2011; 2013; Caloi 2011) and can now shed more light particularly on the more intricate history of the cemetery. The project has been enriched by a detailed study of the vaulted roof problems and the human bones (reburied in the summer of 2009) (Triantaphyllou in this volume; Triantaphyllou and Girella forthcoming; Girella *et al.* 2013).

The aim of this paper is to present some preliminary data on the kinds of social transformation entailed in the history of the cemetery at Kamilari during and after the Protopalatial period and to consider whether or not differences within the community can be identified throughout the periods of occupation. While tholos cemeteries have been viewed within a uniform model, the cemetery at Kamilari offers an opportunity to explore both the paths of the long use of the graves and the variability of mortuary display through time and space.

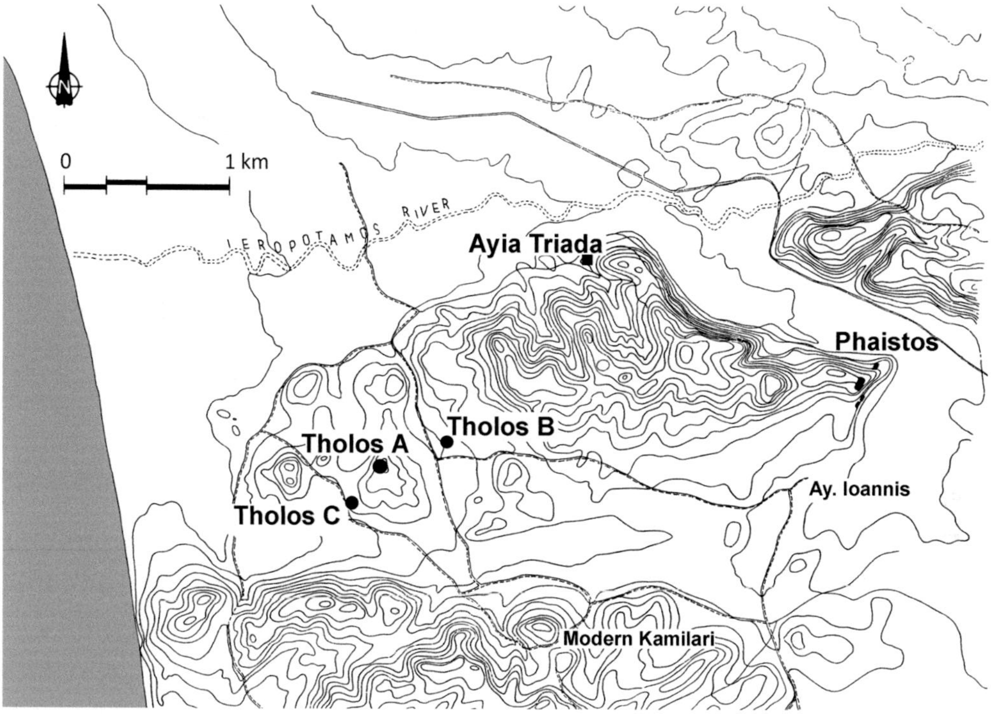

Figure 7.1: Map of the Kamilari area indicating the three tholos tombs.

The tholos cemetery at Kamilari

The tholos cemetery is located north of the modern village of Kamilari and comprises at least three tombs (Figure 7.1): the two larger (A and B) are located approximately 200 metres from each other, while a third, smaller tomb (C) is situated about 150 metres to the east/south-east and was re-used in historical times. These tombs were excavated in 1959 by Levi (1961–62). Alexiou and Branigan reported on Kamilari C and the latter also provided a plan (Alexiou 1957; Branigan 1976).

Tholos A is known by the name of the low hill, Grigori Koryphi, on top of which the tomb is still visible today inside the protective fence (Figure 7.2a). The tomb is composed of three main complexes: a main circular chamber, five external rooms and open-air space to the north (Levi 1961–62: 9–19) (Figure 7.3). The circular chamber has an internal diameter of 7.65 metres with walls constructed of roughly worked blocks and large stones on the interior face. The doorway is located on the East side as in almost all the tholos tombs of southern Crete. Five annexes were built East of the main chamber: a so-called antechamber, room α, which was connected through a corridor with two other rectangular spaces, rooms β and γ. To the South two additional small rooms (δ-ε), the first of which is almost circular, were half built into the rock. Finally, an external courtyard, which was formed by smoothing the natural rock, apparently remained an open space during the whole life of the tholos tomb.

Tholos B, which is half preserved, is located c. 200 metres north-east of Tholos A and 80 metres uphill facing the bigger tomb A (Levi 1961–62: 107–10; 1976: 742–43) (Figure 7.2b). It is constructed, like tomb A, with large stones preserved up to 1.8 metres on the north-east; on the south-east of the tomb the entrance to the tomb is partially preserved.

Tholos C, 150 metres to the east/south-east of the larger tomb, is located on a steep side of a flat plateau (Alexiou 1957: 335; Branigan 1976; 1993: 144; Englezou 1988–89; Pelon 2004: 160) (Figure 7.2c). It has a diameter of c. 3.7 metres, with one quarter of the circuit wall still standing on the north. On its eastern side a rectangular room 3.5 metres long is still visible, built, like the circular chamber, of roughly squared limestone blocks.

With its massive assemblage of finds (over one thousand of complete vessels and several other thousands of sherds and mendable vases, c. 100 stone vessels and 19 seals) the Kamilari cemetery offers the opportunity to explore the stratification and transformation of ritual performances through time (i.e. from MM IB to LM IIIA2). For the present discussion, we will focus on the bigger and better preserved tomb (Tholos A), which

Figure 7.2a: View of Kamilari Tholos A (Grigori Koryphi). (Photo author).

Figure 7.2b: View of Kamilari Tholos B (Mylona Lakkos). (Photo author).

Figure 7.2c: View of Kamilari Tholos C. (Photo N. Cucuzza).

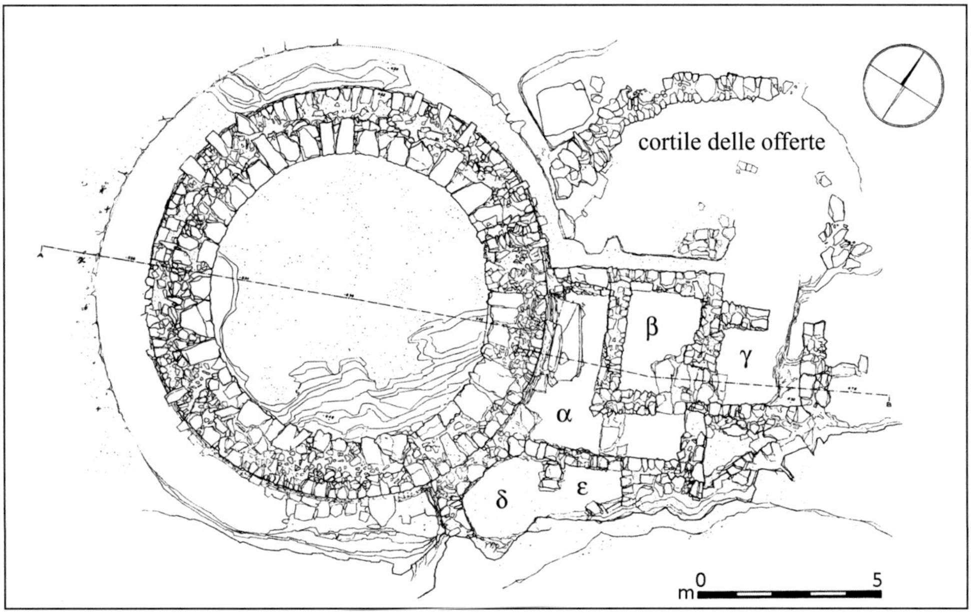

Figure 7.3: Plan of Tholos A. (Adapted from Levi 1961–62: pl. I).

Table 7.1: Table showing the main periods of occupation of the Kamilari tholos tomb cemetery

Tomb	MM IB	MM II	MM III	LM I	LM II-III	Geometric	Classical
A	✧	✧	✧	✧	✧	✧	
B	?	✧	✧	✧			
C	✧	✧	?				✧

allows us to distinguish several phases of human activity at the site (Table 7.1). Combining this with the information taken from the analysis of the ceramic sets and depositional behaviours demonstrates that the cemetery at Kamilari should be viewed as the result of a dynamic process which developed – with Phaistos at the head – during MM IB-II (Watrous and Hadzi–Vallianou 2004: 277–91), and that it later changed alongside the shifts of power that characterised the region. Throughout its history, the main tholos tomb remains a focus of intense activity, but there are indications of changing human perceptions through the different periods. This paper will sidestep other problems connected with the main tholos (e.g. stratigraphy, the vaulted roof, human remains) and will focus on material culture – specifically ceramic sets – to explore the main diachronic changes that affected Tholos A. The aim is to interpret differences in the use of the tombs as elements of the mortuary behaviour of the community which used the cemetery through the centuries. In order to do this, each period of occupation will be presented and compared with the nearby "stories" of the two major settlements: Phaistos and Hagia Triada.

A summary of the stratigraphy

The Kamilari tombs suffered almost complete loss of stratigraphic and anthropological information. Although the thorough examination of the preserved material and the study of its relation to the reconstructed stratigraphic sequence are still ongoing, some preliminary points can be made (Table 7.2). A first attempt (Girella 2003: 312–37) of cross-referencing the stratigraphic information of the position of published vessels and the excavation photographs allowed the identification of several levels, namely in rooms *β* and γ. This preliminary work has now been confirmed and enriched by the reading of the notebooks, which help to reconstruct the sequence of the excavation during the summer of 1959 (Girella 2011: 127–28; 2013: 152). Likewise, find spots were recorded for some of the main and completely preserved finds (Levi 1961–62: fig. 21), though the depths were not regularly recorded for all the objects. In the main chamber, an upper level consists of soil containing a large number of stones related to the collapse of the stone vault. Below this, two burial strata were distinguished: an upper one, thicker and quite irregular; and a lower one, relatively thin, no more than 20 cm, situated directly on the bedrock. Each level was divided into four quarters. The majority of the artefacts, particularly those dating to the Mycenaean period, derived from the upper stratum, but sherds from these two strata join together, and, most strikingly, also with those found in the nearby annexes. Thus, it appears that we are dealing with levels that suffered repeated disturbance caused by cleaning operations. Unpublished plan sketches and pencil drawings from the excavation notebooks help in isolating clusters of grave offerings along the tholos wall (Levi 1961–62: figs. 22–30; Girella 2011: fig. 3), but the prolonged use of the tomb makes it difficult, if not impossible, to associate groups of finds with specific burials.

Room *α*, being a proper antechamber of the tholos tomb was used on several occasions, resulting in the stratigraphy being seriously disturbed. However, the notebooks allow the identification of a surface level of mixed date followed by a deposit of MM III amphoras and jugs (Levi 1961–62: fig. 66; Girella 2003: 322–23).

Table 7.2: Table showing the main stratigraphic data identified in Tholos A

<table>
<tr><th>Tholos</th><th>Room α</th><th>Room β</th><th>Room γ</th></tr>
<tr><td rowspan="5">Upper Level

Lower Level</td><td rowspan="2">Surface Level (MM III-LM IIIA)</td><td>Level V (MM III-LM IIIA)</td><td rowspan="2">Level III (MM III-LM IIIA)</td></tr>
<tr><td>Level IV (MM III-LM IIIA)</td></tr>
<tr><td rowspan="2">MM III Level</td><td>Level III (Amphoras) (MM III)</td><td>Level II (MM III)</td></tr>
<tr><td>Level II (MM II, III)</td><td>Level I (MM II, III)</td></tr>
<tr><td>Protopalatial Level?</td><td>Level I (MM IB, II)</td><td></td></tr>
</table>

Possibly a third, Protopalatial level can be detected underneath, most likely related to the construction and first use of the tholos.

A more complex sequence can be drawn from the notebooks for Room *β* (Girella 2003: 324–29): in the upper level where the clay model with the dancers was found (Levi 1961-62: fig. 72) the pottery dates from MM III to LM IIIA. Directly below it, a second level was isolated (IV) again with MM III, LM I, and LM IIIA pottery. Further deeper, three other levels can be reconstructed from three superimposed levels characterised by distinct groups of vessels, namely Level III represented by a group of MM III jugs and amphoras directly on top of a stratum consisting of human bones (Levi 1961–62: figs. 71, 75), Level II (on the North-east sector of the room) formed by a second group of MM III and MM II vessels associated with the above mentioned bones (Levi 1961–62: figs. 75–6) and finally Level I (identified in the South-west part of the room) corresponding to the basal floor that was quite rich in stone vessels and pottery datable to the Protopalatial period (MM IB–II) (Levi 1961–62: fig. 77).

No levels were identified inside the small Rooms *δ*-*ε* used to keep human bones (mainly skulls and long bones) and ceramic material from MM II to LM I (Levi 1961–62: figs. 97–8). Finally, two levels were distinguished by Levi in Room *γ*: again an upper one (III) represented by the clay models (Levi 1961–62: fig. 87) and a lower one (I) at the rock floor (Levi 1961–62: fig. 88), coinciding with the stone threshold leading to Room *β* via a corridor. The upper level contained MM III, LM I and LM III pottery (confirming a possible disturbance on the surface, probably occurring during the Mycenaean re-occupation), whereas the lower one contains MM II and MM III pottery. Level II, located in between and dating to the MM III, probably corresponds to the level with the amphoras in room *β* (Levi 1961–62: figs. 87, 94).

The external courtyard remains the most problematic area of the tholos tomb in terms of reconstructing stratigraphic information. It is possible to identify a number of spots, where apparently the custom of offering vessels was practised for a longer period (Caloi 2011: pls. XXXIIIa, XXXIVb). These are the area by the wall found on the north/north-west side (Levi 1961–62: fig. 107), the area directly North of Room *β*, corresponding to the well known altar made of stone slabs (Levi 1961–62: fig. 106), the corner between Rooms *β* and *γ* (Levi 1961–62: fig. 108), and the two small spaces south and east of Room *γ*.

Ceramic sets in context

The Protopalatial period

Most concentrations of Protopalatial vessels were found in the main chamber (Levi 1961–62: figs. 61 b–c, 63) and the external courtyard (Levi 1961–62: figs. 114–19; for more information about this period see Caloi 2009; 2011). While there was a wide variety of shapes, a special preference for handleless cups and jugs is evident. Also striking is the extreme variety of shapes recovered outside, which can be linked with the role that the external area played in ritual performances. Ritual activity in this period also entailed the deposition of stone vessels (Levi 1961–62: figs. 120–21) and seals (Platon *et al.* 1977: 5–6, 8–10, 12, 13, 14; Levi 1961–62: figs. 127–30, 134–37; Fiandra 1995).

Although the use of Tholos A began in MM IB, the ceramic assemblage of the subsequent MM II period is wider and shows a special link with Phaistos and Hagia Triada (Caloi 2009). This period in fact displays a significant leap in the economic role of the Palace and probably an increased emphasis on the ritual sphere (Militello 2012). Both the settlements and the tombs exhibit an extraordinary range of pottery and, in particular, a wide variety of wares used for feasting. The presence in the tomb of high quality light-on-dark and polychrome wares (mainly bridge-spouted jars, straight-sided and carinated cups) together with monochrome (consisting mainly of carinated cups), dark-on-light (large plates, bowls, milk jugs and small jugs), plain (handleless cups) and cooking wares, recently identified among the unpublished material, is especially significant (Caloi 2009). Also noteworthy is the existence of possible imports from the Pediada region (Levi 1961–62: fig. 114c), so far only identified macroscopically: a few side-spouted jugs with trefoil spout, characterised by a reddish fine to medium-coarse fabric and surfaces smoothed and dark coated with a slip fired red to dark brown.

It is probable that the level of the rituals could be reflected in the quality of ceramic shapes, and that differences in the quantity of wares might indicate the size of the respective groups, the degree of exclusivity and the status of participants. The composition and nature of the assemblages at Kamilari suggest the existence of interconnected levels of consumption, in which both the circular chamber and the outer space were involved. After MM IB, the outer area played a central role in the performance of collective ceremonies: an example being the well-known paved area on which handleless cups and stone vessels were placed overturned (Levi 1961–62: fig. 106; Caloi 2011: 103, 105–06). In contrast to the frequency of plain or monochrome jugs and cups, access to more restricted intra-group ceremonies is demonstrated by the presence of high quality and strongly individualised vessels in dark-on-light and polychrome wares; this probably hints at the definition of some elite group or head of families, whereas the larger impact of handleless cups and plain ware might reflect the participation of many groups, at least some of lower status. At Hagia Triada Carinci (2003: 115–26) has observed patterns of innovation in the organisation of the funerary area, with pottery assemblages hinting at rites of libation and consumption, based on the quantity of drinking and pouring vessels -handleless cups and jugs- together with a few miniature and rarer shapes. The group of clay figurines representing women worshipping the goddess or waiting for her epiphany (Carinci 2003: fig. 14) is also unique.

A similar picture can be seen at the palace of Phaistos where two levels of consumption are recognised (Militello 2012): the first is highlighted by the presence of elaborately decorated and strongly individualised vessels among more communal ceramic sets in the SW quarter of the Palace (Carinci 2006), in contrast to the plain ware of more "anonymous" drinking sets probably connected with the distribution and sharing of food and drink among a larger number of participants in different palatial locations, such as the archive room 25 (Levi 1976: 271–74; Borgna 2004: 133). Similar cases might be represented in the MM IB Deposit A at Knossos (Knappett and Macdonald 2007: 163) and the Lakkos Deposit at Petras (Haggis 2007), where stylistic and formal variations within standardised ware groups could suggest the existence of either a horizontal or vertical organisation of participants.

The Neopalatial period

The first stage of the Neopalatial period (MM III) is the best represented in the cemetery (Levi 1961–62: figs. 47–53, 55–6, 59–60, 61a, 67–9, 73–4, 79–82, 84, 93, 95–6, 100–04, 109, 113; Girella 2013). Recent thorough studies of MM III ceramics from Phaistos and Hagia Triada now allow us to distinguish MM IIIA from MM IIIB in ceramic terms (Girella 2007; 2010a; 2010b) and it is clear that both MM IIIA and IIIB periods are represented in the tomb (Girella 2013). It is interesting to observe the main role played by the circular chamber and the homogeneous distribution of offerings in other areas (Levi 1961–62: figs. 24–9, 66, 71, 75, 88–9, 97–98, 108) (Figure 7.4).

In addition to ordinary, increasingly frequent handleless cups (Figure 7.5l), drinking and pouring vessels occur basically in monochrome and light-on-dark wares, and, as also observed at Phaistos, they consist of few shapes with a very restricted number of decorative schemes (Girella 2010a: 319–44) (Figure 7.5). Straight-sided cups, bell cups, and bridge-spouted jars regularly occur along with shapes used for storing either

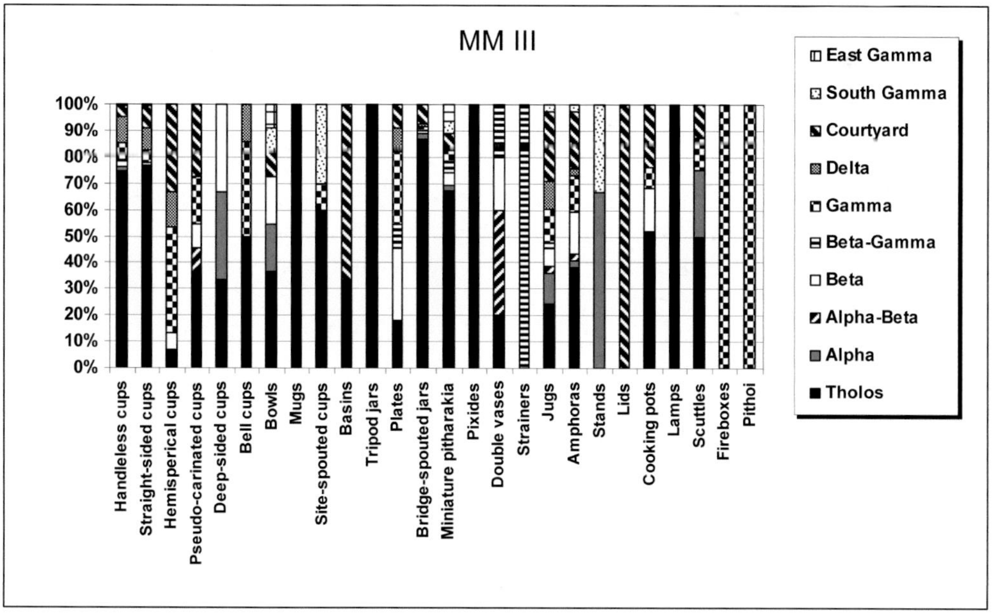

Figure 7.4: Distribution of vessels by room in Tholos A during the MM III.

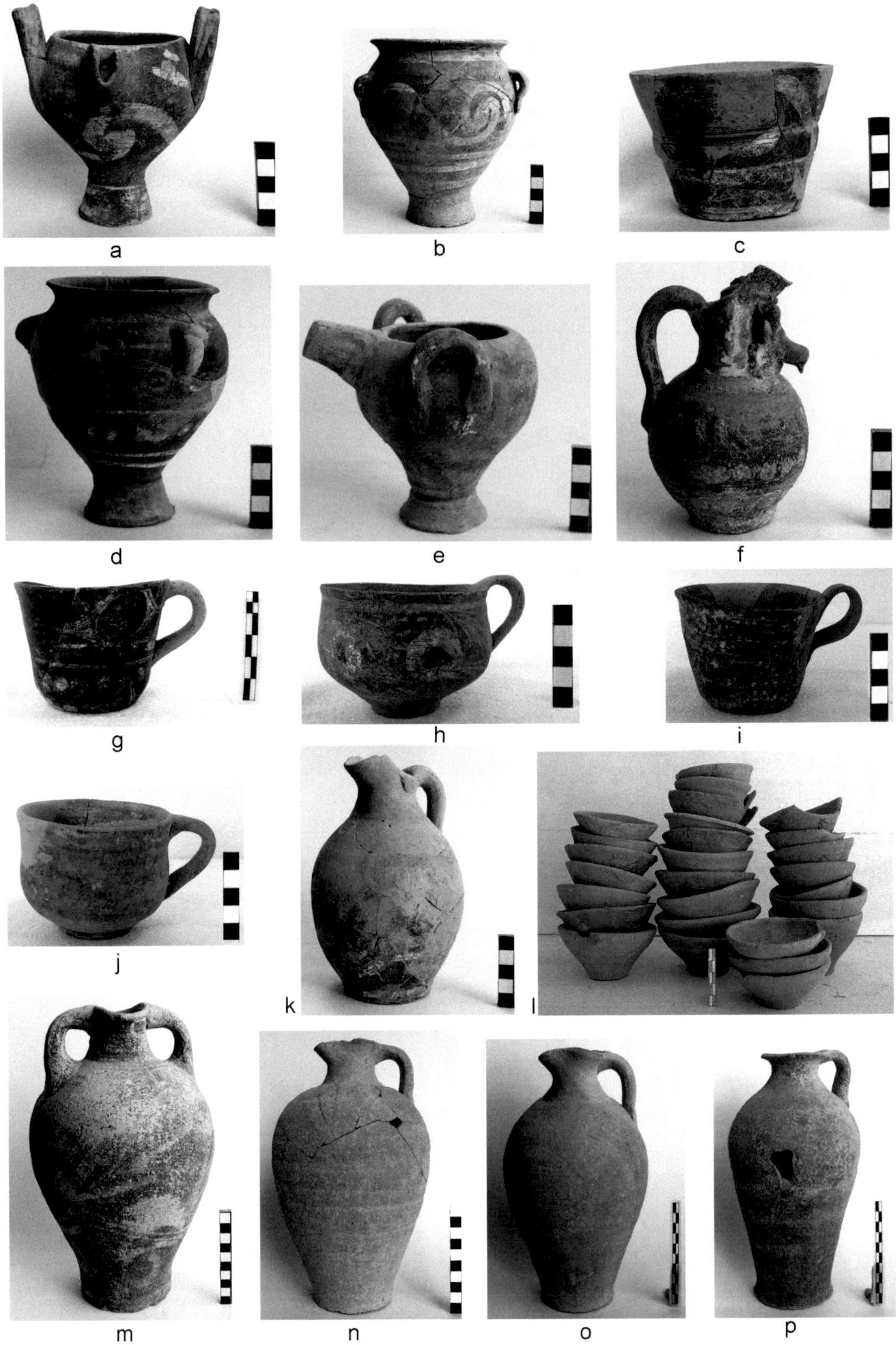

Figure 7.5: Selection of MM III vessels from Tholos A. a = F 2951; b = F 3138; c = F 3202; d = F 3135; e = F 2924; f = F 2638; g = F 3218; h = F 3276; I = F 3264; j = F 3068; k = F 3181; m = 2723; n = F 2721a; o = F 2720; p = F 2787. (Photos author).

liquids or perfumes (small *pitharakia* and two handled footed *stamnoi*). There is also a larger volume of closed shapes mostly for pouring or transport purposes (jugs of medium and large size and oval mouthed amphoras) (Figure 7.5m–p). Cooking ware still occurs with some large specimens of mainly tripod pots (Girella 2011: pl. XLIa). Finally, imports in dark-on-light lustrous ware, probably from North and Eastern Crete, are also found. The deposition of stone vessels, with the exception of a few specimens identified in the outer area (Levi 1961–62: figs. 108, 110), seems not to have been widespread after MM II. In contrast, six of the twenty seals found in the tomb can be dated between MM IIB and MM III (Levi 1961–62: figs. 126.2, 4, 131–32, 139–41; Platon *et al.* 1977: 11, 15, 16–19; Fiandra 1995). Five further MM seals may be related with Tholos A, respectively three included in the Metaxas collection (Sakellarakis and Kenna 1969: CMS IV. 77, 79, 91), a fourth collected during a survey in the area (Platon 1969: 452) and a last one recovered at the stratigraphical museum of Phaistos, possibly dating to the LM IA (Militello 2002: 88, fig. 22).

Judging from the composition of the pottery assemblages in terms of shapes and wares from MM II to III, the number of participants in each ceremony clearly increased towards the end of the period; however, MM III sees only minor changes in the performance of these rituals. Liquid consumption basically continues the earlier trend but there is a growing emphasis on formalised drinking ceremonies: it is important to stress the disappearance from both the palace and tholos tomb of carinated cups and eggshell ware, and the preference for a few shapes, mostly handleless cups and straight-sided cups among the drinking shapes, bridge-spouted jars and juglets for pouring and miniature *pitharakia* for offerings.

Thus far the picture speaks in favour of a general continuity within the MM period (Figure 7.6). It is tempting, however, to envisage a more complex scenario. On the one hand, funerals seem to entail almost the same aspects in terms of the burials practices and the composition of the offerings, suggesting a social organisation with kinship relations based on clans, as was already evident in the late Prepalatial period (Branigan 1991). On the other hand, ware diversities and shape repertoire, as well as the presence of seals accompanying the dead, might attest to differing units of basic production. Not only was seal-owning an important attribute underlying the social position of people, it also stresses for the first time the involvement of owners with palatial affairs (Relaki 2012), and the access to economic resources. Therefore, the progressive affiliation of the Kamilari community with Phaistos illuminates the growing network of social relations operating after MM IB, a network that has been recently advocated on the basis of pottery and seal production and consumption (Todaro 2012; Relaki 2012). Similarly, the strong affinity of fine polychrome Kamares vessels with those found in great numbers at Phaistos likely indicates the existence of internal diversity within the Kamilari community, while shared forms of decoration accentuate communal identity at the settlement level. The above reconstructed picture for the entire MM period might suggest the existence of communities still characterised by groups occupying different social positions where the organisation

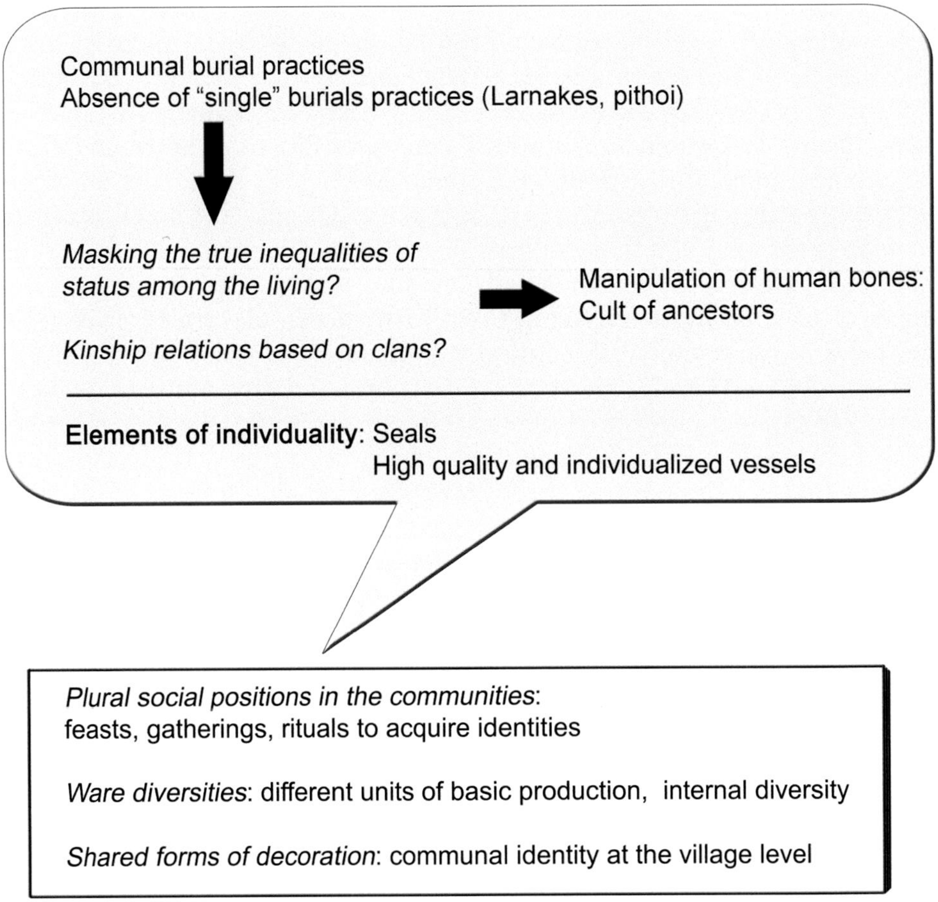

Figure 7.6: Diagram showing the burial and ritual setting of Tholos A in the MM period.

of feasts, gatherings, and rituals was probably an essential part of an ongoing struggle to occupy and define these positions (Branigan 2008).

In LM IA and LM IB the tomb enters a period of a significant change. Not only the quantity, but also the character of the assemblages change (Levi 1961–62: figs. 40, 54, 89–92, 112; Novaro 1999: figs. 1–14) (Figure 7.7). Aside from a well known package of MM III forms (handleless and straight-sided cups, bridge-spouted jars and small *pitharakia*), other shapes are now attested, such as bell and rhytoid cups, strainers, fireboxes as well as new types of *stamnoi* and rhyta. Light-on-dark ware (mostly on bridge-spouted jars and small *pitharakia*) notably persists beyond MM IIIB but dark-on-light lustrous ware becomes more widespread, the latter decorated with wavy lines, tangent spirals, running spirals, also with solid disks, tortoise-shell ripple, nets, quirks, reeds, horizontal and vertical foliate bands, crocuses, double axes, interlock wavy lines, and circles. Significantly, the deposition of seals does not stop in LM I (Levi

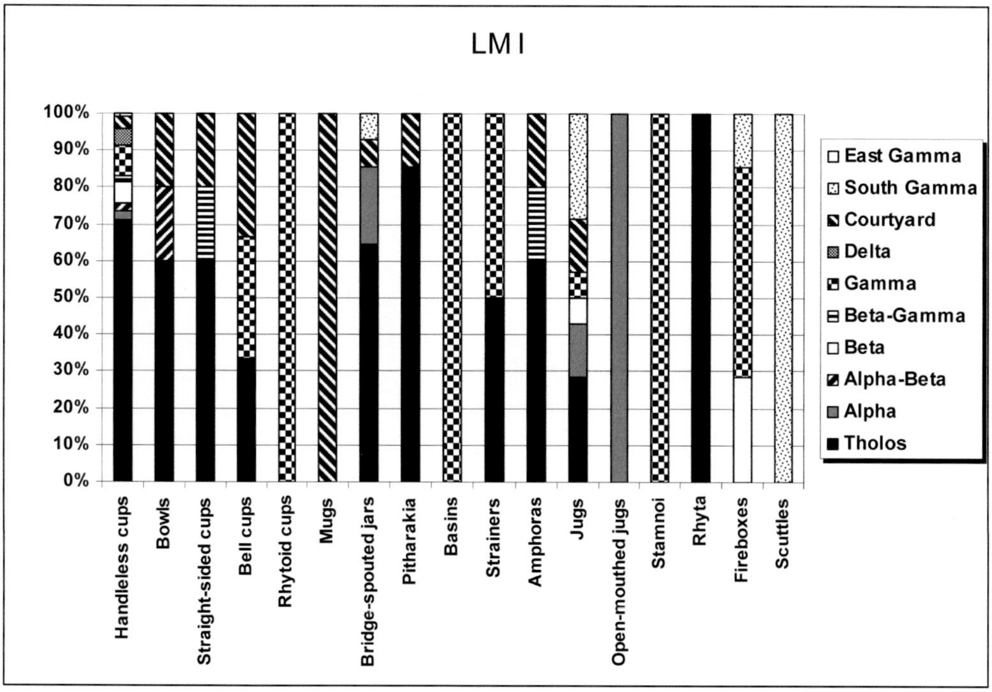

Figure 7.7: Distribution of vessels by room in Tholos A during the LM I.

1961–62: figs. 142–45; Fiandra 1995), suggesting that, although the tomb apparently received far fewer burials than in MM III, it continued to be used as a burial place. The circular chamber remains the preferred area for offering deposition, although room *g* and the outer courtyard are still used too. However, the emphasis on the annex rooms is definitely new. The chronological setting of the extraordinary clay models (Levi 1961–62: figs. 170, 174, 177–78; Lefèvre-Novaro 2001) and the identification in the excavation notebooks of the same depositional level (Novaro 1999: 152–54) enables us to visualise specific actions connected with the funerary ritual in the post-liminal phase or a differently choreographed cult of the dead. In any case, the strengthening of mortuary practices by the reproduction of actions in clay is unique and suggests a different relation between the tomb and its community by means of the plastic embodiment of specific rituals in honour of the dead.

The Post-palatial period

The re-use of the Kamilari cemetery in the Mycenaean period is thus far confirmed only for Tholos A (Levi 1961–62: figs. 32–4, 37–9, 41–5, 57–8; Girella forthcoming: figs. 3–4). This tomb has been used without interruption from LM IB down to LM IIIA2/B, although the existence of a clear LM IIIB ceramic horizon in the tholos is questionable, for the unpublished sherds identified are really few, not very significant and probably hinting at a transitional IIIA2/B phase. Again, there are remarkable changes in the composition of offerings. Although the circular chamber remains the main area of deposition both for ceramic and non-ceramic material, kylikes and bowls are found in the outer area (Girella forthcoming: fig. 3), as well as stirrup jars, suggesting that toasting, libation, or smashing of vessels were carried out as part of a *ritual of separation* (Cavanagh and Mee 1998: 112) (Figure 7.8). Particular emphasis is now paid to the dead body, as one can infer from the use of larnakes within the circular chamber (Levi 1961–62: figs. 22–3, 31) as well as the deposition of vessels likely to have been containers for unguents or perfumed substances (pyxides, alabastra, miniature jugs) (Levi 1961–62: figs. 32–3, 38–9, 42–3; Girella forthcoming: fig. 4), objects for personal adornment of the dead, such as jewellery (Levi 1961-62: pl. IV), and bronze implements (Levi 1961-62: figs. 147–51). This new package of ceramic shapes and other items betray a complex structure of roles within funerary ritual. Finally, the deposition of a LM IIIA Mitannian faience or glass cylinder seal, despite its precise context being unknown (Levi 1961–62: figs. 124.7, 133; Platon *et al.* 1977: 7; Pini 1981: 61, 74, pl. 12.3–4), hints at the possible continuation of this specific custom.

The presence of several LM II (or LM IIIA1) complete (Levi 1961–62: figs. 34, 41, 42a, 57) or mendable vessels among the unpublished material deserves some attention. LM II is, in fact, hardly identifiable at Hagia Triada as well as at Phaistos, although there are several rich secondary deposits at Kommos (Watrous 1992: 20–27, 29–30; Rutter

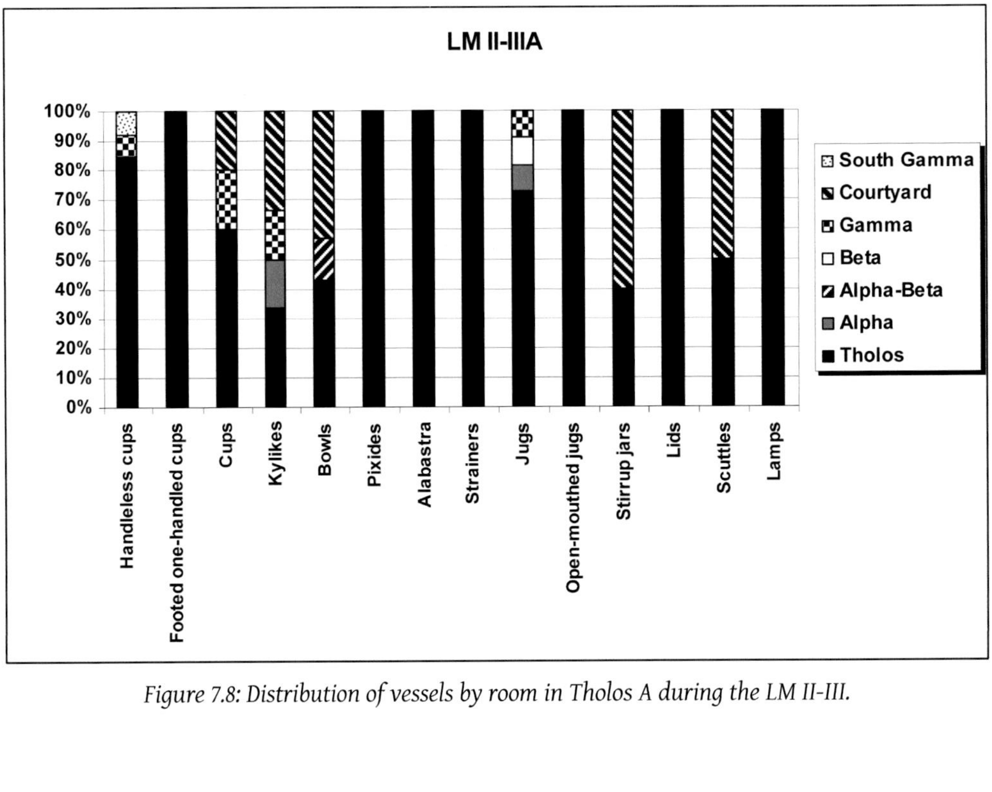

Figure 7.8: Distribution of vessels by room in Tholos A during the LM II-III.

2006: 505–15). However, after the LM IB destructions and the consequent change of the social scenery in the region, Tholos A at Kamilari is now the only tomb that is re-used. Thus, it seems that urban life in the Kamilari area was replaced by small-scale communities (Watrous and Hadzi–Vallianou 2004: 298–300) which very likely led to a retrenchment of collective ceremonies. As we have briefly described, after LM IB, rituals shift from emphasising the *living participants* to stressing the importance of the *dead body*: an emphasis now on personal objects, the small number of feasting/dining implements, and the striking division between the inner chamber and the outer area suggest that the dead were interwoven differently with the rest of the community. The use of Tholos A during LM IIIA corresponds to the *floruit* of the western Mesara when both Hagia Triada and Kommos grew in size and monumentality (Watrous and Hadzi–Vallianou 2004: 300–01). On the other hand, the lack of LM IIIB pottery can be a clear sign of the strong settlement retrenchment that the region underwent (Watrous and Hadzi–Vallianou 2004: 304).

Towards the construction of a funerary landscape

Consolidation and homologation

The long occupation of the cemetery together with the mass of the material collected from Tholos A, in particular, necessitates the consideration of the relationship between the cemetery and its landscape. The accumulation of material from different periods at Kamilari suggests that the community had a very strong sense of place. In particular, Tholos A remains a focus of activity, but the different form of these human additions to the landscape indicates changing perceptions between the present and the past, as well as the role of the dead and the ancestors (Gosden and Head 1994; Ucko and Layton 1999). Admittedly, in our view, the diachronic changes that took place at Kamilari might reflect common social practices based on a largely integrated regional landscape.

The construction of tholos tombs in MM IB at the twilight of tholos-building demands some explanation. On the one hand, it is likely that the setting up of the cemetery represents the conscious "appropriation of a pre-existing EBA *medium* in order to serve different social strategies" (Relaki 2004: 182). On the other hand, spatial aspects highlight a different conception of this tholos cemetery: the study of the unpublished material from Tholos B seems to demonstrate that the earliest material is datable to MM IIB (Caloi 2011: 104); similarly, we know that Tholos C was in use during the Protopalatial period (Branigan 1976: 169, pl. 2). Bearing in mind the poorly preserved state of Tholos B and its architectural similarity with Hagia Triada Tholos B, built during MM IB, one cannot rule out the construction of Kamilari tholos B already within MM IB. If this was the case, one could argue that all three tombs were simultaneously constructed and used in the area. Otherwise, the construction of Kamilari Tholos B and C in MM II would reflect the enlargement of the Kamilari settlement and its consolidation within the Phaistian territory at the acme of Protopalatial period. Significantly, traces of a small settlement have been recognised 150 m South – South-west of Tholos C, apparently not later than MM II (Watrous and Hadzi-Vallianou 2004: 536, site n. 68). Moreover, it is tempting to see a rank-size relationship within the cemetery: Tholos A was the most visible tomb and may have functioned as a proper landmark in the cemetery from the beginning of its construction (Murphy 1998: 27–32), also due to the monumentality of its vaulted roof that must have had a significant impact on the landscape (Girella *et al.* 2013). As with other megalithic tombs, it is highly probable that Tholos A fulfilled the role of a territorial marker (Saxe 1970; Renfrew 1976; Bender 1992). If such interpretation is correct, the cluster of the three tholos tombs suggests that, although at a setting not strictly related to the palace area, the cemetery was still consciously related to the natural landscape around the palace and conceived to control it. Moreover, surveys have demonstrated the existence of an intense settlement density between 2 and 4 km South and South-west of Phaistos. In the area of the Kamilari cemetery, in particular, a small settlement is located West of Tholos A and South of Tholos C within a distance of 100–200 metres (Watrous *et al.* 1993: 225; Watrous and Hadzi–Vallianou 2004: 528, 535, fig. 10.1, sites nos. 7, 68), whereas other traces of settlements are located within almost 1 km West and East of the cemetery (Watrous and Hadzi–Vallianou 2004: 533, 536, fig. 10.1, sites nos. 49, 76).

Within a wider perspective, MM IB is a watershed that sees the end of competition between factions and a coalescence of some factions around the construction of the palace at Phaistos (Warren 1987). It is also the period that sees an exponential increase in the number of known sites in the surrounding region (from 7 to 39 according to the most recent surveys carried out at the Phaistos area: Watrous and Hadzi–Vallianou 2004: 277–84). Likewise, in the cemetery of Hagia Triada, while MM IB is a phase of strong continuity with the earlier ritual traditions: Hagia Triada Tholos A was occupied continuously until MM IIA and Hagia Triada Tholos B, which shows strong architectural similarities with both Kamilari A and B tombs, was built just a few metres away (Paribeni 1904; Carinci 2003: 112–13). Under these circumstances, it is possible to argue that the range of wares (monochrome, barbotine, dark-on-light) and shapes represented at Kamilari is the result of the cultural homologation and the political affiliation of this area to Phaistos.

MM II is an extremely innovative phase, and again the cemetery maintains a special bond with Phaistos and Hagia Triada. The emphasis on the ritual sphere at the Phaistos palace – as suggested by the construction of the North-west building and the *kouloures,* as well as the production of ritual representations in the form of figurines and of figured representation on pottery (Militello 2012) – signals not only a significant increase in the economic role of the palace, but also indicates the spread of a common ritual language in the area.

At Kamilari, Tholos A and B were both functioning and it is highly probable that Tholos C, too, was occupied. However, in MM II, only Tholos A shows signs of very complex rituals: the tomb with its annexes suggests the involvement of both larger and more restricted groups of participants. Both the monumentality and the character of the ceramic material from Tholos A show that this tomb engaged in some form of competition with the other two tombs that made it dominant in the territory. In fact, Tholos B is simpler in its architecture and lacks very high quality ceramic material which seems to reflect some internal division within the cemetery and perhaps in the related settlement. Rather than joining the Kamilari cemetery directly to Hagia Triada or Phaistos, it is altogether more reasonable to believe that both these centres (with Phaistos at the head), may have exercised some influence in the Kamilari area with regard to ritual by means of the possession, circulation, and use/exhibition of high quality and highly decorated vessels (Appadurai 1986). Following in this vein, it is likely that the settlement(s) connected to the Kamilari cemetery must have contributed food and labour to the Phaistian palatial centre. Moreover, by assuming a population of c. 3000 persons, Watrous calculates that an area of 1500-3000 ha was necessary to feed the urban populace (Watrous and Hadzi–Vallianou 2004: 282, fig. 10.5), with the consequence that Kamilari falls approximately along the western border of the hypothetical palace catchment area.

A second and related issue is to understand whether the three tholos tombs were used by a single community which was socially stratified or by three different ones. Significantly, the case of Kamilari finds a good parallel in the Apesokari cemetery, where Tombs I and II were set at several hundred metres from each other (Matz 1951: 13–22; Davaras 1964: 441; Flouda 2011; Vavouranakis 2012), contrary to Platanos or Koumasa (Legarra Herrero 2011). In fact, we can observe a different organisation of the cemeteries, probably hinting at a diverse interaction between cemeteries and settlements after MM IB. The distance between the three tholos tombs may speak in favour of multiple-settlements in the area; however, the dimensions of Tholos A as well as the occurrence of one space devoted to ritual performances concerning the participation of the living suggests the existence of a ranked settlement organisation. It is worth stressing that the complete study on the human remains from both Tholos A and B could also illuminate the composition of groups buried in both tombs, whether, for instance, these reflected or not different population segments based on age or sex criteria (Triantaphyllou and Girella forthcoming).

In any case, the circulation and possession of distinct ceramic styles promoted new social habits and favoured the establishment of central authorities. Also, through the adoption of specific palatial repertoires (mostly the use of handleless cups, jugs, bridge-spouted jars and carinated cups) and by adopting palatial convivial practices, groups outside the palace asserted their nearness to the palatial elites. Following this perspective, the deposition of seals from MM II onwards can aid in the identification of these elite groups, since seals, despite being largely administrative tools, also reflected the status of specific segments of the population (Whitelaw 1983: 343; Karytinos 1998; Relaki 2012: 299–300, 317). More specifically, as already noted by Fiandra (1995) from a formal perspective, it should be stressed that the Protopalatial seals at Kamilari have close comparisons with some seals impressions from Phaistos. The ritual deposition of seals among other offerings may be a sign of individuality within a larger practice that emphasised a "group ideology".

From communal to individual identities

Different patterns are evidenced at the Kamilari cemetery in the Neopalatial period, reflecting a straightforward relation with the historical and social changes that took place in the Phaistos area between MM III and LM IB. In MM III there are only minor changes in the performing of rituals in Tholos A and B. As we have seen, the composition of ceramic sets reflects the Protopalatial custom of drinking, while the monotonous occurrence of specific shapes continues the old ceremonial practices. New aspects include a decreased interest in the deposition of stone vessels and new dimensions of libation connected with symbols such as the *agrimi* (Figure 7.5f). Significantly, in MM III, the deposition of seals might testify to the existence of internal variations among the groups that use Tholos A in MM III. It is perhaps relevant to note that, in addition to continued comparisons with Phaistian seal impressions, other seals emulate Knossian examples.

It has been already noted that Kamilari is very different from other late MM tholos tombs in southern Crete (Girella 2004). The absence of shifts in burial practices, mainly from collective to single inhumations (such as attested at Vorou; Marinatos 1930–31) is worthy of note as this might reflect the absence of major segmentations, such as differences of age, sex, and status. Even more striking are the differences from burial patterns in North-central Crete (Girella 2004; 2013), where a more varied funerary landscape may reflect a more "hierarchical society in a more dynamic and open system of social segmentation" (Girella 2013). One preliminary conclusion is that a different funerary ideology attested in the Kamilari area would reflect a society organised in larger family groups (Girella 2013). In particular, estimation of the minimum number of individuals based on the ongoing human bone analysis from Tholos A (Triantaphyllou in this volume; Triantaphyllou and Girella forthcoming) amounts to some 17 corpses per century, which approaches the composition of a nuclear family of 5 to 7 members (Bintliff 1977). Furthermore, individuals of all age groups – even neonates – and both sexes have been recognised in the human remains. Therefore the hypothesis that family groups have been accommodated in Tholos A can be securely supported by the preliminary results of the osteological study.

It is also important to situate the evidence from the Kamilari cemetery into the political landscape of the region during MM III, when the collapse of the main power centre at Phaistos and the failure of re-building it shifted power and administrative activities towards Hagia Triada after MM IIIB (La Rosa 2002; Girella 2010a: 345–56). Accordingly, the acme of the occupation of Kamilari Tholos A after the two destructions of MM IIB and MM IIIA still requires explanation. This may have been either to connect with the dead after a cataclysm or, after a movement of people toward the coast (Girella 2010a: 350), to initiate the subsequent re-population of the area. In either case, the evidence from Kamilari hints at the persistence of Protopalatial funerary practices that might have served as an ideological strategy to bond the social groups living in the area, perhaps in reaction to the turmoil that undermined the political structure of the region. As observed also for Phaistos (Girella 2010b: 87–88), elites do not necessarily disappear even when there is a striking reduction in the scale of a political centre. However, the record from Kamilari suggests that funerary ideology continues to function albeit at a reduced level of visibility.

After MM III the cemetery of Kamilari seems to have been limited to restricted groups of people. LM I corresponds to another watershed; local histories indicate considerable shifting configurations of political power in the region, starting from a more institutionalised Knossian hegemony (Warren 2004) and continuing into the fully-debated turmoil of LM IB (Driessen and Macdonald 1997: 105–15). Specifically, the birth of autonomous small centres and mansions, such as Selì, Kouses, and, farther away, Pitsidia and Kannia may be signs of a strong renovation of the region which probably started within MM III, soon after the collapse of the palace at Phaistos (Watrous *et al.* 1993; Cucuzza 2001; Watrous and Hadzi–Vallianou 2004: 291–98, fig. 10.9, table 10.2). The funerary context shows a particular strategy to negotiate the social aspects of this period (Figure 7.9): patterns of continuity and diversity suggest the appropriation of the funerary locale to reinforce the social power of groups in a territory that confronted a growing settlement transformation. In fact, this alteration may well have caused specific problems for some groups or extended families, such as access to water or fertile lands, and that this, following the re-establishment of power centres, could have generated competitions among groups.

Finally, Tholos A sheds light on the local histories in the political landscape during the Mycenaean period that first saw its control by the palace at Knossos and then its collapse. The most striking element that emerges from Mycenaean Kamilari is the contrast between the continuous occupation of the same funerary locale and a remarkable lack of uniformity in burial choices (Cucuzza 2002). Larnax burials were adopted inside an older Minoan tholos tomb, i.e. Tholos A at Kamilari, while the chamber tombs at Kalyvia, close to Phaistos have simple inhumations, and at Goudies larnax burials are placed inside a chamber tomb. At Hagia Triada there is a partial re-use of Tholos B (again with larnax burials), as well as the construction of the unique "house tomb" which accommodated the famous stone sarcophagus, only at a distance of a few metres. Despite their geographical proximity these tombs and cemeteries show great differences in architecture, assemblages and burial customs. Although explanations might be found in economy, religion, ethnicity, or gender distinctions, the diversification of tomb and burial types in this region in LM II and IIIA might be part of a process of Mycenaeanisation (Cucuzza 2002; Preston 2004: 333–37). The overall impression is that segments of the community moved on different trajectories by manipulating the mortuary context or emulating the Knossian language.

In conclusion, while awaiting final publication of the Kamilari material and its relation to tomb architecture, this paper argues that the archaeological record shows

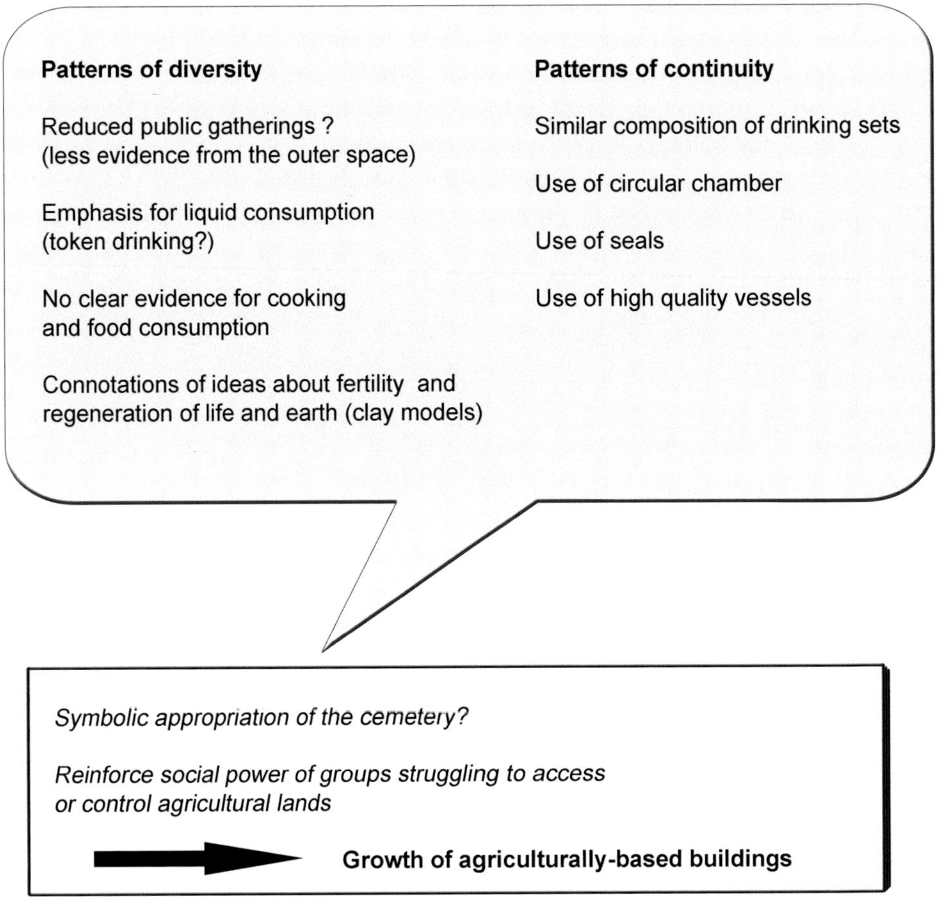

Figure 7.9: Diagram showing the burial and ritual setting of Tholos A in the LM I period.

a spatially continuous pattern within a dynamic social and political context. Thus, the continuity of place together with the diachronic variables that affected the history of the tholos tombs in different periods are essential ingredients in grasping the patterns of transformation within the funerary landscape.

Acknowledgements

I would like to thank the organizers, Maria Relaki and Yiannis Papadatos, for inviting me to the conference and for covering my travel and accommodation expenses. Financial support for this research was generously provided by the Institute of Aegean Prehistory and by the 2007–2009 Progetto di Ricerca Nazionale (PRIN) and the University of Venice, which has funded a post-doctoral position under the supervision of F. Carinci. I am indebted to the late V. La Rosa for granting me permission to study and publish the material from Kamilari. For the permission to study the material stored at the Heraklion Museum I would like to thank the former Director Athanasia Kanta and the former Director of the Italian Archaeological School of Athens, Emanuele Greco, for facilitating my research and accommodation. I am particularly grateful to Peter Warren, Borja Legarra Herrero, Sevi Triantaphyllou and Judith Weingarten who provided useful information and criticisms on an earlier version of this paper. The last one also tries her patience with my English. I am also extremely grateful to Dr. S. Triantaphyllou (Aristotle University of Thessaloniki) for providing me with some preliminary information from her ongoing study of the human bones from the cemetery funded by the Institute of the Aegean Prehistory and the Mediterranean Archaeological Trust. All remaining faults are my own.

Bibliography

Alexiou, S.

1957 Η αρχαιολογική κίνησις εν Κρήτη κατά το έτος 1957, Χρονικά. *Κρητικά Χρονικά* 11: 326–43.

Alexiou, S. and P. M. Warren

2004 *The Early Minoan Tombs of Lebena, Southern Crete* (Studies in Mediterranean Archaeology 30). Sävedalen: Åström.

Appadurai, A.

1986 Introduction: commodities and the politics of value. In A. Appadurai (ed.), *The Social Life of Things. Commodities in Cultural Perspective*: 3–63. Cambridge: Cambridge University Press.

Barrett, J. C.

1988 The living, the dead and the ancestors: Neolithic and Early Bronze Age mortuary practices. In J. C. Barrett and I. A. Kinnes (eds.), *The Archaeology of Context in the Neolithic and Bronze Age: Recent Trends*: 30–56. Sheffield: University of Sheffield.

Belli, P.

1984 Nuovi documenti per lo studio delle tombe circolari cretesi. *Studi Micenei ed Egeo-Anatolici* 25: 91–143.

Bender, B.

1992 Theorising landscape, and the prehistoric landscapes of Stonehenge. *Man* 27: 735–55.

Bintliff, J. L.

1977 *Natural Environment and Human Settlement in Prehistoric Greece* (BAR IS 28). Oxford: British Archaeological Reports.

Borgna, E.

2004 Aegean feasting: a Minoan perspective. In J. C. Wright (ed.), *The Mycenaean Feast* (Hesperia Supplement 73): 127–59. Princeton: American School of Classical Studies at Athens.

Branigan, K.

1970 *The Tombs of Mesara*. London: Duckworth.

1976 A new tholos tomb at Kamilari, Crete. *Studi Micenei ed Egeo-Anatolici* 17: 161–71.

1984 Early Minoan society: the evidence of the Mesara Tholoi revised. In C. Nicolet (ed.), *Aux Origines de l'Hellénisme: La Crète et la Grèce. Hommages à Henri Van Effenterre*: 29–37. Paris: Centres Gustav Glotz.

1991 Funerary ritual and social cohesion in Early Bronze Age Crete. *Journal of Mediterranean Studies* 1: 183–92.

1993 *Dancing with Death: Life and Death in Southern Crete c. 3000–2000 B.C.* Amsterdam: A. M. Hakkert.

1998 The nearness of you: proximity and distance in Early Minoan funerary behaviour. In K. Branigan (ed.), *Cemetery and Society in the Aegean Bronze Age* (Sheffield Studies in Aegean Archaeology 1): 13–26. Sheffield: Sheffield Academic Press.

2008 Communal ceremonies in an Early Minoan tholos cemetery. In C. Gallou, M. Georgiadis and G. Muskett (eds.), *Dioskouroi. Studies Presented to W. G. Cavanagh and C. B. Mee on the Anniversary of Their 30-Year Joint Contribution to Aegean Archaeology* (BAR IS 1889): 15–22. Oxford: Archaeopress.

Caloi, I.

2009 *I Depositi Ceramici MM IB-MM IIB Dalla Tholos di Kamilari Nella Messarà (Creta)*. PhD dissertation, University of Firenze.

2011 Changes and evolution in funerary and non-funerary rituals during the Protopalatial period in the Mesara plain (Crete): the evidence from Kamilari and from the other tholos tombs. *Rivista di Archeologia* XXXV: 97–110.

Campbell-Green, T.

2006 *Cemetery, Ceramics and Space. An Analysis of the Pottery Assemblage from the Early Minoan Cemetery of Moni Odiyitria, South Central Crete, with Specific Reference to its Function*. PhD dissertation, University of Sheffield.

Carinci, F.

2003 Haghia Triada nel periodo medio minoico. *Creta Antica* 4: 97–143.

2006 Circolazione interna e funzioni del settore sud dell'ala occidentale del Primo Palazzo di Festòs. In *Πεπραγμένα του Θ' Διεθνούς Κρητολογικού Συνεδρίου*, vol. A1: 23–39. Ηράκλειο: Εταιρία Κρητικών Ιστορικών Μελετών.

Cavanagh, W. and C. Mee

1998 *A Private Place: Death in Prehistoric Greece* (Studies in Mediterranean Archaeology 125). Jonsered: P. Åström.

Cucuzza, N.

2001 Il sito di Selì in rapporto agli altri centri del circondario. In V. La Rosa and N. Cucuzza (eds.), *L'insediamento di Selì di Kamilari Nel Territorio di Festòs* (Studi di Archeologia Cretese I): 223–28. Padova: Bottega D'Erasmo.

2002 Osservazioni sui costumi funerari dell'area di Festòs ed Haghia Triada nel TM III A1-A2 iniziale. *Creta Antica* 3: 133–66.

Davaras, C.

1964 Αρχαιότητες και μνημεία της Κρήτης. *Αρχαιολογικόν Δελτίον* 19: 441–42.

Driessen, J. and C. F. Macdonald

1997 *The Troubled Island: Minoan Crete before and after the Santorini Eruption* (Aegaeum 17). Liège: University of Liège.

Englezou, M.

1988–89 Τα ειδώλια του Καμηλαρίου. *Κρητικά Χρονικά* 28–29: 64–85.

Fiandra, E.

1995 Change and continuity in the MM III: the tomb of Kamilari. In W. Müller (ed.), *Sceaux Minoens et Mycéniens. IVe Symposium International 10-12 September 1992, Clermont-Ferrand* (CMS Beiheft 5): 77–85. Berlin: Gebr. Mann.

Flouda, G.

2011 Reassessing the Apesokari Tholos A funerary records: preliminary thoughts. *Rivista di Archeologia* XXV: 111–21.

Gerontakou, E.

2003 Δύο Μεσομινωικοί αποθέτες από το νεκροταφείο του Πλατάνου. In A. Vlachopoulos and K. Birtacha (eds.), *ΑΡΓΟΝΑΥΤΗΣ Τιμητικός τόμος για τον Καθηγητή Χρίστο Ντούμα απο τους μαθητές του στο Πανεπιστήμιο Αθηνών (1980-2000)*: 303–30. Athens: Kathimerini A.E.

Girella, L.

2003 *La Produzione Ceramica del Medio Minoico III e L'inizio Dell'età Neopalaziale a Creta*. PhD dissertation, University of Udine.

2004 La *morte ineguale*. Per una lettura delle evidenze funerarie nel Medio Minoico III a Creta. *Annuario della Scuola archeologica di Atene e delle Missioni italiane in Oriente* 80(1): 259–310.

2007 Toward a definition of the Middle Minoan III ceramic sequence in South-Central Crete: returning to the traditional MM IIIA and IIIB division? In F. Felten, W. Gauß and R. Smetana (eds.), *Middle Helladic Pottery and Synchronisms. Proceedings of the International Workshop held at Salzburg, October 31st to November 2nd, 2004*. (Ägina – Kolonna. Forschungen und Ergebnisse, Band 1): 233–55. Wien: Österreichische Akademie der Wissenschaften.

2010a *Depositi Ceramici del Medio Minoico III da Festòs e Haghia Triada* (Studi di Archeologia Cretese VIII). Padova: Bottega D'Erasmo.

2010b A view of MM IIIA at Phaistos: pottery production and consumption at the beginning of the Neopalatial period. *Aegean Archaeology* 9: 49–89.

2011 The Kamilari project publication. *Rivista di Archeologia* XXXV: 123–36.

2013 Exhuming an excavation: preliminary notes on the use of the Kamilari tholos tomb in Middle Minoan III. In C. F. Macdonald and C. Knappett (eds.), *Intermezzo. Intermediacy and Regeneration in Middle Minoan III Crete. Villa Ariadne, Knossos, 3–5 July 2008* (BSA Studies 21): 149–59. London: British School at Athens.

forthcoming The Kamilari Tholos Tombs Project: new light on an old excavation. *Πεπραγμένα του ΙΑ' Διεθνούς Κρητολογικού Συνεδρίου, Ρέθυμνο 21–27 Οκτωβρίου 2011*. Ρέθυμνο: Ιστορική και Λαογραφική Εταιρεία Ρεθύμνης.

Girella, L., A. Marini and G. Palmieri

2013 Problems of roofing of Early Minoan tholos tombs: the case of Kamilari a tholos tomb in the western Mesara plain. *Creta Antica* 14: 69–103.

Goodison, L. and C. Guarita

2005 A new catalogue of the Mesara-type tombs. *Studi Micenei ed Egeo-Anatolici* 47: 171–212.

Gosden, C. and L. Head

1994 Landscape. A usefully ambiguous concept. In L. Head, C. Gosden and J. P. White (eds.), *Social Landscapes*: 113–16. Sydney: Archaeology in Oceania.

Haggis, D. C.

2007 Stylistic diversity and diacritical feasting at Protopalatial Petras: a preliminary analysis of the Lakkos deposit. *American Journal of Archaeology* 111: 715–75.

Hamilakis, Y.

2013 *Archaeology and Senses. Human Experience, Memory, and Affect*. Cambridge: Cambridge University Press.

Karytinos, A.

1998 Sealstones in cemeteries: a display of social status? In K. Branigan (ed.), *Cemetery and Society in the Aegean Bronze Age* (Sheffield Studies in Aegean Archaeology 1): 78–86. Sheffield: Sheffield Academic Press.

Knappett, C. and C. F. Macdonald

2007 *Knossos: Protopalatial Deposits in Early Magazine A and the South-West Houses* (BSA Supplementary Volume 41). Oxford and Northampton: British School at Athens.

La Rosa, V.

2002 Pour une révision préliminaire du Second Palais de Phaistos. In J. Driessen, I. Schoep and R. Laffineur (eds.), *Monuments of Minos. Rethinking the Minoan Palaces. Proceedings of the International Workshop 'Crete of the Hundred Palaces? Louvain-la-Neuve, 14–15 December 2001* (Aegaeum 23): 71–97. Liège: Université de Liège.

Lefèvre-Novaro, D.

2001 Un nouvel examen des modèles réduits trouvés dans la grande tombe de Kamilari (Messarà - Crète). In R. Laffineur and R. Hägg (eds.), *Potnia: Deities and Religion in the Aegean*

Bronze Age. Proceedings of the 8th International Aegean Conference, Göteborg, 12–15 April 2000 (Aegaeum 22): 89–98. Liège: Université de Liège.

Legarra Herrero, B.

2009 The Minoan fallacy: cultural diversity and mortuary behaviour on Crete at the beginning of the Bronze Age. *Oxford Journal of Archaeology* 28.1: 29–57.

2011 The secret lives of the Early and Middle Minoan tholos cemeteries: Koumasa and Platanos. In J. M. A. Murphy (ed.), *Prehistoric Crete: Regional and Diachronic Studies on Mortuary Systems*: 48–84. Philadelphia: INSTAP Academic Press.

2014 *Mortuary Behaviour and Social Trajectories in Pre- and Protopalatial Crete.* (Prehistory Monographs 44). Philadelphia: INSTAP Academic Press.

Levi, D.

1961–62 La tomba a tholos di Kamilari presso a Festòs. *Annuario della Scuola Archeologica di Atene e delle Missioni Italiane in Oriente* 49–50: 7–148.

1976 *Festòs e la Civiltà Minoica. I* (Incunabula Graeca LX). Roma: Edizioni dell'Ateneo.

Marinatos, S.

1930–31 Δύο Πρώιμοι Μινωικοί τάφοι εκ Βορού Μεσαράς. *Αρχαιολογικόν Δελτίον* 13: 137–70.

Matz, F.

1951 *Forschungen auf Kreta, 1942.* Berlin: W. de Gruyter.

Militello, P.

2002 Amministrazione e contabilità a Festòs. II. Il contesto archeologico dei documenti palatini. *Creta Antica* 3: 51–91.

2012 Emerging authority: a functional analysis of the MM II settlement of Phaistos. In I. Schoep, J. Driessen and P. Tomkins (eds.), *Back to the Beginning: Reassessing Social, Economic and Political Complexity in the Early and Middle Bronze Age on Crete, Leuven 1–2 February 2008*: 236–72. Oxford: Oxbow.

Murphy, J. M. A.

1998 Ideologies, rites and rituals: a view of prepalatial Minoan tholoi. In K. Branigan (ed.), *Cemetery and Society in the Aegean Bronze Age* (Sheffield Studies in Aegean Archaeology 1): 27–40. Sheffield: Sheffield Academic Press.

2011 *Prehistoric Crete. Regional and Diachronic Studies on Mortuary Systems*: 48–84. Philadelphia: INSTAP Academic Press.

Novaro, D.

1999 I modellini fittili dalla tomba di Kamilari: il problema cronologico. In V. La Rosa, D. Palermo and L. Vagnetti (eds.), *Epi Ponton Plazomenoi. Simposio Italiano di Studi Egei Dedicato a L. Bernabò Brea e G. Pugliese Carratelli*: 151–60. Roma: Scuola Archeologica Italiana di Atene.

Pader, E.-J.

1982 *Symbolism, Social Relation and the Interpretation of Mortuary Remains* (BAR IS 130). Oxford: British Archaeological Reports.

Panagiotopoulos, D.

2002 *Das Tholosgrab E von Phourni bei Archanes. Studien zu Einem Frühkretischen Grabfund und Seine Kulturellen Kontext* (BAR IS 1014). Oxford: Archaeopress.

Papadatos, Y.

1999 *Mortuary Practices and Their Importance for the Reconstruction of Society and Life in Prepalatial Crete: the Evidence from the Tholos Tomb Gamma in Archanes-Phourni.* PhD dissertation, University of Sheffield.

2005 *Tholos Tomb Gamma: A Prepalatial Tholos Tomb at Phourni, Archanes* (Prehistory Monographs 17). Philadelphia: INSTAP Academic Press.

Paribeni, R.

1904 Ricerche sul sepolcreto di Haghia Triada presso Phaestos. *Monumenti Antici* 14: 677–756.

Parker Pearson, M.
1993 The powerful dead: archaeological relationships between the living and the dead. *Cambridge Archaeological Journal* 3: 203–29.
1999 *The Archaeology of Death and Burial*. Stroud: Sutton.
Pelon, O.
2004 Les tombes circulaires dans l'Égée de l'Âge du Bronze: état des questions. *Topoi* 4: 153–205.
Pini, I.
1981 Spätbronzezeitliche ägäische Glassiegel. *Jahrbuch des Römisch-germanischen Zentralmuseums* 28: 48–81.
Platon, N.
1969 *Corpus der Minoischen und Mykenischen Siegel. Iraklion, Archäologisches Museum. Band II, Teil 1. Die Siegel der Vorpalastzeit*. Berlin: Akademie der Wissenschaften und der Literatur Mainz.
Platon, N., I. Pini and G. Salies
1977 *Corpus der Minoischen und Mykenischen Siegel. Iraklion, Archäologisches Museum. Band II, Teil 2. Die Siegel der Altpalastzeit*. Berlin: Akademie der Wissenschaften und der Literatur Mainz.
Preston, L.
2004 A Mortuary perspective on political changes in Late Minoan II-IIIB Crete. *American Journal of Archaeology* 108: 321–48.
Relaki, M.
2004 Constructing a region: the contested landscapes of Prepalatial Mesara. In J. C. Barrett and P. Halstead (eds.), *The Emergence of Civilisation Revisited* (Sheffield Studies in Aegean Archaeology 6): 170–88. Oxford: Oxbow.
2012 The Social Arenas of Tradition. Investigating collective and individual social strategies in the Prepalatial and Protopalatial Mesara. In I. Schoep, J. Driessen and P. Tomkins (eds.), *Back to the Beginning: Reassessing Social, Economic and Political Complexity in the Early and Middle Bronze Age on Crete, Leuven 1-2 February 2008*: 290–324. Oxford: Oxbow.
Renfrew, C.
1976 Megaliths, territories and populations. In S. J. De Laet (ed.), *Acculturation and Continuity in Atlantic Europe* (Dissertationes Archaeologicae Gandenses): 198–220. Brugge: De Tempel.
Robb, J. E.
1994 Burial and social reproduction in the peninsular Italian Neolithic. *Journal of Mediterranean Archaeology* 7: 27–71.
2007 Burial treatment as transformations of bodily ideology. In N. Laneri (ed.), *Performing Burial*: 287–98. Chicago: Oriental Institute, University of Chicago.
Rutter, J. B.
2006 Minoan Pottery from the southern area: Neopalatial and Late Minoan Pottery. In J. W. Shaw and M. C. Shaw (eds.), *Kommos V. The Monumental Minoan Buildings at Kommos*: 377–630. Princeton and Oxford: Princeton University Press.
Sakellarakis J. A. and V. E. G. Kenna
1969 *Corpus der Minoischen und Mykenischen Siegel. Band IV. Iraklion. Sammlung Metaxas*. Berlin: Akademie der Wissenschaften und der Literatur Mainz.
Saxe, A. A.
1970 *Social Dimensions of Mortuary Practices*. PhD dissertation, University of Michigan.
Shanks, M. and C. Tilley
1984 Ideology, symbolic power and ritual communication: a reinterpretation of Neolithic mortuary practices. In R. Bradley and J. Gardiner (eds.), *Neolithic Studies: A Review of Some Current Research* (BAR 133): 189–218. Oxford: British Archaeological Reports.

Triantaphyllou 2005), the two tholos tombs at Moni Odigitria in the Mesara (Vasilakis and Branigan 2010; Triantaphyllou 2010a), the Kephala Petras rock shelter in Siteia (Tsipopoulou 2007; 2010; 2012b; Triantaphyllou 2009; 2012; 2016; 2017), the Livari cemetery on the South-east coast (Triantaphyllou 2009; Papadatos and Sofianou 2012; 2015), as well as the recently excavated cemetery of Prepalatial house tombs at Sissi on the North coast of Crete (Schoep 2009; Schoep *et al.* 2011; 2012; Crevecoeur and Schmitt 2009; Crevecoeur *et al.* 2015) have given much emphasis on taphonomic factors affecting the burial environment during and after the deposition of the human remains and associated artefacts. Contrary to the study of human bones, scholars of prehistoric funerary archaeology on Crete have expressed greater interest in the investigation of various data sets focusing primarily on the *built environment* – the funerary structures and auxiliary areas – the *material culture* worn, used and carried by the deceased and the living during funerary activities, and to a lesser degree, the *treatment of the deceased* (Branigan 1998; Murphy 1998; Papadatos 1999; 2005; Papadatos and Sofianou 2015; Legarra-Herrero 2009; 2014; 2016; Todaro and Girella 2016; Triantaphyllou 2016; 2017). More than twenty years ago, Keith Branigan in his pioneering article on *Ritual Interference with Human Bones in the Mesara Tholoi* (1987a) was the first to place aspects of manipulation of the deceased in the tholos tombs of the Mesara at the core of a discussion which until then had been largely concerned with the origins of the tombs and the typology of the architecture and associated finds. Drawing on his empirical observations but also on his long-term intensive research in the Mesara and the broader area of the Asterousia mountains, Branigan distinguished five different ways of human interference with the skeletal remains (Branigan 1987a: 45): *clearance* of human remains to dumps either within the tombs or outside them, *fumigation* of either bones or the entire tomb contents, *selected grouping* of certain bones, *selected removal* of certain bones from the tomb and the *breaking or chopping* of some long bones. This paper will discuss Branigan's modes of human interference alongside a critical distinction between primary and secondary burials in Prepalatial assemblages, based on new evidence from recently published and ongoing skeletal studies and will go a step further in exploring the demographic synthesis of the deceased as emerging from the mortuary assemblages discussed here.

Primary versus secondary burials: defining the problem in terminology

Prepalatial mortuary assemblages are predominantly represented by masses of disarticulated human remains housed in specially built collective structures – largely tholos tombs in the South and house tombs on the North coast of the island. The distinction between primary and secondary burial among archaeologists is a critical point in the discussion of the manipulation of the deceased (Bloch and Parry 1982; Metcalf and Huntington 1991; Parker Pearson 1999). The attempt to identify the key characteristics of primary and secondary burials seems to be characterised by some variation between the scientific (forensic) and the ethnographic use of the terminology. The former refers strictly to the location of the disposal of the deceased with minimal consideration of the human activities that may have taken place after burial within the initial disposal area. Following the prevalent forensic terminology therefore, primary burial represents the initial location in which the body was placed, while secondary burial occurs when remains are removed from the primary location (Roksandic 2002: 109; Duday 2006: 33, 45). In ethnographic terms, primary rites involve activities which take place immediately or shortly after death (this time period varies in different cultures from several days to several weeks) of a member of the community, such as the preparation and transfer of the body to the burial location, the mourning, gathering and feasting by the living, as well as the placement of the deceased in the primary area of disposal. Secondary rites which take place between several months to several years after death involve ceremonial activities whose aim is for the living to commemorate the deceased, but also to affirm social bonds between them and between the living and the dead (Parker Pearson 1999: 50; Chesson 1999: 142–43; Chesson 2001a: 13; 2001b: 100).

In this framework, special emphasis should be given to secondary actions, which involve the removal of body parts, such as the cranium or the long bones, from a primary burial, or disturbance of a primary burial as a result of intentional activity. The results of activities such as relocation of skeletal elements or of completely articulated or semi-articulated body parts within the primary area of disposal of the deceased (Andrews and Bello 2006: 17) should be considered as clear evidence of manipulation. The latter should, therefore, be distinguished from primary burials which represent strictly activities that take place immediately or shortly after death. In other words, actions which involve actual physical contact between the living and the remains of the deceased at a stage which varies between several months and several years should be classified as stages of processing for the secondary treatment of the deceased (Schroeder 2001: 82–83). The recognition of secondary activities taking place at the initial disposal area is key to our understanding of what constitutes evidence of manipulation of the deceased in Prepalatial Crete since fully or semi-articulated body parts are not necessarily compatible with primary burials, generally understood to result from disposal immediately after death.

In order to test the above hypothesis, we need to examine the existing information on primary burials provided from preliminary reports and excavation photographs, by taking into account four variables which allow the mode of burial to be classed as primary or secondary: 1) articulation of skeletal elements, 2) burial position and orientation, 3) evidence of *in situ* associated grave goods and identity paraphernalia and 4) representation of skeletal elements. The investigation of old excavations, published either at a very preliminary level, or supported by very little photographic documentation is quite problematic. The evidence for primary burials in Prepalatial tholos tombs in either contracted or extended position is extremely scanty, especially when one considers the large number of excavated assemblages. Most tholos tombs

(Table 8.1) which are reported by their excavators to contain primary burials date to the late Prepalatial period (Branigan 1970: 87; 1987a: 44; 1993: 64–65). Careful examination of the published material, however, reduces the plausible examples to very few. In most cases, we are possibly dealing only with articulated body parts, rather than primary burials. For example, this appears to be the case in Lebena Yerokampos IIa, where an excavation photograph (Alexiou and Warren 2004: Plate 125A) clearly shows an articulated vertebral column lying *in situ* within a layer of heavily burnt disarticulated human bones, and not the remains of a primary burial (Alexiou and Warren 2004: 18). Similarly, evidence from the excavation and skeletal representation at the recently published Moni Odigitria B Ossuary is compatible with a careful collection and storage of articulated body parts, particularly of the lower body, rather than the disposal of primary burials (Triantaphyllou 2010a: 245). With regard to spatial patterning, it is worth mentioning that at Hagia Triada A, Hagios Kyrillos and Apesokari II, where primary burials were reported in preliminary excavation reports only, these seem to come from annexes which were added to the main tholos at a later phase of the construction history of the tombs, suggesting possibly a spatial segregation for the different stages of the processing of the deceased, as already suggested by Branigan (1970: 87).

On the other hand, a larger number of primary burials (totalling 26) (Soles 1992: 244) seems to have been accommodated in the house tombs (Table 8.2), although, with

Table 8.1: Tholos tombs with "primary" burials based on excavation reports (after Branigan 1970: 87)

Tholos tombs	Date	Reference
Apesokari A	MM I	Davaras 1964
Archanes Phourni, Γ	EM IIA-EM III	Papadatos 2005
Hagia Triada A	EM I-MMII	Banti 1930–31
Hagios Kyrillos	MM I	Sakellarakis 1968
Gypsades	MM II	Hood 1958
Lebena Papoura I	EM II-MM I	Alexiou & Warren 2004
Vorou A	MM I	Marinatos 1931

Table 8.2: House tombs with "primary" burials based on excavation reports (after Soles 1992: 244)

House tombs	Date	Reference
Archanes Phourni 3, 5, 7, 18, 19	MM I	Sakellarakis and Sakellaraki 1997; Maggidis 1994
Chrysolakkos II	MM II	Demargne 1945
Mallia eastern ossuaries	MM I	Demargne 1945
Myrtos Pyrgos	MM IIB-LMI	Cadogan 1977–78
Palaikastro V, VI, VII	MM I	Bosanquet & Dawkins 1902
Zakros A, B	MM I-II	Platon 1967

the exception of the house tombs of Phourni cemetery at Archanes, the investigation of photographic material from old excavations is almost impossible. Interestingly, the tomb in Myrtos Pyrgos III-IV revealed nine or ten burials in extended position, some of which show strong evidence for manipulation, suggesting that, although the deceased were not removed from the area of their original deposition, post-mortem activities during or shortly after burial may have taken place (Cadogan 1978; 2011a; 2011b). Moreover, overwhelming support to this suggestion also comes from the human remains in the cist and built graves of the Pseira, Hagia Photia and the recently excavated Gournes cemeteries on the North coast. In particular, close inspection of published excavation photographs from the Pseira (Betancourt and Davaras 2003) and Hagia Photia cemeteries (Davaras and Betancourt 2004) supports the argument for the secondary treatment of the deceased. In neither cemetery is there any clear evidence of articulated skeletal elements or body parts lying down in their physical anatomical position, while with regard to Pseira, Betancourt and Davaras (2003: 137) conclude with confidence that the human remains reflect products of secondary treatment. In Gournes, only one out of thirty-six chamber tombs and pit graves provided scanty fragments of bone material (Galanaki 2006; Nafplioti in press) suggesting, therefore, a lack of any plausible evidence of primary deposition of the deceased.

With regard to the other two criteria of burial position and orientation, and the location of the associated grave goods within the tombs, preliminary reports from Hagia Triada A and Gypsades, as suggested by Branigan (1987a), make reference to a fully contracted position of the dead with knees strongly bent. A published photograph from Gypsades, which, however, represents a late example (Hood 1958), would be consistent with the use of the larnax as a container for secondary, rather than primary burial since no clear evidence of bones with anatomical position can be securely inferred. At Lebena P1, Alexiou and Warren (2004: 12) refer to eight corpses by counting only skulls which were placed in extended position, while at Vorou A, Marinatos describes extended burials in a west–east orientation (Marinatos 1931: 146). Examination of the published photographs, however, reveals that at Vorou A, only long bones were carefully collected, while bones found in pithoi probably belong to secondary burials. Information provided in preliminary reports in relation to burial position and orientation, and the identification of primary burials is extremely dubious. Equally, the association of human remains with specific grave goods is even scantier, as admitted by Alexiou and Warren in their concluding remarks on the Lebena tholos tombs (Alexiou and Warren 2004: 192). Similarly, a list of fourteen primary burials with associated grave goods from burial building 19 of the Phourni cemetery at Archanes, provided by Maggidis (1998: fig. 6.5), is extremely dubious. Observation of published photographic material from building 19 (Sakellarakis and Sapouna-Sakellaraki 1997: fig. 174) as well as the small size of the structure in combination with the large number of the individuals interred therein argue against the likelihood of primary burials and are more compatible with the use of the building as a depository of secondary burials.

Primary versus secondary burials: new evidence from the study of the skeletal remains

Answers to such questions can be given only through the careful recording of the different stages of burial activities. These are being recognised in current excavations thanks to the participation of human bone specialists, as well as through the systematic study of skeletal remains recovered from Prepalatial communal tombs. The evidence of recently examined assemblages (Betancourt *et al.* 2008; Triantaphyllou 2009; 2010; 2012; 2016; Triantaphyllou and Girella forthcoming; Triantaphyllou *et al.* 2017; forthcoming) and reports on the ongoing excavation of the house tomb cemetery at Sissi (Schoep 2009; Schoep *et al.* 2011; 2012; Crevecoeur and Schmitt 2009; Crevecoeur *et al.* 2015) unravel a series of critical issues related to the manipulation of the deceased. The recent analysis and publication of the skeletal material recovered from the two tholos tombs at Moni Odigitria in the Asterousia mountains has established a set of criteria related to the degree of articulation, fragmentation, but also to the body part representation within the assemblage, which help us distinguish between the primary or secondary mode of disposal of the human remains (Triantaphyllou 2010). Although the use of the two tholoi overlapped for a time period of approximately 800 years in EM II and to a lesser degree in EM III/MMIA (Branigan and Campbell-Green 2010: 129–30), there are certain differences in relation to the taphonomic history of the skeletal remains contained in each assemblage. The two skeletal assemblages represent two completely different types of deposition with reference to their spatial arrangement within the tombs: the skeletal material from Tholos A was recovered from within the tholos area, while the Tholos B skeletal material had been deposited in the nearby Ossuary. As regards the degree of articulation, Tholos A produced disarticulated remains only from the tholos area, suggesting continuous and intense removal of the skeletonised material. Tholos B on the other hand, provided different degrees of articulation of the human remains deposited in the Ossuary, indicating therefore a more careful treatment of the remnants of the deceased. In particular, the variable state of articulation of the human remains recovered in the Ossuary of Tholos B ranged from one fully articulated and complete skeleton to partially articulated body parts, especially of the lower skeleton, as well as disarticulated skeletonised human bone material. It is interesting to note that the lower body of a complete skeleton (Skeleton 2) was found prone in a strongly flexed position and folded almost on to the upper body, while the upper body was lying on its back in a fully extended position indicating strongly the removal of human remains in fresh condition and, to a certain degree, the secondary treatment of the deceased shortly after burial (Triantaphyllou 2010: 245; 2016).

Similarly, the degree of fragmentation varied between the two tholoi. Tholos A gave evidence of extreme fragmentation due to intense removal of skeletonised material while the skeletal remains from tholos B showed a more complete state of preservation of the skulls and the long bones, particularly of the lower skeleton. With regard to the representation of different skeletal elements between the two tholoi, in Tholos A, all bone categories occurred, although femurs, mandibles and humeri were slightly better represented, while in Tholos B, there was a clear prevalence of skulls and long bones. In Figures 8.1 and 8.2, the lower black line demonstrates the bone representation of the skeletal material recovered from tholoi A and B respectively, while the superimposed black line equals to the expected skeletal representation according to the estimation of the minimum number of individuals from each tholos tomb (MNI in Tholos A = 133, MNI in Tholos B = 64) (Triantaphyllou 2010: figs. 87, 92). In Tholos A (Fig. 8.1), all major anatomical units are represented, although long bones of the upper and lower skeleton are more frequent, supporting the idea of secondary disposal of the deceased in the form of removed skeletonised remains. This is further supported by the significant deviation of the actual skeletal element representation in Tholos A compared to the expected skeletal element representation based on counts of minimum number of individuals disposed of in the tholos. Long bones, being more robust and therefore more resistant to continuous and intense removal, are often better represented in commingled remains but they too cannot easily escape the attention of the people involved in the clearing operations. In Tholos B (Fig. 8.2), although all major anatomical units are well represented, long bones of the lower skeleton show a significantly higher prevalence, while the actual counts of skeletal elements represented are also closer to expected counts, based on the

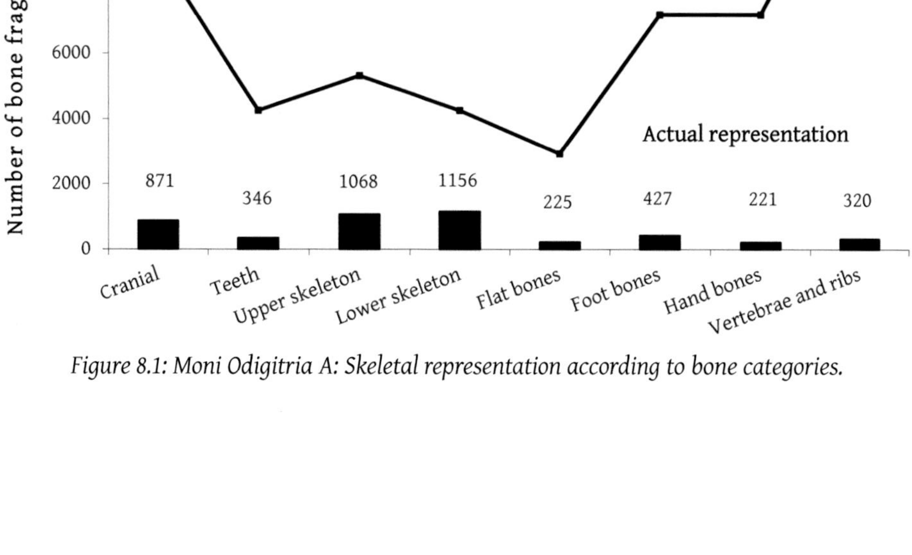

Figure 8.1: Moni Odigitria A: Skeletal representation according to bone categories.

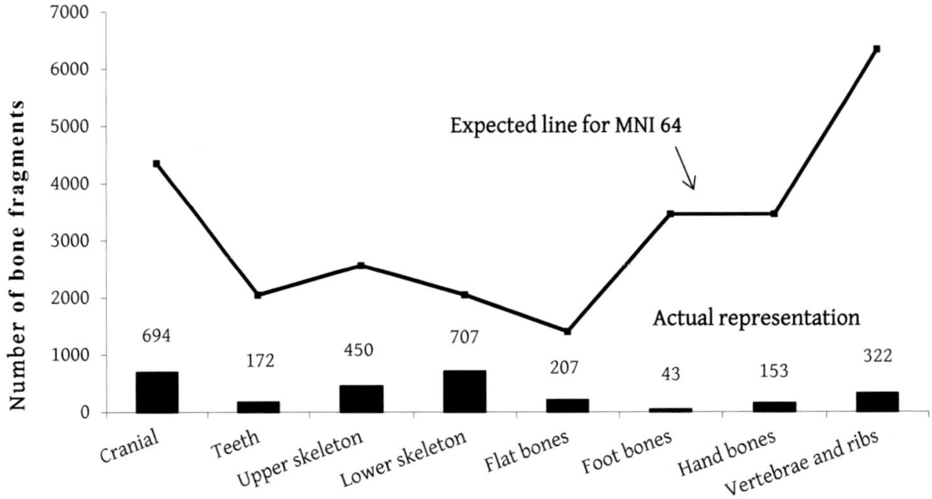

Figure 8.2: Moni Odigitria B: Skeletal representation according to bone categories.

minimum number of individuals calculated for the tholos. This suggests deposition of articulated body parts, in particular of the lower skeleton, rather than deposition of skeletonised remains removed from another location. This picture can be securely verified by excavation photographs (Vasilakis and Branigan 2010: pls. 25, 26).

Preliminary results of the ongoing analysis of the Kephala Petras rock shelter in Siteia, eastern Crete can add important information to the puzzle of the treatment of the deceased in Prepalatial Crete (Tsipopoulou 2007; 2010; Triantaphyllou 2009; 2012; 2016; 2017; Triantaphyllou *et al.* forthcoming). The degree of fragmentation as well as the representation of skeletal elements shed some new light to the type of burial disposal in rock shelters. The Kephala Petras rock shelter produced a considerable number of skulls but also of long and small bones in complete state of preservation. Moreover, Figure 8.3 shows the bone representation of the recorded skeletal elements from Kephala Petras alongside the expected skeletal representation based on the minimum number of the individuals held in the rock shelter (MNI = 165). Although all major anatomical units are well represented, there is a significantly high prevalence of the long bones of the upper and the lower skeleton, as well as of scapulae and the pelves. On the contrary, cranial material is less well represented. This is not an effect of poor preservation, since the recovered skulls are almost complete. Despite the preliminary nature of the ongoing analysis, results from the study of the skeletal material as well as of the associated stratigraphical information are consistent with secondary deposition of human remains which, however, did not only involve defleshed and skeletonised bones, but also body parts which were in fresh condition saving much of their

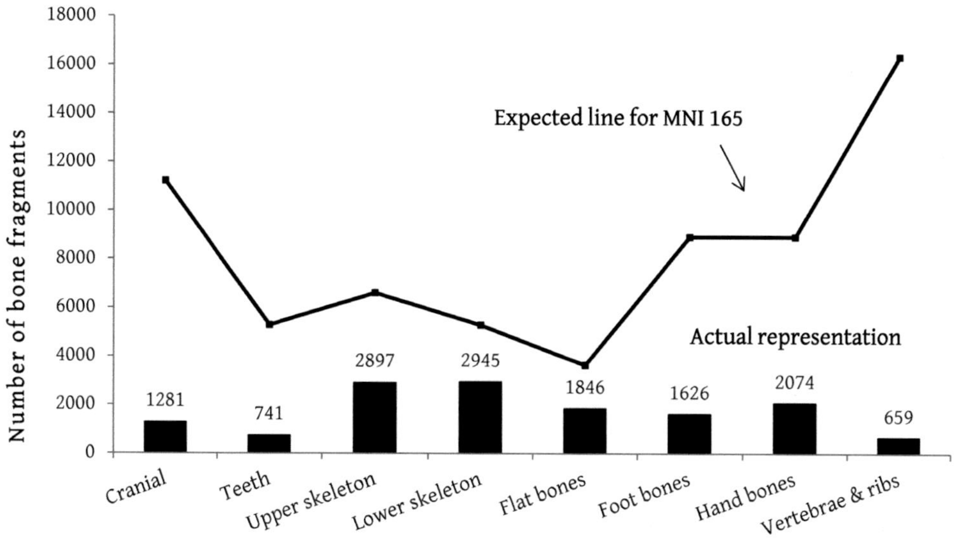

Figure 8.3: Kephala Petras rockshelter: Skeletal representation according to bone categories.

organic components or even their anatomical articulation. Complete long bones and skulls are also common in the skeletal assemblage of the Hagios Charalambos cave which, according to McGeorge, represents the secondary deposition of human skeletal remains (Betancourt *et al.* 2008: 578). The overall picture from rock shelters, based on the analysis of the human skeletal remains, is compatible with the use of such spaces as the final destination of skeletonised bones, as well as of body parts in fresh condition, which, once placed there, they were safely sealed away from further circulation and disturbance from the living community.

The evidence from the ongoing excavations of the house tomb cemetery at Sissi (Schoep 2009; Schoep *et al.* 2011; 2012; Schoep and Tomkins 2016; Crevecoeur and Schmitt 2009; Crevecoeur *et al.* 2015; see also Schoep this volume) and Kephala Petras (Tsipopoulou 2010; 2012a; 2012b; Triantaphyllou 2012; 2016; 2017; Triantaphyllou *et al.* 2017; forthcoming) contributes significantly to our understanding of the various stages of manipulation of the deceased as part of a secondary treatment of human remains. Sissi in particular, gave evidence of both primary and secondary treatment of the deceased (Schoep this volume). It is important, however, to point out that several of the burials recognised by the excavators as "primary burials with evidence of later disturbance", may involve intentional removal of the human remains from within their original disposal area and re-deposition while still fresh and semi-articulated. This seems to be the case in several areas of the Kephala Petras house tomb cemetery as well, suggesting that new excavation projects have the potential to contribute considerably to the reconstruction of mortuary practices of the Prepalatial communities on Crete, which appear to have involved several stages of processing of human remains.

Burning human remains: accidental or deliberate?

Burning has been variously interpreted as an act of fumigation, practical cleansing of the human bones, or symbolic practice (Branigan 1987a: 45 and table 1). Two types of burning can be distinguished: 1) varying degrees of burning affecting the entire tomb, the bone material and the associated artefacts indicating that firing took place *inside* the tomb on a large or small scale and 2) varying degrees of burning of the bone material *only*, indicating that firing took place *outside* the tomb and therefore, the bone material was then transferred inside the disposal area. In most cases burning is localised and has particularly affected the human bones. Tholos A at Kamilari shows clear evidence of extended areas of firing which appears to have taken place only inside the tholos area and not in the auxiliary rooms (Levi 1962: figs. 24–28; Girella 2012; 2013; forthcoming; this volume; Triantaphyllou and Girella forthcoming; Triantaphyllou 2016). It is interesting to note that such fires are totally lacking from the house tombs of the North coast, as well as from the Phourni cemetery at Archanes.

Burnt bones mostly of smoked black and blue/grey colour with minimal severe alterations (e.g., cracking and warping) from the two tholoi at Moni Odigitria in the Asterousia mountains, as well as from the rock shelters of Hagios Charalambos, in Lasithi (Betancourt *et al.* 2008) and Kephala Petras, at Siteia (Triantaphyllou 2010; 2016) would suggest that they are the result of a hasty and short-term process. Moni Odigitria Tholos Tomb A for instance produced only 295 burnt bone fragments out of a total of 6,922 (Triantaphyllou 2010: fig. 88), while Tholos B yielded 60 burnt examples out of the 2,727 bone fragments recovered (Triantaphyllou 2010: fig. 95). It is interesting to note, however, that a few bones from Tholos B in particular gave evidence of alterations on colouring and bone texture which are compatible with a lengthy exposure of the human remains to high temperatures possibly due to the preservation of soft tissue and organic components on the bone, already discussed above. Similarly, in the Kephala Petras rock shelter, only 4% of the human remains provided evidence of burning, primarily of the cranial skeleton with minimal alterations on the bone surface suggesting thus a hasty and short-term exposure to firing conditions of mainly skeletonised human remains (Triantaphyllou 2012). Lightly burnt bones occur also in the Hagios Charalambos cave skeletal assemblage (Betancourt *et al.* 2008: 579). The low frequency of burnt bone fragments in the above assemblages, as well as the slight character of alterations from firing processes, appear to represent short-term activities associated with the burning of the bones outside the area of their secondary and final disposal.

Nevertheless, the study of the recently excavated Prepalatial tholos tomb at Livari Skiadi in south-east Crete (Papadatos and Sofianou 2012; 2015; Triantaphyllou 2016) may change dramatically the prevalent picture of short term burning of human bones reported to date from Prepalatial burial assemblages. The high frequency of bones with evidence of burning from the Livari tholos based on the variety in coloration (black, blue/grey, grey, and white), distortion (slight to severe warping), and cracking (both transverse and longitudinal cracks) on the bone surface (Ubelaker and Rife 2007; Ubelaker 2008; Schmidt and Symes 2008) is striking. In particular, 2,825 out of 4,000 bone fragments of the post-cranial skeleton and 2,670 out of 3,270 fragments of the cranial skeleton show evidence of burning (Triantaphyllou pers. investigation). Furthermore, 284 highly burnt bone fragments demonstrate bronze discoloration, while there are also bone fragments with evidence of melted metal material on their surface suggesting that associated bronze artefacts were exposed at high temperatures for long periods of time. Similarly, the ongoing study of the skeletal material from Kamilari Tholos A (Girella this volume) produced a high frequency of burnt human bones since almost two thirds of the skeletal assemblage demonstrated clear evidence of burning at different temperatures and length of exposure (Triantaphyllou and Girella forthcoming). Furthermore, investigation of the photographic archives (Levi 1962: Figs. 24–28) alongside the recovery of a few large pieces of charcoal mingled with the human bone remains, would suggest that burning at Kamilari was probably the result of deliberate firing associated with the use of fuel in a pyre within the tholos area where a good number of body parts were in fresh condition. Also, a hundred calcined bone fragments showed bronze discoloration, while there is also one case of melted metal material attached on the bone surface. It becomes clear, therefore, that in both Kamilari A and Livari Skiadi tholos tombs, bronze artefacts associated with the human remains were exposed to fire together, although firing must have taken place inside the tomb at Kamilari A and outside the tholos area at Livari Skiadi.

To sum up, different degrees of alterations to the bone surface of human remains recovered in Prepalatial assemblages would be the result of several factors affecting bone elements during burning, e.g., the state of decomposition of the human remains (skeletonised versus fresh bone), contact with fire (direct or indirect) as well as the length of exposure to firing. In many cases it seems that bone parts were still covered with flesh, and the fat and soft tissue facilitated burning at high temperatures. In particular, in the Livari Skiadi Prepalatial tholos tomb, the large number of burnt bones, as well as bone alterations due to firing, appear to be the result of a lengthy and systematic process. The latter would have been achieved through a well-planned and systematic procedure which would evidently require a high amount of energy expenditure and time combined with a large quantity of fuel that would ensure the lengthy exposure of the human remains to high temperatures (McKinley 1997: 132–34; 2000: 407; 2006: 83–85; 2007: 167–68). Ethnographic records as well as experimental work by McKinley report about 700–900 kg of wood necessary for the building of such a pyre (McKinley 2007: 168).

Breakage of the bones: deliberate or taphonomic?

In his 1987 paper on *Ritual Interference with Human Bones in the Mesara Tholoi*, Branigan (1987a: 49–50) recognised the possibility of deliberately broken or chopped human bones from nine tholos tombs located in the Hagiopharango valley with a special reference to the Hagia Kyriaki tholos tomb. This assumption was based primarily on the small size of the bone fragments which often did not exceed 6 cm in length (Branigan 1987a: 49). Besides, a handful of bones produced evidence, according to Branigan, of deliberate chopping by demonstrating very symmetrical and clean edges on both cutting surfaces (Blackman and Branigan 1982: 53; no picture provided). Furthermore, at Kaminospelio tholos tomb, the evidence of deliberate breakage of human bones was further enriched by the surface find of a "quern stone with small fragments of bone adhering to it in the saddle of the quern giving the impression that bones had been pounded or ground on the quern" (Branigan 1987a: 50).

Extremely fragmentary human bones were recognised in the Moni Odigitria Tholos A assemblage in contrast to the almost complete and well preserved skeletal material of the Tholos B ossuary. High fragmentation at Moni Odigitria A appears to have been the result of taphonomic processes which would involve continuous removal of the skeletal remains and trampling since some of the small bone fragments demonstrated rounded edges (Triantaphyllou 2010: 231–32; 2016). More recently, the study of the human remains from the Prepalatial Livari Skiadi tholos tomb revealed a high proportion of small bone fragments with very clean edges (Figs. 8.1–8.5) which could be easily misinterpreted as chopped in fresh condition with a metal tool, probably similar to the ones observed by Branigan in Hagia Kyriaki (Triantaphyllou 2009: 21). It is worth emphasising that this pattern was evident only on long bone shafts which had turned white, with a china-like texture, indicating full oxidisation of the bone (Correia 1997: 276). Careful investigation of specimens with seemingly evidence of chopping at 50–60× magnification (specimens examined by Christidou, Wiener Laboratory, American School of Classical Studies at Athens) would suggest that no deliberate anthropogenic activity was involved in the regularity of the small bone sections as well as in the polished surface of the clean edges. On the contrary, taphonomic processes e.g. continuous removal and trampling of the bone material combined with regular primarily transverse cracks on the bone surface resulting from lengthy exposure to high temperatures appear to have been responsible for the relative regularity of the size of the bone segments, but also of the clean and polished edges on both sides of the bone shafts. It is possible that *in situ* breakage and subsequent trampling caused fragmented surfaces in proximity to rub together causing localised flat and smooth areas along breakage lines. Also, Kamilari Tholos A produced a small amount of very fragmentary human bones with rounded edges or regularly broken in transverse segments with clean edges on both sides of the shaft, which may support intensive trampling during multiple re-openings and removal of the bone material inside the tholos area (Triantaphyllou and Girella forthcoming).

Figure 8.4: Livari Skiadi tholos tomb: Very fragmented bone fragments simulating "chop marks".

In search of a demographic synthesis: how many people?

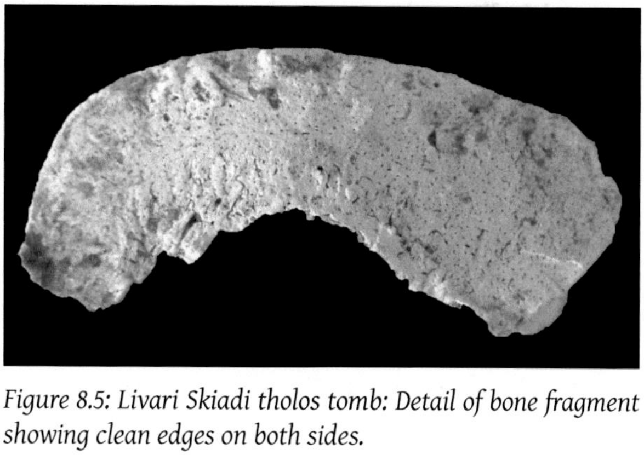

Figure 8.5: Livari Skiadi tholos tomb: Detail of bone fragment showing clean edges on both sides.

The estimate of the *population unit* accommodated inside the tombs has been a controversial issue in the discussion of the Prepalatial burial assemblages. Questions regarding the minimum number of individuals, as well as the composition of the population represented by communal assemblages have been tantalising scholars of Cretan prehistory (for a thorough discussion and survey of different views see Papadatos 1999: 59–63, but also Branigan 1987b; 1993: 84–95; 2010: 262). Calculations proposed by several scholars were based on survey work and the association of the tombs with nearby settlements (Bintliff 1977;

Blackman and Branigan 1977; Branigan 1993), the internal social organisation of the fully excavated EM settlement of Myrtos Phournou Koryphi (Whitelaw 1983; *contra* Warren 1972), the number of skulls recognised during excavation (particularly with regard to house tombs: Soles 1992: 252), but also on the study of artefacts and their distribution within the tombs (Whitelaw 1983).

Recent analysis of skeletal remains offers a unique opportunity to re-evaluate the estimate of population units, but also to investigate the composition of the groups of people buried in Prepalatial communal tombs. A critical factor which needs to be taken into account in this investigation is the length of time that the communal disposal area was in use, although the rate of burial activity may have changed over time as was rightly pointed out by Branigan (1993: 87). The latter cannot be easily defined and therefore the length of use in Table 8.3 follows strictly the time spans for each burial assemblage provided by the associated artefacts. Table 8.3 gives an estimation of population units from skeletal assemblages which have been recently examined (e.g. Tholos tomb Γ, Archanes, Moni Odigitria A and B) or are currently under investigation (e.g. Kamilari A, Livari Skiadi, the Kephala Petras and the Hagios Charalambos rock shelters). The calculation of population units is based on Bintliff's hypothesis that a nuclear family of about five to seven individuals contributes approximately 20 corpses per century (Bintliff 1977: 83), while the duration of the sub-phases in Aegean absolute chronology follows Shelmerdine (2008: fig. 1.1). According to Table 8.3, two preliminary observations can be made here: 1) the minimum number of the individuals represented in communal burial assemblages does not even approach the hundreds of individuals claimed by earlier scholars who based their estimations on the volume of bones per cubic meter of the burial deposit, or on the number of associated artefacts (Bintliff 1977: 83; Branigan 1993: 92–93) and 2) the calculation of population units based on Bintliff's hypothesis would support the idea that usually one nuclear family contributed to communal assemblages except in the case of the Moni Odigitria B and Livari Skiadi tholos tombs which exhibit extremely low values of interred individuals.

Table 8.3: Estimation of population units for recently examined skeletal assemblages (based on Bintliff 1977)

Population	Length of Use	MNI	Skeletons/ 100 yrs	Population Unit
Archanes Phourni, Tholos Γ,	150	30	20	1
Moni Odigitria Tholos A	900	133	14.77	0.73
Moni Odigitria Tholos B	900	64	7.11	0.35
Kamilari Tholos A	500	134	26.8	1.34
Livari Skiadi tholos tomb	700	81	11.57	0.57
Kephala Petras rockshelter	1050	165	15.71	0.78
Hagios Charalambos cave	1800	c. 400	22.22	1.11

Limitations already underlined by scholars who have worked extensively on the size of population units in Prepalatial Crete (Bintliff 1977: 83–84; Whitelaw 1983: 336–39; 2007; 2012; 2015; Branigan 1993: 86–88; for a more recent relevant discussion see Triantaphyllou *et al.* 2015: 4–6 and 15–17) should certainly be taken into consideration and involve: 1) modern looting and multiple disturbance due to the continuous removal of skeletal remains, 2) discontinuous use of the burial ground and 3) differential preservation of different age groups due to taphonomic reasons, more specifically, potential under-representation of sub-adults. Interestingly, the study of the skeletal remains and in particular the distribution of the age groups would support a relative *exclusion* of the sub-adult age categories (Table 8.4) at least in the cases of two tholoi with particularly low values as regards the size of population units. Moni Odigitria B produced four sub-adult versus sixty adult individuals (Triantaphyllou 2010: 236) and Livari Skiadi provided only six sub-adult versus seventy-five adult individuals (Triantaphyllou *et al.* 2015: table 3). This under-representation cannot be explained by the unfavourable preservation of sub-adult bones. Moni Odigitria Tholos A, for instance, which suffered severe modern looting, contained a considerable number of individuals under eighteen years old. The skeletal assemblage from Kamilari A, which suffered from secondary activities, but primarily from harsh post-excavation treatment, produced twenty-three sub-adults out of 103 individuals. Even Archanes Tholos Γ contained sub-adults, albeit few, despite its short-lived – 150 years – use and modest minimum number of individuals recorded (MNI = 30). In other assemblages, where human bones were analysed, sub-adults are well represented, including interestingly even neonates and early infants. It may not be accidental that all three tombs where sub-adults are under-represented – Archanes Tholos Γ, Moni Odigitria B and Livari Skiadi – are located in the vicinity of other tombs which appear to be contemporary: e.g. Tholos tomb E (Panagiotopoulos 2002) and burial buildings 5, 6, 12, 18 and 19 in Archanes (Sakellarakis and Sapouna-Sakellaraki 1997: 387), Moni Odigitria B (Vasilakis and Branigan 2010) and the burial rock shelter at Livari Skiadi (Papadatos and Sofianou 2012; 2015).

Finally, with regard to the two sex groups (Table 8.5), three out of four skeletal assemblages which produced information on sex distribution exhibit

Table 8.4: Distribution of age groups on recently examined skeletal assemblages

Population	0–1 yr	1–6 yrs	6–12 yrs	12–18 yrs	>18 yrs
Archanes Phourni, Tholos Γ,	2	0	2	0	26
Moni Odigitria Tholos A	5	11	9	9	99
Moni Odigitria Tholos B	1	1	1	1	60
Kamilari Tholos A	13	8	4	4	104
Livari Skiadi tholos tomb	0	2	2	2	75
Kephala Petras rockshelter	6	12	11	7	129

Table 8.5: Distribution of sex groups on recently examined skeletal assemblages (sexing is based on skull only)

Population	♂	♀	?
Archanes Phourni, Tholos Γ	8	13	5
Moni Odigitria Tholos A	22	22	55
Moni Odigitria Tholos B	26	15	19
Kephala Petras rockshelter	15	20	65

significant discrepancies between the two sexes suggesting possibly restricted access of particular sexes to mortuary disposal areas. It is important to point out, however, that results regarding sexing should be considered with caution since there is a large number of unsexed individuals owing to a preservational bias. Nevertheless, estimation of the minimum number of individuals combined with the distribution of age and sex groups in the skeletal assemblages under examination would indicate that in certain cases *age*, and to a lesser degree, sex were an important selection criterion.

Conclusions

Much of the work conducted by earlier prominent scholars on aspects of the manipulation of the deceased (Branigan 1987a; 1993), but also on the size of the population units which comprised the Prepalatial communities on Crete (e.g. Warren 1972; Bintliff 1977; Whitelaw 1983; 2007; 2012; 2015; Branigan 1993; 2010) can be further expanded now through a more archaeologically orientated study of the recovered human remains. One of the key issues discussed in this paper involves the different stages of *secondary treatment of the deceased*, ranging from fully articulated skeletons which exhibit some type of deliberate disturbance shortly after death to partly decomposed articulated body parts and completely disarticulated skeletal material in either complete or extremely fragmentary state of preservation. Different stages of manipulation of the deceased may reflect different social, ideological but also political strategies employed by Prepalatial communities in order to negotiate and ascertain individual roles and social identities. Certain stages of the mortuary programme would require high energy expenditure, e.g. extensive and thorough clearance of the primary disposal area in addition to skilled knowledge of particular processes e.g. burning of the human remains and lengthy exposure to high temperatures. It is also possible that certain tasks in managing with death would not only mobilise larger groups of people to help with extensive clearing activities, but would also necessitate particular individuals with specialised knowledge to actually direct the procedure of the removal and careful treatment of partly articulated bodies, or to build up a pyre which would keep burning for several hours at high temperatures in order to achieve complete burning of human bodies.

Death, therefore, when considered a social phenomenon, was an opportunity for communal gathering not only during the immediate instance of the physical loss (biological death), but more importantly during secondary activities taking place shortly after or several months/years after death in order to commemorate members of the community who passed away – i.e. *μνημόσυνα*. The commemoration of the deceased was an obvious occasion, since communal gatherings for secondary rites would have functioned as opportunities for the regulation of social relationships especially within fragmented groups of the broader region, which would require an institutionalised arena for establishing social roles and identities within the communities of the living (Relaki 2004; Legarra-Herrero 2009: 37). It has been suggested that "secondary ceremonies often may require a greater amount of planning than primary rites to ensure cooperation and participation of a large number of people from within and outside of the community (Chesson 1999: 142).

Although a common feature in all Prepalatial skeletal assemblages is the communal character of the deposition, it was possible throughout the above discussion to identify some distinct ways of manipulating the deceased, which could be associated with particular types of disposal areas. Articulated skeletons, body parts or bones in fresh condition occur more frequently in ossuary-type depositions, such as the Ossuary of Moni Odigitria B, the Hagios Charalambos cave and the Kephala Petras rock shelter. It is important to point out here that human remains found in ossuary-type depositions show very little evidence of removal and disturbance once they were placed in their final destination and this seems to be the reason why they remained in articulation. By contrast, fully articulated skeletons and in general body parts in fresh condition which demonstrate secondary treatment shortly after their primary burial occur in house tombs. We should bear in mind, however, that the situation observed in the house tombs would reflect the last use of the mortuary space, since preceding clearing activities would have resulted in the removal of the human remains and their deposition in a nearby cave or rock shelter as this appears to be the case in the house tombs and the rock shelter at Kephala Petras, Siteia (Tsipopoulou 2010). The difference with ossuary-type depositions is that secondary activities in the house tombs take place in the primary area of disposal of the deceased and there is no transportation and therefore actual disturbance of the human remains. Moreover, the re-arrangement of completely disarticulated human remains in the house tombs (e.g. relocation, grouping of bones) would more likely be a matter of internal organisation within the different rooms of the tomb, but certainly would not necessitate their transportation elsewhere. This action would not necessarily require large groups of people to help with managing the human remains as would have been the case in the ossuary-type depositions and therefore, more emphasis appears to have been placed on the *household* than the *kin group*, or the *community*, which appears to have participated more actively in the former case. The link between social units and residential structures may have played an important role in creating identities through mortuary rituals (for more discussion on this issue see Kuijt 2001), as already argued convincingly for the east Cretan tradition of house tombs by Cadogan (2011b), based on the Myrtos Pyrgos house tomb. Furthermore, a large body of ethnographic evidence demonstrates that, when kinship is the principal means of social organisation, secondary burial rites involving certain stages of processing constitute public arenas for the communication and

Betancourt, P. P, C. Davaras, E. Stravopodi, L. Langford-Verstegen, J. D. Muhly, J. Hickman, H. M. C. Dierckx, S. C. Ferrence, D. S. Reese, P. J. P. McGeorge and S. Chlouveraki

2008 Excavations in the Hagios Charalambos cave: a preliminary report. *Hesperia* 77: 539–604.

Bintliff, J. L.

1977 The number of burials in the Mesara tholoi. In D. Blackman and K. Branigan, An archaeological survey of the cower catchment of the Ayiofarango Valley. *Annual of the British School at Athens* 72: 83–4.

Bloch, M. and J. Parry

1982 *Death and the Regeneration of Life*. Cambridge: Cambridge University Press.

Blackman, D. and K. Branigan

1977 An archaeological survey of the lower catchment of the Ayiofarango valley. *Annual of the British School at Athens* 72: 13–84.

1982 The excavation of the EM tholos tomb at Ayia Kyriaki, Ayiofarango, southern Crete. *Annual of the British School at Athens* 77: 1–59.

Bosanquet, R and R. Dawkins

1902 Excavations at Palaikastro, II. *Annual of the British School at Athens* 9: 274–387.

Branigan, K.

1970 *The Tombs of Mesara*. London: Duckworth.

1987a Ritual interference with human bones in the Mesara tholoi. In R. Laffineur (ed.), *Thanatos. Les Coutumes Funeraires en Egée à l'Age du Bronze* (Aegeum 1): 43–51. Liège: Université de Liège.

1987b Body counts in the Mesara tholoi. In *ΕΙΛΑΠΙΝΗ: Τιμητικός τόμος για τον Καθηγητή Νικόλαο Πλάτωνα*: 299–309. Ηράκλειον: Βικελαία Δημοτική Βιβλιοθήκη.

1993 *Dancing with Death: Life and Death in Southern Crete c. 3000–2000 B.C.* Amsterdam: A. M. Hakkert.

1998 The nearness of you: proximity and distance in Early Minoan funerary behaviour. In K. Branigan (ed.), *Cemetery and Society in the Aegean Bronze Age* (Sheffield Studies for Aegean Archaeology 1): 13–26. Sheffield: Sheffield Academic Press.

2010 History and use of the cemetery. In A. Vasilakis and K. Branigan (eds.), *Moni Odigitria: A Prepalatial Cemetery and its Environs in the Asterousia, Southern Crete* (Prehistory Monographs 30): 251–64. Philadelphia: INSTAP Academic Press.

Branigan, K. and T. Campbell-Green

2010 Interpretation of the pottery assemblage. In A. Vasilakis and K. Branigan (eds.), *Moni Odigitria: A Prepalatial Cemetery and its Environs in the Asterousia, Southern Crete* (Prehistory Monographs 30): 127–43. Philadelphia: INSTAP Academic Press.

Branigan, K. and A. Vasilakis

2010 The Hagiopharango in the Early Bronze Age. In A. Vasilakis and K. Branigan (eds.), *Moni Odigitria: A Prepalatial Cemetery and its Environs in the Asterousia, Southern Crete* (Prehistory Monographs 30): 265–69. Philadelphia: INSTAP Academic Press.

Cadogan, G.

1978 Pyrgos, Crete, 1970–77. *Archaeological Reports* 24: 70–84.

2011a A power house of the dead: the functions and long life of the tomb at Myrtos-Pyrgos. In J. M. A. Murphy (ed.), *Prehistoric Crete: Regional and Diachronic Studies on Mortuary Systems*: 103–17. Philadelphia: INSTAP Academic Press.

2011b Myrtos: From Phournou Koryphi to Pyrgos. In K. Glowacki and N. Vogeikoff-Brogan (eds.), *STEGA. The Archaeology of Houses and Households in Ancient Crete from the Neolithic Period through the Roman Era* (*Hesperia* Supplement 44): 39–49. Princeton: American School of Classical Studies at Athens.

Carter, T.

2010 Of blades and burials, flakes and funerals: the chipped stone from Moni Odigitria. In A. Vasilakis and K. Branigan (eds.), *Moni Odigitria: A Prepalatial Cemetery and its Environs in the Asterousia, Southern Crete* (Prehistory Monographs 30): 151–69. Philadelphia: INSTAP Academic Press.

Chesson, M. S.

1999 Libraries of the dead: Early Bronze Age charnel houses and social identity at Urban Babe dh-Dhra, Jordan. *Journal of Anthropological Archaeology* 18: 137–64.

2001a Social memory, identity and death: an introduction. In M. S. Chesson (ed.), *Social Memory, Identity and Death: Ethnographic and Archaeological Perspectives on Mortuary Rituals*: 12–26. Arlington: American Anthropological Association.

2001b Embodied memories of place and people: death and society in an Early Urban community. In M. S. Chesson (ed.), *Social Memory, Identity and Death: Ethnographic and Archaeological Perspectives on Mortuary Rituals*: 100–13. Arlington: American Anthropological Association.

Correia, P.

1997 Fire modification of bone: review of the literature. In U. D. Haglund and M. H. Sorg (eds.), *Forensic Taphonomy: the Forensic Fate of Human Remains*: 275–93. New York: CRC Press.

Crevecoeur, I. and A. Schmitt

2009 Étude archéo-anthropologique de la nécropole (Zone 1). In J. Driessen, I. Schoep, F. Crevecoeur, M. Devolder, F. Gaignerot-Driessen, H. Fiasse, P. Haciguzeller, S. Jusseret, C. Langohr, Q. Letesson, and A. Schmitt (eds.), *Excavations at Sissi. Preliminary Report on the 2007–2008 Campaigns* (Aegis 1): 57–94. Louvain-la-Neuve: Presses Universitaires de Louvain.

Crevecoeur, I., A. Schmitt and I. Schoep

2015 An archaeothanatological approach to the study of Minoan funerary practices: Case-studies from the Early and Middle Minoan cemetery at Sissi, Crete. *Journal of Field Archaeology* 40(3): 283–99.

Davaras, K.

1965 Απεσωκάρι. *Αρχαιολογικόν Δελτίον* 19, B3: 441.

Davaras, C. and P. P. Betancourt

2004 *The Hagia Photia Cemetery I. The Tomb Groups and Architecture* (Prehistory Monographs 14). Philadelphia: INSTAP Academic Press

Demargne, P.

1945 *Nécropoles de Mallia, les Premieres Charniers, l'Ossuaire Principier de Chrysolakkos, Premier Facsicule.* Paris: Études Crétoises VII.

Duday, H.

200 L'archéothanatologie ou l'archéologie de la mort. In R. Gowland and C. Knüsel (eds.), *Social Archaeology of Funerary Remains*: 30–56. Oxford: Oxbow

Galanaki, K.

2006 Πρωτομινωικό ταφικό σύνολο στην πρώην Αμερικανική βάση Γουρνών Πεδιάδος. *Πεπραγμένα του Θ' Διεθνούς Κρητολογικού συνεδρίου*, vol. A2: 227–41. Ηράκλειο: Εταιρεία Κρητικών Ιστορικών Μελετών.

Girella, L.

2012 The Kamilari project publication. *Rivista di Archeologia* XXXV (2011): 123–36.

2013 Exhuming an excavation: preliminary notes on the use of the Kamilari tholos tomb in Middle Minoan III. In C. F. Macdonald and C. Knappett (eds.), *Intermezzo. Intermediacy and Regeneration in Middle Minoan III Crete*, 149–59. (BSA Studies 21) London: British School at Athens.

forthcoming The Kamilari tholos tombs project: new light on an old excavation. *Πεπραγμένα του ΙΑ' Διεθνούς Κρητολογικού Συνεδρίου, Ρέθυμνο, 21-27 Οκτωβρίου 2011.* Ρέθυμνο: Ιστορική και Λαογραφική Εταιρεία Ρεθύμνης.

Hamilakis, Y.

1998 Eating the dead: mortuary feasting and the politics of memory in the Aegean Bronze Age societies. In K. Branigan (ed.), *Cemetery and Society in the Aegean Bronze Age* (Sheffield Studies in Aegean Archaeology 1): 115–32. Sheffield: Sheffield Academic Press.

Hatzaki, E.
2012 Mortuary practices and ideology in Bronze Age–Early Iron Age Crete and Cyprus. In G. Cadogan, M. Iacovou, K. Kopaka, and J. Whitley (eds.), *Parallel Lives: Ancient Island Societies in Crete and Cyprus* (BSA Studies 20): 307–13. London: The British School at Athens.

Hood, M. S. F.
1958 Discoveries during the latest Knossos excavations. *Illustrated London News*: 300–302.

Hutchinson, D. L. and L. V. Aragon
2002 Collective burials and community memories: interpreting the placement of the dead in the southeastern and mid-Atlantic United States with reference to ethnographic cases from Indonesia. In D. B. Small and H. Silverman (eds.), *The Space and Place of Death*: 27–54. Arlington: American Anthropological Association.

Kuijt, I.
2001 Place, death, and the transmission of social memory in early agricultural communities of the near Eastern Pre-pottery Neolithic. In M. S. Chesson (ed.), *Social Memory, Identity and Death: Ethnographic and Archaeological Perspectives on Mortuary Rituals*: 80–99. Arlington: American Anthropological Association.

Levi, D.
1961–62 La tomba a tholos di Kamilari presso a Festòs. *Annuario della Scuola archeologica di Atene e delle Missioni italiane in Oriente* 49–50: 7–148.

Legarra Herrero, B.
2009 The Minoan Fallacy: cultural diversity and mortuary behaviour on Crete at the beginning of the Bronze Age. *Oxford Journal of Archaeology* 28.1: 29–57.
2012 The construction, deconstruction and non-construction of hierarchies in the funerary record of Prepalatial Crete. In I. Schoep, P. Tomkins and J. Driessen (eds.), *Back to the Beginning: Reassessing Social, Economic and Political Complexity in the Early and Middle Bronze Age on Crete*: 325–57. Oxford: Oxbow.
2014 *Mortuary Behavior and Social Trajectories in Pre- and Protopalatial Crete* (Prehistory Monographs 44). Philadelphia: INSTAP Academic Press.

Maggidis, C.
1994 *Burial Building 19 at Archanes: A Study of Prepalatial and Early Protopalatial Funerary Architecture and Ritual*. PhD dissertation, University of Pennsylvania.
1998 From polis to necropolis: social ranking from architectural and mortuary evidence in the Minoan cemetery at Phourni, Archanes. In K. Branigan (ed.), *Cemetery and Society in the Aegean Bronze Age* (Sheffield Studies in Aegean Archaeology 1): 87–102. Sheffield: Sheffield Academic Press.

Marinatos, S.
1931 Δύο Πρωτομινωικοί τάφοι εκ Βωρού Μεσαράς. *Αρχαιολογικόν Δελτίον* 13: 137–76.

McGeorge, P. J. P.
1987a Νέα στοιχεία για το μέσο όρο ζωής στη Μινωική Κρήτη. *Κρητική Εστία* 1: 9–15.
1987b Biosocial evolution in Bronze age Crete. In *ΕΙΛΑΠΙΝΗ: Τιμητικός τόμος για τον Καθηγητή Νικόλαο Πλάτωνα*: 407–16. Ηράκλειον: Βικελαία Δημοτική Βιβλιοθήκη.
1988 Μυθικοί πυγμαίοι και γίγαντες: νέα στοιχεία για το ύψος των Μινωϊτών. *Κρητική Εστία* 2: 9–17.
1990 A comparative study of the mean life expectation of the Minoans. *Πεπραγμένα του ΣΤ' Διεθνούς Κρητολογικού Συνεδρίου, τομ. Α1*: 419–428. Χανιά: Φιλολογικός Σύλλογος "Ο Χρυσόστομος".
1992 The human skeletal remains. In B. P. Hallager and P. J. P McGeorge (eds.), *Late Minoan III Burials at Khania: the Tombs, Finds and Deceased in Odos Palama* (Studies in Mediterranean Archaeology 93): 29–47. Göteborg: Paul Åstroms Förlag.

McKinley, J. I.
1997 Bronze age "barrows" and funerary rites and rituals of cremation. *Proceedings of the Prehistoric Society* 63: 129–45.
2000 The analysis of cremated bone. In M. Cox and S. Mays (eds.), *Human Osteology in Archaeology and Forensic Science*: 403–21. London: Greenwich Medical Media.
2006 Cremation ... the cheap option? In R. Gowland and C. Knüsel (eds.), *Social Archaeology of Funerary Remains*: 81–88. Oxford: Oxbow.
2007 Efficiency of oxidation in Romano–British cremations. In C. W. Schmidt and S. A. Symes (eds.), *The Analysis of Burned Human Remains*: 163–83. New York. Academic Press.

Metcalf, P. and R. Huntington
1991 *Celebrations of Death. The Anthropology of Mortuary Ritual*. Cambridge: Cambridge University Press.

Murphy, J. M.
1998 Ideologies, rites and rituals: a view of Prepalatial Minoan tholoi. In K. Branigan (ed.), *Cemetery and Society in the Aegean Bronze Age* (Sheffield Studies in Aegean Archaeology 1): 27–40. Sheffield: Sheffield Academic Press.

Musgrave, J. H.
1984 The human skeletons. In M. R. Popham (ed.), *The Minoan Unexplored Mansion at Knossos* (British School at Athens Supplement 17): 309–10. London: British School at Athens.

Nafplioti, A.
in press The human skeletal remains (or not). In Galanaki, K., *The Cemetery at Gournes, Vol. 1.* Philadelphia: INSTAP Academic Press.

Panagiotopoulos, D.
2002 *Das Tholosgrab E von Phourni bei Archanes. Studien zu einem frühkretischen Grabfund und seinem kulturellen Kontext* (BAR IS 1014). Oxford: Archaeopress.

Papadatos, Y.
1999 *Mortuary Practices and their Importance for the Reconstruction of Society and Life in Prepalatial Crete: the Evidence from the Tholos Tomb Gamma in Archanes-Phourni*. PhD dissertation, University of Sheffield.
2005 *Tholos Tomb Gamma: A Prepalatial Tholos Tomb at Phourni, Archanes* (Prehistory Monographs 17). Philadelphia: INSTAP Academic Press.

Papadatos, Y. and C. Sofianou
2012 Πολιτισμική ομοιογένεια και διαφοροποίηση στην Προανακτορική Κρήτη: νέα στοιχεία από τις ανασκαφές νεκροταφείων στην επαρχία Σητείας. In M. Andrianakis, P. Varthalitou, and I. Tzachili (eds.), *Archaeological Work in Crete 2, Proceedings of the 2nd meeting, Rethymnon 26-28 November 2010*: 49–59. Rethymnon: University of Crete, Faculty of Letters Publications.
2015 *Livari Skiadi. A Minoan Cemetery in Lefki, Southeast Crete. Volume I: Excavation and Finds* (Prehistory Monographs 50). Philadelphia: INSTAP Academic Press.

Parker Pearson, M.
1999 *The Archaeology of Death and Burial*. Stroud: Sutton.

Platon, N.
1967 Ανασκαφαί Ζάκρου. *Πρακτικά* 20: 162–94.

Relaki, M.
2004 Constructing a region: the contested landscapes of Prepalatial Mesara. In J. C. Barrett and P. Halstead (eds.), *The Emergence of Civilisation Revisited* (Sheffield Studies in Aegean Archaeology 6): 170–88. Oxford: Oxbow Books.

Roksandic, M.
2002 Position of skeletal remains as a key to understanding mortuary behavior. In W. D. Haglund and M. H. Sorg (eds.), *Advances in Forensic Taphonomy: Method, Theory, and Archaeological Perspectives*: 99–118. New York: CRC Press.

Robb, J.
2002 Time and biography: osteobiography of the Italian Neolithic lifespan. In Y. Hamilakis, M. Pluciennik and S. Tarlow (eds.), *Thinking through the Body: Archaeologies of Corporeality*: 153–71. London: Kluewer Academic/Plenum.
2007 Burial treatment as transformations of bodily ideology. In N. Laneri (ed.), *Performing Death: Social Analysis of Funerary Traditions in the Ancient Near East and Mediterranean*: 287–97. Chicago: The Oriental Institute, University of Chicago.
Sakellarakis, Y.
1968 Θολωτός τάφος εις Αγιον Κύριλλον Μεσαράς. *Αρχαιολογικά Ανάλεκτα εξ Αθηνών* 1: 50–53.
Sakellarakis, Y and E. Sapouna-Sakellaraki
1997 *Archanes. Minoan Crete in a New Light*. Athens: Ekdoseis Ammos.
Schmidt, C. W. and S. A. Symes
2008 *The Analysis of Burned Human Remains*. New York. Academic Press.
Schoep, I.
2009 The excavation of the cemetery (Zone 1). In J. Driessen, I. Schoep, F. Crevecoeur, M. Devolder, F. Gaignerot-Driessen, H. Fiasse, P. Haciguzeller, S. Jusseret, C. Langohr, Q. Letesson, and A. Schmitt (eds.), *Excavations at Sissi. Preliminary Report on the 2007–2008 Campaigns* (Aegis 1): 45–56. Louvain-la-Neuve: Presses Universitaires de Louvain.
Schoep, I., A. Schmitt and I. Crevecoeur
2011 The cemetery at Sissi: report of the 2009 and 2010 Campaigns. In J. Driessen and I. Schoep (eds.), *Excavations at Sissi. Preliminary Report on the 2009–2010 Excavations* (Aegis 4): 41–68. Louvain la-Neuve: Presses Universitaires de Louvain.
Schoep, I., A. Schmitt, I. Crevecoeur and S. Déderix
2012 The cemetery at Sissi: Report on the 2011 Campaign. In J. Driessen and I. Schoep (eds.), *Excavations at Sissi. Preliminary Report on the 2011 Excavations* (Aegis 6): 27–50. Louvain-la-Neuve: Presses Universitaires de Louvain.
Schoep, I. and P. Tomkins
2016 Death is not the end. Tracing the manipulation of bodies and other materials in the Early and Middle Minoan cemetery at Sissi. In A. Dakouri-Hild and M. J. Boyd (eds.), *Staging Death: Funerary Performance, Architecture and Landscape in the Aegean*: 227–50. Berlin: de Gruyter.
Schroeder, S.
2001 Secondary disposal of the dead: cross-cultural codes. *World Cultures* 12.1: 77–93.
Shelmerdine, C. W.
2008 Background, sources and methods. In C. W. Shelmerdine (ed.), *The Aegean Bronze Age*: 1–18. Cambridge: Cambridge University Press.
Soles, J. S.
1992 *Prepalatial Cemeteries at Mochlos and Gournia and the House Tombs of Bronze Age Crete* (Hesperia Supplement 24). Princeton: American School of Classical Studies.
Triantaphyllou, S.
2005 The human remains. In Y. Papadatos (ed.), *Tholos Tomb Gamma: A Prepalatial Tholos Tomb at Phourni, Archanes* (Prehistory Monographs 17): 67–76. Philadelphia: INSTAP Academic Press.
2009 EM/MM human skeletal remains from East Crete: the Kephala Petras rock shelter, Siteia, and the Livari tholos tomb, Skiadi. *Kentro, The Newsletter of the INSTAP Study Center for East Crete* 12: 19–23.
2010 The human remains. In A. Vasilakis and K. Branigan (eds.), *Moni Odigitria: A Prepalatial Cemetery and its Environs in the Asterousia, Southern Crete* (Prehistory Monographs 30): 229–48. Philadelphia: INSTAP Academic Press.

2012 Kephala Petras: the human remains and the burial practices in the Rock Shelter. In M. Tsipopoulou (ed.), *Petras, Siteia - 25 years of excavations and studies* (Monographs of the Danish Institute at Athens 16): 161–70. Athens: Danish Institute at Athens.

2016 Staging the manipulation of the dead in Pre- and Protopalatial Crete, Greece (3rd-early 2nd mill. BC): from body wholes to fragmented body parts. *Journal of Archaeological Science*, Reports, (Special Issue for Funerary Taphonomy), 10 (December 2016): 769–79.

2017 'Όσο ψηλά και αν ανεβείς λέξη μην πεις μεγάλη 'πο χώμα σε έφτιαξε ο θεός κι εκειά γυρίζεις πάλι'. In M. Tsipopoulou (ed.), *The Pre- and Protopalatial cemetery in context. 2nd Petras Symposium, 14–15 February 2015*: 271–90 (Monographs of the Danish Institute at Athens 21). Athens: Danish Institute at Athens.

Triantaphyllou, S., Kador, T. and E. Nikita.

2015 Exploring mobility patterns and biological affinities in the southern Aegean: first insights from Early Bronze Age eastern Crete, Greece. *Annual of the British School at Athens*: 1–23.

Triantaphyllou, S., S. Kiorpe and M. Tsipopoulou

2017 House Tomb 5: a preliminary analysis of the human skeletal remains. In M. Tsipopoulou (ed.), *The Pre- and Protopalatial cemetery in context. 2nd Petras Symposium, 14–15 February 2015*: 291–99. (Monographs of the Danish Institute at Athens 21) Athens: Danish Institute at Athens.

Triantaphyllou, S. and L. Girella

forthcoming Η συμβολή της μελέτης των ανθρώπινων οστών στην ερμηνεία του θολωτού τάφου στο Καμηλάρι στην πεδιάδα της Μεσαράς, νομός Ηρακλείου. *Πεπραγμένα του ΙΑ' Διεθνούς Κρητολογικού Συνεδρίου, Ρέθυμνο, 21-27 Οκτωβρίου 2011.* Ρέθυμνο: Ιστορική και Λαογραφική Εταιρεία Ρεθύμνης.

Triantaphyllou, S., M. Tsipopoulou and P. Betancourt

forthcoming Κεφάλα Πετρά Σητείας: ανθρώπινα οστά και ταφικές πρακτικές στην Πρωτομινωική βραχοσκεπή και στο Μεσομινωικό νεκροταφείο. *Πεπραγμένα του ΙΑ' Διεθνούς Κρητολογικού Συνεδρίου, Ρέθυμνο, 21-27 Οκτωβρίου 2011.* Ρέθυμνο: Ιστορική και Λαογραφική Εταιρεία Ρεθύμνης.

Tsipopoulou, M.

2007 The Prepalatial cemetery at Petras, Siteia: preliminary observations. Athens: Minoan Seminar, 2 March 2007, Unpublished manuscript.

2010 Προανακτορική ταφική βραχοσκεπή στον Πετρά Σητείας. In M. Andrianakis and I. Tzachili (eds.), *Archaeological Work in Crete 1, Proceedings of the 1st Meeting*: 121–33. Rethymnon: University of Crete, Faculty of Letters Publications.

2012a Πετράς Σητείας: Προανακτορικό – πρώιμο Παλαιοανακτορικό ταφικό κτίριο 2. In M. Andrianakis, P. Varthalitou, and I. Tzachili (eds.), *Archaeological Work in Crete 2, Proceedings of the 2nd meeting, Rethymnon 26–28 November 2010*: 60–9. Rethymnon: University of Crete, Faculty of Letters Publications.

2012b The Prepalatial-early Protopalatial cemetery at Petras,Siteia: a diachronic symbol of social coherence. In M. Tsipopoulou (ed.), *Petras, Siteia - 25 years of excavations and studies* (Monographs of the Danish Institute at Athens 16): 117–31. Athens: Danish Institute at Athens.

Ubelaker, D. H.

2008 The forensic evaluation of burned skeletal remains: a synthesis. *Forensic Science International* 183: 1–5.

Ubelaker, D. H. and J. L. Rife

2007 The practice of cremation in the Roman-era cemetery at Kenchreai, Greece: the perspective from archaeology and forensic science. *Bioarchaeology of the Near East* 1: 35–57.

Vasilakis, A. and K. Branigan (eds.)
2010 *Moni Odigitria: A Prepalatial Cemetery and its Environs in the Asterousia, Southern Crete* (Prehistory Monographs 30). Philadelphia: INSTAP Academic Press.
Vavouranakis, G.
2007 *Funerary Landscapes East of Lasithi, Crete, in the Bronze Age* (BAR IS 1606). Oxford: Archaeopress.
Vavouranakis, G. and C. Bourbou
2015 Breaking up the past: patterns of fragmentation in Early and Middle Bronze Age tholos tomb contexts in Crete. In K. Harrell and J. Driessen (eds), *Thravsma. Contextualising Intentional Destruction of Objects in the Bronze Age Aegean and Cyprus* (Aegis 9): 167–96. Louvain: Presses Universitaires de Louvain.
Warren, P.
1972 *Myrtos. An Early Bronze Age Settlement in Crete*. London: Thames and Hudson.
Whitelaw, T. M.
1983 The settlement at Fournou Koryfi Myrtos and aspects of Early Minoan social organization. In O. Krzyszkowska and L. Nixon (eds.), *Minoan Society, Proceedings of the Cambridge Colloquium 1981*: 325–45. Bristol: Classical Press.
2007 House, households and community at Early Minoan Fournou Korifi: methods and models for interpretation. In Westgate, R., Fisher, N. and J. Whitley (eds.), *Building Communities: House, Settlement and Society in the Aegean and Beyond:* 65–76. (British School at Athens supplement 15) London: British School at Athens.
2012 The urbanisation of prehistoric Crete: settlement perspectives on Minoan state formation. In Schoep I., Tomkins P. and J. Driessen (eds.), *Back to the Beginning: Reassessing Social, Economic and Political Complexity in the Early and Middle Bronze Age on Crete*: 114–76. Oxford: Oxbow.
2015 The divergence of civilisation: Fournou Korifi and Pyrgos. In Macdonald, C., Hatzaki, E. and Andreou, S. (eds.), *The Great Islands. Studies of Crete and Cyprus presented to Gerald Cadogan:* 41–48. Athens: Kapon Editions.
Xanthoudides, S.
1918 Μέγας Πρωτομινωικός τάφος Πύργου. *Αρχαιολογικόν Δελτίον* 4: 136–70.

Chapter 9

The house tomb in context: Assessing mortuary behaviour in north-east Crete

Ilse Schoep

Introduction

Over the last two decades it has become clear that the island of Crete should no longer be considered a homogenous cultural whole during the Bronze Age, but instead as a series of regions that often reveal very different strategies and dynamics. One of the first areas in which the regional character of the island in the Early and Middle Bronze Age became clear was the mortuary realm, with very obvious differences apparent between the circular tholos tombs in south-central Crete and the house tombs in north-east Crete (Seager 1912; Xanthoudides 1924; Branigan 1993). The picture, however, is more complex than this and, some time ago, Keith Branigan pointed out that tholos tombs also occur in north-east Crete (Branigan 1993: 12), such as for example at Krasi, Knossos and Myrsini. Tomb VIII at Palaikastro also has a semi-circular plan but is not preserved (Soles 1992: 192–93). In addition, some of the tholos cemeteries in south-central Crete also seem to contain some rectangular structures (Koumasa, Ayia Triada, Platanos, although it is by no means clear that they were used in the same way as the house tombs). Maria Relaki (2004) has also argued that different dynamics and patterns can be discerned behind the spread of the tholos tombs, even within the so-called culturally homogenous region of the Mesara plain, suggesting that the dispersal of tholos tombs does not express social and political congruity but is embedded in a web of fierce competition.

In a similar manner to the Mesara plain where people were burying their dead in circular tholos tombs (Branigan 1993: 7; Schoep 1999), north-east Crete is conventionally considered to be a culturally homogenous region because of the distribution of the house tomb. Upon closer inspection the picture of funerary homogeneity in north-east Crete breaks down into different patterns and dynamics and I will argue that the appearance of the house tomb and its associated mortuary behaviour in EM IIA initially restricted to a particular type of community and was the result of a conscious choice that provides insights into social reproduction (Parker Pearson 1982; 2000; Barrett 1990; 1994).

From grave goods to social practice

The earliest mortuary explorations in Crete focused mainly on the recovery of valuable objects from tombs (Evans 1906; Hawes *et al.* 1908; Seager 1912; Xanthoudides 1924), which is reflected in the treatment, or rather the "non-treatment" of the human remains (and palaeo-botanic and faunal remains). The publications of the early excavations are basically catalogues of objects, especially fine pottery and valuable objects (Seager 1912; Xanthoudides 1924). In the early days it was believed that the presence of grave goods reflected the religious beliefs of the deceased, in particular a belief in the afterlife (Morris 1992). New archaeology on the contrary suggested that grave goods can be seen as a direct reflection of the status of the deceased (*isomorphism*). In other words, it was believed that there was a direct correlation between the social rank of the deceased and the number of people with relationships to the deceased and that social rank of the deceased as recognised in funerary rituals corresponds with the social position the deceased held in life (Saxe 1970; Binford 1971; Tainter 1978). The idea that the status of the deceased and the organisation of a society can be read in the funerary record was criticised in the late eighties and nineties (Parker Pearson 2000: 31–34, 83–90). Emphasis shifted from the social role and social persona of the deceased to social practices and mortuary behaviour, while society was now considered to be constituted by agency rather than prescribed roles (Parker Pearson 1982; Barrett 1994). In addition, it was recognised that mortuary practices might embody the workings of power and ideology and that they may have played an important legitimating role (Bloch 1977; Miller and Tilley 1984). Mortuary practices were no longer considered a passive reflection of abstract concepts of society and social structure, but they were thought of as an arena of activity in which the institutions through which social relationships are actively brought into being, transformed and terminated, are moulded (Parker Pearson 1982). Status is not simply reflected at funerals but actively constituted and negotiated (Parker Pearson 2000: 32). This also implies that the funerary record as it is known to us is probably the result of selective rather than inclusive procedures.

Mortuary behaviour, therefore, should be studied within the wider context of social practice because it plays an important role in the reproduction of society (Parker Pearson 2000: 84; Barrett 1994; 2000). Barrett has emphasised the dual transformation of funerary practices: the removal of the corpse from among the living and the re-establishment of the ideal totality of the living community or the reproduction of the statuses and obligations of the living (Barrett 1994: 50–1). It is through these practices that society is produced and reproduced. The material residue of mortuary behaviour is not the by-product of social processes but the means through which people were working and reworking their particular preconceptions about the world (Barrett 1990: 179, 187). Change in mortuary behaviour thus is not the result of a changed social structure, such as the rise of a chiefdom (Renfrew 1972), but it is through mortuary practices that social change may have been introduced. It is not society that induces changes in mortuary rituals, but rather society is carried forward by such practices (Barrett 1990: 182). In accordance with the view that the mortuary material record is a reflection of practices and behaviours rather than an abstract social structure, it becomes problematic to identify Early Minoan society as a chiefdom (Renfrew 1972; Watrous and Hatzi-Vallianou 2004), a tribal society (Parkinson and Galaty 2007), or any other kind of rigid social formation. The fact that a variety of funerary practices are attested in EM II-III Crete as well as the fact that sites and regions follow very different trajectories also cautions against equating funerary data with one island-wide type of social formation.

Characterising and contextualising the appearance of the house tomb in north-east Crete

The meaning of the house tomb cannot be understood without placing it and the mortuary behaviour it represents in a wider geographical and chronological context.

The Early Minoan I background

It is well established that in EM I north-east Crete is characterised by a great variety of mortuary ritual with rock-shelters and caves as well as chamber tombs along the north coast (Legarra Herrero 2009; 2012).

The EM I burial tradition in rock-shelters and caves is attested at Hagios Nikolaos/ Palaikastro (Bosanquet *et al.* 1902–1903: 344–50), Hagios Antonios (Haggis 1993), Petras (Triantaphyllou 2009; 2012) and several caves have also been reported from Lasithi (Hagios Charalambos, Trapeza Cave; see also Betancourt this volume). In Malia, deep rock-crevices along the coast were used from EM I onwards (Demargne 1945: pl. XXVII, 8499). This tradition of burial seems to be grounded in Neolithic mortuary behaviour, particularly a shift in depositional intensity in FN IV (Tomkins 2008; 2012a). These rock-shelters and caves in many cases continue in use in EM II and EM III or even later (see discussion below). In many places in north-east Crete there is no change in burial practices in EM I-EM III.

The FN IV-EM I tradition of burial in caves and rock-shelters, which occurs more or less all over Crete (Legarra Herrero 2009; 2912; Tomkins 2012a), is very different from the EM I mortuary behaviour attested by the late EM I chamber tomb cemeteries at Hagia Photia (Day *et al.* 1998; Davaras and Betancourt 2004) and Gournes (Galanaki 2006). Not only the tomb type, but also the treatment of the dead is different. Whereas chamber tombs were apparently designed to hold the remains of, at most, one or several individuals (Davaras and Betancourt 2004: 238), caves, rock-shelters and tholoi, in contrast, housed larger-scale, collective burials. In the case of Hagia Photia it was suggested that about 15 families contributed bodies over a period of a hundred years. No clusters could be identified and there does not seem to be any pronounced differences between the grave goods of the tombs, mainly lithics and pottery (Davaras and Betancourt 2004). Cist-tombs are reported from Pseira but Betancourt *et al.* (2003: 125) mention multiple burials although the bone material appears to have been very fragmentary.

The presence of chamber tombs and cist-graves does not automatically imply the presence of Cycladic settlers but could point towards emulation of Cycladic mortuary behaviour (Day *et al.* 1998). However, the non-communal nature of these tombs, the different organisation of chamber tomb cemeteries and their sudden disappearance after EM I suggest that the associated communities may have been concerned with marking off different scales and perhaps forms of identity in death to those, often neighbouring, communities whose funerary foci were caves or rock-shelters.

The earliest house tombs

Neither does the disappearance of the Cycladic chamber tombs and cist tombs after EM I imply that EM II mortuary behaviour becomes homogenised in north-east Crete. Indeed, the house tomb is not omnipresent from EM II onwards and forms just one aspect of funerary behaviour in the region, with several cemeteries displaying multiple tomb types (Gournia, Mochlos, Malia, Hagia Triada) (Soles 1992) and some sites perhaps having several cemeteries. The fact that some settlements appear to have had multiple cemeteries (which may display considerable variation in tomb types) may have added an additional level of distinction. Phourni Archanes, for example, is but one of several cemeteries associated with the settlement of Archanes; other cemeteries having been identified at Karnari, Katsoprinias, Anephoros and Kaballaropetra but it is not clear whether EM and MM burials were found here (Sakellarakis and Sapouna-Sakellaraki 1991: 24–5). At EM II Palaikastro tombs were found on Gravel Ridge and Ta Hellenika and additional, new burial sites were developed at Patema and Sarantari from MM I (Soles 1992: 179–193). At Malia, tombs were found at different locations along the coast (*Pièrres Meulières* but also an unpublished "*charnier*" near Building Thita) as well as on *L' ilôt du Christ* (Soles 1992; Olivier and McGeorge 1977). Unlike the tholos tomb, the house tomb seems to represent an innovation of EM IIA, with little in the way of obvious EM I prototypes. The origins of the house tomb have been connected to the small built tombs and the cist graves at Pseira (Betancourt *et al.* 2003; Legarra Herrero 2009; 2012) but, the evidence for *in situ* EM I strata is restricted (see Betancourt *et al.* 2003). At Mochlos, although Seager (1912: 40) mentions EM I material underneath the rough paving of Tombs IV-VI the earliest material in the house tombs dates to EM IIA (Seager 1912; Soles 1992).

Through the deployment of rectangular structures consisting of different compartments (Tombs I-III and IV-VI), EM IIA Mochlos distinguishes itself from contemporary communities in the wider region (Soles 1992: 201). The Alykomouri settlement, which may have been on the most efficient communication route between the plain of Mochlos and Mirabello (Haggis 1993; 2005: 64), continued to use the Hagios Antonios rock-shelter (and perhaps other rock-shelters, Haggis 2005). At Gournia, a house tomb was constructed (Gournia III) in EM IIA, while two rock-shelters (IV and V) were also in use. Tomb III contained 16 skulls and perhaps the eight found in a pit dug in the floor of Tomb I also came from this EM IIA tomb (Soles 1992: 8–9, 31). At EM IIA Sphoungaras, burials were made in rock-shelters I and II (Hall 1912), and in addition inhumations were placed directly in the ground (Sphoungaras Deposit A and B). Besides Mochlos, Gournia and perhaps Pseira, early house tombs were also built at Palaikastro (EM IIA Tomb I and EM IIB Tomb II at *Ta Hellenika*), Sissi and perhaps at Malia (Demargne 1945; Soles 1992).

The other house tombs in the region, with the possible exception of Linares (EM II? Soles 1992: 159), are a later phenomenon: Vasiliki (MMI, Soles 1992: 194–95), Zakros-Pezoules (MM IA-II, Soles 1992: 195–201), Myrtos-Pyrgos (EM III/MMIA-II, Soles 1992: 178), Hagios Georgios (EM III? Soles 1992: 129) and Kalo Khorio (EM III-MMI, Haggis 1996: 681). The house tomb is also adopted further west with clear examples at Malia (MM I or EM III at earliest, *La Maison des Morts*; Chrysolakkos) and Gournes (MM IA-B, Soles 1992: 149). On the North Ridge at Gournia, new tombs were constructed in MM IA (Soles 1992: 201), which coincides with extensive building activities in the settlement (Soles 1979).

West of Malia the earliest house tombs date to EM III (Sakellarakis and Sapouna-Sakellaraki 1997: 199, 202), suggesting that EM II house tombs are entirely an East Cretan phenomenon. At Archanes, two tholos tombs were constructed and used in EM IIA (Panagiotopoulos 2002; Papadatos 2005) and further inland, rock-shelters were used (the Pyrgos Cave and the Kyparissi rock-shelter) (Serpetsidaki 2006). Rectangular structures with several compartments are constructed at Archanes from EM III onwards but a new tholos was also constructed before the end of MM IA (Sakellarakis and Sapouna-Sakellaraki 1997: 169, 198, 199, 204, 210, 214, 215; Soles 1992: 201), underlining the blending of two traditions at this time. Knossos remains the big unknown: are we to expect tholos tombs like at Archanes, house tombs like in East Crete, or perhaps both?

The appearance of the house tomb in EM II is thus far from ubiquitous, even within north-east Crete. It seems that the house tomb and the funerary rituals associated with it were initially restricted to a few coastal settlements, whereas other settlements seem to have continued the older burial tradition in rock-shelters and caves.

House tombs in the wider context of EM II funerary practice in east Crete

The house-type appears to be a distinct tomb-type, but the question is whether this correlates to differences in funerary practices. This is not an easy question to answer because one of the chief weaknesses of the mortuary data currently available is that information about the treatment of human bodies in different tomb types is largely missing from the older publications, although this could provide an interesting perspective on cultural differences between different communities (Hamilakis 2002). In addition, it is impossible to assess diachronic changes in the treatment of bodies. Fortunately, recent excavations provide information on this important aspect (Triantaphyllou 2009; 2012; Crevecoeur and Schmitt 2009; Schoep, Schmitt and Crevecoeur 2011; Schoep, Schmitt, Crevecoeur and Déderix 2012). A preliminary discussion of the material from the rock-shelter at Petras makes clear that the human remains were mainly secondary depositions (Triantaphyllou 2009: 20; 2012; see also this volume), and that all age categories are represented. Study of the human material from the Hagios Charalambos cave also seems to suggest secondary deposition (Betancourt *et al.* 2008: 578). The fact that phalanges of fingers and toes as well as sesamoid and hyoid bones (Betancourt *et al.* 2008: 579) were identified could, however, perhaps suggest that some bodies had not decomposed completely before secondary deposition or that there might also have been some primary depositions. The human remains from the Trapeza cave also appear to be secondary depositions, since some skulls were arranged along the side of the cave and some appear to have been heavily burnt. One hundred and eighteen human skulls or fragments of skulls were noted as well as quantities of other bones and it is stated that "Judging by the fragments of lower jaws (mandible), at least twenty individuals are represented. Among these are youthful, middle-aged, and elderly persons of both sexes. The appearance of the fragments testifies generally to their great antiquity, and some of them look as if they had been almost completely incinerated" (Pendlebury and Money-Coutts 1935–1936: 128).

It may also be suggested that the human remains from the *charniers* in Malia were the result of secondary depositions because the bones are described as pressed together very tightly (suggesting they were deposited in one go), with abundant pottery (Demargne 1945: 1–2). Excavation at Sissi has demonstrated that primary inhumation is accompanied by a few vases only and the presence of "une céramique abondante" in the *charniers* could therefore suggest secondary deposition. Also if the secondary burial took place over a prolonged period of time, one would expect a build-up of earth rather than the bones being pressed closely together.

It seems reasonable then to assume that secondary deposition played a major role in caves and rock-shelters. Whether the remains constitute clearance from (other) tombs or excarnation sites, or were selected after primary deposition and subsequent decomposition in the same location is not clear. Provided that there was enough room for manoeuvre, a cave provides a context in which primary and secondary depositions could have been practiced at the same time, as has been noted for tholoi (Triantaphyllou this volume; Hamilakis 2007) but this is unlikely for contexts such as the *charniers* at Malia and the Haghios Charalambos Cave (Betancourt 2014), which do not offer any space or possibility for the manoeuvring of bones after their final deposition.

Secondary deposition is also a practice that goes back well into the Neolithic and thus appears to be a long tradition on Crete (Tomkins 2012a). Such manipulation would seem to contrast with the individual Cycladic-style tombs that have been excavated on Crete, although it must be noted that the human remains were not well preserved (Galanaki 2006: 229; Davaras and Betancourt 2004).

How do the house tombs fit into this? The information available for the house tombs excavated in the first half of the 20th century, is restricted. At Mochlos, a possible primary burial was found in the northern part of compartment IV (Soles 1992: 57). The few bones that were preserved in compartment V were found scattered about the chamber floor instead of lying together in one heap as was usually the case in other tombs (Seager 1912: 42), while a similar situation is also reported in compartment VI, described as "a confused mass of bones lying on the uneven floor" (Seager 1912: 50). In the right-wing partition of compartment I Seager (1912: 18) mentions 30 skulls and a confused mass of other bones while in compartment II "all the objects seem to have been thrown in promiscuously and were mixed with the fragmentary remains of many bodies" (Seager 1912: 24).

No articulated skeletons were mentioned from Gournia and therefore it may be reasonable to assume that the bones appeared as a non-articulated mass. It is clear that there was significant interference with bones but it is not clear whether we are dealing with secondary burials of selected bones (skulls, long bones) or primary burials that had been disturbed after decomposition. Tomb VI at Palaikastro (*Ta Hellenika*) contained one compartment that was "full of bones, closely packed together" as well as two bodies "in contracted position" and one compartment with a single burial (Dawkins 1903–1904: 202). A contracted (primary?) burial was also found at Patema (Bosanquet *et al.* 1902–1903: 354). The large tomb on Gravel Ridge clearly contained the secondary deposition of selected bones and 65 skulls are marked on the plan (as well as the jar burial of an infant) (Bosanquet 1901–1902: 290–3) but Soles (1992: 191) mentions 97 skulls. Haggis (1996: 651) mentions secondary deposition inside a larnax in the house tombs at Kalo Khorio.

The currently ongoing excavations of house tombs at Sissi have provided evidence for primary and secondary burials (Crevecoeur and Schmitt 2009; Schoep, Schmitt and Crevecoeur 2011; Schoep, Schmitt, Crevecoeur and Déderix 2012) although not usually side-by-side in the same compartment (Fig. 9.1). In the EM II (probably EM IIA late) compartment 1.11, four bodies were primary burials that had been disturbed and some of which had been slightly rearranged after decomposition, probably related to the deposition of a later, fifth, body (Fig. 9.2a + b). Other compartments, however, testify to secondary burial, in which selected bones – mainly long bones and skulls – were carefully deposited (1.9) (Crevecoeur and Schmitt 2009: 79–86) (Fig. 9.3). In compartment 1.10 yet another scenario is attested as this structure contains the densely packed remains of a MNI of 20 individuals (Fig. 9.4). The evidence suggests that here we are dealing with primary burials that were disturbed at a later time and the possibility that certain long bones (but not

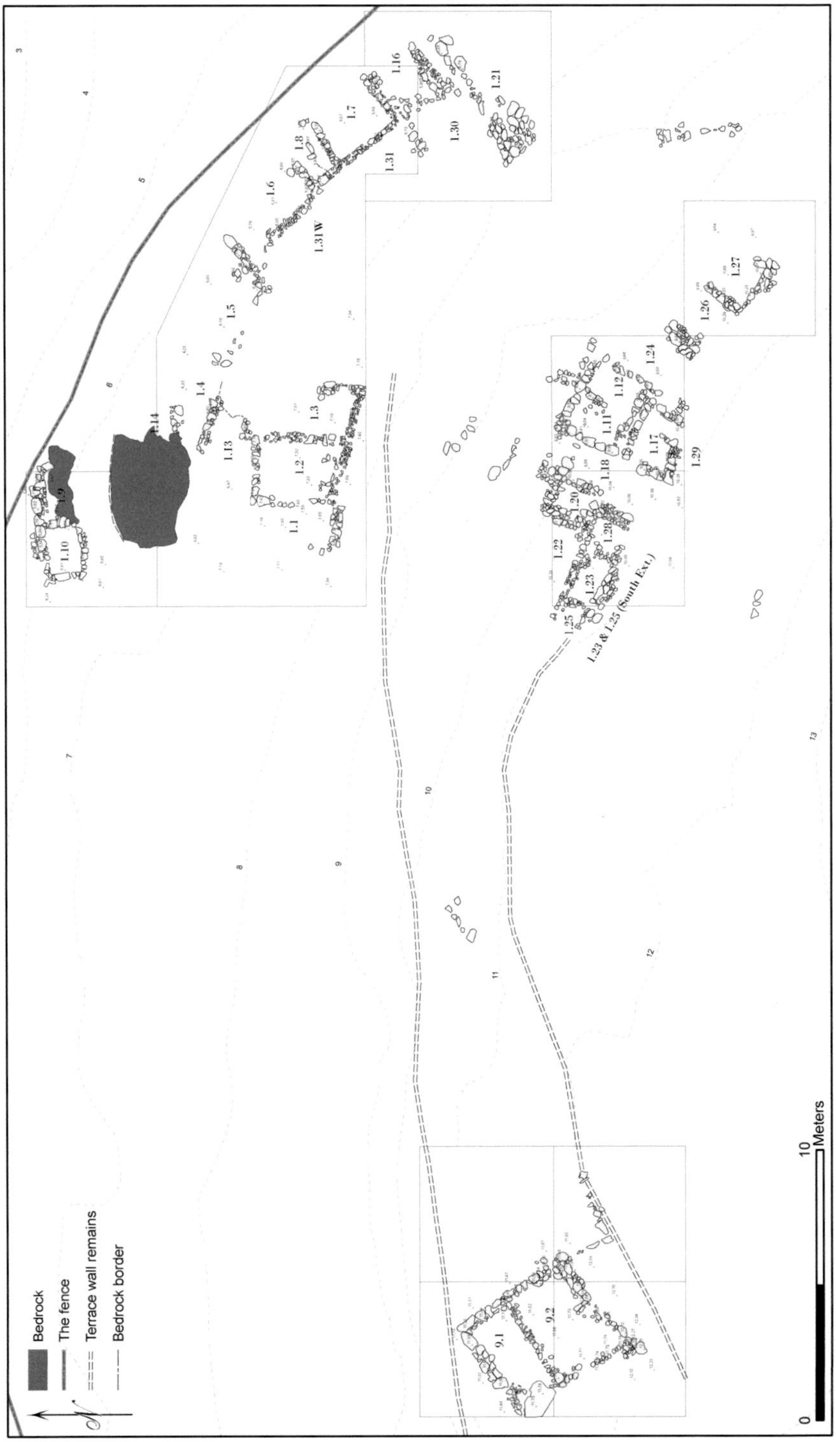

Figure 9.1: Plan of the cemetery at Sissi (P. Haçıgüzeller).

skulls) had been removed after decomposition (Schoep, Schmitt and Crevecoeur 2011). So within a cemetery with a single type of tomb, different treatments of bodies are attested. The question arises as to why some bodies were subjected to secondary burial and others clearly were not (1.11–1.12). There is also evidence at Sissi that some EM III house tombs were cleared out and reused in MM I-II, as suggested by the ca. 0.10m thick stratum of sediment on top of the (cleared) pebble floors in compartments 1.2 and 1.13 (Schoep, Schmitt, Crevecoeur and Déderix 2012: 35). The question as to who used these house tombs and who made decisions about when and how a tomb should be cleared is of crucial importance for the understanding of funerary practices and their social relevance. Equally significant is the temporality of deposition, modification and clearance in tombs and the study of the microstratigraphies preserved inside and outside the tombs will specifically address this question (Carpentier 2015). Obviously, if tombs were regularly cleared out, this has implications for our attempts to use skeletal MNI's in order to study the size of the group contributing to the tombs (see below).

It seems then that the house tombs contained primary as well as secondary depositions of bones. At present it is not possible to identify any significant differences between the house tombs on the one hand and the rock-shelters and caves on the other, but this may be the result of our incomplete knowledge of funerary practices rather than reflecting an ancient reality. Secondary burial in itself needs to be refined as a category, since the recovery of human remains in secondary context does not always attest to the fact of a burial, and there are other strategies which operate with reference to the human corpse and which will result in similar archaeological deposits (Barrett 1994: 51). What is clear is that burial in house tombs has different ideological connotations than burial in rock-shelters and caves (see below).

Problems in correlating tomb type and the size of the contributing group

It has been suggested that the size of the social group constructing and using individual house tombs was smaller in size than the group constructing and using the tholoi (Soles 1992; Branigan 1993; Legarra Herrero 2009). If this were indeed the case, then the use of these tombs could reflect different social structures implying that there would be more to the choice of a tomb type than a cultural preference for a round or rectangular structure (see also Branigan 1993: 7). As to the group who was buried in rock-shelters, Legarra Herrero (2009: 38) argues it to have been smaller than the social group buried in the tholoi but larger than that buried in the cists and chamber tombs.

The conventional approach to estimating the size of the group contributing bodies to a tomb is to set the total number of burials against the length of time a tomb was used. In addition, it is assumed that a nuclear family would contribute about 20 bodies per century to a family tomb (Bintliff 1977: 83). For the Mesara tholoi, Branigan concluded that they were used by groups of two to four families (Branigan 1993: 95). However, it is clear from Branigan's excellent discussion that there are significant

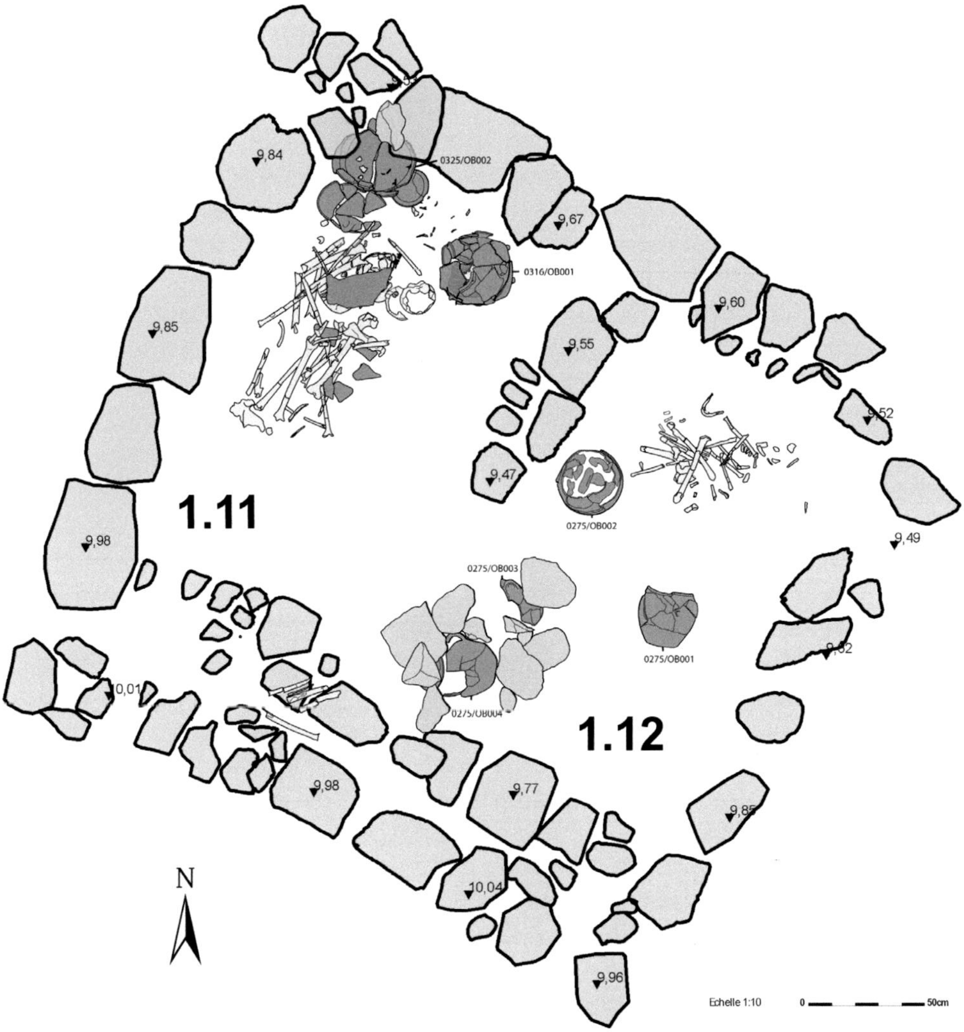

Figure 9.2a: Compartment 1.11–1.12 (I. Crevecoeur).

differences between the various tholoi. Thus Vorou A contained the remains of 55–60 people, whereas tholoi at Lebena and Hagia Triada contained respectively the remains of about 200 and 250 people (Branigan 1993: 90) and Platanos B contained as many as 850 (Branigan 1993: 93). The upper strata in Tholos Γ (EM III/MM IA?) and E at Archanes (MM IA-MM II) contained respectively 44 and 56 skulls, and a group smaller than a nuclear family has been proposed (Panagiotopoulos 2002). Tomb 19 at Phourni was used over a period of about 450 years, giving a MNI of 193, suggesting about 40 burials per 100 years or a population unit of 1.8 to 2 nuclear families (Maggidis 1998: 95). Thus, contemporary tombs within the cemetery of Phourni were used by social groups of different size and this scenario may well apply to other sites.

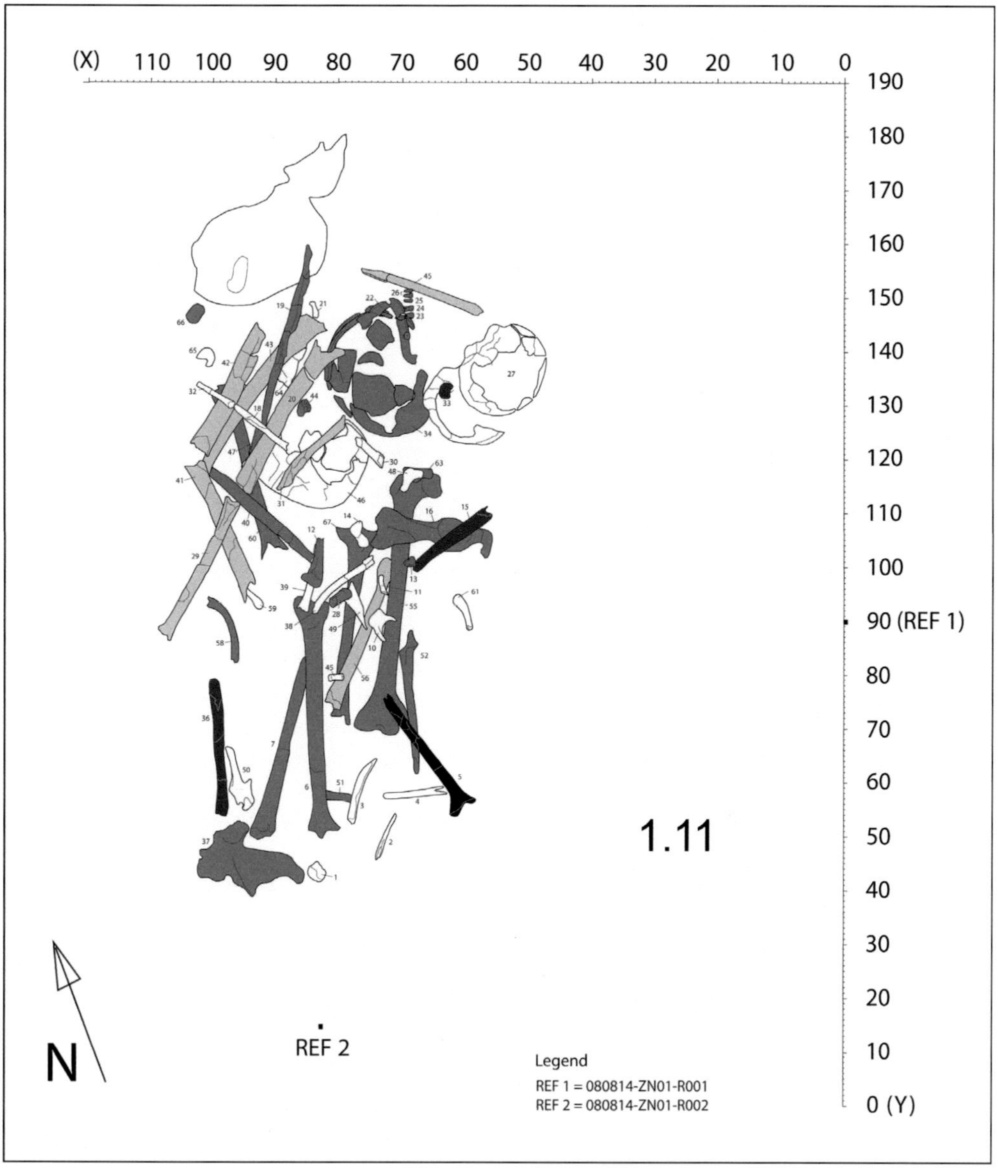

Figure 9.2b: Compartment 1.11–1.12, continued.

For the house tombs (Soles 1992: 253), Soles estimates that the group buried is smaller than or slightly larger than a nuclear family (between 0.4 and 1,4). There is, however, again considerable variation between different house tombs. Thus, 97 skulls are reported from Tomb VII (MM IA and MM IB) at Palaikastro, which was not completely excavated (Soles 1992: 191), and Zakros tombs A and B (MM IA and MM IB/II) contained a MNI of 80 (although according to the excavator, 600, see Soles

Figure 9.3: Compartment 1.9 (A. Schmitt).

1992). Although the compartments of the house tombs in Sissi seem to contain small numbers of people (between 1 and 20), the boundaries of the respective tombs (and the total number per tomb) are at the moment hard to establish.

Thus, the MNI in some house tombs exceeds the MNI in some tholoi, which draws attention to some of the problems associated with this sort of generalised approach. Although in general, the number of individuals from the house tombs seems to be lower than the MNI from the caves and tholoi, there are further problems in estimating accurately the size of the contributing group. What if house tombs were cleared out and reused more often than tholoi? Even if the process of clearing out bones from

Figure 9.4: Compartment 1.10 (A. Schmitt).

house tombs left behind small, chronologically non-diagnostic bones, but dateable sherd material, does the deposition of pottery also imply the deposition of bones? There is a risk involved in assuming that ceramics are a reliable proxy indicator of the date of phases of burial: perhaps burial took place in phases followed by hiatus, perhaps there were phases, such as MM I-II, when deposition involved objects but not bodies? In the absence of independent absolute dating of each MNI there is no way of telling whether the deposition of ceramics went on over longer or shorter periods than the deposition of human skeletal material. A third, possibly complicating, factor is the question of whether everyone had the right to be buried. Is the population unit contributing to the tholos tombs really larger or can the generally larger number of individuals contained in them be explained otherwise: were the tholoi used for a longer period of time or did less restrictions exist as to who had the right to be buried? This is an important factor that has received little attention, although it is unlikely that the cemeteries reflect the entire population of a community, while the right to be buried may differ considerably across time and space. Triantaphyllou (2009) recently noted that some tombs represent all age categories, while others appear not to (Livari tholos tomb *versus* Hagios Charalambos cave and Petras rock-shelter) and so regulations certainly existed.

Understanding the invention/adoption of the house tomb in EM II north-east Crete

In general, the funerary data suggest that tradition and innovation in funerary practices varied contextually between, and perhaps within (see below), different EM II communities in north-east Crete. It seems that change did not occur everywhere at the same time and there may have been considerable differences between the respective communities. This suggests that we should try to understand the introduction/adoption of the house tomb in EM IIA in terms of site-specific conditions and not simply as an island-wide cultural development.

On the basis of the present evidence it would seem that Mochlos played an important and perhaps pioneering role in instituting this new type of funerary practice in EM IIA, at least within the Mirabello region (Mochlos-Gournia-Kavousi). This becomes more likely when considering Mochlos' pivotal role in exchange and trade and its functioning within its region as a "gateway community" for access to new or exotic ideas, objects and practices (Branigan 1991; although the lack of Cycladic material has been emphasised; Carter 2004), most notably in EM II, as suggested by jewellery, stone vases and obsidian blades (Soles 2009: 9).

The construction at Gournia of a single house tomb (Tomb III) in EM IIA, alongside a continuation of burial activity in the rock-shelter at nearby Sphoungaras, would make most sense as a case of emulation of a non-local practice by a specific group within the Gournia community. Given the absence of evidence for use of Tomb III after EM IIA (Soles 1992: 31) and the possibility therefore of a hiatus in house tomb construction and usage at Gournia (Legarra Herrero 2009), this emulation might have been short-lived and ultimately did not succeed in changing the funerary practices of the rest of the community.

Although it is not possible on the basis of the available evidence to see significant differences between the treatment of the dead in rock-shelters, caves and house tombs (for tholoi see Triantaphyllou this volume), it can nevertheless be argued that the introduction and deployment of the house tomb in EM IIA marked a conscious departure from existing, local funerary traditions and had significant ideological implications. First, house tombs, being man-made structures, rather than natural locations like rock-shelters and caves, needed to be constructed and thus involved a more significant degree of planning and building.

Secondly, and perhaps more significantly, EM II house tombs represent multiple funerary foci in their cemeteries at a time when it is more usual to find a single and presumably communal focus (e.g. tholoi, caves and rock-shelters). Although there are numerous problems in defining the specific size and nature of the contributing group, the quantity of house tombs per cemetery and their generally smaller individual size (as opposed to tholoi or caves) does suggest that they were constructed for and by smaller groups of people operating within a community, rather than by the community as a whole. At Mochlos, for example, as many as 13 house tombs were in use by EM IIB (Soles 1992: 201). Through the construction of house tombs, the funerary landscape was transformed and different groups making up the community were able to make their own permanent mark on the landscape. Besides built house tombs, rock-shelters and simple pit graves were also used (Seager 1912; Soles 1992: 42). Such variation within a single cemetery, not only in architecture and grave goods, but perhaps also in the funerary rituals, held great potential for distinguishing between groups of people; it also suggests that funerary practices in such cemeteries were aimed at emphasising the identity of a group within the community (whether nuclear family or lineage group) rather than an overarching communal identity. The construction of the house tomb could be seen as a way of maximising the impact of the funeral and the status of certain intra-communal groups.

Funerary practices and social reproduction

Work on mortuary behaviour in Britain has shown that, at the same time as providing a *locale*, tombs also provide a *medium* for social reproduction (Barrett 1990; 1994). Mortuary practices were one of the means by which society produced and reproduced itself and through which changes may have been brought forward (Barrett 1990). The reason for this is that mortuary symbolism and practices had a dual purpose: the grave not only forms a receptacle for the safe consignment of the dead but becomes a *focal point for the redefinition of genealogical status and for the redefinition of the status of the mourners amongst the living* (Barrett 2000: 184). In order to function as a way of expressing one's own status to a wider audience, mortuary behaviour demands ever more efficient methods of display and extended rites, such as processions, sacrifice and feasting, which draw more people within its influence (Barrett 1990: 186). The construction of house tombs in EM IIA and the (trans)formation of a funerary landscape (i.e. the creation of an architectural setting and a funerary *locale*) might be seen as an attempt to make funerary rituals a more effective medium for social reproduction, specifically the competitive display of difference at an *intra-communal* level, within certain EM II communities in north-east Crete. This is well illustrated by the deposition of extraordinary wealth in some EM II house tombs, most notably those at Mochlos (Seager 1912; Legarra Herrero 2012). In addition, the nature of the grave goods clearly illustrates that these groups were concerned with forging and displaying affiliations with elites elsewhere and it is against this background that the consumption of exotica must be seen (Schoep 2006; Colburn 2008). The limited space in the cemeteries suggests that it was unlikely that the whole community participated in these funerary rites. The size of the courts associated with tomb complexes I/II/III and IV/V/VI at Mochlos suggests that participation was exclusive rather than inclusive.

In this way it may be suggested that the introduction of the house tomb reveals a concern with the ordering of smaller social groups within the community. Through the performance of funerary rituals a particular social order was brought about and/or reinforced amongst the living in these communities. This increased focus on particular intra-communal groups, on their place in the community and on their genealogy represents a departure from the more communal focus that appears to be reproduced by burials in caves, such as Trapeza (Pendlebury *et al.* 1935–1936) and Hagios Charalambos (where remains of over 400 individuals were found) and in the tholos tombs in the Mesara and the Asterousia (Relaki 2004). Although exotic items were also deposited in caves and tholoi, they were consumed in a context that presumably reflected a social group larger than the one that was represented in the house tombs (Branigan 1993; Soles 1992: 251–5). If this is indeed the case (but see discussion above) it could constitute an important difference in EM II between communities using tholos tombs or other communal tombs, on the one hand, and, on the other, those using house tombs, as already suggested by Keith Branigan (1993: 7). However, the tholoi at Phourni/Archanes, where the number of individuals represented in EM III-MM IA seems to be considerably smaller than most tholoi in the Mesara, suggest that the type of tomb is not unequivocally related to the nature of the social group (see above).

What does the early adoption of the house tomb in EM II tell us about the communities that were adopting this funerary behaviour? Most obviously it reveals a concern within some communities to use funerary practices to structure and restructure the status and relationships between specific groups within and beyond the community. Thus the spatial organisation of the Mochlos cemetery, on different terraces with funerary structures varying in size and form, can then be seen as a negotiation between different groups making up the Mochlos community. From this it would seem to follow that within the communities using house tombs in EM II the identities and relationships between *intra-communal* groups were seemingly of greater social concern and more volatile than within contemporary non-house tomb using communities in north-east Crete. Does the continuity in funerary practice apparent in the majority of settlements imply that there was less need to maximise the use of funerary rituals as a political strategy? The Mirabello region is one of the most intensively researched regions on Crete and it is interesting to draw the survey data into this discussion. Haggis emphasises the remarkably long-term adherence of settlement patterns to local social landscapes and highly localised and internal centripetal developments, suggesting that this may be mirrored in the patterns of tomb use (Haggis this volume). Did this adherence to funerary tradition serve an important role in reproducing and maintaining a particular social structure? In the Gournia, Kavousi and Priniatikos Pyrgos areas, the bulk of the sites are hamlets (clusters of houses) and farms with some villages (Gournia, Khalepa, Vasiliki, Kavousi village and Mochlos) (Watrous *et al.* 2012; Haggis this volume). What did the funerary landscape look like and was there a difference between the funerary practices of hamlets and farms on the one hand and villages on the other? Did hamlets and/or farms share cemeteries, as was suggested for settlements without tombs in Agiopharango (Blackman and Branigan 1977: 70)? Did larger places ("villages") develop cemeteries that were specifically associated with them? Keeping in mind Barrett's dual function of funerary rites, the innovations in the funerary domain should not be seen as the result of social change, but as a way of bringing about social change.

Cemeteries and other fields of social discourse

Since funerary behaviour forms part of social practice, the study of cemeteries should ideally be viewed in conjunction with social practice taking place in other locales. One way of structuring this enquiry is by employing Barrett's concept of *fields of discourse* (Barrett 2000). A field is defined as an arena in time-space occupied by virtue of the practice of a particular discourse (Barrett 2000: 28–29). Such fields 'shade off' in time and space and contain material conditions (of which the archaeological evidence is the residue) which contribute towards the structuring of practice. Discourse is a means of communication; it draws upon and reproduces particular structures of knowledge, thus also reproducing relations of dominance between individuals and groups (Barrett 2000: 27). By framing society as composed of multiple such fields of discourse, social practice can be contextualised in time and space. This allows temporal changes in the way these fields were used and perceived to be related to other fields. By examining social practice in this way, it becomes clear that these different but contemporary spatial and temporal arenas fulfilled specific roles in the reproduction of society (Schoep 2012).

The *locales* of the cemeteries, monumental arenas, such as Court Buildings, or other communal arenas and private or residential spaces can be seen as different fields of discourse. Such a perspective on social reproduction undermines the validity of approaches that would extrapolate the structure of a society on the basis of only funerary data, or monumental buildings, or residential space. Such approaches have resulted in very different assessments of Early Minoan society. On the basis of the presence or absence of monumental architecture very different opinions exist about what type of social formation produced these remains, going from an egalitarian and simple one (Cherry 1983; Parkinson and Galaty 2007) to a more complex one often designated a chiefdom (Renfrew 1972; Watrous 1994). It must be stressed that the remains that we study are the result of human practices and not of abstract social formations (Barrett 2000).

Social practices in different fields of discourse, such as monumental buildings, communal spaces (e.g. the court at Vasiliki) and domestic spaces, may have been informed by different concerns and been aimed at reproducing different identities. Thus, although the organisation of the cemetery and funerary practices at Mochlos might have been aimed at defining and negotiating the distinct identities of specific groups within the community (i.e. kinship groups, lineages or nuclear families), practices taking place in a communal context may have been expressing a more communal identity or ideology. Recent research at Phaistos (Todaro 2012) and Knossos (Tomkins 2012b) suggests that during EM II-MM I the Court Buildings were used for ritualised communal gatherings that involved group commensality (Schoep

2012). Practices in these buildings seem to have focused on defining identities at the communal and corporate levels.

By framing the data in terms of fields of discourse one is able to better identify and trace diachronic shifts in practice both within *and* between different fields of discourse. I have suggested elsewhere (Schoep 2012) that, whereas funerary practices formed the main arena for the expression of group identity and status (through the consumption of wealth) in EM II-III, during MM I or early in MM II there is a notable shift in investment by groups into the residential field. Residential spaces become the arena of display and conspicuous consumption, at the same time as there is a tendency for funerary practices to become less conspicuous. In settlements such as Malia and perhaps Knossos there is an unprecedented investment in the architectural elaboration of different elite-complexes. In the case of Quartier Mu at Malia, this even exceeds the investment in the Court Buildings in MM II, a situation which I have suggested reflects increased power on the part of certain groups (lineages?) and perhaps a changed dynamic between these and the Court Building (Schoep 2012).

Acknowledging the existence of different fields of discourse allows for a more subtle and complete view of social reproduction and helps overcome the tendency to read social formations, such as tribes and chiefdoms, from either the "funerary record" or the settlement record (cf. Barrett 1990; 2000).

Conclusions

It has been suggested that EM II funerary practices in north-east Crete vary contextually between and even in some cases within settlements. In most communities the tradition of burial in caves and rock-shelters continues, but in a restricted group of coastal communities a new practice appears in which burial took place in rectangular house-like structures containing multiple compartments. It has been suggested that the new practice of constructing houses for the dead in EM IIA should be seen as a way of maximising the impact of the funeral, mortuary behaviour, and the extension of rites such as processions, sacrifice and feasting (Barrett 1990: 186) that draws more people within its influence. The distribution of the house tomb in EM II is restricted and it was argued that they were adopted in communities, where the status, distinction and ordering of smaller, intra-communal social sub-units had become a particular issue. Such increased focus on specific groups, their place in the community and their genealogy is different from the more communal focus that lies at the heart of burial in caves and the larger rock-shelters. It is well established that funerary monumentality can be linked to moments of political uncertainty (Parker Pearson 2000: 40) and that innovations implemented by high-status groups are frequently emulated later by others (Miller 1985). Both dynamics can be glimpsed operating in the appearance and subsequent spread of house tombs until, by MM I, their usage has spread more widely within and beyond north-east Crete.

Acknowledgements

I would like to thank very warmly Yiannis and Maria for inviting me to the Round Table in honour of Keith Branigan. I would like to offer this article as a small token of gratitude to Keith for the kindness he showed me when I was a visiting post-doctoral researcher and for sharing his office with me. I would also like to thank KU Leuven and the F.W.O-Vlaanderen for funding excavations at the cemetery of Sissi.

Bibliography

Barrett, J.

1990 The monumentality of death: the character of Early Bronze Age mortuary mounds in southern Britain. *World Archaeology* 22: 179–89.

1994 *Fragments from Antiquity: An Archaeology of Social Life 2900–1200 BC*. Oxford: Blackwell.

2000 Fields of discourse: reconstituting a social archaeology. In J. Thomas (ed.), *Interpretive Archaeology: A Reader*: 23–32. London: Leicester University Press.

Betancourt, P. P. and C. Davaras

2003 *Pseira VII: The Pseira Cemetery II. Excavation of the Tombs*. Philadelphia: INSTAP Academic Press.

Betancourt P. P., S. Chlouveraki, C. Davaras, H. M. C. Dierckx, S. C. Ferrence, J. Hickman, P. Karkanas, P. J. P. McGeorge, J. D. Muhly, D. S. Reese, E. Stravopodi and L. Langford-Verstegen.

2008 Excavations in the Hagios Charalambos cave. A preliminary report. *Hesperia* 77: 539–605.

Betancourt, P. P., C. Davaras and E. Stravopodi (eds.)

2014 *Hagios Charalambos: A Minoan Burial Cave in Crete. I Excavation and Portable Objects* (Prehistory Monographs 47). Philadelphia: INSTAP Academic Press.

Binford, L.

1971 Mortuary practices: their study and potential. In J. A. Brown (ed.), *Approaches to the Social Dimensions of Mortuary Practices*: 6–29. Washington D.C.: Society for American Archaeology.

Bintliff, J.

1977 *Natural Environment and Human Settlement in Prehistoric Greece* (BAR IS 28). Oxford: Archaeopress.

Blackman, D. J. and K. Branigan

1977 An archaeological survey of the lower catchment area of the Ayiofarango. *Annual of the British School at Athens* 72: 13–84.

Bloch, M.

1977 The past and the present in the present. *Man* 12: 278–92.

Branigan, K.

1991 Mochlos – An Early Aegean gateway community? In R. Laffineur and L. Basch (eds.), *Thalassa, L'Egee Prehistorique et la Mer* (Aegaeum 7): 97–106. Liège: Universitè de Liège.

1993 *Dancing with Death. Life and death in Southern Crete c. 3000–2000 BC*. Amsterdam: Adolf M. Hakkert.

Bosanquet, R. C.

1901–1902 Excavations at Palaikastro, I. *Annual of the British School at Athens* 9: 286–316.

Bosanquet, R. C., R. M. Dawkins, M. N. Tod, W. L. H. Duckworth, and J. L. Myres.

1902–1903 Excavations at Palaikastro, II. *Annual of the British School at Athens* 9: 274–387.

Carpentier, F.

2015 *Minoans under the Microscope. Archaeological soil micromorphology at the Cretan Bronze Age site of Sissi*. Leuven: Catholic University of Leuven (Unpublished Ph.D).

Cherry, J.
1983 Evolution, revolution and the origins of complex society in Minoan Crete. In O. Krzyszkowska and L. Nixon (eds.), *Minoan Society, Proceedings of the Cambridge Colloquium 1981*: 33–45. Bristol: Bristol Classical Press.

Colburn, C.
2008 Exotica and the Early Minoan elite: Eastern imports in Prepalatial Crete. *American Journal of Archaeology* 112: 203–24.

Crevecoeur, I. and A. Schmitt
2009 Étude archéo-anthropologique de la nécropole (Zone 1). In J. Driessen, I. Schoep, F. Crevecoeur, M. Devolder, F. Gaignerot-Driessen, H. Fiasse, P. Haciguzeller, S. Jusseret, C. Langohr, Q. Letesson, and A. Schmitt (eds.), *Excavations at Sissi. Preliminary Report on the 2007-2008 Campaigns* (Aegis 1): 57–94. Louvain-la-Neuve: Presses Universitaires de Louvain.

Day, D., Wilson, D. E. and E. Kiriatzi
1998 Pots, Labels, and People: Burying ethnicity in the cemetery of Aghia Photia, Siteias. In K. Branigan (ed.), *Cemetery and Society in the Bronze Age Aegean* (Sheffield Studies in Aegean Archaeology 1): 133–49. Sheffield: Sheffield Academic Press.

Davaras, C. and P. P. Betancourt
2004 *The Hagia Photia Cemetery 1: The Tomb Groups and Architecture* (Prehistory Monographs 14). Philadelphia: INSTAP Academic Press.

Dawkins, R.
1903–1904 Excavations at Palaikastro III. *Annual of the British School at Athens* 10: 286–316.

Demargne, P.
1945 *Nécropoles de Mallia, les premiers charniers, l'ossuaire principier de Chrysolakkos* (Études Crétoises VII). Paris: Geuthner.

Evans, A. E.
1906 *The Prehistoric Tombs of Knossos*. London: B. Quaritch.

Galanaki, K.
2006 Πρωτομινωικό ταφικό σύνολο στην πρώην Αμερικανική βάση Γουρνών Πεδιάδος. *Πεπραγμένα του Ι' Διεθνούς Κρητολογικού Συνεδρίου*, vol. A2: 227–35. Χανιά: Φιλολογικός Σύλλογος "Ο Χρυσόστομος".

Haggis, D. C.
1993 The Early Minoan burial cave at Ayios Antonios and some problems in Early Bronze Age chronology. *Studi Micenei ed Egeo-Anatolici* 31: 7–34.
1996 Excavations at Kalo Khorio, East Crete. *American Journal of Archaeology* 100: 645–81.
2005 Kavousi I: The archaeological survey of the Kavousi region. *The Results of the Excavations at Kavousi in Eastern Crete* (Prehistory Monographs 16). Philadelphia: INSTAP Academic Press.

Hall, E.
1912 *Excavations in Eastern Crete, Sphoungaras* (The Museum Anthropological Publications III. ii). Philadelphia: University of Pennsylvania.

Hamilakis, Y.
2002 Introduction. Thinking through the body. In Y. Hamilakis, M. Pluciennik and S. Tarlow (eds.), 2002. *Thinking Through The Body: Archaeologies of Corporeality*: 1–21. New York: Kluwer Academic/Plenum.
2007 Tombs for the living. *Antiquity* 81: 1090–93.

Hawes, H. B., Williams, B. E., Seager, R. B., and E. H. Hall
1908 *Gournia, Vasilike and Other Prehistoric Sites on the Isthmus of Hierapetra*. Philadelphia: The American Exploration Society, Free Museum of Science and Art.

Legarra Herrero, B.
2009 The Minoan Fallacy: cultural diversity and mortuary behaviour on Crete at the beginning of the Bronze Age. *Oxford Journal of Archaeology* 28: 29–57.
2012 The construction, deconstruction and non-construction of hierarchies in the funerary record of Prepalatial Crete. In I. Schoep, P. Tomkins and J. Driessen (eds.), *Back to the Beginning. Reassessing Social, Economic and Political Complexity in the Early and Middle Bronze Age on Crete*: 325–58. Oxford: Oxbow.
Maggidis, C.
1998 From polis to necropolis: social ranking from architectural and mortuary evidence in the Minoan cemetery at Phourni, Archanes. In K. Branigan (ed.), *Cemetery and Society in the Aegean Bronze Age* (Sheffield Studies in Aegean Archaeology 1): 87–102. Sheffield: Sheffield Academic Press.
Miller, D. and C. Tilley (eds.)
1984 *Ideology, Power and Prehistory*. Cambridge: Cambridge University Press.
Morris, I.
1992 *Death-Ritual and Social Structure in Classical Antiquity*. Cambridge: Cambridge University Press.
Olivier, J.-P., and T. McGeorge
1977 Fouille d'urgence de l'entrée du "charnier n°4", en C4/f 5–6. *Bulletin de Correspondance Hellénique* 101: 701–03.
Panagiotopoulos, D.
2002 *Das Tholosgrab E von Phourni bei Archanes: Studien zu einem frühkretischen Grabfund und seinem kulturellen Kontext* (BAR IS 1014). Oxford: Archaeopress.
Papadatos, Y.
2005 *Tholos Tomb Gamma: A Prepalatial Tholos Tomb at Phourni, Archanes* (Prehistory Monographs 17). Philadelphia: INSTAP Academic Press.
Parker Pearson, M.
1982 Mortuary practices, society and ideology: an ethnoarchaeological study. In I. Hodder (ed.), *Symbolic and Structural Archaeology*: 99–113. Cambridge: Cambridge University Press.
2000 *The Archaeology of Death and Burial*. Stroud: Sutton.
Parkinson, W. A. and M. Galaty
2007 Secondary states in perspective: an integrated approach to state formation in the prehistoric Aegean. *American Anthropologist* 109: 113–29.
Pendlebury, J. W. D. S. and M. Money-Coutts
1935–1936 Excavations in the plain of Lasithi. I. The Cave of Trapeza. *Annual of the British School at Athens* 36: 5–131.
Relaki, M.
2004 Constructing a *Region*: the contested landscapes of Prepalatial Mesara. In J. C. Barrett and P. Halstead (eds.), *The Emergence of Civilisation Revisited* (Sheffield Studies in Aegean Archaeology 6): 170–88. Oxford: Oxbow.
Renfrew, C.
1972 *The Emergence of Civilisation*. London: Methuen.
Sakellarakis, Y. and E. Sapouna-Sakellaraki
1991 *Archanes*. Athens: Ekdotike Hellados.
1997 *Archanes. Minoan Crete in a New Light*. Athens: Ammos Editions.
Saxe, A. A.
1970 *Social Dimensions of Mortuary Practices*. PhD dissertation, University of Michigan.
Schoep, I.
1999 The origins of writing and administration on Crete. *Oxford Journal of Archaeology* 18: 265–76.

2006 Looking beyond the First Palaces: elites and the agency of power in EM III-MM II Crete. *American Journal of Archaeology* 110: 37–64.
2012 Bridging the divide between the "Prepalatial" and the "Protopalatial" periods? In I. Schoep, P. Tomkins and J. Driessen (eds.), *Back to the Beginning. Reassessing Social, Economic and Political Complexity in the Early and Middle Bronze Age on Crete*: 403–28. Oxford: Oxbow.

Schoep, I., Schmitt, A. and I. Crevecoeur
2011 *The cemetery of Sissi. Report of the 2011 campaign* (Aegis 5): 41–67 Louvain-la-Neuve: Presses Universitaires de Louvain.

Schoep, I., Schmitt, A., Crevecoeur, I. and S. Déderix
2012 *The cemetery of Sissi. Report of the 2009-2010 campaigns* (Aegis 4): 31–54. Louvain-la-Neuve: Presses Universitaires de Louvain.

Seager, R.
1912 *Explorations in the Island of Mochlos*. Boston, New York: American School of Classical Studies at Athens.

Serpetsidaki, I.
2006 Προανακτορικός σπηλαιώδης τάφος στο Κυπαρίσσι Τεμένους. *Πεπραγμένα του Θ' Διεθνούς Κρητολογικού Συνεδρίου*, vol. A2: 243–58. Ηράκλειο: Εταιρεία Κρητικών Ιστορικών Μελετών.

Soles, J. S.
1979 The Early Gournia town. *American Journal of Archaeology* 83: 149–67.
1992 *The Prepalatial Cemeteries at Mochlos and. Gournia and the House Tombs of Bronze Age Crete* (Hesperia Supplement 24). Princeton: American School of Classical Studies at Athens.
2009 2009 Greek-American excavation at Mochlos. *Kentro* 12: 9–12.

Tainter, J. R.
1978 Mortuary practices and the study of prehistoric social systems. In L. Binford (ed.), *For Theory Building in Archaeology*: 327–51. New York: Academic Press.

Todaro, S.
2012 Craft production and social practices at Prepalatial Phaistos: the background to the First Palace. In I. Schoep, P. Tomkins and J. Driessen (eds.), *Back to the Beginning. Reassessing Social, Economic and Political Complexity in the Early and Middle Bronze Age on Crete*: 195–235. Oxford: Oxbow.

Tomkins, P.
2008 Domesticity by default. Ritual, ritualisation and cave-use in the Neolithic Aegean. *Oxford Journal of Archaeology* 28: 125–53.
2012a Landscapes of ritual, identity, and memory: Reconsidering Neolithic and Bronze Age cave use in Crete, Greece. In H. Moyes (ed.), *Sacred Darkness: A Global Perspective on the Ritual Use of Caves*: 59–79. Boulder: University Press of Colorado.
2012b Behind the horizon. Reconsidering the genesis and function of the "First Palace" at Knossos (Final Neolithic IV-Middle Minoan IB). In I. Schoep, P. Tomkins and J. Driessen (eds.), *Back to the Beginning. Reassessing Social, Economic and Political Complexity in the Early and Middle Bronze Age on Crete*: 32–80. Oxford: Oxbow.

Triantaphyllou, S.
2009 EM/MM skeletal human remains from East Crete: The Kephala Petras rock-shelter, Siteia and the Livari Tholos Tomb, Skiadi. *Kentro* 12: 19–23.
2012 Kephala Petras: the human remains and the burial practices in the Rock Shelter. In M. Tsipopoulou (ed.), *Petras, Siteia - 25 years of excavations and studies* (Monographs of the Danish Institute at Athens 16): 161–70. Athens: Danish Institute at Athens.

Watrous, V. L.
1994 Review of Aegean prehistory III: Crete from earliest prehistory through the Protopalatial Period. *American Journal of Archaeology* 98: 695–753.

Watrous, V. L., D. Hatzi-Vallianou, and H. Blitzer
2004 *The plain of Phaistos: Cycles of complexity in the Messara region of Crete* (Monumenta Archaeologica 23). Los Angeles: Cotsen Institute of Archaeology at UCLA.
Watrous, L. V., Haggis, D., Nowicki, K., Vogeikoff-Brogan, N. and M. Schultz
2012 Early Minoan I-II periods: emergence of a stratified society. In L. V. Watrous, D. Haggis, K. Nowicki, N. Vogeikoff-Brogan and M. Schultz, *An Archaeological Survey of the Gournia Landscape: A Regional History of the Mirabello Bay, Crete, in Antiquity*. (Prehistory Monographs 37). Philadelphia: INSTAP Academic Press.
Xanthoudides, S.
1924 *The Vaulted Tombs of Mesara*. London: Hodder & Stoughton.

Chapter 10

Visible and invisible death. Shifting patterns in the burial customs of Bronze Age Crete

Eleni Hatzaki

Introduction

Nothing could be more different than Cretan burial practices of the Prepalatial (EM-MM IA) from those of the Final Palatial (LM II-IIIA2) and Postpalatial (LM IIIA2-B) periods: the former characterised by many disarticulated bodies (Fig. 10.1) in above ground built tombs (with the exception of the Cycladic inspired cemeteries of north Crete, Davaras and Bentancourt 2004; Galanaki 2006), caves, or rock shelters, the latter by few articulated individuals in underground rock cut or/and stone built tombs (Fig. 10.2). However, both periods are characterised (to a certain extent) by island-wide patterns such as archaeologically visible burial and peaks of ostentatious display, unlike the still largely elusive "middle part", the Protopalatial (MM IB-MM IIB) and Neopalatial (MM IIIA-LM IB) periods, when no island-wide pattern in burial practices can be discerned other than that archaeologically visible burial became over time in different parts of the island extremely rare, if not extinct (Hatzaki 2012). In this paper, this dramatically varied diachronic picture of visibility and invisibility in death at an intra-island level is compared and contrasted with comparable phenomena (or lack of them) in non-funerary contexts. I shall argue that ostentatious display in burial, or the lack of it, in certain cases is directly linked to a shifting emphasis towards other contexts suitable for social and especially public display, associated with the changing social and political setups of Prepalatial, Palatial, and Postpalatial Crete.

Diachronic patterns in ostentatious display at burial and beyond

Prepalatial to Protopalatial: continuity and change in "Minoan" burial practice

Study of human skeletal remains from Prepalatial tombs (Triantaphyllou 2005; 2009; 2010; Cadogan 2011: 107; Triantaphyllou in this volume) suggest that burial generally

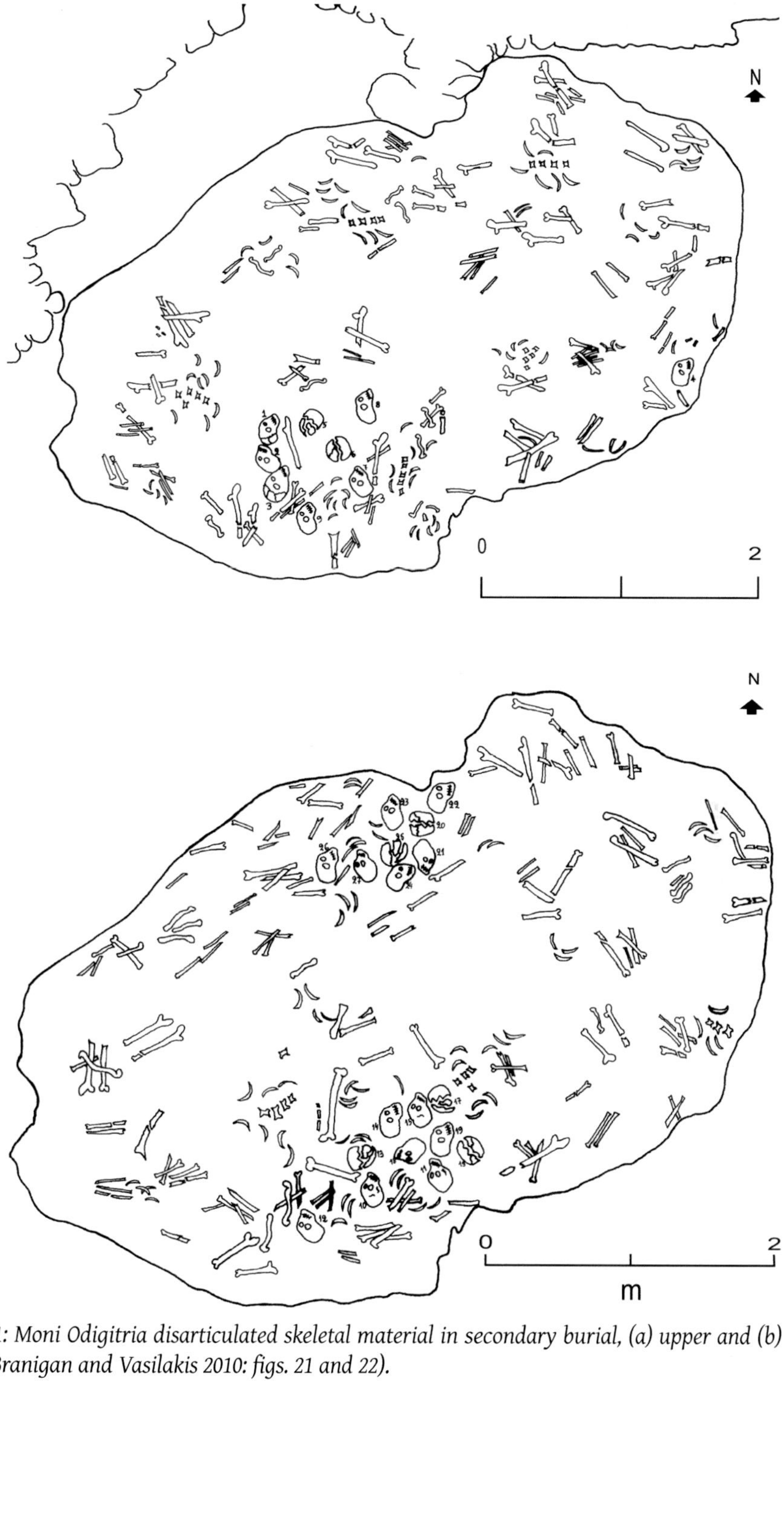

Figure 10.1: Moni Odigitria disarticulated skeletal material in secondary burial, (a) upper and (b) lower stratum (Branigan and Vasilakis 2010: figs. 21 and 22).

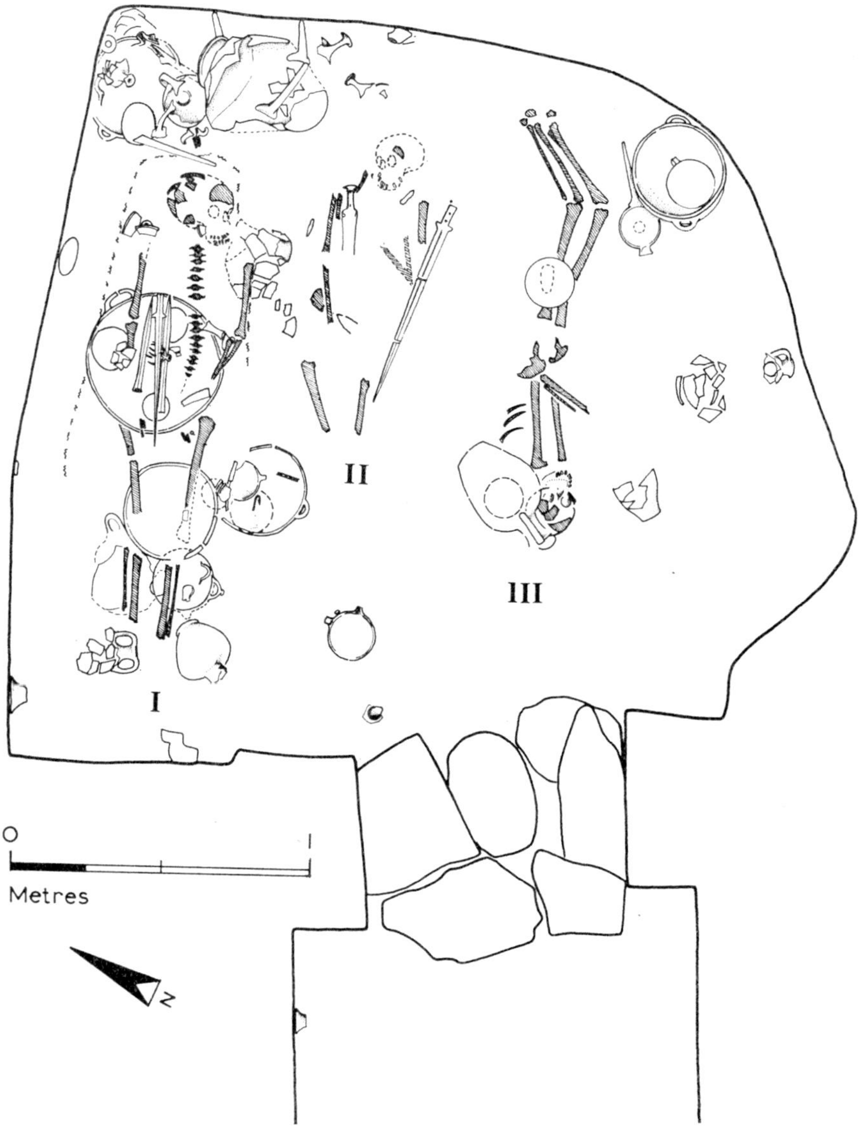

Figure 10.2: Knossos Sellopoulo Tomb 4 articulated skeletal material in primary burial (Popham et al. *1974: 200 fig. 3).*

was inclusive rather than exclusive, since both sexes and all age groups (including infants) are usually represented, implying that archaeologically visible burial was perhaps practiced by a good proportion of the Prepalatial populations of Crete. In a settlement pattern characterised largely by small settlements (such as Phournou Koriphi; Warren 1972; Whitelaw 1983; 2012; Haggis 2002) or even isolated hamlets

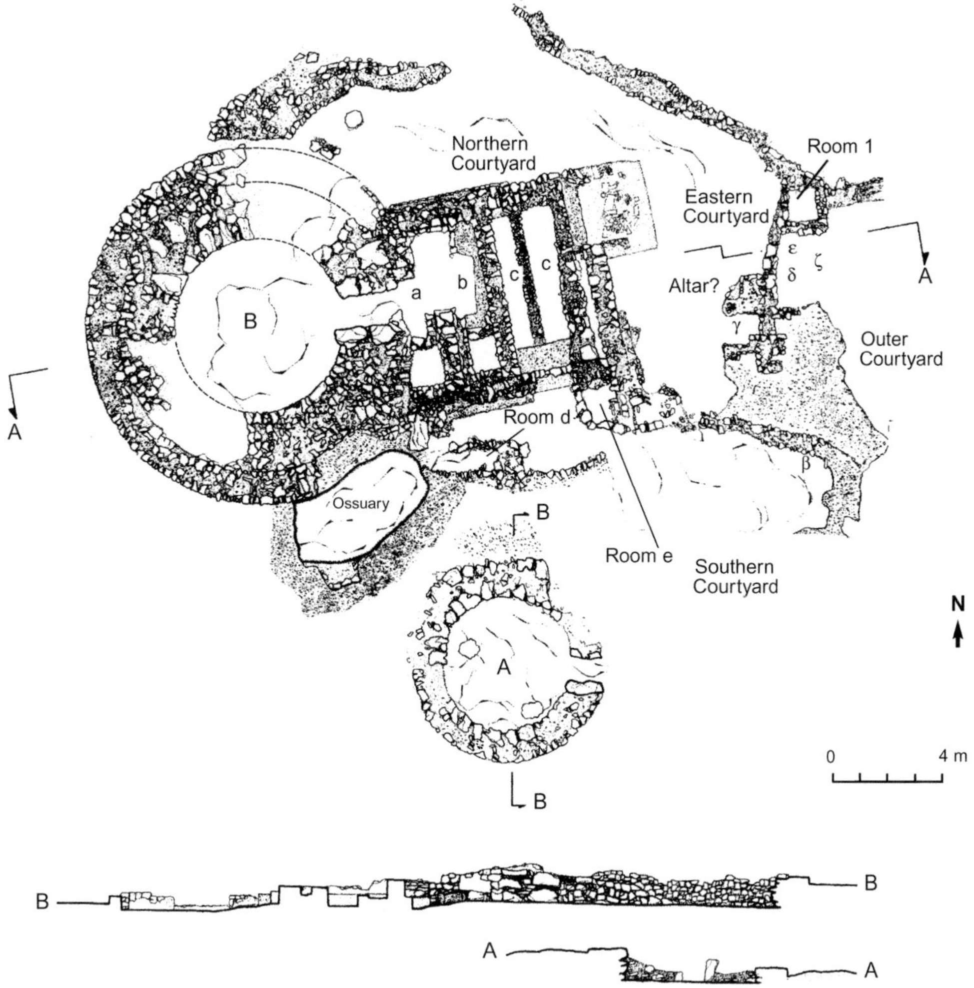

Figure 10.3: Moni Odigitria plan (Branigan and Vasilakis 2010: fig. 14).

diffused within the landscape, as in the Asterousia mountains (Blackman and Branigan 1982; Sbonias in this volume), above ground built tombs not only presented a visually different built environment to that designed for the living, but one that perhaps was the focal point for inter-community gatherings (Fig. 10.3). The fairly consistent association of tholos tombs with dawn alignments (Goodison 2001; 2004) suggests that events other than primary burial also took place, dictated by calendar and ideological practices, indirectly confirmed by evidence for multi-phase treatment of the dead at various stages of decomposition taking place inside, but also outside the tomb (for example at Livari, Triantaphyllou 2009). The inauguration of a built tomb as the focal point for intra-group gatherings started with its construction, a labour intensive activity involving the intentional acquisition of large roughly hewn blocks and their skilful placement within the wall matrix (Xanthoudides 1924: pl. 16) The memory of this laboriously intensive group activity demonstrated through building materials and construction techniques perhaps acted as a form of ostentatious display at an inter-group level, but also aimed at perpetuating intra-group solidarity. With burial in rock shelters and caves such group dynamics were different, perhaps with an emphasis on place over space and the built environment, associated with acts of secondary burial (for example Hagios Charalambos, Betancourt *et al.* 2008; Betancourt 2012). Ostentatious display in the deposition of off-island finished products and/or of objects made locally but of off-island raw materials, while starting in EM I, accelerated by EM IIA (Legarra Herrero 2009; 2011; 2012). Varied regional patterns at intra- or inter-site level suggests that certain types of objects (or/and combinations of) were utilized in different ways due to local conditions including varied appropriation strategies as in the case of the two side by side tholoi at Archanes (Panagiotopoulos 2002; Papadatos 2005; 2007) but also Koumasa and Platanos (Leggara Herrero 2012). The ostentatious display in construction and movable material culture, at least so far, is not paralleled in the albeit sparse Prepalatial settlement contexts. Nevertheless, the dead were brought into the world of the living, testified through the human skull found in Room 89 at Phournou Koriphi (Warren 1972: 135, fig. 28; Driessen 2010).

The subsequent EM IIB-III disrupted picture of burial activity along the north coast of Crete (Legarra Herrero 2009), and the demise of ostentatious display in assorted material culture (with the exception of Mochlos) have been linked to the shrinkage of a Cycladic trade network (Broodbank 2000; 2008) and its ripple effect on Crete. In terms of movable material culture, perhaps the most striking change is the dissemination of a clay container (pithoi and tubs) for burial (Walberg 1987: 58–60; see for example Archanes Phourni Tholos Γ, Papadatos 2005: fig. 5 *a–b*; and Tholos E, Panagiotopoulos 2002: pl. 4). If the appropriation of a vessel type originally designed and used for staple storage suggests intriguing symbolic connotations between actual storage, symbolic storage, and intentional preservation for living and dead alike, the rapid diffusion across the island of clay storage vessels as burial containers may have served several purposes at once. Primary burial within a clay container more or less homogenised appearances and skilfully concealed the apparent lack of any accompanying material culture. The use of clay containers for secondary burial (Triantaphyllou 2005: 71) suggests that perpetuating individuality in terms of a self-contained burial was a short-term phenomenon, which over time lost its social and symbolic importance.

In the changing world of the late Prepalatial period (EM III-MM IA), mortuary behaviour changed dramatically yet again. While the demise of ostentatious display in movable material culture continued, with the notable exception of seals (Sbonias 1999; 2010; 2011; Karytinos 2000; Relaki 2004; 2008; 2012), emphasis shifted to new construction and elaboration of existing burial places with a focus on exterior space. For example, the construction of Apesokari (Branigan 1970: 135), the organisation of the exterior space of the Myrtos Pyrgos House tomb (which involved extensive terracing before laying out the pavement and raised causeway, Cadogan 1978; 2011) (Fig. 10.4), and the architectural elaboration of Archanes Tholos B (Sakellarakis and Sapouna-Sakellaraki 1997: 169–79), all demonstrate the ability of certain social groups to mobilise workforce resources within the community. This phenomenon is paralleled in ceramic datasets, where large concentrations of tableware imply participation in communal feasting activities (for example the 155 pots from the area between Tholos B and Burial Building 6 at Archanes Phourni, Sakellarakis and Sakellaraki 1991: 101, fig. 74; Sakellarakis and Sapouna-Sakellaraki 1997: 396, fig. 347). If the overall picture from the burial record is one of group activities, this is paralleled in non-funerary urban and extra-urban public contexts. Reassessment of Prepalatial architectural remains at later palatial sites such as Knossos, Malia, and Phaistos (Schoep 2006; 2012; Schoep and Tomkins 2007; Todaro 2009) further supports this observation. Notable examples include the north-west terrace at Knossos, a construction of unparalleled scale for late Prepalatial Crete (Tomkins 2011; Macdonald 2011), and the construction of the slightly later (in MM IA) monumental Building V at the mountain sanctuary of Syme (Christakis 2013). The invested interest in public space and place is perhaps best demonstrated in the rising importance of peak sanctuaries, starting to be attested architecturally and artefactually during this period (Nowicki 2001; Briault 2007; Peatfield 2007; 2009).

Protopalatial to Neopalatial: tradition and innovation

The continued use of Prepalatial cemeteries into the Protopalatial obscures any clear cut distinction, but the reproduction of Prepalatial burial architecture during the Protopalatial continues: the case of the Kamilari Tholos (Levi 1962; La Rosa 1992; Girella in this volume) is far from accidental, perhaps the result of micro-regional histories associated with the emulation and perpetuation of past burial practices, in this case in the Mesara, a region littered with Prepalatial tholos tombs. Perhaps the little known Gypsades tholos tomb at Knossos, used at least down to MM IIIA if not LM I (Hood 1960: 169 and pl. 18 *b*), suggests a similar phenomenon occurring at Knossos, although the closest *comparanda*, at Archanes Phourni, ceased to be used during the Prepalatial (Tholos Γ, Papadatos 2005: 163–65) or the Protopalatial (Tholos B, Sakellarakis and Sapouna-Sakellaraki 1997:170; Tholos E, Panagiotopoulos 2002: 134–37) but nevertheless remained visual markers in the landscape.

The continued use of Prepalatial cemeteries into Protopalatial, as at Palaikastro, Gournia, Malia, and Archanes (for a schematic reconstruction of the Phourni cemetery during this period see Papadopoulos 2010: 16 fig. 5), obscures a clear picture of Protopalatial burial practices, but even so, the overall decrease in quantity and quality of material culture from burial contexts is telling. Equally telling are the few occasions where material culture of high quality craftsmanship does occur. While the scale and architectural elaboration of Chryssolakkos (Demargne 1945; Van Effentere and Van Effenterre 1963) is unparalleled within Protopalatial funerary contexts, it is certainly

Figure 10.4: Myrtos-Pyrgos Tomb (Cadogan 1978: 72, fig. 5).

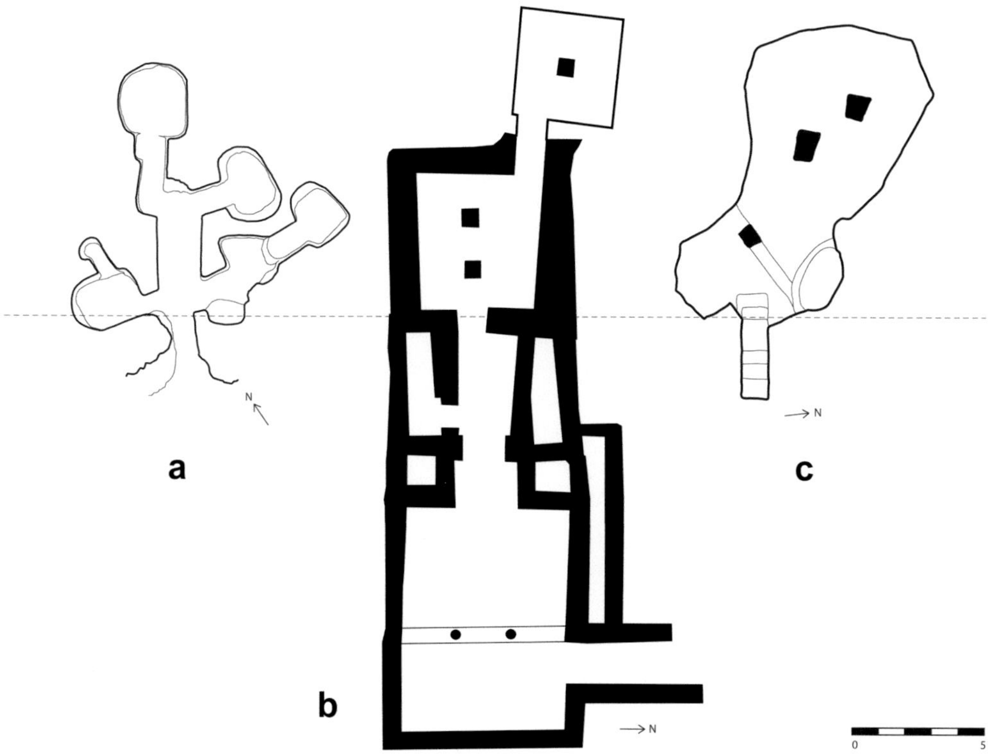

Figure 10.5: (a) Knossos Mavro Spelio Tomb IX (after Forsdyke 1927: fig. 19), (b) Temple Tomb (after Evans 1935, supplemental plan), (c) Poros rock cut tomb, 1967 excavation (Muhly 1992: 30 fig. 1).

compatible with Maliot Protopalatial architecture (for example Crypte Hypostyle and Quartier Mu), a trend mirrored in artefacts with clear Near Eastern prototypes or connotations found at Chryssolakkos (Poursat 1992: 54, fig. 39) and the settlement alike (Poursat 1992: 26, fig. 14–6; Schoep 2006). The systematic evidence for re-deposition of human bones at the Hagios Charalambos cave (where the latest material dates to MM IIB; Betancourt *et al.* 2008; Betancourt 2012) and perhaps Archanes Phourni (Buildings 6, 19), could provide a model for Protopalatial Chryssolakkos (where concentrations of human bones were sparse) especially in relation to other nearby buildings or/ and natural crevices close to the sea (Treuil 2005). The close proximity of certain Prepalatial and Protopalatial cemeteries to the sea, particularly among settlements along the north coast of Crete such as Malia, Gournia (Soles 1992), Sphoungaras (Hall 1912), and Sissi (Schoep 2009; in this volume) perhaps is far from accidental. And while secondary burial seems to have continued, in the cemeteries of Gournia and Sphoungaras one-off burial in pithoi becomes a practice attested until the end of the Neopalatial period (Christakis 2005: 18, 42–43). The adoption of varied burial practices by different social groups could not be more telling than at Gournia, where burial and secondary burial in the House Tombs (Soles 1992: 1–3), where cemetery-site indivisibility was not possible, can be juxtaposed with the group of individuals placed articulated and sitting upwards in upside down pithoi (Hall 1912: pl. 14), in a cemetery that stared meaningfully at the settlement. However, certain things are now absent: ceramic assemblages in large quantities, palatial pottery where display, consumption, and storage were intrinsically combined, for which we have ample evidence from Protopalatial contexts such as the palace at Phaistos and the Kamares cave (Van de Moortel 2006; 2011). Ostentatious display in activities that attract large numbers has clearly moved to settlement and sanctuary contexts, whereas the act of formal burial perhaps becomes in itself an exclusive practice and therefore by definition an act of ostentatious display. Perhaps the most striking example of this trend is in the Proto- and Neopalatial male burials in the Myrtos Pyrgos House Tomb (Cadogan 2011). The demise of formal burial, which accelerates in the Neopalatial, is perhaps one of the most profound social and ideological transformations in the island's prehistory, while ostentatious display in palatial and settlement contexts peaks, and to a certain extent becomes popularised, mass-produced and mass-consumed. For example even the smallest (in square footage) domestic contexts have access to large concentrations of domestic tablewares (see for example Catling *et al.* 1989; Hatzaki 2011a: 253–54), while sealstone production, and therefore ownership, peaks (Krzyszkowska 2005: 120). Yet formal burial becomes a rare (and therefore privileged) commodity, best observed in a site with an unparalleled burial record from the late Prepalatial period onwards. With a population density of up to 18,000 people (Whitelaw 2004), archaeologically visible burial at Neopalatial Knossos and Poros was available to small groups linked by a common identity in burial place and practice. At least since the late Prepalatial period, Knossos (Ailias, Hood 2010) and Poros (Dimopoulou-Rethemiotaki 2004: 367) develop a different form of burial space: underground tombs, marking a spatial, visual and perhaps ideological departure from past customs, and one that will remain consistent throughout prehistory. Primary burial in pithoi (*a la* Sphoungaras and Pachiammos) remains a probability at least until the early Neopalatial period (MM IIIA) but unfortunately one impossible to assess, due to the poor archaeological record (Evans 1928: 554; Preston 2013a). While the use of pithoi and tubs as containers for secondary burial is clearly attested in the Protopalatial Ailias (Hood 2010: 163, fig. 16.2), and Mavro Spelio (Forthsdyke 1927; Alberti 2001; 2006; 2013) and Gypsades tholos (Hood 1960: 169, 173), it dies out from MM IIIB, when pits or/and built special compartments become the standard repository for secondary burial (Dimopoulou 1994: pl. 229 *b*, 231 *a–b*; Muhly 1999: 30, fig. 1, pl. 1 a; Dimopoulou and Rethemiotakis 2000: 39; Dimopoulou-Rethemiotaki 2004: 369, fig. 31.3). If archaeologically visible burial was a major form of ostentatious display, group activities within the tomb area, including feasting, were a restricted activity, open to those with privileged access to the often spacious tomb interiors (the largest of the Poros tombs is 90 m^3; Dimopoulou 1994: 708). Yet despite the evidence for group activities within the burial environment, in terms of scale these remain largely restricted affairs quite different from group activities in palace courts, or extra-urban sanctuaries, such as Kophinas, Syme, and Skotino cave. In the Temple Tomb (Evans 1935: 957–1018), perhaps the most conspicuous example of appropriation and reproduction of Knossian palatial architecture, the rock cut multi-chambered environment of an underground tomb was intentionally translated into a built form, borrowing architectural elements from elite contexts in the palace and settlement alike (Hatzaki in preparation a) (Fig. 10.5). The re-appearance of ostentatious display attested in the burial of gold signet rings in Mavro Spelio (Forthsdyke 1927: pl. 19; Alberti 2013) and Poros (Dimopoulou and Rethemiotakis 2000; Rethemiotakis and Dimopoulou 2003; Dimopoulou 2010) associated with high-ranking individuals (including perhaps administrators), was aimed at intra-group consumption, also attested in the construction of a platform like space to accommodate a high status burial within one of the Poros tombs (Dimopoulou 1994: 708). Perhaps the most striking example of a Neopalatial interest in the performance of activities within a burial environment, which lacks any evidence for primary or secondary burial comes from Building 4 at Archanes Phourni (Sakellarakis and Sapouna-Sakellaraki 1997: 223–29). Textile production attested through weaving, and some other activity involving numerous conical cups (Sakellarakis and Sapouna-Sakellaraki 1997: 228–29, figs. 178–79), perhaps associated with non-archaeologically visible burial, occurred in this ancient burial ground, a place laden with visual memories of past funerary practices. Co-incidentally, large concentrations of disposed conical cups are found in Neopalatial palace, sanctuary, settlement, and cemetery contexts alike, implying multi-contextual use of the same type of vessel, rather than types of tableware used exclusively in certain contexts.

Final Palatial and Postpalatial: Knossoscentrism and departure from the "Minoan" past

At Final Palatial Knossos the departure from the Neopalatial past is marked by a series of profound and abruptly occurring changes in burial place and practice, which form part of a carefully assembled and orchestrated package of material culture change (Hatzaki 2011b). The dissemination of a new burial package beyond Knossos (for example at the "Kouklaki" cemetery Chania, Andreadaki-Vlasaki and Protopapadaki 2010; at Mochlos, Brogan *et al.* 2002; Soles 2008) has been rightly linked to the adoption of the new Knossian (rather than from the Greek Mainland) inspired burial customs throughout the island (Preston 2004a; *contra* Burke 2005). At Knossos and Poros the disrupted picture of burial place suggests a socially fluid setup, whereas the reduction of the interior tomb space to the bare minimum (allowing the burial of 1–4 individuals) essentially excluded that inner group which was so consistently present at intra-tomb activities during the Neopalatial period The absence of large concentrations of tableware from Final Palatial funerary contexts (for example at Zapher Papoura, the most extensively excavated LM III cemetery at Knossos to date; Evans 1906) artefactually confirms this observation. This trend of few active participants and many passive observers in funerary practice in paralleled in public spaces, such as the circular platforms at the Stratigraphical Museum extension site (Warren 1984), and also iconographic evidence, if the Miniature Frescoes belong to this period (*contra* Hood 2005). The intentional focus on the individual is demonstrated in the preservation of the articulated human body, marking a major departure from a thousand year old practice of secondary burial (Hatzaki 2012) (compare Figs. 10.1, 10.2). This special emphasis placed on the individual often accompanied in death by multiple identities staged through the deposition of symbolically charged material culture, includes an assortment of Neopalatial and Final Palatial types of objects, off-island imports, or locally manufactured goods made of local or imported raw materials (see for example Katsambas, Alexiou 1967). While conspicuous consumption of elite architecture is perhaps limited to the palace (with a special emphasis on a newly executed fresco program) and public spaces (circular platforms; Warren 1984; Little Palace North, Hatzaki in preparation b), it is paralleled in funerary contexts. The commission of newly carved ashlar blocks for novel architectural forms and building techniques (such as corbeled masonry) at the Isopata Royal tomb (Evans 1906; Preston 2007) and Kephala tholos (Hutchinson 1956; Preston 2005), suggests that ashlar, so

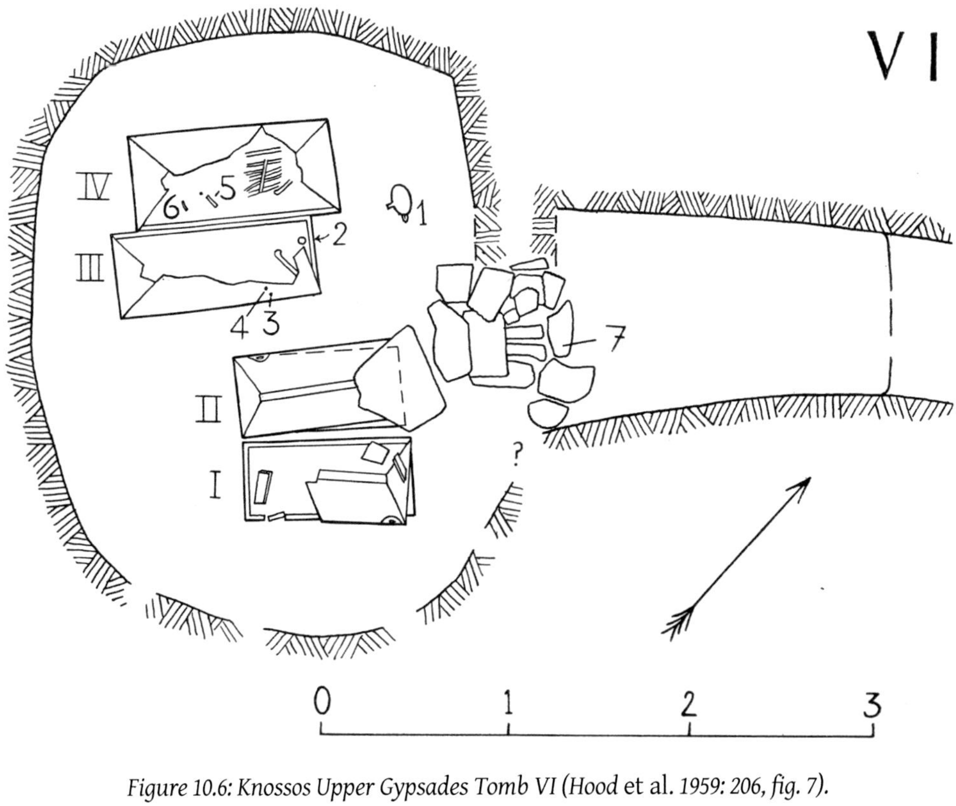

Figure 10.6: Knossos Upper Gypsades Tomb VI (Hood et al. *1959: 206, fig. 7).*

widely utilised in the Neopalatial period (McEnroe 2010: 98–100), had now become a restricted, if not highly exclusive commodity.

With the collapse of Knossos's administrative dominance in LM IIIA2, two patterns appear in the burial record. At Knossos ostentatious display in burial architecture and assorted material culture ceases, perhaps best demonstrated by the adoption of the larnax (Fig. 10.6; Preston 2004b; Hatzaki 2005), a clay container suitable for concealing the human body stripped of rich material culture (Hatzaki in press) – like the pithos and tub larnax earlier. In other parts of the island, especially in the centre (for example Archanes Phourni Tholos A, Sakellarakis 1970; Mycenaean Burial Enclosure, Sakellarakis and Sapouna-Sakellaraki 1997: 189–93; Kallitsaki 1997) and west (for example the tholos tomb at Margarites, Papadopoulou 1997: 140–41; Phylaki, Tzedakis 1988), ostentatious display in tomb architecture and material culture is adopted (Preston 2004a: 341, fig. 9, 343, fig. 10), perhaps triggered by access to previously restricted, Knossos controlled resources. The conspicuous consumption of architecture and movable material culture at Archanes best demonstrates this phenomenon. Finally the dissemination of the tholos tomb particularly in west Crete could have been inspired by Mainland (now the centre of power in the Aegean) rather than Cretan prototypes (Galanakis 2009).

Conclusions

The burial customs of Bronze Age Crete exhibit remarkable continuity and discontinuity of practice through time and space. Some notable patterns are outlined below and summarised on Table 10.1.

The EM IIA and LM II-IIIA are the two most prominent peaks of ostentatious display in the size, quantity, and variability of island and off-island movable material culture. It is perhaps not accidental that in both cases the subsequent period witnesses the demise of ostentatious display in material culture also associated with the appearance of clay containers as a receiver for the human body, perhaps in an attempt to conceal what is now missing from burial practice. For EM III-MM IA this pattern may be associated with the profound changes in the Cycladic trading networks and its knock-on effect on Crete. For the Postpalatial period (LM IIIA2-B) a comparable phenomenon could have followed the collapse of the international network fostered by the palace at Knossos, which post-palatial Cretan elite groups could not maintain at the same scale and level of intensity and credibility, nor could they compete with the rising power of the Mainland.

During the late Prepalatial period ostentatious display shifted from artefacts towards the mobilisation of human resources for building elaborate funerary structures. This trend reappears in the Postpalatial (LM IIIA2-B) particularly with the construction of tholos tombs in west Crete.

Architectural elaboration and the adoption of a palatial architectural vocabulary known from settlement contexts are paralleled, but rare: in Protopalatial Chryssolakkos and the Neopalatial Temple Tomb. But the Final Palatial Isopata Royal Tomb and the Kephala Tholos, while adopting building materials and techniques associated with elite Neopalatial architecture, develop novel architectural designs that no longer borrow from the world of the living.

The involvement of a small group of active participants within the tomb environment remained largely consistent from the Prepalatial to the Neopalatial. In Final Palatial this group seems to have diminished considerably in size, implying a major change is social relations at an intra-group level.

While in late Prepalatial the funerary arena seems to compete with other venues for group activities in terms of number of participants, this pattern changes dramatically in the Protopalatial and continues like this into the Neopalatial with the demise of the burial arena as the focal point for group gatherings. These continue now on a much reduced scale, but become highly exclusive. The popularisation of aspects of elite/palatial material culture does not seem to extend to funerary practice in the Neopalatial.

Tableware in large concentrations as evidence for the occurrence of live participants in funerary related events (feasting or other) is attested throughout the Prepalatial, Protopalatial and in the Neopalatial, but varies in scale and elaboration according to region and context. This practice seems to have abruptly stopped from the Final Palatial period onwards. Also absent from the Protopalatial funerary ceramic tableware are elaborate vessels like those known from palatial, settlement, and some sanctuary contexts.

After the end of the Neopalatial secondary burial ceases, marking an ideological change among social groups buried within the same tomb and cemetery. After the collapse of the palace at Knossos, the custom of secondary burial re-appears but on a much reduced scale. Finally, the practice of formal burial, especially from the Neopalatial period onwards, becomes the exclusive privilege of a few social groups, a form of ostentatious display in its own right. I would argue that this is a trend that continues largely unchanged in the Final Palatial and the Postpalatial, despite the re-appearance of archaeologically visible burial. The mass secondary burials of the Minoan world are now a thing of the past.

The change in burial customs that occurred at Knossos between the late Neopalatial (LM IB) and early Final Palatial (LM II) and their dissemination throughout the island as a Knossos (rather than Mainland) inspired custom, abruptly ended the age old practice of secondary and mass group burial. Preserving the individual after death for posterity was a radically new practice that perpetuated into the Iron Age.

Acknowledgements

The Semple Fund University of Cincinnati is warmly thanked for funding to attend the workshop; Valasia Isaakidou and Paul Halstead for their hospitality at Sheffield; Gerald Cadogan and Sevi Triantaphyllou for encouragement and discussing aspects of this paper; and the editors for their invitation to the workshop and acceptance of a somewhat delayed submission.

Figs 10.1a–b and 10.3 are courtesy of INSTAP Academic Press, Figs 10.2, 10.4, 10.6 are courtesy of the British School at Athens, Keith Branigan, Gerald Cadogan, and Andonis Vasilakis are warmly thanked for permission, and John Wallrodt for preparing Fig 10.5.

Bibliography

Alberti, L.

2001 Costumi funerari Medio Minoici a Cnosso: la necropoli di Mavro Spileo. *Studi Micenei ed Egeo-Anatolici 43*: 163–87.

2006 Μεσομινωικά ταφικά έθιμα στην Κνωσό: Η νεκρόπολη στο Μαύρο Σπήλιο. *Πεπραγμένα του Θ' Διεθνούς Κρητολογικού Συνεδρίου*, vol. A2: 259–69. Ηράκλειο: Εταιρεία Κρητικών Ιστορικών Μελετών.

2013 Middle Minoan III burial customs at Knossos: a "pianissimo" Intermezzo? In C. F. Macdonald and C. Knappett (eds.), *Intermezzo: Intermediacy and Regeneration in Middle Minoan III Crete* (BSA Studies 21): 47–55. London: British School at Athens.

Alexiou, S.

1967 *Υστερομινωικοί τάφοι Λιμένος Κνωσού (Κατσαμπά)* (Library of the Archaeological Society at Athens 56). Athens: Archaeological Society at Athens.

Andreadaki-Vlasaki, M. and E. Protopapadaki

2010 "Kouklaki" excavation (73–77, Igoumenou Gabriel Street). In M. Andreadaki-Vlasaki (ed.), *Khania (Kydonia). A Tour to Sites of Ancient Memory*: 153–65. Khania: Hellenic Ministry of Culture, 25th Ephorate of Prehistoric and Classical Antiquities.

Betancourt, P. P.

2012 Trade and interconnections in Lasithi between EM II and MM I, the evidence from the Ayios Charalambos cave. In I. Schoep, P. Tomkins and J. Driessen (eds.), *Back to the Beginning: Reassessing Social and Political Complexity on Crete during the Early and Middle Bronze Age*: 184–94. Oxford: Oxbow.

Betancourt, P. P., C. Davaras, E. Stravopodi, L. Langford-Verstegen, J. D. Muhly, J. Hickman, H. M. C. Dierckx, S. C. Ferrence, D. S. Reese, P. J. P. McGeorge and S. Chlouveraki

2008 Excavations in the Hagios Charalambos cave: a preliminary report. *Hesperia* 77: 539–604.

Blackman, D. and K. Branigan

1982 The excavation of an Early Minoan tholos tomb at Ayia Kyriaki, Ayiofarango, southern Crete. *Annual of the British School at Athens* 77: 1–57.

Briault, C.

2007 Making mountains out of molehills in the Bronze Age Aegean: visibility, ritual kits, and the idea of a peak sanctuary. *World Archaeology* 39: 122–41.

Branigan, K.

1970 *The Tombs of Mesara. Study of Funerary Architecture and Ritual in Southern Crete, 2800–1700 B.C.* London: Gerald Duckworth.

Brogan, T. M., R. A. K. Smith and J. S. Soles

2002 Mycenaeans at Mochlos? Exploring culture and identity in the Late Minoan IB to IIIA1 Transition. *Aegean Archaeology* 6: 89–118.

Broodbank, C.

2000 *An Island Archaeology of the Early Cyclades*. Cambridge: Cambridge University Press.

2008 The Early Bronze Age in the Cyclades. In C. Shelmerdine (ed.), *The Cambridge Companion to the Aegean Bronze Age*. Cambridge: Cambridge University Press.

Burke, B.
2005 Materialization of Mycenaean ideology and the Ayia Triada sarcophagus. *American Journal of Archaeology* 109: 403–22.
Cadogan, G.
1978 Pyrgos, Crete, 1970–77. *Archaeological Reports* 24: 70–84.
2011 A power house of the dead: The functions and long life of the tomb at Myrtos-Pyrgos. In J. M. A. Murphy (ed.), *Prehistoric Crete: Regional and Diachronic Studies on Mortuary Systems*: 103–118. Philadelphia: INSTAP Academic Press.
Catling, E. A., H. W. Catling, and D. Smyth
1979 Knossos 1975: Middle Minoan III and Late Minoan I houses by the Acropolis. *Annual of the British School at Athens* 74: 1–80.
Christakis, K. S.
2005 *Cretan Bronze Age Pithoi: Traditions and Trends in the Production and Consumption of Storage Containers in Bronze Age Crete*. Philadelphia: INSTAP Academic Press.
2013 The Syme Sanctuary in the transition from the Protopalatial to the Early Neopalatial Period: the evidence of the pottery. In C. F. Macdonald and C. Knappett (eds.), *Intermezzo: Intermediacy and Regeneration in Middle Minoan III Crete* (BSA Studies 21): 169–177. London: British School at Athens.
Davaras, C. and P. P. Betancourt
2004 *The Hagia Photia Cemetery I. The Tomb Groups and Architecture.* Philadelphia: INSTAP Academic Press.
Demargne, P.
1945 *Fouilles exécutées à Mallia. Exploration des nécropoles (1921–1933), premier fascicule* (Études Crétoises 7). Paris: Paul Geuthner.
Dimopoulou, N.
1994 Πόρος Ηρακλείου. *Αρχαιολογικό Δελτίο* 49: 707–11.
2010 A gold discoid from Poros, Herakleion: the guard dog and the garden. In O. Krzyszkowska (ed.), *Cretan Offerings: Studies In Honour Of Peter Warren* (BSA Studies 18): 89–100. London: British School at Athens.
Dimopoulou-Rethemiotaki, N.
2004 Το επίνειο της Κνωσού στον Πόρο-Κατσαμπά. In G. Cadogan, E. Hatzaki, A. Vasilakis (eds.), *Knossos: Palace, City, State* (BSA Studies Studies 12): 365–80. London: British School at Athens.
Dimopoulou, N. and G. Rethemiotakis
2000 The "sacred conversation" ring from Poros. In W. Müller (ed.), *Minoisch-Mykenische Glyptik. Stil, Ikonographie, Funktion*, V. Internationales Siegel-Symposium, Marburg, 23–25 September 1999 (CMS, Beiheft 6): 39–56. Berlin: Gebr. Mann Verlag.
Driessen, J.
2010 The goddess and the skull: some observations on group identity in Prepalatial Crete. In O. Krzyszkowska (ed.), *Cretan Offerings: Studies In Honour Of Peter Warren* (BSA Studies 18): 107–17. London: British School at Athens.
Evans, A. J.
1906 *The Prehistoric Tombs of Knossos*. London: Macmillan.
1928 *The Palace of Minos at Knossos, Volume II*. London: Macmillan.
1935 *The Palace of Minos at Knossos, Volume IV*. London: Macmillan.
Forsdyke, E.J.
1927 The Mavro Spelio cemetery at Knossos. *Annual of the British School at Athens* 28: 243–96.
Galanaki, K.
2006 Πρωτομινωικό ταφικό σύνολο στην πρώην Αμερικανική βάση Γουρνών Πεδιάδος. *Πεπραγμένα του Θ' Διεθνούς Κρητολογικού Συνεδρίου*, vol. A2: 227–41. Ηράκλειο: Εταιρεία Κρητικών Ιστορικών Μελετών.

Galanakis, Y.
2009 A Monumental Death: funerary architecture and social dynamics in the Late Bronze Age Aegean. *Bulletin of the Institute of Classical Studies* 52: 261–62.
Goodison, L.
2001 From tholos tomb to Throne Room: perceptions of the sun in Minoan ritual. In R. Laffineur and R. Hägg (eds.), *Potnia. Deities and Religion in the Aegean Bronze Age* (Aegaeum 22): 77–88. Liège: Université de Liège.
2004 From tholos tomb to Throne Room: some considerations of dawn light and directionality in Minoan buildings. In G. Cadogan, E. Hatzaki and A. Vasilakis (eds.), *Knossos: Palace, City, State.* (BSA Studies 12): 339–50. London: British School at Athens.
Haggis, D. C.
2002 Integration and complexity in the Late Pre-Palatial Period. A View from the countryside in Eastern Crete. In Y. Hamilakis (ed.), *Labyrinth Revisited: Rethinking Minoan Archaeology*: 120–42. Oxford: Oxbow.
Hall, E. H.
1912 *Excavations in Eastern Crete: Sphoungaras* (University of Pennsylvania, the University Museum Anthropological Publications III.ii). Philadelphia: University of Pennsylvania, the University Museum Anthropological Publications.
Hatzaki, E.
2005 Postpalatial Knossos: town and cemeteries from LM IIIA2 to LM IIIC. In A.-L. D'Agata and J. Moody (eds.), *Ariadne's Threads. Connections between Crete and the Greek Mainland in the Postpalatial Period (LM IIIA2 to SM)* (Tripodes 3): 65–95. Athens: Scuola Archeologica Italiana di Atene.
2011a Defining domestic architecture and household assemblages at Late Bronze Age Knossos. In K. Glowacki and N. Vogeikoff-Brogan (eds.), *The Archaeology of Houses and Households in Ancient Crete* (Hesperia Supplement 44): 247–62. Princeton: American School of Classical Studies at Athens.
2011b From LM IB Marine Style to LM II marine motifs. Stratigraphy, chronology and the social context of a ceramic transformation: a response to Maria Andreadaki-Vlazaki. In T. M. Brogan and E. Hallager (eds.), *LM IB pottery. Relative chronology and regional differences. Acts of a workshop held at the Danish Institute at Athens in collaboration with the INSTAP Study Center for East Crete, 27–29 June 2007* (Monographs of the Danish Institute at Athens 11): 75–87. Athens: Danish Institute at Athens.
2012 Mortuary practices and ideology in Bronze–Early Iron Age Crete. In G. Cadogan, M. Iacovou, K. Kopaka and J. Whitley (eds.), *Parallel lives: ancient island societies in Crete and Cyprus* (BSA Studies 20): 307–13. London: British School at Athens.
in press "Pots, frescoes, textiles and people. The social life of decorated pottery at Late Bronze Age Knossos, Crete" in A. Vlachopoulos (ed.), *ΧΡΩΣΤΗΡΕΣ/PAINTBRUSHES. Wall-painting and vase-painting of the 2nd millennium BC in dialogue. Proceedings of an International Conference on the Aegean Iconography Held at Akrotiri, Thera, 24–26 May 2013*, Athens.
Hood, M. S. F.
1960 *Tholos* Tombs of the Aegean. *Antiquity* 34: 166–76.
2005 Dating the Knossos frescoes. In L. Morgan (ed.), *Aegean Wall Painting: A Tribute to Mark Cameron* (BSA Studies 13): 45–81. London: British School at Athens.
2010 The Middle Minoan cemetery on Ailias at Knossos. In O. Krzyszkowska (ed.), *Cretan Offerings: Studies In Honour Of Peter Warren* (BSA Studies 18): 161–68. London: British School at Athens.
Hutchinson, R. W.
1956 A tholos tomb on the Kephala. *Annual of the British School at Athens* 51: 330–42.

Kallitsaki, H.
1997 The Mycenaean burial evidence in Phourni, Archanes. In J. Driessen and A. Farnoux (eds.), *La Crète mycénienne* (BCH Supplément 30): 213–27. Paris.

Karytinos, A.
2000 The stylistic development of seals from Archanes-Phourni throughout the Prepalatial Period – style and social meaning. In W. Müller (ed.), *Minoisch-Mykenische Glyptik. Stil, Ikonographie, Funktion*, V. Internationales Siegel-Symposium, Marburg, 23–25, September 1999 (CMS, Beiheft 6): 123–34. Berlin: Gebr. Mann Verlag.

Krzyszkowska, O.
2005 *Aegean Seals. An Introduction* (BICS Supplement 85). London: Institute of Classical Studies.

La Rosa, V.
1992 Kamilari. In J. W. Myers, E. E. Myers, and G. Cadogan (eds.) *The Aerial Atlas of Ancient Crete*: 112–15. Berkeley: University of California Press.

Legarra Herrero, B.
2009 The Minoan fallacy: cultural diversity and mortuary behaviour on Crete at the beginning of the Bronze Age. *Oxford Journal of Archaeology* 29: 29–57.
2011 The secret lives of the Early and Middle Minoan tholos cemeteries: Koumasa and Platanos. In J. M. A. Murphy (ed.), *Prehistoric Crete: Regional and Diachronic Studies on Mortuary Systems*: 49–84. Philadelphia: INSTAP Academic Press.
2012 The construction, deconstruction and non-construction of hierarchies in the funerary record of Prepalatial Crete. In I. Schoep, P. Tomkins and J. Driessen (eds.), *Back to the Beginning: Reassessing Social and Political Complexity on Crete during the Early and Middle Bronze Age*: 325–57. Oxford: Oxbow.

Levi, D.
1962 La tomba a tholos di Kamilari presso Festos. *Annuario della Scuola archeologica di Atene e delle Missioni italiane in Oriente* 39–40: 7–148.

Macdonald, C. F.
2012 Palatial Knossos: the early years. In I. Schoep, P. Tomkins and J. Driessen (eds.), *Back to the Beginning: Reassessing Social and Political Complexity on Crete during the Early and Middle Bronze Age*: 81–113. Oxford: Oxbow.

McEnroe, J. C.
2010 *Architecture of Minoan Crete: Constructing Identity in the Aegean Bronze Age.* Austin: University of Texas Press.

Muhly, P.
1999 Μινωικός λαξευτός τάφος στον Πόρο Ηρακλείου (Library of the Archaeological Society at Athens 129). Athens: Archaeological Society at Athens.

Nowicki, K.
2001 Minoan peak sanctuaries: reassessing their origins. In R. Laffineur and R. Hägg (eds.), *Potnia: Deities and Religion in the Aegean Bronze Age. Proceedings of the 8th International Aegean Conference, Göteborg, 12-15 April 2000* (Aegaeum 22): 31–37. Liège: Université de Liège.

Panagiotopoulos, D.
2002 *Das Tholosgrab E von Phourni bei Archanes. Studien zu einem frühkretischen Grabfund und seinem kulturellen Kontext* (BAR IS 1014). Oxford: Archaeopress.

Papadatos, Y.
2005 *Tholos Tomb Gamma: A Prepalatial Tholos Tomb at Phourni, Archanes.* (Prehistory Monographs 17) Philadelphia: INSTAP Academic Press.
2007 Beyond cultures and ethnicity: a new look at material culture distribution and inter-regional interaction in the Early Bronze Age Southern Aegean. In S. Antoniadou and A. Pace (eds.), *Mediterranean Crossroads*: 419–51. Oxford: Pierides Foundation.

Papadopoulos, C.

2010 *Death Management and Virtual Pursuits: a Virtual Reconstruction of the Minoan Cemetery at Phourni Archanes* (BAR IS 2082). Oxford: Archaeopress.

Papadopoulou, E.

1997 Μαργαρίτες. *Αρχαιολογικό Δελτίο* 52: 1040–41.

Peatfield, A.

2007 The Dynamics of ritual on Minoan peak sanctuaries. In D. A. Barrowclough and C. Malone (eds.), *Cult in Context: Reconsidering Ritual in Archaeology*: 297–300. Oxford: Oxbow.

2009 The topography of Minoan peak sanctuaries revisited. In A. L. D'Agata and A. Van de Moortel (eds.), *Archaeologies of Cult: Essays on Ritual and Cult in Crete in Honor of Geraldine C. Gesell* (Hesperia Supplement 42): 251–59. Princeton: The American School of Classical Studies at Athens.

Poursat, J.-C.

1992 *Guide de Malia au temps des premiers palais. Le Quartier Mu*. Paris: De Boccard.

Preston, L.

2004a A mortuary perspective on elites in Final and Post-palatial Crete. *American Journal of Archaeology* 108: 321–48.

2004b Contextualising the larnax: tradition, innovation and regionalism in coffin use on Late Minoan II-IIIB Crete. *Oxford Journal of Archaeology* 23: 177–97.

2005 The Kephala Tholos: a study in the re-use of the past. *Annual of the British School at Athens* 100: 61–124.

2007 The Isopata cemetery at Knossos. *Annual of the British School at Athens* 102: 257–314.

2013 The Middle Minoan III funerary landscape in the Knossos valley. In C. F. Macdonald and C. Knappett (eds.), *Intermezzo: Intermediacy and Regeneration in Middle Minoan III Crete* (BSA Studies 21): 67–69. London: British School at Athens.

Relaki, M.

2004 Constructing a region: the contested landscapes of Prepalatial Mesara. In J. C. Barrett and P. Halstead (eds.), *The Emergence of Civilisation Revisited* (Sheffield Studies in Aegean Archaeology 6): 170–88. Oxford: Oxbow.

2008 Community, identity and representation in Prepalatial and Protopalatial Mesara. *Bulletin of the Institute of Classical Studies* 51: 187–88.

2012 The Social arenas of tradition. Investigating collective and individual social strategies in Prepalatial and Protopalatial Mesara. In I. Schoep, P. Tomkins and J. Driessen (eds.), *Back to the Beginning: Reassessing Social and Political Complexity on Crete during the Early and Middle Bronze Age*: 290–324. Oxford: Oxbow.

Rethemiotakis, G. and N. Dimopoulou

2003 The 'Sacred Mansion' ring from Poros, Herakleion. *Mitteilungen des Deutschen Archäologischen Instituts* 118: 1–22.

Sakellarakis, J. A.

1970 Das Kuppelgrab A von Archanes und das kretisch mykenische Tieropferritual. *Prähistorische Zeitschrift* 45: 135–219.

Sakellarakis, Y. and E. Sakellaraki

1991 *Crete. Archanes*. Athens: Ekdotike Athenon.

Sakellarakis, Y. and E. Sapouna-Sakellaraki

1997 *Archanes. Minoan Crete in a New Light*. Athens: Ammos Publications.

Sbonias, K.

1999 Social development, management of production, and symbolic representation in Prepalatial Crete. In A. Chaniotis (ed.), *From Minoan Farmers to Roman Traders: Sidelights on the Economy of Ancient Crete*: 25–52. Stuttgart: Franz Steiner Verlag.

2010 Diversity and transformation. Looking for meanings in the Prepalatial seal consumption and use. In W. Müller (ed.), *Die Bedeutung der minoischen und mykenischen Glyptik: VI. Internationales Siegel-Symposium aus Anlass des 50 jährigen Bestehens des CMS, Marburg, 9–12 Oktober 2008* (CMS, Beiheft 8): 349–62, Mainz am Rhein: Verlag Philipp von Zabern.

2012 Regional elite-groups and the production and consumption of seals in the Prepalatial period. A case-study of the Asterousia region. In I. Schoep, P. Tomkins and J. Driessen (eds.), *Back to the Beginning: Reassessing Social and Political Complexity on Crete during the Early and Middle Bronze Age*: 273–89. Oxford: Oxbow.

Schoep, I.

2006 Looking beyond the First Palaces: elites and the agency of power in EM III-MM II Crete. *American Journal of Archaeology* 110.1: 37–64.

2009 The excavation of the cemetery (Zone 1). In J. Driessen, I. Schoep, F. Crevecoeur, M. Devolder, F. Gaignerot-Driessen, H. Fiasse, P. Haciguzeller, S. Jusseret, C. Langohr, Q. Letesson, and A Schmitt, *Excavations at Sissis. Preliminary Report on the 2007–2008 Campaigns* (Aegis 1): 45–56. Louvain-la-Neuve: Presses Universitaires de Louvain.

2012 Bridging the divide between the "Prepalatial" and the "Protopalatial" periods? In I. Schoep, P. Tomkins and J. Driessen (eds.), *Back to the Beginning: Reassessing Social and Political Complexity on Crete during the Early and Middle Bronze Age*: 403–28. Oxford: Oxbow.

Schoep, I. and P. Tomkins

2007 Prepalatial Crete. In E. H. Cline (ed.), *The Oxford Handbook of the Bronze Age Aegean*. Oxford: Oxford University Press.

Soles, J. S.

1992 *Prepalatial Cemeteries at Mochlos and Gournia and the House Tombs of Bronze Age Crete* (Hesperia Supplement 24). Princeton: American School of Classical Studies.

2008 *Mochlos IIA: Period IV. The Mycenaean Settlement and Cemetery: The Sites.* (Prehistory Monographs 23). Philadelphia: INSTAP Academic Press.

Treuil, R.

2005 Entre morts et vivants à Malia. La "zone des necropolis" et les quartier d'habitation. In I. Bradfer-Burdet, B. Detournay and R. Laffineur (eds.), *ΚΡΗΣ ΤΕΧΝΙΤΗΣ L'artisan crétois. Recueil d'articles en l'honneur de Jean-Claude Poursat, publié à l'occasion des 40 ans de la découverte du Quartier Mu*: 209–20. Liège: Université de Liège.

Todaro, S.

2009 The latest Prepalatial period and the foundation of the first palace at Phaistos: a stratigraphic and chronological re-assessment. *Creta Antica* 10: 105–45.

2012 Craft production and social practices at Prepalatial Phaistos: the background to the First "Palace". In I. Schoep, P. Tomkins and J. Driessen (eds.), *Back to the Beginning: Reassessing Social and Political Complexity on Crete during the Early and Middle Bronze Age*: 32–80. Oxford: Oxbow.

Triantaphyllou, S.

2005 The human remains. In Y. Papadatos, *Tholos Tomb Gamma: A Prepalatial Tholos Tomb at Phourni, Archanes*: 67–76. (Prehistory Monographs 17). Philadelphia: INSTAP Academic Press.

2009 EM/MM human skeletal remains from East Crete: the Kephala Petras rock shelter, Siteia, and the Livari tholos tomb, Skiadi. *Kentro. The Newsletter of the INSTAP Study Center for East Crete* 12: 19–23.

2010 The human remains. In A. Vasilakis and K. Branigan (eds.), *Moni Odigitria: A Prepalatial Cemetery and its Environs in the Asterousia, Southern Crete*: 229–250. (Prehistory Monographs 30). Philadelphia: INSTAP Academic Press.

Tzedakis, Y.

1988 Φυλακή Αποκορώνου. *Αρχαιολογικό Δελτίο* 36: 398–89.

Van de Moortel, A.

2006 A re-examination of the pottery from the Kamares Cave. In M. H. Wiener, J. L. Warner, J. Polonsky and E. E. Hayes (eds.), *Pottery and Society: The Impact of Recent Studies in Minoan Pottery. Gold Medal Colloquium in Honor of Philip P. Betancourt. 104th Annual Meeting of the Archaeological Institute of America, New Orleans, Louisiana, 5 January 2003*: 73–93. Boston: Archaeological Institute of America.

2011 The Phaistos palace and the Kamares cave: A special relationship. In W. Gauß, M. Lindblom, R. A. K. Smith, and J. C. Wright (eds.), *Our Cups Are Full: Pottery and Society in the Aegean Bronze Age. Papers Presented to Jeremy B. Rutter on the Occasion of his 65th Birthday*: 306–18. Oxford: Archaeopress.

Van Effenterre, H. and M. van Effenterre

1963 *Fouilles exécutées à Mallia: Étude du site (1956–1957) et exploration des nécropoles (1915–1928)* (Étude Crétoise 13). Paris: Paul Geuthner.

Walberg, G.

1987 Early Cretan tombs: the pottery. In R. Laffineur (ed.), *Thanatos: les coutumes funéraires en Egée à l'âge du Bronze* (Aegaeum 1): 53–60. Liège: Université de Liège.

Warren, P.

1972 *Myrtos: An Early Bronze Age Site in Crete* (BSA Supplement 7). London: British School at Athens.

1984 Circular platforms at Minoan Knossos. *Annual of the British School at Athens* 79: 307–23.

Watrous, L. V.

2000 Gournia. In J. Muhly and E. Sikla (eds.), *Crete 2000. One Hundred Years of American Archaeological Work on Crete*: 127–31. Athens: American School of Classical Studies at Athens, INSTAP Study Center for East Crete.

Whitelaw, T.

1983 The settlement at Fournou Korifi, Myrtos and aspects of Early Minoan social organization. In O. Krzyszkowska and L. Nixon (eds.), *Minoan Society, Proceedings of the Cambridge Colloquium 1981*: 323–45. Bristol: Bristol Classical Press.

2004 Estimating the population of Neopalatial Knossos. In G. Cadogan, E. Hatzaki and A. Vasilakis (eds.), *Knossos: Palace, City, State* (BSA Studies 12): 147–58. London: British School at Athens.

2012 The Urbanisation of Prehistoric Crete: Settlement Perspectives on Minoan State Formation. In I. Schoep, P. Tomkins and J. Driessen (eds.), *Back to the Beginning: Reassessing Social and Political Complexity on Crete during the Early and Middle Bronze Age*: 114–76. Oxford: Oxbow.

Xanthoudides, S.

1924 *The Vaulted Tombs of Mesara*. London: Hodder & Stoughton.

Chapter 11

Recognising polities in prehistoric Crete

Todd Whitelaw

Reconsidering polities in prehistoric Crete

For most of the first century of Minoan archaeology, a reconstruction of the political structure of palatial period Crete, structured around the three major palaces identified at Knossos, Phaistos and Malia, was universally accepted. This picture became naturalised, generating the expectation that the agrarian Minoan states were necessarily centred on the major lowland basins, in what are today prime agricultural zones (e.g. Renfrew 1972: fig. 14.4). This led to the further expectation that additional palace centres might be discovered in only a few comparable locations, such as the major coastal plains near the medieval and modern centres of Rethymnon and Chania in the archaeologically under-explored west of the island (e.g. Younger and Rehak 2008a: 150; 2008b: 178). Anomalies to these expectations were explained as subordinate centres (Hagia Triada, Gournia), or exceptional (Zakros) (e.g. Warren 1985: 74; Younger and Rehak 2008a: 150–52).

Palaces discovered in recent decades at Petras and Galatas, and elaborate structures at Kommos, Archanes, Mochlos, Protoria, Makrygialos and Chania (and re-investigated at Monastiraki) have generally been subsumed within this accepted structure as either representing subordinate centres, or sidelined as non-canonical centres (e.g. Kommos). However, the chronologies of these newly recognised centres, and detailed re-assessments of the history of the three major palaces (e.g. Macdonald 2010; 2012; La Rosa 2002; 2010a; Pelon 2005; Driessen 2010), have created problems for the temporal as well as spatial reconstruction of Minoan political organisation. As our chronological understanding of individual sites improves, it is increasingly difficult to align the history of any of the palaces with the basic Prepalatial, Protopalatial and Neopalatial temporal scheme, or accept that this encapsulates major island-wide organisational transformations in Cretan political history.

This long-standing framework was constructed on the perceived parallel development of the three major palaces, based far more on assumption than evidence. With limited attention to the Protopalatial levels at the major palatial sites until recently, the final Neopalatial picture (with ideas on the administrative structure retrodicted from the deciphered Linear B tablets from the Final Palatial phase at Knossos) was projected back to the foundation of the palaces at the start of the second millennium. This inevitably created a very static picture of the palaces and palatial society (Bennet 1990: 198) and also required a fundamental transformation at their inception. As the long accepted spatial and temporal frameworks are challenged by new evidence and ideas, debates are increasingly targeting the starting date for the process, the nature and scale of the states which developed, the pace of the transformations, and the universality of these characteristics and processes across the island.

The overall interpretive problem is to document and explain the transformation of Cretan societies from ubiquitous small, independent communities, to at least a limited number of integrated, bureaucratic states during the first half of the second millennium BC. The start and end points of this process are clearest, at least for the polities centred on the three major palaces of central Crete. I have argued elsewhere that the communities at Knossos, Phaistos and Malia, large but not exceptional by Aegean standards in EMII, each witnessed rapid population growth in the final Prepalatial phase (EMIII-MMIA) (Whitelaw 2004; 2012). This corresponds to the evidence now widely accepted for the earliest monumental constructions at each site (Macdonald 2010: 532; La Rosa 2010a: 583–84; Driessen 2010: 559). These dramatic transformations mark, if not the start, then certainly a fundamental step-change in the processes of state formation on Crete.

At the other end of the trajectory, our clearest understanding of the nature of a state on prehistoric Crete comes from the LMIIIA2 period, as documented through the deciphered Linear B tablets recovered from Knossos. These demonstrate the integration of at least the central and western two-thirds of the island into a single polity, administered from the palace at Knossos (Bennet 1985). Debates remain about the dates of establishment and collapse of this polity, and its full extent, since it is anchored in space by only a limited number of toponyms which can be linked convincingly to the names of later Classical cities.

Did this extensive polity represent an inheritance by the LMIIIA administration at Knossos, of a pre-existing LMIB state centred on Knossos, or was this a new creation sometime during the phases LMII-IIIA2? Any answer is complicated by several recent arguments, first, for the preservation of an early Linear B archive in the Room of the Chariot Tablets at Knossos, possibly documenting a smaller, simpler administration, which would then have expanded to the scale documented by the remainder of the archive by the time the place was destroyed (Driessen 2000; 2001b). Support for such an expansion has been built on the changing distribution of ceramics in the Knossian LMII to LMIIIA1 styles (Popham 1980; Bennet 1985: 242–45; Rehak and Younger 2001: 441–42) and perhaps changing burial practices (Preston 2004: 333–37). Secondly, as ceramic assemblages from recent excavations are studied more comprehensively, stylistic regionalism is increasingly being proposed for LMIB (Brogan and Hallager 2011), and now LMII (Arvanitakis 2007). While caught in the problematic equation of pottery style with political affiliation (see below), such regionalism is thought by some to question the assumption of a major Knossos-centred state, and therefore any continuity of political structure from LMIB through LMII to LMIIIA1-2.

Pushing this uncertainty one phase back, we also have to recognise the "Troubled Island" model which interprets the LMIB phase not as the apogee of Minoan Crete, but as a period of crisis and possibly political fragmentation (Driessen and Macdonald 1997). While vigorously disputed, this has usefully questioned a wide range of assumptions which deserve critical attention.

An overall scenario often alluded to, and one that I expect most Minoan archaeologists would broadly agree with, posits that states in central Crete developed at the very start of the Protopalatial period at, and only at, the three centres of Knossos, Phaistos and Malia, which during all or most of the period, divided central Crete amongst them. These were unified into a single polity, controlled by Knossos, by some point within the Neopalatial period (Younger and Rehak 2008a: 150). Debates then revolve around the extent of such a polity, whether just encompassing central Crete, or how far to the east or west it extended. To assess this scenario or propose alternatives, we need to be able to define the territories of polities and track their development in space and time.

While recognising the variety of state societies which have been defined by anthropologists, social and political theorists, within the restricted scope of prehistoric Crete, as an initial step, discussion can usefully focus on the distinction drawn by Trigger between city-states and territorial states (Trigger 2003: 92–119). He explores a wide range of differences between these; the most relevant points here are structure, scale and integration. City-states are essentially single-city political entities, which dominate a restricted hinterland necessary to support the inhabitants of that city, and provide goods and services to the population of the city and its hinterland. Small city-states may have their population wholly resident within the central city, or also distributed across the hinterland in much smaller communities. In larger city-states, subsidiary communities develop to enable more effective exploitation of the larger territory, with resources to support the urban population channelled up through a more developed settlement hierarchy (Steponaitis 1981; Wright 2000). The cities themselves are constrained in scale due to agricultural productivity and the effectiveness of bulk transport technology to provision the city's residents (Falconer 1987; Wilkinson 1994; Bintliff 1999; Whitelaw 2017; in press).

Territorial states are more extensive, will include multiple urban centres, and encompass more territory than the hinterland necessary to support the central city alone. It has been noted cross-culturally that city-states usually develop in the competitive context of similar polities (Price 1977; Renfrew 1975; 1986; Feinman 1998; Nichols and Charlton 1997; Hansen 2000a; Wright 2005), and that territorial states are often created through the unification by alliance or conquest of neighbouring city-states (Trigger 2003: 92–119; Marcus 1998). These larger polities are usually unstable and short-lived, disaggregating into individual city-states which are more effectively integrated social, economic and political entities.

What is far less often explored, is just how difficult it is archaeologically to detect political unification, and therefore to define the extent of territorial states, without written records. In large part, this is because the cultural units that can be defined archaeologically through variability in material culture are usually considerably more extensive than individual city-states. Material culture differences tend to mark broad cultural units (e.g. Yoffee 1991; Lightfoot and Martinez 1995; Emberling 1997; Feinman 1998: 101), but can represent identities at a wide range of social and spatial scales (Jones 1997; Stark 1998; Lucy 2005). Compounding the difficulty of recognition, such political amalgamations are usually dynamic, expanding or contracting more rapidly than material culture distributions change, and crucially, tend to be shorter-lived than the resolution of most archaeological artefact-based chronologies.

A clear illustration of this recognition problem is the contrast in models for Classic Maya territorial organisation proposed before the decipherment of the Mayan glyphs. Some analysts used broad ceramic and architectural styles and the scale of sites, architectural complexes or monuments to infer a small number of large-scale hierarchically-organised polities across the Mayan lowlands (e.g. Adams and Jones 1981; Marcus 1983), whereas others proposed that the dozens of cities were politically independent city-states (e.g. Mathews 1985; Sharer 1994: 494–512). The situation has been considerably clarified, though not entirely resolved (e.g. Flannery 1998: 17–21) through the decipherment of the Mayan glyphs, allowing the reading of genealogies and histories, themselves of course subject to propagandist construction and interpretive ambiguity. These paint a picture of complex and fluid relations among a wide range of small to large independent and quasi-independent city states, with short-term amalgamations and alliances constructed through inter-dynastic marriages and conquests, almost entirely invisible archaeologically (Schele and Mathews 1991; Grube 2000).

In a limited number of archaeological examples, settlement pattern data documenting gaps between clusters of settlements have been argued to represent buffer zones between competing polities (Adams 1981: 63–67; Feinman 1998; Whitelaw 1998). This usually requires a larger scale and finer resolution of survey data than are available for most regions; in these examples, such interpretations were inspired by historical or ethnohistorical accounts of polity independence.

The different nature and scale of city-states and territorial states may require very different approaches for archaeological recognition. A variety of approaches have been used to define polities on prehistoric Crete, usually without explicit theoretical or methodological justification. These will be reviewed, and a further approach explored, assessing its potential strengths and limitations.

Topography and territories

The traditional model of the political structure of Minoan Crete, focused on the three major palaces, assumes they "make sense" in terms of natural divisions of the central Cretan landscape. Most of a century of investigation without revealing additional palatial centres, encouraged the view that these were the only centres, and less explicitly, that all of at least central Crete was divided amongst them (e.g. Warren 1985: 74; Cherry 1986: fig. 2.2; Bennet 1990: 195–98).

In fact, the island has supported a diversity of political divisions (Fig. 11.1), with the four-fold north-coast structured model significant only when the island has been politically dominated from outside, by north Mediterranean-based empires (Bennet 1990). Figure 11.2 schematically represents the scale and number of independent polities on Crete through time. City-states of various sizes were the norm, with territorial states relatively infrequent, and island unification extremely rare, except when the island was incorporated within a much larger state or empire. The one prehistoric episode of large-scale unification, during LMII-IIIA2, was extremely short-lived, probably reflecting the difficulty of establishing and maintaining an indigenous integration of the entire, attenuated island. This documented historical diversity of political entities on Crete suggests that there is no "natural" structure to the political organisation of the island; geography and topography are relevant, but not determining, as is commonly assumed.

Turning from environmental determinism to historical contingency, if we simply accept the locations of the known early palatial centres as given, can these be used to predict the extent of their associated polities? This is what Cherry's well-known map of Thiessen polygons imposed on the distribution of known and potential palaces represents (1986: fig. 2.2).

This has recently been re-examined critically, using GIS techniques to update the Thiessen polygon approach with modelled walking time, dividing central Crete among the three known early and principal palaces (Bevan 2010). But is this how people actually interact across the Cretan landscape? Various categories of social and biological data (e.g. dialects, marriage patterns, genetic data) should document ways in which recent populations have socialised the same landscape. These do not dictate how earlier populations would have behaved, but analogically, may alert us to new possibilities, or challenge our intuitive assumptions. A recently published study of local differences in vocabulary in 1960s–70s Crete (Kontosopoulos 2006), documents variants of 172 words or phrases recorded for 163 communities across the island. The degree of shared usage can arguably be considered a rough index of the intensity of inter-community interaction between residents at different locations, and allows us to investigate the assumed relevance of distance and topography to inter-community interaction on Crete, before the widespread impact of tourism and personal motorised transport on mobility.

To explore the potential division of the central Cretan landscape among the three major palace sites, in Figure 11.3, the degree of similarity in word use is assessed for

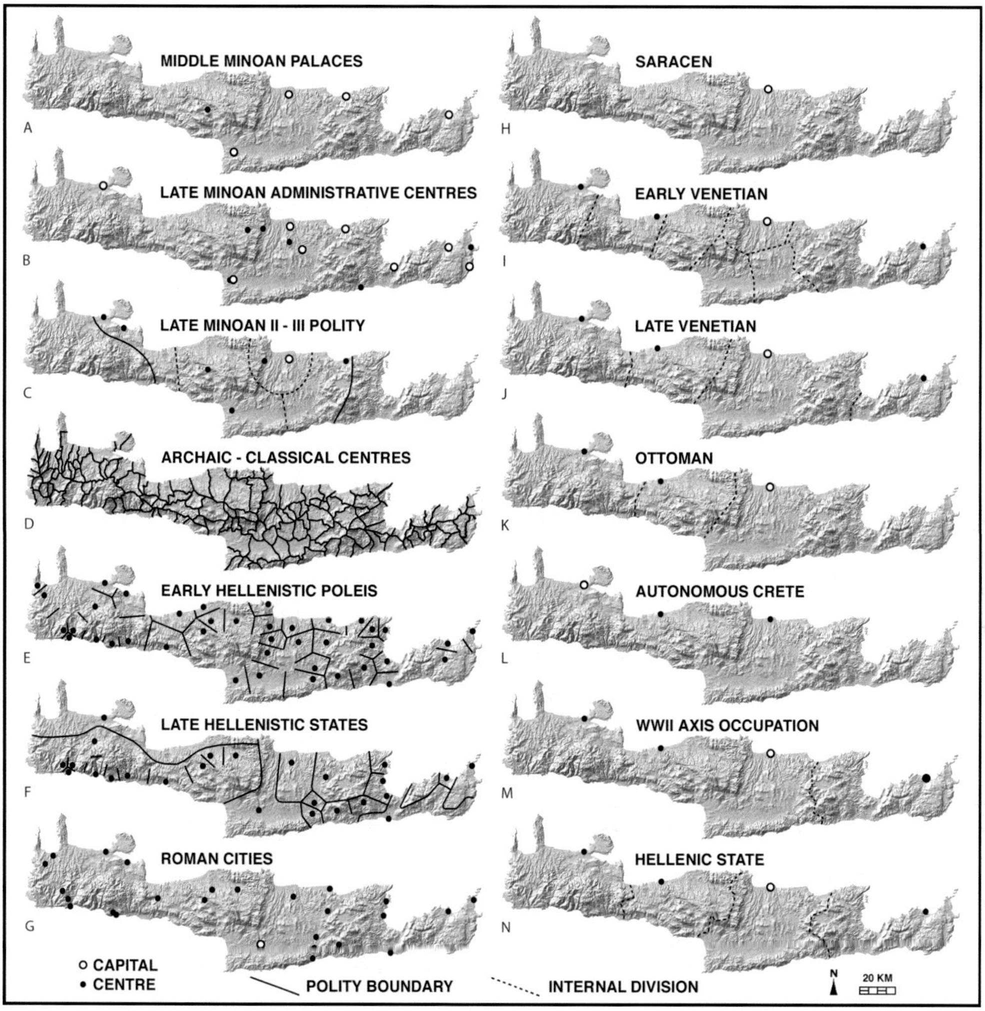

Figure 11.1: The political organisation of Crete, prehistory to the present: A. Principal MM sites; B. LM administrative centres; C. Linear B organisational structure; D. Archaic centres; E. Early Hellenistic cities; F. Late Hellenistic states; G. Roman cities; H. Saracen; I. Early Venetian; J. Late Venetian; K. Ottoman; L. Autonomous Crete; M. Axis occupation; N. Hellenic state.

each community in the study, in relation to the modern communities nearest to each of the three palatial centres. The fourth map compares these datasets to define which communities are most similar in vocabulary to each of these centres.

Overall, this indicates that vocabulary differences increase systematically with distance, providing support for the assumption that GIS walking-time calculations provide a realistic base-line for analysing inter-community interactions. Not surprisingly, the major massifs of Lasithi and Ida represent strong barriers to interaction. More surprisingly, there are only very low levels of differentiation

landscape. But previous studies have mapped additional expectations onto the past landscape which seem unjustifiable, at least viewed against one proxy measure of recent patterns of interaction on the ground.

Of course, this approach to predicting polities from centres only makes sense if we have confidence that we have recognised all the relevant polity centres, which the discoveries of the past few decades should call into question, particularly acknowledging how much of the island has never received systematic or intensive archaeological investigation. Additionally, as a top-down, partitive approach, it can only divide the territory among known centres, it cannot establish whether parts of the landscape lay outside the political control of those or any other centres.

Before leaving geography and topography, it is possible to work in a more exploratory and systematic way, from the bottom up, to define potential landscape units on the island (see also Bevan and Wilson 2013). As pre-industrial societies, agriculture was fundamental to supporting Minoan polities, of whatever scale. While many characteristics will affect agricultural production, surface slope severely constrains the areas available for agriculture in the Mediterranean prior to the widespread construction of agricultural terraces. Figure 11.4 maps areas of less than 10° slope, revealing numerous agriculturally productive landscape blocks at a variety of different scales. As we shall see, the palatial centres could have been supported from fairly limited territories (Figs. 11.5–11.7). Simply taking the Malia plain as an example, we can identify a considerable number of low-slope basins on that sort of scale across

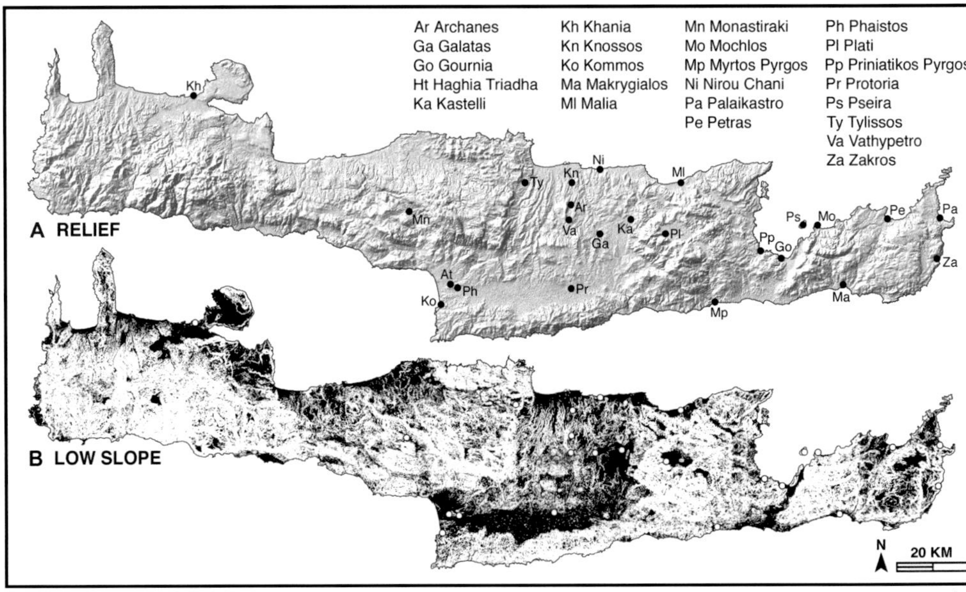

Figure 11.4: Island topography and centres: A. topographic relief and known palaces and other major centres; B. low-slope land.

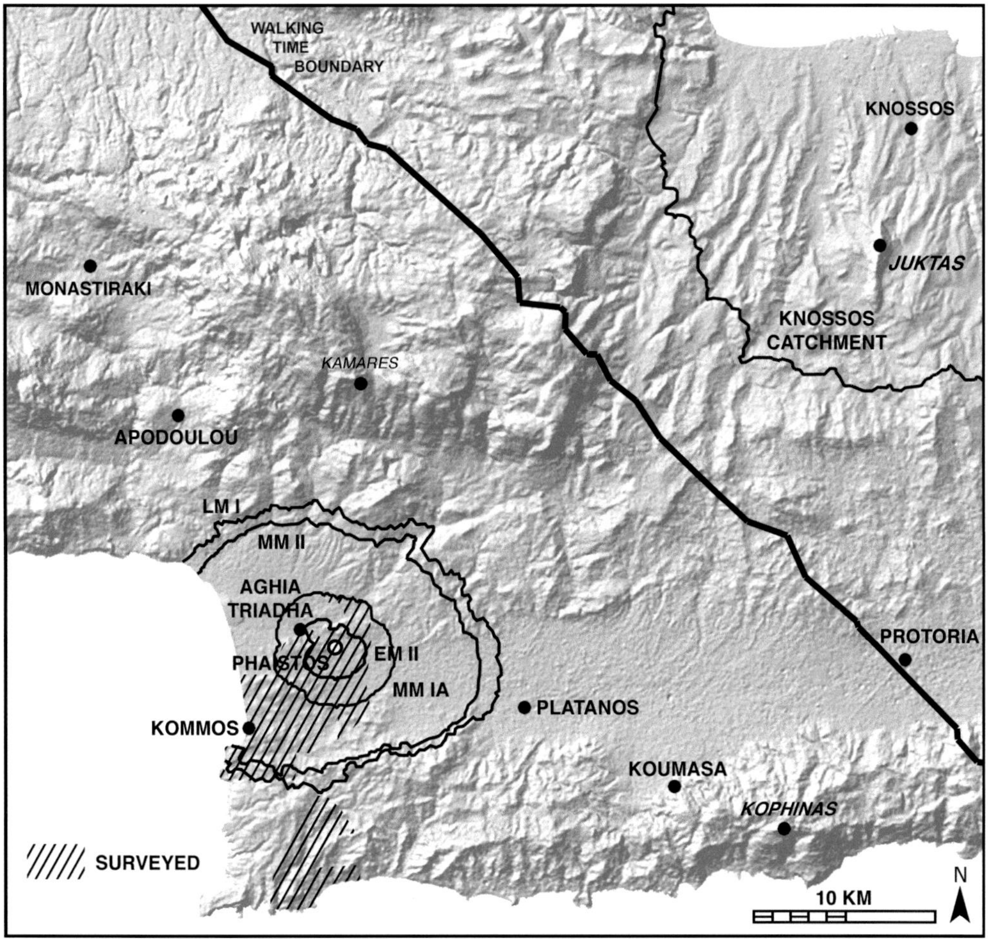

Figure 11.5: Phaistos and the western Mesara: main sites and Phaistos agricultural catchments by phase.[1]

the island, far more than have ever been considered as potential prehistoric palatial territories. While this does not predict that all or even most will have supported a palatial centre, it seems premature to assume that the additional palaces discovered in the past 25 years will not be supplemented by others, when more of Crete receives intensive archaeological investigation.

Over the first century of Minoan archaeology, a model imposed top-down from assumptions about the three major central Cretan palace sites, has generated a remarkably resilient conceptualisation of the Minoan political landscape. This "understanding" in turn encouraged assumptions about the determinist nature of Cretan geography which are not supported by historical patterns, unbiased analyses of topography or patterns of recent social interaction, and have been challenged by recent archaeological discoveries. Island geography and topography, and the

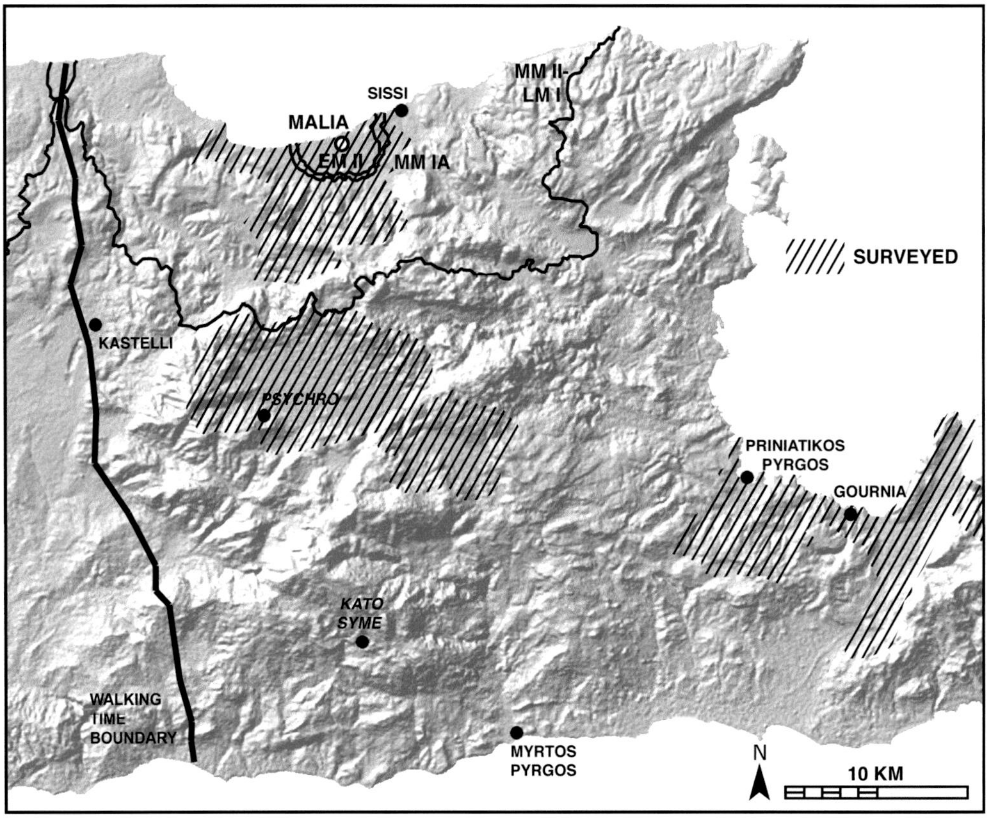

Figure 11.6: Malia and east-central Crete: main sites and Malia agricultural catchments by phase.

mechanical constraints they impose on communication, interaction and transport, will be relevant to how past communities constructed their social and political landscapes, but in far less deterministic ways than have been assumed.

Defining polities through administrative evidence

Administrative systems need to be considered on a sliding scale, and while the nature and content of the existing records are accepted as demonstrating a state level administrative structure in Neopalatial Crete (Schoep 1999; 2002), they only hint at its existence before the end of the Protopalatial period. The very limited Hieroglyphic and Linear A records of that date give little idea of the nature or scale of administration. The control over access to several storerooms documented by the abundant sealings from Phaistos (Weingarten 1986), need not represent a state-level administration, being anticipated by centuries in the sealing system in use at EHII Lerna. The scale of the Protopalatial palace structures themselves (Macdonald 2010; 2012; La Rosa 2010; Militello 2012), and the differentiated society they represent, support an assumption

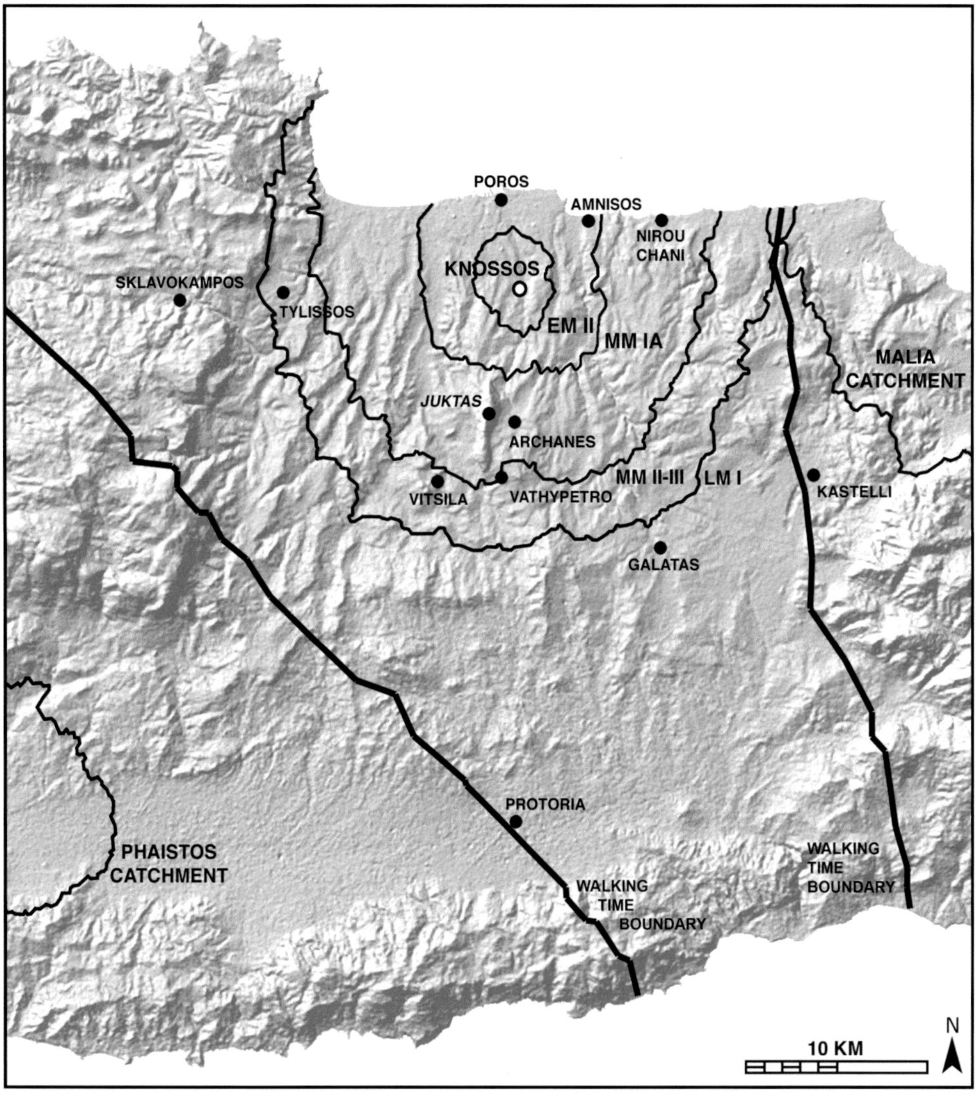

Figure 11.7: Knossos and central Crete: main sites and Knossos agricultural catchments by phase.

of state administration for their construction, maintenance, and the specialised activities they housed, but tell us little about their regional dominance or how they were organised or functioned.

For the Protopalatial period, the use of two different script systems at Phaistos vs Knossos, Malia and Petras, suggests at least two independent administrations, distinguishing Phaistos, though not necessarily differentiating any of the north coast sites.

Turning to the Neopalatial period, where we have considerably more abundant evidence, the political interpretation of the administrative artefacts is far from clear. Differences in administrative practices have been well documented, particularly between Hagia Triada and Zakros, the two sites with substantial samples of administrative artefacts (Weingarten 1986; Hallager 1996; Schoep 1999). Unfortunately, these assemblages largely represent different types of specialised administrative activities, and are not directly comparable for an assessment of differences in overall administrative practices; they simply emphasise how partial our evidence is for administration at each site. There are minor differences in administrative practices at different sites (Weingarten 1986; Schoep 1999), but their significance is difficult to assess without comprehensive documentation of the overall variability within and between each local system. Additionally, is it realistic to expect uniform administrative practices at different centres within the same political system (Schoep 1999: 203–13, 220–1)? If the system works locally, will a newly dominant centre necessarily change it, and even if so, how much standardisation will be imposed, and how long will such changes take to percolate down the levels of the administrative hierarchy? We simply do not know, so whereas identity of practices might be argued as evidence for a common administration, the differences documented to date need not indicate the inverse.

A specific category of administrative artefact is represented by the "look-alike" sealings recovered from a number of sites, and often considered to document the involvement of a Knossian administration across much of the island (Betts 1967; Hallager 1996: 207–13; Wiener 2007: 236), now also documented by sealings at Akrotiri (Weingarten 2010). While a range of arguments is regularly assembled to support the idea of Knossian political hegemony, their ambiguity is usually recognised, and the look-alike sealings have been proposed as the conclusive evidence for political domination (e.g. Niemeier 2004: 394), so they take on exceptional significance. Recent petrographic analyses confirm the similarity of the clay used in the sealings at different sites, and its mineralogical compatibility with central Cretan geology, providing support for the earlier iconographic interpretations (Goren and Panagiotopoulos 2010). While these artefacts document contact between (probably) Knossos and other communities, without being able to read the organic documents they originally sealed, we don't know what, if anything, they indicate about political or administrative organisation (Cherry 1986: 26; Weingarten 1986: 296, n. 26; 1991; 2010; Wiener 1987: 266, n. 46; Schoep 1999: 213–17; Krzyszkowska 2005: 167–68). Were these necessarily official palace-issued administrative documents, and even if so, were they communications between individuals at independent polities (cf. the Amarna letters between Egypt and Hatti), instructions from a dominant power (cf. the Amarna letters from the pharaoh to subordinate rulers in the southern Levant), or different types of communications between individuals at different sites; without the documents themselves, we have no idea.

While administrative artefacts should ideally provide our most direct indications of political integration and polity extent, their interpretation is clear only if the documents themselves can be tied directly to identifiable sites, and provide information about the nature of their interactions. The Knossian Linear B tablets do this, recording administrative transactions linking the centre to a large number of locations through a variety of interactions involving large quantities of materials (documenting the scale and nature of administration), and can be anchored to specific locations by a very small number of toponyms in the centre and west of the island (documenting its minimal extent). Equivalent information is not clearly recorded among the very limited preserved Linear A documents (Bennet 1990: 198–99; Schoep 2001; 2002), nor is it recognisable among the even more limited Hieroglyphic documents.

Defining polities through material culture distributions

Various types and characteristics of Protopalatial and Neopalatial material culture have been invoked to support reconstructions of Minoan political structure and history. Except for the Linear B texts, all other arguments are problematic: theoretically, methodologically and empirically. For reasons of space, not all can be reviewed here, but the examples considered (elite prestige artefacts, ceramic style) outline problems which apply to all attempts to define states in prehistoric Crete on the basis of material culture distributions.

Three types of argument have been developed: 1) specific types or traits document exchange or diffusion from a single source, assumed to indicate political influence or dominance, usually argued or assumed to be Knossian; 2) contrasts are drawn between regional and island-wide styles, usually in ceramics, and the latter are assumed to imply political unification, the former fragmentation; 3) essentially a development from 2, specific ceramic distributions are interpreted as mapping political territories.

The first approach considers the distribution of specific types or styles of material culture as evidence of influence, regularly assumed to represent political dominance, whether the materials are exchanged or locally imitated (Wiener 1987: 266; 1990: 134–43, 150–51; 2007; Niemeier 2004: 393–4). Material culture interpreted this way includes ashlar masonry, mason's marks, lustral basins and Minoan halls (distributions documented by Driessen 1982; 1989–90), figured frescoes (Rehak 1997), and the finest ceramics (Betancourt 2004a; 2004b). A fundamental empirical and methodological problem arises because Knossos is the most intensively investigated palatial site, and documents most fully the range and sequence of development of Minoan elite material culture. It therefore provides abundant *comparanda* for many categories of material evidence, but this does not necessarily demonstrate Knossian precedence, inspiration, production or control, which are usually assumed (however, see Bevan 2010: 40–43). There is an almost inevitable Knossian sampling bias which needs to be acknowledged and assessed critically in each case (see also Knappett 2011: 393–96). Illustrating the compound nature of the assumptions, pictorial fresco fragments recovered at Galatas are identified as the earliest known on the island, but are also assumed to have been painted by artisans trained at Knossos (Rethemiotakis 2002: 57). As other sites are more thoroughly investigated, they may reveal examples which antedate the earliest known Knossian examples, such as the early forms of lustral basin and Minoan Hall at Quartier Mu at Malia (Driessen 1982: 54–55; Poursat 2007), though both are regularly suggested to be evidence for Knossian influence elsewhere on the island (Wiener 1990: 140; 2007: 234).

More fundamentally, even if Knossian precedence can be securely documented, how do we establish that the adoption of such a trait elsewhere represents political imposition or domination, rather than passive diffusion or active emulation? That the spread of such traits can be variously taken to represent Knossian political dominance, cultural hegemony, peer-polity competition (Cherry 1986), or the de-centralisation of elite power (Driessen and Macdonald 1997: 71), indicates the absence of clear theoretical justification for the Knossos-dominance model. While the "Versailles effect" (competitive elite emulation) was coined to apply to Cretan influence in the wider Aegean (Wiener 1984: 17; 1990), it has as much relevance as a process on Crete itself (Wiener 1987: 266; Warren 2002: 204). Aspiring individuals seek to acquire or copy status-enhancing artefacts, material styles and behavioural traits developed in the more competitive context of socially differentiated urban centres. This indicates elite level communication, and illustrates processes of cultural perception and valuation in active identity construction, but how might we actually establish if, or in which cases, such adoptions represent political domination?

A second set of interpretations uses ceramic stylistic uniformity in contrast with regionalism as an indication of the degree of island-wide political unification. The equation of ceramic stylistic similarity with political affiliation is dealt with in more detail below. Here, it is the contrast in relative similarity which is taken to suggest differences in regional political integration. The focus on defining local styles is relatively recent in Minoan ceramic studies, and is highly constrained by recent excavations which have retained and systematically studied significant quantities of material, so the emerging evidence principally concerns a limited number of LMIB assemblages (Brogan and Hallager 2011). Not surprisingly, the more systematically and intensively one looks, the greater the distinctions and local characteristics which can be identified, potentially down to the level of individual potters. The criteria used to define local styles at each site are very mixed, and differ, not allowing systematic comparisons or assessments of degrees of difference among assemblages. Equally problematic, there are no standards against which to calibrate the significance of the differences detected. Interpretively, local styles may represent different production traditions, scales and modes of production, distribution and marketing systems, as well as influence through different types of interactions with other communities. Without having criteria for identifying and distinguishing these different processes, we cannot interpret degrees of regionalism in specifically political terms.

The third approach, using ceramic styles to define political territories, essentially derives from the previous, but has been developed more explicitly with Protopalatial ceramics, and is so directly involved with the question being addressed in this paper, that it requires more detailed exploration.

Distributions defined by artefact style, predominantly pottery because of its abundance, are used world-wide to define archaeological "cultures", to establish our basic time-space frameworks for organising information about the past. How such distributions should be defined, and what they actually represent in human behavioural and social terms, have been fiercely debated for the past 60 years (e.g. Clarke 1968; Whallon and Brown 1982; Dunnell 1971; 1986; Hodder and Orton 1976; Hodder 1978). Approaches to analysing and interpreting such distributions have become increasingly diverse and self-critical in recent decades, with debates about the meaning of artefact style (e.g. Wobst 1977; Conkey and Hastorf 1989; Hegemon 1992), material culture variation and transmission (e.g. Hodder 1978; 1981; Dobres and Hoffman 1994; Stark *et al.* 2008; Gosselain 2000; Hurt and Rakita 2001), and the creation and representation, through material culture, of individual and group identities (e.g. Shennan 1994; Stark 1998; Emberling 1997; Jones 1997; Robb 1999; Green and Perlman 1985; Lightfoot and Martinez 1995; Diaz-Andreu *et al.* 2005). These fundamental and on-going debates about the identification, meaning and significance of material culture variability have received almost no recognition in Minoan archaeology.

Providing evidence for these debates, a wide range of ethnographic and ethnoarchaeological research has established that some characteristics of material culture may mark cultural boundaries whereas others do not, representing economic distribution patterns, technological traditions or learning patterns, among other processes, and others simply represent random variation. Distinguishing among generating processes in ethnographic contexts relies on detailed and systematic analyses, and usually requires other contextual information, observable in the ethnographic present but not necessarily determinable archaeologically.

In Cretan prehistory, without explicit consideration of the assumptions involved, some distributions of artefacts are regularly interpreted, not as defining vague archaeological "cultures", but far more specifically as mapping political entities (e.g. Cadogan 2011). The justification for this seems to be that the spatial units so defined, correspond in location and scale to the political entities we are expecting to find, but this argument is obviously circular. We need to establish why any specific material distributions should be considered to represent political affiliation.

Stylistic distribution studies build from a passive information flow model, in which it is assumed that stylistic similarities between artefacts produced in different communities will decline with the distance between them. The rationale is that producers and consumers in communities which are closer together are likely to interact more regularly with each other, and will be more accepting of (and so, willing to acquire or copy) stylistic variants they are familiar with and accept as appropriate, through regular exposure. So we should normally expect a fall-off in stylistic similarity in material culture with distance (Plog 1980). Deviations from this suggest that something a bit more interesting is going on, for example, factors inhibiting or enhancing interaction between members of the communities, or that specific meanings are attached to the stylistic characteristics which lead to them being differentially accepted or rejected as imports, imitated closely, adapted, or ignored.

A significant analytical problem emerges if, like our vocabulary model, we choose two or more base points and assess the similarity of finds from other points against them. This will invariably define "territories" of influence around the base points, since the stylistic characteristics at any other point will be more similar to one of the original base points than another. Because of the way we have structured the investigation, we will create "territories" centred on our initial base points, even if these are completely arbitrary and there is, in fact, continuous variation across the area.

A systematic and neutral approach would need to give equal weight to the assemblages at all points, to try to define spatial clusters among them, which is the approach ideally used for the definition of archaeological cultures across a region: any groupings in the data emerge through analysis, rather than being imposed from the start. In contrast, Cretan studies have worked from what are presumed to be the most influential centres outwards, with the result that other communities are defined as responsive or subsidiary to those initial points of reference (e.g. "provincial Middle Minoan pottery": Walberg 1983). Unfortunately, because of the way Cretan archaeology has developed, we rarely have either the unbiased substantial samples, nor the quantified documentation of stylistic attributes which are essential for systematic exploratory analyses.

To illustrate the problem, for Protopalatial Crete, we have three palatial sites which have been the principal focus for major investigations, and therefore provide the most abundant samples of Protopalatial pottery. We have assumed they are the major and innovating pottery-producing centres, and so use comparisons with much smaller samples from minor sites, to allocate the latter to the orbit of one assumed territorial centre or another. If style is purely passive, we should expect a regular fall-off in stylistic similarity with distance from a centre, resulting in roughly circular territories around each centre (subject to travel/transport constraints), which is approximately what has been proposed, for example in the territory defined around Knossos (Cadogan 1994). However, since no explicit analysis has been undertaken with the assemblages, we do not know if there is actually a decline in similarity; this is simply a presence/absence distribution of some material resembling that known from the centre. Without knowing the quantities, and whether the dispersed examples are exports from the palatial centres, local copies, or some combination of both, or knowing the different contexts or modes of pottery production or exchange represented in different communities across the region, or contexts of consumption, the processes involved may be economic, social, ideological or political, but we have no basis for determining which, individually or in combination, are responsible for producing the distribution.

Beginning to address such questions was the focus of Knappett's research (1999), though this subtlety is usually ignored, and his study is simply cited as support for the "Malia-Lasithi state" model. It was initially assumed that the stylistic similarity in pottery between Malia and Myrtos Pyrgos was the result of intensive interaction between the communities, with abundant ceramic exchange representing strong economic links (Cadogan 1995; Poursat 2010: 263–64). Knappett's detailed petrographic, technological and stylistic study demonstrated that very little material was actually moving between Malia and Pyrgos, but local fine wares were extremely similar, and it was assumed that those produced at Pyrgos were closely modelled on those of the palatial centre. This was contextualised by the significant contrast with the local and non-standardised styles of the coarse and cooking wares, so the close emulation in fine table wares was identified as a specific elite strategy. This led to his suggestion that while the elites at Pyrgos were sub-ordinate members of the Malia state, the control of that state was principally ideological, rather than economic, and he proposed that the Malia-Lasithi state be considered a de-centralised or segmentary state (1999). But with no demonstrable strong economic links, was Pyrgos actually subordinate to the Malia state, or was it independent, with the local elite simply emulating elite behaviour at the closest major centre, either to facilitate their relations with those elite, or to enhance their prestige at home, or both? We simply don't know: there is no material evidence which clearly supports the view that Myrtos Pyrgos was part of the Protopalatial state centred at Malia.

Stepping back from the specific case, is it possible to recognise archaeologically a politically-determined material culture distribution? Two sets of studies are informative of the problems, but not particularly hopeful about the prospects. Late Iron Age Celtic gold coins in Britain are politically-identified, ideologically-charged artefacts, and are expected to have circulated principally within the boundaries of the political units where they were minted (Collis 1971; Cunliffe 1981; Sellwood 1984). Such politically constrained distributions could be expected to be defined by sharp edges at political boundaries (Collis 1981; Hodder 1977; Kimes *et al.* 1982). While there are regionally defined distributions, there are very considerable overlaps, so they do not produce clear boundaries (Cunliffe 2005). This makes the polities difficult to define on the basis of coinage alone, but given that there are few other bases for doing so (significantly, ceramic stylistic distributions are usually much smaller than the assumed political units: Cunliffe 2005), coinage is used this way (Kimes *et al.* 1982; Cunliffe 2005: 130–79). Even more problematically, similar boundary effects will be generated by economic competition between rival production centres (Hodder and Orton 1976: 195–97), so even if there were clear boundaries, these would not, in themselves, indicate that the material distributions defined political entities. We might expect the economic distribution patterns for different types of goods to vary to some degree (though all may be affected by common constraints on transport, the distribution of consumers, etc.), so detecting the same sharp boundary in a range of types of material culture might be suggestive of a political boundary. This would only apply if that boundary was competitive or hostile, strongly policed, and crucially, stable for a period longer than the resolution of the local archaeological periodisation.

But even political boundaries significant and stable enough to be fortified and patrolled, such as the Roman Germanic *limes*, can be remarkably permeable (Hedeager 1979; Wells 1992).

One of the most relevant studies of ceramic distributions, utilising a substantial, systematically collected sample (6,410 decorated sherds from the survey of 130 sites, in 12 contiguous city-states), considered the effect of political boundaries on both exchange and ceramic styles in the south-east of the Valley of Mexico, in the period immediately before and after Aztec unification, when political boundaries can be reconstructed through ethnohistoric sources (Hodge and Minc 1990; Hodge *et al.* 1993; Minc *et al.* 1994; Minc 2006; 2009). Two levels of political boundaries were considered, those of individual city-states and those defined by alliances among them. While some ceramic distributions were largely concentrated within regions formed by political alliances, none clearly define individual city-states, and all crossed the boundaries, with gradual fall-off in quantities with distance from source. Without previously knowing the polity or alliance boundaries, it is impossible to recognise which distributions are strongly affected by the boundaries and which are not. Following the Aztec conquest of the area, ceramics generally circulated more widely, so political relations did affect exchange patterns, but not in the spatially defined ways which would enable polities to be identified from the ceramic style distributions.

Neither cultural and political boundaries nor material culture distributions appear to conform in any straightforward sense to the assumptions necessary to support the direct interpretation of ceramic or other material culture distributions as political maps, undermining the predominant approach to the definition of polities employed in Cretan prehistory. On the other hand, spatial distributions can inform us about a wealth of processes and behaviours, from the organisation and control of exchange systems, to different types of identity construction. These processes may be affected by political structure and affiliations, but not necessarily in the direct or easily identifiable ways assumed.

Settlement pattern data and political structure

For Crete, an increasing number of intensive surveys are making the island one of the most thoroughly surveyed regions of the Mediterranean, with island-wide coverage and samples from a variety of topographic contexts. However, many projects are published only in preliminary form, and the data are difficult to analyse comparatively, having been collected over several decades by projects with very different approaches to fieldwork, documentation and publication. In addition, many surveys have been very small, often in areas peripheral to the palace centres, and document only a limited segment of a local settlement system.

To date, interpretation has been largely descriptive or focused on the identification of local settlement hierarchies. The model for the latter has been processual settlement pattern archaeology (Flannery 1998: 16–21; Parsons 1972; Wright and Johnson 1975;

Cherry 1987; Kowalewski 2008), aimed primarily at the analysis and interpretation of large regional datasets, for example in Mesopotamia and Mesoamerica (e.g. Adams 1981; Johnson 1972; Wright and Johnson 1975; Sanders *et al.* 1979; Blanton *et al.* 1993). These drew interpretively on the central place models developed for modern industrial societies in Europe and North America (Johnson 1972; 1977; Hodges 1987), though these have been demonstrated also to have relevance to understanding the regional organisation of developing economies (Smith 1974; 1980) and early modern Europe (de Vries 1990).

Because archaeological datasets are invariably only partially preserved, accessible or recorded, represent low resolution data, and exist in a variable landscape, rather than the geographers' idealised isotropic plain, it is accepted that the subtle distinctions in spatial configuration necessary to distinguish among different central place models can rarely be convincingly documented. Instead, the focus is on recognising a hierarchical relationship among sites in a region, and analysing their inter-relationships to understand the degree of integration within the system. The key characteristic for identifying a state level of political integration is usually argued to be a four-level settlement hierarchy, to differentiate such a system from the two to three levels expected for a regional chiefdom (Wright and Johnson 1975; Johnson 1977; Wright 1977), though this is only a "rule of thumb" (Flannery 1998: 16). In the most convincing studies, the settlement data are correlated with archaeological evidence for administrative integration (Wright and Johnson 1975; Johnson 1980a; 1987; Wright 1987; 1998; Marcus 1983), or other data supporting the differential administrative role of specific communities within the postulated settlement hierarchy (e.g. Sanders *et al.* 1979: 52–60; Smith 1979; Blanton *et al.* 1982). More typically, the settlement pattern data alone are relied on, with consequent (usually unacknowledged) uncertainties.

Often ignored, but integrally linked to the subject of this paper, is the difficulty in distinguishing territorial states from multi-polity regions, unless the primary urban centre develops exceptionally in response to its regional administrative role. This depends on factors such as how strongly centralised the system is; there is no single or unambiguous signature (Johnson 1977; 1980b; 1981; Savage 1997; Drennan and Peterson 2004). In practice, many surveys work within naturally defined regions (islands, topographic basins, restricted sections of a river valley), and assume that the study region includes most or all of one past settlement system, but not multiple systems. Other studies simply uncritically analyse a study region as if it was a coherent and integrated whole. Unfortunately, any analysis will be systematically distorted if only part, or parts of more than one system are included in the analysis.

A particular problem in the Aegean and more widely in the Mediterranean, is that requiring a four-level settlement hierarchy to identify a state, rules out most city-states. Even Athens, one of the largest and most politically complex Classical city-states, with its deme centres and dispersed hamlets and farms, had only two administrative levels, three levels overall; community sizes within the largest city-states may fit a rank-size model (Cavanagh 2009), but not the political hierarchical expectation. Most city-states were much smaller (Hansen 2006b), and surveys such as around Koressos on Keos document only two hierarchical levels, the city and rural hamlets or farms (Whitelaw 1998). Some analysts have used the absence of a four-level hierarchy to suggest that the Classical Greek city-state not be considered a state (Marcus 1998: 91). While the nature of Classical city-states is receiving critical and comparative re-assessment (e.g. Berent 2000; Hansen 2006a; Vlassopoulos 2007; Anderson 2009; Gehrke 2009), they should not be rejected as states because they do not fit one very specific spatial model; after all, when it comes to defining the nature of the state, they literally wrote the book. The archaeological models of settlement hierarchies, often applied in a mechanistic fashion, appear to have been formulated principally with reference to territorial states or very large, developed city-states; they are not adequate for recognising or analysing small city-states.

Most diachronic settlement analyses face a similar problem, trying to define the point at which a state can be recognised in a scalar continuum. Settlement data from surveys throughout the East Mediterranean and Near East suggest that developing urban centres from 8–20ha were often surrounded by very small villages or hamlets, with the development of secondary centres as a later phenomenon, as populations expanded under relatively stable conditions (see also Falconer and Savage 1995). At what point in that process one defines the emergence of the state should depend principally on the availability of relevant evidence for the administrative structure of a state, not on what can be a fairly arbitrary exercise in defining site size modes.

The Cretan survey record is particularly problematic; different surveys engage, at best, variable segments of settlement systems, so it is not surprising there is no clear aggregate patterning; this may represent regional diversity (Driessen 2001a), or simply non-comparability of very partial datasets. From the surveys conducted to date on Crete, we have information on core areas of two states, those centred on Phaistos and Malia.

Phaistos and the western Mesara

Taking the 40km^2 of the western Mesara (Watrous *et al.* 2004) and Kommos (Hope Simpson *et al.* 1995) surveys together, these represent the only published intensive survey of a segment of the core of the territory of one of the major palatial centres. The Agiopharango (Blackman and Branigan 1977; Vasilakis 1990), South Coast (Blackman and Branigan 1975) and Odigitria (Branigan and Vasilakis 2010) surveys are assumed to provide smaller peripheral samples of the same polity (Fig. 11.5). Focusing on the core sample, these surveys provide useful, but far from straightforward data. Consistent with other Aegean surveys conducted in the late 1970s–80s, sherd collections were extremely limited and only aggregate site sizes for all periods of occupation are usually documented, masking period-specific changes at sites. Mitigating this, across all prehistoric periods, the only major occupations outside the palatial centre of Phaistos are at the previously known and extensively excavated sites of Hagia Triada and Kommos. Phaistos itself is presently being surveyed (Bredaki *et al.* 2009), but patchy excavations beyond the palace suggest a Neopalatial extent on the order of 55–60 ha (Watrous *et al.* 2004: 294) if occupation was continuous between all the outlying soundings, and a minimum of 32 ha in the Protopalatial period, making a similar assumption (Whitelaw 2012; Militello 2012).

In analysing their data, the project directors define site hierarchies of three (EMII-III) and four levels (MMIB-LMIB), though no clear modes in site size provide any basis for this interpretation. More significantly, despite the over-estimation inevitable with all-period aggregate site size estimates, for the Prepalatial phases, only two sites outside of Phaistos might reach or exceed 1ha (most being much smaller), and for all periods, only Phaistos itself and in the Neopalatial period, Hagia Triada, exceed 2.5ha, when the latter took over from Phaistos as the administrative centre for the region (La Rosa 2010b). The survey data provide no clear evidence for a developed regional settlement hierarchy; the divisions seem imposed on an undifferentiated distribution of very small sites, to meet the expectation of four hierarchical levels for states. However, the absence of clear second-order centres is not entirely surprising, since given the scale of Phaistos itself from MMIA, these should only develop on the order of 4–8 km from the palatial centre, and it is only in the direction of Kommos that the combined intensive survey area extends this far from Phaistos. So if there was a developed settlement hierarchy in the western Mesara, intensive survey has not yet been extensive enough to detect it. On the other hand, we might anticipate that in the area surrounding Phaistos and Gortyn, each investigated fairly continuously for over a century, extensive exploration should have located the major sites, as with Kommos and Hagia Triada.

Taking a different approach to recognise the development of an integrated settlement system, we can use site size, to the degree that it can be calculated from such low-resolution data, to estimate probable community populations, and therefore the notional cultivation areas around each site necessary to support its population. The sites outside Phaistos are so small and well-spaced that there is no overlap of such catchments, suggesting no necessary economic interaction or integration in the Prepalatial periods. The dramatic expansion of Phaistos in the Protopalatial period leads to the complete overlap of the catchment of Phaistos on those of neighbouring hamlets, and indicates the necessity for some sort of inter-site dependency relationships during the Protopalatial period, but not earlier (Whitelaw 2012). On present evidence, Phaistos would have been the centre of a very simple, two or just possibly three-tier settlement system by the end of the Protopalatial period. Such simple, highly centralised, under-developed hierarchies are typical of many East Mediterranean and Near Eastern early urbanising regional systems, and city-states, rather than the well-developed, four-level hierarchically-structured systems characteristic of larger territorial states.

Watrous *et al.* (2004: 286–7, 295), challenging previous assumptions that the Mesara forms a "natural" region (see also Relaki 2004), suggest that Phaistos may never have dominated all of the Mesara plain, let alone all of south-central Crete, based on the argument that the peak sanctuaries of Kophinas and Demati, overlooking the central and eastern Mesara, will have served separate polities. There is no necessary one-to-one relationship between polities and major sanctuaries, and in the absence of any systematic surveys east of Phaistos, this is an interesting but completely speculative proposal. The interpretation of Monastiraki in the Amari valley as a sub-ordinate centre to Phaistos (Kanta 1999; Kanta and Tzigounaki 2000; Watrous *et al.* 2004: 287) in the Protopalatial period, is based solely on stylistic similarities in the ceramics and seals.

The known administrative documents provide minimal information relevant to polity scale. No toponyms can be recognised unambiguously in the Linear A documents from Hagia Triada, giving no idea of its dependent territory (Bennet 1990: 198–99; Schoep 2001: 98–99; 2002: 192). While the quantities of agricultural products listed in the Linear A tablets do not require an extensive dependent territory (Palaima 1994: 318–21; Schoep 2001: 97–99; 2002: 176–92), the small number of recovered tablets is unlikely to document production from the entire territory administered by the site (see also Palaima 1994: 316–17). To date, there are insufficient data with which to define the extent of the territories administered from Phaistos or Hagia Triada in the Protopalatial or Neopalatial periods.

Malia and the Malia-Lasithi state

Intensive survey was initiated at the palatial centre of Malia and expanded to include the coastal plain and neighbouring inland valleys, the only Cretan survey with both urban and hinterland data (Fig. 11.6: Müller 1996; 1997; 1998; 2003; Müller-Celka 2007). To date, preliminary summaries have been published, while analysis of the recovered material continues (Müller-Celka 2007; Puglisi 2007). At the palatial centre, overall sherd density has been recorded, but period-specific material is only reported on a presence/absence basis by survey unit (Müller-Celka 2007: fig. 5; pers comm.). The figure of 50–60 ha for the maximum extent of the site in the Protopalatial period (Müller 1997: 52; Müller-Celka 2007: 856; Driessen 2001a: 61), includes as well as the city, the extensive cemeteries near the shore and the outlying port at Hagia Varvara (Müller-Celka 2007: fig. 5). The urban site surrounding the palace appears to cover 40 ha, with up to another 17 ha of low density occupation in two locations outside the fortification wall on the east. Evidence supporting a contraction of the city in the Neopalatial period (Driessen 2001a: 63), has yet to be published; all the excavated residential areas except Quartier Mu document Neopalatial as well as Protopalatial occupation throughout the core of the site. However, since the distribution of dated Protopalatial ceramics matches well the overall extent of dense surface material (Müller-Celka 2007: fig. 5), the community does not appear to have expanded in the Neopalatial period.

In addition to the coastal plain, survey extended to the inland basins of Mochos and Krasi, in the foothills of Lasithi, in all covering some 40 km^2. The largest sites outside the city appear to be a handful of sites of limited extent, distributed across the coastal plain (Müller 1996; 1998; Puglisi 2007), with no significant subsidiary centres except possibly Sissi (ca. 3 ha) reported within the surveyed territory. The valleys of Mochos and Krasi might be expected to have encouraged the development of at least one sub-ordinate centre in each, as perhaps seen in the Sissi valley.

The Malia survey and other studies in the region provide information not available for the west Mesara, which may help to define the boundaries of the Protopalatial polity. On the southern fringe of the investigated area, well up in the foothills of Lasithi, several small fortified sites originally identified by Evans, have been re-studied and are now dated to the MM period (Müller 2003; Müller-Celka 2007: 859; Nowicki 1995; 1996; 2000). These should indicate some sort of boundary, whether to protect outlying communities of the Malia polity, protect communities outside it from aggression from Malia, or simply reflect instability or limited central control on the periphery of the polity. Whatever specific interpretation, they suggest an effective limit to palatial control on the northern slopes of Lasithi during at least some phases of the MM period.

This obviously raises serious doubts against the argument that the upland plain of Lasithi or areas further south or east were incorporated into a polity centred on Malia. Fortified or defensible sites within and around the Lasithi basin also suggest the area may not have been integrated into any polity during the Protopalatial period (Nowicki 1996). Pottery imports (Betancourt 2007), as well as ceramic dedications from the Malia lowlands at the Psychro cave (Watrous 2004), could have crossed the polity boundary, either episodically or continuously, and do not require political integration.

On the basis of the preliminary published information, the Malia survey appears to present a more comprehensive but comparable picture to the Phaistos region, of a highly centralised settlement system in both the Protopalatial and Neopalatial periods, with a two or just possibly three-level settlement hierarchy. The evidence suggesting a southern polity limit, during at least some part of the MM period, falls approximately where the boundary of the catchment necessary to support the estimated population of the centre should fall (Fig. 11.6), suggesting that Malia in the Protopalatial period was a small city-state, rather than a territorial state.

Knossos: from site to territory

To date, there has been no intensive survey in the wider region around Knossos. On the other hand, over a century of investigations at the palatial centre (Hood and Smyth 1981), supplemented by preliminary observations from an intensive survey of the city (Bredaki *et al.* 2010; Whitelaw *et al.* forthcoming), provide our most detailed understanding of the development of a Cretan palatial centre. The changing occupation area of the site through time can be used to estimate the agricultural catchment necessary to support the centre's resident population.

While this exercise does not define the actual extent of the polity centred on Knossos, it does indicate the approximate scale of the minimum region which must have been controlled by Knossos economically and politically, simply to guarantee subsistence support for its population in each phase (see note 1). The importance of this subsistence-based perspective is that it addresses one of the major uncertainties expressed in alternative explorations: whether the territories defined (by whatever means) were actually dominated economically or politically from the centre (e.g. Knappett 1999; 2007; Knappett and Schoep 2000; Poursat 2008: 195; Warren 2004; Niemeier 2004: 393–94; Müller-Celka 2007).

By the end of the late Prepalatial period (MMIA), occupation at Knossos extended over a minimum of 20 and more likely 40 ha (Whitelaw 2012). Its support catchment will have extended south nearly to Archanes (Fig. 11.7), and I have previously suggested that this may explain the cessation of competitive new construction of burial monuments in the Phourni cemetery after MMIA, as the developing centre at Archanes was subsumed under Knossian control (Whitelaw 2004: 244–45).

A second test point is provided by the foundation of the palace (Rethemiotakis 2002), and re-establishment or very significant expansion of the community (Evely 2008: 104; Whitelaw and Morgan 2009: 94–97; Watrous pers comm.) at Galatas in the Pediada, some 16 km south-east of Knossos. The sparse Protopalatial sites in the region are noted as usually fortified or in defensible locations (Panagiotakis 2003; 2004; Whitley *et al.* 2007: 107; Evely 2008: 105), suggesting that the area was outside any integrated palatial territory at that time. Established in MMIIIA, the palace went through several transformations before abandonment in LMIA (Rethemiotakis 2002). Three alternative scenarios may be considered: 1) the foundation of the palace represents the imposition of Knossian political control in the region, and its abandonment, some change in the exercise of that control (Rethemiotakis 2002); 2) the foundation of the palace represents the emergence of a local elite, and its abandonment either a local collapse, or the suppression of local independence through Knossian expansion (Watrous *et al.* 2004: 287); 3) the foundation of the palace represents the establishment of an independent polity by a cadet or dispossessed line of the Knossian (or Malliote) elite, following the model of Mycenaean peripheral polity formation suggested by Wright (1984).

Held to support the first interpretation, is a shift from stylistically local ceramics, to styles which closely follow Knossian models (Rethemiotakis 2002; Rethemiotakis and Christakis 2004). The nature and comprehensiveness of this stylistic shift has yet to be documented in detail (e.g. some pithoi continue to be produced in the local tradition: Christakis 2006: 125), and the stylistic argument will be subject to all the ambiguities outlined above. In this case, the argument based on ceramics is considered to be strengthened by the contemporary introduction of the palace layout, ashlar masonry (with masons' marks), and frescoes. All of these are elements of Minoan palatial elite culture, so need not document a specifically Knossian origin, and they need not represent an imposition; they could have been adopted by an emerging local elite, asserting their power and seeking legitimation through emulating palatial fashions at pre-existing centres.

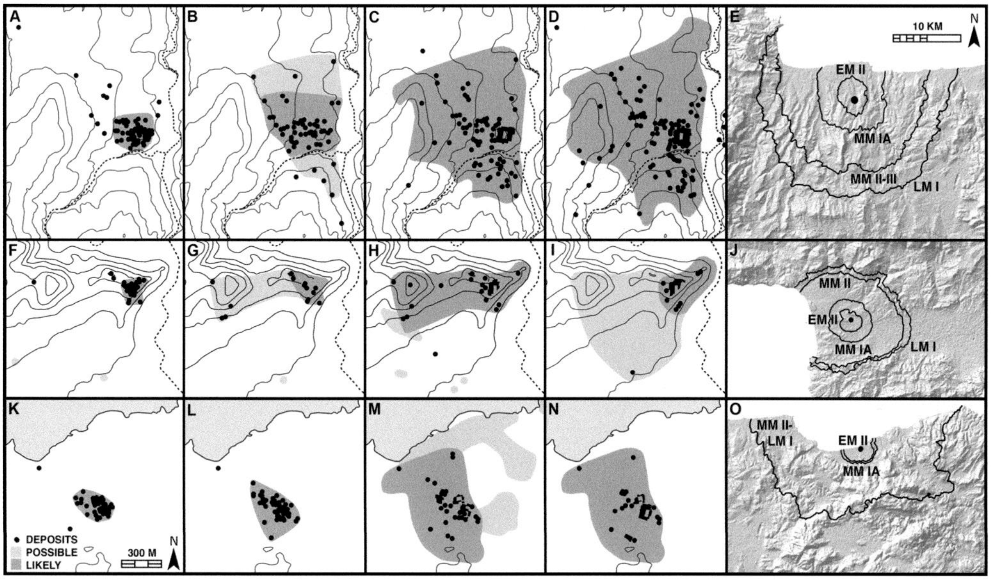

Figure 11.8: The principal palatial sites and their development through time: Knossos: A. EMII; B. EMIII-MMIA; C. MMIB-III; D. LMI; E. catchments; Phaistos: F. EMII; G. EMIII-MMIA; H. MMIB-II; I. MMIII-LMI; J. catchments; Malia: K. EMII; L. EMIII-MMIA; M. MMIB-II; N. MMIII-LMI; O. catchments.

An additional perspective is contributed by preliminary reports on the intensive survey of the immediate hinterland of Galatas, which appears to document the intensive colonisation of a previously under-populated landscape, contemporary with the establishment of the palace (Whitley *et al.* 2006: 107; Whitley *et al.* 2007: 107). This need not rule out the second or third options, but the preliminary evidence seems consistent with a rapid and organised intrusion, and the established Knossian power provides the nearest and most likely source.

Implicating Knossian political expansion in the foundation of the palace at Galatas in MMIIIA, provides a second test point for the city-state model, since the expanding population of Knossos would push its minimum support catchment well into the Galatas region by the end of MMIII, and as far as the site itself in LMI (Fig. 11.9).

Significant changes in the local power structures at Archanes and Galatas correspond broadly to the periods at which the minimum expansion of the Knossian city-state would have impinged on each community's local settlement system. Poros and Amnisos are close enough to have been absorbed within the expanding orbit of Knossos before the end of the later Prepalatial period; the evidence for off-island connections at Poros makes most sense if it was already integrally linked with the significant consuming population at Knossos in EMII (Wilson *et al.* 2004; 2008; Dimopoulou-Rethemiotaki *et al.* 2007). Tylissos and Vitsila will have been integrated into Knossos' political territory within the Neopalatial period, if not earlier. These, with Archanes and Amnisos, are substantial communities which can be suggested as

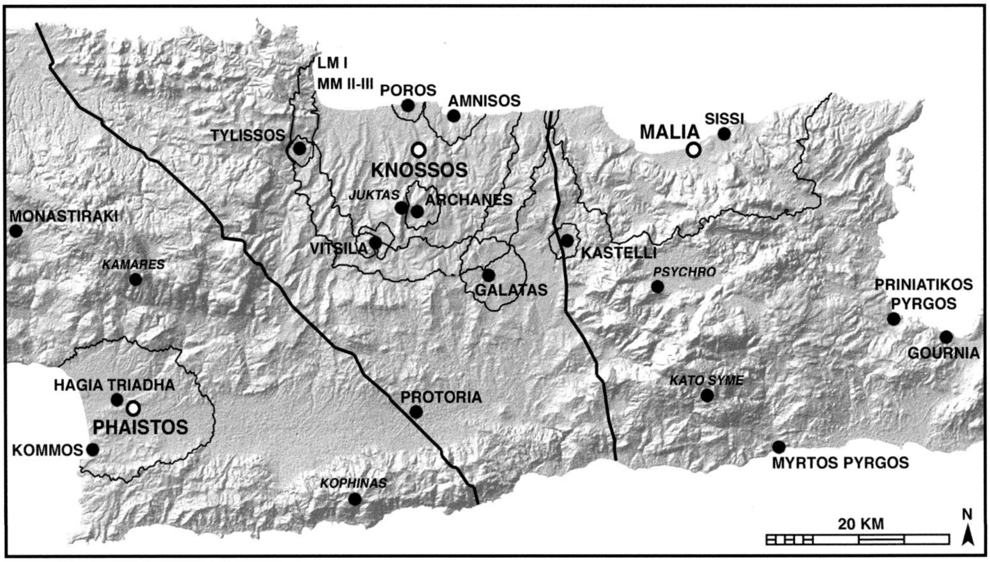

Figure 11.9: Central Crete and the potential expansion of Knossos: principal sites, Neopalatial catchments and walking time boundaries.

subordinate secondary centres within a Neopalatial four-level settlement hierarchy (Whitelaw 2001: 27–29). This would probably involve three levels of administrative hierarchy (e.g. Knossos-Archanes-Vathypetro and Knossos-Tylissos-Sklavokambos), documented through Linear A tablets and sealings. Such a hierarchy cannot, so far, be recognised for Protopalatial city-states, either on the basis of the settlement or preserved administrative evidence.

For Malia, the modelled catchment for the Protopalatial city-state (Fig. 11.6) extends into the foothills of Lasithi to the general area of the fortified sites, consistent with the interpretation that these marked the southern boundary of the Malia polity. These provide a test point for the reconstruction of Malia as a small city-state (Poursat 2008; 2010), rather than territorial state.

Knossos: from city-state to territorial state?

The catchment-based, minimalist definition of territories developed here only applies to city-states, though we cannot yet document any necessary departure from this bottom-up model for any central Cretan palace-centred polity, at least into MMIIIA. This is as far as this model can take us, and arguments for the development of larger territorial states, based at Knossos or any other palatial centre, will have to be established on other, far more ambiguous grounds.

The recent and on-going re-assessments of the construction histories at all palatial sites in the Neopalatial period present a challengingly unsynchronised picture. Whether all or some of these reflect independent and locally contingent histories, or should be choreographed into a drama of Knossian expansion or conquest (e.g. MMIIIA: Galatas; MMIIIB: Phaistos; LMIA: Malia, and LMIB: Lasithi, Zakros), remains unclear (see now Whitelaw in press: figs. 5-6).

If Knossos expanded into a territorial state, this will arguably have post-dated its proposed expansion into the under-populated and unintegrated area around Galatas. Intriguingly, preliminary reports on the Galatas survey suggest that settlements in the region south of the palace retained the nucleated defensible character typical of the Protopalatial period, through the Neopalatial period (Evely 2008: 105), perhaps suggesting that this region remained outside or near the periphery of the expanded polity.

If Galatas was a Knossian imposition in MMIIIA, why was it no longer important to maintain a palatial control centre in the area after LMIA? Did the community at Galatas and its local settlement system also decline, or was administration of the region maintained but re-organised? Did Knossos pull out of the region, or did it relocate its administrative sub-centre in the Pediada elsewhere, perhaps further east to Kastelli (Warren 2004: 163; though the known substantial building is said to decline in parallel with the palace at Galatas: Rethemiotakis 2002: 65; Rethemiotakis and Christakis 2011: 226), possibly reflecting further eastward extension of Knossian control.

Looking east, the evidence for Neopalatial contraction at the urban centre at Malia has yet to be presented, but for the exploration here, a static situation is assumed, so the support catchment estimated for the Protopalatial period is maintained for the Neopalatial period; there is no evidence to suggest expansion into a territorial state in the Neopalatial period (Fig. 11.6). With the expansion of Knossos, its hinterland is likely to have bumped up against that of Malia during the Neopalatial period, at least along the north coastal strip (Fig. 11.9). This convergence may have set the scene for a new type of predatory expansion, involving not just encroachment on, but incorporation of the entire neighbouring city-state at Malia into an expanding Knossian polity.

Does the early LMIA rebuilding of the palace at Malia on a layout resembling that at Knossos, represent its reconstruction as a new second-order centre under Knossian control (Poursat 2008; 2010), or increasing convergence through direct competition with the neighbouring power, and what does the destruction and abandonment of the palace at the end of LMIA or early in LMIB represent in terms of regional political structure (for arguments for a later LMIB destruction, see particularly van de Moortel 2011: 542–45)?

To the south-east, the situation in Lasithi is even less clear. Fortified or defensible sites seem characteristic of the Prepalatial and Protopalatial periods, with the development of sites in non-defensible locations around the plain particularly in the Neopalatial period (Watrous 1982; Nowicki 1996). But whether these communities were ever integrated, or linked politically to a lowland palatial centre, remains unknown. The influx of Knossian ceramic dedications at the Psychro cave in LMIB (Watrous 2004) is intriguing, but need not represent Knossian political dominance.

Looking south, does the shift of administration from Phaistos to Hagia Triada after MMIIIA represent a re-structuring of local power, or (along with the non-reconstruction of the ceremonial palace) a decisive move to cut links with the previous independent elites at the imposition of Knossian dominance (La Rosa 2010a: 590; 2010b: 499)? Does the rebuilding of the palace at Phaistos in LMIB represent some degree of local resurgence in the face of post-Theran eruption Knossian weakness (La Rosa 2010a: 591), or a confident re-inscription of Knossian control (Warren 2004: 163)?

The limited expansion suggested here for Malia, and the gradual expansion of Protopalatial Knossos, raise the prospect that Phaistos, before its eclipse in MMIIIA, may never have expanded to dominate the entire Mesara, and other, as yet undocumented polities may have existed in the Protopalatial and Neopalatial periods in the central and/or eastern Mesara. There may also have been areas, even within central Crete, which were never incorporated into state-level polities based at one of the three main palatial centres.

The suggestion of a southern boundary for Malia in the northern slopes of Lasithi in the MM period, seriously questions whether Malia ever extended its control (as opposed to influence: Müller-Celka 2007; Knappett 2007; Poursat 2008; 2010) as far as the Lasithi plain or beyond to Myrtos Pyrgos. This should also open up a reconsideration of developments around the Gulf of Mirabello, for which the unparalleled settlement data from the combined Vrokastro, Gournia and Kavousi surveys, as well as the extensive recent excavation data from the centres at Gournia, Mochlos, Pseira and Priniatikos Pyrgos, provide a unique resource for studying the development of a region.

In the far east, Petras provides a strong argument for independent local development (Tsipopoulou 1997; 1999; 2002; Tsipopoulou and Papacostopoulou 1997). The history of the palace at Zakros, and any substantial but non-canonical antecedent structure, is under revision (Platon 2002; 2004; 2010). The interpretation that it served as an eastern port for Knossos (Bennet 1990: 196, n.20; Warren 2004: 164; Platon 2004; Wiener 2007: 234–35) seems to rest on the expectation of Knossian dominance, the assumption that it could not have been locally self-sufficient, and Knossian influence in some ceramics, all deserving documentation and critical appraisal.

To the west, the patterns of recent interaction (Fig. 11.3), as well as the evidence for Hellenistic conquests and alliances (Fig. 11.1), question whether central Cretan polities should be expected to have had any significant political impact in west or west-central Crete. The integration documented by the Knossian Linear B archive is clearly an exception, perhaps accounting for its short duration and instability. Even this control may have been more restricted and strategic than is usually assumed (Driessen 2001b), fitting better a network (Smith 2005) rather than territorial state model.

Recognising polities: problems and prospects

The questions outlined above all deserve exploration, but none of the speculative suggestions warrant the certainty with which particular political interpretations are regularly espoused in the literature. The latter have almost all been framed with an expectation of Knossian dominance. It is refreshing when the political status of a site or local region is considered in its own terms (e.g. Andreadaki-Vlasaki 2002; 2010; Tsipopoulou 1997; 2002; Shaw 2006; Cunningham and Driessen 2004), and then in the context of a range of wider regional possibilities.

Many of the assumptions which structure present approaches to interpretation go back to the origins of Minoan archaeology, and are so fundamentally ingrained that they are difficult to recognise, let alone unpack and examine critically. Underlying nearly all conceptualisations of Minoan political landscapes has been the naturalisation of a pattern of palatial centres in central Crete, originally constructed on extremely limited information. This has discouraged investigations which might test the assumed understanding, and tended to focus our attention on spatial scales and landscape units which are not necessarily appropriate for the entities we are trying to recognise. A longer-term historical perspective makes it clear that Cretan geography is far less deterministic of political structures than has been assumed by prehistorians. Looking at the relatively small territory required to support a major palatial centre like Protopalatial Phaistos, we can realistically expect there to have been more, whether like Petras, developing locally, or Galatas, perhaps representing an intrusive colonisation of relatively unpopulated territory. There are also numerous agriculturally suitable areas, not hitherto considered, which could have supported independent polities (not necessarily all states) of various scales in the Protopalatial or Neopalatial periods. While the island has been relatively well investigated when compared with most Mediterranean landscapes, it is easy to forget how little of Crete has been systematically or intensively investigated archaeologically.

If we cannot rely on geographical "givens", we need to use period-specific archaeological evidence to define and track changes in contingent and dynamic political formations. A first step has to be to accept how difficult it is to recognise the territories of individual states archaeologically. A fundamental problem arises because states are dynamic: they expand and contract through conquest and alliance, often combining individual small-scale city-states or incorporating non-state territories beyond their borders, into larger, less stable, regional territorial states. These processes will often take place on time-scales shorter than can be monitored using our material culture chronologies, and constant changes will blur any boundaries we might hope to detect in material distributions.

Material culture analyses have tremendous potential for informing us about interactions between the residents of different communities, and their motivations for doing so, but interpreting these directly in terms of politics is rarely attempted elsewhere in world archaeology, with good reason. We are considerably more experienced at interpreting individual processes, such as exchange; comparisons of multiple patterns may then be suggestive of the political contexts within which different types of exchanges took place, pointing towards the actors, their potential motivations, and constraints. If we wish to use material culture distributions for such analyses, we need to consider a wide range of material culture, and document large and reliable samples systematically using standardised criteria, to allow detailed comparisons and robust spatial analyses.

In a similar way, settlement data need to be approached more subtly, as there are no diagnostic patterns that will allow us to define the limits of states on the ground with confidence. Rather, we can compare site types and their distributions (e.g. site sizes, spacing, clustering, relative population nucleation), as these pattern against landscape characteristics (e.g. resources, agricultural and other productive potential, defensible locations, routes), and track changes in relationships and configurations through time. These patterns can then be explored interpretively, in terms of what they may indicate about the nature and organisation of relations between communities, and the locations and configurations of sites may suggest the limits of integrated settlement systems, or the re-structuring of local systems when communities become incorporated into (or drop out of) larger regional systems. Such studies have begun (e.g. Haggis 2005: 59–81; Hayden 2004: 35–137; Nowicki 2000; Cunningham and Driessen 2004), though interpretations and larger-scale pattern recognition are inhibited by the small scale of individual surveys and the limited and non-comparable recording and presentation of data by different projects.

The catchment-based approach to the definition of polities explored here attempts several things. It tries to define what sort of data can be used most effectively to address very specific questions, in this case, to define the agricultural hinterlands of city-state polities. It also recognises that, logical as the approach may seem, it cannot simply be asserted, but needs to be tested against archaeologically recoverable data. The patterns generated can also help support specific interpretations of other evidence, so that while the material culture arguments for the palace at Galatas as a Knossian foundation are not conclusive, that the hinterland necessary to support the expanding population of Knossos is likely to have imposed on the western Pediada at about the same time as these characteristics appear in the area, provides a different line of support for that political interpretation of the material culture changes.

Comparatively, the catchment approach also raises interesting questions about the differential constraints on expansion faced by each of the central Cretan polities. In Figure 11.8, settlement size and catchment estimates are mapped, by phase, for the three palatial centres at the same scale, facilitating comparisons. Phaistos, at the western end of the Mesara plain, will have had direct access to abundant prime agricultural land, and its minimum necessary catchment will only have reached the foothills north and south by the end of the Protopalatial period. Further expansion will have been easiest and most productive east, down the plain, but only if there were no competing polities in the central or eastern Mesara. Any attenuated expansion of the polity will have required significant second-order centres, perhaps incorporating previously independent local centres.

In contrast, the hinterland of Protopalatial Malia would have required expansion into the small inland valleys, and by the time of the maximum documented extent of the city, in MMII, would have been strongly circumscribed by relatively unproductive uplands. Intriguingly, its estimated MMII catchment borders hit against the hills separating it from the Pediada plain, the Lasithi basin, and the Mirabello coastal lowlands. To incorporate these more distant areas would probably have required the development of a more decentralised form of administration, probably also resulting in weaker control.

Between these two extremes, expansion from Knossos was through fairly dissected but largely productive terrain, all fairly comparable both in terms of agricultural productivity and transport constraints. A pattern of control developed for the immediate territory might be extended, with no natural impediments or boundaries. Despite no intensive regional survey within its territory, Knossos is the only region of Crete for which we know of significant likely second-order centres, at Archanes, Tylissos, Poros, Amnisos and potentially Vitsila. The expansion of Knossos to approximately double the size of the other central Cretan palatial centres, suggests that it did indeed develop a significant regional administrative role, to a degree that the other central Cretan palatial centres never did. While I have argued elsewhere for multiple pathways to complexity among Cretan Prepalatial communities (Whitelaw 2004), these need to be pursued beyond the common elements of small-scale state origins (Whitelaw 2012), to document the divergent individual histories of each polity which we are increasingly confronted by, through the on-going re-assessments at each palatial centre.

The approach developed here works from the known to the unknown, exploring regional structures from the bottom up. But this is most relevant to the scale of city-state polities. To move beyond this and confirm whether there were any territorial states in Crete before that documented by the Knossos Linear B tablets, and develop an understanding of their nature, requires that we figure out how to work more effectively with a wider range of material data, with more explicit recognition and critical assessment of the assumptions we are making, realistic assessment of sample biases, and engagement with the full range of interpretive possibilities.

We will also need to work out how to use material distributions to monitor different types of inter-community and inter-individual interactions, which themselves may be subject to political influence, organisation or control. To do this, we need to identify appropriate, theoretically-justified approaches to interpreting the material record, and to develop methodologically-sound, empirically-supported interpretations. What is clear from the evidence of new centres and re-assessments at those long known, is that political developments on the island are far more locally varied, fluid and dynamic than our traditional approaches allowed us to recognise or interpret.[2]

Acknowledgements

I am very happy to offer this paper to Keith, in recognition of 37 years of encouragement, support and friendship. For decades he was almost a lone voice asking interpretive questions about Prepalatial and particularly Protopalatial societies. I am grateful to the editors for the invitation to participate in the Round Table. I am also grateful to the other participants for their comments and their own stimulating contributions, to Glynis Jones for her hospitality in Sheffield, and to Andrew Bevan for comments on a draft. I owe a significant debt to Andrew Bevan for running a range of GIS analyses for me; they were more time consuming then either of us anticipated when I asked and he agreed. I would also like to thank Andonis Vasilakis and Maria Bredaki, co-directors of the Knossos Urban Landscape Project, for allowing me to draw on some preliminary data from that project. The project is a collaboration between the British School at Athens and the Herakleion Archaeological Ephoreia of the Hellenic Ministry of Culture and Tourism. Principal funding has been provided by the Institute for Aegean Prehistory and the British Academy, with additional funds and support from the BSA, Herakleion Ephoreia and the Institute of Archaeology, UCL. This paper was written while on sabbatical, and I would also like to thank my colleagues at UCL who covered my teaching and administrative duties during that time.

Notes

1 For calculating catchments in Figures 11.5–11.9, only land of 10° slope or less is included, and distance away from the site is assessed in terms of walking time, so the catchments include all low slope land within an equivalent walking time from the site, sufficient to support the estimated population in each phase, allowing 0.5 ha to support each individual. This allowance is fairly conservative, thereby defining minimum catchments. The mapped catchments also incorporate the areas necessary to support the populations estimated for subsidiary sites within the catchment, calculated from the regional population density estimated from the MM and LM rural sites in the Western Mesara and Kommos surveys (100 persons/km^2). For Neopalatial Knossos, the estimated catchments for the major sites at Tylissos, Archanes, Poros and Amnisos are incorporated, as well as a purely notional figure for the known but unstudied centre at Vitsila. For calculations, Prepalatial and Protopalatial site areas and reconstructed populations follow Whitelaw (2012), with the area for Protopalatial Phaistos estimated at 40 ha, given the patchy distribution of excavations across the site and the suggestions of wider occupation from the on-going survey, and for Malia 50 ha, incorporating also the evidence from the survey. For the Neopalatial period, Phaistos is estimated at 55 ha (Watrous *et al.* 2004: 294), and Malia kept stable at 50 ha.

2 This paper was submitted in April 2011, with minor clarifications following review in August 2013. Publications, particularly of the Galatas, Gournia, Malia and Phaistos surveys are relevant to, but do not significantly affect the arguments presented here. Some aspects of the arguments explored here have been developed further in subsequent publications (Whitelaw 2014; 2017; in press). Further analyses of the Cretan vocabulary dataset are reported in Bevan and Wilson 2013; Bevan and Crema 2014 and Paliou and Bevan 2017.

Bibliography

Adams, R. E. and R. Jones,
1981 Spatial patterns and regional growth among Classic Maya cities. *American Antiquity* 46: 301–22.

Adams, R. M.
1981 *Heartland of Cities: Surveys of Ancient Settlement and Land Use on the Central Floodplain of the Euphrates.* London: University of Chicago Press.

Anderson, G.
2009 The personality of the Greek state. *Journal of Hellenic Studies* 129: 1–22.

Andreadaki-Vlasaki, M.
2002 Are we approaching the Minoan palace of Khania? In J. Driessen, I. Schoep and R. Laffineur (eds.), *Monuments of Minos. Rethinking the Minoan Palaces* (Aegaeum 23): 157–66. Liège: Université de Liège.
2010 Khania (Kydonia). In E. Cline (ed.), *The Oxford Handbook of the Bronze Age Aegean (ca. 3000-1000 BC)*: 518–28. Oxford: Oxford University Press.

Arvanitakis, J.
2007 Evidence for ceramic regionalism in early Final Palatial Crete: new perspectives. In P. P. Betancourt, M. Nelson and H. Williams (eds.), *Krinoi kai Limenes: Studies in Honor of Joseph and Maria Shaw* (Prehistory Monographs 22): 243–49. Philadelphia: INSTAP Academic Press.

Bennet, J.
1985 The structure of the Linear B administration at Knossos. *American Journal of Archaeology* 89: 231–49.
1990 Knossos in context: comparative perspectives on the Linear B administration of LM II-III Crete. *American Journal of Archaeology* 94: 193–212.

Berent, M.
2000 Anthropology and the Classics: war, violence, and the stateless *polis*. *Classical Quarterly* 50: 257–89.

Betancourt, P. P.
2004a Knossian expansion in Late Minoan IB: the evidence of the Spirals and Arcading Group. In G. Cadogan, E. Hatzaki and A. Vasilakis (eds.), *Knossos: Palace, City, State* (BSA Studies 12): 295–98. London: British School at Athens.
2004b Pseira and Knossos: the transformation of an East Cretan seaport. In L. Preston Day, M. Mook and J. Muhly (eds.), *Crete Beyond the Palaces: Proceedings of the Crete 2000 Conference* (Prehistory Monographs 10): 21–8. Philadelphia: INSTAP Academic Press.
2007 Lasithi and the Malia-Lasithi state. In P. P. Betancourt, M. Nelson and H. Williams (eds.). *Krinoi kai Limenes: Studies in Honor of Joseph and Maria Shaw* (Prehistory Monographs 22): 209–19. Philadelphia: INSTAP Academic Press.

Betts, J.
1967 New light on Minoan bureaucracy. A re-examination of some Cretan sealings. *Kadmos* 6: 15–40.

Bevan, A.
2010 Political geography and palatial Crete. *Journal of Mediterranean Archaeology* 23: 27–54.

Bevan, A. and A. Wilson
2013 Models of settlement hierarchy based on partial evidence. *Journal of Archaeological Science* 40: 2415–27.

Bevan, A. and E. Crema
2014 Une modélisation geographiquement explicite d'interaction culturelle. Dialectes crétois modernes, archéologie de lâge du Bronze. *Les nouvelles de l'archéologie* 135: 450–50.

Bintliff, J.
1999 Settlement and territory. In G. Barker (ed.), *The Companion Encyclopaedia of Archaeology, Vol. 1*: 505–45. London: Routledge.

Blackman, D. and K. Branigan
1975 An archaeological survey of the south coast of Crete, between the Ayiofarango and Chrisostomos. *Annual of the British School at Athens* 70: 17–36.
1977 An archaeological survey of the lower catchment of the Ayiofarango valley. *Annual of the British School at Athens* 72: 13–84.

Blanton, R., S. Kowalewski, G. Feinman and J. Appel
1982 *Monte Alban's Hinterland. Part I: The Prehispanic Settlement Patterns of the Central and Southern Parts of the Valley of Oaxaca, Mexico* (Museum of Anthropology Memoir 15). Ann Arbor: University of Michigan.
Blanton, R., S. Kowalewski, G. Feinman and L. Finsten
1993 *Ancient Mesoamerica: a Comparison of Change in Three Regions 2nd ed.* Cambridge: Cambridge University Press.
Branigan, K. and A. Vasilakis
2010 Survey of the environs around the tholos cemetery. In A. Vasilakis and K. Branigan (eds.), *Moni Odigitria: A Prepalatial Cemetery and Its Environs in the Asterousia, Southern Crete* (Prehistory Monographs 30): 3–46. Philadelphia: INSTAP Academic Press.
Bredaki, M., F. Longo, M. Benzi, S. Foresta, A. Rossi, V. Achilli, V. Amato, D. Bragagnolo, M. Fabris, V. Lenuzza, A. Menin, E. Santaniello, M. Spiridakis and G. Targa
2009 Progetto Festòs. Ricognizioni archeologiche di superficie: le campagne 2007–2009. *Annuario della Scuola archeologica di Atene e delle Missioni italiane in Oriente* 87: 935–78.
Bredaki, M., T. Whitelaw and A. Vasilakis
2010 Πρόγραμμα επιφανειακής έρευνας περιοχής Κνωσού. Προκαταρκτική έκθεση για την εργασία των ετών 2005–2007. In, M. Andrianakis and I. Tzachili (eds.). *Archaiologiko Ergo Kritis 1*: 294–301. Rethymnon: Philosophical School, University of Crete.
Brogan, T. and E. Hallager (eds.)
2011 *LM IB Pottery: Relative Chronology and Regional Differences* (Monographs of the Danish Institute at Athens 11). Athens: Danish Institute at Athens.
Cadogan, G.
1994 An Old Palace period Knossos state? In D. Evely, H. Hughes-Brock and N. Momigliano (eds.), *Knossos: A Labyrinth of History. Papers Presented in Honour of Sinclair Hood*: 57–69. Oxford: Oxbow.
1995 Mallia and Lasithi: a palace-state. *Πεπραγμένα του Ζ' Διεθνούς Κρητολογικού Συνεδρίου, Vol. A1*: 97–104. Ρέθυμνο: Ιστορική και Λαογραφική Εταιρεία.
2011 Behind the façade: what social and political realities are behind the cultural regionalities of Middle Minoan Crete? *Πεπραγμένα του Ι' Διεθνούς Κρητολογικού Συνεδρίου (Χανιά 1-8 Οκτωβρίου 2006), Vol A1*: 127–39. Χανιά: Φιλολογικός Σύλλογος "Ο Χρυσόστομος".
Cavanagh, W.
2009 Settlement structure in Laconia and Attica at the end of the Archaic period: the fractal dimension. *American Journal of Archaeology* 113: 405–21.
Cherry, J.
1986 Politics and palaces: some problems in Minoan state formation. In C. Renfrew and J. Cherry (eds.), *Peer Polity Interaction and Socio-political Change*: 19–45. Cambridge: Cambridge University Press.
1987 Power in space: archaeological and geographical studies of the state. In J. M. Wagstaff (ed.), *Landscape and Culture. Geographical and Archaeological Perspectives*: 146–72. Oxford: Blackwell.
Christakis, K.
2006 Traditions and trends in the production and consumption of storage containers in Protopalatial and Neopalatial Crete. In M. Wiener, J. Warner, J. Polonsky and E. Hayes (eds.). *Pottery and Society: The Impact of Recent Studies in Minoan Pottery*: 119–37. Boston: Archaeological Institute of America.
Clarke, D.
1968 *Analytical Archaeology*. London: Methuen.
Collis, J.
1971 Functional and theoretical interpretations of British coinage. *World Archaeology* 3: 71–84.
1981 A typology of coin distributions. *World Archaeology* 13: 122–8.

Conkey, M. and C. Hastorf (eds.)

1989 *The Uses of Style in Archaeology.* Cambridge: Cambridge University Press.

Cunliffe, B.

1981 Money and society in pre-Roman Britain. In B. Cunliffe (ed.), *Coinage and Society in Britain and Gaul: Some Current Problems.* (CBA Research Report 38): 29–39. London: Council for British Archaeology.

2005 *Iron Age Communities in Britain: an Account of England, Scotland and Wales from the Seventh Century BC Until the Roman Conquest. 4th ed.* London: Routledge.

Cunningham, T., and J. Driessen

2004 Site by site: combining survey and excavation data to chart patterns of socio-political change in Bronze Age Crete. In S. Alcock and J. Cherry (eds.), *Side-by-Side Survey: Comparative Regional Studies in the Mediterranean World*: 101–13. Oxford: Oxbow.

de Vries, J.

1990 Problems in the measurement, description and analysis of historical urbanization. In A. van der Woude, A. Hayami and J. de Vries (eds.), *Urbanization in History. A Process of Dynamic Interactions*: 43–60. Oxford: Clarendon Press.

Diaz-Andreu, M., S. Lucy, S. Babic and D. Edwards

2005 *The Archaeology of Identity: Approaches to Gender, Age, Status, Ethnicity and Religion.* London: Routledge.

Dimopoulou-Rethemiotaki, N., D. Wilson and P. M. Day

2007 The earlier Prepalatial settlement of Poros-Katsambas: craft production and exchange at the harbour town of Knossos. In P. M. Day and R. C. P. Doonan (eds.), *Metallurgy in the Early Bronze Age Aegean* (Sheffield Studies in Aegean Archaeology 7): 84–97. Oxford: Oxbow.

Dobres, M.-A. and C. Hoffman

1994 Social agency and the dynamics of prehistoric technology. *Journal of Archaeological Method and Theory* 1: 211–58.

Drennan, R. and C. Peterson

2004 Comparing archaeological settlement systems with rank-size graphs: a measure of shape and statistical confidence. *Journal of Archaeological Science* 31: 533–49.

Driessen, J.

1982 The Minoan Hall in domestic architecture on Crete: to be in vogue in Late Minoan IA? *Acta Archaeologica Lovaniensia* 21: 27–92.

1989–90 The proliferation of Minoan palatial architectural style: (I) Crete. *Acta Archaeologica Lovaniensia* 28–29: 3–23.

2000 *The Scribes of the Room of the Chariot Tablets at Knossos: An Interdisciplinary Approach to the Study of a Linear B Deposit* (Minos Supplement 15). Salamanca: Ediciones Universidad de Salamanca.

2001a History and hierarchy. Preliminary observations on the settlement pattern in Minoan Crete. In K. Branigan (ed.), *Urbanism in the Aegean Bronze Age* (Sheffield Studies in Aegean Archaeology 4): 51–71. London: Sheffield Academic Press.

2001b Centre and periphery: some observations on the administration of the kingdom of Knossos. In S. Voutsaki and J. Killen (eds.), *Economy and Politics in the Mycenaean Palace States* (Cambridge Philological Society Supplementary Volume 27): 96–112. Cambridge: Cambridge Philological Society.

2010 Malia. In E. Cline (ed.), *The Oxford Handbook of the Bronze Age Aegean (ca. 3000–1000 BC)*: 556–70. Oxford: Oxford University Press.

Driessen, J. and C. Macdonald

1997 *The Troubled Island: Minoan Crete Before and After the Santorini Eruption* (Aegaeum 17). Liège: Université de Liège.

Dunnell, R.

1971 *Systematics in Prehistory.* London: Free Press.

1986 Methodological issues in Americanist artifact classification. In M. Schiffer (ed.), *Advances in Archaeological Method and Theory* 9: 149–207. New York: Academic Press.

Emberling, G.

1997 Ethnicity in complex societies: archaeological perspectives. *Journal of Archaeological Research* 5: 295–344.

Evely, D.

2008 Crete. In C. Morgan (ed.), Archaeology in Greece 2007–2008. *Archaeological Reports* 54: 94–112.

Falconer, S.

1987 *Heartland of Villages: Reconsidering Early Urbanism in the Southern Levant.* P.h.D. Dissertation, University of Arizona. Ann Arbor: University Microfilms International.

Falconer, S. and S. Savage

1995 Heartlands and hinterlands: alternative trajectories of early urbanization in Mesopotamia and the southern Levant. *American Antiquity* 60: 37–58.

Feinman, G.

1998 Scale and social organization: perspectives on the archaic state. In G. Feinman and J. Marcus (eds.), *Archaic States*: 95–134. Santa Fe: School of American Research Press.

Flannery, K.

1998 The ground plans of archaic states. In G. Feinman and J. Marcus (eds.), *Archaic States*: 15–58. Santa Fe: School of American Research Press.

Gehrke, H.-J.

2009 States. In K. Raaflaub and H. van Wees (eds.), *A Companion to Archaic Greece*: 395–410. London: Wiley-Blackwell.

Goren, Y. and D. Panagiotopoulos

2010 The "Lords of the Rings": an analytical approach to the riddle of the "Knossian replica rings". *Bulletin of the Institute of Classical Studies* 52: 257–58.

Gosselain, O.

2000 Materializing identities: an African perspective. *Journal of Archaeological Method and Theory* 7: 187–217.

Green, S. and S. Perlman (eds.)

1985 *The Archaeology of Frontiers and Boundaries.* New York: Academic Press.

Grube, N.

2000 The city-states of the Maya. In M. H. Hansen (ed.), *A comparative study of thirty city-state cultures. An investigation conducted by the Copenhagen Polis Centre*: 547–65. Copenhagen: Reitzels Forlag.

Haggis, D. C.

2005 *Kavousi. The Results of the Excavations at Kavousi in Eastern Crete I. The Archaeological Survey of the Kavousi Region* (Prehistory Monographs 16). Philadelphia: INSTAP Academic Press.

Hallager, E.

1996 *The Minoan Roundel and Other Sealed Documents in the Neopalatial Linear A Administration.* (Aegaeum 14). Liège: Université de Liège.

Hansen, M. (ed.)

2000a *A Comparative Study of Thirty City-state Cultures: An Investigation Conducted by the Copenhagen Polis Centre* (Historisk-filosofiske skrifter, Det Kongelige Danske videnskabernes selskab 21). Copenhagen: Royal Danish Academy of Sciences and Letters.

2006a *Polis: An Introduction to the Ancient Greek City-state.* Oxford: Oxford University Press.

2006b *The Shotgun Method. The Demography of the Ancient Greek City-state Culture.* London: University of Missouri Press.

Hayden, B.
2004 *Reports on the Vrokastro Area, Eastern Crete, Vol. 2. The Settlement History of the Vrokastro Area and Related Studies* (University Museum Monograph 119). Philadelphia: University of Pennsylvania Museum of Archaeology and Anthropology.

Hedeager, L.
1979 A quantitative analysis of Roman imports in Europe north of the Limes (0–400 AD), and the question of Roman-Germanic exchange. In K. Kristiansen and C. Paludan-Müller (eds.), *New Directions in Scandinavian Archaeology* (Studies in Scandinavian Prehistory and Early History 1): 191–216. Copenhagen: National Museum of Denmark.

Hegemon, M.
1992 Archaeological research on style. *Annual Review of Anthropology* 21: 517–36.

Hodder, I.
1977 How are we to study the distributions of Iron Age material? In J. Collis (ed.), *The Iron Age in Britain: a Review*: 8–16. Sheffield: Department of Prehistory and Archaeology, University of Sheffield.
1978 (ed.) *The Spatial Organisation of Culture.* London: Duckworth.
1981 *Symbols in Action: Ethnoarchaeological Studies of Material Culture.* Cambridge: Cambridge University Press.

Hodder, I. and C. Orton
1976 *Spatial Analysis in Archaeology.* Cambridge: Cambridge University Press.

Hodge, M. and L. Minc
1990 The spatial patterning of Aztec ceramics: implications for Prehispanic exchange systems in the Valley of Mexico. *Journal of Field Archaeology* 17: 415–37.

Hodge, M., H. Neff, M. Blackman and L. Minc
1993 Black-on-orange ceramic production in the Aztec empire's heartland. *Latin American Antiquity* 4: 130–57.

Hodges, R.
1987 Spatial models, anthropology and archaeology. In J. M. Wagstaff (ed.), *Landscape and Culture. Geographical and Archaeological Perspectives*: 118–33. Oxford: Blackwell.

Hood, M. S. F. and D. Smyth
1981 Archaeological Survey of the Knossos Area, 2nd ed. (BSA Supplementary Volume 14). London: British School at Athens.

Hope Simpson, R., P. P. Betancourt, P. Callaghan, D. Harlan, J. Hayes, J. Shaw, M. Shaw, and L. V. Watrous
1995 The archaeological survey of the Kommos area. In J. Shaw and M. Shaw (eds.), *Kommos 1. Part I: The Kommos Region, Ecology, and Minoan Industries*: 325–402. Princeton: Princeton University Press.

Hurt, T. and G. Rakita (ed.)
2001 *Style and Function. Conceptual Issues in Evolutionary Archaeology.* London: Bergin and Garrey.

Johnson, G.
1972 A test of the utility of central place theory in archaeology. In P. Ucko, R. Tringham and G. Dimbleby (eds.), *Man, Settlement and Urbanism*: 769–85. London: Duckworth.

Johnson, G.
1977 Aspects of regional analysis in archaeology. *Annual Review of Anthropology* 6: 479–508.
1980a Spatial organization of early Uruk settlement systems. In M.-T. Barrelet (ed.), *L' Archeologie de l' Iraq du Debut se l' epoque Neolithique à 333 avant Notre Ere: Perspectives et Limites de L'interpretation Anthropologique des Documents*: 233–63. Paris: Centre National de la Recherche Scientifique.
1980b Rank-size convexity and system integration: a view from archaeology. *Economic Geography* 56: 234–47.

1981 Monitoring complex system integration and boundary phenomena with settlement size data. In S. van der Leeuw (ed.), *Archaeological Approaches to the Study of Complexity*: 144–88. Amsterdam: University of Amsterdam.

1987 The changing organization of Uruk administration on the Susiana plain. In F. Hole (ed.), *The Archaeology of Western Iran. Settlement and Society from Prehistory to the Islamic Conquest*: 107–39. Washington DC: Smithsonian Institution.

Jones, S.

1997 *The Archaeology of Ethnicity: Constructing Identities in the Past and Present*. London: Routledge.

Kanta, A.

1999 Monastiraki and Phaistos: elements of Protopalatial history. In P. P. Betancourt, V. Karageorghis, R. Laffineur, and W.-D. Niemeier (eds., *Meletemata: Studies in Aegean Archaeology Presented to Malcolm H. Wiener as He Enters His 65th Year. Vol. II.* (Aegaeum 20): 387–93. Liège: Université de Liège.

Kanta, A. and A. Tzigounaki

2000 The Protopalatial multiple sealing system. New evidence from Monastiraki. In M. Perna (ed.), *Administrative Documents in the Aegean and Their Near Eastern Counterparts*: 193–205. Torino: Centro Internazionale di Ricerche Archeologiche Antropologiche e Storiche.

Kimes, T., C. Haselgrove and I. Hodder

1982 A method for the identification of the location of regional cultural boundaries. *Journal of Anthropological Archaeology* 1:113–31.

Knappett, C.

1999 Assessing a polity in Protopalatial Crete: the Malia-Lasithi state. *American Journal of Archaeology* 103: 615–39.

2007 Malia et ses relations régionales à l' époque du Minoen Moyen: les échanges céramiques à travers trois siècles (2000–1700 av. J.-C.). *Bulletin de Correspondence Hellénique* 131: 861–64.

2011 Time, place and practice in the East Mesara: the case of Skinias. A response to Stella Mandalaki. In T. Brogan and E. Hallager (eds.), *LM IB Pottery: Relative Chronology and Regional Differences* (Monographs of the Danish Institute at Athens 11): 393–96. Athens: Danish Institute at Athens.

Knappett, C. and I. Schoep

2000 Continuity and change in Minoan palatial power. *Antiquity* 74: 365–71.

Kontosopoulos, N.

2006 *Γλωσσικός Ἀτλας της Κρήτης*. Herakleion: University of Crete Press.

Kowalewski, S.

2008 Regional settlement pattern studies. *Journal of Archaeological Research* 16: 225–85.

Krzyszkowska, O.

2005 *Aegean Seals. An Introduction* (BICS Supplement 85). London, Institute of Classical Studies.

La Rosa, V.

2002 Pour une révision préliminaire du second palais de Phaistos. In J. Driessen, I. Schoep and R. Laffineur (eds.), *Monuments of Minos. Rethinking the Minoan Palaces* (Aegaeum 23): 71–97. Liège: Université de Liège.

2010a Phaistos. In E. Cline (ed.), *The Oxford Handbook of the Bronze Age Aegean (ca. 3000–1000 BC)*: 582–95. Oxford: Oxford University Press.

2010b Ayia Triada. In E. Cline (ed.), *The Oxford Handbook of the Bronze Age Aegean (ca. 3000–1000 BC)*: 495–508. Oxford: Oxford University Press.

Lightfoot, K. and A. Martinez

1995 Frontiers and boundaries in archaeological perspective. *Annual Review of Anthropology* 24: 471–92.

Lucy, S.
2005 Ethnic and cultural identities. In M. Diaz-Andreu, M., S. Lucy, S. Babic and D. Edwards (eds.), *The Archaeology of Identity: Approaches to Gender, Age, Status, Ethnicity and Religion.* London: Routledge: 86–109.

Macdonald, C.
2010 Knossos. In E. Cline (ed.), *The Oxford Handbook of the Bronze Age Aegean (ca. 3000-1000 BC)*: 529–42. Oxford: Oxford University Press.
2012 Palatial Knossos: the early years. In I. Schoep, P. Tomkins and J. Driessen (eds.), *Back to the Beginning: Reassessing Social and Political Complexity on Crete During the Early and Middle Bronze Age*: 81–113. Oxford: Oxbow.

Marcus, J.
1983 Lowland Maya archaeology at the crossroads. *American Antiquity* 48: 454–88.
1998 The peaks and valleys of ancient states: an extension of the dynamic model. In G. Feinman and J. Marcus (eds.), *Archaic States:* 59–94. Santa Fe: School of American Research Press.

Mathews, P.
1985 Maya early Classic monuments and inscriptions. In G. Willey and P. Mathews (eds.), *A Consideration of the Early Classic Period in the Maya Lowlands* (Institute for Mesoamerican Studies 10): 5–54. Albany: State University of New York.

Militello, P.
2012 Emerging authority: a functional analysis of the MM II settlement of Phaistos. In I. Schoep, P. Tomkins and J. Driessen (eds.), *Back to the Beginning: Reassessing Social and Political Complexity on Crete During the Early and Middle Bronze Age*: 236–72. Oxford: Oxbow.

Minc, L.
2006 Monitoring regional market systems in prehistory: models, methods and metrics. *Journal of Anthropological Archaeology* 25: 82–116.
2009 Style and substance: evidence for regionalism within the Aztec market system. *Latin American Antiquity* 20: 343–74.

Minc, L., M. Hodge and M. J. Blackman
1994 Stylistic and spatial variability in Early Aztec ceramics. In M. Hodge and M. Smith (eds.), *Economies and Polities in the Aztec Realm* (Studies on Culture and Society 6): 133–73. Albany: University of Albany.

Müller, S.
1996 Malia: Prospection archéologique de la plaine de Malia. *Bulletin de Correspondence Hellénique* 120: 921–8.
1997 Malia et la Crète de l'âge du bronze: L'organisation d'un territoire minoen. *Dossiers d'Archéologie* 222: 52–53.
1998 Malia: Prospection archéologique de la plaine de Malia. *Bulletin de Correspondence Hellénique* 114: 548–52.
2003 Malia: Prospection archéologique de la plaine de Malia. *Bulletin de Correspondence Hellénique* 127: 456–69.

Müller-Celka, S.
2007 Terroir et territoire à Malia à l'époque protopalatiale. *Bulletin de Correspondence Hellénique* 131: 855–60

Nichols, L. and T. Charlton (eds.)
1997 *The Archaeology of City-states: Cross-cultural Approaches.* Washington, D.C: Smithsonian Institution Press.

Niemeier, W.-D.
2004 When Minos ruled the waves: Knossian power overseas. In G. Cadogan, E. Hatzaki A. Vasilakis (eds.), *Knossos: Palace, City, State.* (BSA Studies 12): 393–98. London: British School at Athens.

Nowicki, K.
1995 Report on investigations in Greece. X. Studies in 1993 and 1994. *Archeologia* 46: 63–70.
Nowicki, K.
1996 Lasithi (Crete): one hundred years of archaeological research. *Aegean Archaeology* 3: 27–47.
2000 *Defensible Sites in Crete c. 1200–800 B.C. (LM IIIB/IIIC through Early Geometric)* (Aegaeum 21). Liège: Université de Liège.
Palaima, T.
1994 Seal-users and script-users/nodules and tablets at LMIB Hagia Triada. In P. Ferioli, E. Fiandra, G. Fissore and M. Frangipane (eds.), *Archives Before Writing*: 307–30. Rome: Centro Internazionale di Ricerche Archeologiche Antropologiche e Storiche.
Paliou, E. and A. Bevan
2017 Computational approaches to Minoan settlement interaction and growth. In Q. Letesson and C. Knappett (eds.), *Minoan Architecture and Urbanism. New Perspectives on Ancient Built Environment*: 266–88. Oxford: Oxford University Press.
Panagiotakis, N.
2003 L'évolution archéologique de la Pédiada (Crète centrale): premier bilan. *Bulletin de Correspondence Hellénique* 127: 327–430.
2004 Contacts between Knossos and the Pediada region in central Crete. In G. Cadogan, E. Hatzaki A. Vasilakis (eds.). *Knossos: Palace, City, State.* (BSA Studies 12): 177–86. London: British School at Athens.
Parsons, J.
1972 Archaeological settlement patterns. *Annual Review of Anthropology* 1: 127–50.
Pelon, O.
2005 Les deux destructions du palais de Malia. In I. Bradfer-Burdet, B. Detournay and R. Laffineur (eds.), *ΚΡΗΣ ΤΕΧΝΙΤΗΣ. L'Artisan Crétois: Recueil d'articles en l'honneur de Jean-Claude Poursat, publié à l'occasion des 40 ans de la découverte du Quartier Mu* (Aegaeum 26): 185–97. Liège: Université de Liège.
Platon, L.
2002 The political and cultural influence of the Zakros palace on nearby sites and in a wider context. In J. Driessen, I. Schoep and R. Laffineur (eds.), *Monuments of Minos. Rethinking the Minoan Palaces* (Aegaeum 23): 145–56. Liege: Université de Liège.
2004 Το Υστερομινωικό Ι ανάκτορο της Ζάκρου: μια "Κνωσός" έξω απο την Κνωσό. In G. Cadogan, E. Hatzaki A. Vasilakis (eds.), *Knossos: Palace, City, State.* (BSA Studies 12): 381–92. London: British School at Athens.
2010 Kato Zakros. In E. Cline (ed.), *The Oxford Handbook of the Bronze Age Aegean (ca. 3000–1000 BC)*: 509–17. Oxford: Oxford University Press.
Plog, S.
1980 *Stylistic Variation in Prehistoric Ceramics: Design Analysis in the American Southwest.* Cambridge: Cambridge University Press.
Popham, M.
1980 Cretan sites occupied between c. 1450 and 1400 B.C. *Annual of the British School at Athens* 75: 163–67.
Poursat, J.-C.
2007 Un "Petit Palais" au Quartier Mu? Organisation de l'espace et répartition fonctionnelle. *Bulletin de Correspondence Hellénique* 131: 831–33.
2008 Minoan palaces and polities: a view from Malia. *Bulletin of the Institute of Classical Studies* 51: 195–96.
2010 Malia: palace, state, city. In O. Krzyszkowska (ed.), *Cretan Offerings. Studies in Honour of Peter Warren.* (BSA Studies 18): 259–67. London: British School at Athens.

Preston, L.
2004 A mortuary perspective on political changes in Late Minoan II-IIIB Crete. *American Journal of Archaeology* 108: 321–48.
Price, B.
1977 Shifts in production and organization: a cluster-interaction model. *Current Anthropology* 18: 209–33.
Puglisi, D.
2007 Le territoire de Malia a l'epoque neopalatiale: premieres données de la prospection. *Bulletin de Correspondence Hellénique* 131: 865–9.
Rehak, P.
1997 The role of religious painting in the function of the Minoan villa: the case of Ayia Triadha. In R. Hägg (ed.), *The Function of the "Minoan Villa"* (Swedish Institute in Athens, Series in 4° 46): 163–75. Stockholm: Paul Åström.
Rehak, P. and J. Younger
2001 Neopalatial, Final Palatial, and Postpalatial Crete. In T. Culllen (ed.), *Aegean Prehistory: A Review* (AJA Supplement I): 383–465. Boston: Archaeological Institute of America.
Relaki, M.
2004 Constructing a region: the contested landscapes of Prepalatial Mesara. In J. Barrett and P. Halstead (eds.). *The Emergence of Civilisation Revisited* (Sheffield Studies in Aegean Archaeology 6): 170–88. Oxford: Oxbow.
Renfrew, C.
1972 *The Emergence of Civilisation. The Cyclades and the Aegean in the Third Millennium B.C.* London: Methuen.
1975 Trade as action at a distance. Questions of integration and communication. In J. Sabloff and C. Lamberg-Karlovsky (eds.), *Ancient Civilizations and Trade*: 3–59. Albuquerque: University of New Mexico Press.
1986 Introduction: peer polity interaction and socio-political change. In C. Renfrew and J. Cherry (eds.), *Peer Polity Interaction and Socio-Political Change*: 1–18. Cambridge: Cambridge University Press.
Rethemiotakis, G.
2002 Evidence on social and economic changes at Galatas and Pediada in the New Palace period. In J. Driessen, I. Schoep and R. Laffineur (eds.), *Monuments of Minos. Rethinking the Minoan Palaces* (Aegaeum 23): 55–69. Liège: Université de Liège.
Rethemiotakis, G., and K. Christakis
2004 Cultural interaction between Knossos and Pediada: the evidence from the Middle Minoan IB pottery. In G. Cadogan, E. Hatzaki A. Vasilakis (eds.), *Knossos: Palace, City, State.* (BSA Studies 12): 169–75. London: British School at Athens.
2011 LM I pottery groups from the palace and the town of Galatas, Pediada. In T. Brogan and E. Hallager (eds.), *LM IB Pottery: Relative Chronology and Regional Differences* (Monographs of the Danish Institute at Athens 11): 205–27. Athens: Danish Institute at Athens.
Robb, J. (ed.)
1999 *Material symbols: culture and economy in prehistory.* (Occasional paper of the Center for Archaeological Investigations, Southern Illinois University at Carbondale 26). Carbondale: Southern Illinois University at Carbondale.
Sanders, W., J. Parsons and R. Santley
1979 *The Basin of Mexico: the Ecological Processes in the Evolution of a Civilization.* New York: Academic Press.
Savage, S.
1997 Assessing departures from log-normality in the rank-size rule. *Journal of Archaeological Science* 24: 233–44.

Schele, L. and P. Mathews
1991 Royal visits and other intersite relationships among the Classic Maya. In T. P. Culbert (ed.), *Classic Maya Political History: Hieroglyphic and Archaeological Evidence*: 226–52. Cambridge: Cambridge University Press.

Schoep, I.
1999 Tablets and territories? Reconstructing Late Minoan IB political geography through undeciphered documents. *American Journal of Archaeology* 103: 201–21.
2001 Managing the hinterland: the rural concerns of urban administration. In K. Branigan (ed.), *Urbanism in the Aegean Bronze Age* (Sheffield Studies in Aegean Archaeology 4): 87–102. London: Sheffield Academic Press.
2002 *The Administration of Neopalatial Crete. A Critical Assessment of the Linear A Tablets and their Role in the Administrative Process* (MINOS Supplement 17). Salamanca: Ediciones Universidad de Salamanca.

Sellwood, L.
1984 Tribal boundaries viewed from the perspective of numismatic evidence. In B. Cunliffe and D. Miles (eds.), *Aspects of the Iron Age in Central Southern Britain*: 191–204. Oxford: Oxford University Committee for Archaeology.

Sharer, R.
1994 *The Ancient Maya. 5th ed.* Stanford: Stanford University Press.

Shaw, J.
2006 Kommos in the Mesara landscape. In J. Shaw and M. Shaw (ed.), *Kommos. Vol. V. The Monumental Minoan Buildings at Kommos*: 863–78. Princeton: Princeton University Press.

Shennan, S. (ed.)
1994 *Archaeological Approaches to Cultural Identity.* London: Routledge.

Smith, C.
1974 Economics of marketing systems. Models from economic geography. *Annual Review of Anthropology* 3: 167–201.
1990 Types of city-size distributions. A comparative analysis. In A. van der Woude, A. Hayami and J. de Vries (eds.), *Urbanization in History. A Process of Dynamic Interactions*: 20–42. Oxford: Clarendon Press.

Smith, M.
1979 The Aztec marketing system and settlement patterns in the Valley of Mexico: a central place analysis. *American Antiquity* 44: 110–25.
2005 Networks, territories, and the cartography of ancient states. *Annals of the Association of American Geographers* 95: 832–49.

Stark, M. (ed.)
1998 *The Archaeology of Social Boundaries.* Washington D. C.: Smithsonian Institution Press.

Stark, M., B. Bowser and L. Horne (eds.)
2008 *Cultural Transmission and Material Culture: Breaking Down Boundaries.* Tucson: University of Arizona Press.

Steponaitis, V.
1981 Settlement hierarchies and political complexity in non-market societies: the Formative period of the Valley of Mexico. *American Anthropologist* 83: 320–63.

Trigger, B.
2003 *Understanding early civilizations: a comparative study*. Cambridge: Cambridge University Press.

Tsipopoulou, M.
1997 Palace-centered polities in eastern Crete: Neopalatial Petras and its neighbors. In W. Aufrecht, N. Mirau and S. Gauley (eds.), *Urbanism in Antiquity: From Mesopotamia to Crete* (Journal for the Study of the Old Testament Supplement Series 244): 263–77. Sheffield: Sheffield Academic Press.

1999 From local centre to palace: the role of fortification in the economic transformation of the Siteia Bay area, east Crete. In R. Laffineur (ed.), *POLEMOS: Le contexte guerrier en Égée á l 'âge du* Bronze (Aegaeum 19): 179–89. Liège: Université de Liège.
2002 Petras, Siteia: the palace, the town, the hinterland and the Protopalatial background. In J. Driessen, I. Schoep and R. Laffineur (eds.), *Monuments of Minos. Rethinking the Minoan Palaces* (Aegaeum 23): 133–44. Liège: Université de Liège.

Tsipopoulou, M., and A. Papacostopoulou
1997 "Villas" and villages in the hinterland of Petras, Siteia. In R. Hägg (ed.), *The Function of the "Minoan Villa"* (Swedish Institute in Athens, Series in 4° 46): 203–14. Stockholm: Paul Åström.

Van de Moortel, A.
2011 Late IB ceramic phases at Palaikastro and Malia: a response to Sean Hemingway, J. Alexander MacGillivray and L. Hugh Sackett. In T. Brogan and E. Hallager (eds.), *LM IB Pottery: Relative Chronology and Regional Differences* (Monographs of the Danish Institute at Athens 11): 531–45. Athens: Danish Institute at Athens.

Vasilakis, A.
1990 Προϊστορικές θέσεις στη Μονή Οδηγητρία – Καλούς Λιμένες. *Κρητική Εστία* 3: 11–79.

Vlassopoulos, K.
2007 *Unthinking the Greek Polis. Ancient Greek History Beyond Eurocentrism.* Cambridge: Cambridge University Press.

Walberg, G.
1983 *Provincial Middle Minoan Pottery.* Mainz am Rhein: Von Zabern.

Warren, P.
1985 Minoan Palaces. *Scientific American* 253(1): 205–11.
2002 Political structure in Neopalatial Crete. In J. Driessen, I. Schoep and R. Laffineur (eds.), *Monuments of Minos. Rethinking the Minoan Palaces* (Aegaeum 23): 201–05. Liège: Université de Liège.
2004 Terra cognita? The territory and boundaries of the early Neopalatial Knossian state. In G. Cadogan, E. Hatzaki and A. Vasilakis (eds.), *Knossos: Palace, City, State* (BSA Studies 12): 159–68. London: British School at Athens.

Watrous, L. V.
1982 *Lasithi: a History of Settlement on a Highland Plain in Crete* (Hesperia Supplement 18). Princeton: American School of Classical Studies at Athens.
2004 New pottery from the Psychro Cave and its implications for Minoan Crete. *Annual of the British School at Athens* 99: 129–47.

Watrous, L. V., D. Hadzi-Vallianou and H. Blitzer
2004 *The Plain of Phaistos: Cycles of Social Complexity in the Mesara Region of Crete* (Monumenta Archaeologica 23). Los Angeles: The Cotsen Institute of Archaeology.

Weingarten, J.
1986 The sealing structures of Minoan Crete: MM II Phaistos to the destruction of the palace of Knossos. Part I: the evidence until the LMIB destructions. *Oxford Journal of Archaeology* 5: 279–98.
1991 Late Bronze Age trade within Crete: the evidence of seals and sealings. In N. Gale (ed.), *Bronze Age Trade in the Mediterranean* (Studies in Mediterranean Archaeology 90): 303–24. Jonsered: Paul Astrom.
2010 Corridors of power: a social network analysis of the Minoan "replica rings". In W. Miller (ed.), *Die Bedeutung der Minoischen und Mykenischen Glyptik* (CMS Beiheft 8): 395–412. Mainz am Rhein: von Zabern.

Wells, P.
1992 Tradition, identity and change beyond the Roman frontier. In E. Schortman and P. Urban (eds.), *Resources, Power and Interregional Interaction*: 175–88. London: Plenum.

Whallon, R. and J. Brown (eds.)
1982 *Essays on Archaeological Typology* (Kampsville Seminar in Archeology). Evanston: Center for American Archaeology.

Whitelaw, T.
1998 Colonisation and competition in the polis of Koressos: the development of settlement in North-West Keos from the Archaic to the Late Roman periods. In L. Mendoni and A. Mazarakis Ainian (eds.), *Kea-Kythnos: History and Archaeology. Proceedings of an International Symposium Kea-Kythnos. 22–25 June 1994.* (Meletimata 27): 227–57. Paris: Diffusion de Boccard.
2001 From sites to communities: defining the human dimensions of Minoan urbanism. In K. Branigan (ed.), *Urbanism in the Aegean Bronze Age* (Sheffield Studies in Aegean Archaeology 4): 15–37. London: Sheffield Academic Press.
2004 Alternative pathways to complexity in the southern Aegean. In J. Barrett and P. Halstead (eds.), *The Emergence of Civilisation Revisited* (Sheffield Studies in Aegean Archaeology 6): 232–56. Oxford: Oxbow.
2012 The urbanisation of prehistoric Crete: settlement perspectives on Minoan state formation. In I. Schoep, P. Tomkins and J. Driessen (eds.), *Back to the Beginning: Reassessing Social and Political Complexity on Crete during the Early and Middle Bronze Age*: 114–76. Oxford: Oxbow.
2014 Political formations in Prehistoric Crete. *Bulletin of the Institute of Classical Studies* 57(2):148–49.
2017 The development and character of urban communities in Prehistoric Crete in their regional context: a preliminary study. In Q. Letesson and C. Knappett (eds.), *Minoan Architecture and Urbanism. New Perspectives on Ancient Built Environment*: 114–80. Oxford: Oxford University Press.
In press Feeding Prehistoric Knossos: exploring economic and logistical implications of urbanisation in prehistoric Crete. In D. Garcia, R. Orgeolet, M. Pomadère and J. Zurbach (eds.), *The Country in the City.* Oxford: Archaeopress.

Whitelaw, T., M. Bredaki and A. Vasilakis
forthcoming Prehistoric Knossos: tracing its long-term history through its surface record. *Πεπραγμένα του ΙΑ' Διεθνούς Κρητολογικού Συνεδρίου, Ρέθυμνο 21-27 Οκτωβρίου 2011.* Ρέθυμνο: Ιστορική και Λαογραφική Εταιρεία Ρεθύμνης.

Whitelaw, T. and C. Morgan
2009 Crete. In C. Morgan (ed.), Archaeology in Greece 2008–2009. *Archaeological Reports* 55: 79–100.

Whitley, J., S. Germanidou, D. Urem-Kotsou, A. Dimoula, I. Nikolakopoulou, A. Karnava and E. Hatzaki
2006 Archaeology in Greece 2005–2006. *Archaeological Reports* 52: 1–112.

Whitley, J., S. Germanidou, D. Urem-Kotsou, A. Dimoula, I. Nikolakopoulou, A. Karnava and D. Evely
2007 Archaeology in Greece 2006–2007. *Archaeological Reports* 53: 1–121.

Wiener, M.
1984 Crete and the Cyclades in LMI: the tale of the conical cups. In R. Hagg and N. Marinatos (eds.), *The Minoan Thalassocracy Myth and Reality* (Swedish Institute in Athens, Series in 4° 32): 17–25. Stockholm: Swedish Institute in Athens.
1987 Trade and rule in palatial Crete. In R. Hägg and N. Marinatos (eds.), *The Function of the Minoan Palaces* (Swedish Institute in Athens, Series in 4°, 35): 261–7. Stockholm: Swedish Institute in Athens.
1990 The isles of Crete? The Minoan thalassocracy revisited. In D. Hardy, C. Doumas, J. Sakellarakis and P. Warren (eds.), *Thera and the Aegean World III. Vol. 1: Archaeology*: 128–61. The Thera Foundation: London.
2007 Neopalatial Knossos: rule and role. In P. P. Betancourt, M. Nelson and H. Williams (eds.), *Krinoi kai Limenes: Studies in Honor of Joseph and Maria Shaw* (Prehistory Monographs 22): 231–42. Philadelphia: INSTAP Academic Press.

Wilkinson, T.

1994 The structure and dynamics of dry-farming states in Upper Mesopotamia. *Current Anthropology* 35: 483–520.

Wilson, D., P. M. Day, and N. Dimopoulou-Rethemiotaki

2004 The pottery from Early Minoan I-IIB Knossos and its relations with the harbour site of Poros-Katsambas. In G. Cadogan, E. Hatzaki and A. Vasilakis (eds.), *Knossos: Palace, City, State* (BSA Studies 12): 67–74. London: British School at Athens.

2008 The gateway port of Poros-Katsambas: trade and exchange between north-central Crete and the Cyclades in EB I-II. In N. Brodie, J. Doole, G. Gavalas and C. Renfrew (eds.), *Horizon. Ορίζων: A colloquium on the prehistory of the Cyclades* (McDonald Institute Monographs): 261–70. Cambridge: McDonald Institute for Archaeological Research.

Wobst, H. M.

1977 Stylistic behavior and information exchange. In. C. Cleland (ed.), *For the Director: Essays in Honor of James B. Griffin* (Anthropological Papers 61): 317–41. Ann Arbor: Museum of Anthropology, University of Michigan.

Wright, H.

1977 Recent research on the origin of the state. *Annual Review of Anthropology* 6: 379–97.

1987 The Susiana hinterlands during the era of primary state formation. In F. Hole (ed.), *The Archaeology of Western Iran. Settlement and Society from Prehistory to the Islamic Conquest*: 141–55. Washington DC: Smithsonian Institution.

1998 Uruk states in southwestern Iran. In J. Marcus and G. Feinman (ed.), *Archaic States*: 173–97. Santa Fe: School of American Research.

2000 Modeling tributary economies and hierarchical polities. In G. Feinman and L. Manzanilla (eds.), *Cultural Evolution. Contemporary Viewpoints*: 197–213. London: Plenum.

2005 The polycentricity of the archaic civilizations. In V. Scarborough (ed.), *A Catalyst for Ideas. Anthropological Archaeology and the Legacy of Douglas Schwartz*: 149–67. Santa Fe: School of American Research Press.

Wright, H. and G. Johnson

1975 Population, exchange, and early state formation in southwestern Iran. *American Anthropologist* 77: 267–89.

Wright, J.

1984 Umpiring the Mycenaean empire. In P. P. Betancourt (ed.), *The Scope and Extent of the Mycenaean Empire* (Temple University Aegean Symposium 9): 58–70. Philadelphia: Temple University.

Yoffee, N.

1991 Maya elite interaction: through a glass, sideways. In T. P. Culbert (ed.), *Classic Maya Political History: Hieroglyphic and Archaeological Evidence*: 285–310. Cambridge: Cambridge University Press.

Younger, J. and P. Rehak

2008a The material culture of Neopalatial Crete. In C. Shelmerdine (ed.), *The Cambridge Companion to the Aegean Bronze Age*: 140–64. Cambridge: Cambridge University Press.

2008b Minoan Culture: Religion, Burial Customs, and Administration. In C. Shelmerdine (ed.), *The Cambridge Companion to the Aegean Bronze Age*: 165–85. Cambridge: Cambridge University Press.

Chapter 12

The relevance of survey data as evidence for settlement structure in Prepalatial Crete

Donald C. Haggis

Introduction

The results of intensive archaeological surveys published over the past decade have been slow to affect the current discourse on Prepalatial Crete. While there is some understandable reluctance by excavators to accept chronologies and attributes of sites derived principally from the distribution of surface sherds, the recent intensity of excavation, stratigraphic studies, and material analyses in Prepalatial areas has encouraged vivid site histories and social models which are used to extrapolate compelling regional generalisations. Such complexly detailed and interwoven narratives seem to find little place for survey, except as an occasional and tangential corroboration of narratives (e.g. Tomkins and Schoep 2010: 72–73). Survey results by and large have been ignored, perhaps in part because they are seen as too obtuse or imprecise to affect interpretations of site-specific data. Even so, the tendency to trust implicitly the excavation sample – even the narrow stratigraphic component, building, or assemblage – is probably because of its concreteness, vividness, and level of analytical rigour and contextual detail, in contrast to the ambivalent and discursive conclusions of most survey publications. On the one hand, the brush-strokes of survey are too broad, the resolution of the picture is too coarse, and we seem to be more wary of the uncontrolled biases of the survey sample (and the meaning of sherds on the ground), than we are of equally ambiguous data sets derived from excavation. On the other hand, even if we trust the Prepalatial survey data, we still want to link integration to a hierarchical and centrifugal expansion of settlement from a notional centre, into a hinterland whose hypothetical carrying capacity determines the extent of viable geopolitical identity and complexity. In a sense we demand of survey the identification of normative site hierarchies and primary centres that indicate degrees of structural complexity; in this line of thought, the results of survey generally show little meaningful settlement development of this sort until MM IA or later (Driessen 2001: 60–61; Tomkins and Schoep 2010: 73).

My intention here is to review recent interpretations of survey data that pertain to the visualisation of settlement structure in Prepalatial Crete, looking for recurring patterns that could inform our view of regional histories. The idea is to begin exploring the potential of macro-regional and multi-regional perspectives that might be useful to single-site contextually-focused studies derived from excavation. That is, by looking at general trends across a number of landscapes – in a sense, pasting together a number of small-scale surveys as opposed to summarising local narratives shaped from preconceived synchronic territories or hypothetical developmental trajectories – we might begin to see commonalities in the diachronic structure of settlement that could suggest some general cultural practices or processes.

Even if surveys generate Prepalatial data that seem to fail our preconceptions of structure (formally stratified or hierarchical interrelationships), or compress chronological and cultural variables, and conflate the complex layers of the post-processual discourse, it is perhaps not because of the quality or comparability of the data sets published by each project, but in the initial questions we are asking of that data (cf. Terrenato 2004); the effective analytical scale of fieldwork; the over-arching interpretative framework; and the assumed behavioural scales of the apparent structures. If we change the scale of analysis, stepping back momentarily from implicit functions of agricultural geography, hierarchy and proximity, as *a priori* predictors of small-scale interdependence, complexity and territoriality (cf. Relaki 2004: 172–73), looking instead more broadly at large-scale, if not island-wide, patterns, we might come closer to discerning some basic and culturally-predicated configurations in the landscape.

I am not at all suggesting that we abandon local narratives derived from excavation and survey, or questions of regional variability and diversity derived from micro-regional patterns. I do think however that it might be useful to examine the language and implications of the concluding narratives of published surveys in grappling with the meaning of macro-scalar settlement patterns and problematic incongruities of settlement structure.

Mesara, Vrokastro (Kalo Chorio-Meseleroi), and Gournia

Mesara

In 1983, John Cherry, perhaps for the first time, confronted the Prepalatial settlement data, extrapolating from Myrtos and Vasiliki to the "...scores of other EM settlements, whose small scale and autonomy clearly represent the norm at this time" (1983: 39–40). The survey data available seemed to support this view. Blackman and Branigan's (1977) now famous Agiopharango map provided for Cherry "a clear picture of a wholly undifferentiated social landscape, comprising very small scale, autonomous, local units". Localism, subsistence-based economies and parochial autonomy characterised the pattern, fitting well with a growing processual reaction to persistent materialist and evolutionary paradigms that showed excavated EM settlements (and individual architectural features) to be formal predecessors of palatial buildings and institutions (cf. Watrous 1982: 9–11; 2001: 175). Of course, Keith Branigan's pioneering work in both survey and excavation was instrumental in shaping both of these apparently opposing views of the same data.

Even though Cherry had not seen the survey data available to us now, I doubt that his view then or the picture would have really changed very much. In fact, Vance Watrous's (2001: 167) first reading of the western Mesara data in 1994, about a decade after Cherry, saw very little dynamic settlement growth throughout the Prepalatial period, with a weak three-level hierarchy remaining fairly constant. His not-so-surprising summary statement in 1994 reflected the null case, arguing that there was really no evidence for a ranked society in EM II that anticipated the apparent complexities of palatial organisation (Watrous 2001: 179, 221–22; Watrous and Hadzi-Vallianou 2004: 233).

In light of new excavation and analyses of various complex configurations of material, involving ceramic and metallurgical production, exchange, and ceremonial consumption (e.g. Day and Wilson 2002; Day and Doonan 2007); early and interregional use of sealing systems (e.g. Sbonias 1999; Schoep 1999; Relaki 2009); and the regional and social-ceremonial significance of tombs and burial practices (Branigan 1998; Murphy 1998; Relaki 2004; Papadatos 2007: 164; Legarra Herrero 2009), the picture began to change. Settlement studies kept up with the new perspectives, but a decade later, in 2004, Watrous's narrative had changed only a little with the western Mesara becoming only "more hierarchical in EM II" (Watrous and Hadzi-Vallianou 2004: 237; Watrous 2001: 221), an ambivalent view of moderate complexity shared by most (cf. Driessen 2001; Tomkins and Schoep 2010). Even so, the presumably centrifugal dispersal of lower-level sites apparently around the ridge of Hagia Triada and Phaistos had previously existed in EM I if not earlier (Todaro 2012), as did a widely dispersed and fairly even spread of settlements (Fig. 12.1). Apparently new in EM II was a tendency toward greater diversity of exploited areas by farms and field sites, especially in marginal land (Watrous and Hadzi-Vallianou 2004: 239; cf. Watrous 1982: 10–11), supporting a vivid case of differentiated agricultural dependence. The results, however subtle, indicated to Watrous an economic ranking centring on Phaistos and its privileged access to the best arable land in contrast, for example, to that of the ridge south of Kamilari or the more distant Agiopharango. New sites, even as distant as the Kommos zone, lacked tholoi and were thus conceivably part of the territory of Phaistos (Watrous and Hadzi-Vallianou 2004: 238). For Watrous, the only real central place was perhaps Phaistos itself with a vaguely drawn catchment of about two to five km radius, marked roughly by Kommos, Sivas, and Sopata Kouse (Watrous and Hadzi-Vallianou 2004: 244; cf. Relaki 2004; Todaro 2012).

In this picture of slowly growing hinterlands, there is some ambivalence about the change from EM I to II and the actual disposition of the central places and the shifting emphasis of their regional functions. Watrous visualised a group of families at Phaistos and Hagia Triada who would have controlled the territory along the ridge south of Kamilari; the sites further afield were smaller rural communities, apparently independent, and controlling their own tholoi and ceremonial centres. What is interesting in Watrous's narrative is that in order to demonstrate hierarchical

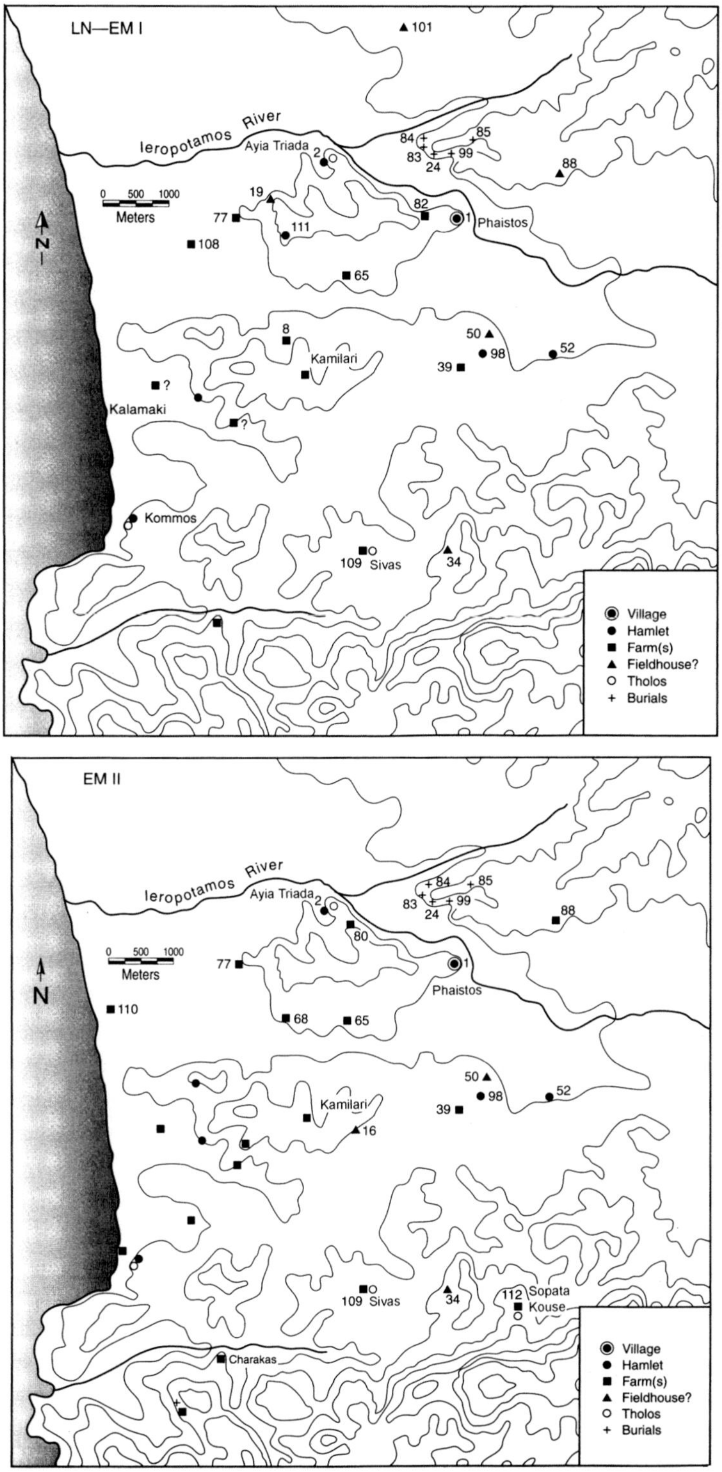

Figure 12.1: LN-EM II settlement patterns in west Mesara (after Watrous and Hadzi-Vallianou 2004).

dependence or local autonomy, he departs almost completely from discussion of the settlement structure itself, using a bilateral centre-periphery exchange model derived from excavations and the contents of individual tholos tombs (Watrous and Hadzi-Vallianou 2004: 243–45). Hagia Triada and Platanos traded agricultural products for prestige goods from the north coast; or derived specialised goods like pottery from peripheral Mesara sites in exchange for agricultural surplus, with the marginal sites collecting prestige goods down the line from the centres. Thus, a kind of typical staple/wealth finance model, rather than the form of settlement structure *per se*, determined a satisfactory hierarchical organisation, and therefore, integrated structure, in turn, predicting a ranked society. That is, he presents parallel systems rather than a disaggregation of economic and social patterns, and the picture of settlement structure, while clear enough, loses its explanatory force or even relevance to the discussion.

Vrokastro

A similar ambivalence about settlement structure exists at Vrokastro (Fig. 12.2), which was also published in 2004, where there is a doubling of sites between FN-EM I and EM II-III; the growth in my view has to do for a large part with the choice of chronological divisions, making it actually very difficult to isolate or disaggregate EM I and II patterns. Although site sizes fall into what seems an overly complex four-tiered range, it is important that Hayden (2004: 72–73) is careful to point out that size divisions might have little relationship to differentiation of status or function, though the coastal zone, and particularly Priniatikos Pyrgos, is tentatively favoured as a possible centre by EM II (Fig. 12.2). In Vrokastro, like in the western Mesara, EM II sees a tendency to expand into marginal areas of the hinterland, with remarkable stability and continuity from FN or EM I; the coastal zone and the immediate Istron river catchment actually show little significant change in settlement structure *per se*, for the better part of 1000 years (Fig. 12.2). Also like with Phaistos/Hagia Triada and Platanos in the Mesara, on a regional scale, the identification of a primary centre at Priniatikos Pyrgos does not easily map directly onto the material patterns derived from survey, which fail to reveal a coherent hierarchical structure taking us much beyond Cherry's prognostic observations of the Agiopharango two decades ago.

There are two observations that emerge from these interpretations of settlement patterns: first, there is a remarkable consistency in structure, that is distribution, sizes, and perceived chronology and longevity, if not of individual sites, of microenvironments, even if we are able through excavation or refined ceramic chronologies to demonstrate discontinuous occupation sequences (Figs. 12.1, 12.2). The second, which I think is equally significant, is that the researchers' response to the data implies a kind of ambivalence, or even vagueness, about the structure suggested by the site distributions, at least as they relate to ideas of social and economic dynamics. The dominant pattern, apparently an even spread of hamlets or small villages, in Agiopharango, Lasithi, the western Mesara and Vrokastro, is reflected also in the more recent examples from Kavousi and Gournia. In Kavousi, FN-EM sites cluster in three areas, around the modern village of Kavousi (north

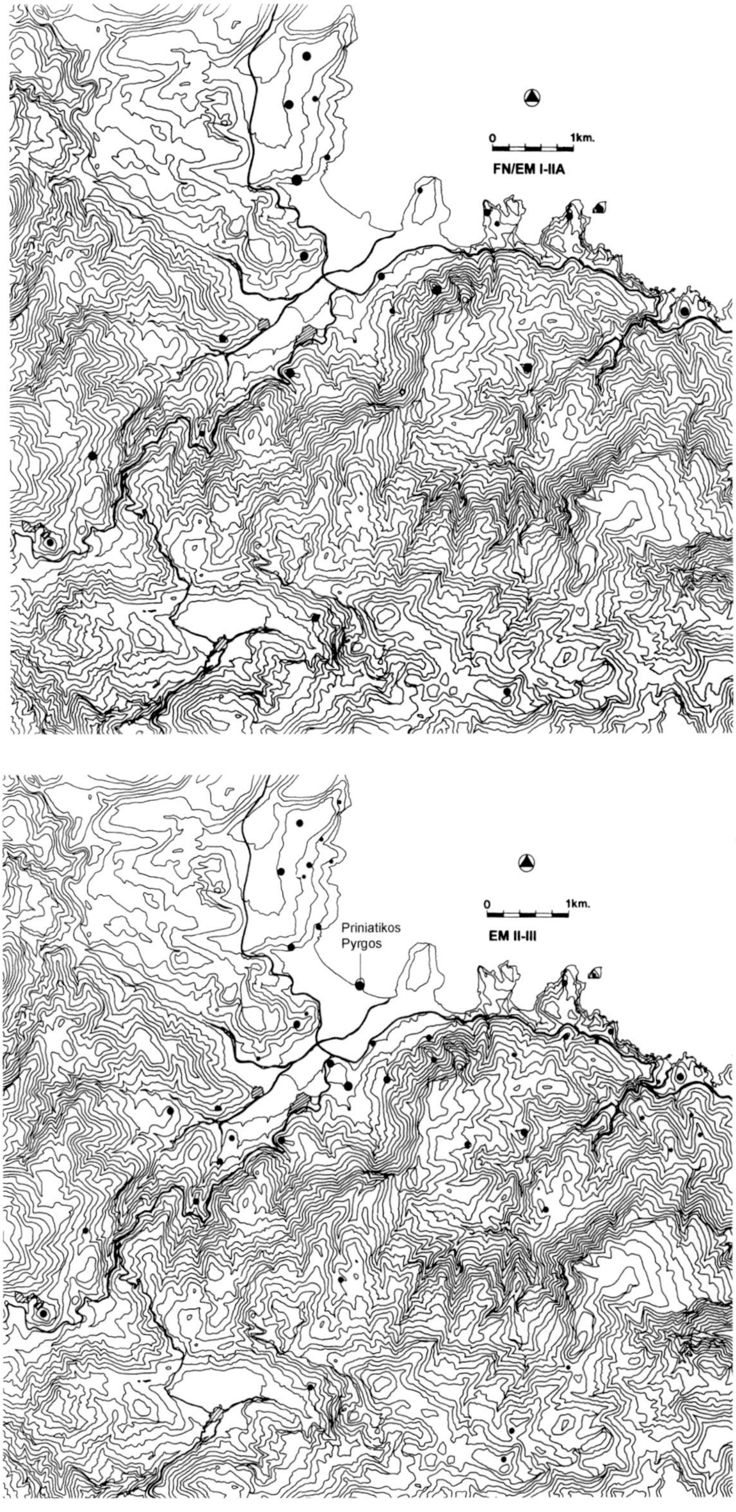

Figure 12.2: FN-EM III settlement patterns in Vrokastro (after Hayden 2004).

Papoura catchment), in Hagios Antonios, and in Khordakia (Chrysokamino), with one hamlet or village identifiable in each group (Haggis 2005). In the cases of Vrokastro, Gournia, and Mesara, arguably the best data we have to date, there is an unusually consistent spacing of these sites at regular intervals of about 0.5 to 2 km, and nearly identical site-size ranking with notional farms and hamlets dominating the pattern in comparable area samples (Fig. 12.3). Though I find the comparability of results

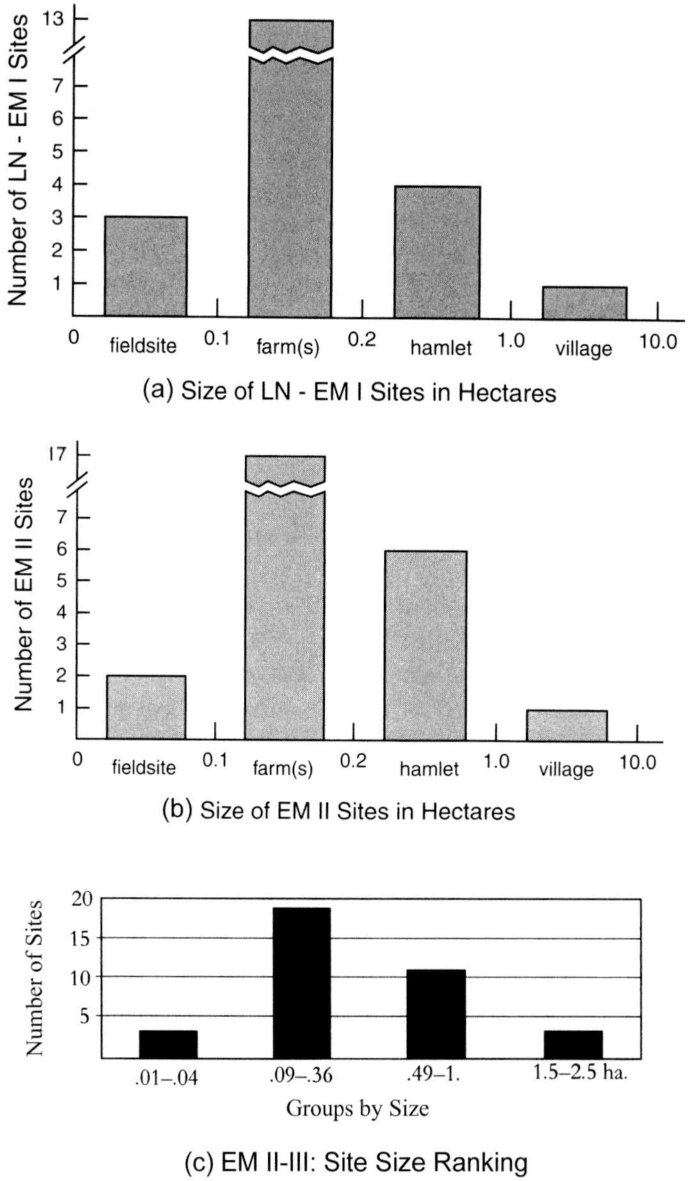

Figure 12.3: Prepalatial site hierarchies in Mesara (a and b) (after Watrous and Hadzi-Vallianou 2004), and Vrokastro (c) (Hayden 2004) regions.

and similarity of patterns frankly surprising given the differences in geomorphology, sampling and recovery methods, and knowledge of local ceramic sequences (especially coarse wares), I remain intrigued by the consistent size ranking and the primacy of hamlets in the pattern. Continuity, longevity, and the existence of localised clusters of sites echo many of Watrous and Cherry's initial impressions of the Prepalatial landscape, though the hamlets, by their very existence and replication, suggest a highly integrated structure (Haggis 2002).

What is perhaps most interesting is the constancy of the structure and that similar or identical configurations are found in diverse contexts in different areas of the island, suggesting a strong social component, that is, motives of cultural production and social practice rather than merely agricultural dependence, environmental variability, or population growth (cf. Legarra Herrero 2009). The bulk of the sites are hamlets and so-called farms, and I would agree with Hayden (2004) that there are probably no meaningful social distinctions to be made between the first two or three levels of settlement in any area, although differences in the chronology of population growth and adaptive accommodation to diverse environments are to be expected.

Gournia

Localisation and entrenchment characterise the pattern, which is fundamentally the same at Gournia and the north Ierapetra isthmus (Watrous and Schultz 2012) (Fig. 12.4). Here too we might reconstruct the gradual growth and dispersal of lower-order sites (again the hamlets and farms) but there is little compelling evidence to suggest a centrifugal process of concentric settlement expansion from higher-order centres, such as the first order "villages", filling out a centre-periphery model. What we see instead is entrenchment in the use of specific localities – that is a connectedness to specific places – conceivably for hundreds of years and probably discontinuously for the better part of the third millennium. A second characteristic of the pattern is the consistent ranking, with little distinction between lower-order sites, the vast majority being hamlets or clusters of houses (Fig. 12.4). This persistent lower-level expansion, continued reuse, or growth from within specific micro-regions seems structurally unrelated to, or at least spatially disconnected from the nearest primary or first order centres. The latter are frankly hard to define and show few significant changes in size or function throughout the period. In this even distribution, the field sites and villages seem to interact no differently than the fuzziest categories of farms and hamlets in between: the size-ranking in and of itself does not effectively predict the structure of settlement in the region.

Although we recognise ranking of sites as a critical material correlate for complexity (cf. Haggis 1999; Driessen 2001), the practice of ordering such units actually does little to help us model the meaning of the structure of the settlement, or to relate that structure to other forms of data, such as the distribution and character of contexts, ceramics, metals, prestige goods, and so on. Though Watrous uses rank-size distinctions to show an emerging hierarchy in the Mesara, he is hesitant to link the pattern of dispersed settlement in the broader region directly to the motivation of

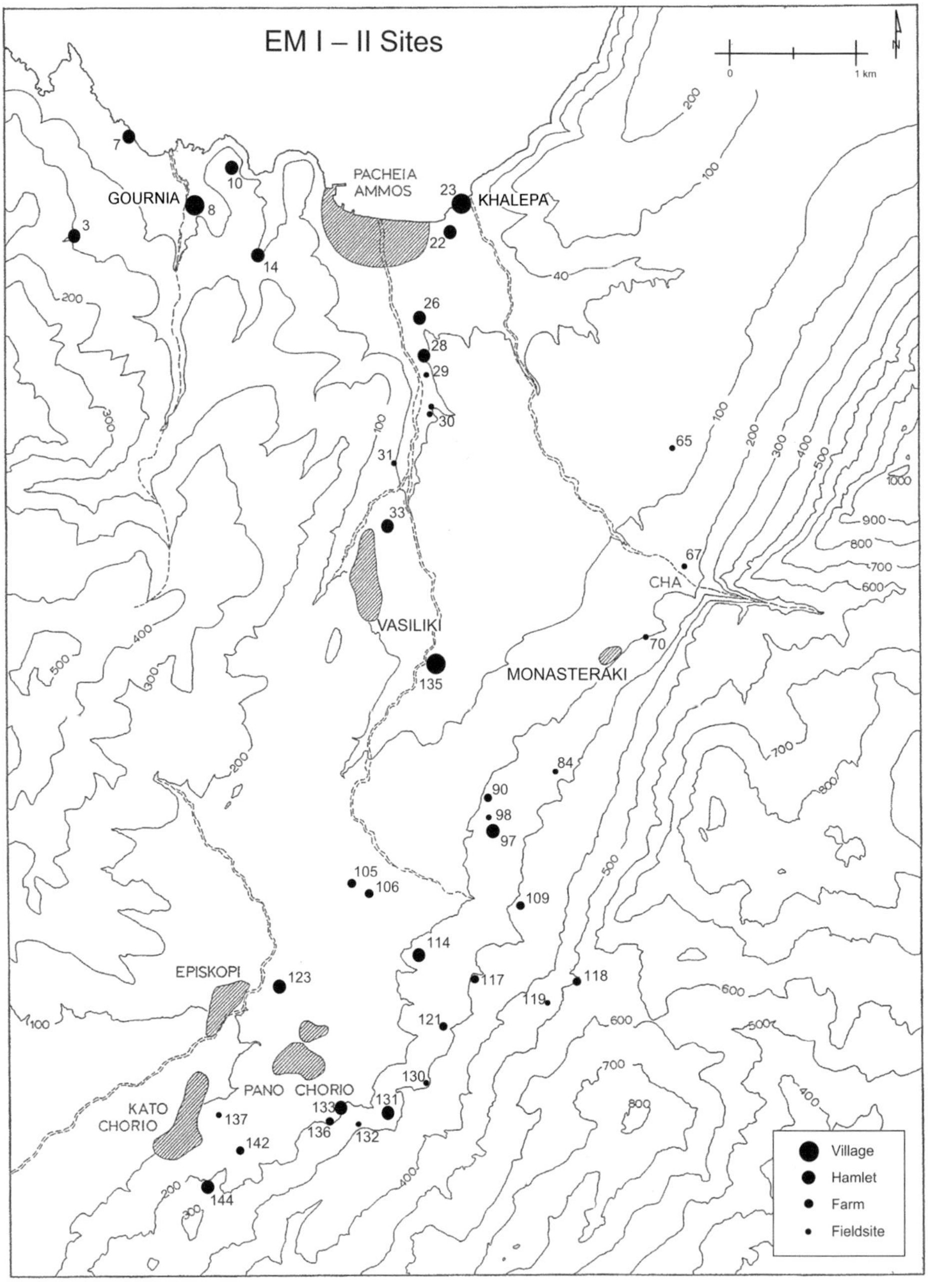

Figure 12.4: EM settlement patterns in Gournia and north Isthmus of Ierapetra (after L. V. Watrous and M. Schultz 2012).

primary centres. This is to say, Phaistos or variously Hagia Triada (cf. Relaki 2004: 181; Todaro 2012) and Platanos might be first order centres, even centres of territories, but the structure of their territories does not seem easy to visualise through a neat chronologically measurable ranking of sites in the hinterland (Fig. 12.1). Similarly, in the north Isthmus, the so-called "villages", if this is valid or socially-distinctive term at all, seem disconnected from the distribution of hamlets and farms, operating or interacting with other sites in the same way as hamlets.

Gournia, Khalepa, and Vasiliki follow this disengaged village pattern, as does perhaps Kavousi village (Site 24) and Mochlos (Figs. 12.4, 12.5). The real regional growth (increase in sites) (Watrous and Schultz 2012) is in the category of hamlets, and localised clustering is the dominant pattern. The actual process of hierarchisation correlates apparently more to hamlets than to villages, and Watrous emphasises that the even spacing and dispersal suggest relatively independent agriculturally-based populations with little centralised control in the region (Watrous and Schultz 2012; cf. Watrous 2001: 221, 223).

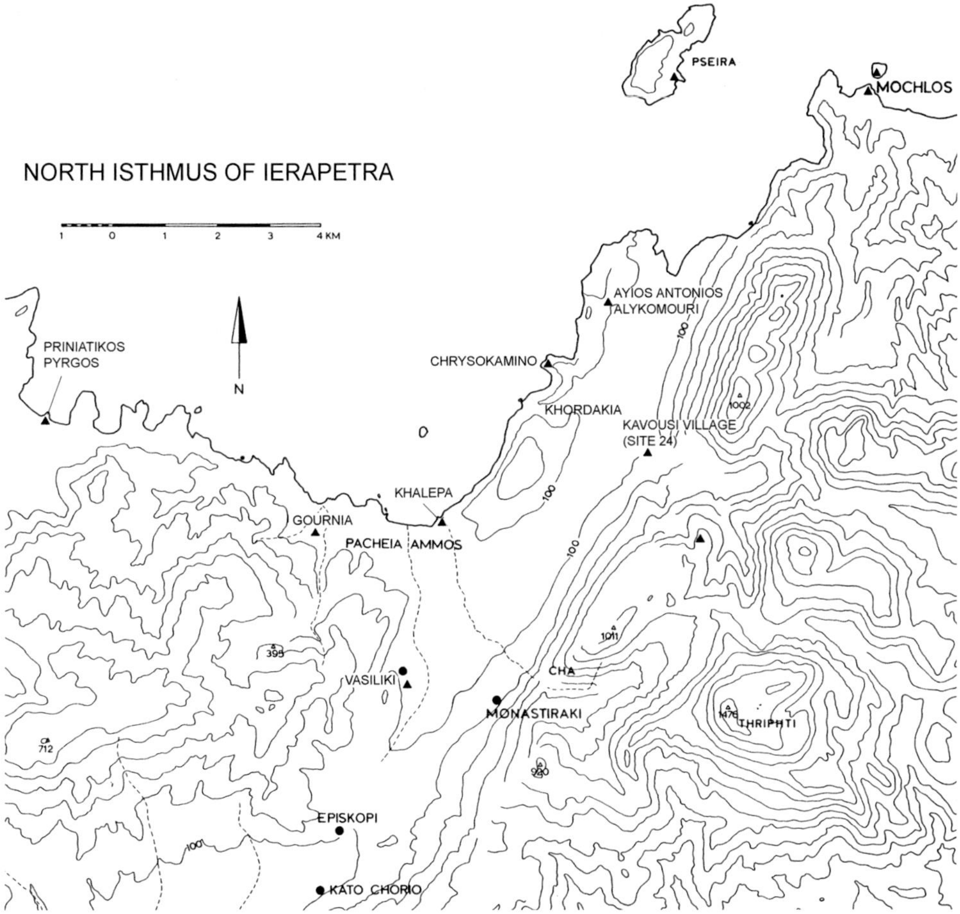

Figure 12.5: North Isthmus of Ierapetra (courtesy, Gournia Project).

Although Vasiliki could be the base of a chiefdom in EM IIB (Watrous 2001: 223), better exceptions might be Gournia itself, which, like Hayden's view of Priniatikos Pyrgos, shows evidence of centrifugal hierarchy, but we need to understand the meaning of the sizes of Gournia or Priniatikos Pyrgos, and their relationship to similarly large hamlets in the immediate vicinity (within 0.5 to 2 km distance) (Fig. 12.4). The coastal orientation of sites like Priniatikos Pyrgos, Khalepa, Gournia, and Mochlos, exchange patterns, and differentiation of grave goods from known excavated contexts (Watrous and Schultz 2012) seem dissociated from the settlement structure in the hinterland. Thus, I am not saying that Phaistos, Hagia Triada, Platanos, Gournia and Priniatikos Pyrgos are not different from the hamlets, or important special-function sites; I just do not think that they all functioned in the same way at the same time (Tomkins and Schoep 2010: esp. 72–74), or that there is a meaningful rural pattern of concentric or systemic dependence of the smaller sites, that points to a clear territorial interdependence. While they might have sociopolitical or economic importance in the region, the apparent structure of settlement in the hinterland is probably not a result of their function; although for the Mesara, Todaro (2012) has suggested that at the end of EM I the substantial Prepalatial buildings at Phaistos were abandoned presumably for hamlets in the vicinity, only to be revisited for ceremonial purposes. In east Crete, however, the coastal sites (Khalepa, Mochlos, Gournia, Priniatikos Pyrgos) look like examples of Branigan's (1991) gateway communities (Fig. 12.5), or transshipment, trading, or industrial centres, Poros-like towns, operating with a degree of independence of in-land centres (cf. Day and Wilson 2002; Tomkins and Schoep 2010: 72).

As in the western Mesara, none of the assumed primary centres in the north Isthmus shows significant diachronic settlement development in a spatially-ordered hierarchy of emerging centrifugal dispersal and dependence. Even in the Gournia valley itself, the difference in the pattern looks more like a matter of scale: the individual units are bigger, operating in a proportionately larger micro-region (Fig. 12.4). The socioeconomic patterns of trade, differentiation of wealth in excavated cemeteries (Mochlos and Gournia), and even the position of villages (Vasiliki, Alykomouri, or Kavousi) do not map easily onto the settlement structure in a way that suggests regional integration that we associate with linear hierarchies (Fig. 12.5). So what do the patterns tell us?

They strongly suggest highly localised and internal centripetal developments; entrenched and static structures exploiting micro-regions, and remarkably long-term adherence to local social landscapes that are reproduced or replicated, almost identically, across the sample areas. This kind of long-lived localisation might be reflected in the patterns of tomb use as well, perhaps mirroring aspects of settlement development.

Other relevant material patterns

Lack of clear hierarchies, as well as consistent and homogeneous mortuary behaviour, characterise the distribution of tombs in the Mesara (Relaki 2004; Legarra Herrero

2009). Branigan has pointed out not only the close relationship between settlement sites and cemeteries, but also the stability and integrity of the local communities maintaining funerary cults (Branigan 1998: 21). Joanne Murphy (1998: 28–31) goes a step further in stressing the longevity and continuity of tomb use, as well as its relationship to a physical locale. Though she recognises evidence of chronological discontinuity, she argues convincingly for a continuous ideology of community, a consciousness of the place itself, which must take into account the development of lineage groups and real social relationships on variable scales (cf. Relaki 2004: 172–73; Legarra Herrero 2009: 33–34). Such modes of interaction are complicated and are harder to measure or identify archaeologically, than, for example, predictive models of normal bilateral population growth of nuclear families within hypothetical agricultural catchment areas, or the assumed, but yet weakly modelled, social implications of topographic proximity and hierarchy of settlement sizes.

More recently, Maria Relaki (2004:181–183) has emphasised this localised pattern in the Mesara, seeing collective identities marked by increased competition and factionalism in EM II. While I do not disagree with the potential importance of the proliferation of tombs and increased elaboration of social competition, I am not convinced of the lack of post-funerary or extra-funerary rituals at tomb sites in EM I, nor that the trend (if we are really comfortable with the chronology of tomb use) necessarily indicates a new pattern of fragmentation *per se* or lack of regional integration in EM II. The developed EM II pattern could, to the contrary, emphasise the continuity, importance, and perhaps enhanced articulation of local identities on an expanding regional scale, which might correspond to intensified social contacts and regional interaction, perhaps a growing complexity of regional or supra-local social bonds, connections, and of course kinship ties that would lead to increased formalisation and expression of local cult practices and social rituals. Similarly, Legarra Herrero's (2009) analysis of regional mortuary cultures in the Prepalatial presents the Mesara as a coherent and homogeneous cultural landscape, in which intraregional links would have formed integrated structures.

This ambivalence or incongruity of interpretations of settlement data discussed above is I think essential to the inherent structures demonstrated by the patterns. So while Watrous wants to see greater integration in EM II based on a slightly more developed settlement hierarchy and economic differentiation of primary centres, Relaki paints a picture of increased localism and fragmentation of community identities. While I have argued before that a way of getting around the incongruity is to radically reshape our definition and rethink the nature of integration (Haggis 2002), Relaki's picture of the Mesara is nevertheless compelling; the pattern of both settlement and cemeteries could tell us however that there was increased interaction between pre-existing social regions or communities. That is we might visualise the pattern as resulting from competitive emulation, a kind of peer-polity interaction, but on multiple and replicated small scales. A proliferation of tholoi in the Mesara in EM IIA would then mean less a formation or consolidation of a new structure, than an intensification of inter- and intra-regional interaction. But even in those instances where we can define new settlement development and tomb construction, and discontinuous re-use of settlements and tombs, we are probably seeing a re-articulation of long-established identities in the landscape (in Murphy's terms an "ideology of community"), a reassertion of local claims to the landscape, its history and resources, in response to an intensification of wider concentric but variable social interactions.

The question still remains as to the meaning of the dispersed pattern, if the functional relationships between small settlement groups are not likely to have been an economically-ranked centrifugal dispersal of sites dependent on primary centres. This notion of primary centres is formed from presumed redistributive functions of staple-finance and surplus management; the centralisation of power hierarchies that mobilised resources and population, developed and monopolised wealth finance, and redirected labour toward strategies of various kinds of economic specialisation and intensification. In the cases discussed here, such a system would centre on sites poised for access to external exchange, like in east Crete (Figs. 12.4, 12.5); or in the Mesara (Fig. 12.1), sites located to control the best arable. The weakness of the model (and the ultimate effectiveness of the interpretations derived from survey) is perhaps that the resultant settlement patterns in the hinterlands are very similar if not identical throughout the island, and do little to inflect a dominant top-down hierarchical model.

The main problem is that the pattern is static, and growth, if it is really significant at all, is local and localised, centring on hamlets, about 0.2 to 0.5 ha in size, which in my view are probably functionally indistinguishable from some of the farms and even many of the so-called villages. It may be that, in survey, we do not really know how to deal with such small-scale and localised configurations or to model regional or interregional integration without evidence of larger-scale differentiation of units that is, to model real complexity, integrated and multilateral social/cultic, and political/economic interactions on multiple scales.

In spite of nearly a half century of intensive survey we still tend to look at the site itself, the partially excavated site or individual building, as a basic diagnostic unit, whose definition becomes an analytical template with an exclusive identity (and explanatory force), normally functioning in our narratives without specific social models. That is to say, the problem may not be in the identification of the basic social unit, but in modelling the relationships between basic units on variable organisational and spatial scales. The other problem is of course the notion of hierarchy (Haggis 2002). In the diachronically static structures at Gournia, Vrokastro, and Mesara, ranking suggests spatial relationships between sites with very little dependency beyond two levels at any scale. This is not to say that definition of domestic units on the local scale, and analyses of hierarchical relationships on a regional scale are not without value. I just think that we lack a developed body of theory or realm of analogy to expose the real social complexities of the patterns and therefore the structure.

The essential static pattern may also appear in other effective scales of analysis. Similar to the problem of hierarchy in the region, we have long struggled with the lack of clear distinctions in the differentiation of social units within Prepalatial settlements. What we normally see in the excavated sample is a kind of integrated built environment with a vaguely-defined communal character that finds parallel expression in collective burials in the mortuary sphere. Early on Branigan pictured Myrtos Phournou Koriphi, like Vasiliki, as a "mansion" of sorts, an architecturally unified household of a leader (1970: 48–49). A decade or so later, following Todd Whitelaw's articulation of individual domestic units in 1983 (cf. Whitelaw 2007), the excavator Peter Warren (1987: 52) remained surprisingly steadfast in his view that Phournou Koriphi represented a collective of interrelated groups, "an extended family or clan", emphasising the "close knit, interdependent, communal character..." of the settlement. Although Branigan, Warren and Whitelaw's very different impressions of the site, and indeed of Vasiliki, were never necessarily mutually exclusive, – at least without a scale-dependent and reductive social model to predict material correlates of our notional terms village, hamlet, mansion, or house – what was compelling about the site to the excavator was its essential agglomerative form, its tightly constructed cellular structure, indeed the lack of freestanding houses. Warren's point is interesting and emphasises the essential static nature of Prepalatial settlement; in the landscape this could then manifest itself in various scales and sizes of individual kinship-corporate groups, notional households or broadly conceptual *oikoi*. The few excavated Prepalatial settlements that we have seem to reflect the same kind of slow growth and static – in my view constant, long-lived, entrenched, and integrated – structure that is apparent in the regional patterns. Archaeological and ethnographic analogies present diverse and complex potentially valid models, such as "established houses", and "multilocal house-groups" (Driessen 2010), or similarly-structured agglomerative compounds indicating the corporate exploitation of land that is reflected in both the structure of settlement and the palaeobotanical and landscape data for Early Iron Age and Archaic Greece, where we are perhaps on firmer ground (Foxhall 2003: esp. 83–85).

A few years ago in the Langford Conference, Jan Driessen (2010), applied the idea of the "established house" to Minoan Crete as a social-conceptual term, arguing that Minoan agglutinative compounds could represent intergenerational and locus-bound groups; he stressed the continuity and permanence suggested by the architectural forms; the localisation of the social group, continuity of place, and the connection between the physical locus of building and the surrounding landscape as a condition engendering and sustaining ideas of kinship and social identities. Relevant to our discussion here is that Driessen visualised Vasiliki as representing two or three such houses, and Myrtos, a single house. Along very similar lines, Knappett (2009) understood different Minoan house sizes to reflect different effective scales of kinship structure; that is, different levels of similarly-structured units within regional hierarchies. The fractal-like replication of structures in the Prepalatial patterns echoes Knappett's developed palatial landscape, but on smaller scale, or perhaps earlier stage;

palatial integration, if we continue to use this term (Haggis 2002), might be seen as a continuous and gradual scaling up of basic organisational units that manifest initially in the hamlets and villages of early Prepalatial.

I am not suggesting that Prepalatial settlements do not grow or contract in size, go out of use or be re-used and rebuilt, but they adhere to regular patterns of agglomerative and integrated structuring of space, and the orientation and juxtaposition of units over long periods of time. While wall abutment and bonding are wholly unreliable indicators of long-term phasing of settlement development, if lacking stratigraphic corroboration (cf. Whitelaw 1983; restated in 2007), the use of contiguous construction, superimposed orientation of wall lines, and even respect for common spaces, such as the paved courts at Vasiliki, suggest a consciousness of space and perhaps continuity of use of space, and an awareness of the community as a historically constant and unified built environment. As an aside, I would contrast the Minoan *static* form with mainland "prepalatial" patterns (such as Lerna, Eutresis, Hagios Stephanos, or Asine) which are distinctly *dynamic* in character, chronologically variable, if not perpetually interrupted, emphasising a constant and inter-generational transmission and negotiation of social space by intramural burial, and the placement and demarcation of individual freestanding houses, courtyards, and household units in a kind of emphatic and strategic reassertion and articulation of social barriers of different nuclear households within the settlement.

On Crete, the static installations in the landscape are the hamlets and villages of the dispersed regional patterns derived through survey, and maybe our real problem is first in attributing social, economic, or political significance to such small-scale social units (Whitelaw's [1983] five or six families), sites that normally, in a top-down approach, appear to us as the lower- (if not lowest-) level in-filling of the countryside; residual symptoms of the political and economic centralisation, that we imagine for large sites like Knossos, Hagia Triada or Phaistos; or the villages in east Crete that seem to be the top of the replicated hierarchies in the survey data presented here. In diachronic analyses, we insist that smaller sites should be an outgrowth of bigger sites, and the result of settlement dispersal, rather than a form of primary settlement development.

Conclusions

In order to understand settlement structure as a long-term social process, rather than a result of economic expansion or sociopolitical centralisation, we need to sort out what constitutes distinctive assemblages that could help to explain regional functions, comparing or contrasting them with that of communal tombs, and putative scaled-up, regional, or ceremonial centres (Tomkins and Schoep 2010; Tomkins, this volume; Todaro 2009; 2012). Indeed we may be faced with evidence of the replication of activities in hamlets, centres, and cemeteries, showing considerable fluidity of social behaviour; and differences in the scale or type of the occasion, rather than clearly or neatly differentiated functions. At this juncture, it is important to keep in mind that assemblages that we associate with communal or diacritical ceremonial activities, such as pottery and special drinking vessels (Day and Wilson 2002; Catapoti 2011); kernoi; seals and sealings (Relaki 2009; 2012); copper implements, and objects with presumably necrotaphic contexts of consumption and meanings (cf. Papadatos 2007; Dimopoulou-Rethemiotaki, Wilson and Day 2007) appear in diverse contexts in settlement sites as well, including the smallest hamlet-sized communities.

For one example, Relaki (2009: 361–62; 2012) has shown that seal iconography in Prepalatial has both emblematic and assertive functions in multiple ritualised venues. As both group and individual emblems, seals were deposited in tombs as a form of ritual rationing, impeding the diffusion of symbolic value away from corporate groups and their connections to specific locales in the landscape; that is, the process of deposition was an active process of cultural localisation. The localising tendency of iconographic clusters in the Mesara (Sbonias 1999), where seals are connected with specific social groups and their claims to land and resources (Relaki 2009), accords well with the conservatism and longevity of the dispersed pattern of small-scale settlement. The social dynamics of interaction (competition, *vel sim*) on a regional scale could be visualised as a deliberate process of displaying and reaffirming connections to places, perhaps a local dynamic that was replicated by peer communities on various scales. If the essential group was the household, then we might expect that it would establish modes of interaction and create patterns of behaviour around and between such units, catalysing and reinforcing the entrenchment, continuity, and replication of local social groups through time and space, resulting in the apparently durable, stable and undifferentiated settlement patterns observable in the survey data.

What we will probably find in the first instance is repeated kinds of assemblages suggesting activities operating in different scales of participation, with social meanings that are recreated in various forms across the landscape. I would like to see them centring at the most basic level, perhaps the smallest social unit, at these hamlets, with their tombs and dependent farms and field sites. That is, we will need to remodel the social identity and political and economic significance of these hamlet-sized settlements and their farms, and their relationship with the wider region.

On the regional scale, the uniform spacing and clustering of lower-level sites, indeed even the proliferation of so-called farm and field sites, suggest a localised development of social groups of various sizes, probably kinship groups, over long periods time; these are not necessarily unbroken contiguous lineages, but interrelated configurations with common connections to specific real or reinvented lineages centring on specific locales in the landscape. The process of growth, if we could measure it, would probably have been centripetal, internal, and internalising, in a sense accruing population within a vast number of micro-regions. Growth and dispersal, such as the continual creation and reproduction of hamlets, farms and field sites, would have happened irrespective of primary centres, but in direct response to social interaction with similarly-configured groups across the regions. Such interactions, even competitive negotiations, would have shaped, maintained, and perhaps even contained the spatial boundaries of the EM community.

Bibliography

Blackman, D. and K. Branigan

1977 An archaeological survey of the lower catchment of the Ayiofarango Valley. *Annual of the British School at Athens* 72: 13–84.

Branigan, K.

1970 *The Foundations of Palatial Crete. A Survey of Crete in the Early Bronze Age*. London: Routledge and Paul Kegan.

1991 Mochlos: An early Aegean "gateway community"? In R. Laffineur and L. Basch (eds.), *Thalassa. L'Egée préhistorique et la mer* (Aegaeum 7): 97–105. Liège: Université de Liège.

1998 The nearness of you: Proximity and distance in Early Minoan funerary behaviour. In K. Branigan (ed.), *Cemetery and Society in the Aegean Bronze Age*. (Sheffield Studies in Aegean Archaeology 1): 13–26. Sheffield: Sheffield Academic Press.

Catapoti, D.

2011 Rise to the occasion: An insight into the "Politics of Drinking" at the Prepalatial settlement of Myrtos-Phournou Koryfi, South Crete. *Πεπραγμένα του Ι' Διεθνούς Κρητολογικού Συνεδρίου, Χανιά 1-8 Οκτωβρίου* 2006: 197–210. Χανιά: Φιλολογικός Σύλλογος "Ο Χρυσόστομος".

Cherry, J. F.

1983 Evolution, revolution, and the origins of complex society in Minoan Crete. In O. Krzyszkowska and L. Nixon (eds.), *Minoan Society. Proceedings of the Cambridge Colloquium 1981*: 33–45. Bristol: Bristol Classical Press.

Day, P. M. and R. C. P. Doonan (eds.)

2007 *Metallurgy in the Early Bronze Age Aegean* (Sheffield Studies in Aegean Archaeology 7). Oxford: Oxbow.

Day, P. M. and D. E. Wilson

2002 Landscapes of memory, craft and power in Pre-Palatial and Proto-Palatial Knossos. In Y. Hamilakis (ed.), *Labyrinth Revisited. Rethinking "Minoan" Archaeology*: 143–66. Oxford: Oxbow.

Dimopoulou-Rethemiotaki, N., D. E. Wilson and P. M. Day

2007 The earlier Prepalatial settlement of Poros-Katsambas: Craft production and exchange at the harbour town of Knossos. In P. M. Day and R. C. P. Doonan (eds.), *Metallurgy in the Early Bronze Age Aegean* (Sheffield Studies in Aegean Archaeology 7): 84–97. Oxford: Oxbow.

Driessen, J.

2001 History and hierarchy. Preliminary observations on the settlement pattern in Minoan Crete. In K. Branigan (ed.), *Urbanism in the Aegean Bronze Age* (Sheffield Studies in Aegean Archaeology 4): 51–71. London: Sheffield Academic Press.

2010 Spirit of Place: Minoan Houses as Major Actors. In D. J. Pullen (ed.), *Political Economies of the Aegean Bronze Age. Papers from the Langford Conference, Florida State University, Tallahassee, 22-24 February 2007*: 35–65. Oxford: Oxbow.

Foxhall, L.

2003 Cultures, landscapes, and identities in the Mediterranean world. *Mediterranean Historical Review*18: 75–92.

Haggis, D. C.

1999 Staple finance, peak sanctuaries, and economic complexity in late Prepalatial Crete. In A. Chaniotis (ed.), *From Minoan Farmers to Roman Traders: Sidelights on the Economy of Ancient Crete*: 53–85. Stuttgart: Franz Steiner Verlag.

2002 Integration and complexity in the late Pre-Palatial period. A view from the countryside in Eastern Crete. In Y. Hamilakis (ed.), *Labyrinth Revisited. Rethinking "Minoan" Archaeology*: 120–42. Oxford: Oxbow.

2005 *Kavousi. The Results of the Excavations at Kavousi in Eastern Crete I. The Archaeological Survey of the Kavousi Region* (Prehistory Monographs 16). Philadelphia: INSTAP Academic Press.

Hayden, B. J.

2004 *Reports on the Vrokastro Area, Eastern Crete, Vol. 2. The Settlement History of the Vrokastro Area and Related Studies* (University Museum Monograph 119). Philadelphia: University of Pennsylvania Museum of Archaeology and Anthropology.

Knappett, C.

2009 Scaling up: From household to state in Bronze Age Crete. In S. Owen and L. Preston (eds.), *Inside the City in the Greek World: Studies of Urbanism from the Bronze Age to the Hellenistic Period* (University of Cambridge Museum of Classical Archaeology Monographs 1): 14–26. Oxford: Oxbow.

Legarra Herrero, B.

2009 The Minoan fallacy: cultural diversity and mortuary behaviour on Crete at the beginning of the Bronze Age. *Oxford Journal of Archaeology 28*: 29–57.

Murphy, J. M.

1998 Ideology, rites and rituals: A view of Prepalatial Minoan tholoi. In K. Branigan (ed.), *Cemetery and Society in the Aegean Bronze Age* (Sheffield Studies in Aegean Archaeology 1): 27–40. Sheffield: Sheffield Academic Press.

Papadatos, Y.

2007 The beginning of metallurgy in Crete: New evidence from the FN-EM I settlement at Kephala Petras, Siteia. In P. M. Day and R. C. P. Doonan (eds.), *Metallurgy in the Early Bronze Age Aegean* (Sheffield Studies in Aegean Archaeology 7): 154–67. Oxford: Oxbow.

Relaki, M.

2004 Constructing a region: The contested landscapes of Prepalatial Mesara. In J. C. Barrett and P. Halstead (eds.), *The Emergence of Civilisation Revisited* (Sheffield Studies in Aegean Archaeology 6): 170–88. Oxford: Oxbow.

2009 Rethinking administration and seal use in third millennium Crete. *Creta Antica* 10: 353–72.

2012 The social arenas of tradition. Investigating collective and individual social strategies in the Prepalatial and Protopalatial Mesara. In P. Tomkins, I. Schoep, and J. Driessen (eds.), *Back to the Beginning. Reassessing Social, Economic and Political Complexity in the Early and Middle Bronze Age on Crete. Proceedings of an International Workshop, Leuven 1-2 February 2008*: 290–324. Oxford: Oxbow.

Sbonias, K.

1999 Social development, management of production, and symbolic representation in Prepalatial Crete. In A. Chaniotis (ed.), *From Minoan Farmers to Roman Traders: Sidelights on the Economy of Ancient Crete*: 25–51. Stuttgart: Franz Steiner Verlag.

Schoep, I.

1999 The origins of writing and administration in Crete. *Oxford Journal of Archaeology* 18: 265–76.

Terrenato, N.

2004 Sample size matters! The paradox of global trends and local surveys. In S. Alcock and J. Cherry (eds.), *Side-by-Side Survey: Comparative Regional Studies in the Mediterranean World*: 36–48. Oxford: Oxbow.

Todaro, S.

2009 The latest Prepalatial period and the foundation of the first Palace at Phaistos: A stratigraphic and chronological re-assessment. *Creta Antica* 10: 105–45.

2012 Craft production and social practices at Prepalatial Phaistos: The background to the first "Palace". In P. Tomkins, I. Schoep, and J. Driessen (eds.), *Back to the Beginning. Reassessing*

Social, Economic and Political Complexity in the Early and Middle Bronze Age on Crete. Proceedings of an International Workshop, Leuven 1–2 February 2008: 195–235. Oxford: Oxbow.

Tomkins, P. and I. Schoep

2010 Early Bronze Age. Crete. In E. H. Cline (ed.), *The Oxford Handbook of the Bronze Age Aegean*: 66–82. Oxford: Oxford University Press.

Warren, P. M.

1987 The genesis of the Minoan palace. In R. Hägg and N. Marinatos (eds.), *The Function of the Minoan Palaces. Proceedings of the Fourth International Symposium at the Swedish Institute in Athens, 10–16 June, 1984*. (Swedish Institute in Athens, Series in 4°, 35): 47–56. Stockholm: Swedish Institute in Athens.

Watrous, L. V.

1982 *Lasithi. A History of a Settlement on a Highland Plain in Crete* (Hesperia Supplement 18). Princeton: American School of Classical Studies at Athens.

2001 Crete from earliest prehistory through the Protopalatial period. In T. Cullen (ed.), *Aegean Prehistory: A Review* (*AJA Supplement* I): 157–215. Boston: Archaeological Institute of America (reprint of *AJA* 98.4 [1994]: 695–753).

Watrous, L. V. and D. Hadzi-Vallianou

2004 Emergence of a ranked society (Early Minoan II-III). In L. V. Watrous, D. Hadzi-Vallianou and H. Blitzer (eds.) *The Plain of Phaistos: Cycles of Social Complexity in the Mesara Region of Crete* (Monumenta Archaeologica 23): 233–52. Los Angeles: The Cotsen Institute of Archaeology at UCLA.

Watrous, L. V. and M. Schultz

2012 Early Minoan I–II period: Emergence of a stratified society. In L. V. Watrous, D. Haggis, K. Nowicki, N. Vogeikoff-Brogan, and M. Schultz, *An Archaeological Survey of the Gournia Landscape: A Regional History of the Mirabello Bay, Crete, in Antiquity* (Prehistory Monographs 37): 21–31. Philadelphia: INSTAP Academic Press.

Whitelaw, T. M.

1983 The settlement at Fournou Korifi, Myrtos and aspects of Early Minoan social organization. In O. Krzyszkowska and L. Nixon (eds.) *Minoan Society. Proceedings of the Cambridge Colloquium 1981*: 323–45. Bristol: Bristol Classical Press.

2007 House, households and community at Early Minoan Fournou Korifi: methods and models for interpretation. In R. Westgate, N. Fisher and J. Whitley (eds.), *Building Communities: House, Settlement and Society in the Aegean and Beyond, Proceedings of a Conference held at Cardiff University, 17–21 April 2001* (BSA Studies 15): 65–76. London: British School at Athens.

Chapter 13

Comparative issues in archaeological field survey in the Asterousia region

Andonis Vasilakis and Kostas Sbonias

In the early 1970s a new wave of survey research was inaugurated in Greece with two survey projects in small peripheral areas. Jameson's survey in the south-west Argolid in 1972 (Jameson *et al.* 1994) and Blackman and Branigan's survey of the Agiopharango valley in Crete in 1971–72 (Blackman and Branigan 1977). Although they were both small-scale projects in backwater areas, the crucial novelty was the application of an intensive methodology without preconceptions about favourable locations for site recovery. By limiting the geographical scope of the older topographic tradition, this new generation of surveys could reveal information missed by less detailed approaches, fill in the gaps in the archaeological record and create a basis for analyzing processes at the local level (cf. Cherry 1983; 1994; Bintliff 1994; 2000; Barker and Mattingly 1999–2000; Alcock and Cherry 2004).

Blackman and Branigan's choice to study a small and self-contained geographical unit, the lower catchment of the Agiopharango valley, arose from the looting of the area and the necessity to protect the sites due to road construction activities. Along with the previous work of Branigan on the Mesara tombs (Branigan 1970), it pioneered regional research in Crete and transferred the discussion to processes at the local level. In terms of methodology, rather than choosing a sampling strategy the lower catchment of the Agiopharango was conceived as a unit of research, on the basis of environmental and geographical criteria, with the goal to study changing social and economic patterns in the valley through time and establish the natural environment of this occupation (Blackman and Branigan 1977: 13). Full recovery of sites to the extent that it is possible by intensive survey, study of the recorded sites in their physical landscape, association of burial sites with neighbouring habitation and potential cultivable land, and discussion of the changing patterns of human settlement and demography in the valley were the main topics of the report that appeared in 1977.

The aim of the present paper is to look in a comparative way at the archaeological surface surveys that were undertaken in the area focusing on the Bronze Age and to discuss issues raised by Blackman and Branigan in their first paper. Comparative data, apart from the Agiopharango survey and the short survey of the south coast in the area of Kaloi Limenes and Lasaia (Blackman and Branigan 1975), are offered by the extensive reconnaissance research of Vasilakis in the western part of the Asterousia region (Vasilakis 1989–90), Vasilakis' and Branigan's intensive survey at Moni Odigitria in the upper catchment of the Agiopharango valley (Branigan and Vasilakis 2010: 3–27) and finally, the recent intensive survey in the Trypiti gorge by Sbonias and Vasilakis.

A review of archaeological survey research in the Asterousia region

A main characteristic of the Asterousia region back in the 1970s, and to a large extent even today, is its remote character and the lack of modern development and infrastructure which could have altered the landscape. This resulted in a high degree of preservation of the archaeological record on the surface, but on the other hand, led to an enormous degree of looting which destroyed the archaeological context of many sites (Sakellarakis 1965: 562–64; Alexiou 1967a: 482–84), leaving in many cases simple dots on a map to represent badly dated tholos cemeteries (Fig. 13.1). Information on settlement was almost non-existent (for the association of cemetery and settlement sites, see Branigan 1998: 14–19, table 1). Archaeological rescue excavations followed in most cases illicit tomb robbing, e.g. by Alexiou at Hagia Kyriaki, Megaloi Skinoi, Kaloi Limenes and Lebena (Alexiou 1967a), by Davaras at Kaloi Limenes, Lasaia and Skaniari Lakkos (Alexiou 1963: 312; Davaras 1968: 405–06), by Sakellarakis at Agiopharango and Hagia Kyriaki (Sakellarakis 1965: 562–64), by Dimopoulou and Vasilakis at Moni Odigitria (Vasilakis and Branigan 2010), and by Vasilakis at Krotos (Vasilakis 1983) and Skaniari Lakkos (Vasilakis 1994–96). Yet with the exception of the Lebena (Alexiou and Warren 2004) and the Moni Odigitria cemeteries (Vasilakis and Branigan 2010), the Hagia Kyriaki burial complex (Blackman and Branigan 1982) and the more recent excavation at Skaniari Lakkos by Vasilakis (Vasilakis 1989–90: 50–56; Saltos 2000), this work neither resulted in full excavation and publication of the sites, nor did it put an end to the illicit excavations.

The survey of the lower catchment of the Agiopharango valley (Blackman and Branigan 1977) was thus the first attempt to place the Early Minoan sites, some of them already known by previous research, within a context and to investigate the settlements and social units associated with the graves. By studying the physical environment and the distribution of graves and potential cultivable land, it became clear that the valley could be divided into smaller landscape units, each one associated with several related families sharing the use of a single communal tholos tomb. A number of dispersed settlement units, farmsteads and/or hamlets, and a larger village in the area of Megaloi Skinoi were associated with each individual cemetery (Fig. 13.1).

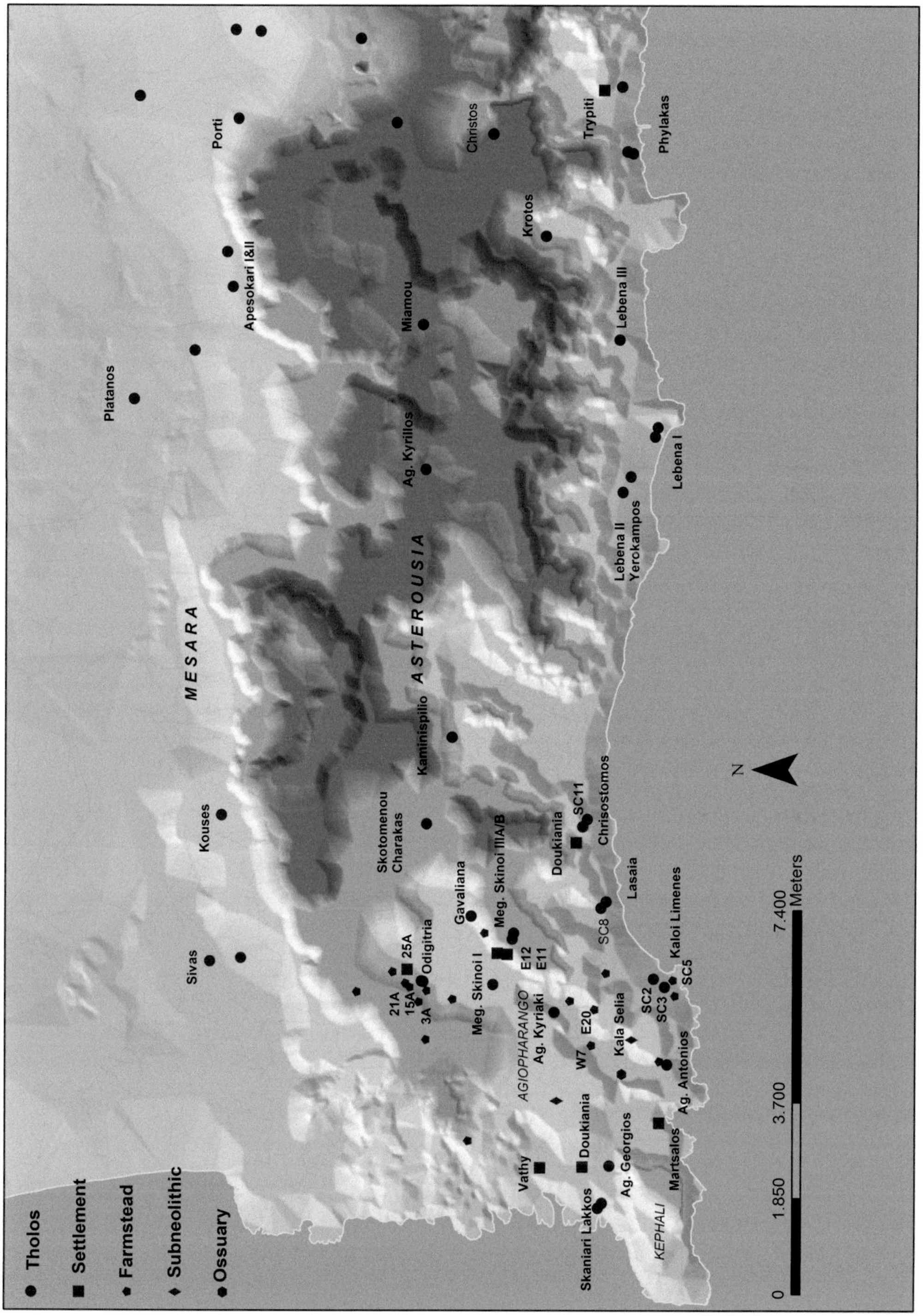

Figure 13.1: The western Mesara and Asterousia region, showing Minoan sites mentioned in the text (figure produced by the authors).

Part of the work undertaken was also the excavation of the looted burial complex at Hagia Kyriaki (Blackman and Branigan 1982), with three farms ascribed to it (Fig. 13.1: E5, E20 and W7). The excavation enriched our knowledge of the Prepalatial period in the Asterousia region and documented the earliest phases of permanent settlement in the valley. Structures which underlay the tholos included Final Neolithic and EM I wares and the appearance of similar isolated sherds on sites occupied by EM I tholoi suggested the first occupation of the Agiopharango should be placed in the Final Neolithic period.

This approach of surveying small landscape units on the basis of topographic criteria was continued by Blackman and Branigan in a complementary brief survey of the south coast between the Agiopharango and Chrysostomos in September 1971, which recorded three tholos cemeteries in the harbours of Kaloi Limenes and Lasaia (Fig. 13.1; Blackman and Branigan 1975). Two tholoi (SC2 and SC3) associated with a small farmstead (SC5) were recorded at Kaloi Limenes and two further examples (SC8) were located east of Kaloi Limenes, on the hillside of Lasaia (excavated by Davaras 1968: 405–06). Two more tholoi (SC11) were excavated near Chrysostomos (Blackman and Braninigan 1975: 32–34), in close proximity to the Minoan settlement of Doukiania. This settlement, which is located above the Greco-Roman town of Lasaia, was soon after investigated by Hatzi-Vallianou and Vasilakis in 1978, before it was totally destroyed by illegal excavators (Hatzi-Vallianou 1979a: 382–83). Further east the excavation of the Lebena tombs by Alexiou produced a comparable distribution of tholos cemeteries in association with strips of cultivable land along the coast near Lebena (Alexiou and Warren 2004).

Vasilakis' work in the wider area of the Asterousia started in 1978 with a series of rescue excavations in the Prepalatial cemeteries of Kouses (with Vallianou in 1978–9, cf. Hatzi-Vallianou 1979b), Moni Odigitria in 1980 (Vasilakis and Branigan 2010), Krotos in 1983 (Vasilakis 1983) and a short excavation at the settlement of Megaloi Skinoi in the same year (Vasilakis 1989–90: 39–45). The aim of his reconnaissance work was to compile an archaeological map of the prehistoric sites of the area, revisiting sites recorded by Blackman and Branigan in the south coast and the lower catchment of the Agiopharango and extending his topographic work to the north, to the upper catchment of the Agiopharango and the interior of the mountains, and to the west along the coast up to the Lithino promontory and the bay of Vathy (Fig. 13.1).

The results of this work, which can be characterised as a "one-man survey" were published in 1989 (Vasilakis 1989–90). On the basis of the topography and natural barriers, Vasilakis divided the area into six sub-regions which created suitable niches for habitation, characterised by small gorges and the bays into which they flow, their valleys and the surrounding slopes and hills (Vasilakis 1989–90: 68). He discussed the areas of Kaloi Limenes, lower Agiopharango, Hagia Kyriaki, Megaloi Skinoi, Moni Odigitria and Kephali-Vathy and identified the areas of Megaloi Skinoi, Kephali-Vathy and Moni Odigitria as the main foci of habitation. This approach had been followed already by Blackman and Branigan who had tried to relate burial sites to their neighbouring habitation sites and potential cultivable land and to identify territorial units, or catchment areas associated with "a number of clan or extended family holdings, each of which contained not only the group's communal tomb, but also either scattered farmsteads or small hamlets", with a small village community at Megaloi Skinoi (Blackman and Branigan 1977: 71).

Vasilakis' work confirmed the early habitation of the area through the identification of six new sites of the Final Neolithic (cf. Vasilakis 1987 for the publication of the house at Kala Selia). Of particular importance was the excavation of the settlement at Martsalos (Vasilakis 1996: 643–44) and of the settlement at Doukiania in 2001 (Vasilakis 1989–90: 56–58), close to the Pre- and Proto-palatial cemetery of Skaniari Lakkos, which was excavated during 1994/95 (Fig. 13.1). These sites indicated a divergent trajectory in this part of the south coast, characterised by a new cycle of development in the Proto- and Neo-palatial periods, in contrast to the picture of declining human occupation in the lower Agiopharango valley recorded by Blackman and Branigan between the MM I and LM I periods.

The Moni Odigitria area and processes at the local level

The next step in the archaeological research was to look more intensively at the various sub-regions by situating individual excavated sites in the context of their micro-region, creating windows into the landscape through systematic field survey. The excavation of the tholos cemeteries at Moni Odigitria and Skaniari Lakkos and of the settlements at Trypiti, Martsalos and Doukiania by Vasilakis provided more detailed in-depth information on selected sites of the region. Two intensive surveys, by Branigan and Vasilakis in 2002 at Moni Odigitria and a second one by Sbonias and Vasilakis at Trypiti in 2007 and 2008 attempted to link the evidence from these excavations with the surrounding landscape.

Considering the pattern and nature of human settlement in the western Asterousia, the Agiopharango survey had made important observations by recording evidence of contemporary settlement near every tomb or group of tombs (Branigan 1998: 15). The Moni Odigitria survey, which was organised as part of the publication of the Moni Odigitria cemetery, clarified further issues of habitation and occupation density in relation to the Prepalatial cemetery (Branigan and Vasilakis 2010: 3–27). It seems that dense agglomerate architecture is lacking from the area of the Moni Odigitria tholos graves in the Prepalatial period. Four localities of Prepalatial habitation (EM IIA) were identified in the immediate area north, north-west and south-west of the Prepalatial cemetery indicating a scatter of houses, some of them in small clusters of households (Fig. 13.1: sites 3A, 15A, 25A; cf. Branigan and Vasilakis 2010: 14–20, 26–27, fig. 3). Sites 3A and 25A seem to have been inhabited by several households, Site 15A appears to represent a single house and some additional EM occupation appears to have been south of the cemetery and close to the Moni Odigitria monastery itself. Overall it is suggested that 7–12 households were associated with these localities in the EM II period and a much smaller number in the FN-EM I, when the distribution of the material was much more restricted (Branigan and Vasilakis 2010: 26–27).

This scatter of houses agrees with the picture from the lower Agiopharango valley where dispersed farmsteads where associated with individual round tombs. Even in the vicinity of Megaloi Skinoi, which forms the largest habitation focus in the area, the surface material seems to have spread over a large area of 3.25 hectares, encircled by a wall which seems to have enclosed the scattered houses and some of the settlement's fertile land (Fig. 13.1 site E11; cf. Blackman and Branigan 1977: 41). At Megaloi Skonoi, another focus of habitation, interpreted initially by Blackman and Branigan as a peak sanctuary (site E12), is located on a conical hill to the north of the cemetery and, on the basis of the surface finds, seems to represent another focus of dispersed habitation in the area (Vasilakis 1989–90: 45–46: Megaloi Skinoi IV).

A scatter of houses with a low density of habitation was thus the usual form of settlement in this region. Yet despite their small size, these peripheral communities of the Asterousia appear in EM II to have hosted craft production involving a range of artefact types and media with a variety of morphological and decorative characteristics (Sbonias 2012: 276). As one of the authors has argued elsewhere on the basis of the occurrence of ivory seals at Moni Odigitria in the EM III-MM IA period, Moni Odigitria seems to have strengthened its character as a regional focus in the western Asterousia, participating in conspicuous consumption and power legitimation strategies practised by kinship groups in the wider region of south-central Crete (Sbonias 2010a; 2010b: 357–62; 2012: 280). Subsequently, in the MM I period, it appears as an agent of change and innovation, with the introduction of a new technique and style in seal production, characterised by the use of a white material imitative of Egyptian faience (Pini 1990; Sbonias 1995: 113–18; Krzyszkowska 2005: 72–74; Sbonias 2010a: 216–18). This new style encompasses Moni Odigitria as an obvious centre (i.e., 18 seals from the excavation and 24 from the Mitsotakis collection probably originating from the Odigitria tombs; see Sbonias 2010a: 216–18) and also the wider Kaloi Limenes area (seals from the Metaxas collection published by Sakellarakis and Kenna [1969] with the indication "Kaloi Limenes"). The association of certain communities with the production of a distinctive style of seals might reflect the integrative role of these communities at the local level as well as the absence of a strong influence from Phaistos on the Asterousia region. Access to external, long-distance trade networks via the south coast by agents related to the local elites might have been one factor influencing the distinct position of the western Asterousia in the MM I period (Sbonias 2012: 280–86).

This strengthening of particular communities at the end of the Prepalatial period and during the transition to the Protopalatial is also reflected in the nucleation trends observed in the settlement pattern. At Moni Odigitria the several Prepalatial foci of habitation were abandoned and habitation was restricted in two of them (Fig. 13.1: sites 3A and 25A) which expanded in the Protopalatial period. Site 25A at Aloniou Kephali seems to have grown into the main settlement with structures well spaced over an area of over 1.5 ha, while at site 21A a single significant building was erected (Branigan and Vasilakis 2010: 18–20, 26–27).

On the other hand, the Moni Odigitria burial complex seems to have gone out of use by the end of MM IB. This agrees with the picture drawn by Blackman and Branigan in the lower catchment of the Agiopharango, where two key sites, Megaloi Skinoi and Hagia Kyriaki, were also abandoned in this period (Blackman and Branigan 1977: 68). Blackman and Branigan suggested a two-stage process: a first stage of gradual abandonment in MM I-II and a second phase over MM III-LM I, when ties with the land were progressively weakened (Blackman and Branigan 1977: 68–69). They suggested that this decline may be explained by social and economic developments during this period, symbolised by the rise of the palaces. They also drew attention to the coastal towns of Crete that grew rapidly in the MM period, as part of these economic changes that were taking place. The evidence from Moni Odigitria survey does not suggests a decline, but rather nucleation processes taking place at certain settlement sites, which expanded during the MM period, while rapid decline in the area is observed after MM III (Branigan and Vasilakis 2010: 27). Yet in other areas of the Asterousia these trends were followed by a new cycle of transformation of the landscape, which involved settlement growth in coastal areas and selected harbour sites. The recent survey at Trypiti threw additional light on these processes.

The Trypiti survey

The Trypiti survey gave us the opportunity to consider more fully the periods succeeding the Prepalatial habitation of the region (Fig. 13.2). Here we surveyed a small landscape unit associated with the Prepalatial settlement of Trypiti (Vasilakis 1990; 1995; 2010). The survey, apart from identifying the limits of the Prepalatial settlement with the addition of habitation terraces surrounding the main peak, showed that the excavated settlement at Adami Korphali was only one element in a complex landscape, which involved many communities in a diachronic pattern of habitation. The lower part of the Trypiti gorge, the surrounding mountain slopes, the upper and especially the lower terraces by the coast which represent the available areas of arable land and the small bay into which the gorge flows, create a landscape unit around the small sheltered bay of Trypiti that was inhabited and exploited in several periods in antiquity, from the EM to the Hellenistic period. Today the area is deserted and totally oriented to pastoralism.

In terms of methodology we followed an intensive non-site approach with a continuous recording of the remains on the surface by teams of field walkers. Pottery was recorded in 50m long transects with regular distances between the field walkers (usually 15m) and a collection grid of 10×10m was applied in areas with structural remains (Fig. 13.2). The circumstances at Trypiti are ideal for this kind of research because of the lack of modern occupation, the low vegetation and the wind erosion that brings to the surface not only sherd scatters, but also structural remains

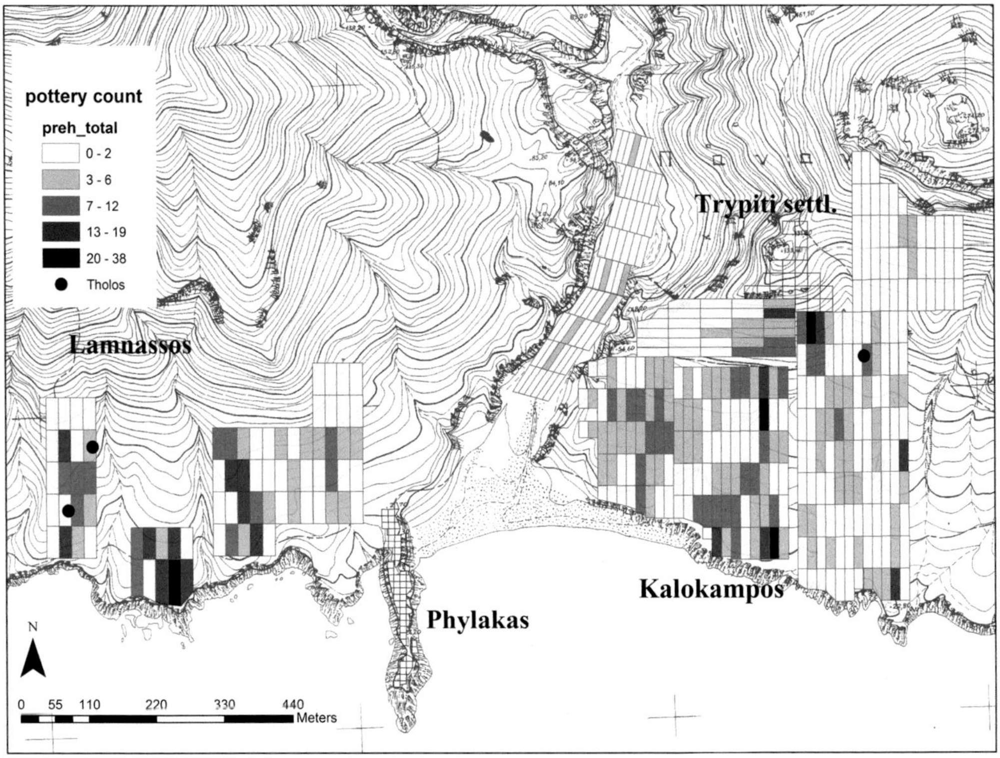

Figure 13.2: The distribution of prehistoric pottery in the Trypiti survey (figure produced by the authors on the basis of the archaeological field survey conducted by Sbonias and Vasilakis). Map densities indicate ranges of raw count of sherds collected in 50m long and 1m wide transects.

(Fig. 13.3). Figure 13.2 displays the distribution of pottery characterised broadly as prehistoric in the preliminary study and consists, with the exception of some foci of Prepalatial pottery, mainly of MM-LM material (raw counts in 50m long and 1m wide transects).

We started the research in the area of Kalokampos, known in the bibliography as the location of the Prepalatial tholos tomb of Trypiti (Fig. 13.2). It is an extended, relatively flat plateau that starts immediately south of the Prepalatial settlement and reaches to the coast where it falls abruptly into the sea. The survey revealed a wide distribution of Minoan pottery in the form of an almost continuous carpet of material in an area of approximately 17 ha, which indicates a shift in habitation after the abandonment of the Prepalatial settlement. The pottery density and the distinct scatters of material indicate a scatter of houses over the entire area of the plateau, with gaps between the houses for agricultural exploitation. The visible architectural remains that were recorded confirm the association of areas with high density of material with the location of houses (Fig. 13.3). The visible remains of the buildings are usually 10–12m long and half as wide, with two visible rooms in some cases. A

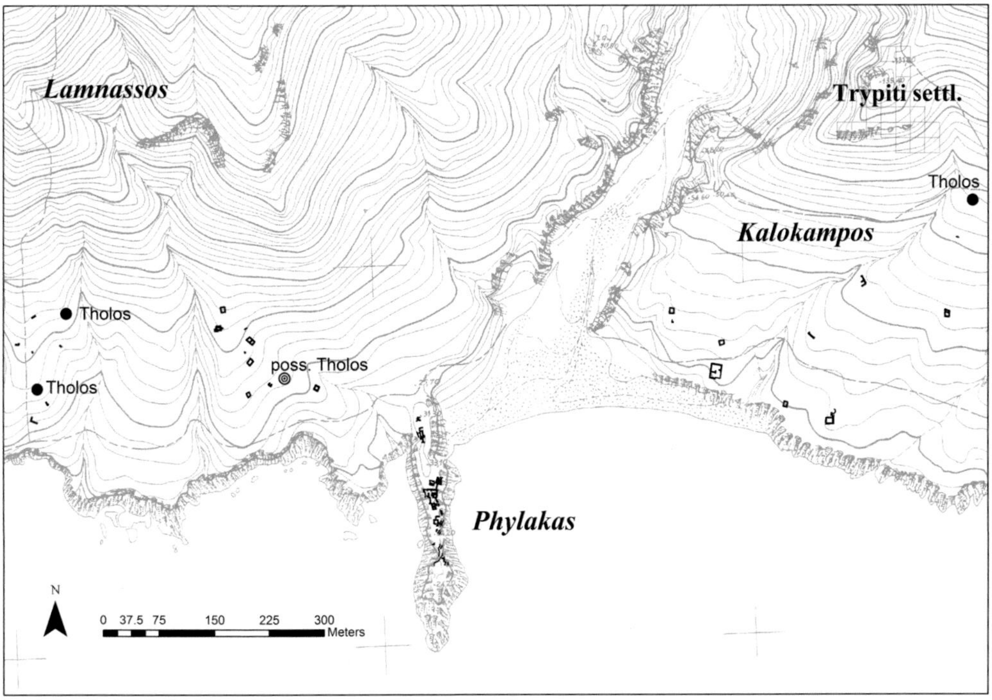

Figure 13.3: Structural remains visible on the surface in the Trypiti area (topographic recording by Emeri Farinetti).

larger structure, built on the lower terraces of the plateau near the cliff measures 20 × 15m. As many buildings have been destroyed by cultivation in the past, it is the distribution of the pottery that gives an indication of the size of the settlement and the actual habitation density. The scatter of material is characterised broadly as MM-LM, with recognisable MM and especially LM pottery associated with many structures. Prepalatial material is confined to the upper slopes close to the Prepalatial settlement and the tholos tomb and is generally absent from the lower slopes of the Kalokampos plateau. There is therefore a clear spatial separation between the dense Prepalatial habitation at Trypiti Adami Korphali and the dispersed houses of the Palatial periods across the entire plateau.

Continuation of the research in 2008 brought to light further evidence of dense habitation in the area of Trypiti. On the west side of the Trypiti gorge, on the mountain slopes above and to the west of the promontory of Phylakas, an extended distribution of Minoan pottery is recorded associated with a dispersed arrangement of rectangular buildings on the slopes and the lower terraces by the coast, similar to that at Kalokampos (Fig. 13.2). Here the architectural remains on the slope are better preserved and indicate a distance of 20 to 30–35 m between the buildings (Fig. 13.3). The pottery associated with the buildings is mainly MM and LM but EM I and EM II material was also found on the surrounding slopes. A circular structure in this area might also indicate the existence of a possible tholos.

This distribution of pottery seems to have continued to the east around the spring on the slope above the promontory of Phylakas, today a bulldozed area which was not covered by the survey. In this area Evans had recorded MM II and LM I pottery and had found a fragment of a clay larnax inscribed with Linear A signs (Evans 1928: 83–84 and figs. 39–40). The presence of burials in this area cannot be excluded, yet the main character of the finds on the slopes north-west of Phylakas indicates rather dispersed habitation of a comparable nature to that recorded at the plateau of Kalokampos. It seems that two foci of habitation were developed on either side of the gorge with similar features: clusters of houses, well spaced buildings, positioned on the lower slopes and terraces towards the coastal cliff. The gorge seems to create a boundary, as is also the case today with the two modern villages sharing the bay of Trypiti.

This fragmentation of the landscape goes back certainly to the Pre-palatial period. The Trypiti settlement at Adami Korfali as well as the Pre-palatial tholos tomb at Kalokampos create a distinct focus of presence in this period east of Trypiti gorge. On the west side of the gorge EM I-II pottery occurs on the slopes northwest of Phylakas. A further 300 m to the west two more tholos tombs are located on the slopes of the same ridge with a distance of around 100 m between them, investigated by Vasilakis in the past (Vasilakis 2000: 124). Scattered houses in relation to these graves were recorded by the survey (Fig. 13.3). These architectural remains, which are less well preserved on the surface, in comparison to the buildings of the palatial periods at Kalokampos and above Phylakas, seem to form two clusters. If related to the tholos tombs, they may support the suggestion of proximity of cemetery and settlement in the Prepalatial period. This picture of dispersed habitation agrees with the evidence from Moni Odigitria and the lower catchment of Agiopharango, and differs from the dense agglomeration of houses at the Prepalatial settlement of Trypiti.

In the Protopalatial period, apart from the scattered MM presence on both sides of the Trypiti bay, a remarkable development took place on the rocky promontory of Phylakas on the west side of Trypiti bay, where a harbour settlement was established (Figs. 13.2–3). A trial trench by Vasilakis in one of the houses suggested MM II as the main period of development, continuing in MM III (Vasilakis 1991–93: 295–96). During the survey the whole promontory was gridded and both MM and LM pottery was recorded and collected. The settlement follows the dense agglomeration of houses, also known from other palatial settlements on Crete. The distribution of the surface material and the recording of the architectural remains, which are preserved remarkably well on the surface, cover an area of approximately 1 ha and the site falls in the lower edge of the third level of urban hierarchy proposed by Branigan (2001: 40–41), which includes coastal settlements such as Mochlos, Pseira, Priniatikos Pyrgos and others. We could suppose a link of this area with wider political structures and the use of Phylakas as harbour for trade networks along the south coast.

Settlement trends along the south coast in the MM and LM periods

Summarising the settlement trends in the Asterousia region, we could suggest that the regression in the MM and LM periods recorded in the surveys of the western Asterousia may reflect actual social processes. The evidence seems to indicate that in inland areas there was indeed a gradual regression with nucleation processes taking place during the MM, followed by a rapid decline in settlement numbers in the LM period. Both the abandonment of many tholos tombs in the Agiopharango, the nucleation at Megaloi Skinoi and Moni Odigitria and their succeeding abandonment after MM III point towards this. On the other hand, divergent trajectories can be noticed in the coastal areas. The Trypiti survey indicates a remarkable continuation of habitation in the area and the relocation of settlement closer to the sea in less defensible positions after the abandonment of the Trypiti settlement. Such shifts in habitation (combined with the growth of the Neopalatial settlement of Doukiania in the Kephali area of western Asterousia: see below) as well as a change in burial customs with the abandonment of the tholos cemeteries and the adoption of rectangular ossuaries/house-tombs (Skaniari Lakkos, possible ossuaries at Moni Odigitria at Kephali Hagios Ioannis and at Agiopharango) might be a factor behind the picture of gradual abandonment of the Prepalatial settlement sites and circular tombs in the Asterousia region. Furthermore, it seems that a new cycle of development took place along the south coast during the advanced Protopalatial period, which involved the coastal areas and selected harbour sites. In the Trypiti bay the prominent harbour settlement of Phylakas was established at least in the MM II period and continues in the Neo-palatial period. The surrounding slopes on both sides of the bay bear further evidence for scattered habitation at the same time.

Phylakas seems to be just one point in a chain of coastal settlements that appear to prosper in this period (Fig. 13.4). In the western Asterousia the settlement of Doukiania (Vasilakis 2000: 117), which existed in the Pre- and Protopalatial periods, grew particularly large in the Neopalatial period in a new location (comprising approximately 30 houses), becoming the main focus of habitation in the western Asterousia up to the LM III period. Although not by the coast, it was orientated towards the sea and controlled topographically two natural harbours in the area, Vathy and Martsalos. At Vathy Neopalatial finds and a LM III house are reported (Davaras 1968: 405). At Martsalos a harbour site with close parallels to Phylakas has been partially investigated (Vasilakis 1996: 643–44; 2000: 117). Two rooms of a large building were excavated (approximately 150 sq. m) dated from MM IB to LM IB. The finds include a stone anchor and MMIIB pottery that shows affinities with material from Phaistos.

Further evidence suggests the growth in such coastal areas (Fig. 13.4). Around six kilometres to the east, at Lasaia, MM III and LM finds of the same character as at

Figure 13.4: The south coast of Crete, showing sites occupied in the Palatial period from the western Mesara to Viannos regions (figure produced by the authors).

Martsalos are reported (Vasilakis 2000: 119). At Loutra, twelve kilometres east of Lasaia, possible remains of a MM settlement can be found (Vasilakis, personal investigation). The harbour settlement on the rocky promontory of Phylakas, discussed above, is situated another 2.5 km to the east. Two kilometres east of Trypiti, at Salamias, LM finds have been located. Seven kilometres east of Phylakas, at Hagios Ioannis Kapetanianon, Minoan buildings were discovered on two capes, Ponta and Plaka. The buildings on Plaka, mapped by Hadjidaki in 1999 (Hadjidaki 2004: 54–59; Blackman 2000: 139) constitute a Minoan harbour site with likely occupation in the EM II and MM III periods. Twenty-one surveyed seaside buildings were recorded. The remains of a structure interpreted as a possible man-made mole or breakwater indicate the presence of a possible Minoan harbour installation. Around 300 m to the east, on the promontory of Ponta, a Neopalatial settlement was surveyed (Kanta and Galanaki, 2011). Further coastal sites are recorded at Treis Ekklisies (Pre- and Protopalatial finds at the location Tragopiastis), and in the Viannos region at Tsoutsouras (Neopalatial settlement at the location Aliori excavated by Antonakaki), Dermatos (MM-LM settlement at the location Mitatoulia), Keratokambos Plaka Aï Gianni (MM III-LM I settlement: cf. Rethemiotakis 1981: 390; Banou 2004: 187–88), Trapeza Keratokambou (mainly LM surface finds: cf. Banou 2004: 187), Phaphlagos and Psari Phorada (Alexiou 1967b) up to Myrtos Pyrgos (Cadogan 2006).

Thus along the southern coast of the Asterousia region, from Martsalos and Doukiania in the west to the harbour settlements of Phylakas and Hagios Ioannis Kapetanianon and a series of other sites further east in the Viannos region, a new cycle of development seems to have taken place during the Proto- and Neopalatial periods, associated probably with maritime communications along the southern coast. Thus, the initial proposal by Blackman and Branigan of the gradual abandonment of the Asterousia in the Protopalatial period and afterwards needs to be reconsidered, as divergent trajectories between the inland and coastal areas of the Asterousia seem to exist. The results from the Trypiti survey demonstrate the complex nature of these settlement cells and suggest that the southern coast of the Asterousia region participated in similar developments taking place in the coastal areas of Crete, related to the rapid growth of maritime trade from the second millennium onwards (cf. Wiener 1991; Van de Moortel 2007; Legarra Herrero 2011). In the Asterousia the similarities of the pottery at the harbour settlements of Martsalos and Phylakas with the Phaistos material indicate possible links at a supra-regional level. This is in accordance with the results of recent excavations at Phaistos which suggest that in the advanced Protopalatial period (MM II) the palace experienced significant growth and consolidation (Todaro 2009; Sbonias 2012: 286–87). More intensive research in the particular micro-environments of the southern coast will allow in the future a truly comparative approach and synthesis of the changing pattern of settlement in the Bronze Age and the evaluation of the role of these coastal communities in maritime interconnections.

Acknowledgements

We would like to thank the organisers of the conference for inviting us to participate. Many thanks to all the participants of the Trypiti survey as well as to Tim Campbell-Green and Borga Legarra Herrero for the preliminary sorting of the pottery. Many thanks also are due to Emeri Farinetti for the topographic recording of the architectural remains on the surface. The Trypiti survey was supported by INSTAP.

Bibliography

Alcock, S. E. and J. F. Cherry

2004 *Side-by-Side Survey: Comparative Regional Studies in the Mediterranean Region*. Oxford: Oxbow.

Alexiou, S.

1963 Αρχαιότητες και μνημεία της Κρήτης. *Αρχαιολογικόν Δελτίον* 18, B2: 309–16.

1967a Αρχαιότητες και μνημεία Κεντρικής και Ανατολικής Κρήτης. *Αρχαιολογικόν Δελτίον* 22, B2: 480–88.

1967b Μικραί ανασκαφαί και περισυλλογή αρχαιοτήτων εις Κρήτην. *Πρακτικά της εν Αθήνης Αρχαιολογικής Εταιρείας*: 212.

Alexiou, S. and P. Warren
2004 *The Early Minoan Tombs of Lebena, Southern Crete* (Studies in Mediterranean Archaeology 30). Sävedalen: Paul Åströms Förlag.

Banou, E. S.
2004 Νέα στοιχεία για τις σχέσεις της Βιάννου με την Κνωσό κατά την Υστερομινωική ΙΙΙΑ εποχή. In G. Cadogan, E. Hatzaki and A. Vasilakis (eds.), *Knossos: Palace, City, State* (BSA Studies 12): 187–206. London: British School at Athens.

Barker. G. and Mattingly, D. (series eds.)
1999–2000 *The Archaeology of the Mediterranean Landscapes* (5 vols.). Oxford: Oxbow.

Bintliff, J.
1994 The history of the Greek countryside: As the wave breaks, prospects of future research. In P. N. Doukellis and L. G. Mendoni (eds.), *Structures Rurales et Sociétés Antiques*: 7–15. Paris: Les Belles Lettres.
2000 Beyond dots on the map: the future of artifact survey in Greece. In J. Bintliff, M. Kuna and N. Venclova (eds.), *The Future of Archaeological Field Survey in Europe*: 3–20. Sheffield: Sheffield Academic Press.

Blackman, D.
2000 Archaeology in Greece 1999–2000. *Archaeological Reports* 46: 3–151.

Blackman, D. J. and K. Branigan
1975 An archaeological survey on the south coast of Crete, between the Ayiofarango and the Chrisostomos. *Annual of the British School at Athens* 70: 17–36.
1977 An archaeological survey of the lower catchment of the Ayiofarango Valley. *Annual of the British School at Athens* 72: 13–84.
1982 The excavation of an Early Minoan tholos tomb at Ayia Kyriaki, Ayiofarango, southern Crete. *Annual of the British School at Athens* 77: 1–57.

Branigan, K.
1970 *The Tombs of Mesara. A Study of Funerary Architecture and Ritual in Southern Crete, 2800–1700 B.C.* London: Duckworth.
1998 The nearness of you: proximity and distance in Early Minoan funerary behaviour. In K. Branigan (ed.) *Cemetery and Society in the Aegean Bronze Age* (Sheffield studies in Aegean Archaeology 1): 13–26. Sheffield: Sheffield Academic Press.

Branigan, K. and A. Vasilakis
2010 Survey in the environs around the tholos cemetery. In A. Vasilakis and K. Branigan 2010, *Moni Odigitria. A Prepalatial Cemetery and Its Environs in the Asterousia, Southern Crete* (Prehistory Monographs 30): 3–27. Philadelphia: INSTAP Academic Press.

Cadogan, G.
2006 A long-lived south coast community. *Πεπραγμένα του Θ' Διεθνούς Κρητολογικού Συνεδρίου*, τομ. 161–66. Ηράκλειο: Εταιρεία Κρητικών ιστορικών μελετών.

Cherry, J. F.
1983 Frogs round the pond: perspectives on current archaeological survey projects in the Mediterranean region. In D. R. Keller and D. W. Rupp (eds.), *Archaeological Survey in the Mediterranean Area* (BAR IS 155): 375–416. Oxford: British Archaeological Reports.
1994 Regional survey in the Aegean: the "New Wave" (and After). In P. N. Kardulias (ed.), *Beyond The Site: Regional Studies in the Aegean*: 91–102. Lanham, Rowman and Littlefield.

Davaras, K.
1968 Περιοχή Μονής Οδηγήτριας (Νομός Ηρακλείου). Αρχαιολογικόν Δελτίον 23, Β2: 405–06.

Driessen, J.
2001 History and hierarchy. Preliminary observations on the settlement pattern in Minoan Crete. In K. Branigan (ed.), *Urbanism in the Aegean Bronze Age* (Sheffield Studies in Aegean Archaeology 4): 51–71. London, Sheffield Academic Press.

Evans, A.
1928 *The Palace of Minos at Knossos, Vol. II*. London, MacMillan.

Hatzi-Vallianou, D.
1979a Λασαία. *Αρχαιολογικό Δελτίο* 34, B2: 382–83.
1979b Σώπατα Κουσέ. *Αρχαιολογικό Δελτίο* 34, B2: 384.

Hadjidaki, E.
2004 A possible Minoan harbor of South Crete. In L. Preston Day, M. S. Mook, J. D. Muhly (eds.), *Crete Beyond the Palaces: Proceedings of the Crete 2000 Conference* (Prehistory Monographs 10): 53–60. Philadelphia: INSTAP Academic Press.

Jameson, M. H., C. R. Runnels and T. H. van Andel
1994 *A Greek Countryside. The Southern Argolid from Prehistory to the Present Day*. Stanford: Stanford University Press.

Kanta, A. and K. Galanaki
2011 Στοιχεία Μινωικής μνημειακής τοπογραφίας απο τον Άη Γιάννη Καπετανιανών του Δήμου Κόφινα. *Πεπραγμένα του ΙΑ' Διεθνούς Κρητολογικού Συνεδρίου*, τομ. A1 (abstracts). Ρέθυμνο: Ιστορική και Λαογραφική Εταιρεία Ρεθύμνης.

Krzyszkowska, O.
2005 *Aegean Seals. An Introduction* (BICS Supplement 85). London: Institute of Classical Studies.

Legarra Herrero, B.
2011 New kid on the block: the nature of the first systemic contacts between Crete and the eastern Mediterranean around 2000 BC. In T. C. Wilkinson, S. Sherratt and J. Bennet (eds.), *Interweaving Worlds: Systemic Interactions in Eurasia, 7th to 1st Millennia BC*: 266–81. Oxford and Oakville: Oxbow.

Pini, I.
1990 Eine frühkretische siegelwerkstatt? *Πεπραγμένα του ΣΤ' Διεθνούς Κρητολογικού Συνεδρίου*, τομ. A2 115–27. Χανιά: Φιλολογικός Σύλλογος "Ο Χρυσόστομος".

Rethemiotakis, G.
1981 Περιοδείες. *Αρχαιολογικό Δελτίο* 36, B2: 389–90.

Sakellarakis, J.
1965 Αρχαιότητηες και μνημεία Κεντρικής και Ανατολικής Κρήτης. Μονή Οδηγήτριας. *Αρχαιολογικό Δελτίο* 20, B3: 562–64.

Sakellarakis, J. and V. E. G. Kenna
1969 *Corpus der Minoischen und Mykenischen Siegel. Band IV. Iraklion, Sammlung Metaxas*. Berlin: Akademie der wissenschaften und der literatur mainz.

Saltos, V.
2000 Ζητήματα ταφικής αρχιτεκτονικής στη Νότια Κρήτη κατά την Προανακτορική περίοδο. *Πεπραγμένα του Η' Διεθνούς Κρητολογικού Συνεδρίου*, τομ. A2: 193–200. Ηράκλειο: Εταιρεία Κρητικών ιστορικών μελετών.

Sbonias, K.
1995 *Frühkretische Siegel. Ansätze Für Eine Interpretation Der Sozial-politischen Entwicklung auf Kreta Während der Frühbronzezeit* (BAR IS 620). Oxford: Tempus Reparatum.
2010a Seals from the cemetery. In A. Vasilakis and K. Branigan, *Moni Odigitria. A Prepalatial Cemetery and Its Environs in the Asterousia, Southern Crete* (Prehistory Monographs 30): 201–25. Philadelphia, INSTAP Academic Press.
2010b Diversity and transformation. Looking for meanings in the prepalatial seal consumption and use. In W. Müller (ed.), *Die Bedeutung der Minoischen und Mykenischen Glyptik* (CMS Beiheft 8), 349–62. Mainz am Rhein: Philipp von Zabern.
2012 Regional elite-groups and seal production and consumption in the Prepalatial period. A case-study of the Asterousia region. In I. Schoep, P. D. Tomkins and J. Driessen (eds.), *Back to the Beginning: Reassessing Social, Economic and Political Complexity in the Early and Middle Bronze Age on Crete*: 273–89. Oxford: Oxbow.

Todaro, S.

2009 The latest prepalatial period and the foundation of the first palace at Phaistos: a stratigraphic and chronological re-assessment. *Creta Antica* 10: 105–45.

Van de Moortel, A.

2007 Kommos and its east Mediterranean connections in the Protopalatial period. In P. P. Betancourt, M. C. Nelson and H. Williams (eds.), *Krinoi kai Limenes. Studies in Honor of Joseph and Maria Shaw* (Prehistory Monographs 22): 177–84. Philadelphia: INSTAP Academic Press.

Vasilakis, A.

1987 Ανασκαφή Νεολιθικού σπιτιού στους Καλούς Λιμένες της Νότιας Κρήτης. In *ΕΙΛΑΠΙΝΗ, τιμητικός τόμος για τον καθηγητή Νικόλαο Πλάτωνα*: 45–53. Ηράκλειο: Βικελαία Δημοτική Βιβλιοθήκη.

1983 Κρότος Καινουρίου. *Αρχαιολογικό Δελτίο* 38, Β2: 355.

1989–90 Προϊστορικές θέσεις στη Μονή Οδηγήτριας-Καλούς Λιμένες. *Κρητική Εστία* 3: 11–79.

1990 Ο Πρωτομινωικός οικισμός της Τρυπητής. *Αρχαιολογία* 30: 52–56.

1991–93 Αρχαιολογικές Ειδήσεις 1989–1991 (Φύλακας). *Κρητική Εστία* 4: 295–96.

1994–96 Αρχαιολογικές Ειδήσεις 1992–1994, Μονή Οδηγήτριας (Σκανιάρη Λάκκος). *Κρητική Εστία* 5: 336–37.

1996 Καλοί Λιμένες Μάρτσαλος. *Αρχαιολογικό Δελτίο* 51, Β2; 643–44.

1995 Τρυπητή 1986–1991. *Πεπραγμένα του Ζ' Διεθνούς Κρητολογικού Συνεδρίου*, τομ. Α1 69–74. Ρέθυμνο: Ιστορική και Λαογραφική Εταιρεία Ρεθύμνης.

2000 Αστερούσια: από τα Νεολιθικά σπίτια και τους Προανακτορικούς τάφους στους οικισμούς/καταφύγια της αρχής της Εποχής του Σιδήρου. In A. Vasilakis (ed.), *Η Μεσαρά μέσα από τα μνημεία της. Πρώτη Αρχαιολογική Συνάντηση Μεσαράς 5-7.11.1996*: 111–40. Moires: Dapani.

2010 Myrtos Fournou Korifi and Trypiti Adami Korfali: similarities and differences in two Prepalatial settlements in southern Crete. In O. Krzyszkowska (ed.), *Cretan Offerings: Studies in Honour of Peter Warren* (BSA Studies 18): 353–58. London: British School at Athens.

Vasilakis, A. and K. Branigan

2010 *Moni Odigitria. A Prepalatial Cemetery and Its Environs in the Asterousia, Southern Crete* (Prehistory Monographs 30). Philadelphia: INSTAP Academic Press.

Wiener, M. H.

1991 The nature and control of Minoan foreign trade. In N. H. Gale (ed.) *Bronze Age Trade in the Mediterranean* (Studies in Mediterranean Archaeology 90): 325–50. Göteborg: Paul Åströms Förlag.

Chapter 14

Beyond the collective ... The Minoan Palace in action

Jan Driessen

Introduction: dual strategies

From M(iddle) M(inoan) IB onwards, we witness a dramatic transformation of Crete's social landscape. Large, monumental complexes are built along and around existing courts, and investment in funerary complexes, which received the bulk of the attention before, rapidly diminishes (Devolder 2009). Although courts used as cohesion-enhancing devices seem already to have been the norm in many a Prepalatial (if not earlier) settlement (Todaro and Di Tonto 2006; Driessen 2007; Tomkins 2012), the architectural elaboration of the subsidiary buildings was unprecedented and now included ashlar or orthostate masonry, standardised room types (Minoan Hall, lustral basin), wall facings, and a scale that, for several hundred years, would remain essential to the Minoan architectural canon. Many scholars assume this development to have been accompanied by increased hierarchy. They advocate that political power, wealth and production were centralised in the hands of a single ruler and his personal network, a more exclusionary mode. However, an alternative perspective is possible, one that sees the palaces as community structures with power, wealth and production distributed in a corporate mode and shared as a product of group membership. In this paper I will specifically argue that Minoan palaces result from an inclusionary social process with the voluntary involvement of different social groups. I shall draw upon cross-cultural work in anthropological archaeology, particularly the dual-processual model developed by Blanton *et al.* (1996) and Feinman (2000b), but it follows ideas originally proposed by Renfrew (1974), distinguishing between individualising and group-oriented forms of chiefdoms. Renfrew already placed emphasis where corporate chiefdoms were concerned on communal activities and group rituals, interpreting societies with henge monuments and Prehistoric Malta as such group-oriented chiefdoms. Minoan

Crete, in his view, however, was seen as an individualising form of chiefdom and this is why Feinman (2000a: 36), when characterising the individualising form of chiefdom, used a series of elements put forward by Renfrew (1974). These included the circumstance that specific individuals were differentiated and privileged, that a marked disparity in personal possessions existed, that the residences and tombs of rulers were far grander than those of the bulk of the population, that exotic trade wealth had a significant role in prestige accumulation, that some exchanged goods were crafted by specialists and that there was less evidence for communal ritual and public construction. Still, as already noted by Feinman (2000a: 35), many societies mix elements of corporate-based and network-based strategies, opposing a too categorical classification. Since wealth accumulation is said to be more distinctive in network-based strategies, we may perhaps combine these ideas with the two alternative strategies suggested by Whitelaw (2004: 244), i.e. trade-based or agricultural-based, with corporate societies keener to control agricultural production and surplus. Very much in the same vein as Feinman and Blanton did for American archaeology, Schoep and Knappett (2004: 24) also argued for a dual process on Minoan Crete in which heterarchical developments emerged as well as hierarchical aspects. They were especially interested in illustrating how bottom-up processes could lead to complexity, countering the common assumption that complexity implies the existence of central authority. By highlighting bottom-up dynamics in administrative practices, craft production and architecture, they stress that "changes in heterarchical structures *prefigured* any major hierarchical developments" (Schoep and Knappett 2004: 25, their italics), arguing that heterarchical developments were important into MM II but less explicit afterwards whereas hierarchical developments, although present before, became more explicit from MM II onwards. Perhaps our hesitation when facing the archaeological material can also be expressed by the dichotomy *domination* or *collaboration* (cf. Blanton and Fargher 2008: 12; cf. also Mills 2000; see also Haggis 1999 and 2002 on *integration* and *connectedness*). Interestingly, Blanton and colleagues (1996) observed that societies mainly pursuing corporate leadership strategies aim to suppress openly shown competition by developing an ethos of reciprocity between the society's different sodalities, also arguing that ritual systems may have played a pivotal role in promoting community solidarity by emphasising cyclical, repetitive obligations to the community as a whole and by removing wealth from the control of individuals (Blanton *et al.* 1996; Wills 2000: 33). It is this line of approach which is further developed in this paper. Elsewhere (Driessen 2002), I have already argued against the ruler-centric model (for a review see, most recently, Bevan 2010 for Minoan Crete) since it is hard to reconcile with the absence of prestigious individual burials, the "faceless" iconography and the architectural layout of the main central buildings. I have also underlined the scarcity of evidence for the Pre- and Proto-palatial period connecting elements of aggrandising, whether in the shape of domestic and funerary architecture, portable wealth or craft specialisation, with *specific* individuals rather than serving to distinguish between *different social* groups (Driessen 2010a). In the present paper, I explore the extent to which group membership can be identified in Minoan society and how it operated.

Corporate communities

Very much like V. G. Childe was reconstructing people while digging pots, archaeologists immediately tend to associate sherd scatters with human groups, often conflating community with site, with each spatially localised co-residential group of people called a community (cf. Hare 2000). Isbell (2000: 244) has shown the inherent dangers of such a definition since people can reside together without experiencing solidarity whereas some people not residing together may feel strongly about their belonging to some specific community (Marcus 2000: 235–36). Whereas Yeager and Canuto (2000: 6) favour an interactionist perspective and the frequent co-presence of community members, Wolfe (2006: 24) argued that a community was "certainly much more than a set of relations among individuals". Their ideas, combined with the more operational and functionalist approach of Kolb and Snead's (1997), would highlight social reproduction, subsistence production and self-identification/ social recognition as three archaeologically visible functions that can be attached to communities (cf. Yeager and Canuto 2000: 4–5). With Isbell (2000: 248), we may assume some kind of identity between a "natural" community and an "imagined" community with the implication that the material domain, as argued by Soja (1989: 129), was simultaneously "the means, medium, and outcome of social reproduction". "Natural" communities are more static, fixed in place within a settlement or locale while "imagined" communities can take different forms, are more fluid and are not based on proximity but on relationships and on broader perceptions of identity: here there is less direct equivalence of "community" and "site" (Driessen and Frankel 2012). This makes it also possible to identify spatial units in the field that were *smaller* than the settlement but *larger* than the nuclear family and which acted as moral persons, some kind of fractal personhood (Fowler 2004: 21, 48) in which proximate spatial residency would reflect an imagined community, fulfilling a specific social role within a larger community. Anthropological parallels show that a residential structure forming a single household may be occupied by a single nuclear family, by multiple nuclear families or by an extended family. Within a single residential structure, multiple nuclear families may also sometimes form different households. Similarly, multiple residential structures may be occupied by multiple nuclear families forming multiple households but a single extended family forming a single household may have occupied different residential structures. We mostly lack sufficient archaeological correlates to identify such social units but it would be unwise to exclude their potential existence *a priori*.

Hayden and Cannon (1982) in their seminal paper, *The Corporate Group as Archaeological Unit*, stress that these are "groups that function as individuals in relation to property" and add that these were formed because "of strong economic or environmental pressures, and which, as a result, exhibit a recognisable degree of residential coherency among two or more nuclear families within the community" (Hayden and Cannon 1982: 135). As such they are termed residential corporate groups, which "are much more closed and exert a pervasive influence on all aspects of individuals' lives, including their marriage, their post-marital residence, their economic production, their feasting and celebrations, and their pastimes and pleasures" (Hayden and Cannon 1982: 135).

To identify corporate groupings, a series of archaeological variables can be used amongst which architecture (plan, size and complexity) remains the main criterion. Stylistic homogeneity versus variability within and between corporate groups within the same community may also be a potentially interesting criterion (Hayden and Cannon 1982: 147). Indeed, attached craft production may result in a specific style, underlining the coherence of the corporate group, and eventually be used emblematically. Some other criteria may be relevant. Certain critical resources, resulting from trade, hunt or exploitation, may have been linked to specific corporate groups in a more or less exclusionary way.

The Minoan *House*

Without discounting the existence of nuclear families (for which see especially Whitelaw 2001; 2007) and following the spatial data discussed by Hayden and Cannon (1982: 142), to which I add some elements provided by Stanish (1989), I propose the hypothetical reconstruction of three different types of corporate groups for Minoan Crete: the *co-residential corporate group*, the *proximate residential corporate group* and the *dispersed corporate group*. In the first two cases, single households may have been formed whereas the third probably implied separate households.

I have argued that *co-residential corporate groupings* formed the core of Minoan society from the Neolithic period onwards (Driessen 2010a; 2010b). My main argument, then and now, remains the size of many Minoan residential structures which, I infer, would have been dictated by a hypothetical matrilineal and matrilocally organised social system (Driessen 2012; 2013). I put forward the hypothesis that some residences reflected specific, isomorphic social groups corresponding with what anthropologists call *House Societies*. Factions (and even sodalities) compete, *Houses* cooperate, both within and with others. The longevity and size of the residence both underline the intergenerational and corporate nature of this association. At the level of a small site, this corresponds with what Tomkins (2004) has called *submerged* households with the community as a whole being a social actor and with agricultural surplus being pooled and its storage organised at a higher, perhaps communal level. He sees this as a characteristic for Early Neolithic and Middle Neolithic Knossos (Tomkins 2004: 43) with a development towards more individualised households by the Late Neolithic. I would rather argue that the size of these Late Neolithic residences suggests that they contained social groups larger than the nuclear family, reflecting a system which, *mutatis mutandis*, would still be operational at the end of the Bronze Age and very likely beyond. The large residential complexes that abound in Minoan archaeology during its different cultural periods would exemplify this type of social structure (cf. Romanou 2007). In the economic field, these *Houses* pooled labour and production and acted as a single economic unit. In small settlements, a single *House* may have existed but in larger settlements, several of these may have formed the larger community (Driessen 2010a).

Proximate residential corporate groupings imply that members of a single social group occupy closely located residences and share certain areas in which specific integrative functions took place. Often the partition walls between the different residences are difficult to distinguish, resulting in an agglutinative plan. The patterned individual residences making up the complex, quarter or block are usually interpreted as representing nuclear families, which may be true for some, but sufficient complementary features suggest that the different components sometimes acted as a single body, perhaps sometimes only sporadically and on an occasional basis e.g. when cohesion and integration may have been pursued through the ritual and ceremonial role of the residence. In such cases, the physical structure was at the same time the symbol and the screen against which the solidarity of its members was expressed through many collective ceremonies and rituals. Within settlements, barrios, sectors or quarters, spatially delineated by walls or streets, may be identifiable but sometimes they are simply defined by interaction patterns of multiple households (Chesson 2003). Neopalatial Gournia and Pseira may be examples of such more loosely organised corporate structures where each quarter may have had its own specialised structures for artisanal production, cult and administration (Driessen 2010a: 36 for references). This type of corporate structure may be regarded as the frailest since the components probably mostly formed multiple autonomous households. In other cases, it may also have involved an internal but mutual organisation of production, exchange and consumption with the different components acting as a single household. Myrtos Phournou Koriphi, but also the different blocks (B, Γ and Δ) in central Palaikastro would correspond to such an organisation. At Palaikastro, the quarters are sometimes distinguished by specific boundaries such as walls or streets. Typical here too is redistributed wealth and reduplicated service structures linked to neighbourhoods. Sometimes the flow of materials can link households with their proximate neighbourhood (Hutson *et al.* 2007).

Where the *co-residential corporate group* and the *proximate residential corporate group* are concerned, it is possible to argue for the existence of some kind of internal hierarchy, illustrated through weighed architectural elaboration, access and circulation of portable finds. Moreover, the same features may have been used to express some kind of hierarchy or difference in status between the different corporate groups.

Although spatial solidarity of the members of a *House* may have been pursued, it may not always have been possible or desirable for reasons of procurement of special resources or mating partners. Moreover, stasis or internal stress may have been averted through the departure of some members and the creation of subsidiaries of the *House* elsewhere, in nearby or distant places. With *dispersed corporate groupings*, I envisage a social grouping that occupies residential structures in different proximate and non-proximate settlements acting only occasionally as a single household but still forming a strong, imagined community. The specific, seemingly random patterning of identical or related material culture (e.g. seals and pottery styles) throughout the Cretan countryside may suggest such networks (Driessen and Frankel 2012). The members of such a dispersed *House* mostly gather on occasion of special feasts related to rites of passage (births, weddings, funerals) but this type of corporation could perhaps also be a mechanism through which trading associates (both where resources and mating partners were concerned) were preferentially integrated within the social group and be treated as fictive kin (Marcus 2000: 239). In such a hypothesis, members of a single social group or *House* would occupy residential structures both at, e.g. Malia and Myrtos Pyrgos (Protopalatial) or Knossos and Myrtos Pyrgos (Neopalatial). It would also open the possibility that certain highly ritualised structures (South-East House, Royal Villa, House of the Chancel Screen, etc.) in the cosmological centre which Knossos must have been, acted as some kind of embassies or subsidiaries for groups that usually or mostly resided elsewhere. Special links, again attested through material culture, may suggest such networks that reinforced regional and interregional cohesion (cf. Van Gijseghem and Vaughn 2008). The implication of such a suggestion is that social networks may have crisscrossed regional circumscriptions hypothetically reconstructed through territorial modelling (Bevan 2010).

Corporate performance. The iconography of solidarity

Although a full discussion of corporate iconography falls outside the scope of this paper, its omnipresence may be underlined. A single example may suffice: the Harvester Vase from Hagia Triada depicts a procession of men, carrying forked sticks, perhaps for shaking olive trees, accompanied by musicians. It clearly represents the idea of a successful expedition of a group of men. Similar themes, mostly involving men but also women, form the core of Minoan human representation. Cunningham (2007) underlined the preponderance of "crowd scenes (Grandstand and Sacred Grove frescos), communal activities (Boxer and Harvester Rhyta), and representations of towns (Town Mosaic, Master Impression). Along with the lack of individual aggrandisement, these iconographic preoccupations suggest the importance of community and communal functions" (Cunningham 2007: 106–07). Even the dangerous bull hunt/game seems to imply that it is only through union and mutual aid, through *collective action*, that a result could be achieved. As noted by Chapin (2011: 519), "Aegean power and authority relied on coalitional success ...neither male nor female forms of gendered social relations express authority individually ...power and prestige in Aegean Neopalatial society seem to derive from the strength of its successful coalitions". Male coalitions – sodalities or fraternities – are still typical for historical Crete as illustrated in the

3rd cent. BC oath of the 180 ephebes of Dreros. Nevertheless, Minoan art is at least to some degree to be understood as ideology rendered visual which may imply that successful coalitions were aspired to but perhaps not always corresponding to real life situations. What also seems clear is that certain acts of solidarity and corporate performance which, from MM IB onwards, would incrementally be concentrated at peak sanctuaries and palaces were first centred on the funerary domain. Interestingly, *Dancing with Death* was both the title of and the chapter within one of the books written by Keith Branigan. He underlined the communal or public aspects of the tombs in the Messara and suggested that the open spaces outside were especially used for dancing (Branigan 1993: 130), as illustrated by the Kamilari and other terracotta models. Branigan connected dancing with rituals and ceremonies that were concerned with the vegetation cycle and fertility and the tombs as such "a focus for kin-group and village expressions of communality and stability" (Branigan 1993: 137). Since *Dancing with Death*, several authors, including Senta German (2005), Alexandra Liveri (2008) and Stella Mandalaki (2004), have discussed Minoan dances as performances, listing the many Minoan examples from the Pre-, Proto- and Neopalatial period. An element which to my mind has not received sufficient attention but which was developed by Yosef Garfinkel for the Near East is the importance of dancing as a communal action, the moving of many as one, the solidarity and cohesion enhancing aspects of the performance (now also Soar 2010: 151). Dancing, Garfinkel (1997; 2003) argues, installs solidarity within people and as such, traditional dancing still remains a major expression of Cretan collectivity. Dancing (but also pilgrimages) may be viewed as a natural and self-organising structure in which complexity develops through spontaneous and coherent movement of people (cf. Malville 2009), serving to inscribe corporate behaviour in its youngest members.

Collective action and common pool resources

Why form a corporate group rather than a nuclear family? Hayden and Cannon (1982) only considered economic, environmental and defence aspects as compelling people to live together. Tomkins (2004), following earlier work by Halstead (1995), defends a similar approach where Early and Middle Neolithic households are concerned. "Households", he argues "if truly isolated, risk extinction... In order to offset their inviability, individual households must have relied on periodic, external assistance that was ensured by the cultivation of social interactions beyond the household, which probably took the form of networks of exchange, alliances and obligations that included food and probably exotic materials, such as obsidian or ceramic vessels" (Tomkins 2004: 40). In his opinion too, economic necessity may have forced people to live in larger social units. In this he was following Byrd (1994) who suggested similar constraints for Neolithic villages in Jordan. What I would like to add is that specific ecological conditions (type of crops and landscape) on Crete may have benefitted the development of certain types of kin relations – in our case corporate groupings based on matrilineal descent and matrilocal residence – from the start rather than as an outcome. Hayden and Cannon (1982: 151) already noted that "restricted economic control over important resources (land, trade, fishing sites, cattle, etc.)... may explain why residential corporate groups among upper class families persist... even where corporate groups disappear almost entirely among lower classes". If ecological conditions forced Minoans to adopt a societal organisation that was more viable, the different types of corporate groupings – co-residential, proximate and dispersed – would be its cultural and material expression. This is the idea already behind the production process recognised by Tomkins (2004: 47) for Early Neolithic and Middle Neolithic Knossian pottery, which, he argues "may be compared to agriculture, which similarly requires group co-operation at certain stages in the production process (e.g. sowing, threshing, weeding" (Tomkins 2004: 49)). Cereals, vines and olives demand considerable investment and pooling of resources essential for survival (cf. Harvester's vase). The seasonality of these practices would have necessitated *collective action*, the "group behaviour of individuals united by particular life experiences, existential anxieties, and strategic interests" (Saitta 2007: XVII), which, according to Hodder, is some different way of individual agency (cited in Saitta 2007: 24). In Blanton and Fargher's 2008 study "Collective Action in the Formation of Pre-Modern States", collective action is linked to public goods, bureaucratisation and principal control. Their cross-cultural study includes all types of collective polities with which they understand complex societies "in which the government... provide services... in exchange for revenues... provided by compliant taxpayers" (Blanton and Fargher 2008: 13). In their scheme, cooperation develops between rulers and taxpayers but they fail to address what are known as *grassroot organisations* (or self-organisations), bottom-up collective action resulting from solidarity based on some specific identity that defines a community of individuals. In social theory, the concept of self-organisation was introduced by Niklas Luhmann (1984). In recent periods, this is often class-based or related to ethnicity as illustrated by Dean Saitta's "Archaeology of Collective Action" (2007) but in the past self-organisation developed within communities most often along specific kinship links to allow *collective activities on land owned communally*. If we follow Hayden and Cannon (1982: 150) in assuming that corporate groups are more likely to emerge under conditions of moderate land shortages and other resource scarcities (e.g. obsidian, metal), Crete may be a case in point. Land being the most critical resource in all agriculture-based societies, it will be imperative to maintain cohesive land tracts to make production profitable and to provide a sufficient labour force. This is imperative, criss-crossing scales, or types of social organisation. What I want to suggest is that Crete may have represented what has been called a *communal ownership of property* (COP), a model introduced by Fleming (1985) and applied by different scholars (e.g. Chapman *et al.* 1996: 273) to explain prehistoric subsistence in societies in which the scale of seasonal agricultural work exceeded the labour force availability put at the disposal of average nuclear families. *Communal ownership of property* is a model often related to commons or *common-pool resources*, natural resources used by many individuals in common. Commons were widespread in all European medieval towns (e.g. Béaur 2006; Bowden *et al.* 2009) but it is a misconception that commons were limited to grazing lands nor should commons be confused with open access (Gibson 2008: 47). Commons were in fact used for many different activities such as fishing, foraging, horticulture, agriculture, arboriculture, grazing, hunting, and mining, and seasonality (cf. transhumance) may also have played a role. As Gibson (2008: 48) explains "Useful distinctions have been made between communal, common, and private forms of land tenure... Members can restrict access to land held in *common*, but cannot dictate how it is to be used by individual households. Under *communal* land tenure, a community can both restrict access to land and also dictate how it is to be used. The owners of *private* property can exclude others from the land, and dispose of it without restrictions". Common-pool resources in general, but also in the context of this paper, comprise a series of renewable and non-renewable resources on which people depend heavily for their subsistence and are hence more typical for *marginal* environments such as reconstructed for the island of Crete (on marginality see Halstead 2008; on coping with uncertainty, Halstead 1981). Conventional solutions typically involve either centralised governmental regulation or privatisation of the resource. Hardin's (1968) objection ("the tragedy of the commons") arguing that people would deplete natural resources or prevent others from using these has been effectively countered especially by Elinor Ostrom (1990), 2009 Nobel prize winner of economics. She has noted that communities often practice specific rules that protect the commons through the design of *durable cooperative institutions that are organised and governed by the resource users themselves*, i.e. a kind of institutionalised self-organisation or bottom-up action. These common pool resources or CPR are organised communally because the advantages of such a system exceed the individual exploitation (and the risk of encountering violence) and state intervention through coercion (even if the tithe is usually at least partially invested in the common good). The cases of self-organisation studied by Ostrom usually affect a relatively low number of individuals (from 50 to 15,000 people), small-scale communities such as we reconstruct for Minoan Crete. To some degree, this line of thought picks up the ideas on social storage or the relief redistribution system explored by Halstead (1981; 1988) and Branigan (1988a; 1988b: 65) but without immediately assuming a hierarchical development and a palatial elite divorced from its societal setting. Indeed, Ostrom (1990) identifies eight "design principles" of stable local common-pool resource management, especially operational in non-hierarchical conditions. These are: (1) clearly defined boundaries (effective exclusion of external unentitled parties), (2) rules regarding the appropriation and provision of common resources are adapted to local conditions, (3) collective-choice arrangements allow most resource appropriators to participate in the decision-making process, (4) effective monitoring by monitors who are part of, or accountable to the appropriators, (5) a scale of graduated sanctions for resource appropriators who violate community rules, (6) mechanisms of conflict resolution are cheap and of easy access, (7) the self-determination of the community is recognised by higher-level authorities, and (8) in the case of larger common-pool resources, organisation in the form of multiple layers of nested enterprises, with small local CPRs at the base level.

Where Crete is concerned, communal pasture zones for summer and winter grazing existed in historical times and still today so they may also be assumed for the Bronze Age (Chaniotis 1999: 191, 197). In fact, the increase of land boundaries as implied by early Cretan epigraphic evidence can be explained as reflecting intensified pressure on access of communal lands. Such frontiers often follow limits between specific land use zones that eventually develop into real political boundaries (Chapman *et al.* 1996: 276; Chaniotis 1999: 199). We may also connect such grassroots organisation to renewable resources as inshore fisheries, hunting grounds, forests etc. and to the occasional adaptations of the natural environment as implied by irrigation systems and dams, as seen at Pseira and Gournia for example, water provisioning (as presented by well-digging in common ground at Palaikastro) and to non-renewable resources comprising the exploitation of minerals (such as quarried stone for building and vases, obsidian and various portable objects but also metals; see Devolder 2009: 192). It may also imply the creation of *specific infrastructures related to such resources*. In the case of Chalcolithic Palestine, Levy (1998: 239) has argued that cult centres, shrines, monumental buildings and formal cemeteries should foremost be seen as regulating institutions that developed as a reflection of formalised behaviour codes that were related to common pool resources. Is such a scheme envisagable for Prepalatial and Protopalatial Minoan Crete?

Are the Minoan palaces the result of collective action?

Has mythological Minos forced us into seeing the palace as a hierarchical construct intimately connected to a ruler? Two quotes, from works by Italian archaeologists of the pioneer days of Minoan archaeology, illustrate that initially the evidence was interpreted along other lines. F. Halbherr, undoubtedly having read Aristotle's views on the Cretan *politeia*, remarked when first encountering the Knossian ruins before Evans excavated these: "The largeness of the building makes me think that it must have been one of the chief public edifices of the city, and the large jars for storing grain, wine or oil remind us of the Andreion in which the citizens of Crete used to come together for their public meals or syssitia, to which also were invited any distinguished persons who happened to be visiting their city" (Halbherr 1893: 111). A decade later, another internationally acclaimed scholar, Angelo Mosso, stated: "The very architecture of the palaces of Knossos and Phaestos may testify to the power of the democracy. The liberal supply of seats in the palaces of Phaestos and Knossos was an expense forced on the architect by the crowding of a large public in the hall and the courts, and by the freedom with which the people could enter the palace ..." (Mosso 1907: 163). In fact, Chapter 8 in Mosso's *Palaces of Crete*, published in London in 1907, was entitled "Prehistoric Socialism" (*sic*) partly because he followed Stillman who, already in 1866, had claimed to have found "the great building for public assemblies, the so-called Sissitia (Sussitia), where the earliest Socialists ate in common. ...The soup kitchens, free meals for school children, and municipal bakehouses of the present day are trifles, for at that time men, women and children were all fed at the expense of the State" (Mosso 1907: 161). In the opinion of both scholars, bottom-up driven collective actions were operational in the organisation and function of the Minoan palaces. Is the Minoan palace in fact a durable cooperative institution that was organised and governed by the resource users themselves, an original institution regulating or governing the commons? Was it a building that resulted out of a voluntary community decision and act? I pursue this line of approach by asking two questions: who *built* the palaces and who *used* the palaces? Where the second question is concerned, more evidence has been brought forward in recent years underlining the possibility that the palace was used by different groups and by the larger community, or at least selected members of the latter. The permeability of its access system, the essence of its circulation pattern in which the central court and other courts formed poles of convergence, and the presence of different entrances linked with specific functional zones within the complex all seem to suggest not only a variety of non-resident users but also the importance of interaction for which the building was specifically constructed (Palyvou 2002; Driessen 2004; Letesson 2006; Letesson & Vansteenhuyse 2006). The involvement of different groups may also be reconstructed on the basis of other, portable evidence. Both Weingarten (1986) and Relaki (2009; 2012) have shown how the sealing pattern represented by the Phaistos *Vano 25 archivio di cretule* is indicative of a non-resident sealing pattern. Day and Wilson (2004) for Prepalatial Knossos and Macdonald and Knappett (2007) for Protopalatial Knossos have reconstructed ceremonies taking place within the palace involving many participants. Recently excavated palaces such as those at Petras and Galatas have yielded evidence suggesting ceremonies implying large groups (Tsipopoulou 2002; Rethemiotakis 2002). All this corroborates the evidence of the iconography and the importance of mass meetings through which solidarity and integration were enhanced. Where Postpalatial Crete is concerned, it may be informative that Tsipopoulou (2009) has recently suggested that the presence of identical sets of terracotta figures with upraised arms and snake tubes of different clays within the shrine at Chalasmenos could be related to the fact that different groups each dedicated their set. Perhaps we will be able to propose a similar hypothesis for the palaces in the future but since most buildings, apart from that at Zakros, were found largely empty on excavation, there is little evidence to proceed on (Fig. 14.1). Koehl (2006) invites us to consider the so-called Treasuries within the palaces of Zakros and Knossos as storing ritual equipment to be used communally, with rhyta meant to be distributed during communal ceremonies. He notes how these rhyta were often found in clusters and, taking into account the Procession Frescoes, argues that rhyta were distributed from storerooms to participants to be used in processions (Koehl 2006: 331–332). He remarks, however, how sometimes pairs of almost identical rhyta occur in a single deposit but that, at Gournia, two

Figure 14.1: Artist reconstruction of crowd gathering in the Central Court of the palace of Malia from the original drawing by the late Bernard Warren, by kind permission of his family.

separated pairs occurred respectively in House Bb r11 and House Cm r58. "These separated pairs might have commemorated a link that was forged between families of groups within the community. Perhaps the pairs were divided at the conclusion of a ceremony in which members of both groups, or a single representative from each one, participated" (Koehl 2006: 331). Future work may perhaps also show who was actually using the palace or even which specific area within the building and for what activity since certain selection processes may have been operational related to specific rites or age, ritual experience, or gender (Driessen 2009). Large-scale storage accessible from the outside could be an additional indication (Garfinkel *et al.* 2009) and the best illustrations for this remain the Protopalatial *kouloures* at Knossos and Phaistos or the Neopalatial battery of silos found outside the Malia palace.

The second question, who built the Minoan palaces, is now impossible to answer. Studies especially by Graham (1963), Preziosi (1983), Palyvou (2002), Shaw (2009) and Letesson (2009) have underlined the planned nature of the building and the possibility that an original square covering the west wing and the central court formed the basis of the construction, undoubtedly dictated by ritual at every moment of its conception, construction, elaboration, decoration, and perhaps even destruction if the layer of *calcestruzzo* poured over the Protopalatial remains at Phaistos can be interpreted in this way. Planning such a building is one thing, and mythical Daedalos is usually given credit, but actually building it is another. A basic observation needs to be our point of departure: the monumentality of the Minoan palace, because of its scale, elaboration, longevity or plan, mirrors an investment of energy that is unparalleled by other aspects in Minoan society. It compares well with the Archaic investment in immense temples at Samos, Didyma and Athens. As such it reflects a power and an ability to mobilise a work force. Traditionally, this has been seen as reflecting hierarchy. In our bottom-up approach, we may envision a hypothesis seeing the palaces as the materialisation of a corporate strategy and a collective action aiming to reduce open tension or competition between the different corporate groups that made up society. What if the construction itself of such a *great house* would be essential in promoting solidarity through its emphasis on the involvement of the different groups, perhaps on a cyclical basis? Was the act as or more important than the result? If the building act itself was a ritual activity, linked to specific time and place constraints, then participating in the construction was perhaps also considered to fulfil religious or ritual obligations. This is a hypothesis proposed for Chacoan Great Houses (Wills 2000: 38) and Neolithic megalithic monuments (Renfrew 1974) but some features of Minoan building practices may actually reinforce such a hypothesis. I am especially thinking of the repetition in the plan and orientations of the palaces as shown by Shaw (1973; 2010), Preziosi (1984) and Palyvou (2002), but also by the importance of equinox and solstice alignments effectively illustrated by Goodison (2004), and especially by the incremental discovery of foundation or building deposits (e.g. Herva 2005). Add to these the attention given to architecture, both where its realisation in the miniature (with faience façades, clay models, fresco and seal depictions) and in large scale construction are concerned, and the ritual element behind Minoan architecture cannot be underestimated. If through participation in the construction of such a major monumental public building a right of access could be acquired by corporate groupings or their representatives (cf. Wills 2000: 43), then a communal investment may perhaps be envisaged. At present we lack sufficient methodological approaches to answer this question positively but there are some elements which may be highlighted. If we take a processual approach to understanding the Minoan palaces, two elements that need discussion are labour and communication, both essential in the organisation of their production (Wills 2000: 21). Mobilising a work force and making sure it constructs the building according to some specific prescriptions implies that task coordination would be critical to construction success (Wills 2000: 36). This can be achieved through self-organisation and what is sometimes called a small-world network in which *patching* took place, an effective way through which non-literate societies would have handled the complex coordination problems presented by the construction of such large complexes (Wills 2000: 37). This said, even if the palace was the result of collective action, it must not imply necessarily that it was built by the community at large: in Archaic Greece, whatever the political system, the polis constructed the temple as a sign for the collectivity, but the actual work was done by privately contracted gangs.

Seeing the construction and reconstruction of palaces as part of corporate obligations with a sequential, cyclical involvement by the different *Houses* would have reduced potential tensions and coordination requirements and would also have resulted in a learning process of a large specialist task force which could then also explain the regional proliferation of styles and techniques, channelled through the network of our hypothetical dispersed corporative group. As noted by Wills (2000: 38), the result of such a collective process could be quite striking but need not have involved a heavy institutionalised structure or an elaborate political organisation.

A few additional observations may perhaps render this hypothesis, in which there is an obvious link between the palaces and the communities that build these, more attractive. First of all, it may be noted that moments of palace building correspond to moments of population increase (at least as evidenced by survey data) following periods of stress (EM III, MM IIB-III) so that a connection is more than likely and that the building as such may have acted as a release of stress (cf. Malville 2009: 40 on pilgrimages as stress release) for the community at large rather than as an aggrandising monument celebrating a ruler. If this stands a chance of being correct, the palaces as such may suggest a *coalescent* society, a new social formation formed through the integration of groups coming from different places, or the incoming of new groups (Kowalewski 2006; Haggis pers. com.). I have suggested such a process for the formation of the Malia palace (Driessen 2001) and both Relaki and Todaro assume a similar process for Late Neolithic and Early Minoan Phaistos (Relaki 2004; Todaro and Di Tonto 2006).

Secondly, by hypothesising the number of people involved and the time it took to construct Minoan palaces and major buildings considering that only during the two or three agriculturally low months people invested in constructing large monumental buildings, Devolder (2008; 2009) was able to suggest that the energy input represented reflected larger work groups than those potentially and proportionally represented by the residents of these structures. In cases such as Kommos and Gournia, the construction clearly implied a large workforce if the work was finished in a reasonable time, too large to have been supplied by the residents of the buildings. The investment therefore suggests collaboration. Thirdly, as shown by Schoep (2004), Protopalatial architectural innovations seem to show up first in domestic residential structures and only afterwards in central architecture. This could also imply that those who had built more impressive group-related constructions acquired the expertise first which was only later put into practice in communal buildings. Fourthly, all palace buildings took time to build, and thus reflect a gradual process. The progressive construction of the palaces is clearest where Protopalatial Phaistos is concerned but must also apply to most other buildings. Partly related to this is finally the within-structure variability that exists in each building. Often this is interpreted as reflecting different architectural phases but it may be suggested that the variations reflect the work of distinctive socio-political groups (cf. Hastings and Moseley 1975 and Moseley 1975 for an interesting example of such practices in Peru). Related to this, we may consider mason's marks. As Shaw recently noted (2009: n. 482), mason's marks indicate that a structure was a communal building since they occur almost exclusively in palaces, large potentially public structures and shrines (e.g. Palaikastro Building 5, Zeus Thenatas shrine at Amnissos). Is it possible that palatial mason's marks reflect the involvement of different groups in the construction of these buildings? In a recent study, Begg underlines that "The signs assert a collective claim to the creation or ownership of workmanship, either for payment or to commemorate what that particular team had accomplished, in the manner of the signs on the blocks deep inside the pyramid of Khufu. Their use was either temporary, if intended to document payment, or permanent, if commemorative. If the Protopalatial signs served a similar purpose, a strong possibility given the comparative evidence, then the explanation for their different appearance might lie in the nature or organisation of the groups engraving them" (Begg 2004: 20). There are three elements in favour of seeing the marks as signatures for different groups: the signs are often located on parts of blocks that were not visible, most major signs are represented in almost equal numbers and concentrations of similar signs cluster in specific areas of major buildings. Especially this last feature is telling and could suggest that each zone was produced by a different group. Did the people who built the Hall of the Double Axes at Knossos belong to a different group than those who constructed the Court of the Distaffs or the North Entrance Passage with its tridents or the Magazines with its window signs? Begg (2004: 20) further notes: "An economical proposal to account for the number of mason's marks would be a system of associations or groups of workers who were permanently organised on a standing basis and who were called upon to provide the required labour, either in a *corvée* system or by their own decision. The identity of these groups could be symbolised by their distinctive marks. Each group could have provided the material from start to finish in a vertically integrated system. Members of the groups operated throughout Neopalatial Crete, where they sometimes contributed work to other upper-class structures having ashlar walls, such as villas. At the various sites the relative proportions of the various groups might have varied, with the trident club being most active at Phaistos, for example. The groups represent an aspect of Minoan social organisation not necessarily found on the Mycenaean mainland."

Beyond the collective

In this paper, I have put forward elements allowing a reconstruction of a corporate organisation of Minoan society with the *House* as a basic element, an enduring social group centring on a residential structure of which the longevity and size underline the intergenerational and corporate nature of this association. The coalitions and co-operative labour forces as suggested by our iconographic material find a good reflection in the way Minoan residences and settlements were structured. By reconstructing three types of corporate groupings (co-residential, proximate and dispersed), I propose a kin network encompassing large regions of the island, resulting in integration and cohesion which culminated in the construction of the palaces. I have hypothesised these as the results of community related practices, bottom-up processes and collective corporate actions in which self-organisation was important with the act of building serving to reinforce group cohesion and installing solidarity, stability as well as a specific identity and hence ethnicity in the related community and region, acts which before may well have primarily centered around funerary complexes. The palaces were monumental communal structures, mechanisms that were put in place in the first place to promote the cohesion between different coalescent groups, the *Houses*. They were a formal *Great House* for integrative practices where disputes were settled, feasts were held and where power may have been held by house representatives, perhaps chosen for their age, gender or ritual experience. They may, moreover, be indicative of a coalescent society. The ritual associations of Minoan architecture may suggest a pattern of collective commitment, involving large numbers of participants that was most pronounced during the construction, but may have been re-enacted through calendrical or cyclical rites.

Acknowledgements

I thank F. Gaignerot, T. F. Cunningham, A. Chapin, M. Devolder, J. Malville, Q. Letesson, J. Wright, M. Dorban and R. Koehl for references, hard to find articles and valuable input. C. Knappett is thanked for improving the structure of my thoughts and D. Haggis for forcing me to express them better. Finally, I would like to thank K. Branigan and the editors for making the drawing by the late Bernard Warren available.

Bibliography

Béaur, G.

2006 En un débat douteux. Les communaux, quels enjeux dans la France des XVIIIe–XIXe siècles? *Revue d'histoire moderne et contemporaine* 53.1: 89–114.

Begg, D. J. I.

2004 An archaeology of palatial mason's marks on Crete. In A. P. Chapin (ed.), *ΧΑΡΙΣ: Essays in Honor of Sara A. Immerwahr* (Hesperia Supplements 33): 1–25. Athens: American School of Classical Studies.

Bevan, A.

2010 Political geography and palatial Crete. *Journal of Mediterranean Archaeology* 23.1: 27–54.

Blanton, R. E. and L. F. Fargher

2008 *Collective Action in the Formation of Pre-Modern States*. New York: Springer.

Blanton, R. E., G. M. Feinman, S. A. Kowalewski and P. N. Peregrine

1996 A dual-processual theory for the evolution of Mesoamerican Civilization. *Current Anthropology* 37: 1–14, 65–68.

Bowden, M., G. Brown and N. Smith

2009 *An Archaeology of Town Commons in England*. English Heritage.

Branigan, K.
1988a Social security and the state in Middle Bronze Age Crete. In R. *Laffineur* (ed.), *Annales d'archéologie égéenne de l'Université de Liège* (Aegaeum 2): 11–16. Liège: Université de Liège.
1988b Some observations on state formation in Crete. In E. B. French and K. A. Wardle (eds.), *Problems in Greek Prehistory. Papers Presented at the Centenary Conference of the British School of Archaeology at Athens, Manchester, April 1986*: 63–72. Bristol: Bristol Classical Press.
1993 *Dancing with Death. Life and Death in Southern Crete c. 3000–2000 BC*. Amsterdam: A. M. Hakkert Publisher.
Byrd, B. F.
1994 Public and private. Domestic and corporate: The emergence of the Southwest Asian village. *American Antiquity* 59.4: 639–66.
Canuto, M. A. and J. Yaeger (eds.)
2000 *The Archaeology of Communities. A New World Perspective.* London and New York: Routledge.
Chapin A. P.
2011 Gender and coalitional power in the miniature frescoes of Crete and the Cycladic islands. In *Πεπραγμένα του Ι' Διεθνούς Κρητολογικού Συνεδρίου, vol. A3*: 507–22. Χανιά: Φιλολογικός Σύλλογος "Ο Χρυσόστομος".
Chaniotis, A.
1999 Milking the mountains. Economic activities on the Cretan uplands in the Classical and Hellenistic periods. In A. Chaniotis (ed.), *From Minoan Farmers to Roman Traders: Sidelights on the Economy of Ancient Crete*: 181–220. Stuttgart: Franz Steiner Verlag.
Chapman J., R. Shiel and S. Batovic
1996 *The Changing Face of Dalmatia. Archaeological and Ecological Studies in a Mediterranean Landscape (Reports of the Research Committee of the Society of Antiquaries of London*, 54). Leicester: Leicester University Press.
Chesson, M. S.
2003 Households, houses, neighbourhoods and corporate villages. *Journal of Mediterranean Archaeology* 16(1): 79–102.
Cunningham, T. F.
2007 In the shadows of Kastri: An examination of domestic and civic space at Palaikastro (Crete). In R. Westgate, N. Fisher and J. Whitley (eds.), *Building Communities: House, Settlement and Society in the Aegean and Beyond. Proceedings of a Conference held at Cardiff University, 17-21 April 2001* (BSA Studies 15): 99–110. London: British School at Athens.
Day, P. M. and D. E. Wilson
2002 Landscapes of memory, craft and power in Pre-palatial and Proto-palatial Knossos. In Y. Hamilakis (ed.), *Labyrinth Revisited. Rethinking "Minoan" Archaeology*: 143–66. Oxford: Oxbow.
Devolder, M.
2008 Investment and prestige at Neopalatial Knossos. In O. Menozzi, M. Di Marzio and D. Fossataro (eds.), *SOMA 2005: Proceedings of the IX Symposium on Mediterranean Archaeology, Chieti (Italy), 24-26 February, 2005* (BAR IS 1739): 351–55. Oxford: Archaeopress.
2009 *Composantes et Interactions Sociales en Crète Néopalatiale (1700–1450 av. J.-C.). Investigation des Données Archéologiques.* PhD dissertation, Université Catholique de Louvain.
Driessen, J.
2001 History and Hierarchy. Preliminary observations on the settlement pattern of Minoan Crete. In K. Branigan (ed.), *Urbanism in the Aegean Bronze Age* (Sheffield Studies in Aegean Archaeology 4): 51–71. London and New York: Sheffield Academic Press.
2002 The King must die. Some observations on the use of Minoan Court Compounds. In J. Driessen, I. Schoep and R. Laffineur (eds.), *Monuments of Minos. Rethinking the Minoan Palaces. Proceedings of the International Workshop "Crete of the Hundred Palaces?" held at the*

Université Catholique de Louvain, Louvain-la-Neuve, 14–15 December 2001 (Aegaeum 23): 1–13. Liège: Université de Liège.

2004 The central court of the Palace at Knossos. In G. Cadogan, E. Hatzaki, A. Vasilakis (eds.), *Knossos: Palace, City, State: Proceedings of the Conference in Herakleion organised by the British School at Athens and the 23rd Ephoreia of Prehistoric and Classical Antiquities of Herakleion, in November 2000* (BSA Studies 12): 75–82. London: British School at Athens.

2007 IIb or not IIb: On the beginnings of Minoan monument building. In J. Bretschneider, J. Driessen and K. van Lerberghe (eds.), *Power and Architecture: Monumental Public Architecture in the Bronze Age Near East and Aegean* (Orientalia Lovaniensia Analecta 156): 73–92. Leuven: Peeters Publishers.

2009 Daidalos' Designs and Ariadne's Threads: Minoan towns as places of interaction. In S. Owen and L. Preston (eds.), *Inside the City in the Greek World. Studies of Urbanism from the Bronze Age to the Hellenistic Period* (University of Cambridge Museum of Classical Archaeology Monograph 1): 41–54. Oxford: Oxbow.

2010a Spirit of place: Minoan *Houses* as major actors. In D. J. Pullen (ed.), *Political Economies of the Aegean Bronze Age: Papers from the Langford Conference, Florida State University, Tallahassee, 22–24 February 2007*: 35–65. Oxford: Oxbow.

2010b The Goddess and the Skull. Some observations on group identity in Prepalatial Crete. In O. Krzyszkowska (ed.), *Cretan Offerings: Studies in Honour of Peter Warren* (BSA Studies 18): 107–17. London: British School at Athens.

2012 A matrilocal *House* society in Pre-and Protopalatial Crete? In I. Schoep, P. D. Tomkins and J. Driessen (eds.), *Back to the Beginning. Reassessing Social, Economic and Political Complexity on Crete during the Early and Middle Bronze Age*: 358–83. Oxford: Oxbow.

2013 Chercher la Femme. Identifying Minoan gender relations in the built environment. In D. Panagiotopoulos and U. Günkel-Maschek (eds.), *Minoan Realities. Proceedings of the Heidelberg Workshop* (Aegis 5): 141–64. Louvain-la-Neuve: Presses Universitaires.

Driessen, J. and D. Frankel

2012 Mines and Minds. Settlement networks and the diachronic use of space on Cyprus and Crete. In G. Cadogan, M. Iacovou, K. Kopaka and J. Whitley (eds.), *Parallel Lives: Ancient Island Societies in Crete and Cyprus. International Symposium Organised by the Universities of Crete and Cyprus and the British School at Athens, Nicosia, 30 November-2 December 2006* (BSA Studies 20): 61–84. London: British School at Athens.

Feinman, G. M.

2000a Corporate/Network: New perspectives on models of political action and the Puebloan Southwest. In M. B. Schiffer (ed.), *Social Theory in Archaeology* (*Foundations of Archaeological Enquiry*): 31–51. Salt Lake City: The University of Utah Press.

2000b Dual-processual theory and social formations in the Southwest. In B. J. Mills (ed.), *Alternative Leadership Strategies in the Prehispanic Southwest*: 207–24. Tucson: University of Arizona Press.

Fleming, A.

1985 Land tenure, productivity and field systems. In G. Barker and C. Gamble (eds.), *Beyond Domestication in Prehistoric Europe*: 129–46. New York: Academic Press.

Fowler, C.

2004 *The Archaeology of Personhood. An Anthropological Approach* (*Themes in Archaeology*). London and New York: Routledge.

Garfinkel, Y.

1998 Dancing and the beginning of art scenes in the Near East and South-East Europe. *Cambridge Archaeological Journal* 8: 207–37.

2003 *Dance at the Dawn of Agriculture*. Austin: Texas University Press.

Garfinkel, Y., D. Ben-Shlomo and T. Kuperman

2009 Large-scale storage of grain surplus in the sixth millennium BC: The silos of Tel Tsaf. *Antiquity* 83: 309–25.

German, S.

2005 *Performance, Power and the Art of the Aegean Bronze Age* (BAR IS 1347). Oxford: Archaeopress.

Gibson, B. D.

2008 Chiefdoms and the emergence of private property in land. *Journal of Anthropological Archaeology* 27: 46–62.

Goodison, L.

2004 From tholos tomb to Throne Room: Some considerations of dawn light and directionality in Minoan buildings. In G. Cadogan, E. Hatzaki and A. Vasilakis (eds.), *Knossos: Palace, City, State: Proceedings of the Conference in Herakleion organised by the British School at Athens and the 23rd Ephoreia of Prehistoric and Classical Antiquities of Herakleion, in November 2000* (BSA Studies 12): 339–50. London: British School at Athens.

Graham, J. W.

1963 *The Palaces of Crete*. Princeton: University Press.

Haggis, D.

1999 Staple Finance, peak sanctuaries, and economic complexity in Late Prepalatial Crete. In A. Chaniotis (ed.), *From Minoan Farmers to Roman Traders: Sidelights on the Economy of Ancient Crete*: 53–85. Stuttgart: Franz Steiner Verlag.

2002 Integration and complexity in the Late Pre-Palatial Period. A view from the countryside in Eastern Crete. In Y. Hamilakis (ed.), *Labyrinth Revisited. Rethinking "Minoan" Archaeology*: 120–42. Oxford: Oxbow.

Halbherr, F.

1893 Researches in Crete. VIII. Cnossos. *The Antiquary* 28, September 1893: 110–12.

Halstead, P.

1981 From determinism to uncertainty: Social storage and the rise of the Minoan Palace. In A. Sheridan and G. Bailey (eds.), *Economic Archaeology* (BAR IS 96): 187–213. Oxford: British Archaeological Reports.

1988 On redistribution and the origin of Minoan-Mycenaean palatial economies. In E. B. French and K. A. Wardle (eds.), *Problems in Greek Prehistory. Papers Presented at the Centenary Conference of the British School of Archaeology at Athens, Manchester, April 1986*: 519–29. Bristol: Bristol Classical Press.

1995 From sharing to hoarding: The Neolithic foundations of Aegean Bronze Age Society? In R. Laffineur and W.-D. Niemeier (eds.), *Politeia: Society and State in the Aegean Bronze Age. Proceedings of the 5th International Aegean Conference, University of Heidelberg, Archäologisches Institut, 10-13 April 1994* (Aegaeum 12): 11–21. Liège: Université de Liège.

2008 Between a rock and a hard place: Coping with marginal colonisation in the Later Neolithic and Early Bronze Age of Crete and the Aegean. In P. Tomkins and V. Isaakidou (eds.), *Escaping the Labyrinth: The Cretan Neolithic in Context* (Sheffield Studies in Aegean Archaeology 8): 229–57. Oxford: Oxbow.

Harding, G.

1968 The tragedy of the commons. *Science* 162: 1243–48.

Hare, T. S.

2000 Between the household and the empire. Structural relationships within and among Aztec communities and polities. In M. A. Canuto and J. Yaeger (eds.), *The Archaeology of Communities. A New World Perspective*: 78–101. London and New York: Routledge.

Hastings, C. M. and M. E. Moseley

1975 The adobes of Huaca del Sol and Huaca de La Luna. *American Antiquity* 40.2:196–203.

Hayden, B. and A. Cannon
1982 The corporate group as an archaeological unit. *Journal of Anthropological Archaeology* 1:2: 132–58.
Herva, V.-P.
2005 The life of buildings: Minoan building deposits in an ecological perspective. *Oxford Journal of Archaeology* 24.3: 215–27.
Hutson, S. R., T. W. Stanton, A. Magnoni, R. Terry and J. Craner
2007 Beyond the buildings. Formation processes of Ancient Maya houselots and methods for the study of non-architectural space. *Journal of Anthropological Archaeology* 26:3: 442–73.
Isbell, W. H.
2000 What we should be studying: the "imagined community" and the "natural community". In M. A. Canuto and J. Yaeger (eds.), *The Archaeology of Communities. A New World Perspective*: 243–66. London and New York: Routledge.
Koehl, R.
2006 *Aegean Bronze Age Rhyta*. Philadelphia: INSTAP Academic Press.
Kolb, M. J. and J. E. Snead
1997 It is a small world after all: Comparative analyses of community organization in archaeology. *American Antiquity* 62.4: 609–28.
Koster, H. A.
1997 Yours, mine, and ours: Private and public pasture in Greece. In N. Kardulias and M. T. Shutes (eds.), *Aegean Strategies: Studies of Culture and Environment on the European Fringe*: 141–85. Lanham, Maryland: Rowman and Littlefiled Publishers, Inc.
Koster, H. A. and H. A. Forbes
2000 The "Commons" and the Market: Ecological effects of communal land tenure and market integration on local resources in the Mediterranean. In S. Buck Sutton (ed.), *Contingent Countryside: Settlement, Economy, and Land Use in the Southern Argolid Since 1700*: 262–74. Stanford: Stanford University Press.
Kowalewski, S. A.
2006 Coalescent societies. In T. J. Pluckhahn and R. Etheridge (eds.), *Light on the Path. The Anthropology and History of the Southeastern Indians*: 94–122. Tuscaloosa: The University of Alabama Press.
Letesson, Q.
2006 Reconstructing Minoan monumentality. In J. Day, C. Greenlaw, H. Hall, A. Kelly, L. Matassa, K. McAleese, E. Saunders and D. Stritch (eds.), *Symposium on Mediterranean Archaeology (SOMA 2004): Proceedings of the eighth annual meeting of postgraduate researchers, School of Classics, Trinity College, Dublin. 20–22 February 2004* (BAR IS 1514): 95–100. Oxford: Archaeopress.
2009 *Du phénotype au génotype. Analyse de la syntaxe spatiale en architecture minoenne (MMIIIB – MRIB)* (Aegis 2). Louvain-la-Neuve: Presses Universitaires.
Letesson, Q. and K. Vansteenhuyse
2006 Towards an archaeology of perception: "Looking" at the Minoan Palaces. *Journal of Mediterranean Archaeology* 19.1: 91–119.
Levy, T. E.
1998 *The Archaeology of Society in the Holy Land*. London and New York: Leicester University Press.
Liveri, A.
2008 Representations and interpretations of dance in the Aegean Bronze Age. Ritual dances in Cycladic and Minoan religions. *Mitteilungen des Deutschen Archäologischen Instituts* 123: 1–38.

Luhmann, N.

1984 *Soziale Systeme: Grundriß einer allgemeinen Theorie*. Frankfurt: Suhrkamp.

Macdonald, C. F. and C. Knappett

2007 *Knossos: Protopalatial Deposits in Early Magazine A and the South-West Houses* (BSA Supplementary Volume 4). London: British School at Athens.

Malville, J. M.

2009 Complexity and self-organization in pilgrimage systems. In J. M. Malville and B. N. Saraswati (eds.), *Pilgrimage: Sacred Landscapes and Self-Organized Complexity*: 32–51. New Delhi: Indira Gandhi National Center for the Arts and DK Printworld.

Mandalaki, S.

2004 Ο χορός στη Μινωική Κρήτη. *Αρχαιολογία και Τέχνες* 90: 15–20 http://www.arxaiologia.gr/assets/media/PDF/migrated/90_15-20.pdf (accessed on January 8th, 2010).

Marcus, J.

2000 Toward an archaeology of communities. In M. A. Canuto and J. Yaeger (eds.), *The Archaeology of Communities. A New World Perspective*: 231–42. London and New York: Routledge.

Mills, B. J.

2000 Alternative models, alternative strategies: Leadership in the Prehispanic Southwest. In B. J. Mills (ed.) *Alternative Leadership Strategies in the Prehispanic Southwest*: 3–18. Tucson: University of Arizona Press.

Moseley, M. E.

1975 Prehistoric principles of labor organization in the Moche valley, Peru. *American Antiquity* 40.2: 191–96.

Mosso, A.

1907 *The Palaces of Crete and Their Builders*. London: T. Fisher Unwin.

Ostrom, E.

1990 *Governing the Commons: The Evolution of Institutions for Collective Action*. New York: Cambridge University Press.

Palyvou, C.

2002 Central courts: The supremacy of the void. In J. Driessen, I. Schoep and R. Laffineur (eds.), *Monuments of Minos. Rethinking the Minoan Palaces. Proceedings of the International Workshop "Crete of the Hundred Palaces?" held at the Université Catholique de Louvain, Louvain-la-Neuve, 14–15 December 2001* (Aegaeum 23): 167–78. Liège: Université de Liège.

Preziosi, D.

1983 *Minoan Architectural Design. Formation and Signification*. Berlin: Mouton.

Relaki, M.

2004 Constructing a region: the contested landscapes of Prepalatial Mesara. In J. C. Barrett and P. Halstead (eds.), *The Emergence of Civilisation Revisited* (Sheffield Studies in Aegean Archaeology 6): 170–88. Oxford: Oxbow.

2009 Rethinking administration and seal use in third millennium BC Crete. *Creta Antica* 10(2): 353–72.

2012 The Social Arenas of Tradition. Investigating collective and individual social strategies in the Prepalatial and Protopalatial Mesara. In I. Schoep, P. Tomkins & J. Driessen (eds.), *Back to the beginning. Reassessing social and political complexity on Crete during the Early and Middle Bronze Age*: 290-324. Oxford: Oxbow.

Renfrew, C.

1974 Beyond a subsistence economy: The evolution of social organization in prehistoric Europe. In C. B. Moore (ed.), *Reconstructing Complex Societies* (Supplement to the Bulletin of the American Schools of Oriental Research 20): 69–85. Cambridge, MA: American Schools of Oriental Research.

Rethemiotakis, G.
2002 Evidence on social and economic changes at Galatas and Pediada in the New-Palace period. In J. Driessen, I. Schoep and R. Laffineur (eds.), *Monuments of Minos. Rethinking the Minoan Palaces. Proceedings of the International Workshop "Crete of the Hundred Palaces?" held at the Université Catholique de Louvain, Louvain-la-Neuve, 14–15 December 2001* (Aegaeum 23): 55–70. Liège: Université de Liège.

Romanou, D.
2007 Residence design and variation in residential group structure: a case study, Mallia. In R. Westgate, N. Fisher and J. Whitley (eds.), *Building Communities: House, Settlement and Society in the Aegean and Beyond. Proceedings of a Conference held at Cardiff University, 17–21 April 2001* (BSA Studies 15): 77–90. London: British School at Athens.

Saitta, D. J.
2007 *The Archaeology of Collective Action. The American Experience* (Archaeological Perspective Series). Gainesville, FL: University Press of Florida.

Shaw, J. W.
1973 The orientation of the Minoan Palaces. *Antichità Cretesi: Studi in onore di Doro Levi 1. Chroniche di Archeologia* 12: 47–59.
2009 *Minoan Architecture: Materials and Techniques* (Studi di archeologia cretese). Padova: Bottega d'Erasmo.
2010 Setting in the Palaces of Minoan Crete: A review of how and when. In O. Krzyszkowska (ed.), *Cretan Offerings: Studies in Honour of Peter Warren* (BSA Studies 18): 303–14. London: British School at Athens.

Schoep, I.
2004 Assessing the role of architecture in conspicuous consumption in the Middle Minoan I–II Periods. *Oxford Journal of Archaeology* 23(3): 243–69.

Schoep, I. and C. Knappett
2004 Dual Emergence: Evolving heterarchy, exploding hierarchy. In J. C. Barrett and P. Halstead (eds.), *The Emergence of Civilisation Revisited* (Sheffield Studies in Aegean Archaeology 6): 21–37. Oxford: Oxbow.

Soar, K.
2010 Circular dance performances in the prehistoric Aegean. In A. Michaels (ed.), *Dynamics and the Science of Ritual*: 137–56. Wiesbaden: Harrassowitz Verlag.

Soja, E. W.
1989 *Postmodern Geographies: The Reassertion of Space in Critical Social Theory*. London: Verso Press.

Stanish, C.
1989 Household archaeology: Testing models of zonal complementarity in the South Central Andes. *American Anthropologist* 91: 7–24.

Todaro, S. and S. Di Tonto
2006 The Neolithic settlement of Phaistos revisited: Evidence for ceremonial activity on the eve of the Bronze Age. In V. Isaakidou and P. D. Tomkins (eds.), *Escaping the Labyrinth: New perspectives on the Neolithic of Crete* (Sheffield Studies in Aegean Archaeology 8): 177–90. Oxford: Oxbow.

Tomkins, P. D.
2004 Filling in the "Neolithic Background": social life and social transformation in the Aegean before the Bronze Age. In J. C. Barrett and P. Halstead (eds.), *The Emergence of Civilisation Revisited* (Sheffield Studies in Aegean Archaeology 6): 38–63. Oxford: Oxbow.
2012 Behind the horizon. Reconsidering the genesis and function of the "First Palace" at Knossos (Final Neolithic IV-Middle Minoan IB). In I. Schoep, P. D. Tomkins and J. Driessen (eds.), *Back to the Beginning. Reassessing Social, Economic and Political Complexity on Crete during the Early and Middle Bronze Age*: 32–80. Oxford: Oxbow.

Tsipopoulou, M.
2002 Petras, Siteia: The Palace, the town, the hinterland and the Protopalatial background. In J. Driessen, I. Schoep and R. Laffineur (eds.), *Monuments of Minos. Rethinking the Minoan Palaces. Proceedings of the International Workshop "Crete of the Hundred Palaces?" held at the Université Catholique de Louvain, Louvain-la-Neuve, 14-15 December 2001* (Aegaeum 23): 133–44. Liège: Université de Liège.
2009 Goddesses for "Gene"? The Late Minoan IIIC Shrine at Halasmenos, Ierapetra. In A. L. D' Agata and A. Van de Moortel (eds.), *Archaeologies of Cult: Essays on Ritual and Cult in Crete in Honor of Geraldine C. Gesell* (Hesperia Supplement 42): 121–36. Princeton: The American School of Classical Studies at Athens.
Van Gijseghem, H. and K. J. Vaughn
2008 Regional integration and the built environment in Middle-Range societies: Paracas and Early Nasca houses and communities. *Journal of Anthropological Archaeology* 27(1): 111–30.
Weingarten, J.
1986 The sealing structures of Minoan Crete: MM II Phaistos to the destruction of the Palace of Knossos. Part I: The evidence until the LM IB destructions. *Oxford Journal of Archaeology* 5(3): 279–98.
Whitelaw, T. M.
2001 From sites to communities: Defining the human dimensions of Minoan urbanism. In K. Branigan (ed.), *Urbanism in the Aegean Bronze Age* (Sheffield Studies in Aegean Archaeology 4): 15–37. London and New York: Sheffield Academic Press.
2004 Alternative pathways to complexity in the Southern Aegean. In J. C. Barrett and P. Halstead (eds.), *The Emergence of Civilisation Revisited* (Sheffield Studies in Aegean Archaeology 6): 232–56. Oxford: Oxbow.
2007 House, households and community at Early Minoan Fournou Korifi: Methods and models for interpretation. In R. Westgate, N. Fisher and J. Whitley (eds.), *Building Communities: House, Settlement and Society in the Aegean and Beyond. Proceedings of a Conference held at Cardiff University, 17-21 April 2001* (BSA Studies 15): 65–77. London: British School at Athens.
Wills, W. H.
2000 Political leadership and the construction of Chacoan great houses. In B. J. Mills (ed.), *Alternative Leadership Strategies in the Prehispanic Southwest*: 19–44. Tucson: University of Arizona Press.
Wolfe, A. W.
2006 Network perspectives on communities. Structure and Dynamics 1(4): 1–25. Retrieved from: http://escholarship.org/uc/item/8184j9bq
Yaeger, J. and M. A. Canuto
2000 Introducing an archaeology of communities. In M. A. Canuto and J. Yaeger (eds.), The Archaeology of Communities. A New World Perspective: 1–15. London and New York: Routledge.

Chapter 15

The "emergence of the individual" revisited: Memory and trans-corporeality in the mortuary landscapes of Bronze Age Crete[1]

Yannis Hamilakis

Introduction

What is a person and how is personhood constituted in various contexts? Is personhood an exclusive attribute of humans, or can we have non-human (e.g. animal) persons? Can we talk of personhood in the abstract sense? To what extent is the rigid separation between persons, and between a person and her embodied constitution, appropriate and legitimate? What other expressions and materialisations of personhood are there, beyond our own, modernist notion of the individual? These are some of the questions that have generated wide and fruitful discussion in various fields in recent years, including in anthropology and social archaeology. Despite some recent interesting attempts, however, these themes are hugely underrepresented in the discussions within Aegean prehistory. And yet for some of these areas of inquiry, the Aegean archaeological material offers extremely rich and diverse "food for thought".

In this short chapter, obviously I will not be able to tackle all these themes, but I hope to open the discussion on one specific facet, and that is the assumed "emergence of the individual" towards the end of the Early Bronze Age. The archaeological realm of Bronze Age Crete (and the mortuary arena in particular) would be my main focus, but with comparative excursions to other regional archaeological and ethnographic locales. In exploring this issue, I will also offer some alternative suggestions on how to re-conceptualise mortuary landscapes and practices, the main material evidence deployed in such discussions. These suggestions will be based on notions of corporeality, on the dialectic between remembering and forgetting, and on alternative conceptions of space and time (and the fusion between the two).

"The emergence of the individual"? Elements of doubt

Reading and re-reading Keith Branigan's *Dancing with Death* (1993) one is reminded of its richness in insights and observations, and of the author's ability to produce a captivating interpretative picture out of a diverse, and mostly rudimentarily recorded empirical dataset. Branigan was also one of the first to discuss extensively patterns such as the appearance of larnakes and funerary pithoi in communal burials, thought to have happened at the end of the Early Bronze Age. He prompted researchers to think about the possible social implications of the phenomenon, suggesting, with some degree of scepticism and ambivalence, that we may be observing the decline - in importance - of the clan, and the emergence of the notion of individuality:

> "At some time in EM III or MM I a change of burial practice seems to have been initiated. Rectangular clay coffins and large jars (pithoi) begin to appear inside the tholos tombs with remains of burials inside them...On the face of it, the appearance of larnax and pithos burials in the tombs would seem to point to a developing trend for individual inhumations, though initially at least they were still made in the communal context of the tholos tomb. Later Middle and Late Minoan pithos burials were found outside some of the tholoi, as if to confirm that the concept of the burial of the individual had at last broken free from the demands of the communal burial" (Branigan 1993: 65–66).

To be fair, Branigan refers here explicitly to the "concept of the burial of the individual" as opposed to the concept of the individual in the abstract sense, but it is clear throughout the book that he attributes to this perceived development wider implications. For example, he returns to this theme in the final page of his book, where he notes:

> "The idea of utilising a burial container to emphasise one's individuality, whilst being buried within the communal tomb to emphasise one's communality, is an interesting development in the EM III-MM I and to some extent it must represent a weakening of the kin-group traditions, and a period when stress was emerging between the demands of the kin-groups on the one hand and the ever-larger nucleated communities on the other" (Branigan 1993: 141).

This has become the standard and accepted view by most researchers (e.g. McEnroe 2010: 32, for a recent textbook, with references), but note in the first passage above the ambivalence implied in the phrase "On the face of it"; immediately afterwards, Branigan outlines some of the evidence which underscores his scepticism:

> "This may be a correct interpretation of the evidence, but if the intention of the larnax and pithos burials was to express individuality rather than communality, then it was an intention that was subverted. In tholos E [Epsilon] at Arkhanes, for example, the thirty-one larnakes and two pithoi contained the remains of thirty-six individuals, whilst in the nearby tholos C [Gamma] the larnakes near the entrance to the tomb had each received multiple burials... Similarly three of the pithoi from tomb A at Vorou each held two burials..." (1993: 67).

It is clear thus that while standing by his initial statement and interpretation, he considered it fair to list some of the evidence that points to a different direction, interpreting this as a subversion of the intended emphasis on the individual. It is this implied scepticism and ambivalence that I find most fruitful and rewarding, and I take them as a departure point in my own exploration in this chapter. Does evidence such as the assumed appearance of larnakes and funerary pithoi at the end of the Early Bronze Age indeed indicate an emphasis on individuality, after almost a thousand years of communality? More importantly, are terms such as individuality, and the dialectic between individuality and communality, the appropriate conceptual tools for the Early Bronze Age of Crete or for prehistoric contexts in general? I am not, of course, the first to cast doubts on this interpretation. Papadatos (1999) and Catapoti (2005) in their unpublished PhDs have questioned the link. Based partly on their work and the work of others, I want to continue the discussion and suggest some alternative interpretations.

Individuals and personhood in archaeology

Before I try to tackle in some detail these issues with regard to the Cretan context, it may be worth reminding ourselves that the relevance of the concept of the individual in prehistory or indeed in any pre-modern context has been one of the hotly debated questions in recent archaeological thinking. Very briefly, certain strands of interpretative archaeology, especially the ones inspired by the early (and not-so-early) work of Ian Hodder (e.g. 2000 for a recent reflection) have called for the search for the individual and his and her role and agency, in the remote as well as in the recent past. They saw this as a necessary, if not essential, corrective to the marginalisation of the individual, caused by the emphasis on processes, structures, systems and power hierarchies, characteristic of "new archaeology". In other words, they saw this as an essential humanising move. Other strands, however, have claimed that such a call introduces modernist modes of thinking into the past: the individual, they claim, is a figure of western capitalist modernity, and its implied bounded and indivisible nature contrasts sharply with non-western ethnographic data that reveal different conceptions of personhood (e.g. Thomas 2002; Fowler 2002). Melanesian ethnography, especially the work of Strathern (1988), who has analysed and helped popularise a non-western conception of personhood which, according to her, is dividual, relational and composite, as opposed to the individual and bounded western one, has become a standard supporting device for this archaeological argument. Strathern's work has inspired numerous archaeological re-interpretations of data, from the fragmentation studies by John Chapman and Bisserka Gaydarska in the Balkan Neolithic (Chapman 2000; Chapman and Gaydarska 2007) to the re-interpretation of disarticulated and re-assembled skeletal material, often involving fragments from human bodies, as well as from animals and objects, in British prehistory (e.g. Fowler 2002). Incidentally, an argument similar to the one on Crete was proposed in the early 1980s for British prehistory: some researchers saw in the shift from communal to single burials in the Later Neolithic and the Bronze Age, the emergence of the individual. The partibility phenomenon, especially the handling, manipulation and circulation of human skeletal *parts*, has been used as a counter-argument against this idea (cf. Thomas 2002: 39).

More recent takes by both ethnographers and archaeologies, however, have exposed the complexity of the phenomenon. Another Melanesian ethnographer, LiPuma, has criticised Strathern's arguments as well as other studies that talk of the incommensurability of Melanesian and western personhood, on several grounds (1998):

> "First, they [these studies] compare Melanesian notions of the person not to the Western reality of personhood but to Western ideology, itself a highly contested product. Second, they tend to see Melanesian notions as the inverse of Western ideology, thereby winding up defining the former as the negative image of the latter. Third, to argue that these forms of personhood are incommensurable rules out the possibility of ethnography which presumes that there are points of commensurability...Fourth, to argue for total cultural relativity is politically disempowering insofar as it underscores the ground of critique..." (1998: 75).

LiPuma concludes that "the ontological form is the dual person delineated by dividual and individual facets. Universally, then, the person emerges from the tension, itself always variable and culturally/historically shaped, between these two aspects of personhood and the ways in which they are objectified and embodied" (1988: 75).

The archaeological discussion on this issue has been extremely valuable in helping us move away from the naturalisation of the "individual" as the sole and exclusive model of personhood, and in allowing us to explore the diversity of pre-modern and non-western perceptions of the self, but the debate has become somehow polarised and sterile. Recent interventions, however, such as the one by Fowler (2004) who, taking on board LiPuma and others' criticism, draws attention to non-human personhood, to bodily boundaries, and to the transmission and circulation of substances, or the one by Knapp and van Dommelen who argue for a shift of emphasis from typologies of personhood to social practice (2008), are much more fruitful and promising.

Nevertheless, there are still several problems that need to be addressed. Despite recent attempts, the philosophical principle that makes a sharp distinction between person/self and body still underscores much of the discussion, forgetting that personhood is a matter of physical and corporeal expression and performance. Furthermore, whenever the discussion on persons, individuals and selves moves onto the terrain of embodiment, this is seen mainly as discourse, and the body is treated primarily, if not exclusively, as a representational and discursive construct, rather than the material, existential ground of selfhood (cf. Hamilakis 2002; Hamilakis *et al.* 2002). I thus propose here to shift the discussion to *corporeality* in order to signal the primacy of the sensory and sensual engagement in the continuous constitution and re-constitution of the various forms of personhood and selfhood (Hamilakis 2011; 2012; 2013). And I talk here of corporeality and not of the body deliberately, since I want to avoid the connotations of stasis and boundedness that the term "body" may at times imply, and foreground instead the fluid processes of corporeal existence, thinking and practice. In addition, corporeality is less about bodily boundaries and more about relationships, bodily movement, and circulation *through* bodies, variously conceived. Personhood and selfhood in their turn, should be seen as the assemblage not of permanent and unchanging types (individuals versus dividuals, for example), but of transient, corporeally expressed, performative states. Finally, since much of this discussion concerns mortuary practices, it is worth reminding ourselves that burial rites do not reflect or represent in a direct and unproblematic way ideas on personhood, and that the generation of remembering and forgetting, the field of memory, is perhaps the most fruitful and most promising interpretative horizon open to us (Hamilakis 1998; 2010; 2013; Hamilakis and Labanyi 2008; Jones 2007).

From individuals to trans-corporeality in Bronze Age Crete

So how do the data from Bronze Age Crete contribute to this discussion? Can we talk about individuals becoming visible at the end of the Early Bronze Age? In the passages by Branigan cited above we saw that the key evidence for the emergence of individuality is the presence of burial containers. Yet these same passages also give several examples of burial containers that did not hold individual burials: Tholoi E and Γ at Archanes Phourni, and Tholos A at Vorou. At Archanes Tholos Γ, for example, in the EM III, "[T]hree larnakes contained the remains of one burial...three coffins had two burials...one larnax had three burials, and finally, the pithos and one more larnax contained the remains of four individuals" (Papadatos 2005: 57). While Papadatos believes that larnakes were used for primary burials and not as ossuaries, at other sites there is clear evidence that they were seen as containers for both "primary" burials, and partial skeletons and loose body parts, as well as for objects and artefacts. The examples from Vorou are particularly instructive (Marinatos 1930–31). This is an MM I site where, according to the excavator, the use of larnakes and pithoi constitutes its most prominent feature; here a container from tholos A held a well-preserved skeleton without skull, whereas a pithos from the same tomb contained a well-preserved skeleton but with two skulls, one of which was that of a child. At the same site, outside tholos B, a pithos contained an un-burnt skeleton, as well as other burnt bones, and cups and other objects. This last example reminds us that the find spots of burial containers are diverse: they were found inside the tombs, in built enclosures and antechambers around them, as well as outdoors in the surrounding area, but in association with the main mortuary structures. Rather than seeing containers such as larnakes and pithoi as distinctive, highly idiosyncratic, and individualised and individualising objects thus, they should be seen as one of many material strategies for the arrangement and organisation of mortuary space, alongside other compartments, such as antechambers, enclosures, pits and so on. The outer rooms and antechambers in particular are not simply *post hoc* practical solutions to the need for more space, as it is often the temptation to interpret them. For if that was the case, why is it that in many tombs (e.g. Apesokari A, and B, Platanos B, Hagios Kyrillos, Kamilari C, Sopata Kouse, possibly Platanos C) these rooms were part of the original design?

I would add that in this set of practices to do with the rearrangement and organisation of space we should also include the selection and the grouping of body parts into discrete piles. This well-documented strategy has been more easily recognisable with regard to skulls, which often receive special treatment and care: examples here include Agia Triada A, Koumasa B, Platanos B, Vorou A, Archanes Phourni Γ, and Moni Odigitria, where in the "ossuary", skulls were arranged into groups of five or ten (cf. Branigan 1987; 2010: 257; Papadatos 2005; Xanthoudides 1924: 7).

Interestingly, even at Hagios Charalambos cave in the Lasithi mountains, a cave which in MM IIB was used as an ossuary for the deposition of a large number of mixed skeletons and objects dating from the Neolithic period onwards, strategies of compartmentalisation are present: the natural galleries of the cave were used as separate compartments, but in one of them, two walls were constructed, dividing further the space into discrete areas (Betancourt *et al.* 2008; Betancourt, this volume). While when deposited, bones and objects were mixed, there seemed to be a need to keep some skeletons and objects separate from others.

And the question then becomes, to what extent the compartmentalisation and subdivision of mortuary space and the grouping of body parts are features that appear first at the end of the "pre-palatial" period, or whether such strategies can be detected much earlier. In much of the literature on the matter, we read that features such as antechambers and enclosures appear, along with burial containers, towards the end of the Prepalatial, as a response to developing needs and to changes in funerary ceremonies (Branigan 1993: 63). This is based on the observation that in a number of cases, these antechambers seemed to have been added onto the main tomb gradually and in an organic manner, rather than being built as part of the original design in one go. So in this rather functionalist neo-evolutionist narrative, in both cases, that of the ante-chambers and of the larnakes, we are supposed to see a progressive development from the homogenous to the heterogeneous, from the unified, undifferentiated space to the compartmentalised and subdivided one, and of course from the communal to the individual (cf. Hamilakis 2002b for a broader critique). Yet as I mentioned earlier, there are several cases where these antechambers were part of the original design, and while some or perhaps most of these cases date to the MM I, in at least one case, that of Platanos B, these features are dated to the EM II, making the argument of gradual compartmentalisation seem weak.

A further look at other data would confirm that this strategy for compartmentalisation and subdivision, and of grouping, arrangement, and re-deposition of body parts and objects in discrete locales has been there all along; it can be detected even in the earlier contexts. Let me offer some examples: Branigan has noted the existence of some unusual tholoi such as Kaminospelios (Blackman and Branigan 1973), and Merthies and Plakoura (Pendlebury 1935). All three of them possess walls that divide the interior of the tholos into two, and in the case of Kaminospelios the published report implies that this wall was part of the original construction of the tomb in EM I-II (Fig. 15.1). There is another smaller wall, which, if part of the original architecture, would have subdivided the tholos even further, creating more discrete locales. Dating for the

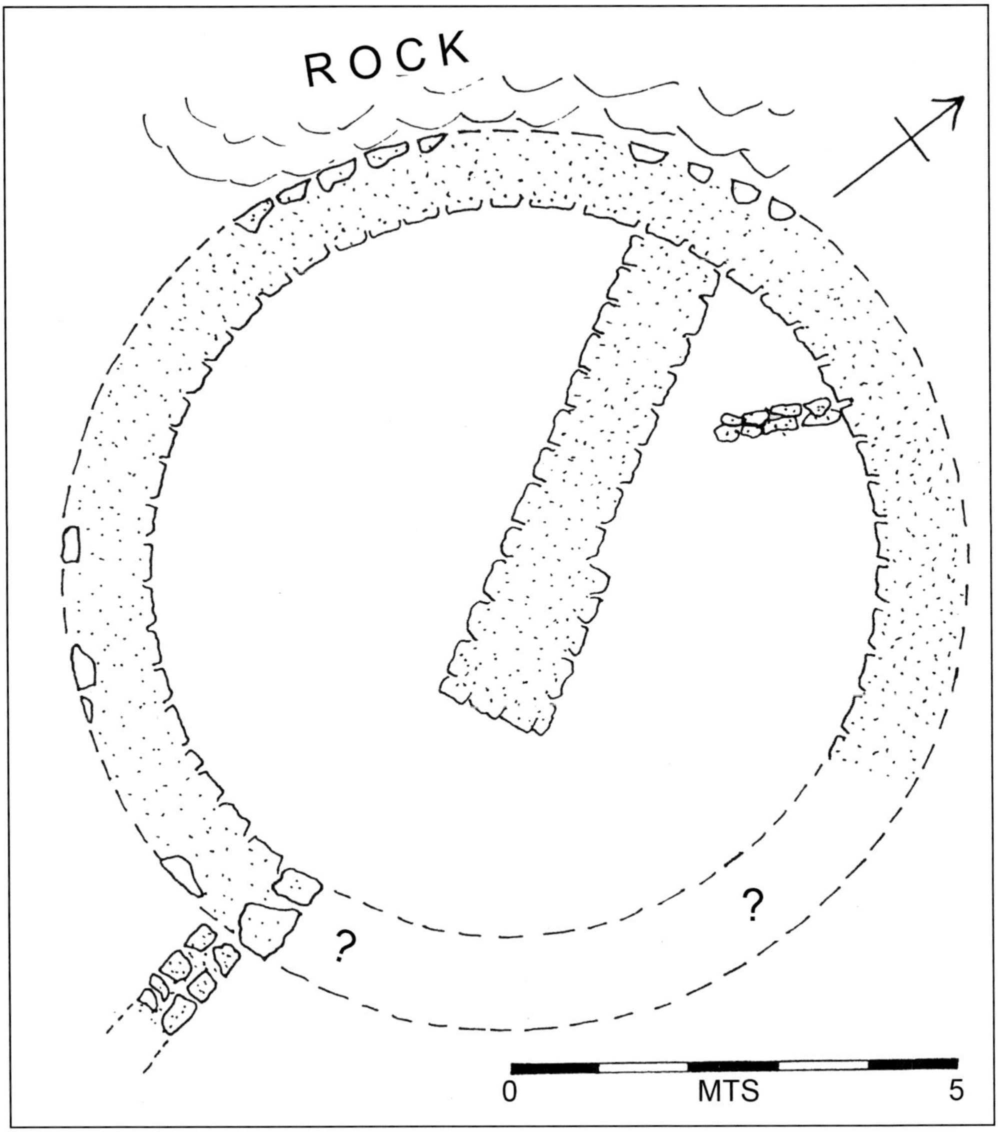

Figure 15.1: Plan of the tholos tomb at Kaminospelio (modified from Blackman and Branigan 1973).

other two tombs is uncertain, but the report notes EM sherds. In Lebena Yerokampos II, a stone-made, box-like compartment, called by the excavator θήκη (*thiki* – niche), had been built against the wall using upright, long and narrow stones, and with an open front into the tomb (Alexiou and Warren 2004: 56), thus dividing the open space of the tholos (Fig. 15.2). It contained gathered bones and skulls, EM I pottery and a marble figurine (Fig. 15.3). Compartmentalisation is also evident from early on in house tombs, as, for example, in the case of EM II tombs at the Sissi cemetery,

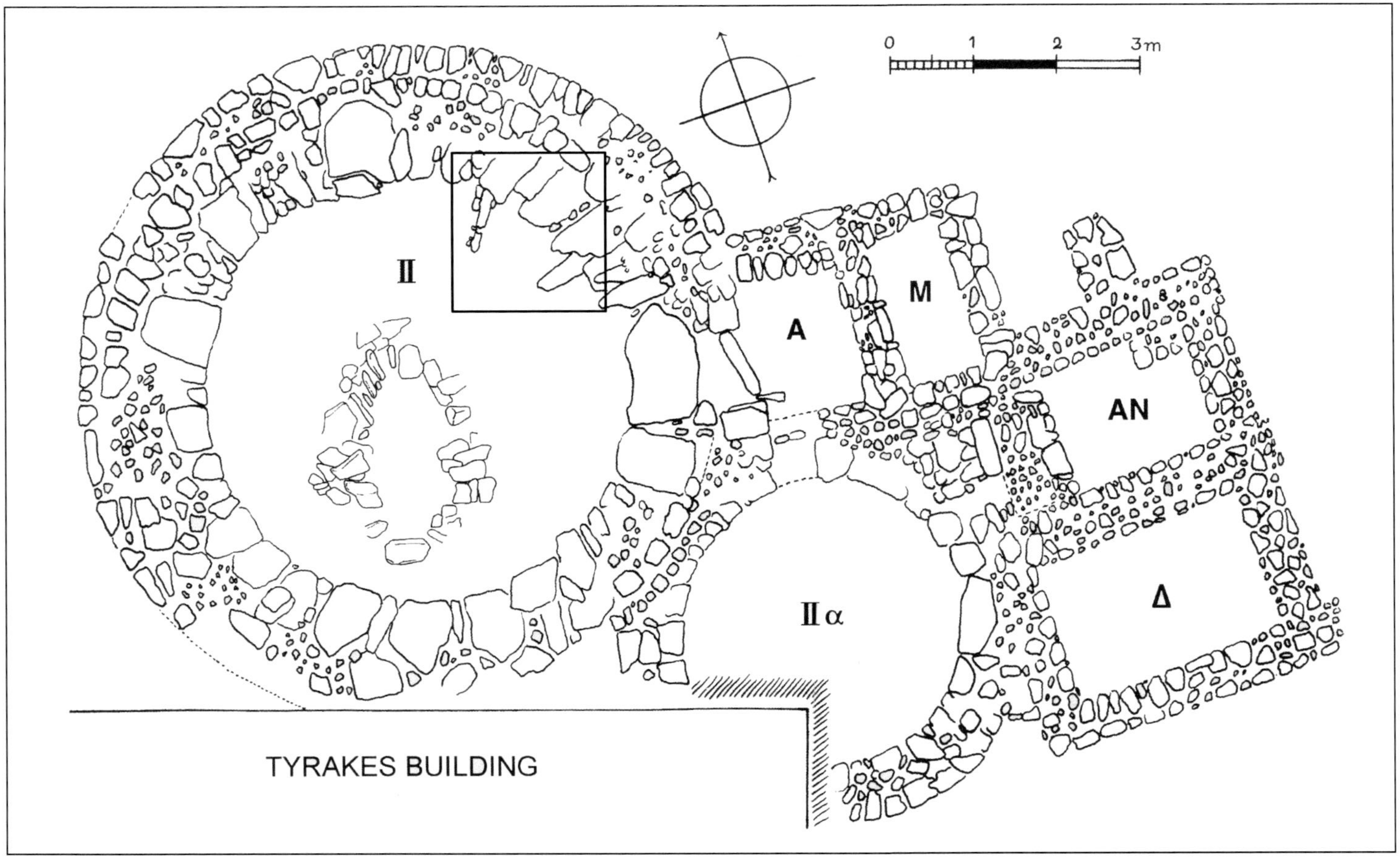

Figure 15.2: Plan of tholos II at Lebena Yerokampos with the θήκη (niche) highlighted (modified from Alexiou and Warren 2004, fig. 12).

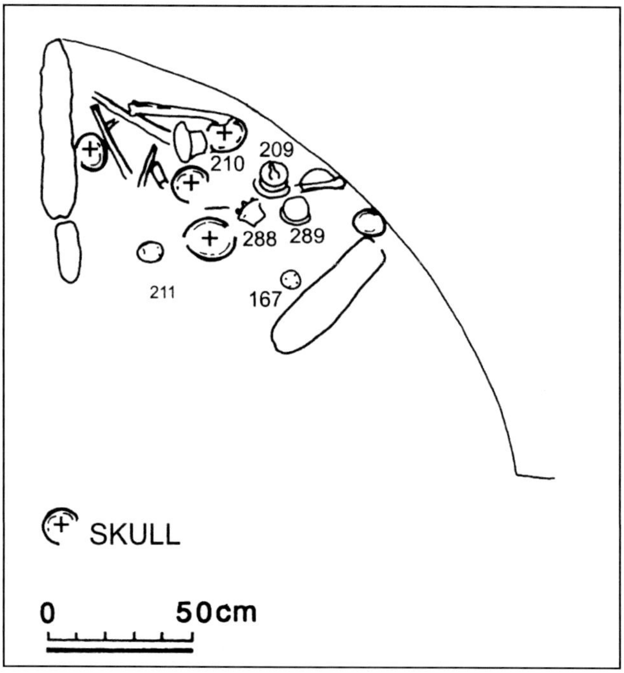

Figure 15.3: Lebena Yerokampos II: detail, showing the θήκη (niche) at "stage" C, containing human remains and artefacts (modified from Alexiou and Warren 2004, fig. 15a).

where walls and other features (e.g. burial containers such as jars) subdivided the space (Schoep, this volume).

As for the collection of body parts and objects, Archanes Tholos Γ offers perhaps the most unambiguous evidence. Three skulls from EM IIA burials were collected and deposited carefully, together with objects and artefacts, in a fissure of the bedrock outside the tholos (Papadatos 2005). Beyond south-central Crete, evidence for the collection and re-deposition of certain body parts in the early Prepalatial period, especially skulls, is found in other contexts such as the house tombs at Mochlos and Gournia (Soles 1992), at Sissi (Schoep, this volume), and elsewhere.

Even the presence of larnakes, pithoi and other mobile burial containers is encountered in at least four early, and mostly communal burial contexts: at Archanes Tholos E where the lids of two larnakes were found, dating to EM II (Panagiotopoulos 2002); at Sissi, where in an EM IIA tomb, jars containing the bones of foetuses were found (Schoep, pers.comm.); at Nopigeia in the west, where an EM II pithos-like receptacle contained a child burial (Karantzali 1992-93: 66–67), although in this case it is not clear whether we are dealing with a cemetery or an isolated burial; and at the important Pyrgos cave in the north-central part of the island, Xanthoudides (1918) has found remnants of more than twenty larnakes of EM date, in a context with communal burials, and which in pottery terms is EM I-II. In the same report,

Xanthoudides also raises the possibility, which we should not take lightly, that in other contexts, wooden coffins might have been used (1918: 167; cf. also 1924: 92).

Space limitations do not allow me to discuss the regional diversity of this picture (cf. Hamilakis 2013; 2014; Leggara Herrero 2009), and the possible regional origins of specific material forms. For example, it is clear that in the "Cycladic", cist-grave cemeteries of the north coast (such as Hagia Photia; Davaras and Betancourt 2004), with their relative invisibility, restricted space, and the small number of corpses, the engagements between the living and the dead would have been much different from ones in the tholos tombs, the caves, and the house tombs. But here I am more interested in the broad trends in material practices, evident in most contexts. And based on the data I have briefly mentioned here, it is clear that neither in the early Prepalatial, nor in the late Prepalatial and first palatial phase are we justified in talking about the material expression of the emergence of individuality, nor do we see, at least in the mortuary record, an interplay between the communal and the individual. We are rather dealing with an extremely fluid corporeal landscape, where bodies alive, bodies dead, odorous, decomposing, whole or parts, articulated or disarticulated, commingled and interacted with each other and with objects, and passed through various transitory stages in relatively quick succession. It is clear that our terminology of "primary" and "secondary" burial is unable to express this corporeal fluidity (cf. Triantaphyllou, this volume). While this "messy" picture is often attributed to the recent looting of these tombs, it is now becoming increasingly clear that it was primarily the people of the Bronze Age who were likely to have been responsible for this constant interference. These locales were far from being resting places.

At certain moments, perhaps at the initial stages of deposition, a dead body was *temporarily individuated* but still within the collective arena of the corporeal landscape. In its temporarily individuated state, that body continued to exercise agency and act as a social person, even if it was through the sensorial impact emanating from its decomposing corpse. Before long however, that body, now perhaps having lost most of its flesh, was reunited with other bodies or body parts, even in the seemingly solitary larnakes. And more often than not, body parts, having lost their temporary boundedness and coherence, ended up in anonymous piles, were pushed aside, their bones broken, covered with a layer of sand or soil (cf. Branigan 1987; Hamilakis 1998) becoming thus invisible, or even immersed in and thus partially deformed and destroyed by fire (most prominently, in the recently discovered tholos tomb at Livari, east Crete, where most of the recovered bones were found burnt; cf. Papadatos and Sofianou 2012; Triantaphyllou 2009). Some bones at least, and perhaps the skulls especially, were removed from the burial arena altogether and were perhaps circulating in settlements and other locales: in some cases, the number of skulls and skull parts is much lower than the actual number of burials (Branigan 1987), and in at least one settlement, that of Myrtos Phournou Koriphi, a skull was found (Warren 1972). As for objects, some were perhaps rendered ritually dead by deformation or fragmentation (Hamilakis 1998), some were placed with the regrouped bones and skulls, but many others were dispersed (cf. Xanthoudides 1924: 8), starting a new life as they re-entered the world of the living, either whole or as fragments, enchaining thus the participants to the mortuary locales, to the ceremonies witnessed, and to each other (cf. Chapman and Gaydarska 2007). I have claimed elsewhere that many of these practices which resulted in the mixing, covering, destruction, deformation and fragmentation of bones and objects signal that this was the time for forgetting, so that positively valued space for new remembering can be generated. Communal eating and drinking, mortuary feasting, was a crucial component in these ceremonies (Hamilakis 1998; see also now the example of Moni Odigitria – Branigan 2010: 258).

Burning as a distinctive strategy in this process requires a brief comment. While the evidence was plentiful in the earlier reports, little attention was paid to it, and the conventional explanation was that of fumigation (and thus accidental burning of bones), a modernist and simplistic argument which takes our own western attitudes towards the corpse and towards bodily odours as universal and cross-cultural. Branigan (1987), while initially in favour of the fumigation idea, has concluded that the burning "was not fumigation at all, but was used to cleanse, symbolically or otherwise, the bones of one or a handful of individuals" (1987: 45). The extent of burning is becoming gradually recognised, thanks to the specialist studies of skeletal material (cf. Triantaphyllou 2009, for Moni Odigitria, and especially Livari). It seems, however, that the intention was not to completely destroy the corpses, a practice which we conventionally associate with cremation, but to destroy the remaining flesh of specific bodies; otherwise why the *localised* pattern of burning inside some of the tombs (Branigan 1987: 45), and why we have so many *surviving* bones with signs of burning, in various colourations, many of them charred in fact, rather than completely burnt? The destruction of the flesh but also of any items of clothing would have had the effect of eliminating any remaining signs of individuality, but the act itself, the lighting of fire and the burning of human flesh and fat, would have produced a highly memorable performative event and a strong olfactory sensory experience. Paradoxically, it would have been the very attempt to erase the memory of that specific individual as an active social agent which would have created strong bodily memories of the occasion, and potentially of that person as well. Absence, and the act of rendering something absent can at times be much more evocative and mnemonically important than continuous presence (cf. Forty and Küchler 1999).

While we are thus witnessing in the mortuary record a series of material practices which may signify efforts to forget individuals as active social agents in order to remember them as members of the collective of the ancestors (thus creating space for new memories), remembering is much more complex and can spring up in the most unexpected of occasions, and often in an involuntary manner. Furthermore, there is evidence in this mortuary context that there was a need, an impulse, for that remembering to be pro-longed, for the time of oblivion to be postponed, and for the living who used to visit and re-visit the mortuary arena, to have a focal point to relate to, identify and reconnect with; a visible, tactile, and odorous corpse of bones and objects to experience. This would have been a locale where genealogical links could be traced, where time could be reckoned with, memories triggered by bones and objects, re-collected, and familial bonds reaffirmed. I suggest that this need was present from the start of the Early Bronze Age, although perhaps not with the same urgency, intensity and force everywhere, and throughout this period. This was a need which was expressed with diverse material means, be they subdivisions and compartmentalisation of the communal space, carefully collected body parts deposited in discrete locales, or rooms, antechambers, and containers such as larnakes and pithoi.

Rather than talking of a tension between the individual and the collective thus, we should talk instead of the tension or even clash between remembering and forgetting. And the words tension and clash here are not accidental: even larnakes and pithoi were not permanent and secure material devices, guaranteeing eternal remembering. At Vorou some pithoi were found empty (Marinatos 1930–31) suggesting that bones were periodically removed, joining perhaps anonymous piles. More importantly, recall that many of these containers were found in fragments, even in unrobbed contexts. And that in the case of Porti, Xanthoudides reports a pit enclosed by a wall (trench γ) that "was filled to the brim with bones, among which were a few bits of Middle Minoan pithoi" (1924: 56). Forgetting was eventually unavoidable, but perhaps some people had insisted or even made sure, if necessary by force, that this should take place as soon as possible.

It seems, however, that at the end of the Early Bronze Age, remembering was expressed in new, and perhaps more costly but inevitably more durable material means, whether it was the more frequent use of clay coffins, or the now routine use of stone-built antechambers. This is also the period when we are witnessing "more tombs per cemetery than ever before" (Leggara Herrero 2012: 342), another spatial strategy which would have resulted in the compartmentalisation of the burial arena. Whether the increase in the number of tombs per cemetery signifies an emphasis on "co-residential" social groups as opposed to the broader community (*ibid.*) is hard to tell. What it is clear, however, is its mnemonic effects, the grouping and deposition of certain bodies, body parts and objects in discreet and materially durable and sensorially impressive locales, enabling remembering and re-collection. Other sensory mnemonic practices such as feasting and drinking also became more important at the same time, and involved more people than before (Hamilakis 1998; Legarra Herrero 2012: 351). Drinking too, now mostly from individual cups rather than communal chalices, was another expression of a temporary, collective individuation. Memory as a resource seems at this time to have become more politically expedient than before, and the need to materialise mnemonic connections in a firm, unambiguous and durable manner more important.

Trans-corporeality seems to have been a fundamental feature of these mortuary landscapes. By this I mean the condition of corporeal fluidity whereby co-jointed and commingled, dead or alive bodies, body parts and objects, occupy temporary and transient positions, and whereby movement of bodies and objects but also movement and circulation of substances *through* bodies, become paramount. This is evident not only in the absence of any permanent, bounded individual burials, but also in the constant movement and re-arrangement and manipulation of body parts, and in constant interaction between the living and the dead, and in the collective rituals centred around the circulation and consumption of food and drink. Whatever notions of personhood and selfhood would have been produced and negotiated in this landscape, they would have been done so in this trans-corporeal arena (cf. Bird-David 2004).[2] This trans-corporeal selfhood, however, was mediated by the processes of remembering and forgetting and the interplay between the two.

The mortuary landscape as a chronotopic map

The Russian literary theorist Mikhail Bakhtin, in order to denote the fusion or rather the inseparability of time and space, defined his concept of *chronotope* in the context of his 1937-38 essay, "Forms of time and of the chronotope in the novel: notes towards a historical poetics". He defined it as follows:

> "In the literary artistic chronotope, spatial and temporal indicators are fused into one carefully thought-out, concrete whole. Time, as it were, thickens, takes on flesh, becomes artistically visible; likewise, space becomes charged and responsive to the movements of time, plot and history. This intersection of axes and fusion of indicators characterizes the artistic chronotope." (Bakhtin 1981: 84).

Despite its literary origins, Bakhtin insisted that the concept is of generic significance (1981: 84–85), and has been since used in may other contexts. The anthropologist Keith Basso, for example, has used it to describe and analyse perceptions of landscape amongst the Western Apache, where certain locales embody the fusion of time and space, locales which become alive through stories and historical tales (1984: 44–45). This concept resonates with my argument here. The mortuary landscapes I have been talking about can be seen not simply as mnemo-scapes but also as trans-corporeal, chronotopic maps. As "deep maps" (cf. Pearson and Shanks 2001: 64–65) that were constantly produced and reproduced, always in the process of becoming, maps that required embodied practices in order to be deciphered and re-enacted. Maps where the specific points and locales corresponded perhaps to specific familial and genealogical groupings, and where mnemonic stratigraphies had to be re-traced in every visit.

There are two important further features that need emphasising here. The first is movement. Activating these maps and deciphering their mnemonic stratigraphies required a kinaesthetic experience, the movement of the participants through the specific micro-locales, more or less in a regulated manner. Note how the presence of additional tombs, and more so of enclosures, rooms and antechambers did not only compartmentalise space, but also defined human movement: most of antechambers in fact block the entrance of the tholos tomb, thus dictating to the participants a specific

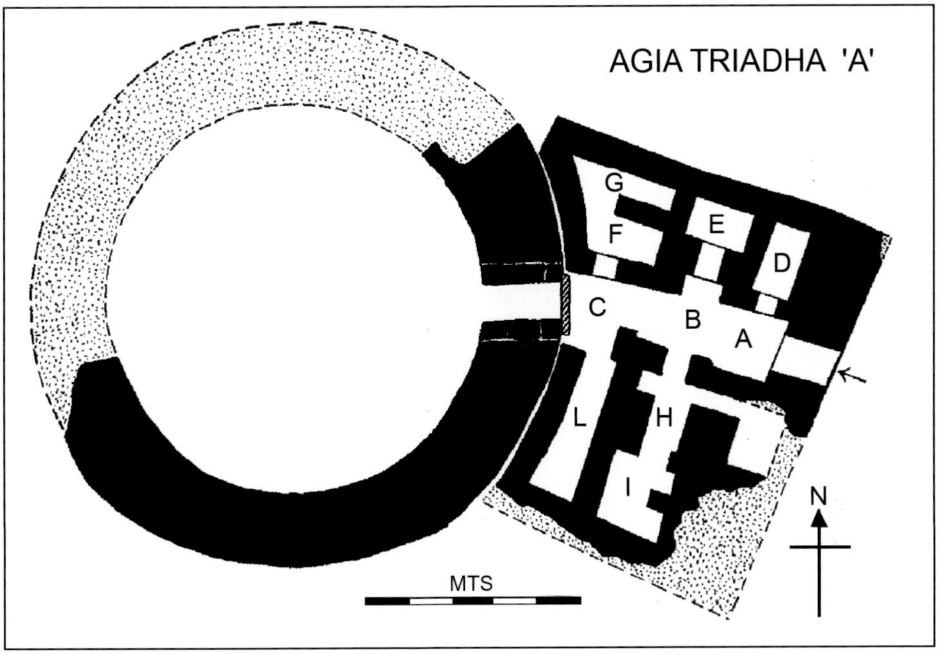

Figure 15.4: Plan of tholos tomb A at Hagia Triada (modified from Branigan 1976, p. 9).

itinerary: people had to pass through specific locales and witness concentrations of bones and artefacts, corresponding perhaps to distinctive times, places, and/or familial/ clan ties (e.g. at Hagia Triada A – Fig. 15.4). This was an act of sensorially acknowledging time/space links and associations, of deciphering genealogical stratigraphies.

The second feature, which resonates with the original, literary context of the notion of the chronotope, and one that was stressed by Basso in the Western Apache case, is that of story-telling. The act of immersing oneself in this chronotopic map, the journey that one would have taken every time she/he visited the mortuary landscape, would have evoked stories and legends of past people and events, stories that would have gradually acquired mythical proportions. Rare and unusual objects which would have been deposited with the bones in specific micro-locales would have acted as memory props for these stories. While it would be difficult to find concrete physical evidence for the act of communal story-telling and the performance of genealogical and mythical narratives, well-documented feasting and drinking events and the open spaces and platforms which were provided for these public gatherings in front of some tombs, would have offered the social and spatial contexts for these performances.

Conclusion

While the exploration of this topic has barely begun, based on the evidence and the discussion presented here we can conclude that, at least as far as the mortuary arena is concerned, there are no safe material grounds for talking of the emergence of the individual and of individuality in the Early and the Middle Bronze Age of Crete (the Prepalatial and the Protopalatial periods). There is, however, good evidence that the people of Crete at the time were engaging in a series of material and spatial strategies to do with their own attempts at producing and negotiating familial time, and at coming to terms with remembering and forgetting. I have examined here a series of diverse material evidence, and have suggested that larnakes and funerary pithoi should not be viewed in isolation but they should instead be grouped together with the use of rooms, antechambers, pits, and other features of the mortuary landscape (including the selection and grouping of bones and skulls) as material strategies for the organisation of the mortuary landscape and the creation of distinctive, spatial micro-locales. These practices of segmentation and subdivision of mortuary space are not expressions of individuality but rather materialisations of remembering, attempts at prolonging and maintaining mnemonic connections and associations, transient moments in the dialectic and clash between remembering and forgetting.

I have also made two further points that are hopefully of wider relevance. The first is that in our efforts to move beyond typologies of personhood, and static, unchanging categories of the self, we should explore the processes of *collective individuation* (cf. Hamilakis 2013), materially expressed in ways such as the use of individual drinking vessels in communal drinking rituals, or the temporary isolation of a dead body within a communal burial space; we should also investigate the processes of *trans-corporeality* placing emphasis neither on individuality nor on dividuality/partibility, nor on multiple bounded selves, but on the condition of corporeal fluidity, on trans-bodily engagements, and on the movement and circulation of substances and objects through bodies. My second point relates to our efforts to understand conceptions of time and space in the past. I have suggested that in the context of mortuary landscapes, and perhaps more widely, the concept of the chronotope, which denotes the inseparability of time and space, may be of significant interpretative potential. I have developed this concept here by suggesting that, in dealing with the dialectic of remembering and forgetting, people may have organised and experienced mortuary landscapes as chronotopic maps, three-dimensional, experiential maps which required bodily movement and intense trans-corporeal interaction in order to be continually produced and activated. It is hoped that other studies will explore further the potential (and limitations) of this idea.

Acknowledgements

It is with great pleasure and affection that I contribute this chapter to the volume honouring Keith Branigan. Keith has been an invaluable academic advisor and mentor, a source of inspiration over the years, and a person who offered much needed support at a crucial time. Above all, he has been an open-minded scholar who has recognised the importance of allowing new ideas, however challenging and provocative, to be heard and flourish.

I am grateful to the editors of this volume, to the audience of the Sheffield Round Table in which an early version of this paper was presented, and to an anonymous referee for comments, suggestions, and access to unpublished work. Constance von Rüden also discussed aspects of this paper with me providing illuminating commentary, as well as help with some of the illustrations.

Note

1 The text for this chapter was written in 2010 and its revised form was submitted to the editors in 2011; sections from this text were subsequently incorporated in Hamilakis 2013.

2 Nurit Bird-David evokes the concept of trans-corporeality in analysing perceptions of illness among the Nayaka people of India today. She does so in order to critique western notions of inter-corporeality (e.g. Weiss 1999) which, despite their intended use to move beyond the individual, still maintain the kernel of bounded bodily entities, albeit in a plural form. Among the Nayaka, she writes, illnesses "are not thought to 'invade' the 'skin-bounded body' but rather to come 'between' body-subjects and jeopardise their joining and dealing with each other" (2004: 335).

Bibliography

Alexiou, S. and P. M. Warren

2004 *The Early Minoan tombs of Lebena, southern Crete* (Studies in Mediterranean Archaeology 30). Sävedalen: Paul Åström Förlag.

Bakhtin, M.

1981 *The Dialogic Imagination: Four Essays*. Edited by M. Holquist and translated by C. Emerson and M. Holquist. Austin: University of Texas Press.

Basso, K. H.

1984 "Stalking with stories": names, places and moral narratives among the western Apache. In E. M. Bruner (ed.), *Text, Play, and Story: The Construction and Reconstruction of Self and Society*: 19–55. Washington, DC: The American Ethnological Society.

Bird-David, N.

2004 Illness-images and joined beings: a critical/Nayaka perspective on intercorporeality. *Social Anthropology* 12.3: 325–39.

Blackman, D. J. and K. Branigan

1973 An unusual tholos tomb at Kaminospilio, south Crete. *Κρητικά Χρονικά* 25.1: 199–206.

Branigan, K.

1987 Ritual interference with human bones in the Mesara tholoi. In R. Laffineur (ed.), *Thanatos: Les coutumes funéraires en Egée à l'âge de Bronze* (Aegaeum 1): 43–51. Liège: Université de Liège.

1993 *Dancing with Death: Life and Death in Southern Crete c. 3000–2000 BC*. Amsterdam: Adolf M. Hakkert.

2010 History and use of the cemetery. In A. Vasilakis and K. Branigan (eds.), *Moni Odigitria: A Prepalatial Cemetery and its Environs in Asterousia, Southern Crete*: 251–69. (Prehistory Monographs 30) Philadelphia: INSTAP Academic Press.

Catapoti, D.

2005 *From Power to Paradigm: Rethinking the Emergence of the "Palatial Phenomenon" in Bronze Age Crete*. Unpublished PhD dissertation, University of Sheffield.

Chapman, J.

2000 *Fragmentation in Archaeology: People, Places and Broken Objects on the Prehistory of South-Eastern Europe*. London: Routledge.

Chapman, J. and B. Gaydarska
2007 *Parts and Wholes: Fragmentation in Prehistoric Context*. Oxford: Oxbow.
Davaras, C. and P. P. Betancourt
2004 *The Hagia Photia Cemetery I: The Tomb Groups and Architecture* (Prehistory Monographs 14). Philadelphia: INSTAP Academic Press.
Fowler, C.
2002 Body parts: personhood and materiality in the earlier Manx Neolithic. In Y. Hamilakis, M. Pluciennik and S. Tarlow (eds.), *Thinking Through the Body: Archaeologies of Corporeality*: 47–69. New York: Kluwer.
2004 *The Archaeology of Personhood: An Anthropological Approach*. London: Routledge.
Forty, A. and S. Küchler (eds.)
1999 *The Art of Forgetting*. Oxford: Berg.
Hamilakis, Y.
1998 Eating the dead: mortuary feasting and the political economy of memory in the Bronze Age Aegean. In K. Branigan (ed.), *Cemetery and Society in the Aegean Bronze Age* (Sheffield Studies in Aegean Archaeology 1): 115–32. Sheffield: Sheffield Academic Press.
2010 Recollecting the fragments: archaeology as mnemonic practice. In K. Lillios and V. Tsamis (eds.), *Material Mnemonics and Everyday Memory in European Prehistory*: 188–199. Oxford: Oxbow.
2011 Archaeologies of the senses. In T. Insoll (ed.), *The Oxford Handbook on the Archaeology of Ritual and Religion*: 208–225. Oxford: Oxford University Press.
2012 Eleven theses on the archaeology of the senses. In Day, J. (ed.), *Making Senses of the Past: Towards a Sensory Archaeology* (Center for Archaeological Investigations, Occasional Paper 40): 409–19. Carbondale: Southern Illinois University.
2013 *Archaeology and the Senses: Human Experience, Memory, and Affect*. Cambridge: Cambridge University Press.
2014 Sensuous memory, history, and the "rise of the palaces" in Bronze Age Crete. In P. van Dommelen and B. Knapp (eds.), *The Cambridge Handbook on the Bronze and Iron Age Mediterranean*: 320–36. Cambridge: Cambridge University Press.
Hamilakis, Y. and J. Labanyi
2008 Time, materiality, and the work of memory. *History and Memory* 20.2: 5–17.
Hamilakis, Y., M. Pluciennik, and S. Tarlow
2002 Thinking through the body: introduction. In Y. Hamilakis, M. Pluciennik and S. Tarlow (eds.), *Thinking Through the Body: Archaeologies of Corporeality*: 121–36. New York: Kluwer.
Hodder, I.
2000 Agency and individuals in long-term processes. In J. E. Robb and M. A. Dobres (eds.), *Agency in Archaeology*: 21–33. London: Routledge.
Karantzali, E.
1992–93 Στοιχεία Πρωτομινωικής κατοίκησης στα Νοπήγεια Κισσάμου. *Αρχαιολογικό Δελτίο* B 47-48: 65–82.
Knapp, B. and P. van Dommelen
2008 Past practices: rethinking individuals and agents in archaeology. *Cambridge Archaeological Journal* 18.1: 15–34.
Legarra Herrero, B.
2009 The Minoan fallacy: cultural diversity and mortuary behaviour on Crete at the beginning of the Bronze Age. *Oxford Journal of Archaeology* 28: 29–57.
2012 The construction, deconstruction and non-construction of hierarchies in the funerary record of Prepalatial Crete. In I. Schoep, P. Tomkins and J. Driessen (eds.), *Back to the Beginning: Reassessing Social and Political Complexity on Crete during the Early and Middle Bronze Age*: 325-57. Oxford: Oxbow.

LiPuma, E.
1998 Modernity and forms of personhood in Melanesia. In M. Lambek and A. Strathern (eds.), *Bodies and Persons: Comparative Perspectives from Africa and Melanesia*: 53-79. Cambridge: Cambridge University Press.
Marinatos, S.
1930–31 Δύο Πρώιμοι Μινωικοί τάφοι εκ Βωρού Μεσαράς. *Αρχαιολογικόν Δελτίον* 13: 18–170.
McEnroe, J.
2010 *The Architecture of Minoan Crete: Constructing Identity in the Aegean Bronze Age*. Austin: The University of Texas Press.
Panagiotopoulos, D.
2002 *Das Tholosgrab E von Phourni bei Archanes. Studien zu einem frühkretischen Grabfund und seinem kulturellen Kontext* (BAR IS 1014). Oxford: Archaeopress.
Papadatos, Y.
1999 *Mortuary Practices and their Importance for the Reconstruction of Society and Life in Prepalatial Crete: The Evidence from Tholos Tomb Gamma in Archanes-Phourni*. Unpublished PhD Dissertation: University of Sheffield.
2005 *Tholos Tomb Gamma: A Prepalatial Tholos Tomb at Phourni, Archanes* (Prehistory Monographs 17). Philadelphia: INSTAP Academic Press.
Papadatos, Y. and C. Sofianou
2012 Πολιτισμική ομοιογένεια και διαφοροποίηση στην Προανακτορική Κρήτη: νέα στοιχεία από τις ανασκαφές νεκροταφείων στην επαρχία Σητείας. In M. Andrianakis, P. Varthalitou and I. Tzachili (eds.), *Archaeological Work in Crete 2, Proceedings of the 2nd meeting, Rethymnon 26-28 November 2010*: 49–59. Rethymnon: University of Crete, Faculty of Letters Publications.
Pearson, M. and M. Shanks
2001 *Theatre/Archaeology*. London: Routledge.
Pendlebury, J. D. S.
1935 Journeys in Crete 1934. *Annual of the British School at Athens* 33: 80–100.
Platon, N.
1959 Η αρχαιολογική κίνησις εν Κρήτη κατά το έτος 1959. *Κρητικά Χρονικά* 13.3: 359–93.
Strathern, M.
1988 *The Gender of the Gift: Problems with Women and Problems with Society in Melanesia*. Berkeley: University of California Press.
Thomas, J.
2002 Archaeology's humanism and the materiality of the body. In Y. Hamilakis, M. Pluciennik and S. Tarlow (eds.), *Thinking Through the Body: Archaeologies of Corporeality*: 29–45. New York: Kluwer.
Triantaphyllou, S.
2009 EM/MM human skeletal remains from East Crete: The Kephala Petras rock shelter, Siteia, and the Livari Tholos Tomb, Skiadi. *Kentro* 12: 19–23.
Warren, P. M.
1972 *Myrtos: An Early Bronze Age Site in Crete* (BSA Supplementary Volume 7). London: Thames and Hudson.
Weiss, G.
1999 *Body Images: Embodiment as Intercorporeality*. London: Routledge.
Xanthoudides, S.
1918 Μέγας Πρωτομινωικός τάφος Πύργου. *Αρχαιολογικόν Δελτίον* 4: 136–70.
1924 *The Vaulted Tombs of Mesara*. London: Hodder & Stoughton.